Welcome to the Nerd Farm!

Doonesbury Books by G. B. Trudeau

Recent Collections

Read My Lips, Make My Day, Eat Quiche and Die!
Give Those Nymphs Some Hooters!
You're Smokin' Now, Mr. Butts!
I'd Go with the Helmet, Ray
Welcome to Club Scud!
What Is It, Tink, Is Pan in Trouble?
Quality Time on Highway 1
Washed Out Bridges and Other Disasters
In Search of Cigarette Holder Man
Doonesbury Nation
Virtual Doonesbury
Planet Doonesbury
Buck Wild Doonesbury
Duke 2000: Whatever It Takes
The Revolt of the English Majors
Peace Out, Dawg!
Got War?
Talk to the Hand
Dude: The Big Book of Zonker
Heckuva Job, Bushie!

Special Collections

The Doonesbury Chronicles
Doonesbury's Greatest Hits
The People's Doonesbury
Doonesbury Dossier: The Reagan Years
Doonesbury Deluxe: Selected Glances Askance
Recycled Doonesbury: Second Thoughts on a Gilded Age
Action Figure!
The Portable Doonesbury
Flashbacks: Twenty-Five Years of Doonesbury
The Bundled Doonesbury
The Long Road Home: One Step at a Time
The War Within: One More Step at a Time
Doonesbury.com's The Sandbox: Dispatches from Troops in Iraq and Afghanistan

A DOONESBURY BOOK

Welcome to the Nerd Farm!

BY G. B. TRUDEAU

Andrews McMeel
Publishing, LLC
Kansas City

DOONESBURY is distributed internationally by Universal Press Syndicate.

07 08 09 10 11 BAM 10 9 8 7 6 5 4 3 2 1

ISBN-13: 978-0-7407-6850-7
ISBN-10: 0-7407-6850-6

Library of Congress Control Number: 2007925787

www.andrewsmcmeel.com

DOONESBURY may be viewed on the Internet at
www.doonesbury.com and www.GoComics.com.

"Getting an education from MIT is like taking a drink from a fire hose."

—Jerome Wiesner

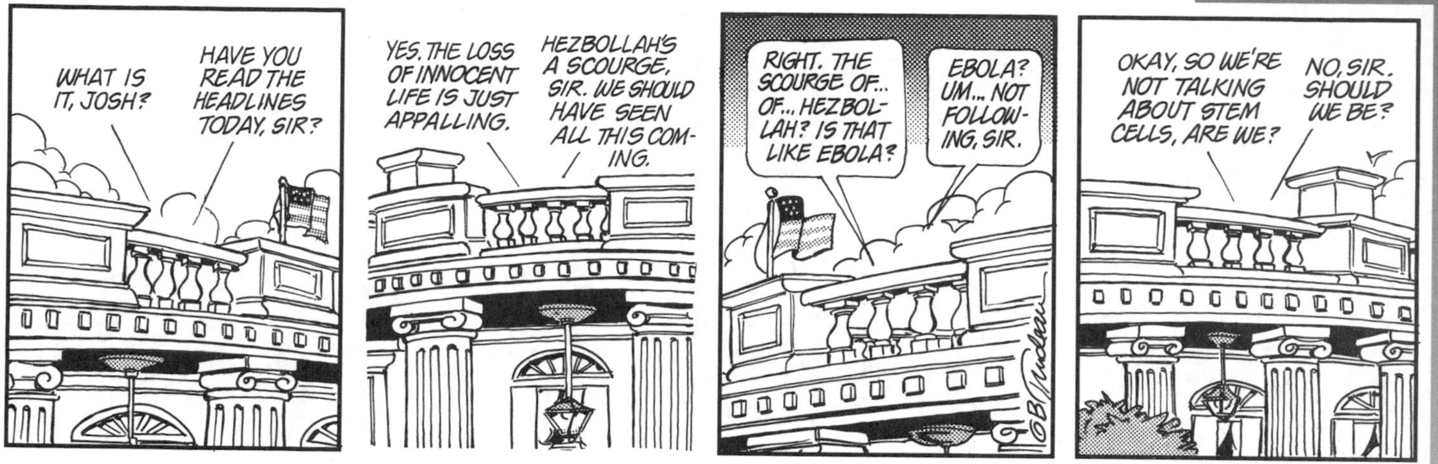
WHAT IS IT, JOSH?
HAVE YOU READ THE HEADLINES TODAY, SIR?
YES. THE LOSS OF INNOCENT LIFE IS JUST APPALLING.
HEZBOLLAH'S A SCOURGE, SIR. WE SHOULD HAVE SEEN ALL THIS COM-ING.
RIGHT. THE SCOURGE OF... OF... HEZBOL-LAH? IS THAT LIKE EBOLA?
EBOLA? UM... NOT FOLLOW-ING, SIR.
OKAY, SO WE'RE NOT TALKING ABOUT STEM CELLS, ARE WE?
NO, SIR. SHOULD WE BE?

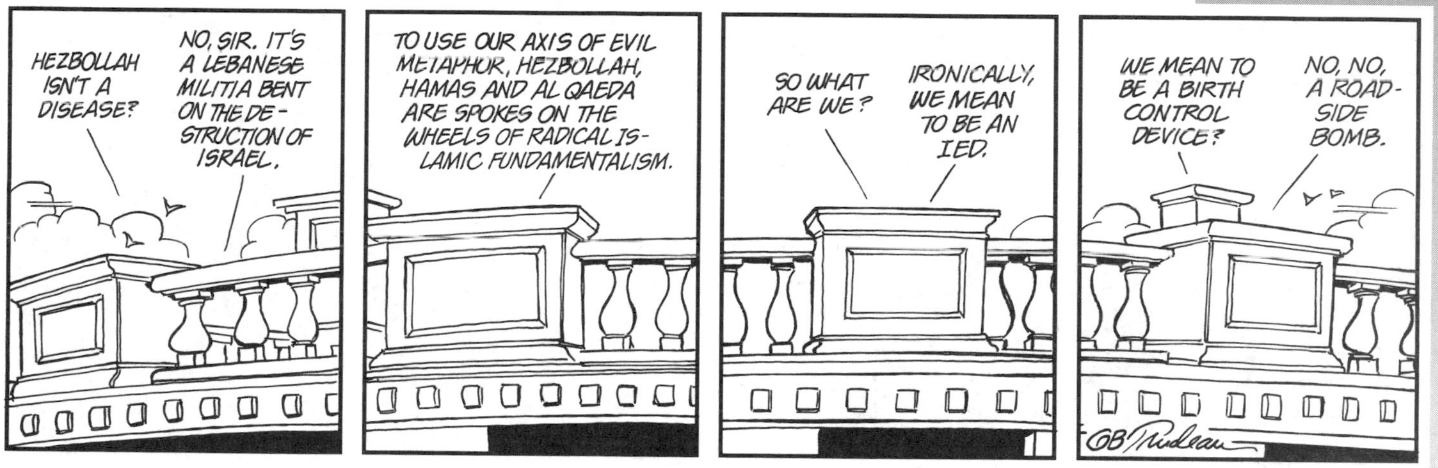
HEZBOLLAH ISN'T A DISEASE?
NO, SIR. IT'S A LEBANESE MILITIA BENT ON THE DE-STRUCTION OF ISRAEL.
TO USE OUR AXIS OF EVIL METAPHOR, HEZBOLLAH, HAMAS AND AL QAEDA ARE SPOKES ON THE WHEELS OF RADICAL IS-LAMIC FUNDAMENTALISM.
SO WHAT ARE WE?
IRONICALLY, WE MEAN TO BE AN IED.
WE MEAN TO BE A BIRTH CONTROL DEVICE?
NO, NO, A ROAD-SIDE BOMB.

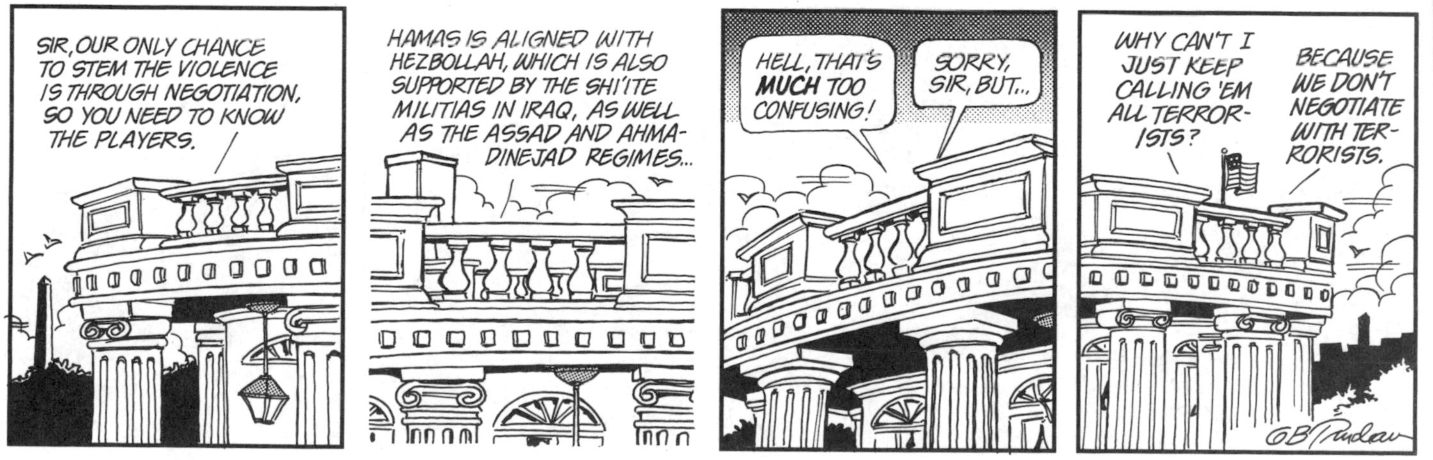
SIR, OUR ONLY CHANCE TO STEM THE VIOLENCE IS THROUGH NEGOTIATION, SO YOU NEED TO KNOW THE PLAYERS.
HAMAS IS ALIGNED WITH HEZBOLLAH, WHICH IS ALSO SUPPORTED BY THE SHI'ITE MILITIAS IN IRAQ, AS WELL AS THE ASSAD AND AHMA-DINEJAD REGIMES...
HELL, THAT'S MUCH TOO CONFUSING!
SORRY, SIR, BUT...
WHY CAN'T I JUST KEEP CALLING 'EM ALL TERROR-ISTS?
BECAUSE WE DON'T NEGOTIATE WITH TER-RORISTS.

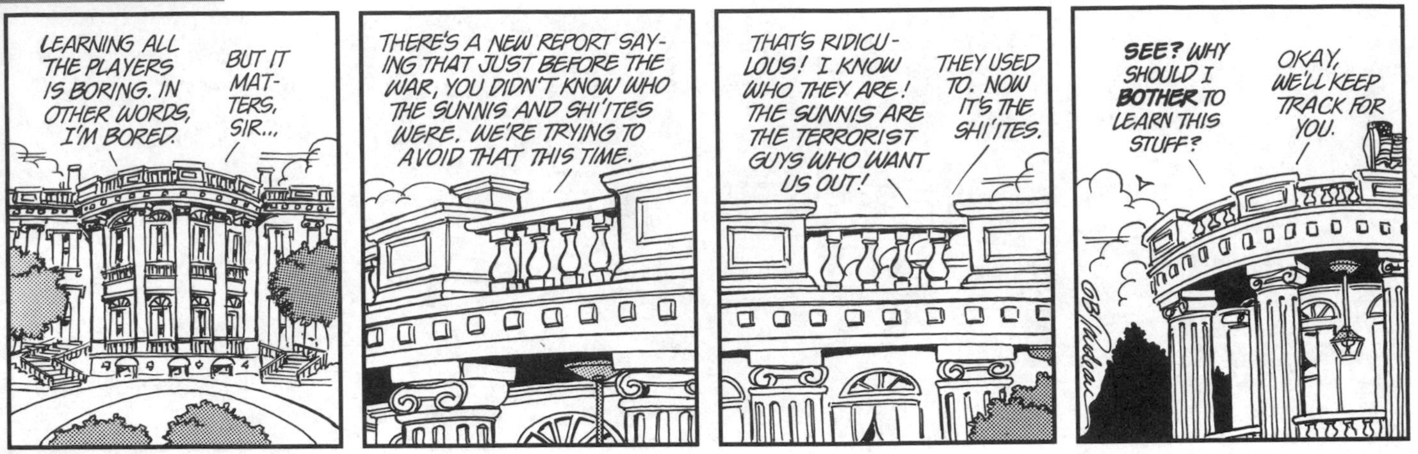
LEARNING ALL THE PLAYERS IS BORING. IN OTHER WORDS, I'M BORED.
BUT IT MATTERS, SIR...
THERE'S A NEW REPORT SAYING THAT JUST BEFORE THE WAR, YOU DIDN'T KNOW WHO THE SUNNIS AND SHI'ITES WERE. WE'RE TRYING TO AVOID THAT THIS TIME.
THAT'S RIDICULOUS! I KNOW WHO THEY ARE! THE SUNNIS ARE THE TERRORIST GUYS WHO WANT US OUT!
THEY USED TO. NOW IT'S THE SHI'ITES.
SEE? WHY SHOULD I BOTHER TO LEARN THIS STUFF?
OKAY, WE'LL KEEP TRACK FOR YOU.

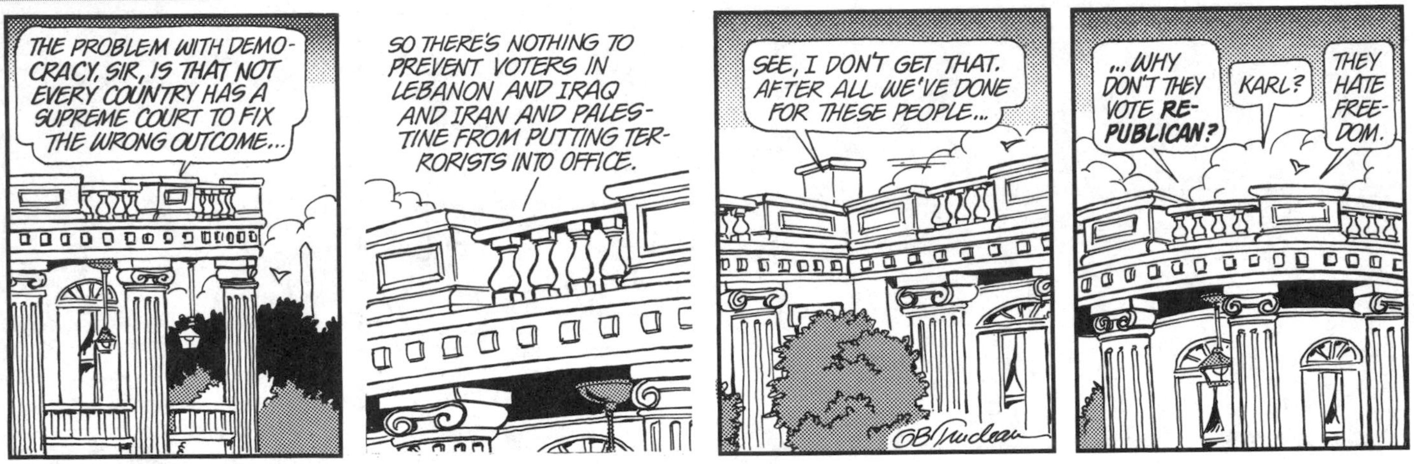
THE PROBLEM WITH DEMOCRACY, SIR, IS THAT NOT EVERY COUNTRY HAS A SUPREME COURT TO FIX THE WRONG OUTCOME...
SO THERE'S NOTHING TO PREVENT VOTERS IN LEBANON AND IRAQ AND IRAN AND PALESTINE FROM PUTTING TERRORISTS INTO OFFICE.
SEE, I DON'T GET THAT. AFTER ALL WE'VE DONE FOR THESE PEOPLE...
...WHY DON'T THEY VOTE REPUBLICAN?
KARL?
THEY HATE FREEDOM.

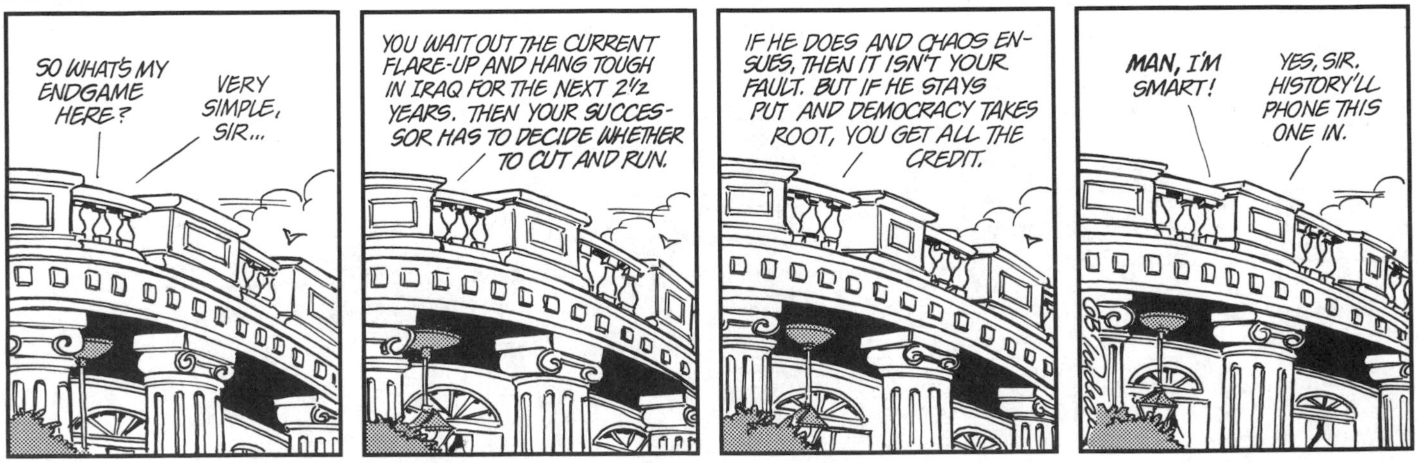
SO WHAT'S MY ENDGAME HERE?
VERY SIMPLE, SIR...
YOU WAIT OUT THE CURRENT FLARE-UP AND HANG TOUGH IN IRAQ FOR THE NEXT 2½ YEARS. THEN YOUR SUCCESSOR HAS TO DECIDE WHETHER TO CUT AND RUN.
IF HE DOES AND CHAOS ENSUES, THEN IT ISN'T YOUR FAULT. BUT IF HE STAYS PUT AND DEMOCRACY TAKES ROOT, YOU GET ALL THE CREDIT.
MAN, I'M SMART!
YES, SIR. HISTORY'LL PHONE THIS ONE IN.

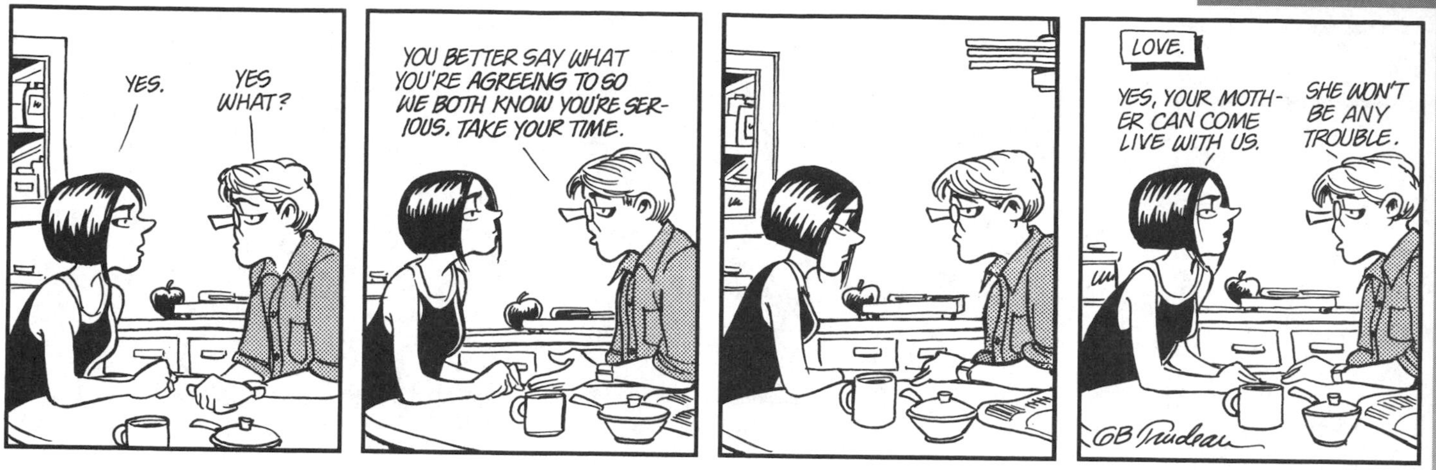
YES.
YES WHAT?
YOU BETTER SAY WHAT YOU'RE AGREEING TO SO WE BOTH KNOW YOU'RE SERIOUS. TAKE YOUR TIME.
LOVE.
YES, YOUR MOTHER CAN COME LIVE WITH US.
SHE WON'T BE ANY TROUBLE.

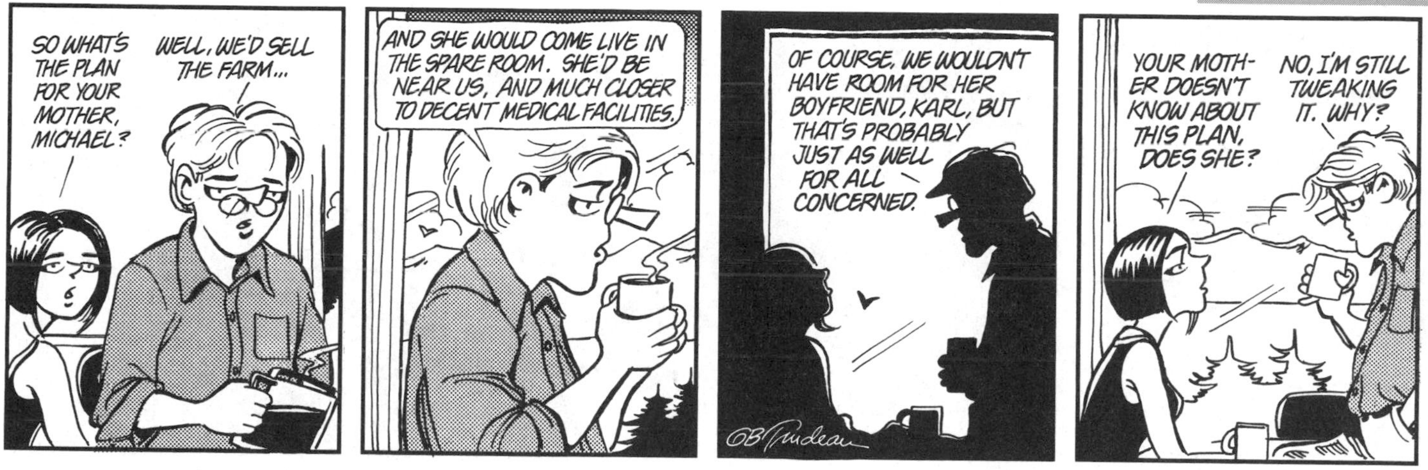
SO WHAT'S THE PLAN FOR YOUR MOTHER, MICHAEL?
WELL, WE'D SELL THE FARM...
AND SHE WOULD COME LIVE IN THE SPARE ROOM. SHE'D BE NEAR US, AND MUCH CLOSER TO DECENT MEDICAL FACILITIES.
OF COURSE, WE WOULDN'T HAVE ROOM FOR HER BOYFRIEND, KARL, BUT THAT'S PROBABLY JUST AS WELL FOR ALL CONCERNED.
YOUR MOTHER DOESN'T KNOW ABOUT THIS PLAN, DOES SHE?
NO, I'M STILL TWEAKING IT. WHY?

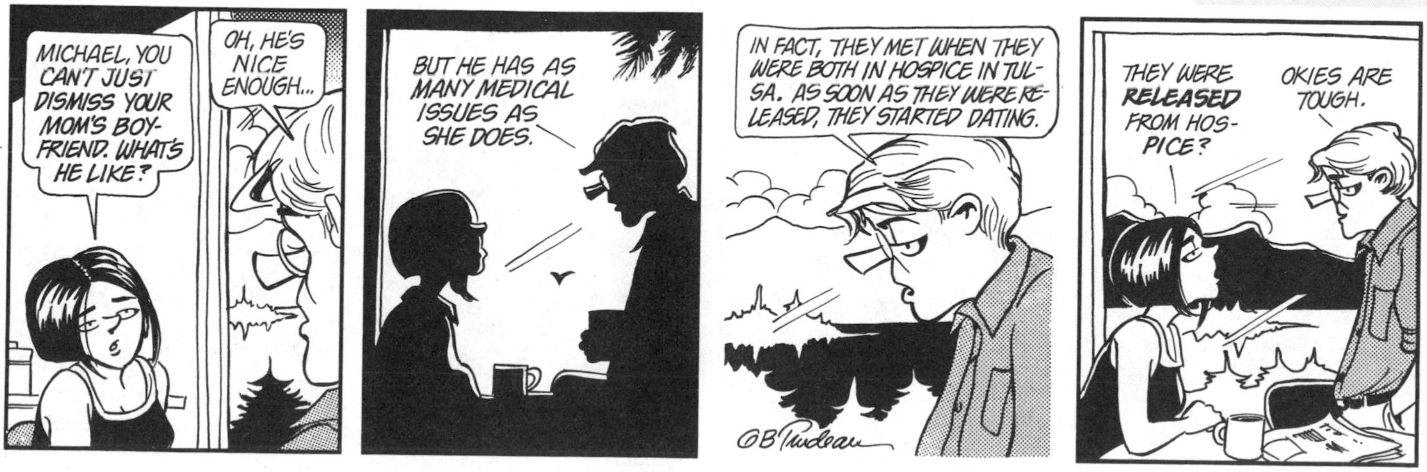
MICHAEL, YOU CAN'T JUST DISMISS YOUR MOM'S BOYFRIEND. WHAT'S HE LIKE?
OH, HE'S NICE ENOUGH...
BUT HE HAS AS MANY MEDICAL ISSUES AS SHE DOES.
IN FACT, THEY MET WHEN THEY WERE BOTH IN HOSPICE IN TULSA. AS SOON AS THEY WERE RELEASED, THEY STARTED DATING.
THEY WERE **RELEASED** FROM HOSPICE?
OKIES ARE TOUGH.

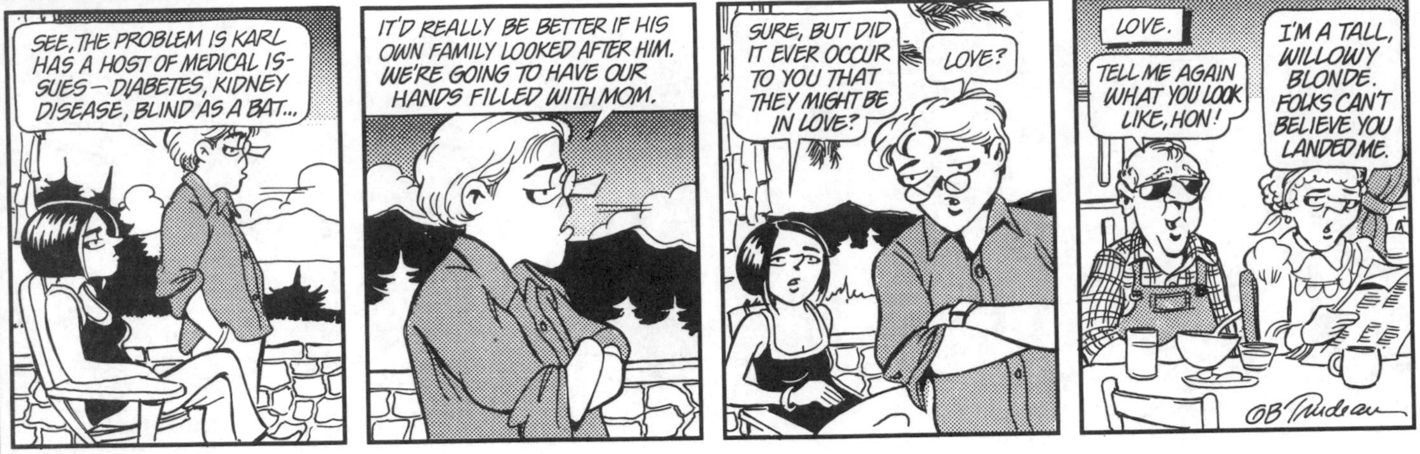
SEE, THE PROBLEM IS KARL HAS A HOST OF MEDICAL ISSUES — DIABETES, KIDNEY DISEASE, BLIND AS A BAT...
IT'D REALLY BE BETTER IF HIS OWN FAMILY LOOKED AFTER HIM. WE'RE GOING TO HAVE OUR HANDS FILLED WITH MOM.
SURE, BUT DID IT EVER OCCUR TO YOU THAT THEY MIGHT BE IN LOVE?
LOVE?
LOVE.
TELL ME AGAIN WHAT YOU LOOK LIKE, HON!
I'M A TALL, WILLOWY BLONDE. FOLKS CAN'T BELIEVE YOU LANDED ME.

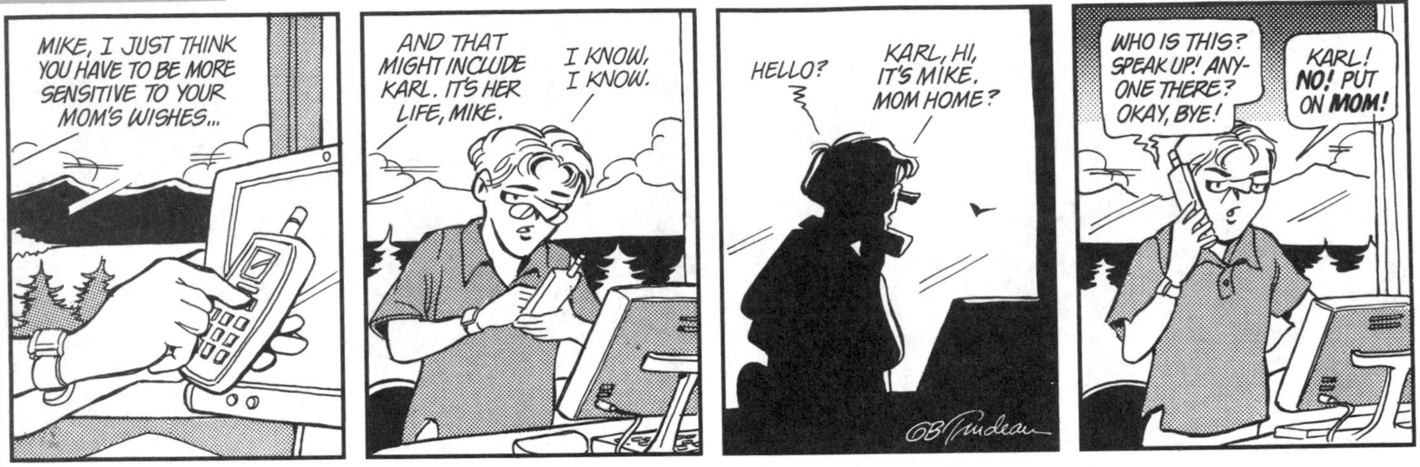
MIKE, I JUST THINK YOU HAVE TO BE MORE SENSITIVE TO YOUR MOM'S WISHES...
AND THAT MIGHT INCLUDE KARL. IT'S HER LIFE, MIKE.
I KNOW, I KNOW.
HELLO?
KARL, HI, IT'S MIKE. MOM HOME?
WHO IS THIS? SPEAK UP! ANYONE THERE? OKAY, BYE!
KARL! **NO!** PUT ON **MOM!**

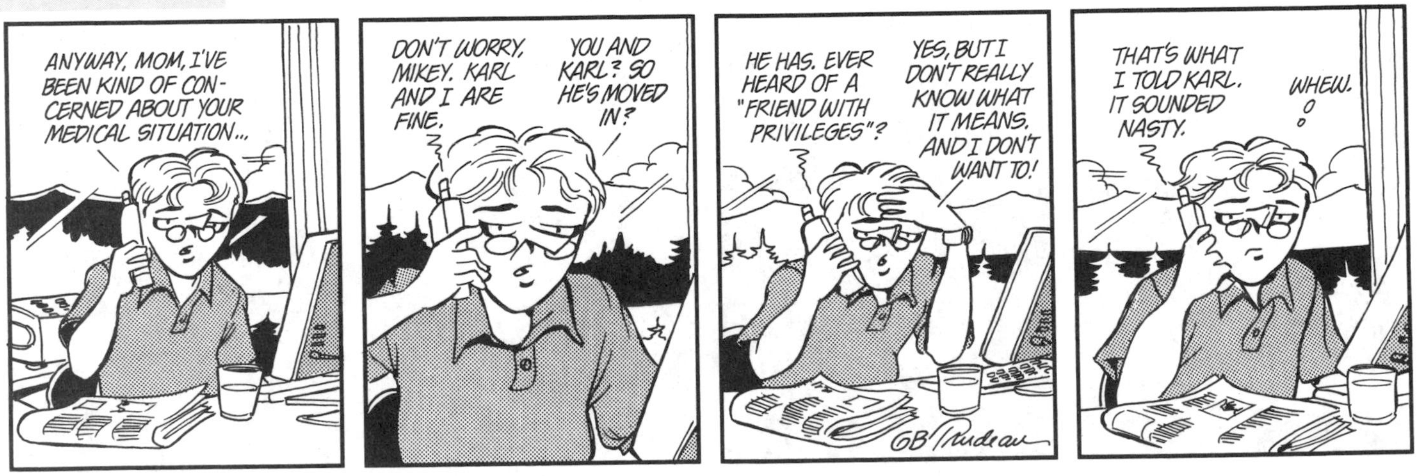
ANYWAY, MOM, I'VE BEEN KIND OF CONCERNED ABOUT YOUR MEDICAL SITUATION...
DON'T WORRY, MIKEY. KARL AND I ARE FINE.
YOU AND KARL? SO HE'S MOVED IN?
HE HAS. EVER HEARD OF A "FRIEND WITH PRIVILEGES"?
YES, BUT I DON'T REALLY KNOW WHAT IT MEANS, AND I DON'T WANT TO!
THAT'S WHAT I TOLD KARL. IT SOUNDED NASTY.
WHEW.

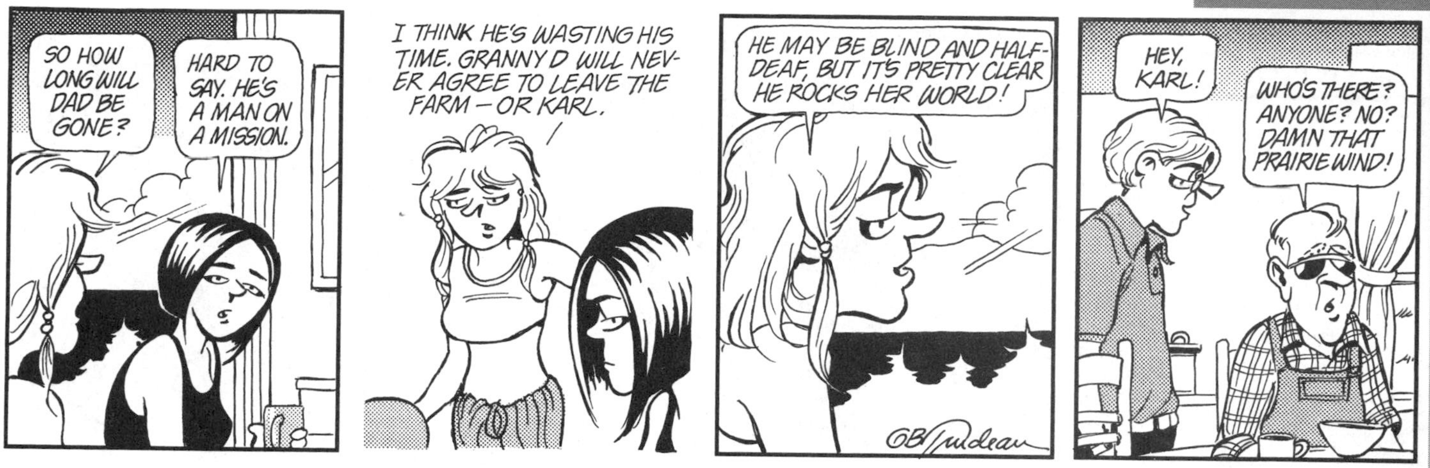
SO HOW LONG WILL DAD BE GONE?
HARD TO SAY. HE'S A MAN ON A MISSION.
I THINK HE'S WASTING HIS TIME. GRANNY D WILL NEVER AGREE TO LEAVE THE FARM — OR KARL.
HE MAY BE BLIND AND HALF-DEAF, BUT IT'S PRETTY CLEAR HE ROCKS HER WORLD!
HEY, KARL!
WHO'S THERE? ANYONE? NO? DAMN THAT PRAIRIE WIND!

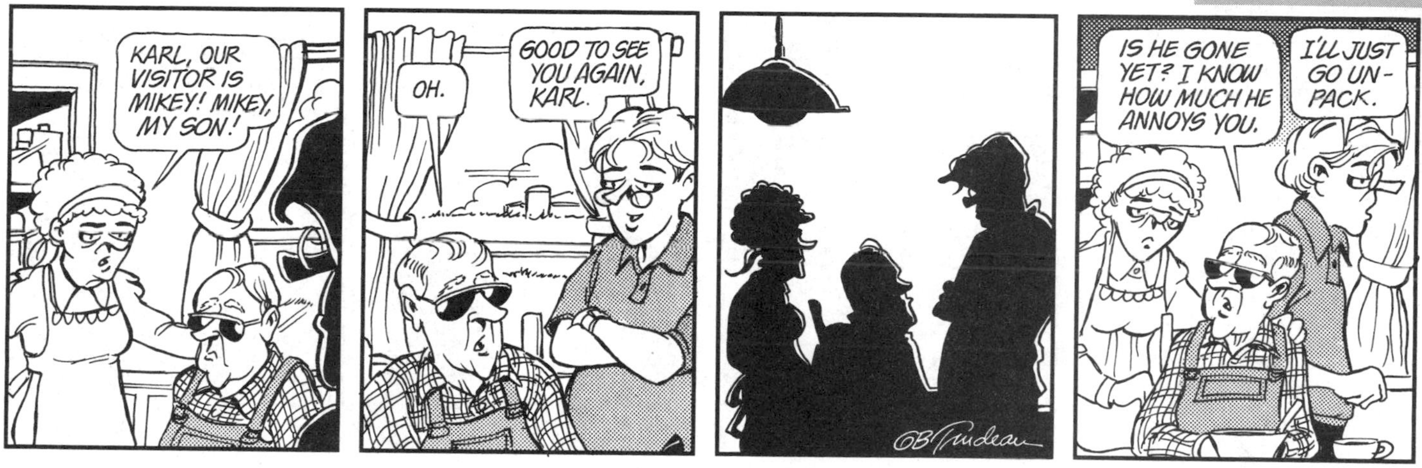
KARL, OUR VISITOR IS MIKEY! MIKEY, MY SON!
OH.
GOOD TO SEE YOU AGAIN, KARL.
IS HE GONE YET? I KNOW HOW MUCH HE ANNOYS YOU.
I'LL JUST GO UNPACK.

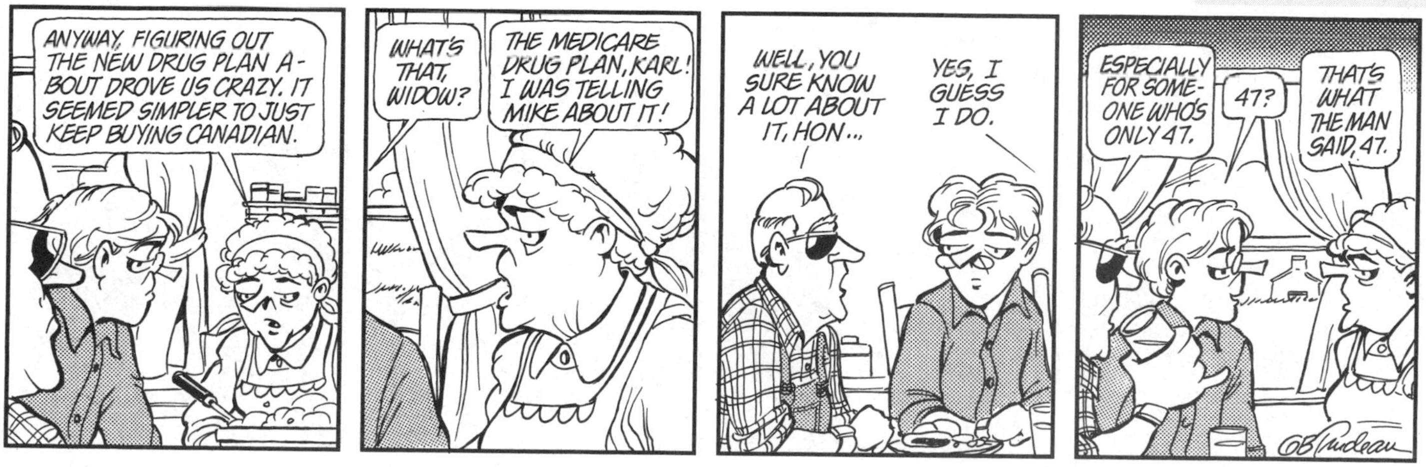
ANYWAY, FIGURING OUT THE NEW DRUG PLAN ABOUT DROVE US CRAZY. IT SEEMED SIMPLER TO JUST KEEP BUYING CANADIAN.
WHAT'S THAT, WIDOW?
THE MEDICARE DRUG PLAN, KARL! I WAS TELLING MIKE ABOUT IT!
WELL, YOU SURE KNOW A LOT ABOUT IT, HON...
YES, I GUESS I DO.
ESPECIALLY FOR SOMEONE WHO'S ONLY 47.
47?
THAT'S WHAT THE MAN SAID, 47.

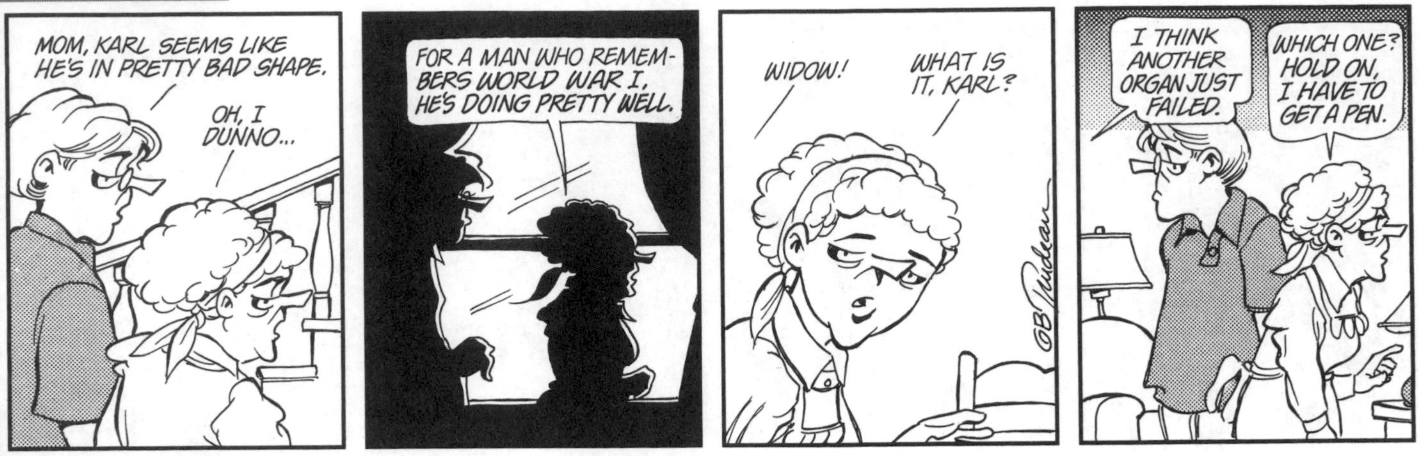
MOM, KARL SEEMS LIKE HE'S IN PRETTY BAD SHAPE.
OH, I DUNNO...
FOR A MAN WHO REMEMBERS WORLD WAR I, HE'S DOING PRETTY WELL.
WIDOW!
WHAT IS IT, KARL?
I THINK ANOTHER ORGAN JUST FAILED.
WHICH ONE? HOLD ON, I HAVE TO GET A PEN.
GB Trudeau

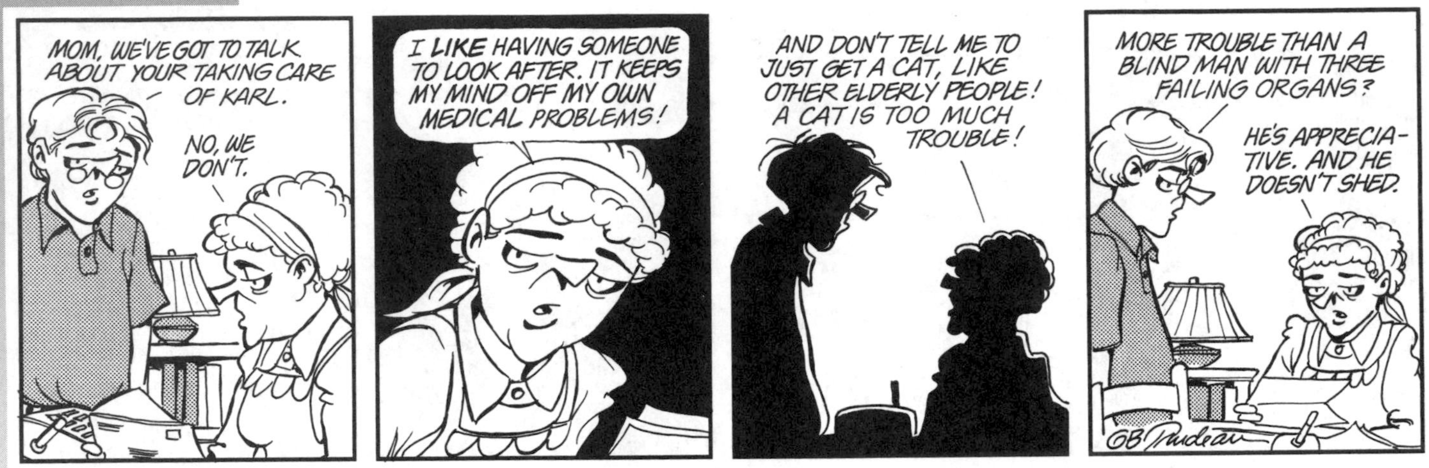
MOM, WE'VE GOT TO TALK ABOUT YOUR TAKING CARE OF KARL.
NO, WE DON'T.
I LIKE HAVING SOMEONE TO LOOK AFTER. IT KEEPS MY MIND OFF MY OWN MEDICAL PROBLEMS!
AND DON'T TELL ME TO JUST GET A CAT, LIKE OTHER ELDERLY PEOPLE! A CAT IS TOO MUCH TROUBLE!
MORE TROUBLE THAN A BLIND MAN WITH THREE FAILING ORGANS?
HE'S APPRECIATIVE. AND HE DOESN'T SHED.
GB Trudeau

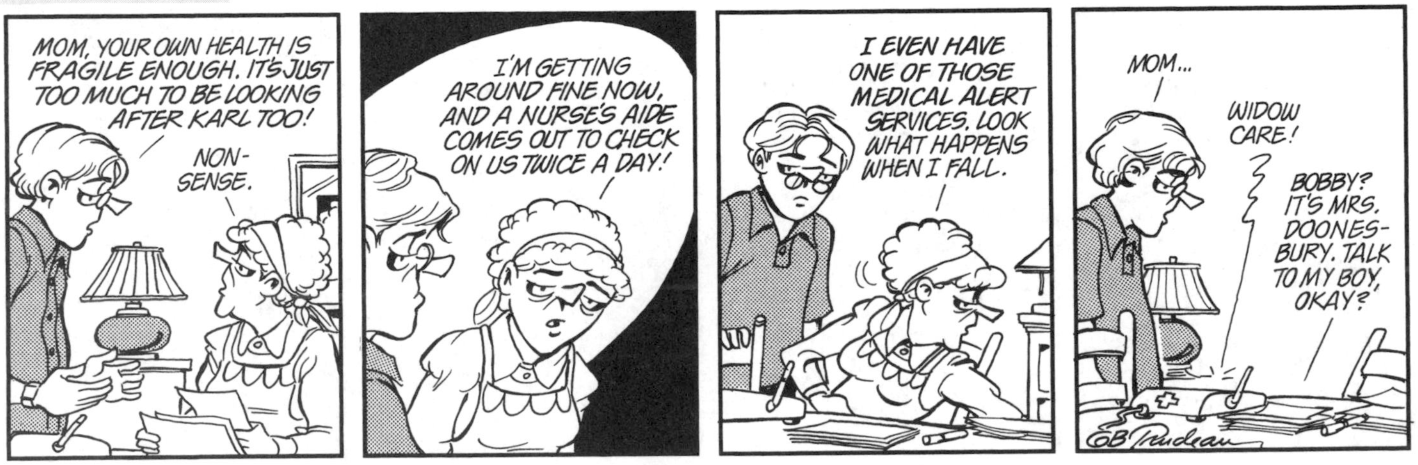
MOM, YOUR OWN HEALTH IS FRAGILE ENOUGH. IT'S JUST TOO MUCH TO BE LOOKING AFTER KARL TOO!
NONSENSE.
I'M GETTING AROUND FINE NOW, AND A NURSE'S AIDE COMES OUT TO CHECK ON US TWICE A DAY!
I EVEN HAVE ONE OF THOSE MEDICAL ALERT SERVICES. LOOK WHAT HAPPENS WHEN I FALL.
MOM...
WIDOW CARE!
BOBBY? IT'S MRS. DOONESBURY. TALK TO MY BOY, OKAY?
GB Trudeau

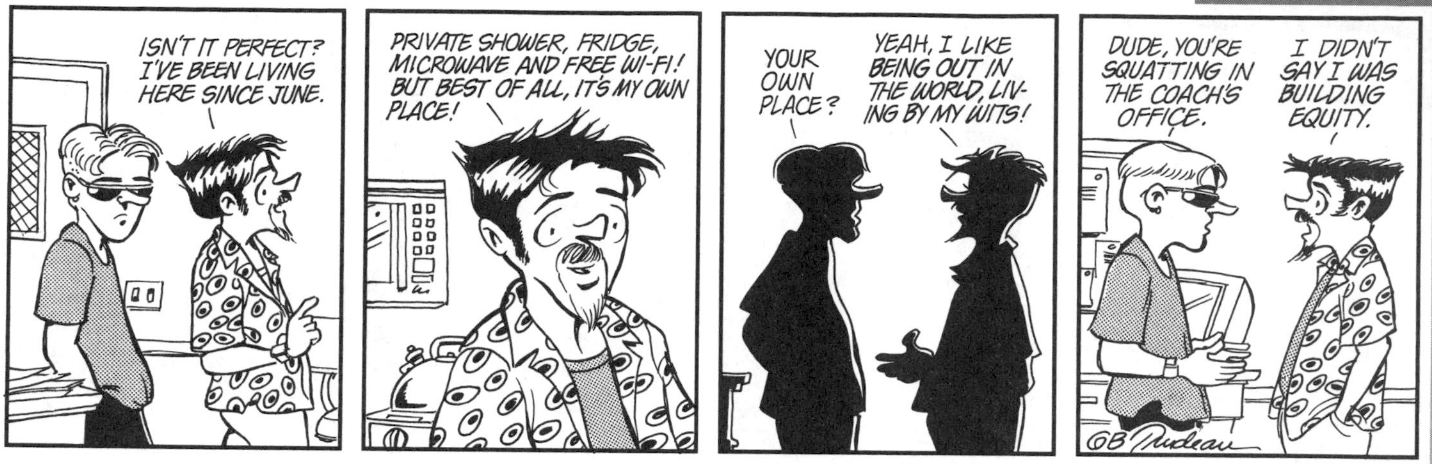
ISN'T IT PERFECT? I'VE BEEN LIVING HERE SINCE JUNE.
PRIVATE SHOWER, FRIDGE, MICROWAVE AND FREE WI-FI! BUT BEST OF ALL, IT'S MY OWN PLACE!
YOUR OWN PLACE?
YEAH, I LIKE BEING OUT IN THE WORLD, LIVING BY MY WITS!
DUDE, YOU'RE SQUATTING IN THE COACH'S OFFICE.
I DIDN'T SAY I WAS BUILDING EQUITY.
©B Trudeau

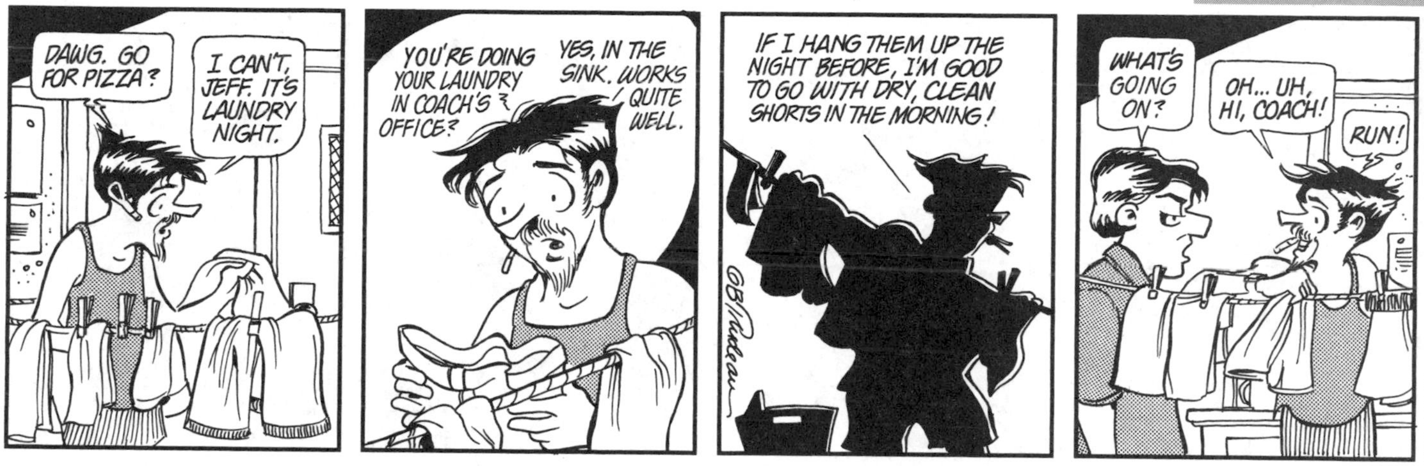
DAWG. GO FOR PIZZA?
I CAN'T, JEFF. IT'S LAUNDRY NIGHT.
YOU'RE DOING YOUR LAUNDRY IN COACH'S OFFICE?
YES, IN THE SINK. WORKS QUITE WELL.
IF I HANG THEM UP THE NIGHT BEFORE, I'M GOOD TO GO WITH DRY, CLEAN SHORTS IN THE MORNING!
©B Trudeau
WHAT'S GOING ON?
OH... UH, HI, COACH!
RUN!

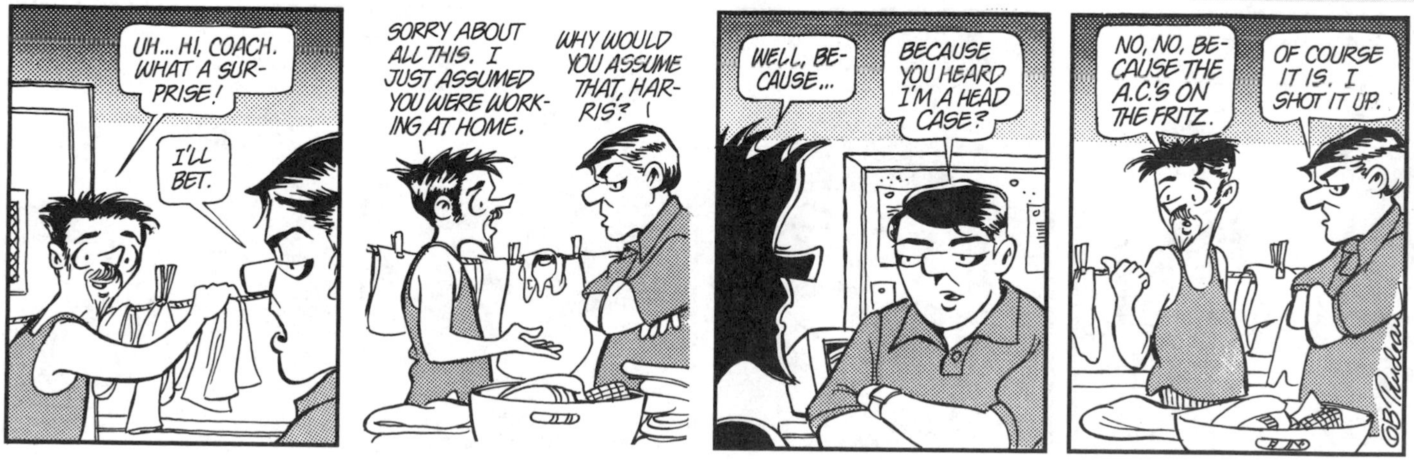
UH... HI, COACH. WHAT A SURPRISE!
I'LL BET.
SORRY ABOUT ALL THIS. I JUST ASSUMED YOU WERE WORKING AT HOME.
WHY WOULD YOU ASSUME THAT, HARRIS?
WELL, BECAUSE...
BECAUSE YOU HEARD I'M A HEAD CASE?
NO, NO, BECAUSE THE A.C.'S ON THE FRITZ.
OF COURSE IT IS. I SHOT IT UP.
©B Trudeau

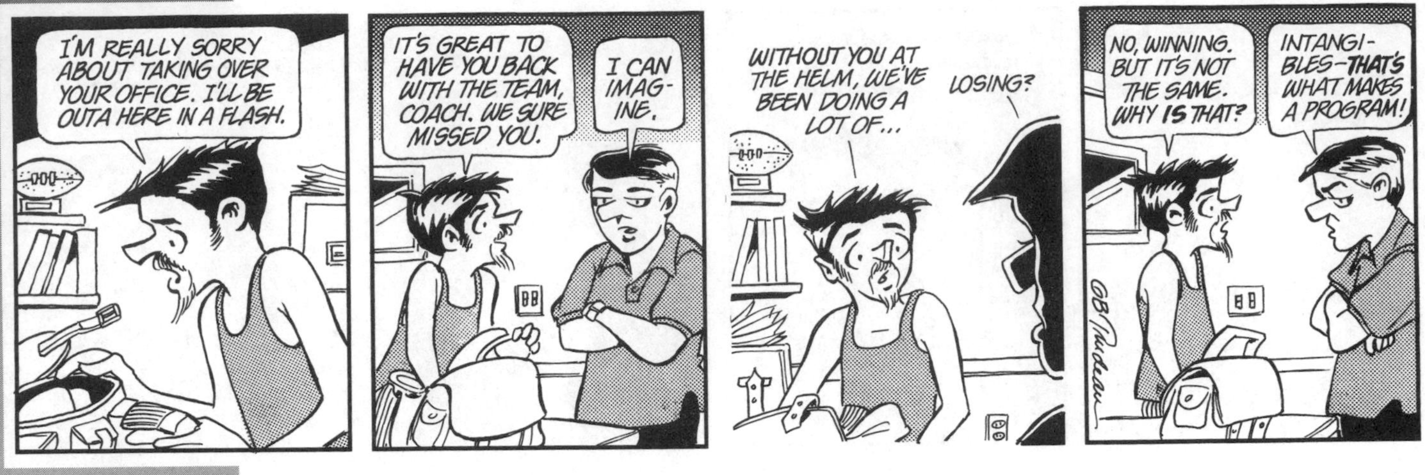
I'M REALLY SORRY ABOUT TAKING OVER YOUR OFFICE. I'LL BE OUTA HERE IN A FLASH.
IT'S GREAT TO HAVE YOU BACK WITH THE TEAM, COACH. WE SURE MISSED YOU.
I CAN IMAGINE.
WITHOUT YOU AT THE HELM, WE'VE BEEN DOING A LOT OF...
LOSING?
NO, WINNING. BUT IT'S NOT THE SAME. WHY **IS** THAT?
INTANGIBLES—**THAT'S** WHAT MAKES A PROGRAM!

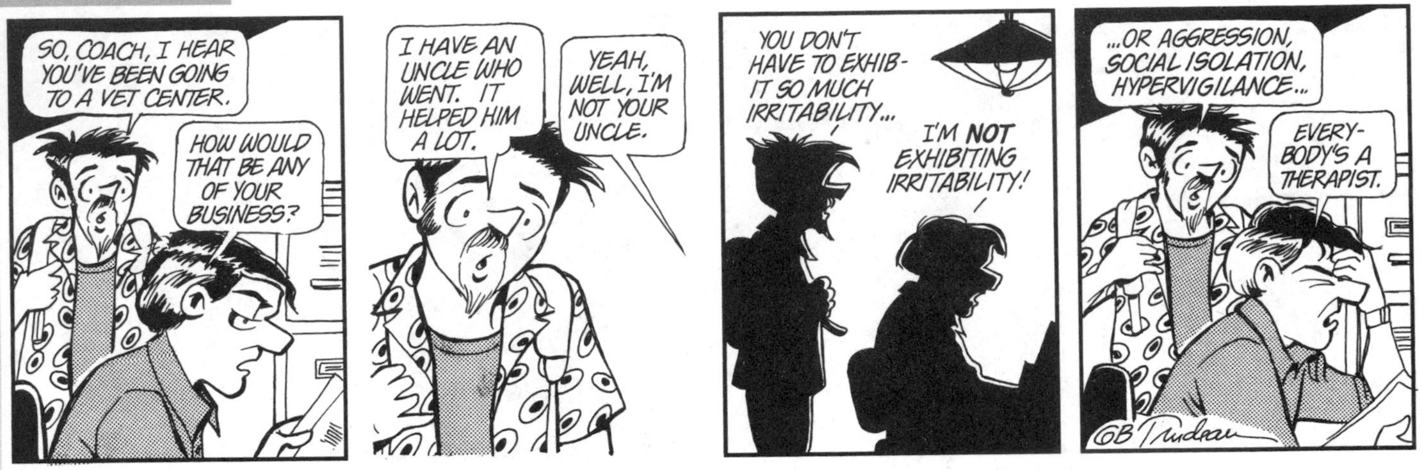
SO, COACH, I HEAR YOU'VE BEEN GOING TO A VET CENTER.
HOW WOULD THAT BE ANY OF YOUR BUSINESS?
I HAVE AN UNCLE WHO WENT. IT HELPED HIM A LOT.
YEAH, WELL, I'M NOT YOUR UNCLE.
YOU DON'T HAVE TO EXHIBIT SO MUCH IRRITABILITY...
I'M **NOT** EXHIBITING IRRITABILITY!
...OR AGGRESSION, SOCIAL ISOLATION, HYPERVIGILANCE...
EVERYBODY'S A THERAPIST.

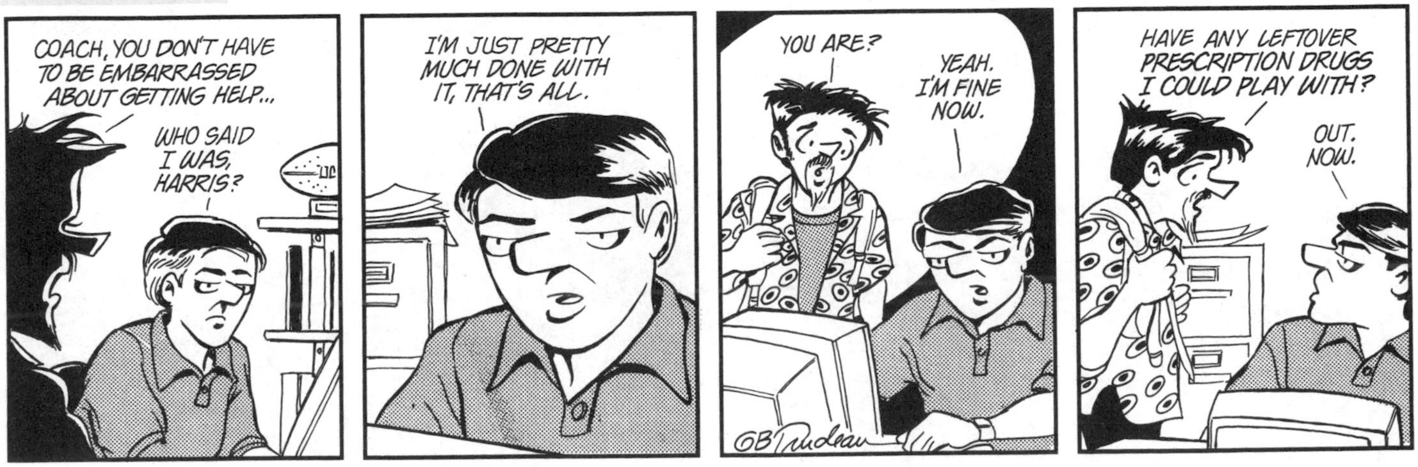
COACH, YOU DON'T HAVE TO BE EMBARRASSED ABOUT GETTING HELP...
WHO SAID I WAS, HARRIS?
I'M JUST PRETTY MUCH DONE WITH IT, THAT'S ALL.
YOU ARE?
YEAH. I'M FINE NOW.
HAVE ANY LEFTOVER PRESCRIPTION DRUGS I COULD PLAY WITH?
OUT. NOW.

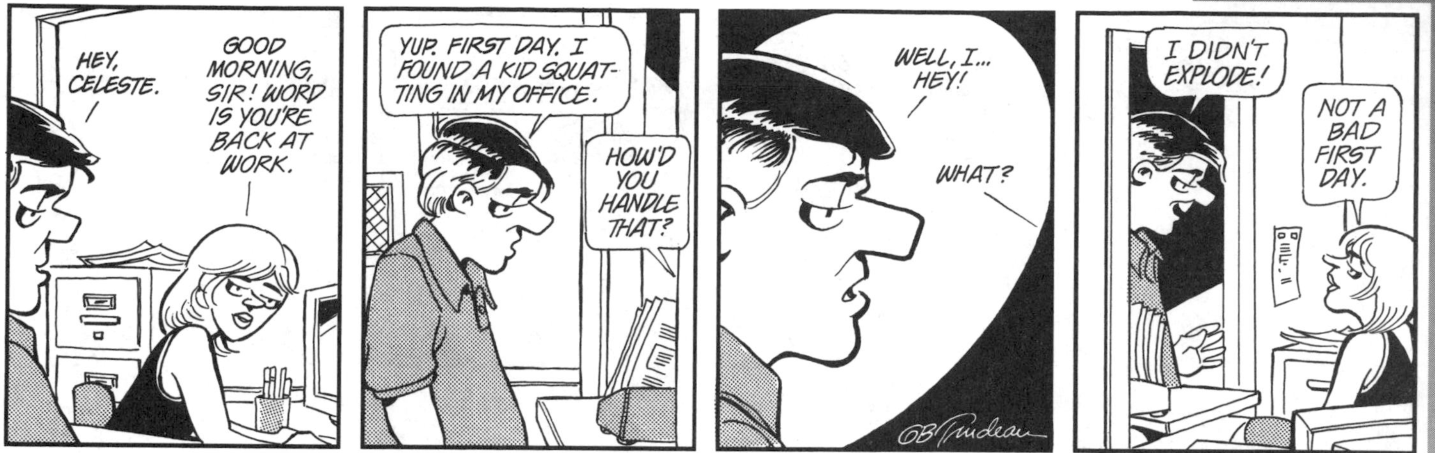
HEY, CELESTE.
GOOD MORNING, SIR! WORD IS YOU'RE BACK AT WORK.
YUP. FIRST DAY. I FOUND A KID SQUATTING IN MY OFFICE.
HOW'D YOU HANDLE THAT?
WELL, I... HEY!
WHAT?
I DIDN'T EXPLODE!
NOT A BAD FIRST DAY.
©B Trudeau

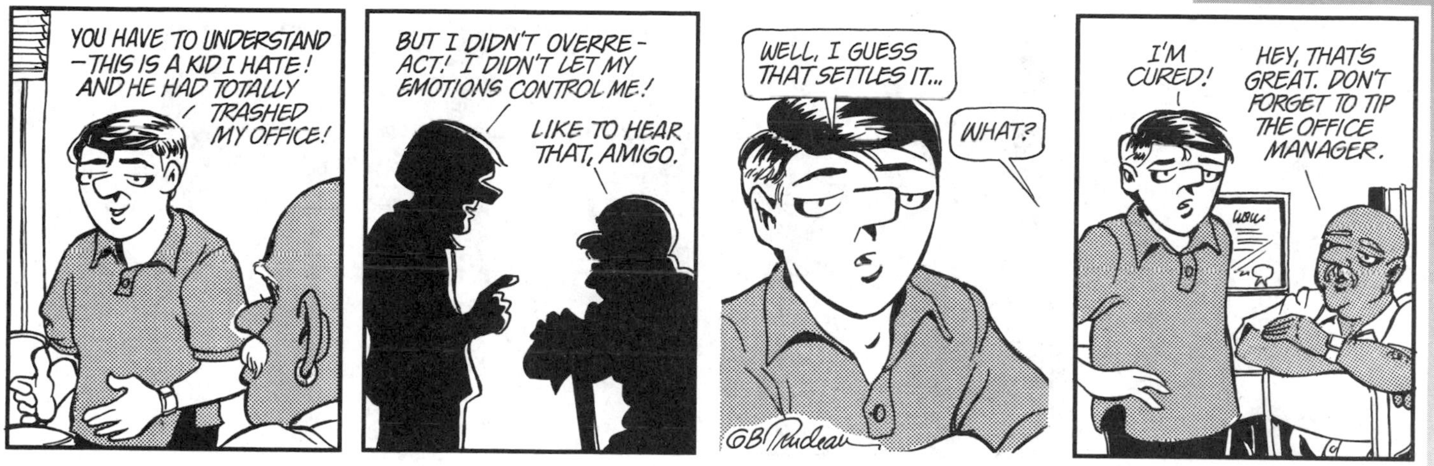
YOU HAVE TO UNDERSTAND—THIS IS A KID I HATE! AND HE HAD TOTALLY TRASHED MY OFFICE!
BUT I DIDN'T OVERREACT! I DIDN'T LET MY EMOTIONS CONTROL ME!
LIKE TO HEAR THAT, AMIGO.
WELL, I GUESS THAT SETTLES IT...
WHAT?
©B Trudeau
I'M CURED!
HEY, THAT'S GREAT. DON'T FORGET TO TIP THE OFFICE MANAGER.

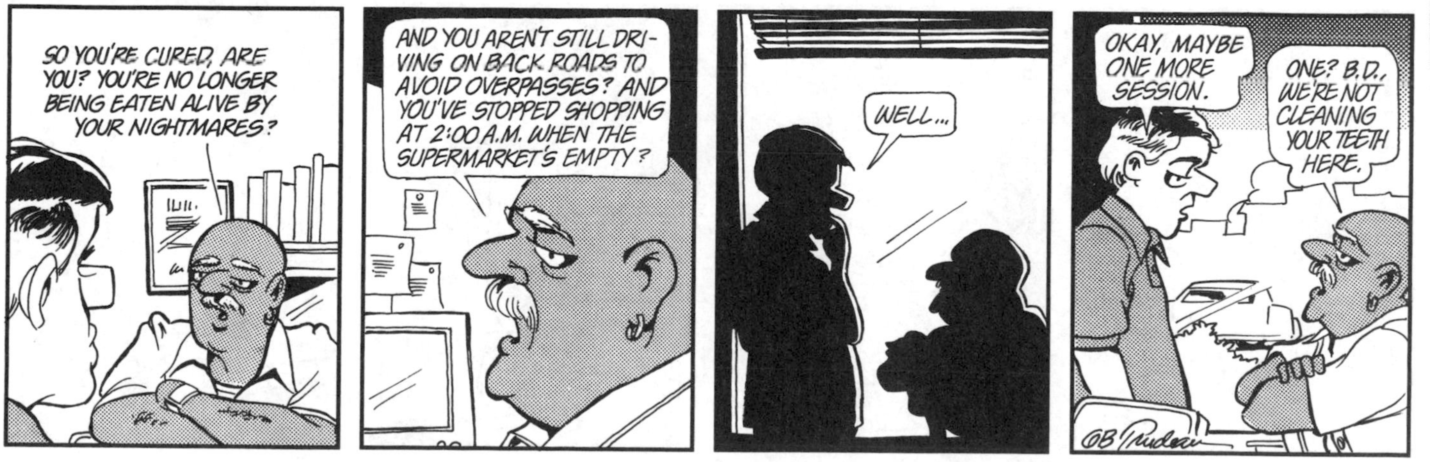
SO YOU'RE CURED, ARE YOU? YOU'RE NO LONGER BEING EATEN ALIVE BY YOUR NIGHTMARES?
AND YOU AREN'T STILL DRIVING ON BACK ROADS TO AVOID OVERPASSES? AND YOU'VE STOPPED SHOPPING AT 2:00 A.M. WHEN THE SUPERMARKET'S EMPTY?
WELL...
OKAY, MAYBE ONE MORE SESSION.
ONE? B.D., WE'RE NOT CLEANING YOUR TEETH HERE.
©B Trudeau

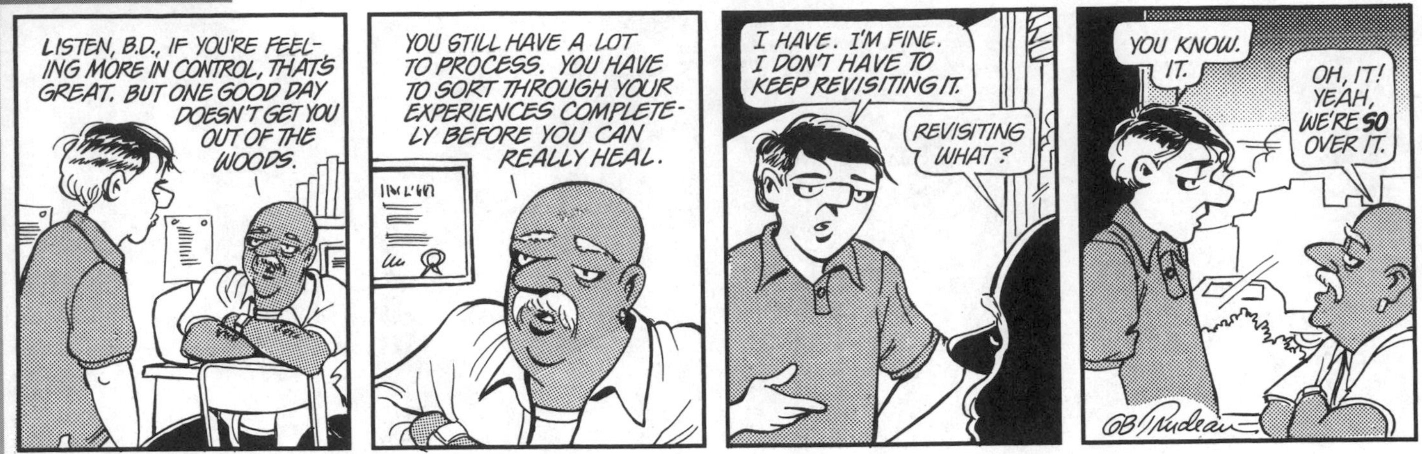

LISTEN, B.D., IF YOU'RE FEELING MORE IN CONTROL, THAT'S GREAT. BUT ONE GOOD DAY DOESN'T GET YOU OUT OF THE WOODS.
YOU STILL HAVE A LOT TO PROCESS. YOU HAVE TO SORT THROUGH YOUR EXPERIENCES COMPLETELY BEFORE YOU CAN REALLY HEAL.
I HAVE. I'M FINE. I DON'T HAVE TO KEEP REVISITING IT.
REVISITING WHAT?
YOU KNOW. IT.
OH, IT! YEAH, WE'RE SO OVER IT.

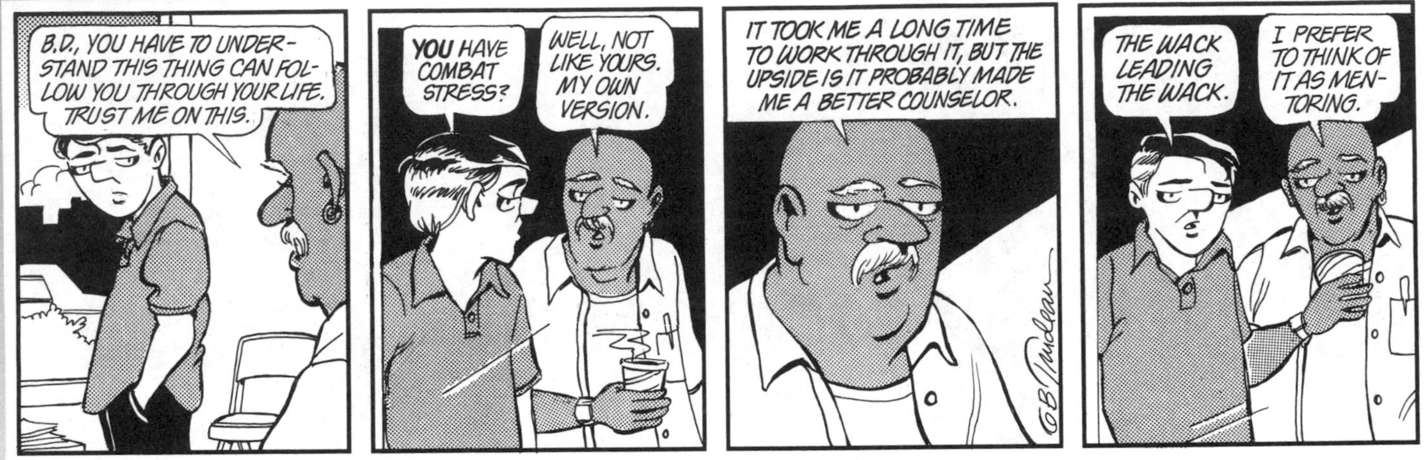

B.D., YOU HAVE TO UNDERSTAND THIS THING CAN FOLLOW YOU THROUGH YOUR LIFE. TRUST ME ON THIS.
YOU HAVE COMBAT STRESS?
WELL, NOT LIKE YOURS. MY OWN VERSION.
IT TOOK ME A LONG TIME TO WORK THROUGH IT, BUT THE UPSIDE IS IT PROBABLY MADE ME A BETTER COUNSELOR.
THE WACK LEADING THE WACK.
I PREFER TO THINK OF IT AS MENTORING.

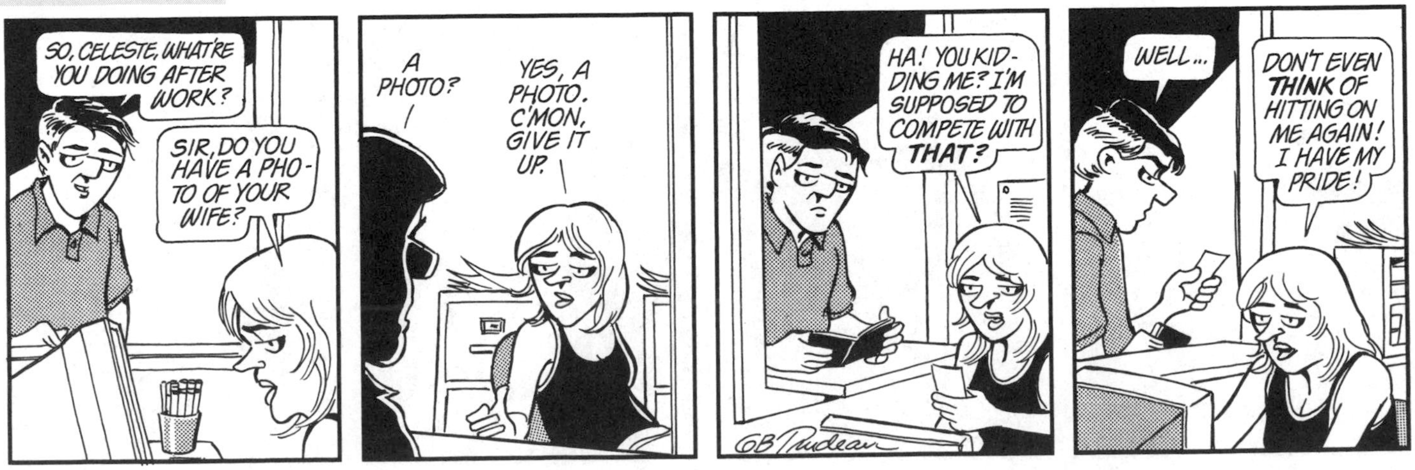

SO, CELESTE, WHAT'RE YOU DOING AFTER WORK?
SIR, DO YOU HAVE A PHOTO OF YOUR WIFE?
A PHOTO?
YES, A PHOTO. C'MON, GIVE IT UP.
HA! YOU KIDDING ME? I'M SUPPOSED TO COMPETE WITH THAT?
WELL...
DON'T EVEN THINK OF HITTING ON ME AGAIN! I HAVE MY PRIDE!

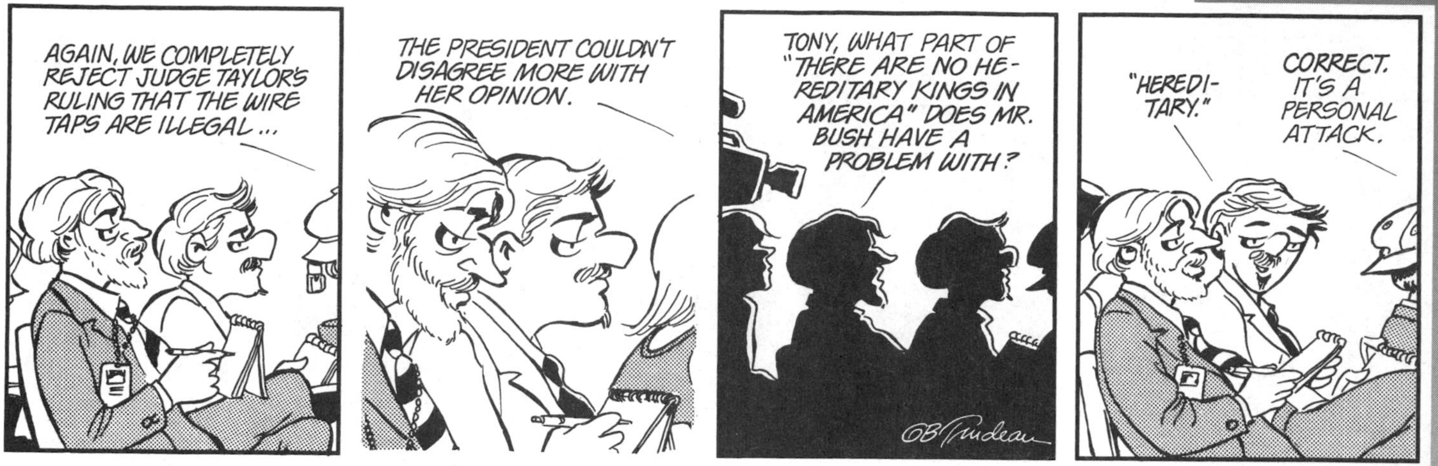
AGAIN, WE COMPLETELY REJECT JUDGE TAYLOR'S RULING THAT THE WIRE TAPS ARE ILLEGAL ...
THE PRESIDENT COULDN'T DISAGREE MORE WITH HER OPINION.
TONY, WHAT PART OF "THERE ARE NO HEREDITARY KINGS IN AMERICA" DOES MR. BUSH HAVE A PROBLEM WITH?
"HEREDITARY."
CORRECT. IT'S A PERSONAL ATTACK.

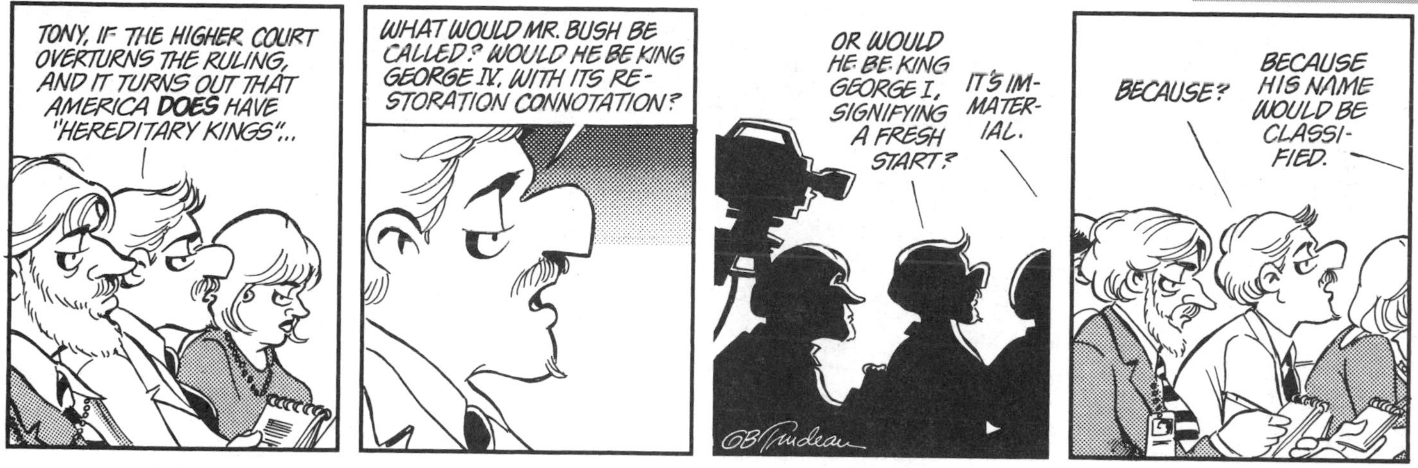
TONY, IF THE HIGHER COURT OVERTURNS THE RULING, AND IT TURNS OUT THAT AMERICA DOES HAVE "HEREDITARY KINGS"...
WHAT WOULD MR. BUSH BE CALLED? WOULD HE BE KING GEORGE IV, WITH ITS RESTORATION CONNOTATION?
OR WOULD HE BE KING GEORGE I, SIGNIFYING A FRESH START?
IT'S IMMATERIAL.
BECAUSE?
BECAUSE HIS NAME WOULD BE CLASSIFIED.

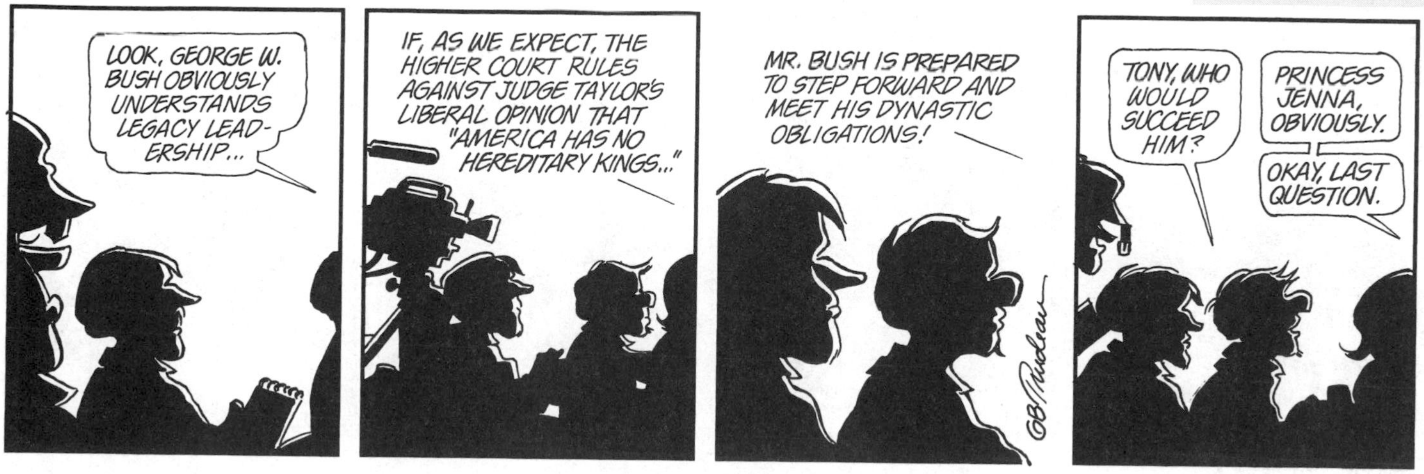
LOOK, GEORGE W. BUSH OBVIOUSLY UNDERSTANDS LEGACY LEADERSHIP...
IF, AS WE EXPECT, THE HIGHER COURT RULES AGAINST JUDGE TAYLOR'S LIBERAL OPINION THAT "AMERICA HAS NO HEREDITARY KINGS..."
MR. BUSH IS PREPARED TO STEP FORWARD AND MEET HIS DYNASTIC OBLIGATIONS!
TONY, WHO WOULD SUCCEED HIM?
PRINCESS JENNA, OBVIOUSLY.
OKAY, LAST QUESTION.

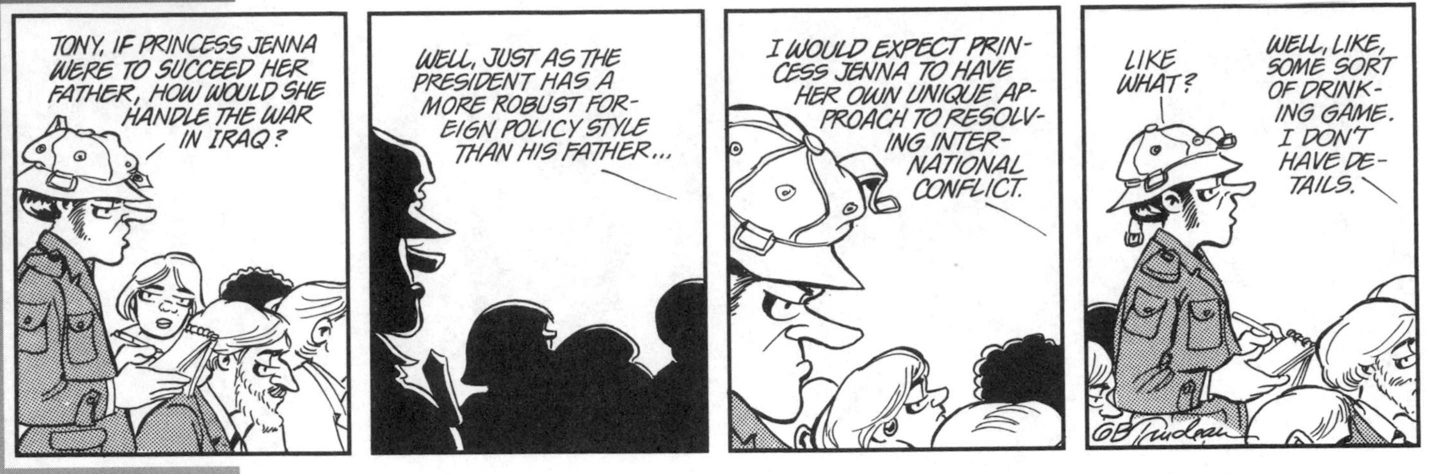
TONY, IF PRINCESS JENNA WERE TO SUCCEED HER FATHER, HOW WOULD SHE HANDLE THE WAR IN IRAQ?
WELL, JUST AS THE PRESIDENT HAS A MORE ROBUST FOREIGN POLICY STYLE THAN HIS FATHER...
I WOULD EXPECT PRINCESS JENNA TO HAVE HER OWN UNIQUE APPROACH TO RESOLVING INTERNATIONAL CONFLICT.
LIKE WHAT?
WELL, LIKE, SOME SORT OF DRINKING GAME. I DON'T HAVE DETAILS.
GB Trudeau

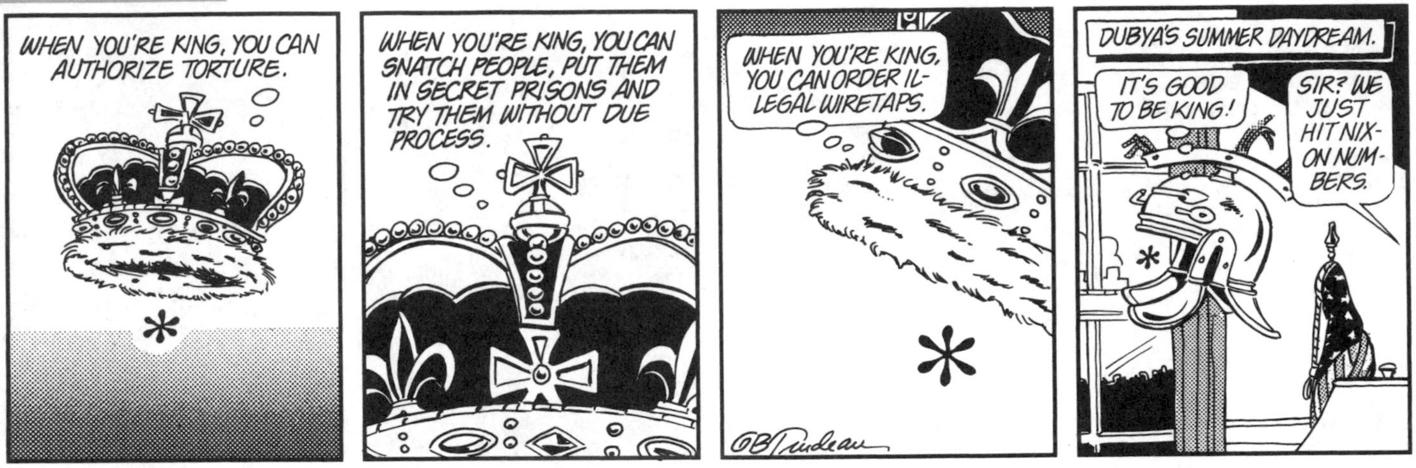
WHEN YOU'RE KING, YOU CAN AUTHORIZE TORTURE.
WHEN YOU'RE KING, YOU CAN SNATCH PEOPLE, PUT THEM IN SECRET PRISONS AND TRY THEM WITHOUT DUE PROCESS.
WHEN YOU'RE KING, YOU CAN ORDER ILLEGAL WIRETAPS.
GB Trudeau
DUBYA'S SUMMER DAYDREAM.
IT'S GOOD TO BE KING!
SIR? WE JUST HIT NIXON NUMBERS.

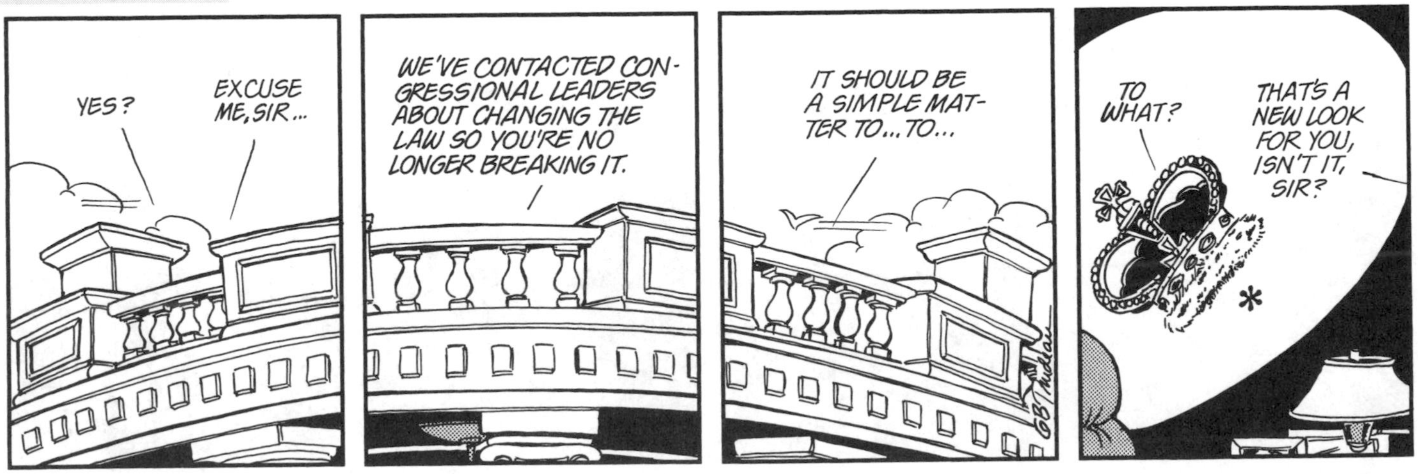
YES?
EXCUSE ME, SIR...
WE'VE CONTACTED CONGRESSIONAL LEADERS ABOUT CHANGING THE LAW SO YOU'RE NO LONGER BREAKING IT.
IT SHOULD BE A SIMPLE MATTER TO... TO...
GB Trudeau
TO WHAT?
THAT'S A NEW LOOK FOR YOU, ISN'T IT, SIR?

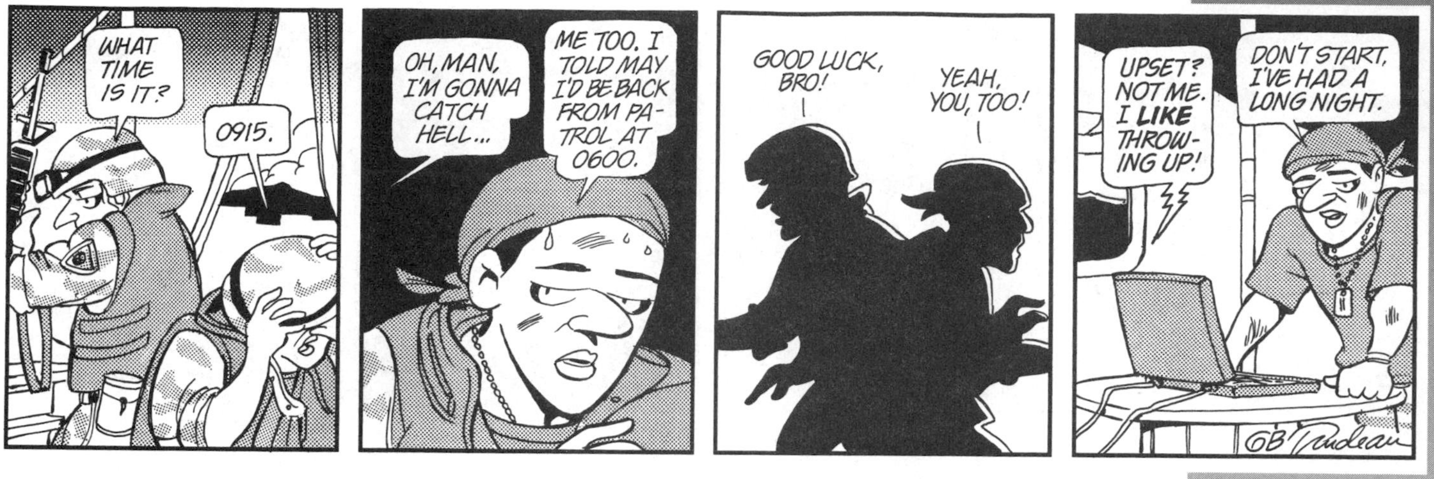
WHAT TIME IS IT?
0915.
OH, MAN, I'M GONNA CATCH HELL...
ME TOO. I TOLD MAY I'D BE BACK FROM PATROL AT 0600.
GOOD LUCK, BRO!
YEAH, YOU, TOO!
UPSET? NOT ME. I **LIKE** THROWING UP!
DON'T START, I'VE HAD A LONG NIGHT.
©B Trudeau

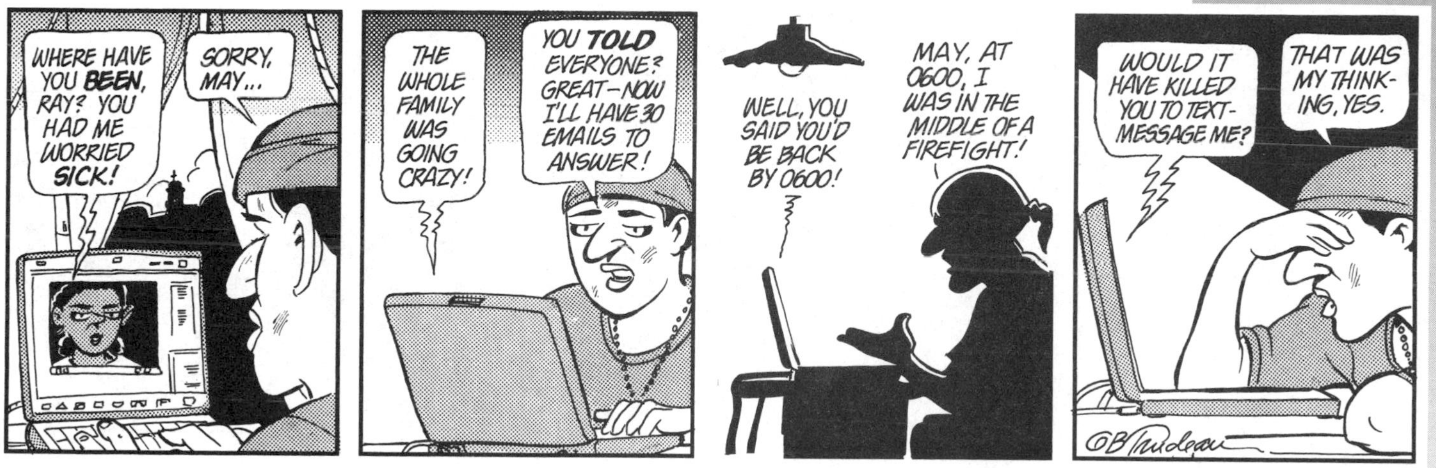
WHERE HAVE YOU **BEEN**, RAY? YOU HAD ME WORRIED **SICK**!
SORRY, MAY...
THE WHOLE FAMILY WAS GOING CRAZY!
YOU **TOLD** EVERYONE? GREAT—NOW I'LL HAVE 30 EMAILS TO ANSWER!
WELL, YOU SAID YOU'D BE BACK BY 0600!
MAY, AT 0600, I WAS IN THE MIDDLE OF A FIREFIGHT!
WOULD IT HAVE KILLED YOU TO TEXT-MESSAGE ME?
THAT WAS MY THINKING, YES.
©B Trudeau

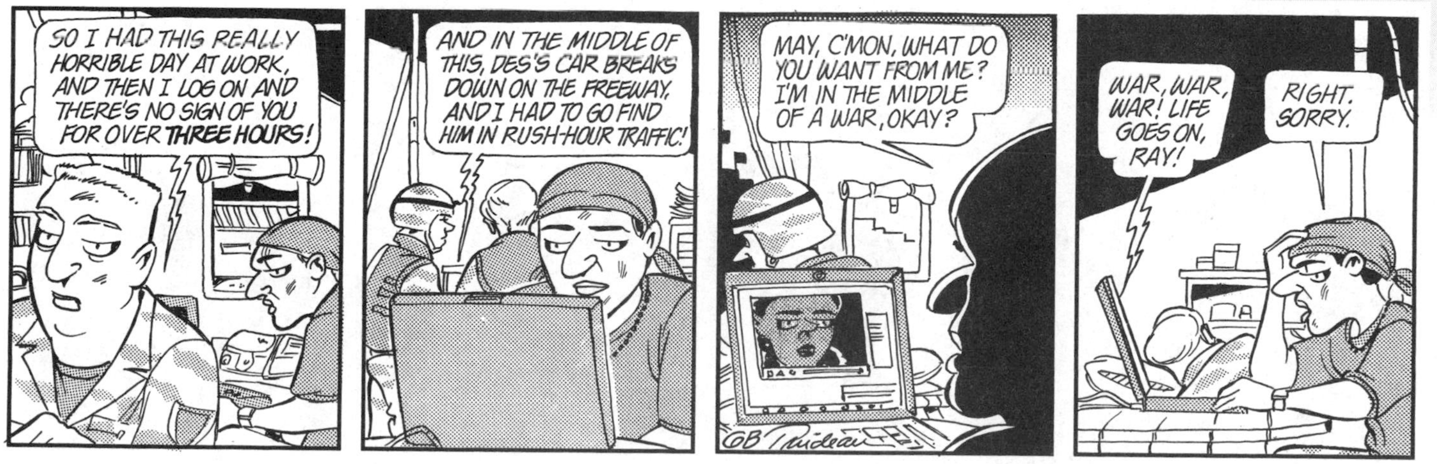
SO I HAD THIS REALLY HORRIBLE DAY AT WORK, AND THEN I LOG ON AND THERE'S NO SIGN OF YOU FOR OVER **THREE HOURS**!
AND IN THE MIDDLE OF THIS, DES'S CAR BREAKS DOWN ON THE FREEWAY, AND I HAD TO GO FIND HIM IN RUSH-HOUR TRAFFIC!
MAY, C'MON, WHAT DO YOU WANT FROM ME? I'M IN THE MIDDLE OF A WAR, OKAY?
WAR, WAR, WAR! LIFE GOES ON, RAY!
RIGHT. SORRY.
©B Trudeau

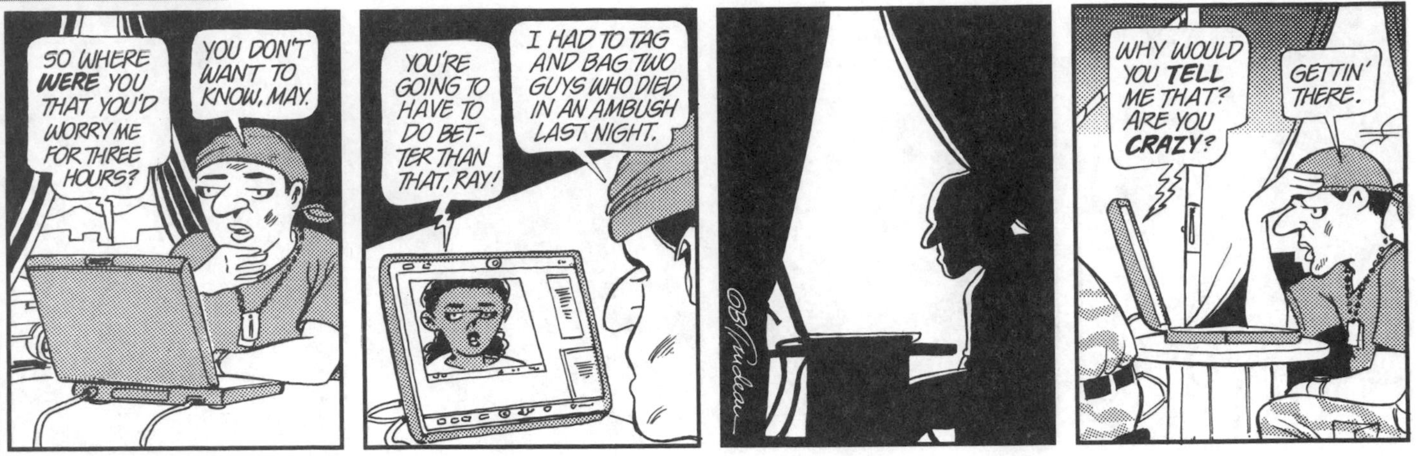
SO WHERE WERE YOU THAT YOU'D WORRY ME FOR THREE HOURS?
YOU DON'T WANT TO KNOW, MAY.
YOU'RE GOING TO HAVE TO DO BETTER THAN THAT, RAY!
I HAD TO TAG AND BAG TWO GUYS WHO DIED IN AN AMBUSH LAST NIGHT.
WHY WOULD YOU TELL ME THAT? ARE YOU CRAZY?
GETTIN' THERE.

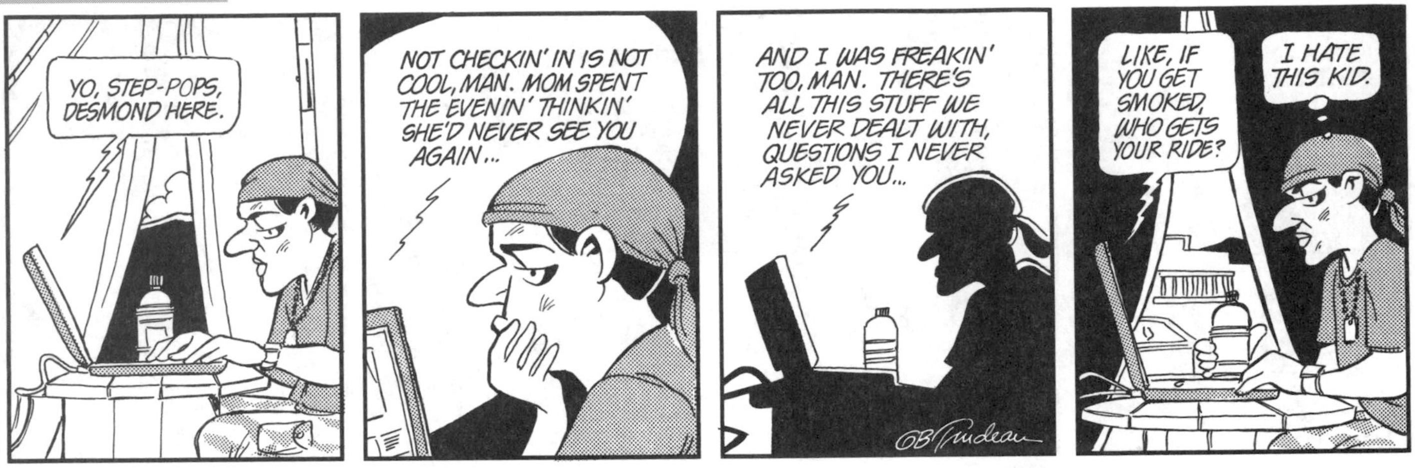
YO, STEP-POPS, DESMOND HERE.
NOT CHECKIN' IN IS NOT COOL, MAN. MOM SPENT THE EVENIN' THINKIN' SHE'D NEVER SEE YOU AGAIN...
AND I WAS FREAKIN' TOO, MAN. THERE'S ALL THIS STUFF WE NEVER DEALT WITH, QUESTIONS I NEVER ASKED YOU...
LIKE, IF YOU GET SMOKED, WHO GETS YOUR RIDE?
I HATE THIS KID.

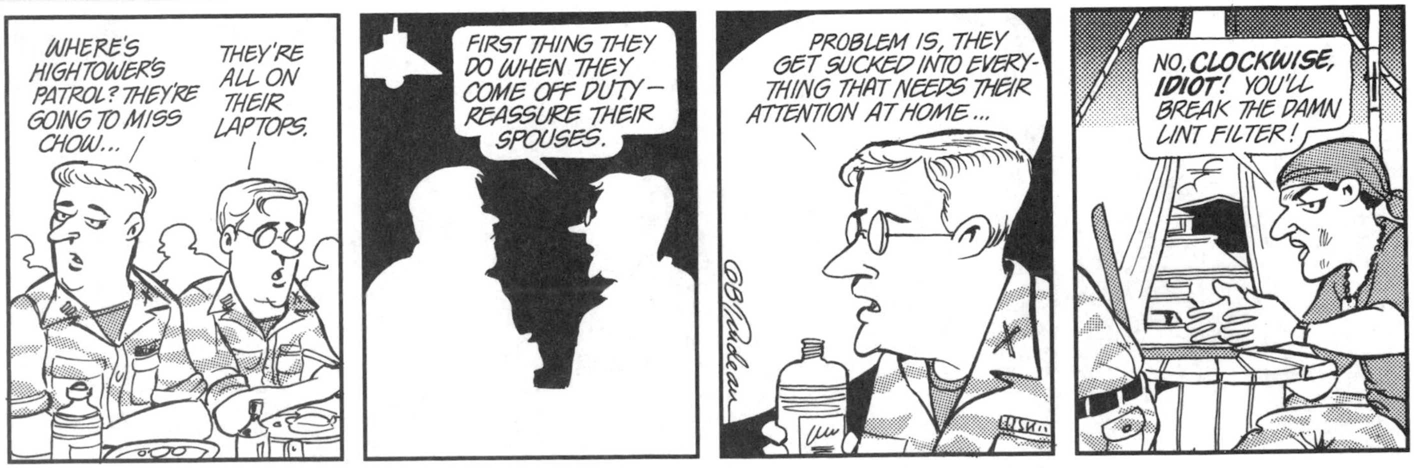
WHERE'S HIGHTOWER'S PATROL? THEY'RE GOING TO MISS CHOW...
THEY'RE ALL ON THEIR LAPTOPS.
FIRST THING THEY DO WHEN THEY COME OFF DUTY — REASSURE THEIR SPOUSES.
PROBLEM IS, THEY GET SUCKED INTO EVERYTHING THAT NEEDS THEIR ATTENTION AT HOME...
NO, CLOCKWISE, IDIOT! YOU'LL BREAK THE DAMN LINT FILTER!

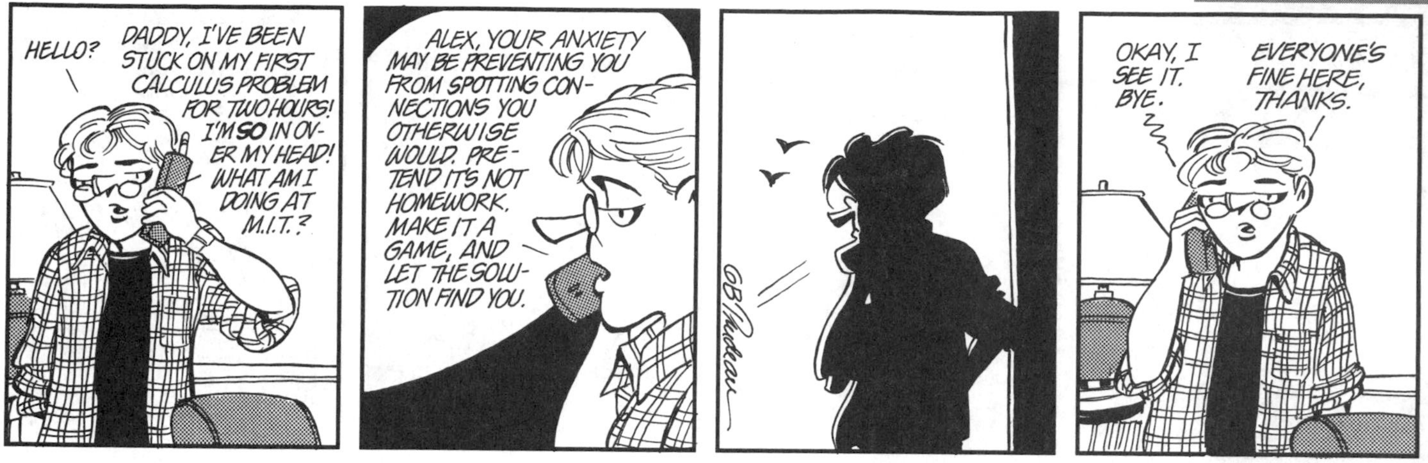
HELLO?
DADDY, I'VE BEEN STUCK ON MY FIRST CALCULUS PROBLEM FOR TWO HOURS! I'M SO IN OVER MY HEAD! WHAT AM I DOING AT M.I.T.?
ALEX, YOUR ANXIETY MAY BE PREVENTING YOU FROM SPOTTING CONNECTIONS YOU OTHERWISE WOULD. PRETEND IT'S NOT HOMEWORK. MAKE IT A GAME, AND LET THE SOLUTION FIND YOU.
OKAY, I SEE IT. BYE.
EVERYONE'S FINE HERE, THANKS.

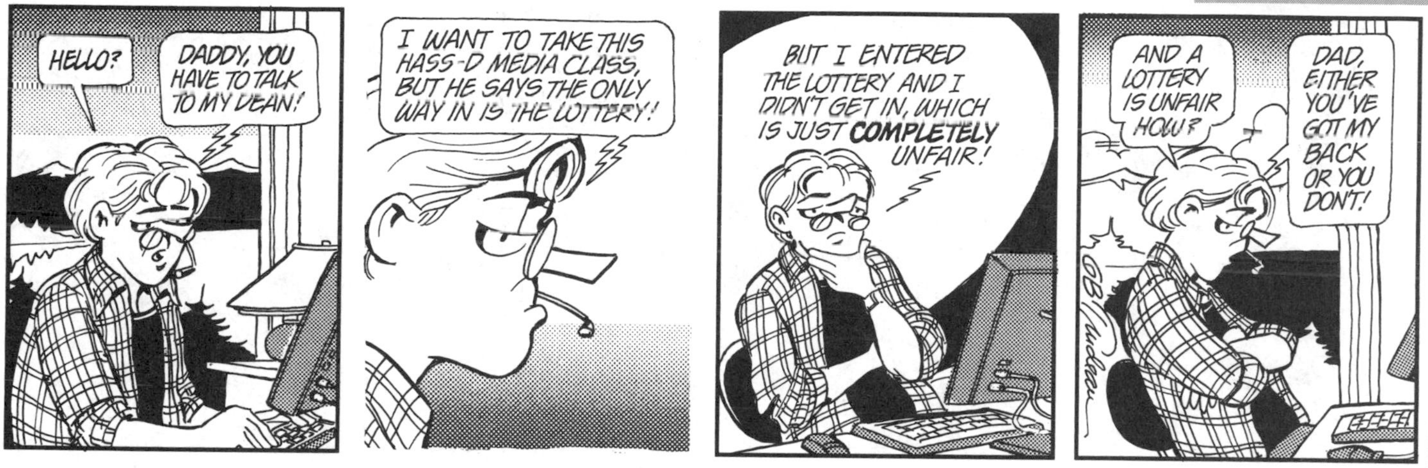
HELLO?
DADDY, YOU HAVE TO TALK TO MY DEAN!
I WANT TO TAKE THIS HASS-D MEDIA CLASS, BUT HE SAYS THE ONLY WAY IN IS THE LOTTERY!
BUT I ENTERED THE LOTTERY AND I DIDN'T GET IN, WHICH IS JUST COMPLETELY UNFAIR!
AND A LOTTERY IS UNFAIR HOW?
DAD, EITHER YOU'VE GOT MY BACK OR YOU DON'T!

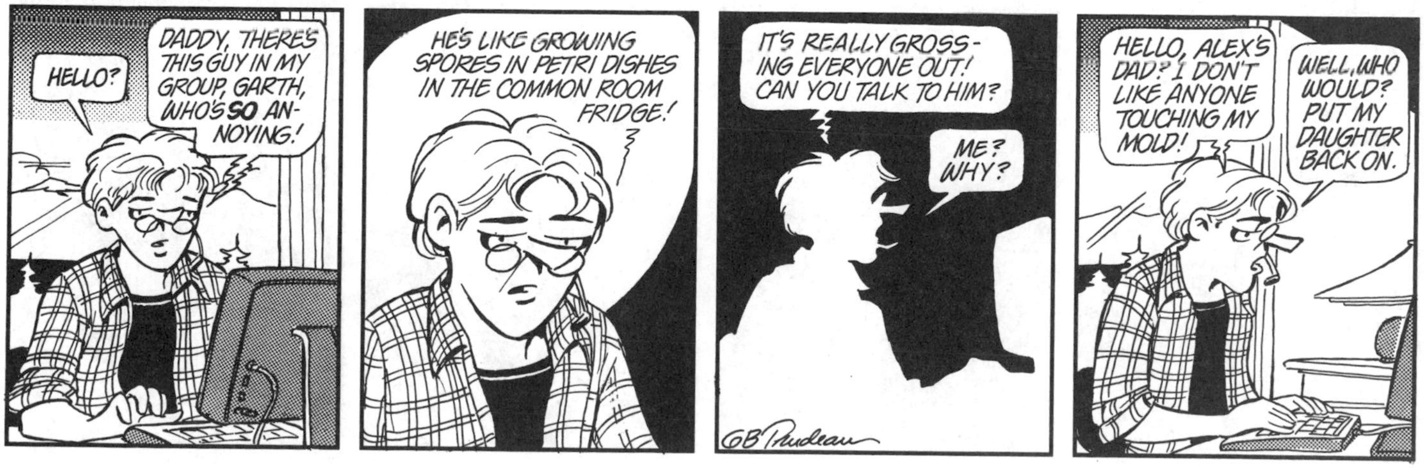
HELLO?
DADDY, THERE'S THIS GUY IN MY GROUP, GARTH, WHO'S SO ANNOYING!
HE'S LIKE GROWING SPORES IN PETRI DISHES IN THE COMMON ROOM FRIDGE!
IT'S REALLY GROSSING EVERYONE OUT! CAN YOU TALK TO HIM?
ME? WHY?
HELLO, ALEX'S DAD? I DON'T LIKE ANYONE TOUCHING MY MOLD!
WELL, WHO WOULD? PUT MY DAUGHTER BACK ON.

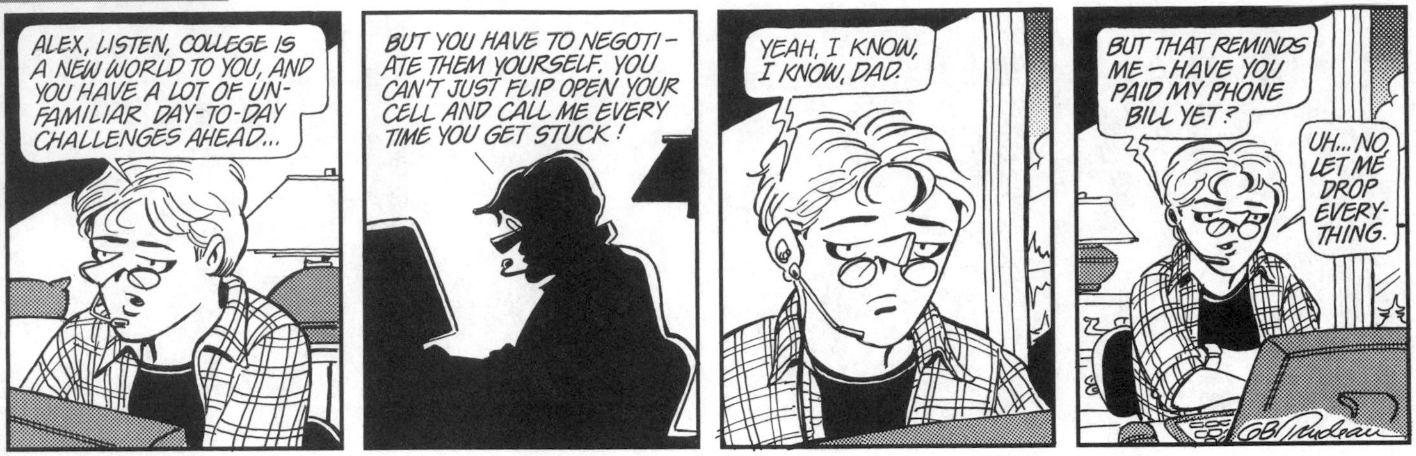
ALEX, LISTEN, COLLEGE IS A NEW WORLD TO YOU, AND YOU HAVE A LOT OF UN-FAMILIAR DAY-TO-DAY CHALLENGES AHEAD...
BUT YOU HAVE TO NEGOTI-ATE THEM YOURSELF. YOU CAN'T JUST FLIP OPEN YOUR CELL AND CALL ME EVERY TIME YOU GET STUCK!
YEAH, I KNOW, I KNOW, DAD.
BUT THAT REMINDS ME – HAVE YOU PAID MY PHONE BILL YET?
UH... NO, LET ME DROP EVERY-THING.

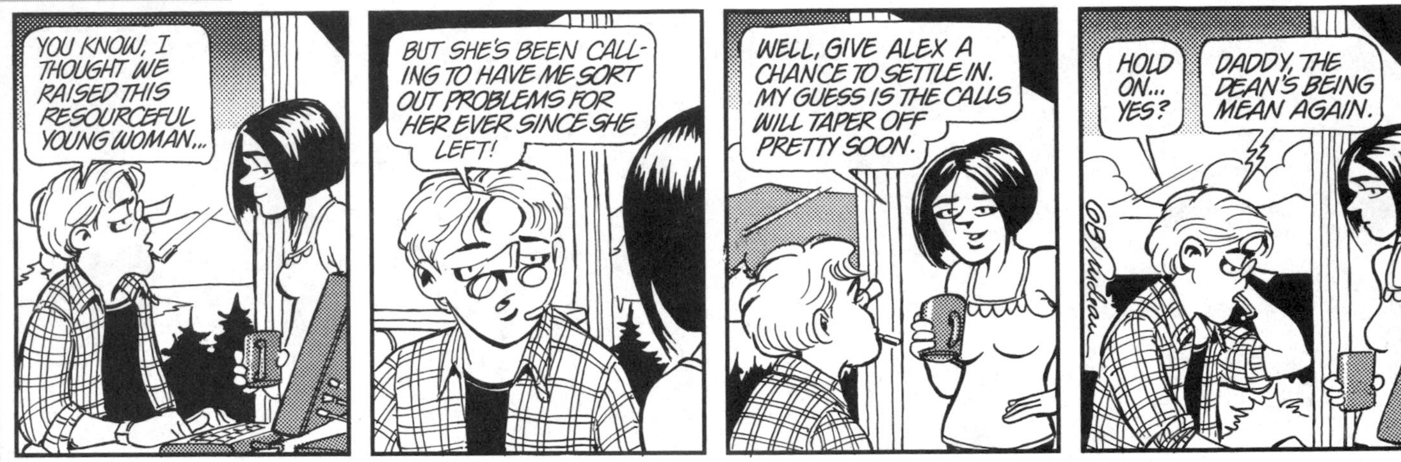
YOU KNOW, I THOUGHT WE RAISED THIS RESOURCEFUL YOUNG WOMAN...
BUT SHE'S BEEN CALL-ING TO HAVE ME SORT OUT PROBLEMS FOR HER EVER SINCE SHE LEFT!
WELL, GIVE ALEX A CHANCE TO SETTLE IN. MY GUESS IS THE CALLS WILL TAPER OFF PRETTY SOON.
HOLD ON... YES?
DADDY, THE DEAN'S BEING MEAN AGAIN.

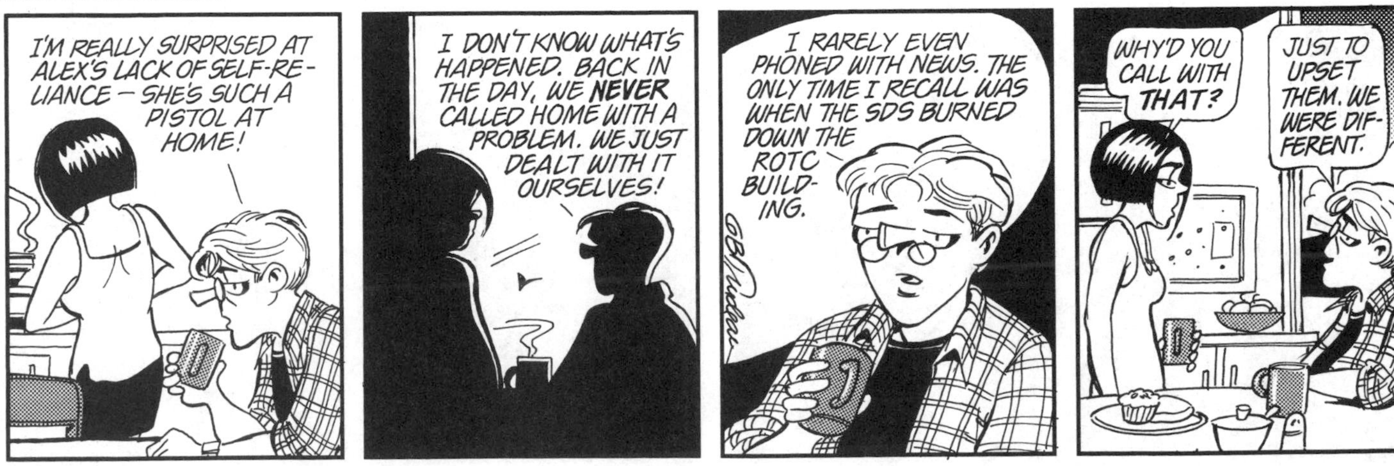
I'M REALLY SURPRISED AT ALEX'S LACK OF SELF-RE-LIANCE – SHE'S SUCH A PISTOL AT HOME!
I DON'T KNOW WHAT'S HAPPENED. BACK IN THE DAY, WE NEVER CALLED HOME WITH A PROBLEM. WE JUST DEALT WITH IT OURSELVES!
I RARELY EVEN PHONED WITH NEWS. THE ONLY TIME I RECALL WAS WHEN THE SDS BURNED DOWN THE ROTC BUILD-ING.
WHY'D YOU CALL WITH THAT?
JUST TO UPSET THEM. WE WERE DIF-FERENT.

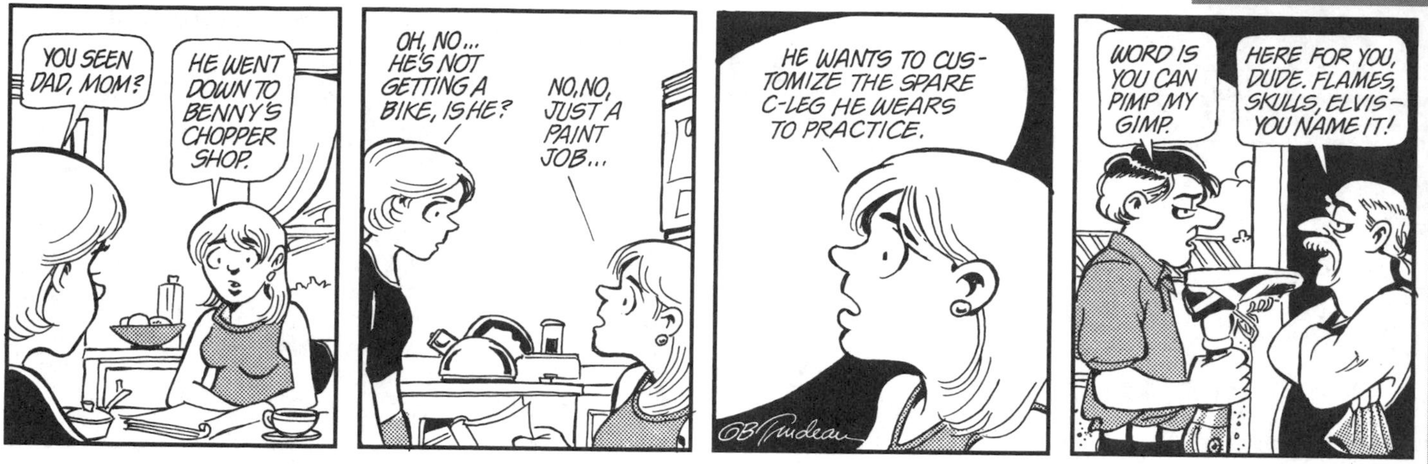
YOU SEEN DAD, MOM?
HE WENT DOWN TO BENNY'S CHOPPER SHOP.
OH, NO... HE'S NOT GETTING A BIKE, IS HE?
NO, NO, JUST A PAINT JOB...
HE WANTS TO CUS- TOMIZE THE SPARE C-LEG HE WEARS TO PRACTICE.
WORD IS YOU CAN PIMP MY GIMP.
HERE FOR YOU, DUDE. FLAMES, SKULLS, ELVIS- YOU NAME IT!

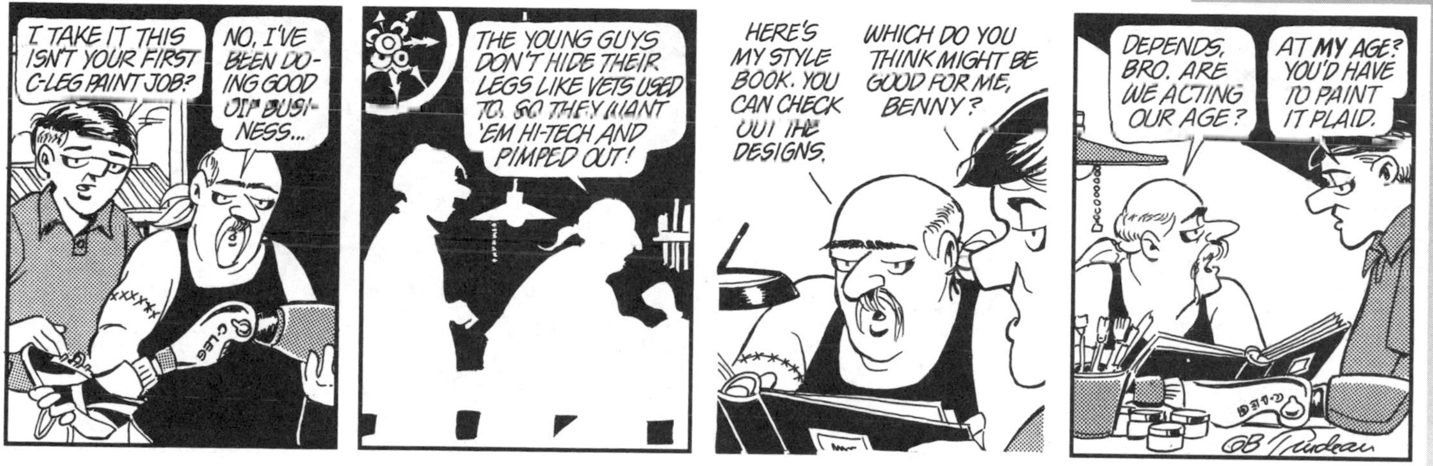
I TAKE IT THIS ISN'T YOUR FIRST C-LEG PAINT JOB?
NO, I'VE BEEN DO- ING GOOD OL' BUSI- NESS...
THE YOUNG GUYS DON'T HIDE THEIR LEGS LIKE VETS USED TO, SO THEY WANT 'EM HI-TECH AND PIMPED OUT!
HERE'S MY STYLE BOOK. YOU CAN CHECK OUT THE DESIGNS.
WHICH DO YOU THINK MIGHT BE GOOD FOR ME, BENNY?
DEPENDS, BRO. ARE WE ACTING OUR AGE?
AT MY AGE? YOU'D HAVE TO PAINT IT PLAID.

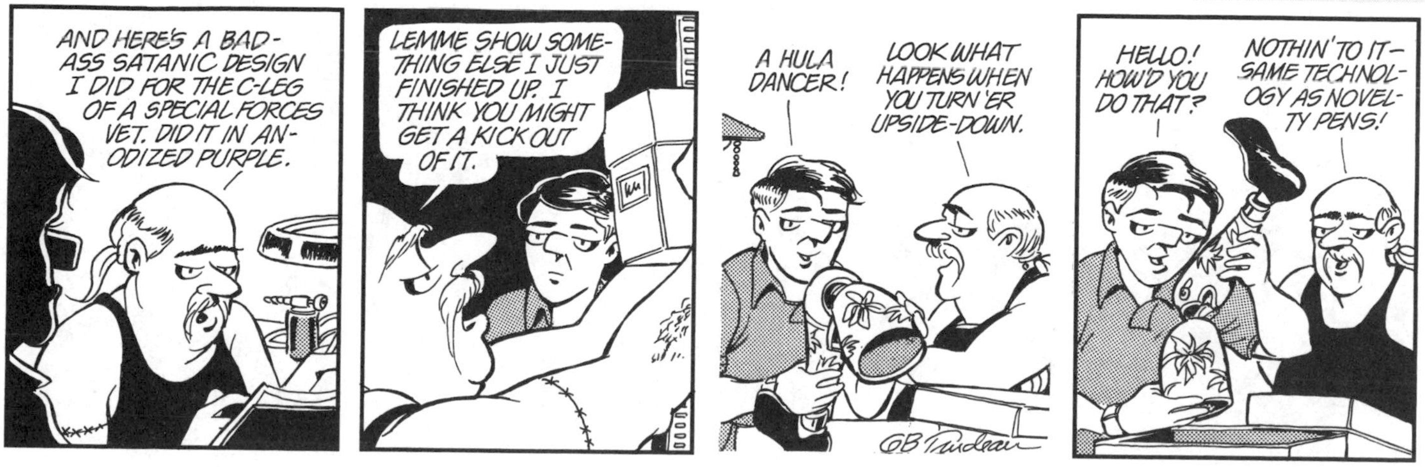
AND HERE'S A BAD- ASS SATANIC DESIGN I DID FOR THE C-LEG OF A SPECIAL FORCES VET. DID IT IN AN- ODIZED PURPLE.
LEMME SHOW SOME- THING ELSE I JUST FINISHED UP. I THINK YOU MIGHT GET A KICK OUT OF IT.
A HULA DANCER!
LOOK WHAT HAPPENS WHEN YOU TURN 'ER UPSIDE-DOWN.
HELLO! HOW'D YOU DO THAT?
NOTHIN' TO IT- SAME TECHNOL- OGY AS NOVEL- TY PENS!

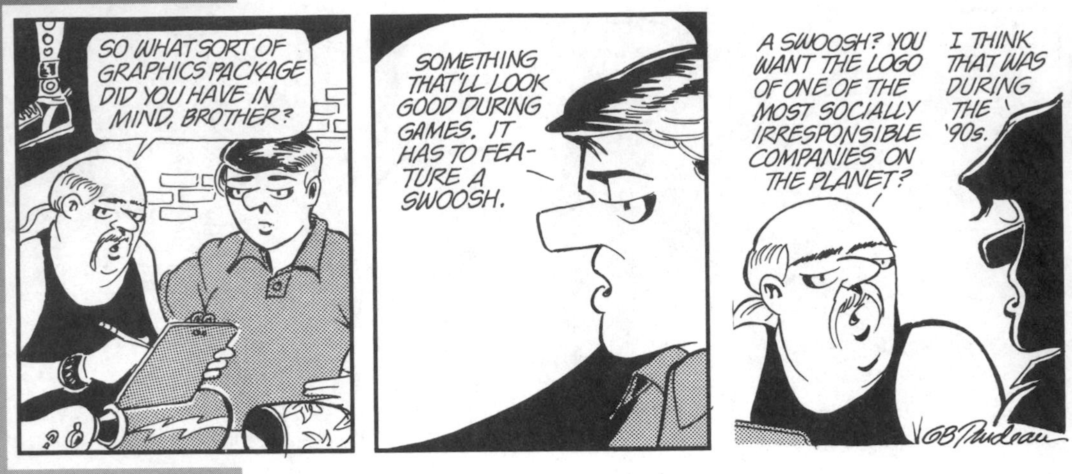
SO WHAT SORT OF GRAPHICS PACKAGE DID YOU HAVE IN MIND, BROTHER?
SOMETHING THAT'LL LOOK GOOD DURING GAMES. IT HAS TO FEATURE A SWOOSH.
A SWOOSH? YOU WANT THE LOGO OF ONE OF THE MOST SOCIALLY IRRESPONSIBLE COMPANIES ON THE PLANET?
I THINK THAT WAS DURING THE '90s.
OH, OKAY. TEAL, GOLD OR PURPLE?
TEAL WITH MAGNESIUM TRIM.

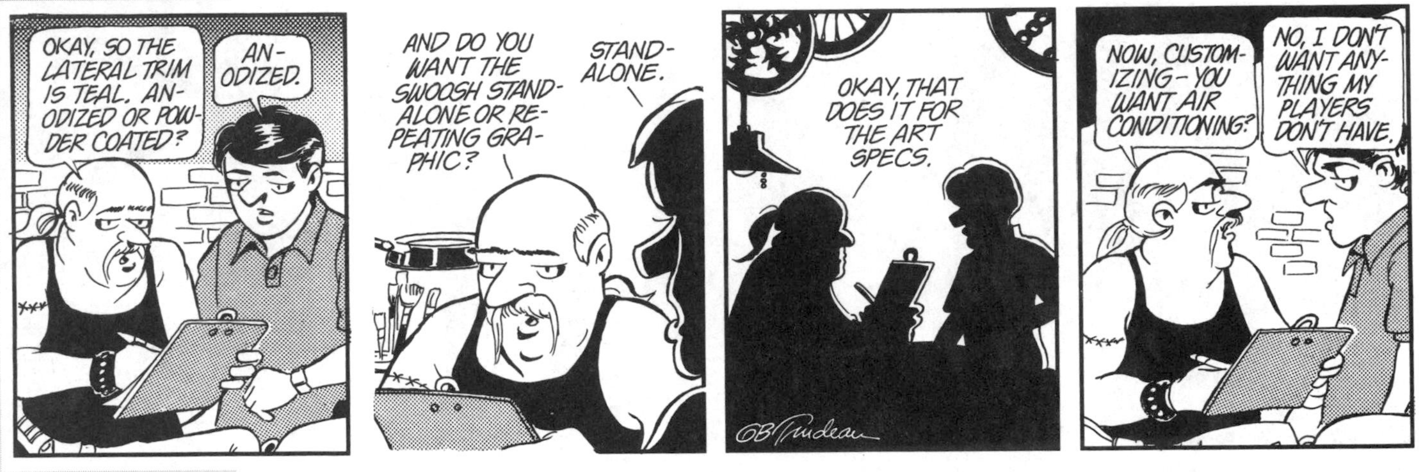
OKAY, SO THE LATERAL TRIM IS TEAL. ANODIZED OR POWDER COATED?
ANODIZED.
AND DO YOU WANT THE SWOOSH STAND-ALONE OR REPEATING GRAPHIC?
STAND-ALONE.
OKAY, THAT DOES IT FOR THE ART SPECS.
NOW, CUSTOMIZING – YOU WANT AIR CONDITIONING?
NO, I DON'T WANT ANYTHING MY PLAYERS DON'T HAVE.

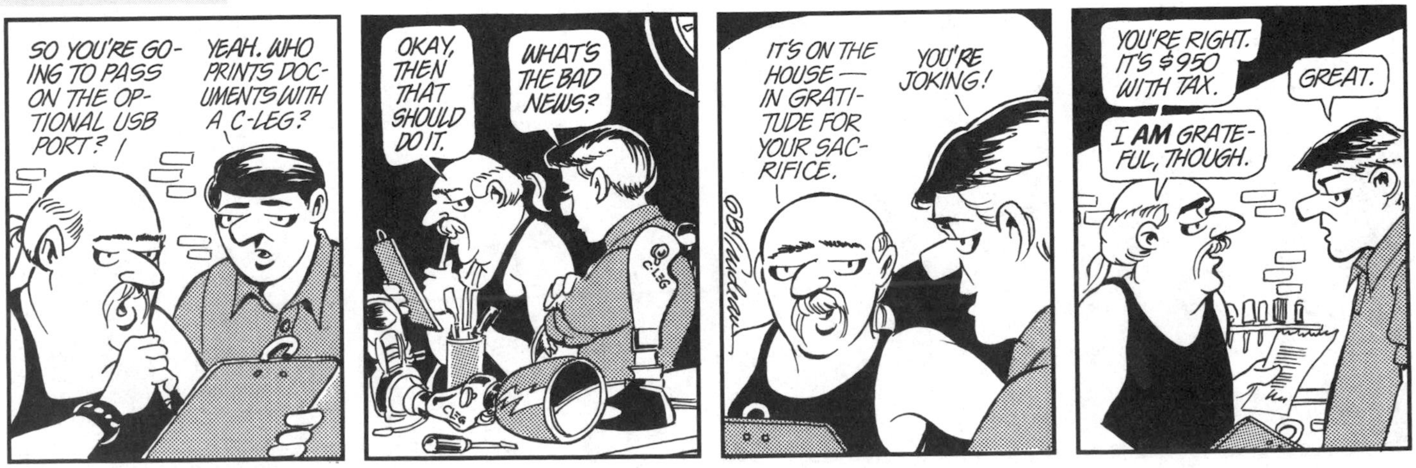
SO YOU'RE GOING TO PASS ON THE OPTIONAL USB PORT?
YEAH. WHO PRINTS DOCUMENTS WITH A C-LEG?
OKAY, THEN THAT SHOULD DO IT.
WHAT'S THE BAD NEWS?
IT'S ON THE HOUSE – IN GRATITUDE FOR YOUR SACRIFICE.
YOU'RE JOKING!
YOU'RE RIGHT. IT'S $950 WITH TAX.
GREAT.
I AM GRATEFUL, THOUGH.

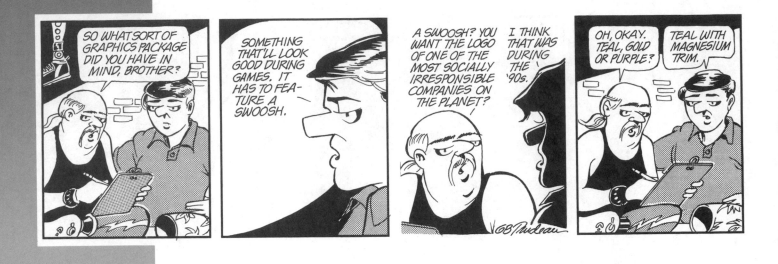

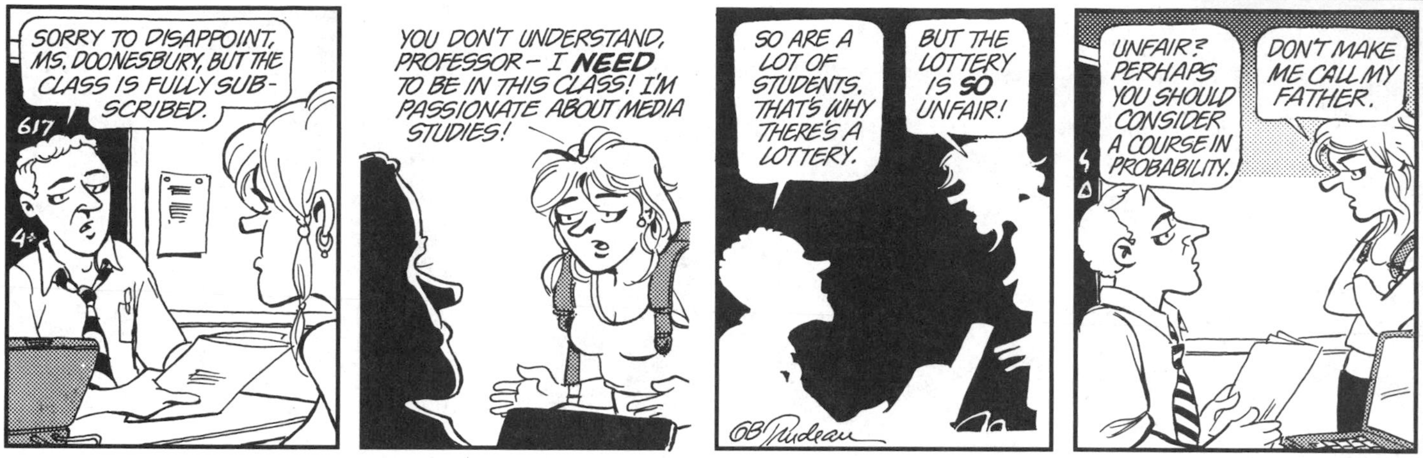
SORRY TO DISAPPOINT, MS. DOONESBURY, BUT THE CLASS IS FULLY SUB-SCRIBED.
YOU DON'T UNDERSTAND, PROFESSOR – I **NEED** TO BE IN THIS CLASS! I'M PASSIONATE ABOUT MEDIA STUDIES!
SO ARE A LOT OF STUDENTS. THAT'S WHY THERE'S A LOTTERY.
BUT THE LOTTERY IS **SO** UNFAIR!
UNFAIR? PERHAPS YOU SHOULD CONSIDER A COURSE IN PROBABILITY.
DON'T MAKE ME CALL MY FATHER.

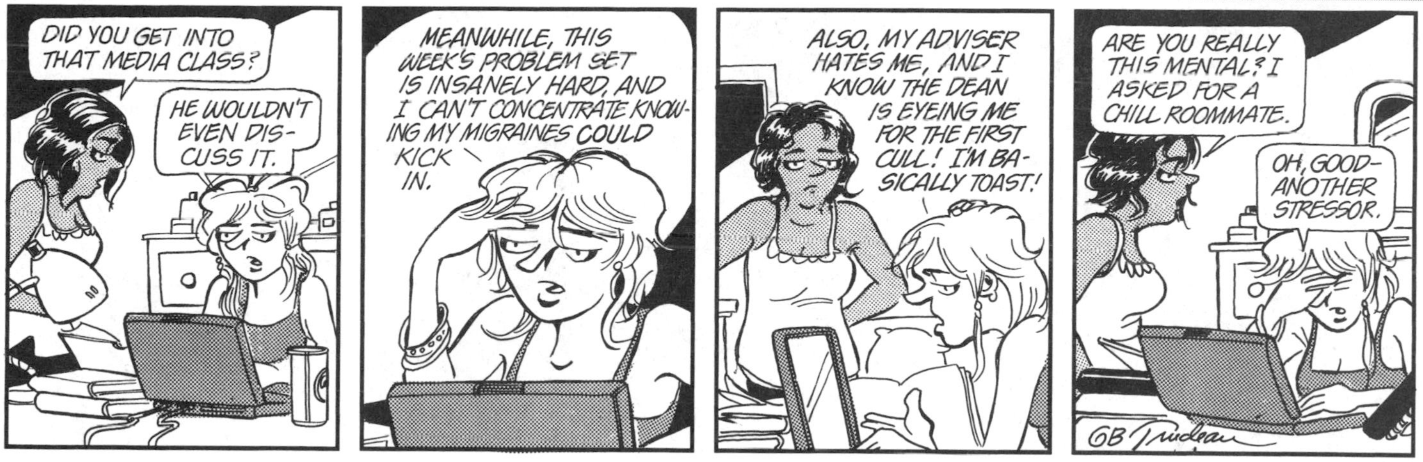
DID YOU GET INTO THAT MEDIA CLASS?
HE WOULDN'T EVEN DIS-CUSS IT.
MEANWHILE, THIS WEEK'S PROBLEM SET IS INSANELY HARD, AND I CAN'T CONCENTRATE KNOW-ING MY MIGRAINES **COULD** KICK IN.
ALSO, MY ADVISER HATES ME, AND I KNOW THE DEAN IS EYEING ME FOR THE FIRST CULL! I'M BA-SICALLY TOAST!
ARE YOU REALLY THIS MENTAL? I ASKED FOR A CHILL ROOMMATE.
OH, GOOD– ANOTHER STRESSOR.

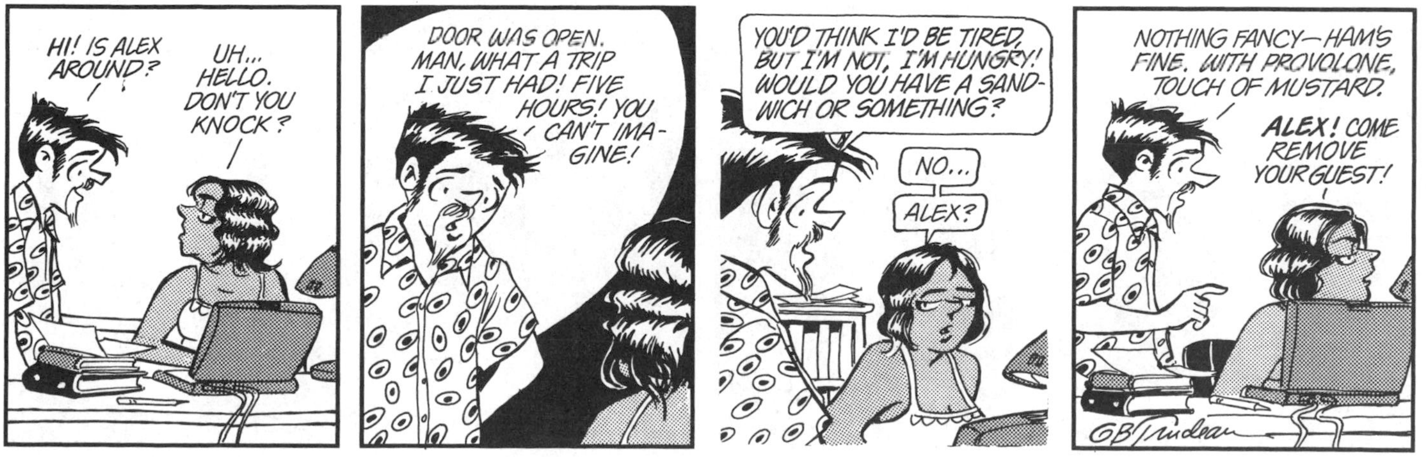
HI! IS ALEX AROUND?
UH... HELLO. DON'T YOU KNOCK?
DOOR WAS OPEN. MAN, WHAT A TRIP I JUST HAD! FIVE HOURS! YOU CAN'T IMA-GINE!
YOU'D THINK I'D BE TIRED, BUT I'M NOT, I'M HUNGRY! WOULD YOU HAVE A SAND-WICH OR SOMETHING?
NO...
ALEX?
NOTHING FANCY—HAM'S FINE. WITH PROVOLONE, TOUCH OF MUSTARD.
ALEX! COME REMOVE YOUR GUEST!

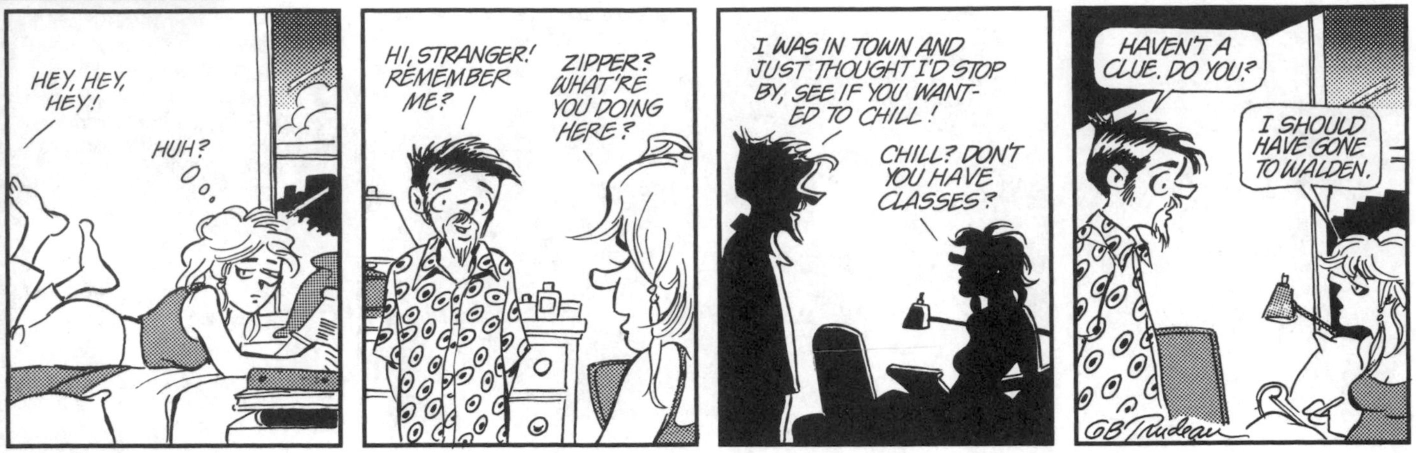
HEY, HEY, HEY!
HUH?
HI, STRANGER! REMEMBER ME?
ZIPPER? WHAT'RE YOU DOING HERE?
I WAS IN TOWN AND JUST THOUGHT I'D STOP BY, SEE IF YOU WANTED TO CHILL!
CHILL? DON'T YOU HAVE CLASSES?
HAVEN'T A CLUE. DO YOU?
I SHOULD HAVE GONE TO WALDEN.
GB Trudeau

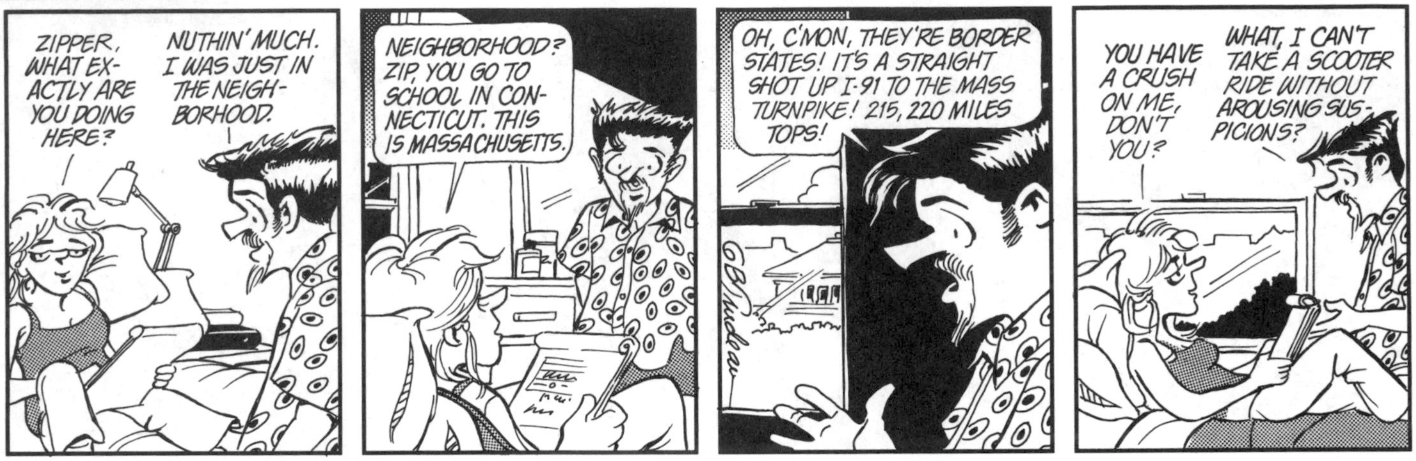
ZIPPER, WHAT EXACTLY ARE YOU DOING HERE?
NUTHIN' MUCH. I WAS JUST IN THE NEIGHBORHOOD.
NEIGHBORHOOD? ZIP, YOU GO TO SCHOOL IN CONNECTICUT. THIS IS MASSACHUSETTS.
OH, C'MON, THEY'RE BORDER STATES! IT'S A STRAIGHT SHOT UP I-91 TO THE MASS TURNPIKE! 215, 220 MILES TOPS!
GB Trudeau
YOU HAVE A CRUSH ON ME, DON'T YOU?
WHAT, I CAN'T TAKE A SCOOTER RIDE WITHOUT AROUSING SUSPICIONS?

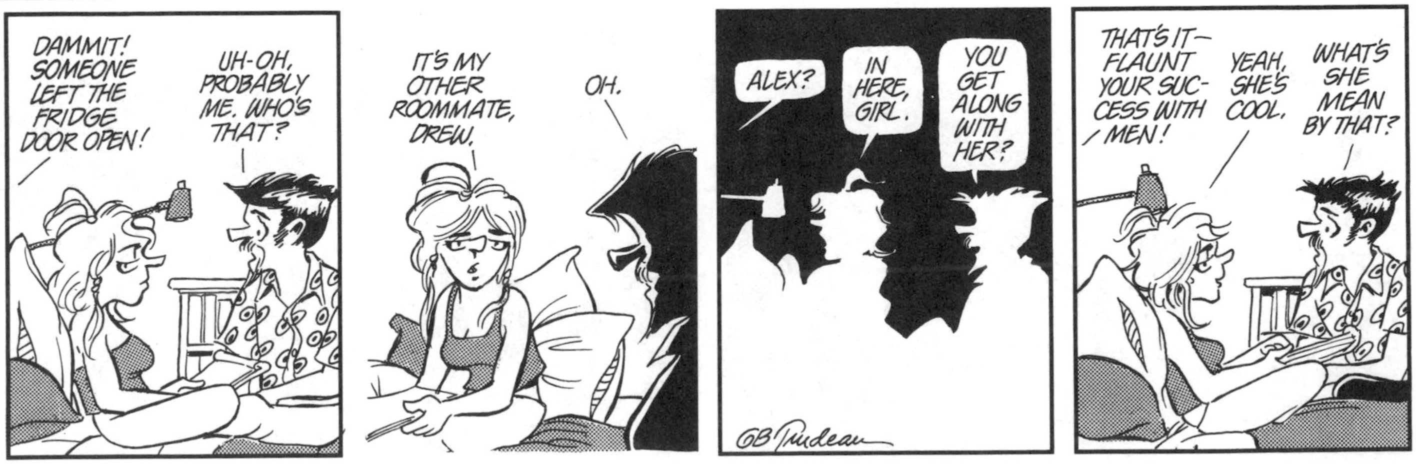
DAMMIT! SOMEONE LEFT THE FRIDGE DOOR OPEN!
UH-OH, PROBABLY ME. WHO'S THAT?
IT'S MY OTHER ROOMMATE, DREW.
OH.
ALEX?
IN HERE, GIRL.
YOU GET ALONG WITH HER?
GB Trudeau
THAT'S IT— FLAUNT YOUR SUCCESS WITH MEN!
YEAH, SHE'S COOL.
WHAT'S SHE MEAN BY THAT?

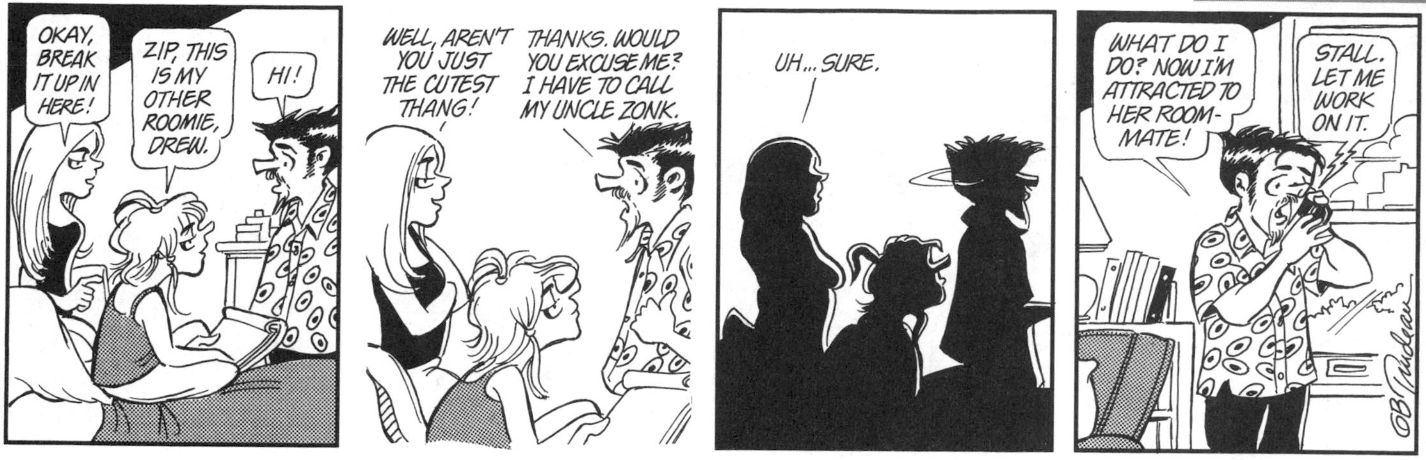
OKAY, BREAK IT UP IN HERE!
ZIP, THIS IS MY OTHER ROOMIE, DREW.
HI!
WELL, AREN'T YOU JUST THE CUTEST THANG!
THANKS. WOULD YOU EXCUSE ME? I HAVE TO CALL MY UNCLE ZONK.
UH... SURE.
WHAT DO I DO? NOW I'M ATTRACTED TO HER ROOM-MATE!
STALL. LET ME WORK ON IT.

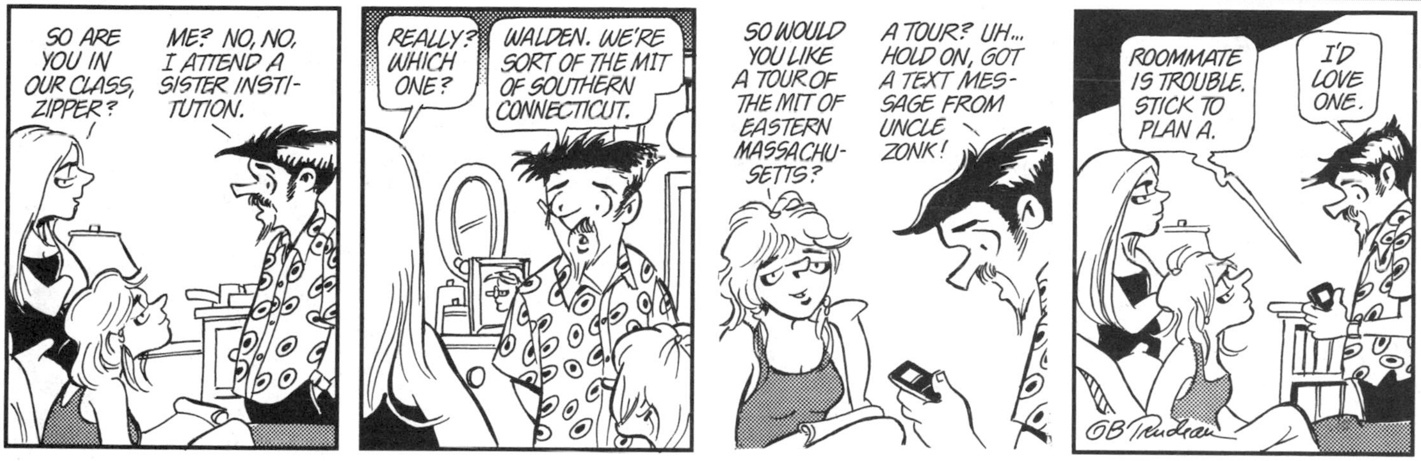
SO ARE YOU IN OUR CLASS, ZIPPER?
ME? NO, NO, I ATTEND A SISTER INSTI-TUTION.
REALLY? WHICH ONE?
WALDEN. WE'RE SORT OF THE MIT OF SOUTHERN CONNECTICUT.
SO WOULD YOU LIKE A TOUR OF THE MIT OF EASTERN MASSACHU-SETTS?
A TOUR? UH... HOLD ON, GOT A TEXT MES-SAGE FROM UNCLE ZONK!
ROOMMATE IS TROUBLE. STICK TO PLAN A.
I'D LOVE ONE.

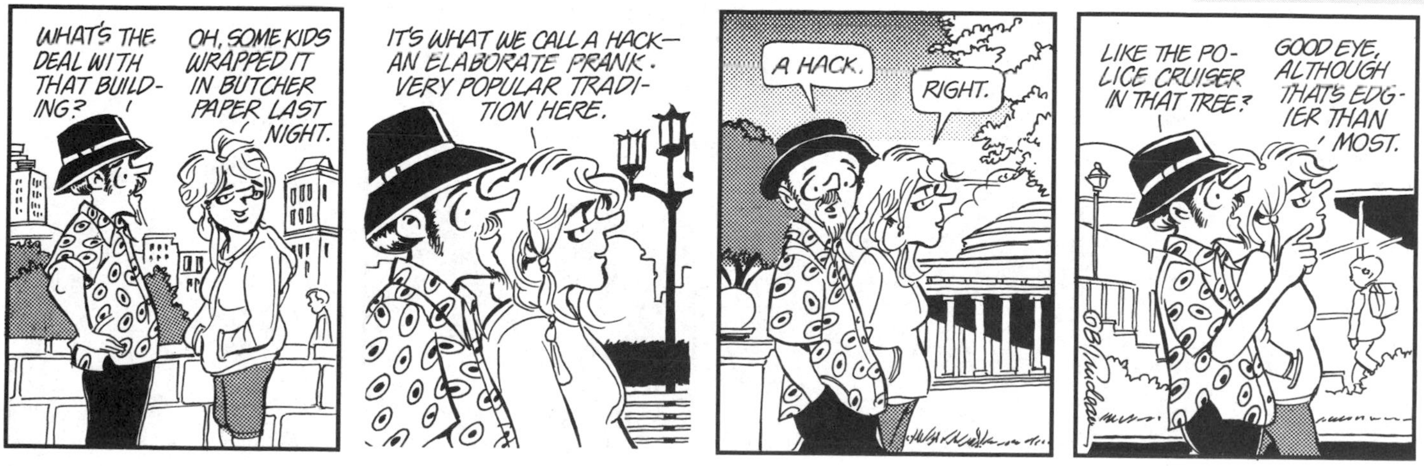
WHAT'S THE DEAL WITH THAT BUILD-ING?
OH, SOME KIDS WRAPPED IT IN BUTCHER PAPER LAST NIGHT.
IT'S WHAT WE CALL A HACK— AN ELABORATE PRANK. VERY POPULAR TRADI-TION HERE.
A HACK.
RIGHT.
LIKE THE PO-LICE CRUISER IN THAT TREE?
GOOD EYE, ALTHOUGH THAT'S EDG-IER THAN MOST.

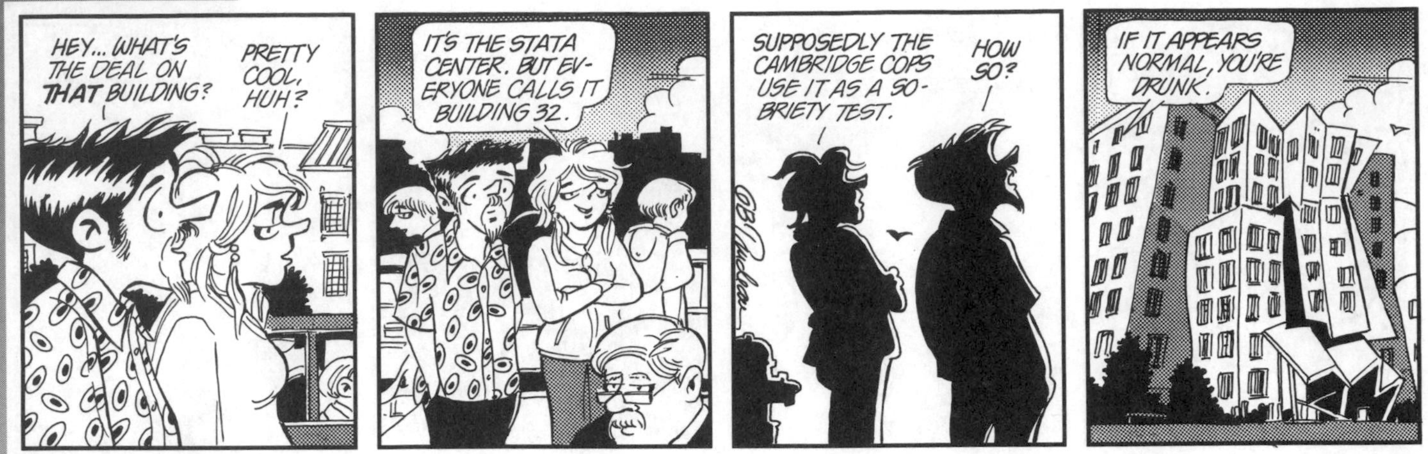
HEY... WHAT'S THE DEAL ON **THAT** BUILDING?
PRETTY COOL, HUH?
IT'S THE STATA CENTER. BUT EV-ERYONE CALLS IT BUILDING 32.
SUPPOSEDLY THE CAMBRIDGE COPS USE IT AS A SO-BRIETY TEST.
HOW SO?
IF IT APPEARS NORMAL, YOU'RE DRUNK.

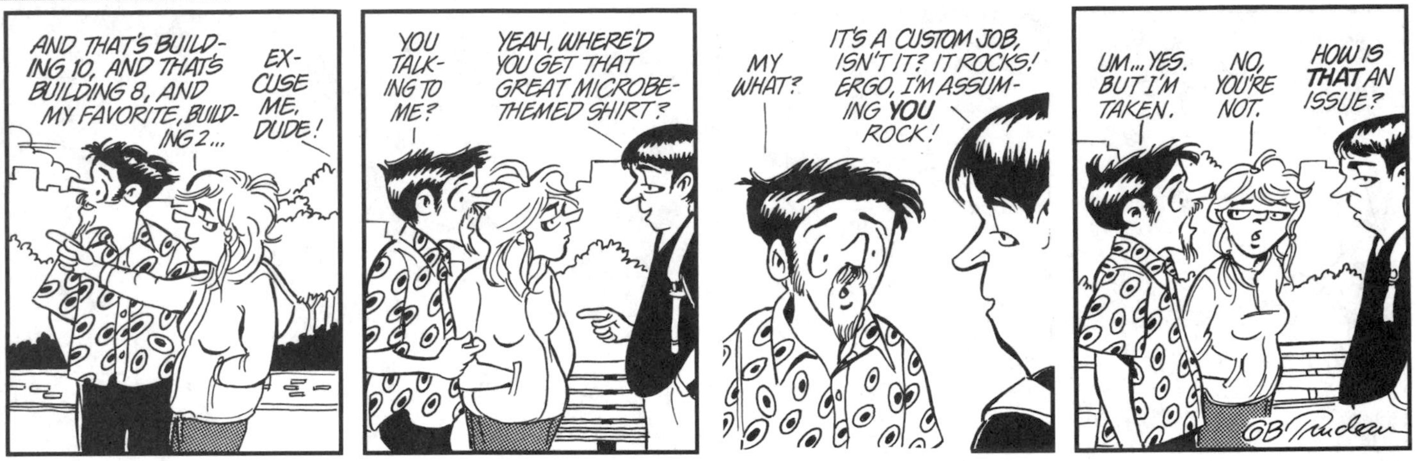
AND THAT'S BUILD-ING 10, AND THAT'S BUILDING 8, AND MY FAVORITE, BUILD-ING 2...
EX-CUSE ME, DUDE!
YOU TALK-ING TO ME?
YEAH, WHERE'D YOU GET THAT GREAT MICROBE-THEMED SHIRT?
MY WHAT?
IT'S A CUSTOM JOB, ISN'T IT? IT ROCKS! ERGO, I'M ASSUM-ING **YOU** ROCK!
UM... YES. BUT I'M TAKEN.
NO, YOU'RE NOT.
HOW IS **THAT** AN ISSUE?

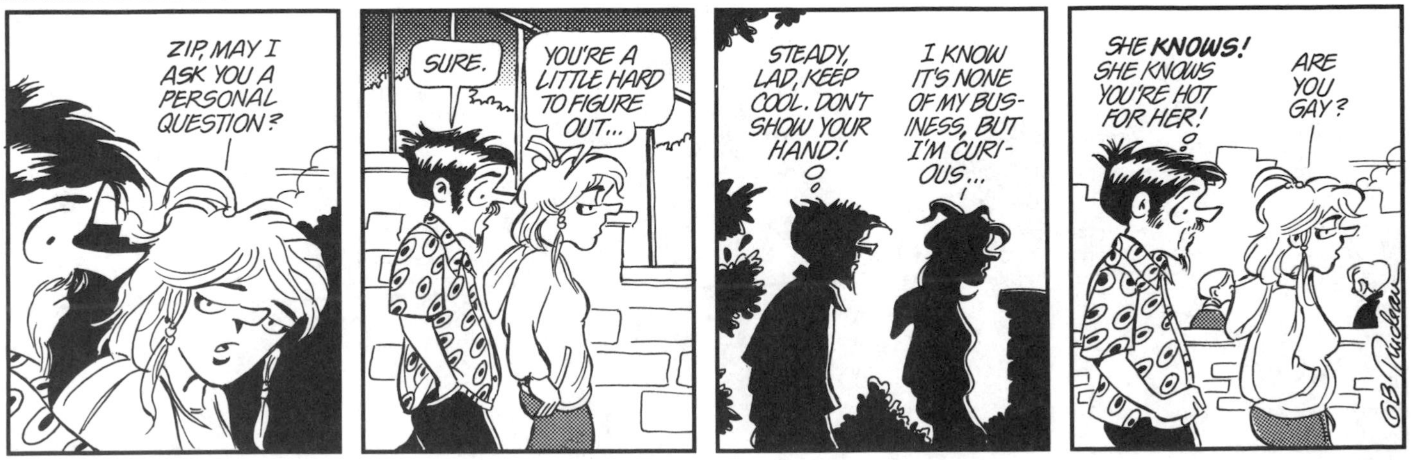
ZIP, MAY I ASK YOU A PERSONAL QUESTION?
SURE.
YOU'RE A LITTLE HARD TO FIGURE OUT...
STEADY, LAD, KEEP COOL. DON'T SHOW YOUR HAND!
I KNOW IT'S NONE OF MY BUS-INESS, BUT I'M CURI-OUS...
SHE **KNOWS!** SHE KNOWS YOU'RE HOT FOR HER!
ARE YOU GAY?

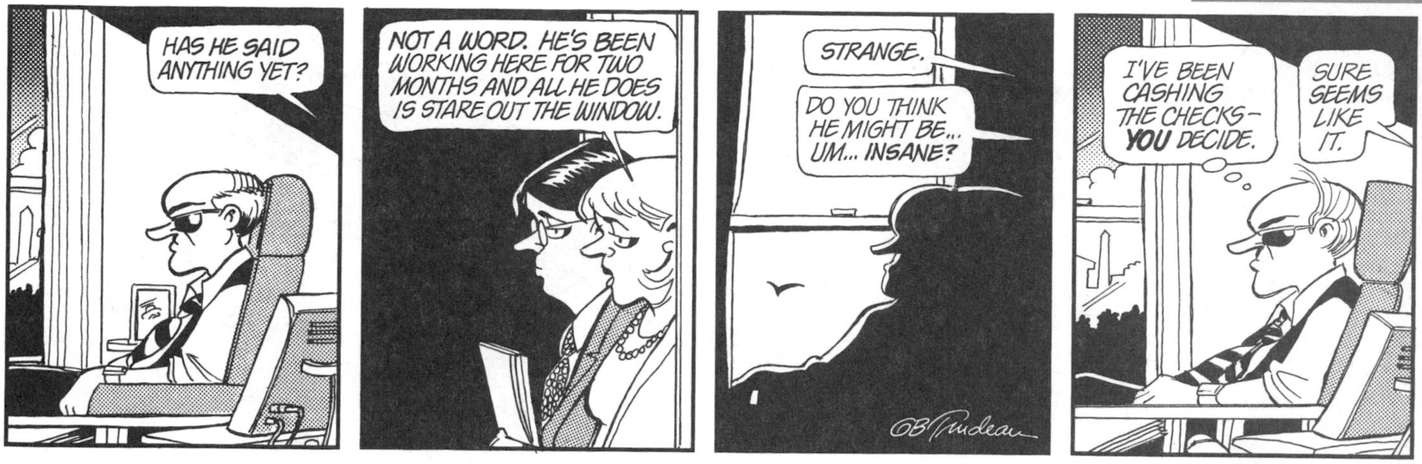
HAS HE SAID ANYTHING YET?
NOT A WORD. HE'S BEEN WORKING HERE FOR TWO MONTHS AND ALL HE DOES IS STARE OUT THE WINDOW.
STRANGE.
DO YOU THINK HE MIGHT BE... UM... INSANE?
I'VE BEEN CASHING THE CHECKS– **YOU** DECIDE.
SURE SEEMS LIKE IT.
GBTrudeau

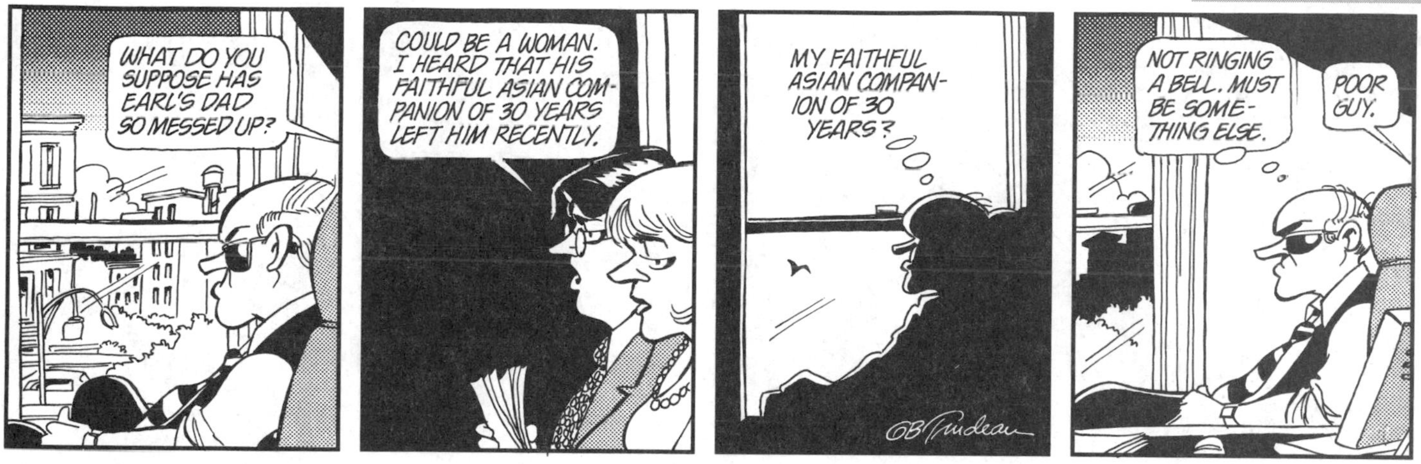
WHAT DO YOU SUPPOSE HAS EARL'S DAD SO MESSED UP?
COULD BE A WOMAN. I HEARD THAT HIS FAITHFUL ASIAN COMPANION OF 30 YEARS LEFT HIM RECENTLY.
MY FAITHFUL ASIAN COMPANION OF 30 YEARS?
NOT RINGING A BELL. MUST BE SOMETHING ELSE.
POOR GUY.
GBTrudeau

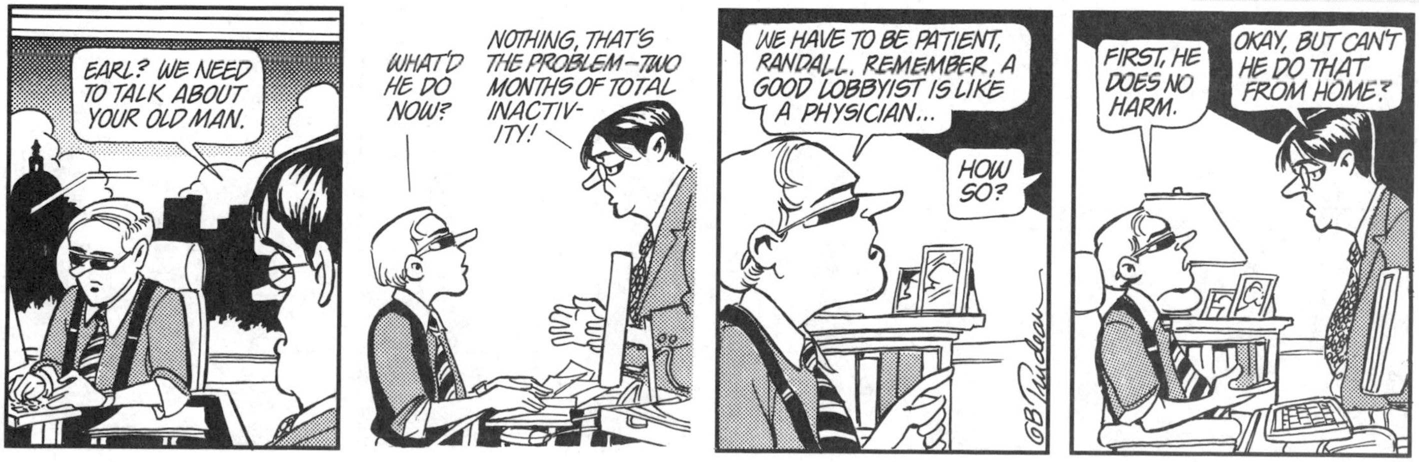
EARL? WE NEED TO TALK ABOUT YOUR OLD MAN.
WHAT'D HE DO NOW?
NOTHING, THAT'S THE PROBLEM—TWO MONTHS OF TOTAL INACTIVITY!
WE HAVE TO BE PATIENT, RANDALL. REMEMBER, A GOOD LOBBYIST IS LIKE A PHYSICIAN...
HOW SO?
GBTrudeau
FIRST, HE DOES NO HARM.
OKAY, BUT CAN'T HE DO THAT FROM HOME?

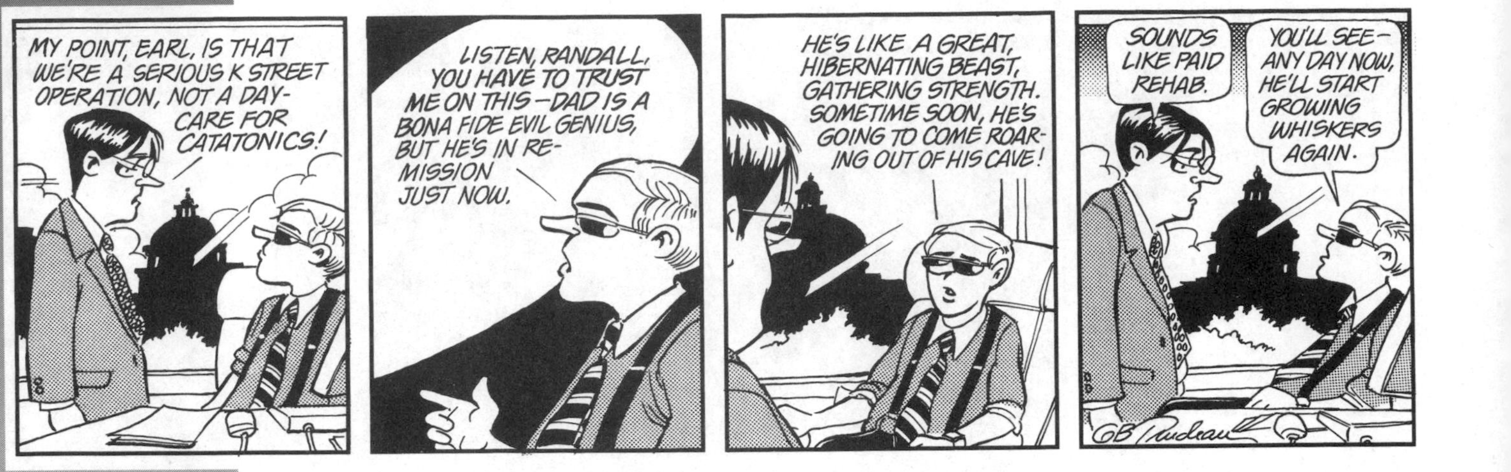
MY POINT, EARL, IS THAT WE'RE A SERIOUS K STREET OPERATION, NOT A DAY-CARE FOR CATATONICS!
LISTEN, RANDALL. YOU HAVE TO TRUST ME ON THIS—DAD IS A BONA FIDE EVIL GENIUS, BUT HE'S IN RE-MISSION JUST NOW.
HE'S LIKE A GREAT, HIBERNATING BEAST, GATHERING STRENGTH. SOMETIME SOON, HE'S GOING TO COME ROAR-ING OUT OF HIS CAVE!
SOUNDS LIKE PAID REHAB.
YOU'LL SEE—ANY DAY NOW, HE'LL START GROWING WHISKERS AGAIN.

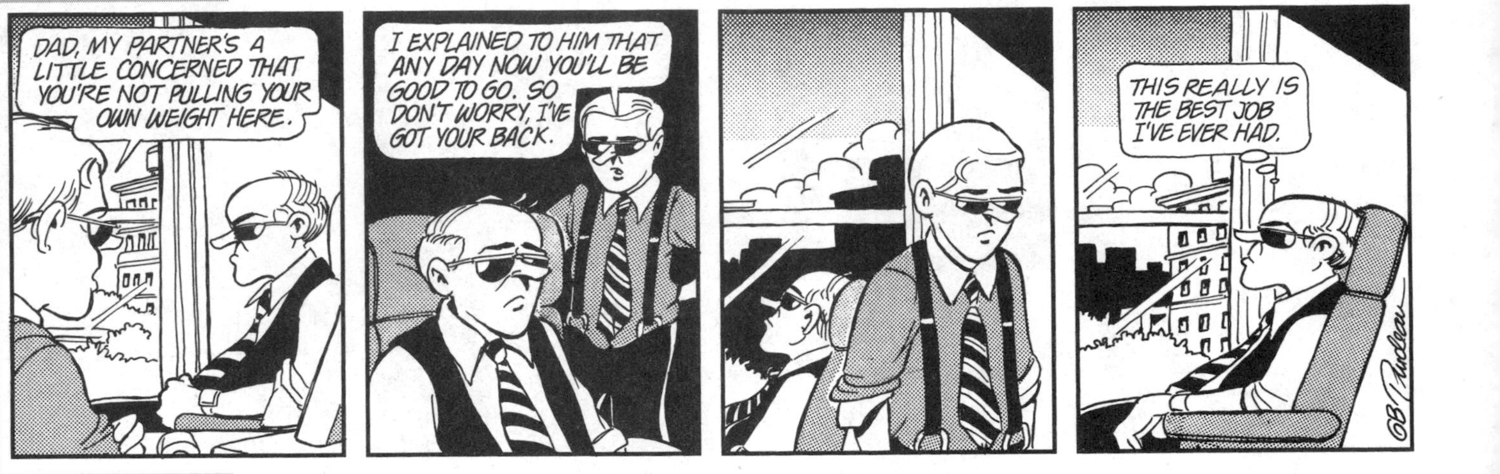
DAD, MY PARTNER'S A LITTLE CONCERNED THAT YOU'RE NOT PULLING YOUR OWN WEIGHT HERE.
I EXPLAINED TO HIM THAT ANY DAY NOW YOU'LL BE GOOD TO GO. SO DON'T WORRY, I'VE GOT YOUR BACK.
THIS REALLY IS THE BEST JOB I'VE EVER HAD.

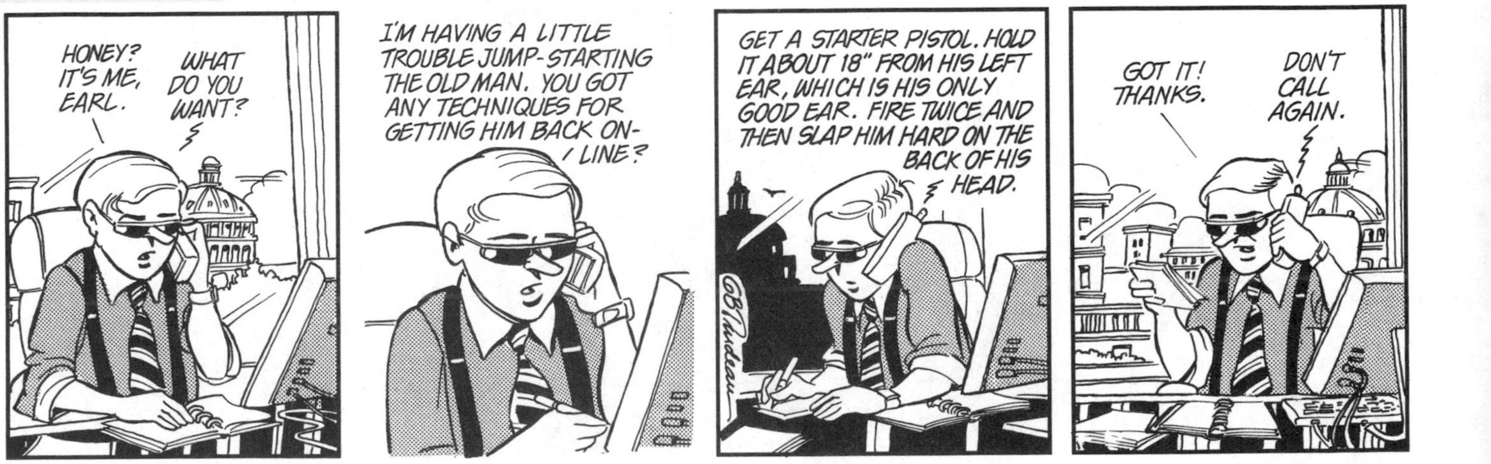
HONEY? IT'S ME, EARL.
WHAT DO YOU WANT?
I'M HAVING A LITTLE TROUBLE JUMP-STARTING THE OLD MAN. YOU GOT ANY TECHNIQUES FOR GETTING HIM BACK ON-LINE?
GET A STARTER PISTOL. HOLD IT ABOUT 18" FROM HIS LEFT EAR, WHICH IS HIS ONLY GOOD EAR. FIRE TWICE AND THEN SLAP HIM HARD ON THE BACK OF HIS HEAD.
GOT IT! THANKS.
DON'T CALL AGAIN.

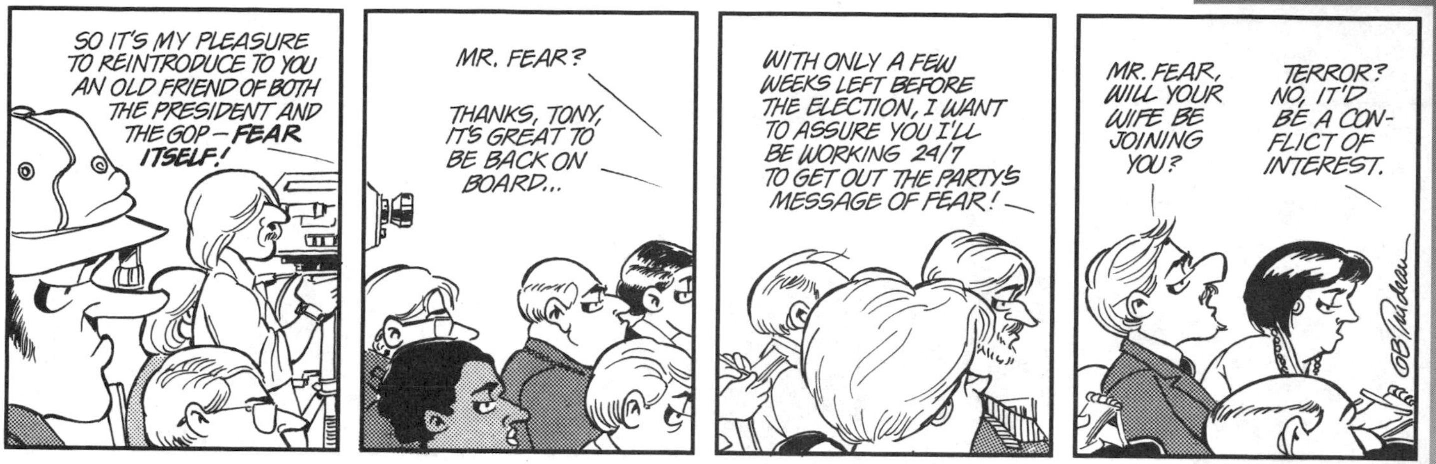
SO IT'S MY PLEASURE TO REINTRODUCE TO YOU AN OLD FRIEND OF BOTH THE PRESIDENT AND THE GOP — FEAR ITSELF!
MR. FEAR?
THANKS, TONY, IT'S GREAT TO BE BACK ON BOARD...
WITH ONLY A FEW WEEKS LEFT BEFORE THE ELECTION, I WANT TO ASSURE YOU I'LL BE WORKING 24/7 TO GET OUT THE PARTY'S MESSAGE OF FEAR!
MR. FEAR, WILL YOUR WIFE BE JOINING YOU?
TERROR? NO, IT'D BE A CON-FLICT OF INTEREST.

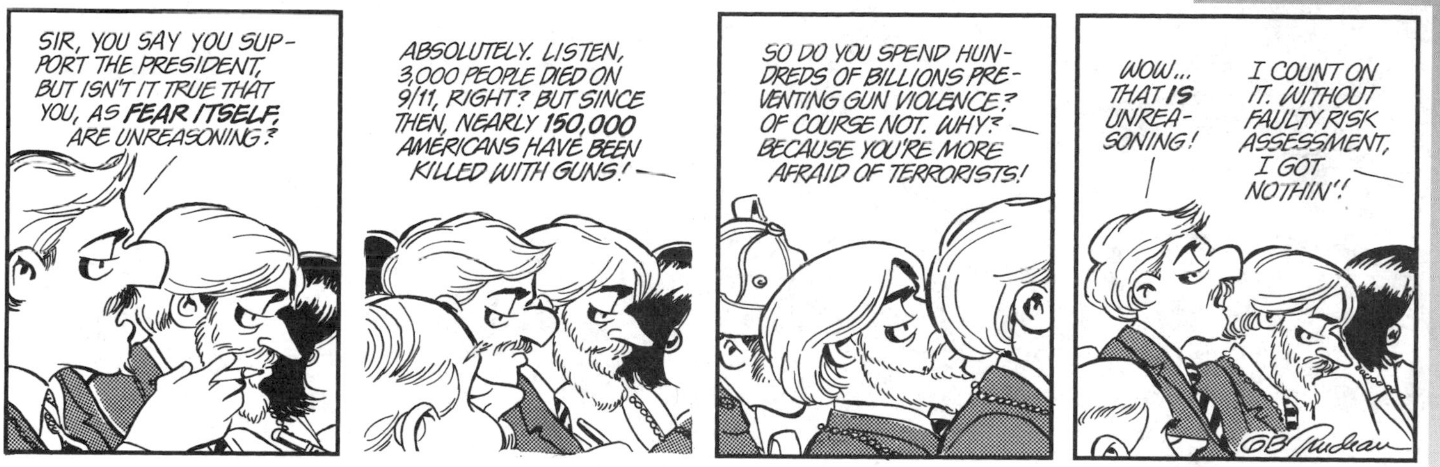
SIR, YOU SAY YOU SUP-PORT THE PRESIDENT, BUT ISN'T IT TRUE THAT YOU, AS FEAR ITSELF, ARE UNREASONING?
ABSOLUTELY. LISTEN, 3,000 PEOPLE DIED ON 9/11, RIGHT? BUT SINCE THEN, NEARLY 150,000 AMERICANS HAVE BEEN KILLED WITH GUNS!
SO DO YOU SPEND HUN-DREDS OF BILLIONS PRE-VENTING GUN VIOLENCE? OF COURSE NOT. WHY? BECAUSE YOU'RE MORE AFRAID OF TERRORISTS!
WOW... THAT IS UNREA-SONING!
I COUNT ON IT. WITHOUT FAULTY RISK ASSESSMENT, I GOT NOTHIN'!

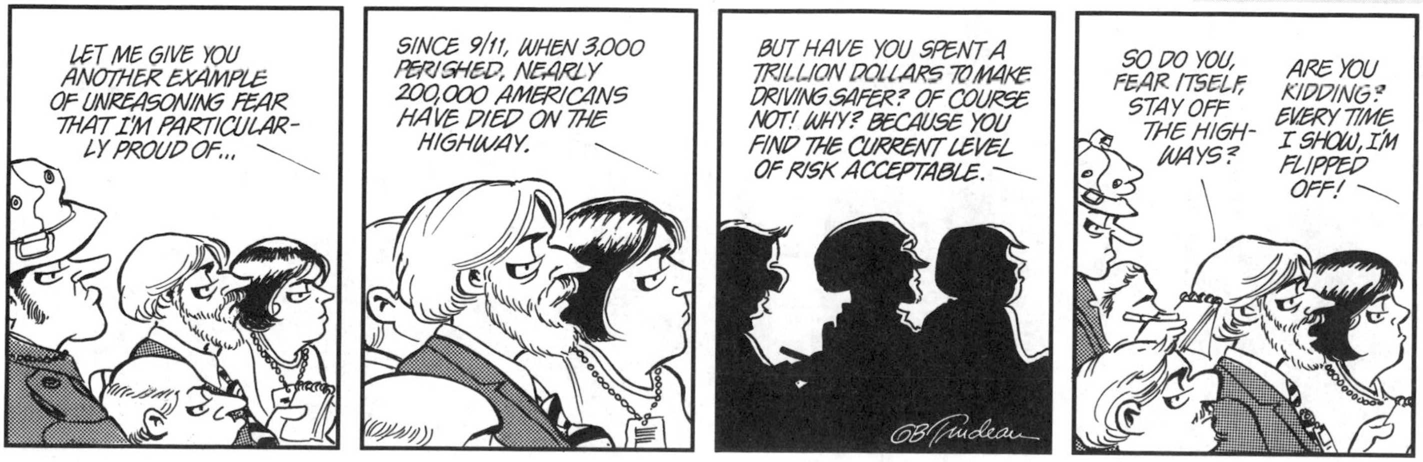
LET ME GIVE YOU ANOTHER EXAMPLE OF UNREASONING FEAR THAT I'M PARTICULAR-LY PROUD OF...
SINCE 9/11, WHEN 3,000 PERISHED, NEARLY 200,000 AMERICANS HAVE DIED ON THE HIGHWAY.
BUT HAVE YOU SPENT A TRILLION DOLLARS TO MAKE DRIVING SAFER? OF COURSE NOT! WHY? BECAUSE YOU FIND THE CURRENT LEVEL OF RISK ACCEPTABLE.
SO DO YOU, FEAR ITSELF, STAY OFF THE HIGH-WAYS?
ARE YOU KIDDING? EVERY TIME I SHOW, I'M FLIPPED OFF!

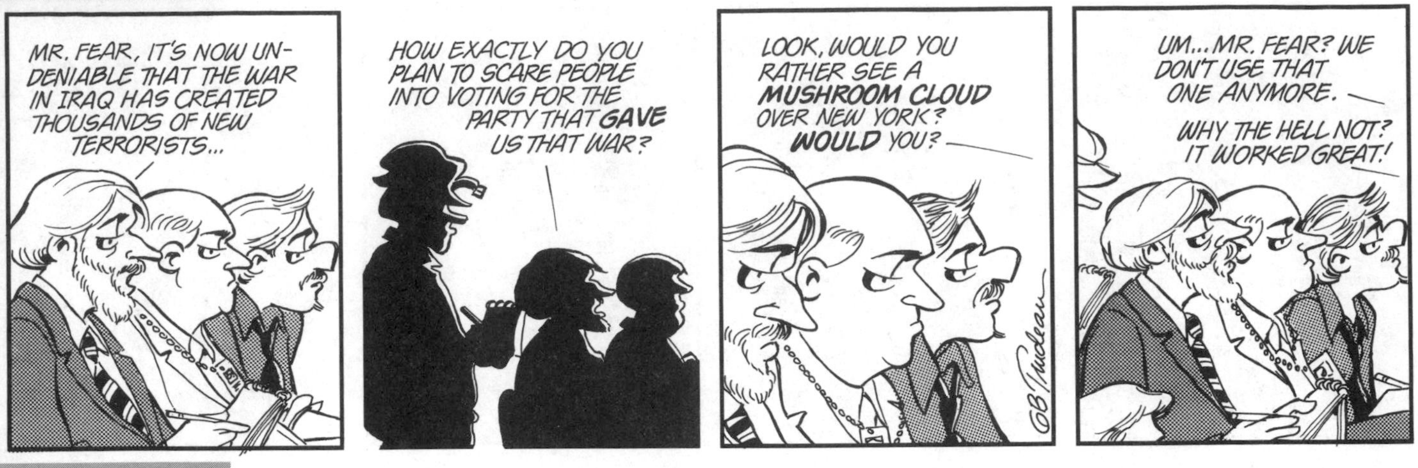
MR. FEAR, IT'S NOW UNDENIABLE THAT THE WAR IN IRAQ HAS CREATED THOUSANDS OF NEW TERRORISTS...
HOW EXACTLY DO YOU PLAN TO SCARE PEOPLE INTO VOTING FOR THE PARTY THAT **GAVE** US THAT WAR?
LOOK, WOULD YOU RATHER SEE A **MUSHROOM CLOUD** OVER NEW YORK? **WOULD** YOU?
UM... MR. FEAR? WE DON'T USE THAT ONE ANYMORE.
WHY THE HELL NOT? IT WORKED GREAT!

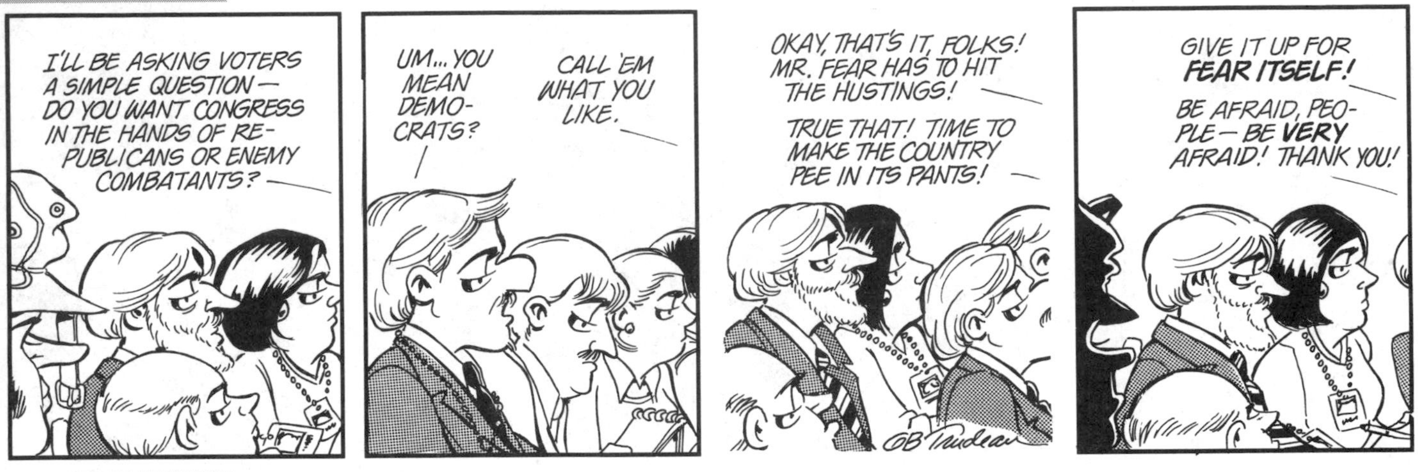
I'LL BE ASKING VOTERS A SIMPLE QUESTION— DO YOU WANT CONGRESS IN THE HANDS OF REPUBLICANS OR ENEMY COMBATANTS?
UM... YOU MEAN DEMOCRATS?
CALL 'EM WHAT YOU LIKE.
OKAY, THAT'S IT, FOLKS! MR. FEAR HAS TO HIT THE HUSTINGS!
TRUE THAT! TIME TO MAKE THE COUNTRY PEE IN ITS PANTS!
GIVE IT UP FOR **FEAR ITSELF!**
BE AFRAID, PEOPLE— BE **VERY** AFRAID! THANK YOU!

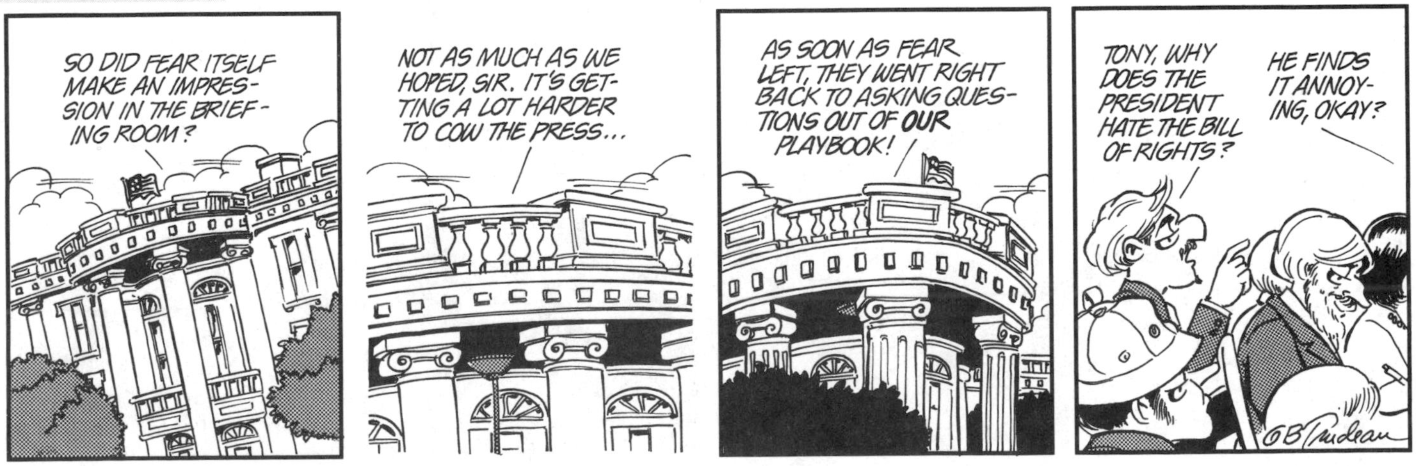
SO DID FEAR ITSELF MAKE AN IMPRESSION IN THE BRIEFING ROOM?
NOT AS MUCH AS WE HOPED, SIR. IT'S GETTING A LOT HARDER TO COW THE PRESS...
AS SOON AS FEAR LEFT, THEY WENT RIGHT BACK TO ASKING QUESTIONS OUT OF **OUR** PLAYBOOK!
TONY, WHY DOES THE PRESIDENT HATE THE BILL OF RIGHTS?
HE FINDS IT ANNOYING, OKAY?

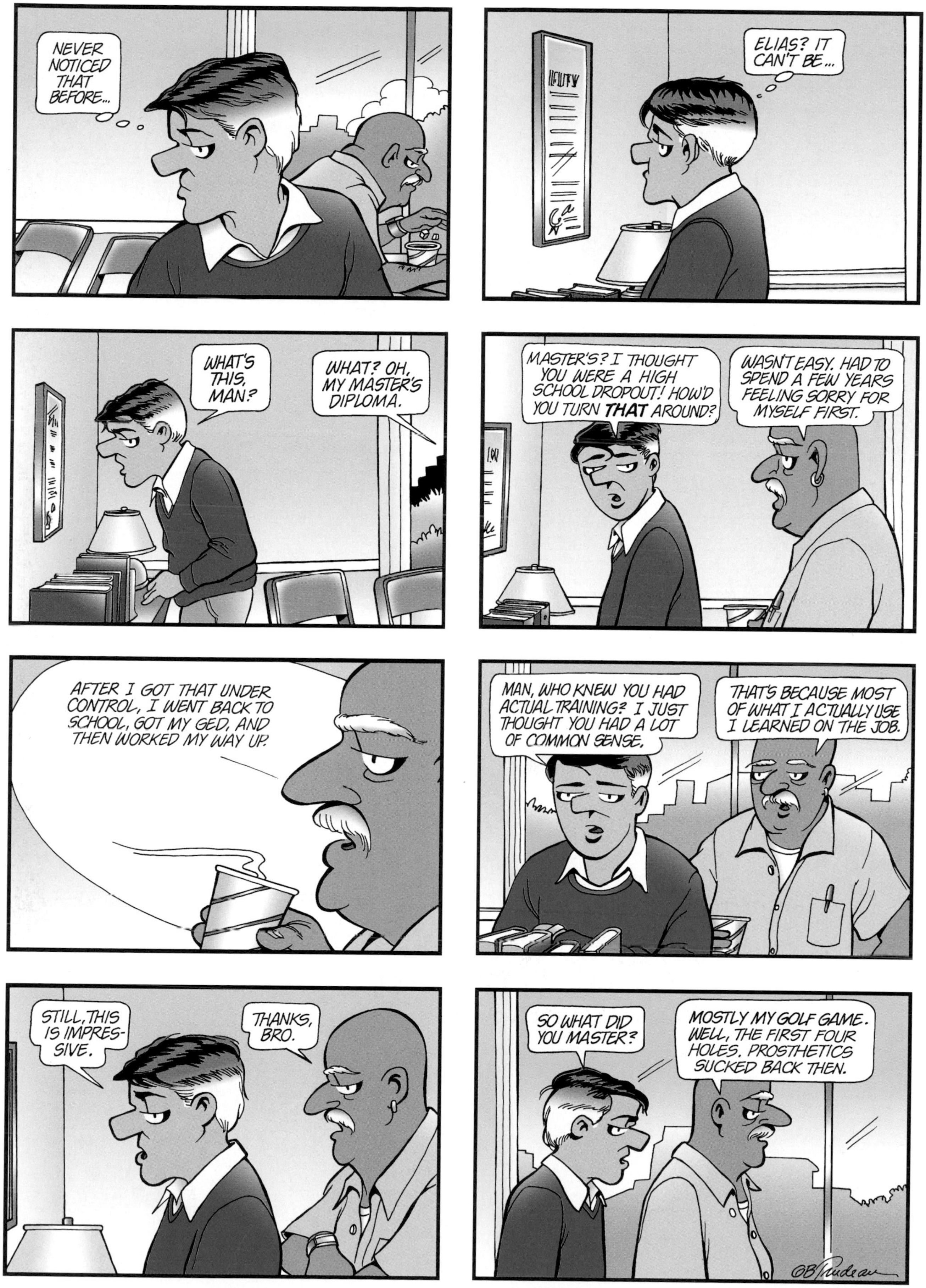
NEVER NOTICED THAT BEFORE...
ELIAS? IT CAN'T BE...
WHAT'S THIS, MAN?
WHAT? OH, MY MASTER'S DIPLOMA.
MASTER'S? I THOUGHT YOU WERE A HIGH SCHOOL DROPOUT! HOW'D YOU TURN THAT AROUND?
WASN'T EASY. HAD TO SPEND A FEW YEARS FEELING SORRY FOR MYSELF FIRST.
AFTER I GOT THAT UNDER CONTROL, I WENT BACK TO SCHOOL, GOT MY GED, AND THEN WORKED MY WAY UP.
MAN, WHO KNEW YOU HAD ACTUAL TRAINING? I JUST THOUGHT YOU HAD A LOT OF COMMON SENSE.
THAT'S BECAUSE MOST OF WHAT I ACTUALLY USE I LEARNED ON THE JOB.
STILL, THIS IS IMPRES-SIVE.
THANKS, BRO.
SO WHAT DID YOU MASTER?
MOSTLY MY GOLF GAME. WELL, THE FIRST FOUR HOLES. PROSTHETICS SUCKED BACK THEN.
©B. Trudeau

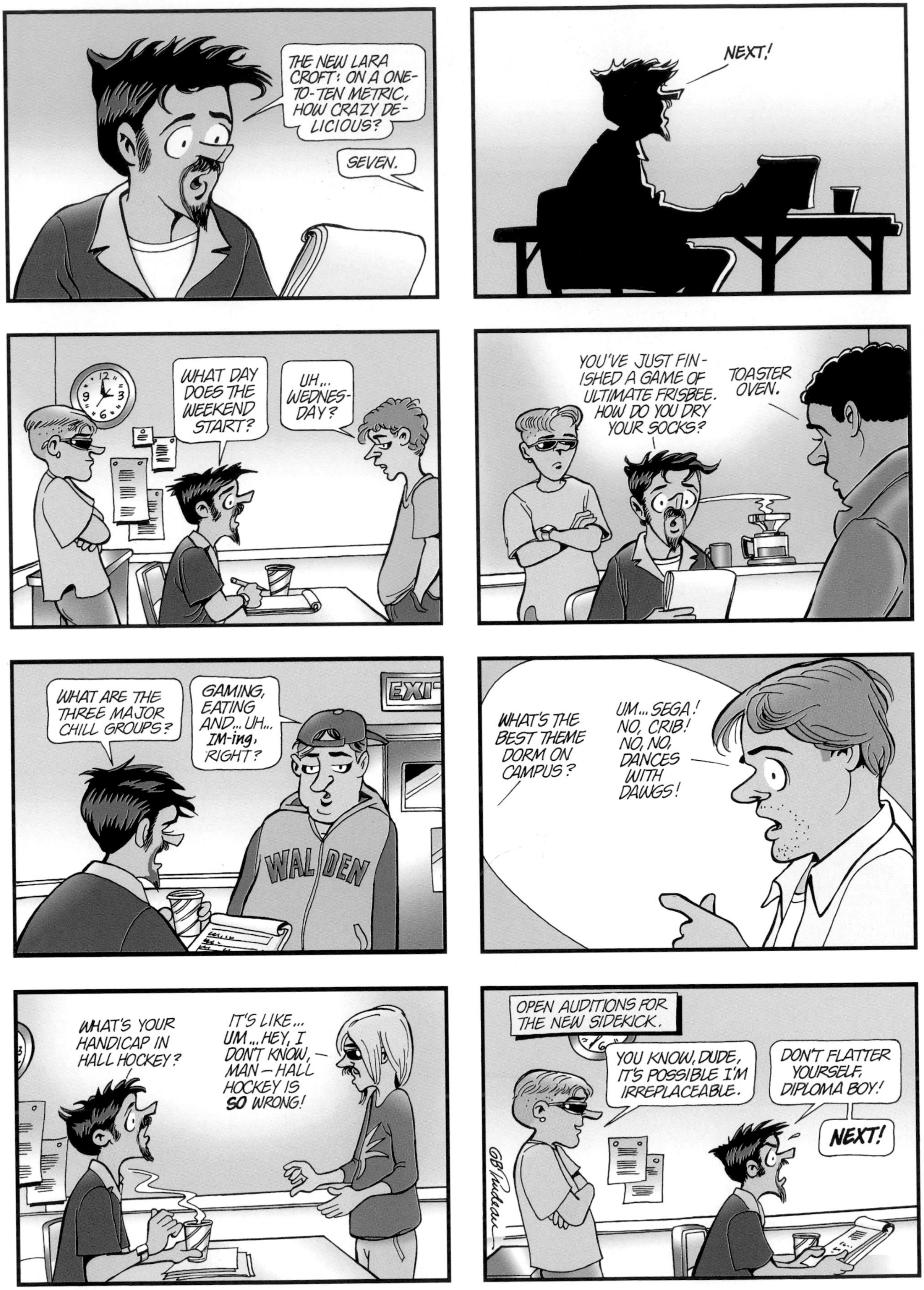
THE NEW LARA CROFT: ON A ONE-TO-TEN METRIC, HOW CRAZY DE-LICIOUS?
SEVEN.
NEXT!
WHAT DAY DOES THE WEEKEND START?
UH... WEDNES-DAY?
YOU'VE JUST FIN-ISHED A GAME OF ULTIMATE FRISBEE. HOW DO YOU DRY YOUR SOCKS?
TOASTER OVEN.
WHAT ARE THE THREE MAJOR CHILL GROUPS?
GAMING, EATING AND... UH... IM-ing, RIGHT?
EXIT
WALDEN
WHAT'S THE BEST THEME DORM ON CAMPUS?
UM... SEGA! NO, CRIB! NO, NO, DANCES WITH DAWGS!
WHAT'S YOUR HANDICAP IN HALL HOCKEY?
IT'S LIKE... UM... HEY, I DON'T KNOW, MAN — HALL HOCKEY IS SO WRONG!
OPEN AUDITIONS FOR THE NEW SIDEKICK.
YOU KNOW, DUDE, IT'S POSSIBLE I'M IRREPLACEABLE.
DON'T FLATTER YOURSELF, DIPLOMA BOY!
NEXT!

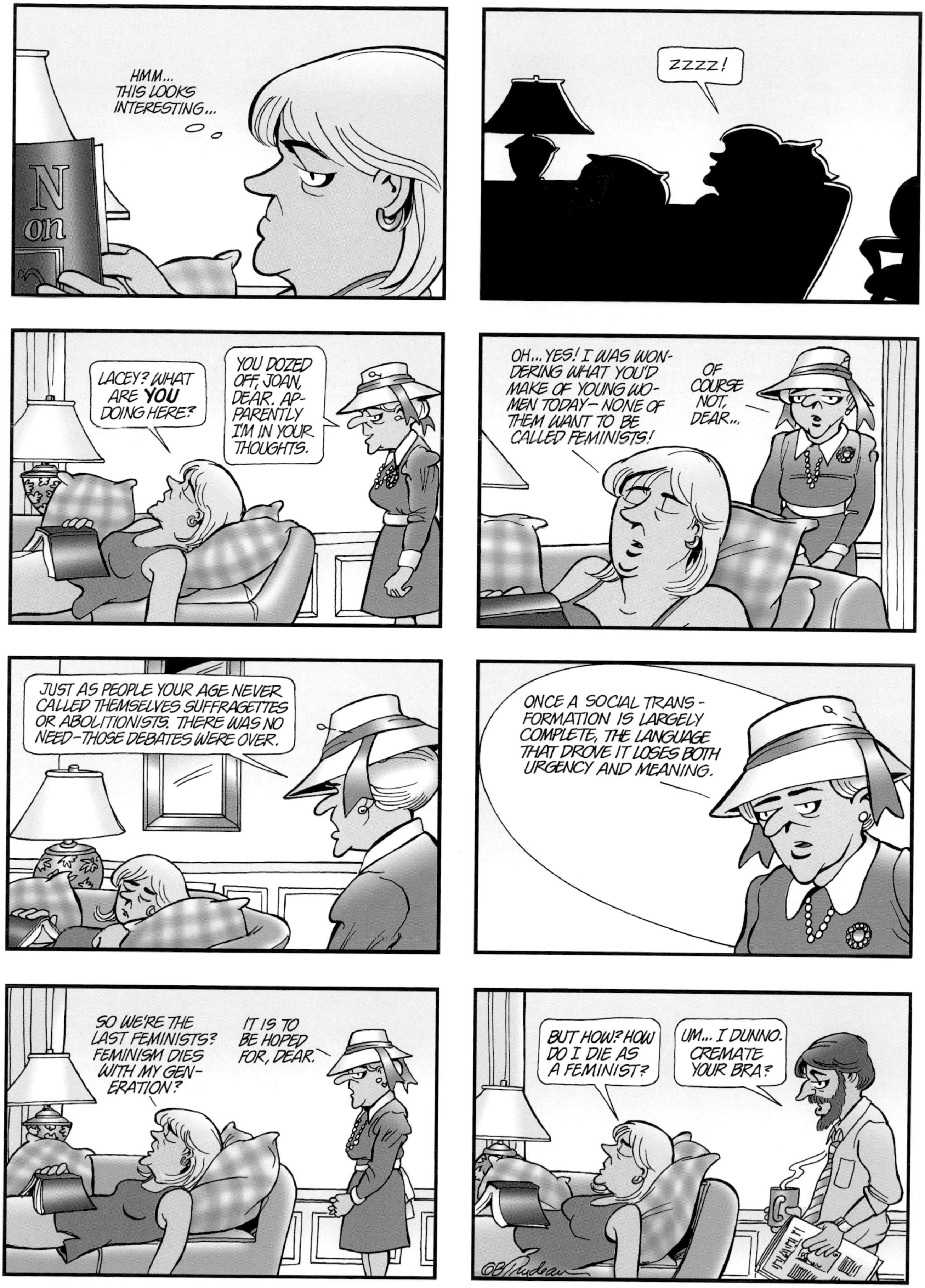
HMM... THIS LOOKS INTERESTING...
ZZZZ!
LACEY? WHAT ARE **YOU** DOING HERE?
YOU DOZED OFF, JOAN, DEAR. APPARENTLY I'M IN YOUR THOUGHTS.
OH... YES! I WAS WONDERING WHAT YOU'D MAKE OF YOUNG WOMEN TODAY— NONE OF THEM WANT TO BE CALLED FEMINISTS!
OF COURSE NOT, DEAR...
JUST AS PEOPLE YOUR AGE NEVER CALLED THEMSELVES SUFFRAGETTES OR ABOLITIONISTS. THERE WAS NO NEED—THOSE DEBATES WERE OVER.
ONCE A SOCIAL TRANSFORMATION IS LARGELY COMPLETE, THE LANGUAGE THAT DROVE IT LOSES BOTH URGENCY AND MEANING.
SO WE'RE THE LAST FEMINISTS? FEMINISM DIES WITH MY GENERATION?
IT IS TO BE HOPED FOR, DEAR.
BUT HOW? HOW DO I DIE AS A FEMINIST?
UM... I DUNNO. CREMATE YOUR BRA?
©B Trudeau

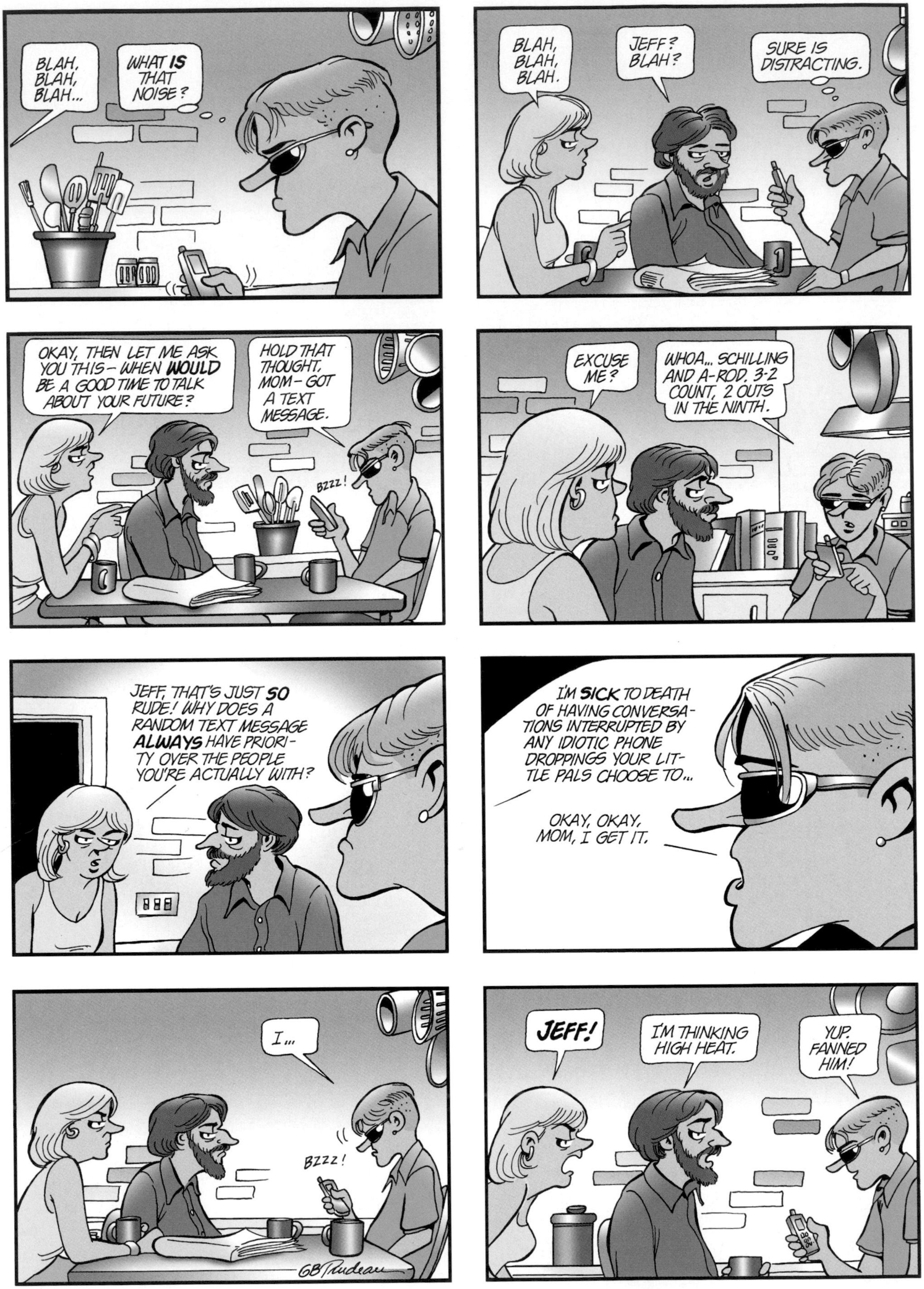
BLAH, BLAH, BLAH...
WHAT IS THAT NOISE?
BLAH, BLAH, BLAH.
JEFF? BLAH?
SURE IS DISTRACTING.
OKAY, THEN LET ME ASK YOU THIS– WHEN WOULD BE A GOOD TIME TO TALK ABOUT YOUR FUTURE?
HOLD THAT THOUGHT, MOM– GOT A TEXT MESSAGE.
BZZZ!
EXCUSE ME?
WHOA... SCHILLING AND A-ROD, 3-2 COUNT, 2 OUTS IN THE NINTH.
JEFF, THAT'S JUST SO RUDE! WHY DOES A RANDOM TEXT MESSAGE ALWAYS HAVE PRIORITY OVER THE PEOPLE YOU'RE ACTUALLY WITH?
I'M SICK TO DEATH OF HAVING CONVERSATIONS INTERRUPTED BY ANY IDIOTIC PHONE DROPPINGS YOUR LITTLE PALS CHOOSE TO...
OKAY, OKAY, MOM, I GET IT.
I...
BZZZ!
GBTrudeau
JEFF!
I'M THINKING HIGH HEAT.
YUP. FANNED HIM!

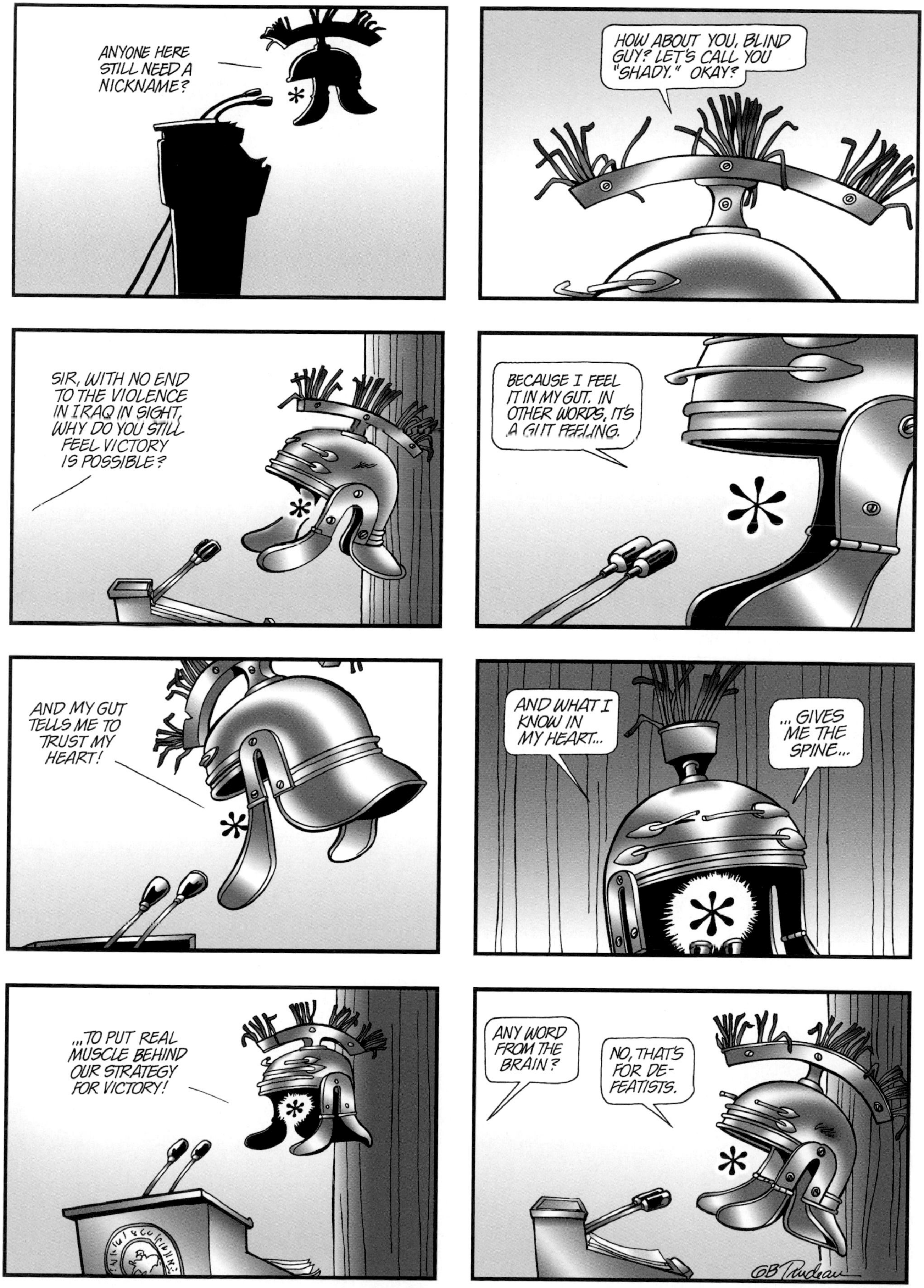
ANYONE HERE STILL NEED A NICKNAME?
HOW ABOUT YOU, BLIND GUY? LET'S CALL YOU "SHADY." OKAY?
SIR, WITH NO END TO THE VIOLENCE IN IRAQ IN SIGHT, WHY DO YOU STILL FEEL VICTORY IS POSSIBLE?
BECAUSE I FEEL IT IN MY GUT. IN OTHER WORDS, IT'S A GUT FEELING.
AND MY GUT TELLS ME TO TRUST MY HEART!
AND WHAT I KNOW IN MY HEART...
...GIVES ME THE SPINE...
...TO PUT REAL MUSCLE BEHIND OUR STRATEGY FOR VICTORY!
ANY WORD FROM THE BRAIN?
NO, THAT'S FOR DEFEATISTS.
GB Trudeau

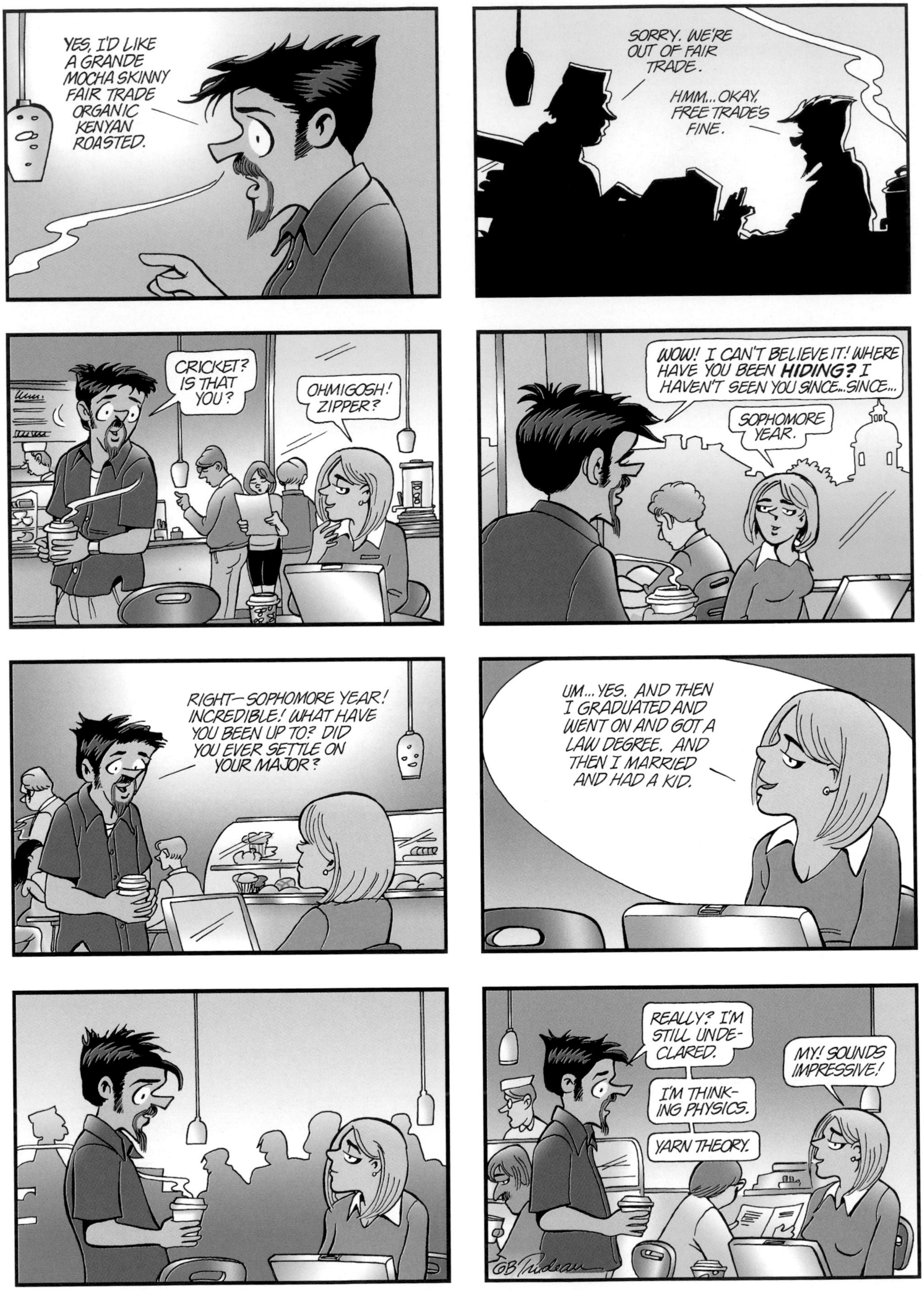
YES, I'D LIKE A GRANDE MOCHA SKINNY FAIR TRADE ORGANIC KENYAN ROASTED.
SORRY. WE'RE OUT OF FAIR TRADE.
HMM... OKAY. FREE TRADE'S FINE.
CRICKET? IS THAT YOU?
OHMIGOSH! ZIPPER?
WOW! I CAN'T BELIEVE IT! WHERE HAVE YOU BEEN **HIDING?** I HAVEN'T SEEN YOU SINCE... SINCE...
SOPHOMORE YEAR.
RIGHT—SOPHOMORE YEAR! INCREDIBLE! WHAT HAVE YOU BEEN UP TO? DID YOU EVER SETTLE ON YOUR MAJOR?
UM... YES. AND THEN I GRADUATED AND WENT ON AND GOT A LAW DEGREE. AND THEN I MARRIED AND HAD A KID.
REALLY? I'M STILL UNDE-CLARED.
I'M THINK-ING PHYSICS.
YARN THEORY.
MY! SOUNDS IMPRESSIVE!

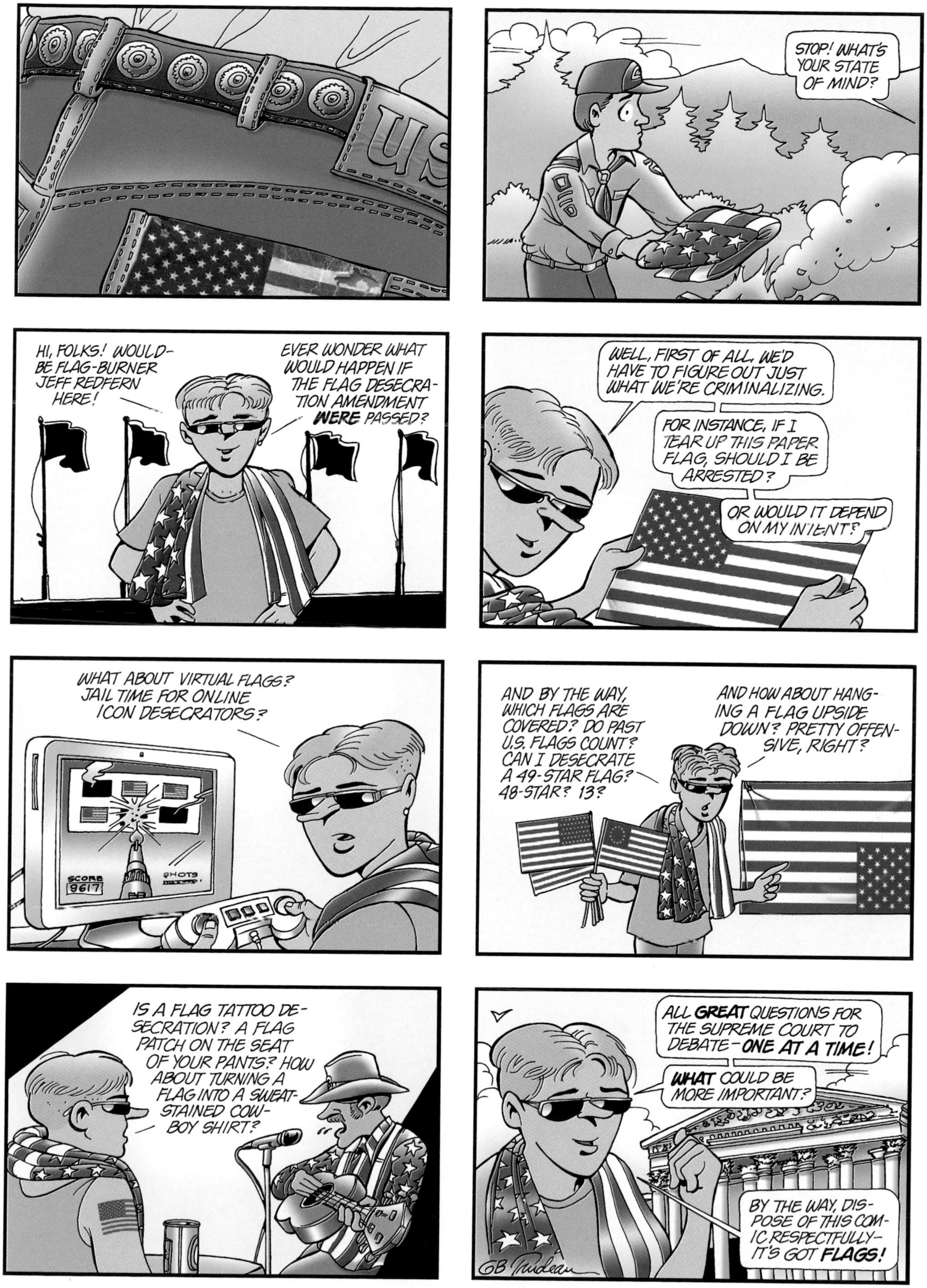
STOP! WHAT'S YOUR STATE OF MIND?
HI, FOLKS! WOULD-BE FLAG-BURNER JEFF REDFERN HERE!
EVER WONDER WHAT WOULD HAPPEN IF THE FLAG DESECRATION AMENDMENT WERE PASSED?
WELL, FIRST OF ALL, WE'D HAVE TO FIGURE OUT JUST WHAT WE'RE CRIMINALIZING.
FOR INSTANCE, IF I TEAR UP THIS PAPER FLAG, SHOULD I BE ARRESTED?
OR WOULD IT DEPEND ON MY INTENT?
WHAT ABOUT VIRTUAL FLAGS? JAIL TIME FOR ONLINE ICON DESECRATORS?
SCORE
9617
SHOTS
AND BY THE WAY, WHICH FLAGS ARE COVERED? DO PAST U.S. FLAGS COUNT? CAN I DESECRATE A 49-STAR FLAG? 48-STAR? 13?
AND HOW ABOUT HANGING A FLAG UPSIDE DOWN? PRETTY OFFENSIVE, RIGHT?
IS A FLAG TATTOO DESECRATION? A FLAG PATCH ON THE SEAT OF YOUR PANTS? HOW ABOUT TURNING A FLAG INTO A SWEAT-STAINED COWBOY SHIRT?
ALL GREAT QUESTIONS FOR THE SUPREME COURT TO DEBATE—ONE AT A TIME!
WHAT COULD BE MORE IMPORTANT?
BY THE WAY, DISPOSE OF THIS COMIC RESPECTFULLY—IT'S GOT FLAGS!
GB Trudeau

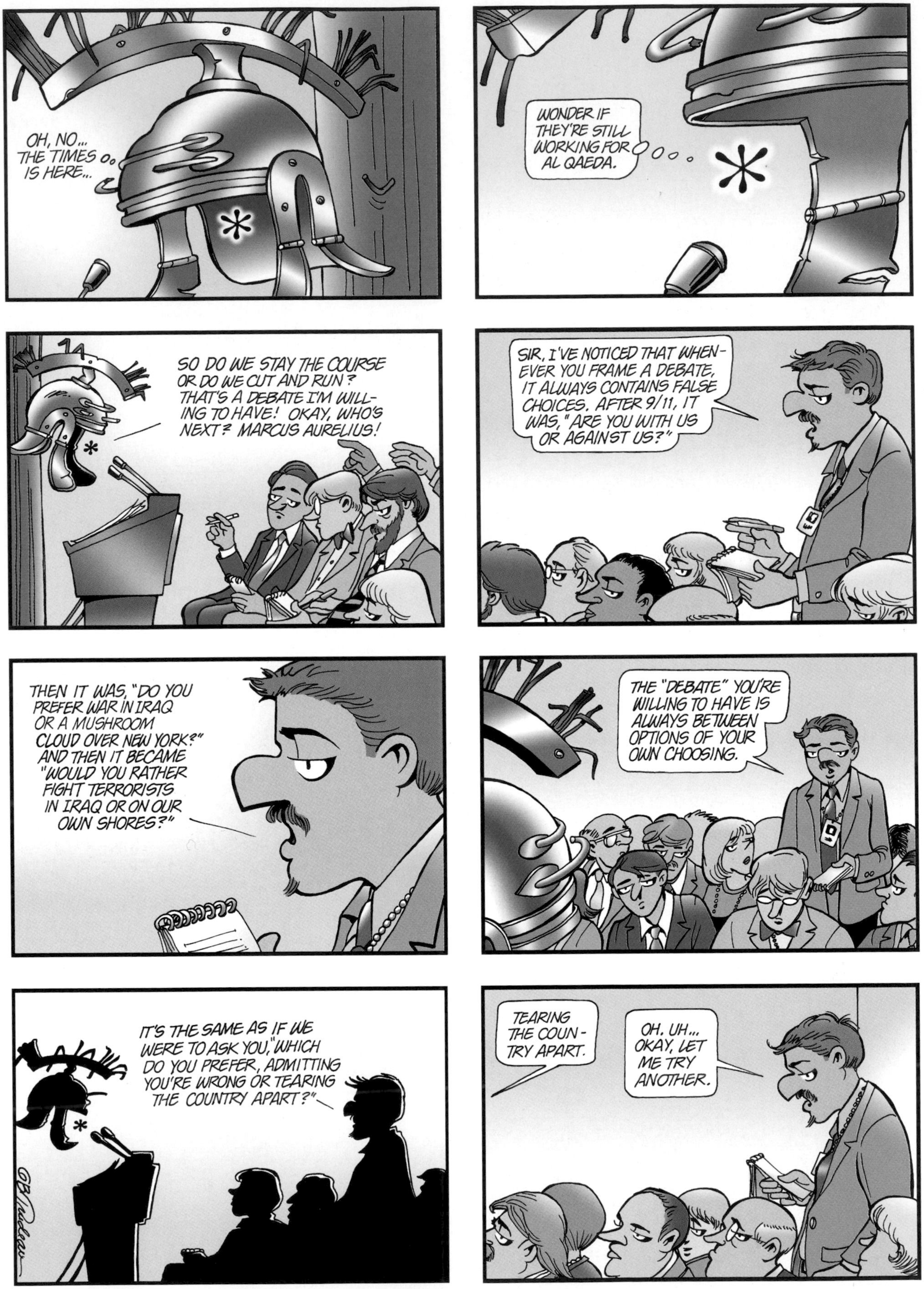
OH, NO... THE TIMES IS HERE...
WONDER IF THEY'RE STILL WORKING FOR AL QAEDA.
SO DO WE STAY THE COURSE OR DO WE CUT AND RUN? THAT'S A DEBATE I'M WILLING TO HAVE! OKAY, WHO'S NEXT? MARCUS AURELIUS!
SIR, I'VE NOTICED THAT WHENEVER YOU FRAME A DEBATE, IT ALWAYS CONTAINS FALSE CHOICES. AFTER 9/11, IT WAS, "ARE YOU WITH US OR AGAINST US?"
THEN IT WAS, "DO YOU PREFER WAR IN IRAQ OR A MUSHROOM CLOUD OVER NEW YORK?" AND THEN IT BECAME "WOULD YOU RATHER FIGHT TERRORISTS IN IRAQ OR ON OUR OWN SHORES?"
THE "DEBATE" YOU'RE WILLING TO HAVE IS ALWAYS BETWEEN OPTIONS OF YOUR OWN CHOOSING.
IT'S THE SAME AS IF WE WERE TO ASK YOU, "WHICH DO YOU PREFER, ADMITTING YOU'RE WRONG OR TEARING THE COUNTRY APART?"
TEARING THE COUNTRY APART.
OH, UH... OKAY, LET ME TRY ANOTHER.

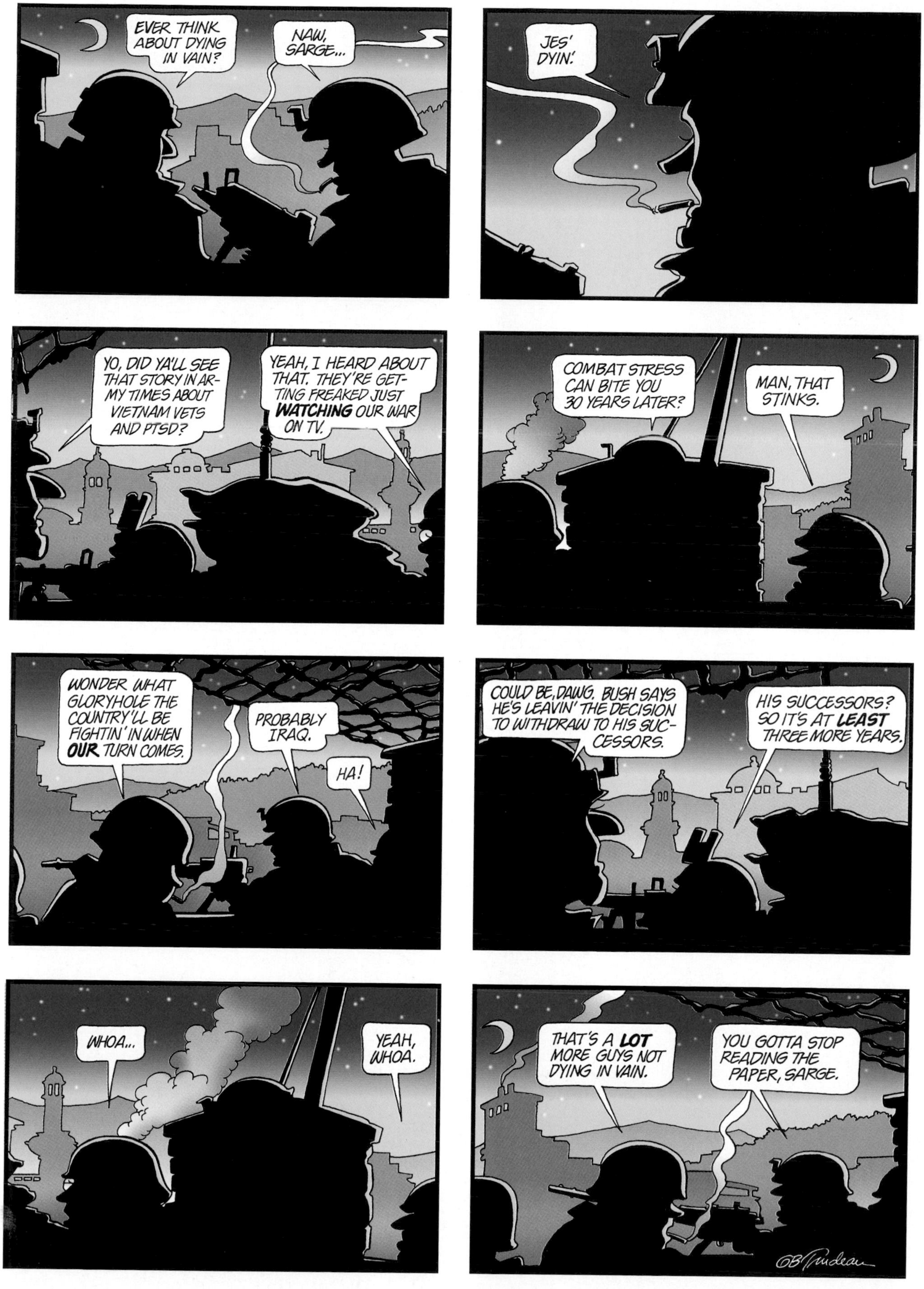
EVER THINK ABOUT DYING IN VAIN?
NAW, SARGE...
JES' DYIN'.
YO, DID YA'LL SEE THAT STORY IN ARMY TIMES ABOUT VIETNAM VETS AND PTSD?
YEAH, I HEARD ABOUT THAT. THEY'RE GETTING FREAKED JUST WATCHING OUR WAR ON TV.
COMBAT STRESS CAN BITE YOU 30 YEARS LATER?
MAN, THAT STINKS.
WONDER WHAT GLORYHOLE THE COUNTRY'LL BE FIGHTIN' IN WHEN OUR TURN COMES.
PROBABLY IRAQ.
HA!
COULD BE, DAWG. BUSH SAYS HE'S LEAVIN' THE DECISION TO WITHDRAW TO HIS SUCCESSORS.
HIS SUCCESSORS? SO IT'S AT LEAST THREE MORE YEARS.
WHOA...
YEAH, WHOA.
THAT'S A LOT MORE GUYS NOT DYING IN VAIN.
YOU GOTTA STOP READING THE PAPER, SARGE.
GB Trudeau

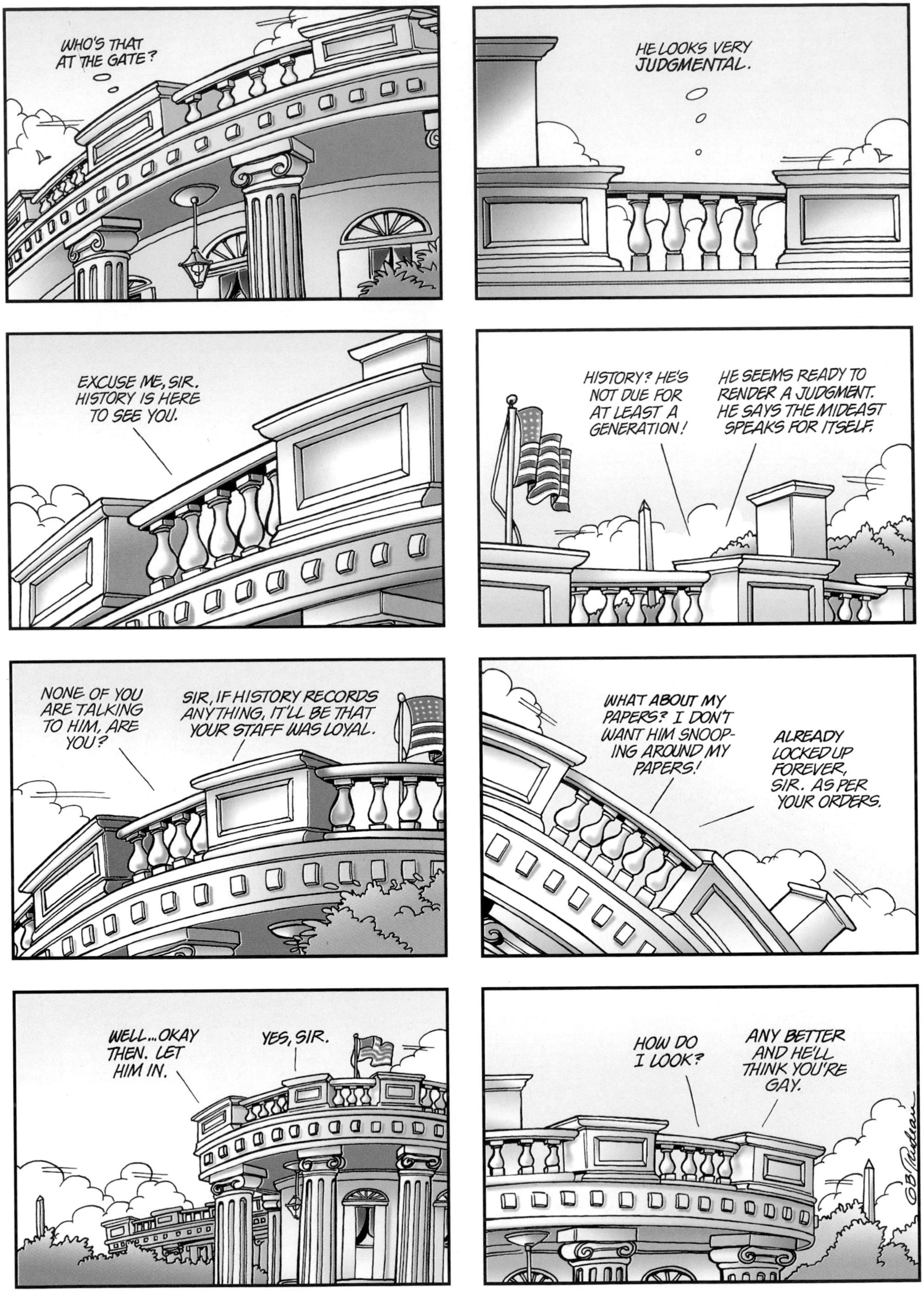
WHO'S THAT AT THE GATE?
HE LOOKS VERY JUDGMENTAL.
EXCUSE ME, SIR. HISTORY IS HERE TO SEE YOU.
HISTORY? HE'S NOT DUE FOR AT LEAST A GENERATION!
HE SEEMS READY TO RENDER A JUDGMENT. HE SAYS THE MIDEAST SPEAKS FOR ITSELF.
NONE OF YOU ARE TALKING TO HIM, ARE YOU?
SIR, IF HISTORY RECORDS ANYTHING, IT'LL BE THAT YOUR STAFF WAS LOYAL.
WHAT ABOUT MY PAPERS? I DON'T WANT HIM SNOOPING AROUND MY PAPERS!
ALREADY LOCKED UP FOREVER, SIR. AS PER YOUR ORDERS.
WELL...OKAY THEN. LET HIM IN.
YES, SIR.
HOW DO I LOOK?
ANY BETTER AND HE'LL THINK YOU'RE GAY.
©B Trudeau

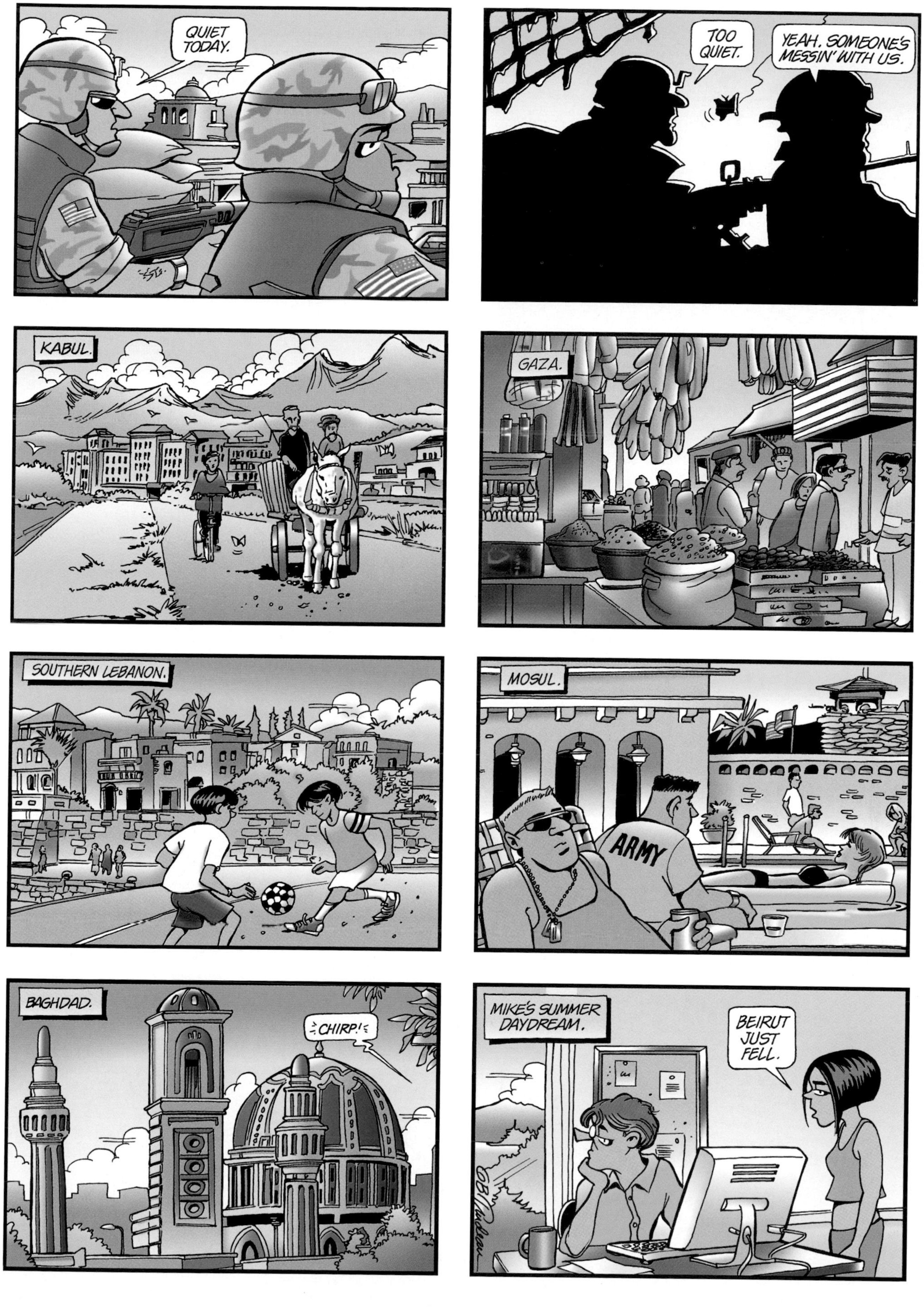
QUIET TODAY.
TOO QUIET.
YEAH. SOMEONE'S MESSIN' WITH US.
KABUL.
GAZA.
SOUTHERN LEBANON.
MOSUL.
ARMY
BAGHDAD.
CHIRP!
MIKE'S SUMMER DAYDREAM.
BEIRUT JUST FELL.

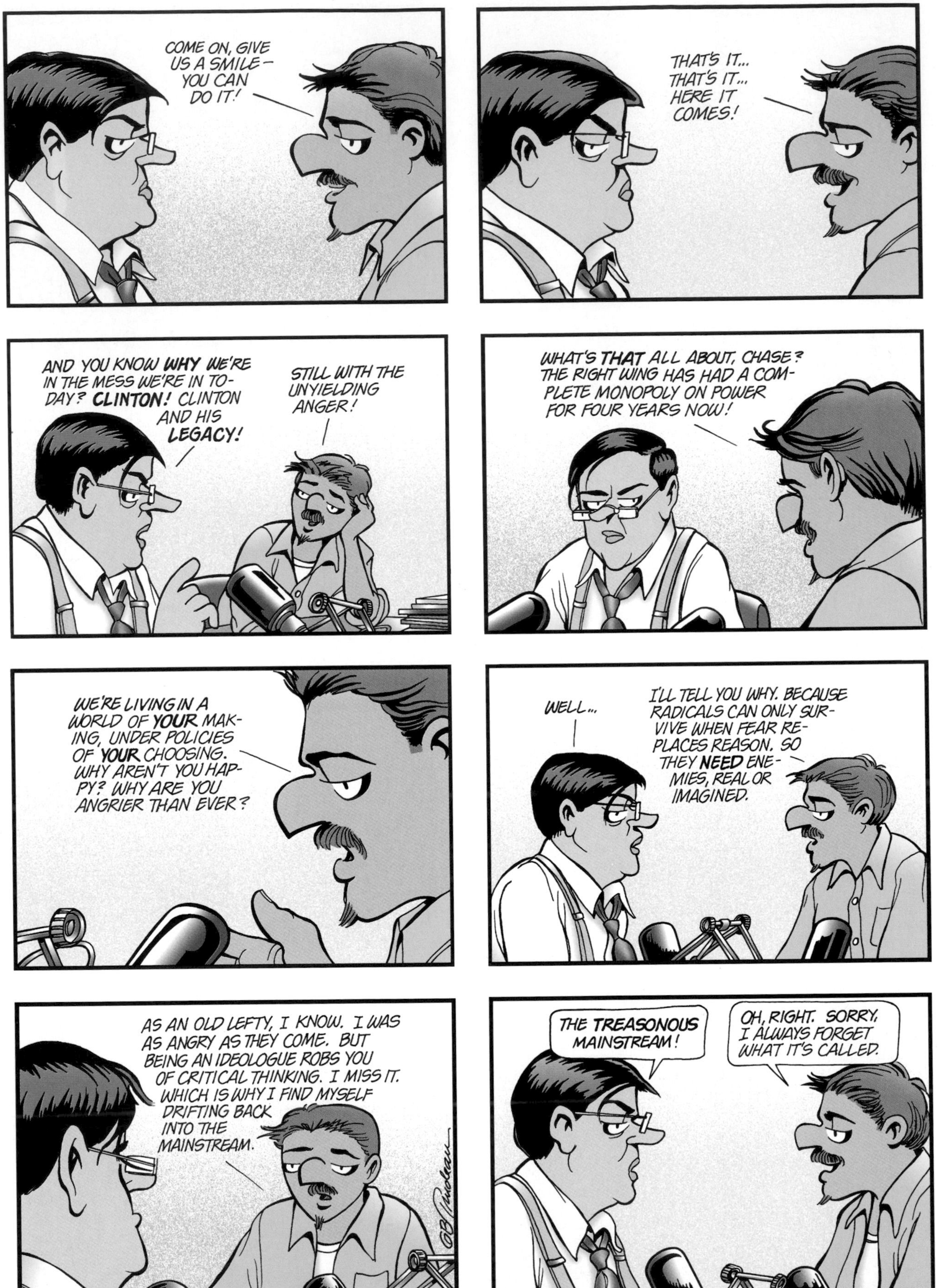
COME ON, GIVE US A SMILE– YOU CAN DO IT!
THAT'S IT... THAT'S IT... HERE IT COMES!
AND YOU KNOW WHY WE'RE IN THE MESS WE'RE IN TODAY? CLINTON! CLINTON AND HIS LEGACY!
STILL WITH THE UNYIELDING ANGER!
WHAT'S THAT ALL ABOUT, CHASE? THE RIGHT WING HAS HAD A COMPLETE MONOPOLY ON POWER FOR FOUR YEARS NOW!
WE'RE LIVING IN A WORLD OF YOUR MAKING, UNDER POLICIES OF YOUR CHOOSING. WHY AREN'T YOU HAPPY? WHY ARE YOU ANGRIER THAN EVER?
WELL...
I'LL TELL YOU WHY. BECAUSE RADICALS CAN ONLY SURVIVE WHEN FEAR REPLACES REASON. SO THEY NEED ENEMIES, REAL OR IMAGINED.
AS AN OLD LEFTY, I KNOW. I WAS AS ANGRY AS THEY COME. BUT BEING AN IDEOLOGUE ROBS YOU OF CRITICAL THINKING. I MISS IT. WHICH IS WHY I FIND MYSELF DRIFTING BACK INTO THE MAINSTREAM.
THE TREASONOUS MAINSTREAM!
OH, RIGHT. SORRY. I ALWAYS FORGET WHAT IT'S CALLED.

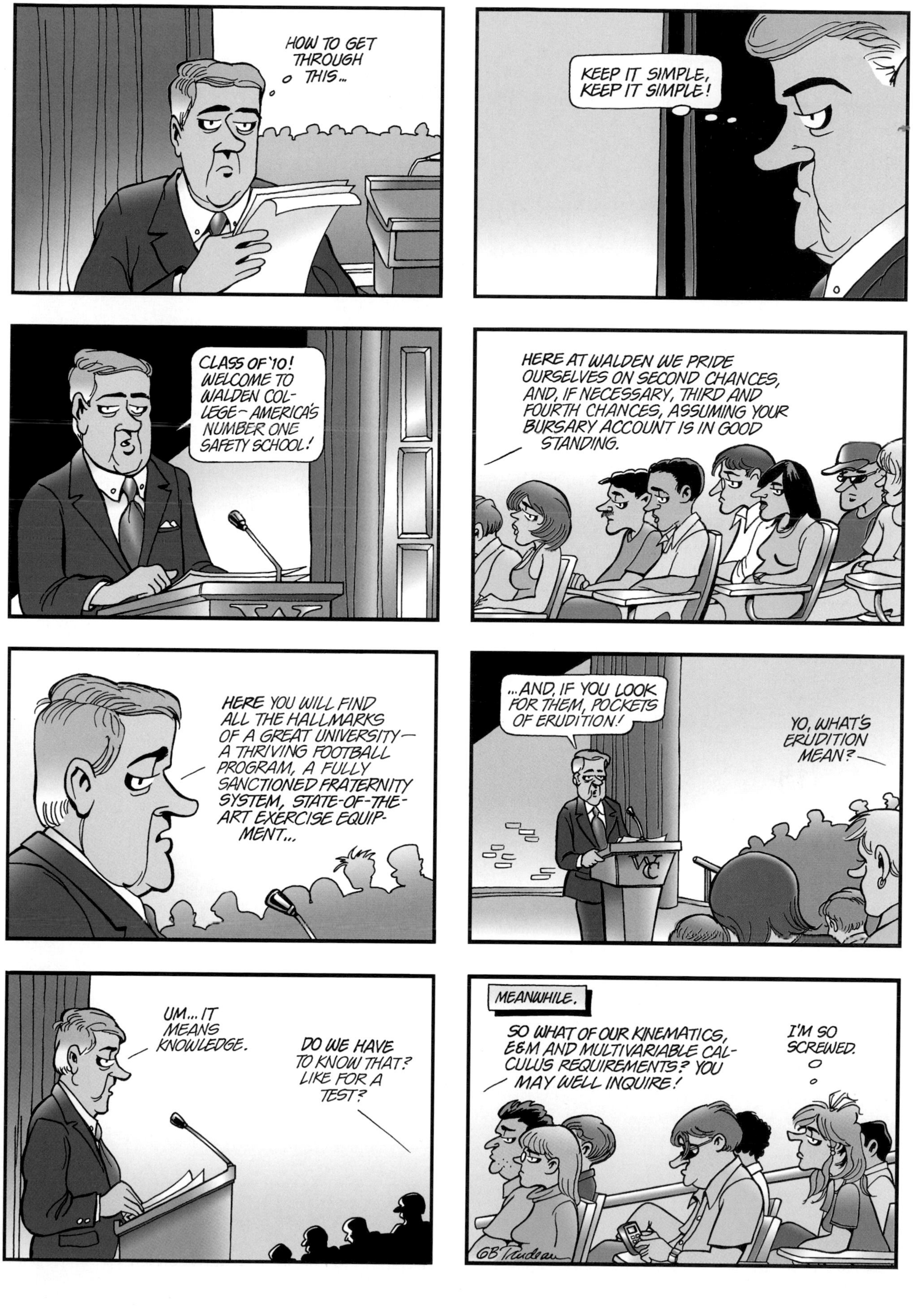
HOW TO GET THROUGH THIS...
KEEP IT SIMPLE, KEEP IT SIMPLE!
CLASS OF '10! WELCOME TO WALDEN COLLEGE—AMERICA'S NUMBER ONE SAFETY SCHOOL!
HERE AT WALDEN WE PRIDE OURSELVES ON SECOND CHANCES, AND, IF NECESSARY, THIRD AND FOURTH CHANCES, ASSUMING YOUR BURSARY ACCOUNT IS IN GOOD STANDING.
HERE YOU WILL FIND ALL THE HALLMARKS OF A GREAT UNIVERSITY—A THRIVING FOOTBALL PROGRAM, A FULLY SANCTIONED FRATERNITY SYSTEM, STATE-OF-THE-ART EXERCISE EQUIPMENT...
...AND, IF YOU LOOK FOR THEM, POCKETS OF ERUDITION!
YO, WHAT'S ERUDITION MEAN?
UM... IT MEANS KNOWLEDGE.
DO WE HAVE TO KNOW THAT? LIKE FOR A TEST?
MEANWHILE.
SO WHAT OF OUR KINEMATICS, E&M AND MULTIVARIABLE CALCULUS REQUIREMENTS? YOU MAY WELL INQUIRE!
I'M SO SCREWED.
GB Trudeau

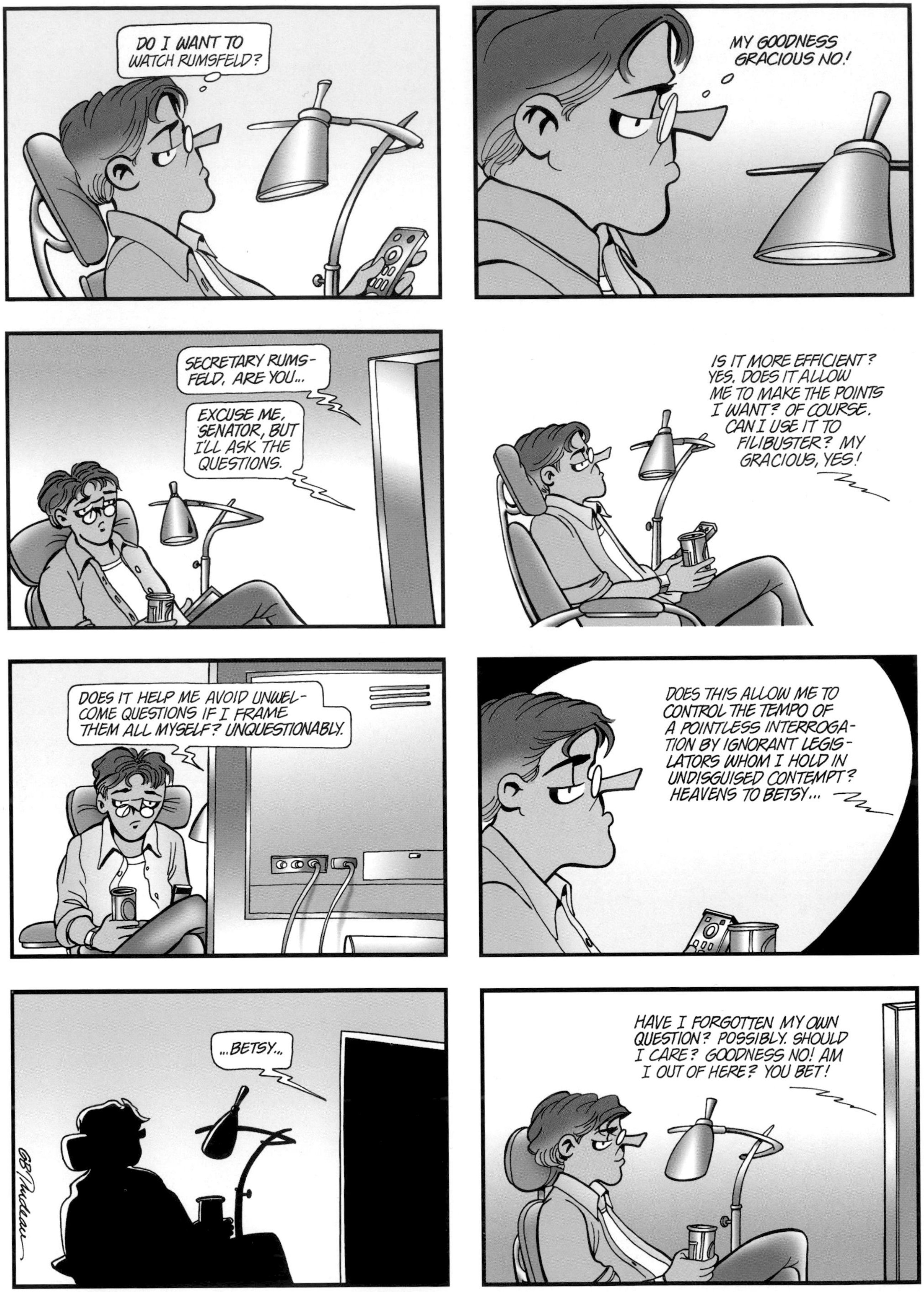
DO I WANT TO WATCH RUMSFELD?
MY GOODNESS GRACIOUS NO!
SECRETARY RUMSFELD, ARE YOU...
EXCUSE ME, SENATOR, BUT I'LL ASK THE QUESTIONS.
IS IT MORE EFFICIENT? YES. DOES IT ALLOW ME TO MAKE THE POINTS I WANT? OF COURSE. CAN I USE IT TO FILIBUSTER? MY GRACIOUS, YES!
DOES IT HELP ME AVOID UNWELCOME QUESTIONS IF I FRAME THEM ALL MYSELF? UNQUESTIONABLY.
DOES THIS ALLOW ME TO CONTROL THE TEMPO OF A POINTLESS INTERROGATION BY IGNORANT LEGISLATORS WHOM I HOLD IN UNDISGUISED CONTEMPT? HEAVENS TO BETSY...
...BETSY...
HAVE I FORGOTTEN MY OWN QUESTION? POSSIBLY. SHOULD I CARE? GOODNESS NO! AM I OUT OF HERE? YOU BET!

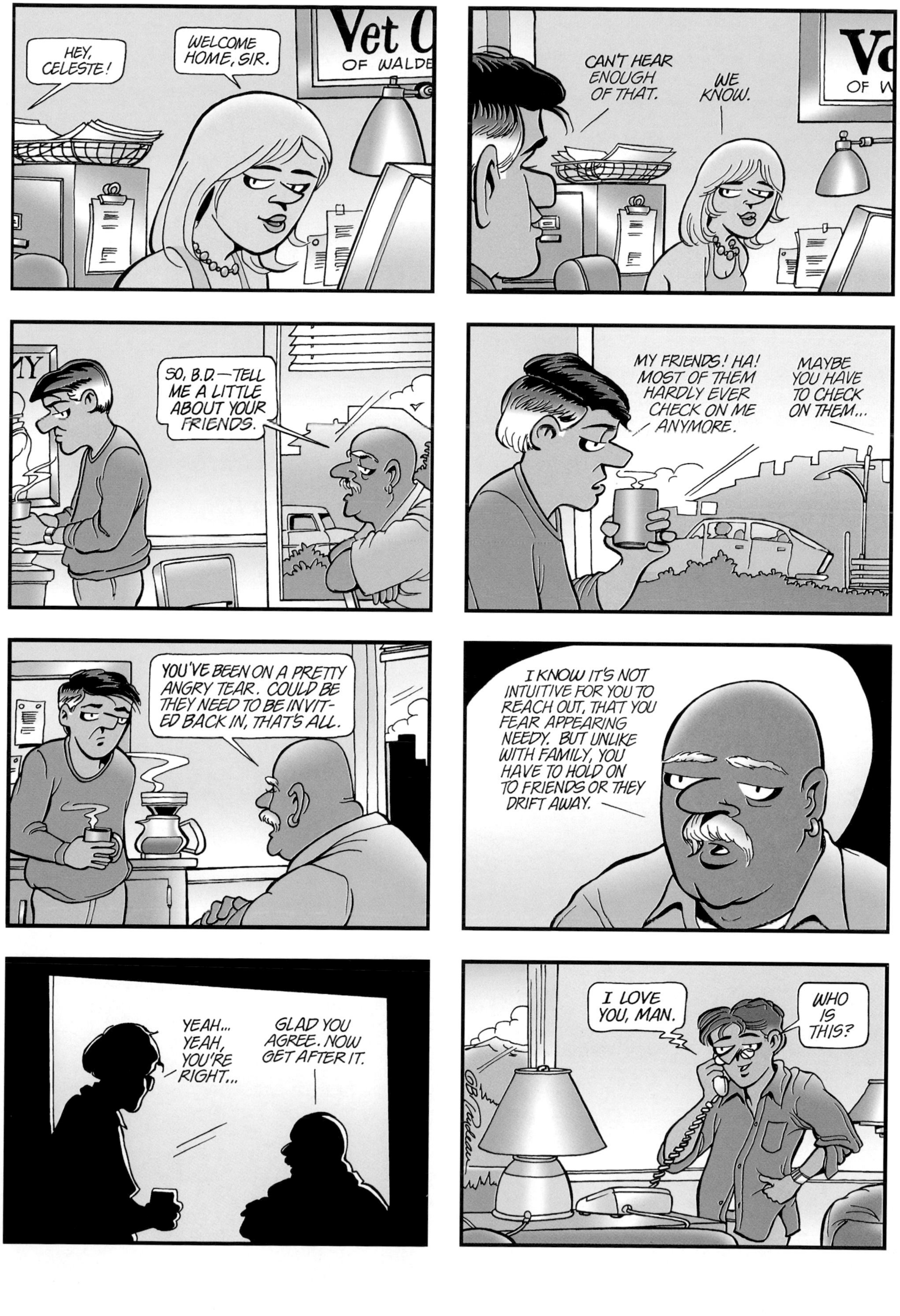

HEY, CELESTE!
WELCOME HOME, SIR.
Vet C
OF WALDE
CAN'T HEAR ENOUGH OF THAT.
WE KNOW.
SO, B.D.—TELL ME A LITTLE ABOUT YOUR FRIENDS.
MY FRIENDS! HA! MOST OF THEM HARDLY EVER CHECK ON ME ANYMORE.
MAYBE YOU HAVE TO CHECK ON THEM...
YOU'VE BEEN ON A PRETTY ANGRY TEAR. COULD BE THEY NEED TO BE INVIT-ED BACK IN, THAT'S ALL.
I KNOW IT'S NOT INTUITIVE FOR YOU TO REACH OUT, THAT YOU FEAR APPEARING NEEDY. BUT UNLIKE WITH FAMILY, YOU HAVE TO HOLD ON TO FRIENDS OR THEY DRIFT AWAY.
YEAH... YEAH, YOU'RE RIGHT...
GLAD YOU AGREE. NOW GET AFTER IT.
I LOVE YOU, MAN.
WHO IS THIS?

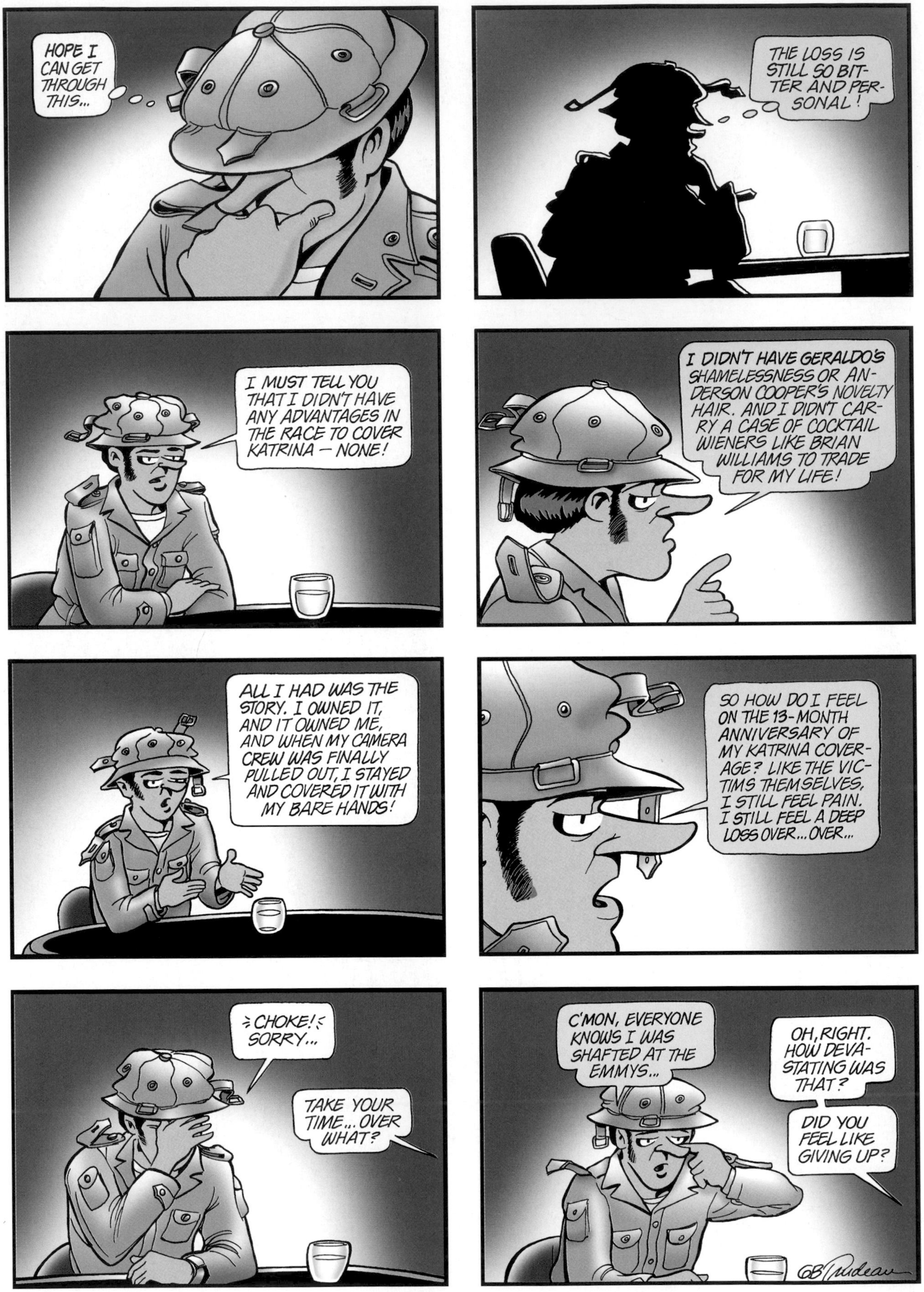
HOPE I CAN GET THROUGH THIS...
THE LOSS IS STILL SO BITTER AND PERSONAL!
I MUST TELL YOU THAT I DIDN'T HAVE ANY ADVANTAGES IN THE RACE TO COVER KATRINA — NONE!
I DIDN'T HAVE GERALDO'S SHAMELESSNESS OR ANDERSON COOPER'S NOVELTY HAIR. AND I DIDN'T CARRY A CASE OF COCKTAIL WIENERS LIKE BRIAN WILLIAMS TO TRADE FOR MY LIFE!
ALL I HAD WAS THE STORY. I OWNED IT, AND IT OWNED ME, AND WHEN MY CAMERA CREW WAS FINALLY PULLED OUT, I STAYED AND COVERED IT WITH MY BARE HANDS!
SO HOW DO I FEEL ON THE 13-MONTH ANNIVERSARY OF MY KATRINA COVERAGE? LIKE THE VICTIMS THEMSELVES, I STILL FEEL PAIN. I STILL FEEL A DEEP LOSS OVER... OVER...
CHOKE! SORRY...
TAKE YOUR TIME... OVER WHAT?
C'MON, EVERYONE KNOWS I WAS SHAFTED AT THE EMMYS...
OH, RIGHT. HOW DEVASTATING WAS THAT?
DID YOU FEEL LIKE GIVING UP?
GB Trudeau

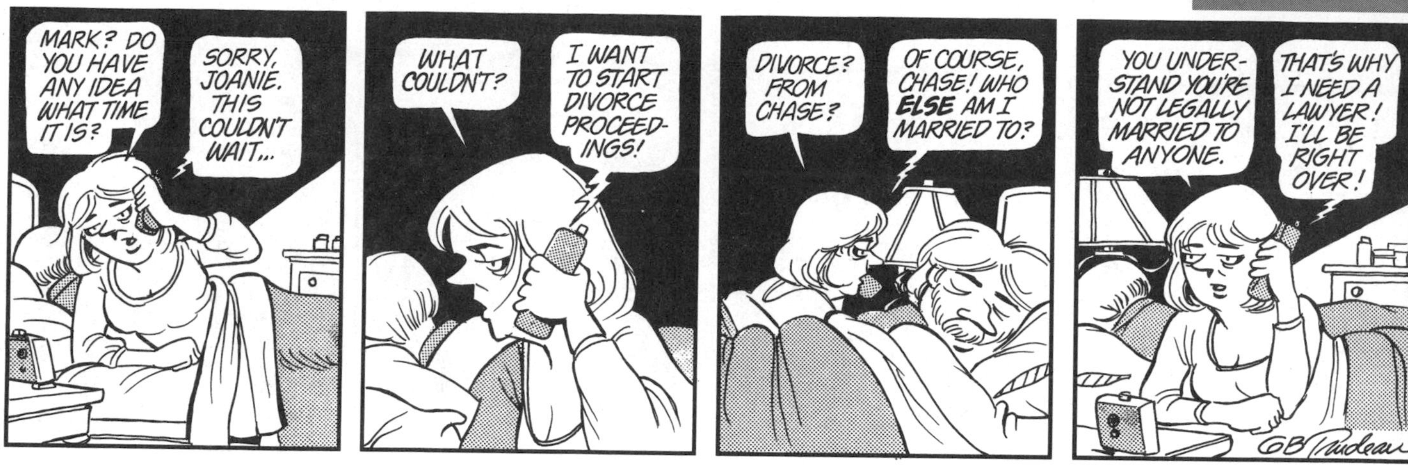
MARK? DO YOU HAVE ANY IDEA WHAT TIME IT IS?
SORRY, JOANIE. THIS COULDN'T WAIT...
WHAT COULDN'T?
I WANT TO START DIVORCE PROCEEDINGS!
DIVORCE? FROM CHASE?
OF COURSE, CHASE! WHO ELSE AM I MARRIED TO?
YOU UNDERSTAND YOU'RE NOT LEGALLY MARRIED TO ANYONE.
THAT'S WHY I NEED A LAWYER! I'LL BE RIGHT OVER!
GB Trudeau

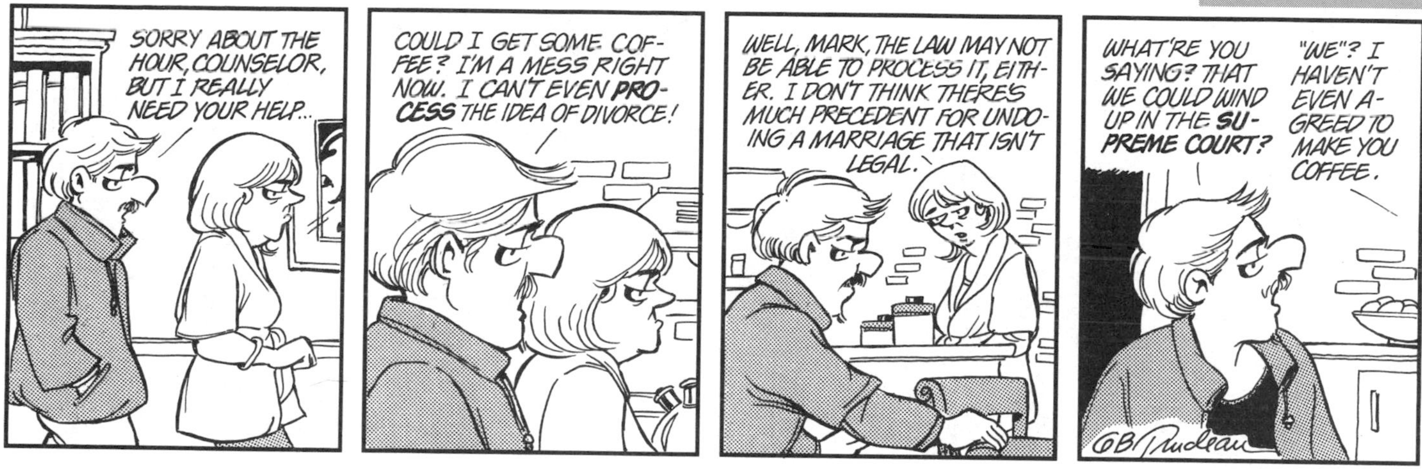
SORRY ABOUT THE HOUR, COUNSELOR, BUT I REALLY NEED YOUR HELP...
COULD I GET SOME COFFEE? I'M A MESS RIGHT NOW. I CAN'T EVEN PROCESS THE IDEA OF DIVORCE!
WELL, MARK, THE LAW MAY NOT BE ABLE TO PROCESS IT, EITHER. I DON'T THINK THERE'S MUCH PRECEDENT FOR UNDOING A MARRIAGE THAT ISN'T LEGAL.
WHAT'RE YOU SAYING? THAT WE COULD WIND UP IN THE SUPREME COURT?
"WE"? I HAVEN'T EVEN AGREED TO MAKE YOU COFFEE.
GB Trudeau

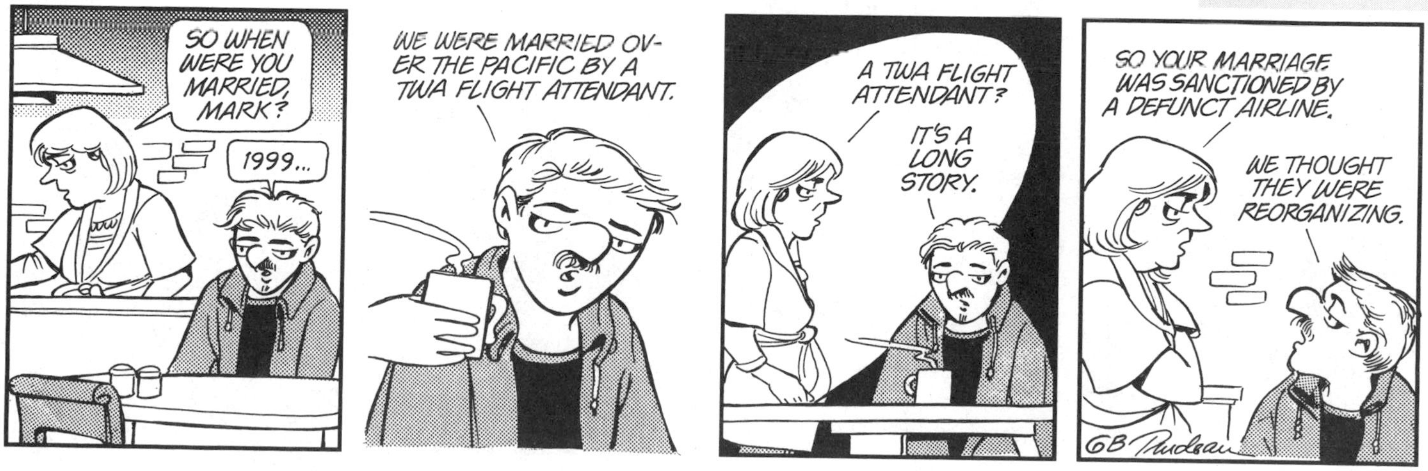
SO WHEN WERE YOU MARRIED, MARK?
1999...
WE WERE MARRIED OVER THE PACIFIC BY A TWA FLIGHT ATTENDANT.
A TWA FLIGHT ATTENDANT?
IT'S A LONG STORY.
SO YOUR MARRIAGE WAS SANCTIONED BY A DEFUNCT AIRLINE.
WE THOUGHT THEY WERE REORGANIZING.
GB Trudeau

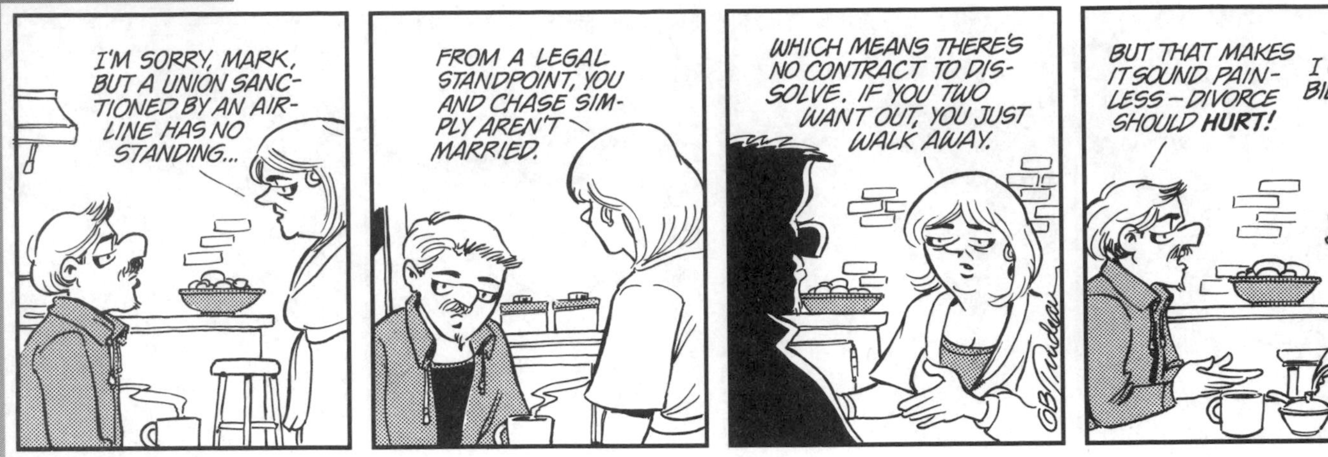
I'M SORRY, MARK, BUT A UNION SANCTIONED BY AN AIRLINE HAS NO STANDING...
FROM A LEGAL STANDPOINT, YOU AND CHASE SIMPLY AREN'T MARRIED.
WHICH MEANS THERE'S NO CONTRACT TO DISSOLVE. IF YOU TWO WANT OUT, YOU JUST WALK AWAY.
BUT THAT MAKES IT SOUND PAINLESS — DIVORCE SHOULD **HURT!**
I COULD BILL YOU.

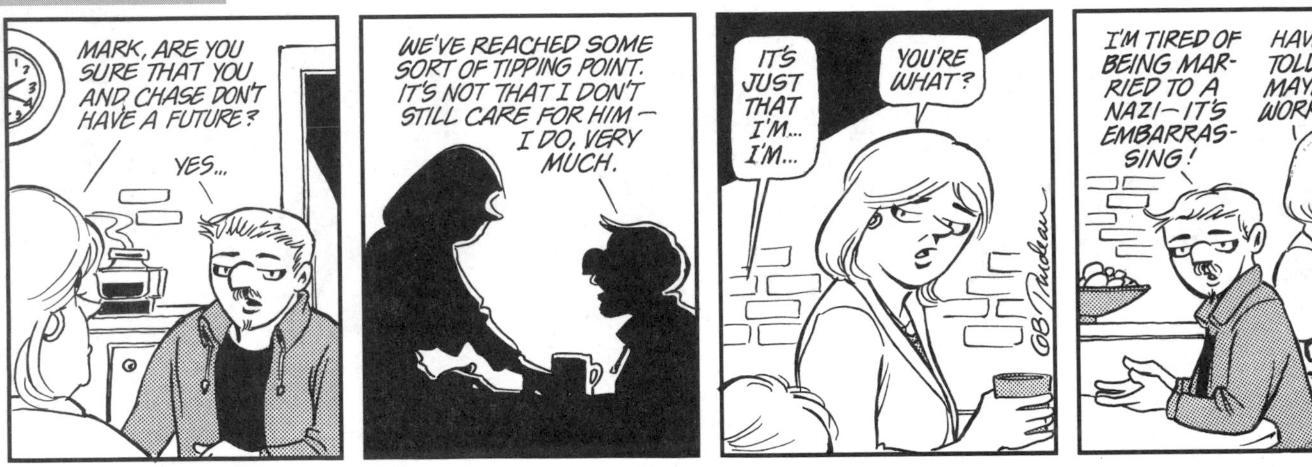
MARK, ARE YOU SURE THAT YOU AND CHASE DON'T HAVE A FUTURE?
YES...
WE'VE REACHED SOME SORT OF TIPPING POINT. IT'S NOT THAT I DON'T STILL CARE FOR HIM — I DO, VERY MUCH.
IT'S JUST THAT I'M... I'M...
YOU'RE WHAT?
I'M TIRED OF BEING MARRIED TO A NAZI — IT'S EMBARRASSING!
HAVE YOU TOLD HIM? MAYBE HE'D WORK ON IT.

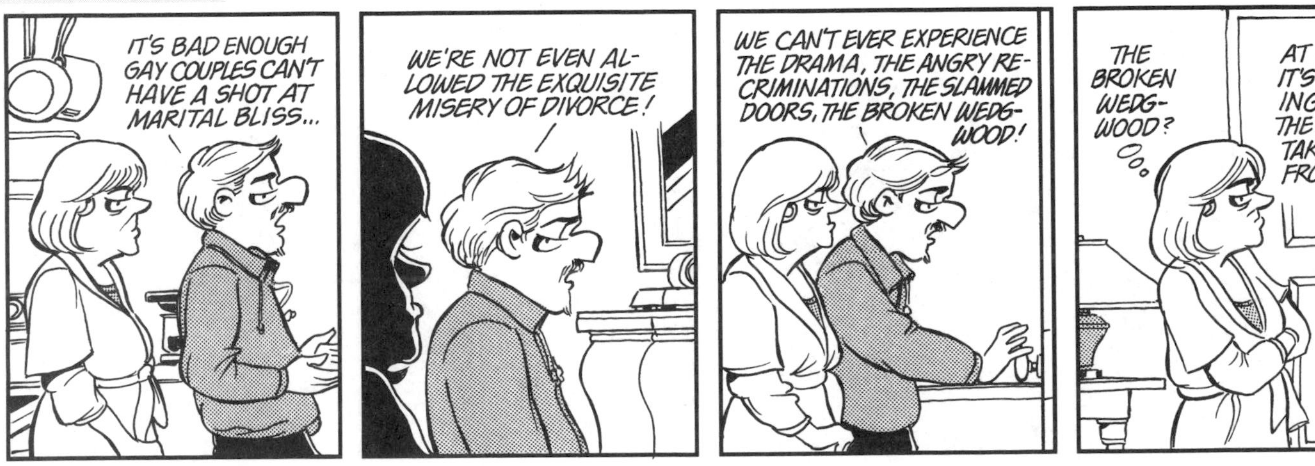
IT'S BAD ENOUGH GAY COUPLES CAN'T HAVE A SHOT AT MARITAL BLISS...
WE'RE NOT EVEN ALLOWED THE EXQUISITE MISERY OF DIVORCE!
WE CAN'T EVER EXPERIENCE THE DRAMA, THE ANGRY RECRIMINATIONS, THE SLAMMED DOORS, THE BROKEN WEDGWOOD!
THE BROKEN WEDGWOOD?
AT LEAST IT'S RAINING OUT. THEY CAN'T TAKE THAT FROM ME.

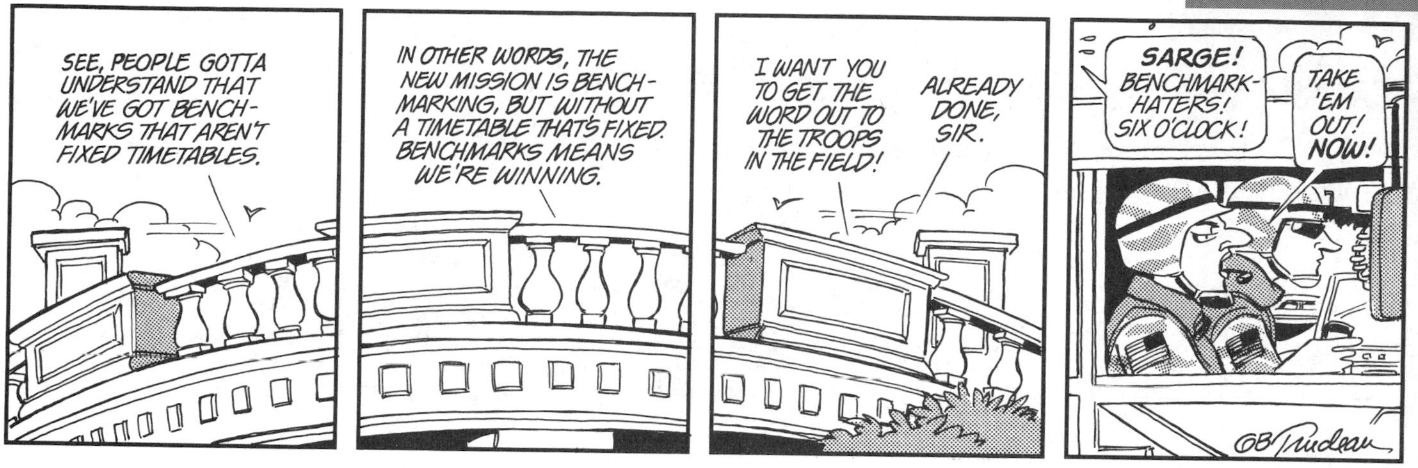
SEE, PEOPLE GOTTA UNDERSTAND THAT WE'VE GOT BENCH-MARKS THAT AREN'T FIXED TIMETABLES.
IN OTHER WORDS, THE NEW MISSION IS BENCH-MARKING, BUT WITHOUT A TIMETABLE THAT'S FIXED. BENCHMARKS MEANS WE'RE WINNING.
I WANT YOU TO GET THE WORD OUT TO THE TROOPS IN THE FIELD!
ALREADY DONE, SIR.
SARGE! BENCHMARK-HATERS! SIX O'CLOCK!
TAKE 'EM OUT! NOW!

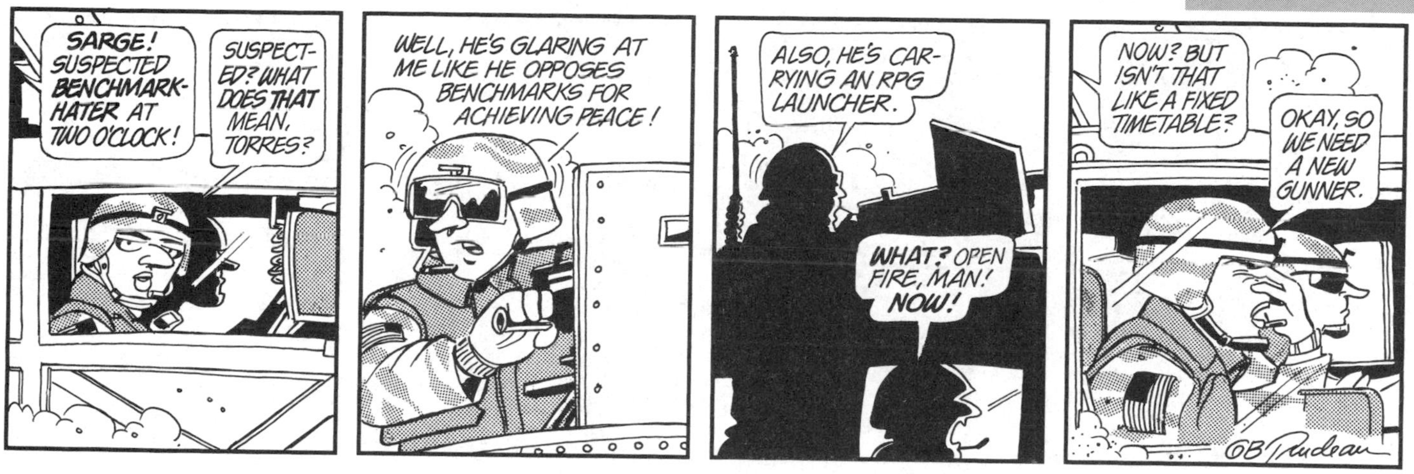
SARGE! SUSPECTED BENCHMARK-HATER AT TWO O'CLOCK!
SUSPECT-ED? WHAT DOES THAT MEAN, TORRES?
WELL, HE'S GLARING AT ME LIKE HE OPPOSES BENCHMARKS FOR ACHIEVING PEACE!
ALSO, HE'S CAR-RYING AN RPG LAUNCHER.
WHAT? OPEN FIRE, MAN! NOW!
NOW? BUT ISN'T THAT LIKE A FIXED TIMETABLE?
OKAY, SO WE NEED A NEW GUNNER.

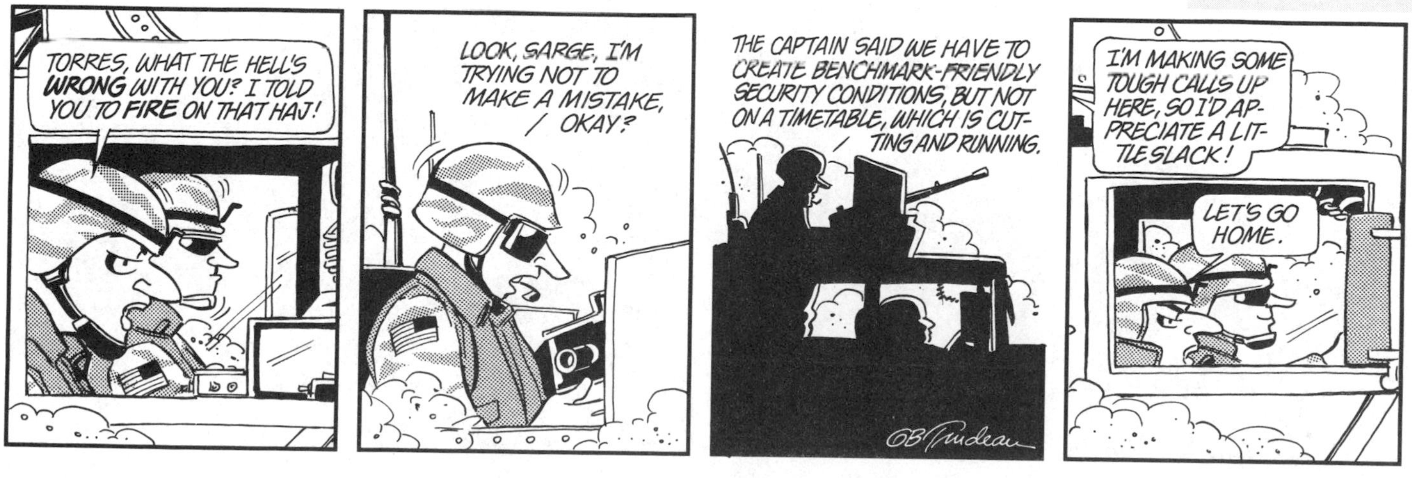
TORRES, WHAT THE HELL'S WRONG WITH YOU? I TOLD YOU TO FIRE ON THAT HAJ!
LOOK, SARGE, I'M TRYING NOT TO MAKE A MISTAKE, OKAY?
THE CAPTAIN SAID WE HAVE TO CREATE BENCHMARK-FRIENDLY SECURITY CONDITIONS, BUT NOT ON A TIMETABLE, WHICH IS CUT-TING AND RUNNING.
I'M MAKING SOME TOUGH CALLS UP HERE, SO I'D AP-PRECIATE A LIT-TLE SLACK!
LET'S GO HOME.

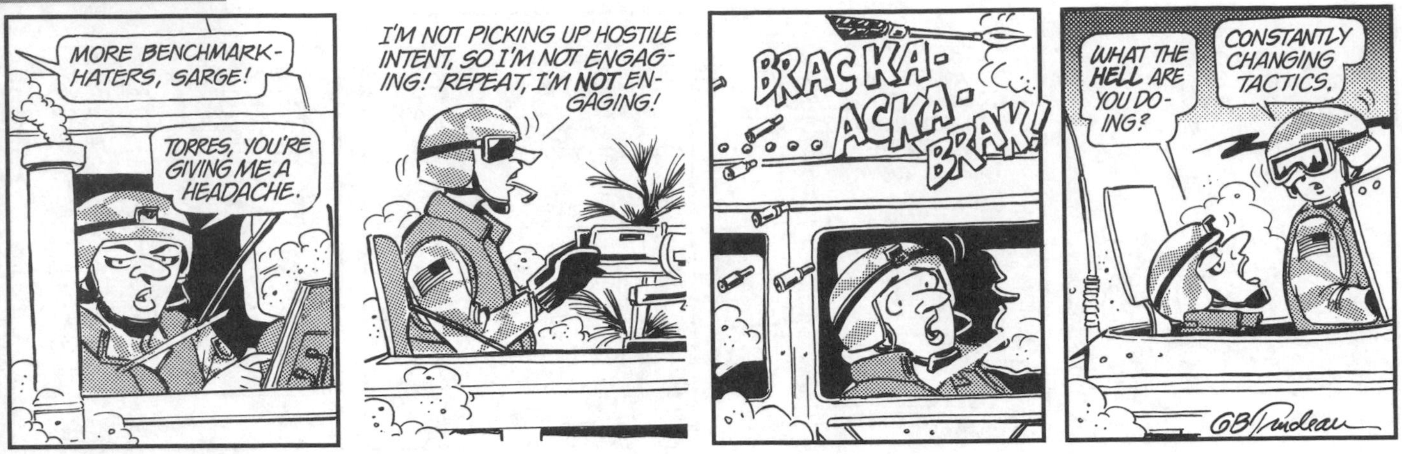
MORE BENCHMARK-HATERS, SARGE!
TORRES, YOU'RE GIVING ME A HEADACHE.
I'M NOT PICKING UP HOSTILE INTENT, SO I'M NOT ENGAGING! REPEAT, I'M NOT ENGAGING!
BRAC KA-ACKA-BRAK!
WHAT THE HELL ARE YOU DOING?
CONSTANTLY CHANGING TACTICS.
GB Trudeau

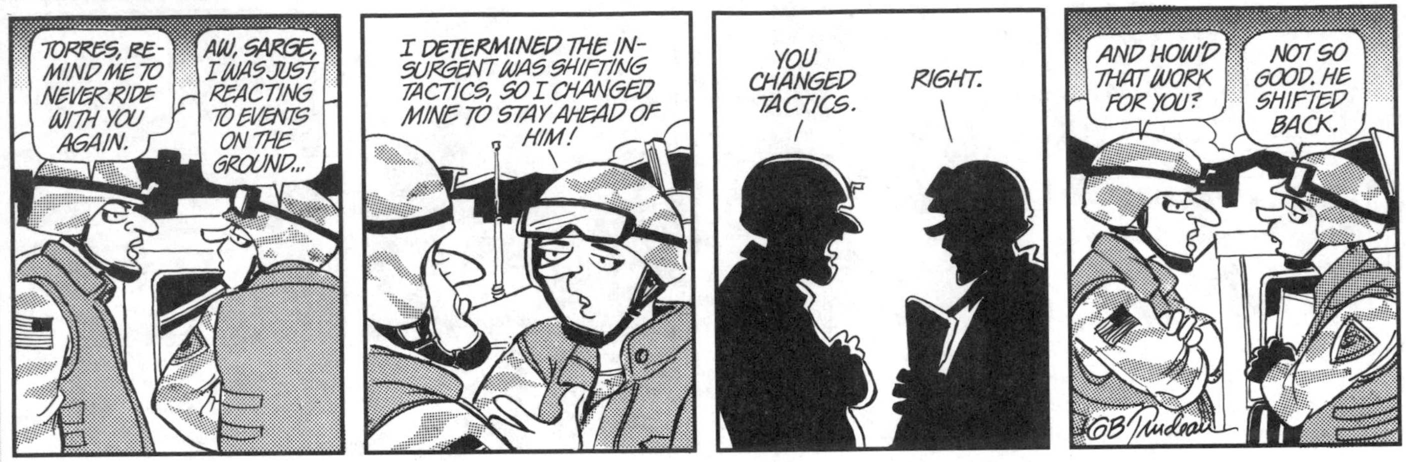
TORRES, REMIND ME TO NEVER RIDE WITH YOU AGAIN.
AW, SARGE, I WAS JUST REACTING TO EVENTS ON THE GROUND...
I DETERMINED THE INSURGENT WAS SHIFTING TACTICS, SO I CHANGED MINE TO STAY AHEAD OF HIM!
YOU CHANGED TACTICS.
RIGHT.
AND HOW'D THAT WORK FOR YOU?
NOT SO GOOD. HE SHIFTED BACK.
GB Trudeau

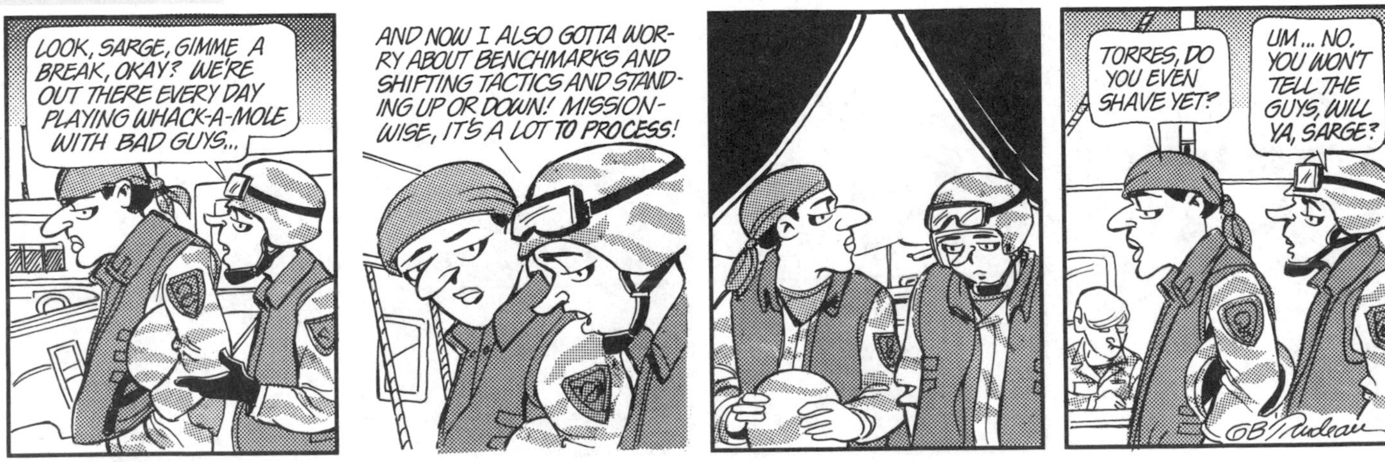
LOOK, SARGE, GIMME A BREAK, OKAY? WE'RE OUT THERE EVERY DAY PLAYING WHACK-A-MOLE WITH BAD GUYS...
AND NOW I ALSO GOTTA WORRY ABOUT BENCHMARKS AND SHIFTING TACTICS AND STANDING UP OR DOWN! MISSION-WISE, IT'S A LOT TO PROCESS!
TORRES, DO YOU EVEN SHAVE YET?
UM ... NO. YOU WON'T TELL THE GUYS, WILL YA, SARGE?
GB Trudeau

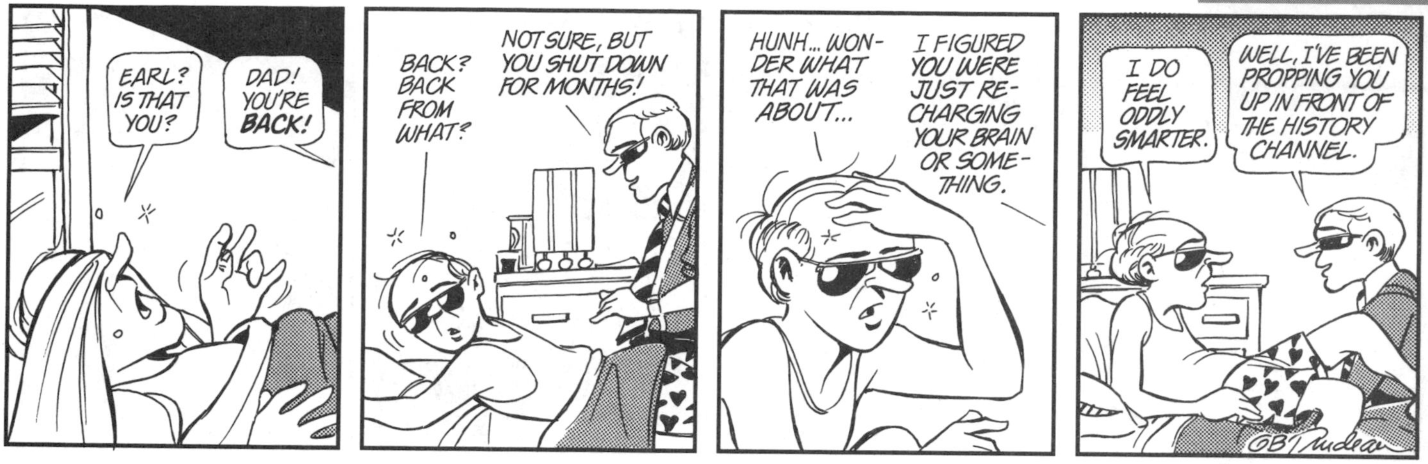
EARL? IS THAT YOU?
DAD! YOU'RE BACK!
BACK? BACK FROM WHAT?
NOT SURE, BUT YOU SHUT DOWN FOR MONTHS!
HUNH... WONDER WHAT THAT WAS ABOUT...
I FIGURED YOU WERE JUST RECHARGING YOUR BRAIN OR SOMETHING.
I DO FEEL ODDLY SMARTER.
WELL, I'VE BEEN PROPPING YOU UP IN FRONT OF THE HISTORY CHANNEL.
GBTrudeau

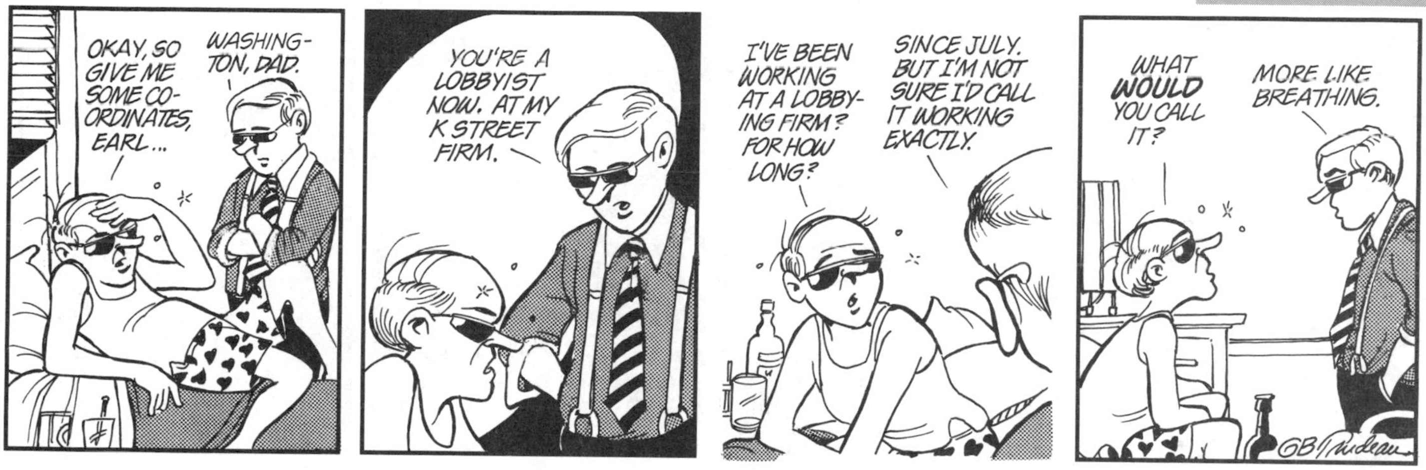
OKAY, SO GIVE ME SOME COORDINATES, EARL...
WASHINGTON, DAD.
YOU'RE A LOBBYIST NOW. AT MY K STREET FIRM.
I'VE BEEN WORKING AT A LOBBYING FIRM? FOR HOW LONG?
SINCE JULY. BUT I'M NOT SURE I'D CALL IT WORKING EXACTLY.
WHAT WOULD YOU CALL IT?
MORE LIKE BREATHING.
GBTrudeau

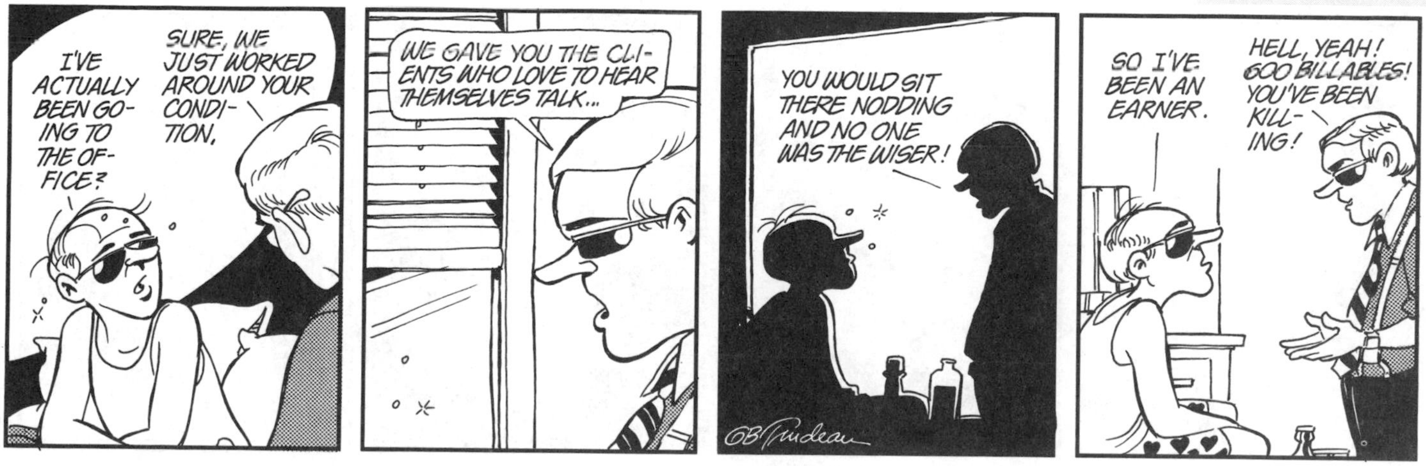
I'VE ACTUALLY BEEN GOING TO THE OFFICE?
SURE, WE JUST WORKED AROUND YOUR CONDITION.
WE GAVE YOU THE CLIENTS WHO LOVE TO HEAR THEMSELVES TALK...
YOU WOULD SIT THERE NODDING AND NO ONE WAS THE WISER!
GBTrudeau
SO I'VE BEEN AN EARNER.
HELL, YEAH! 600 BILLABLES! YOU'VE BEEN KILLING!

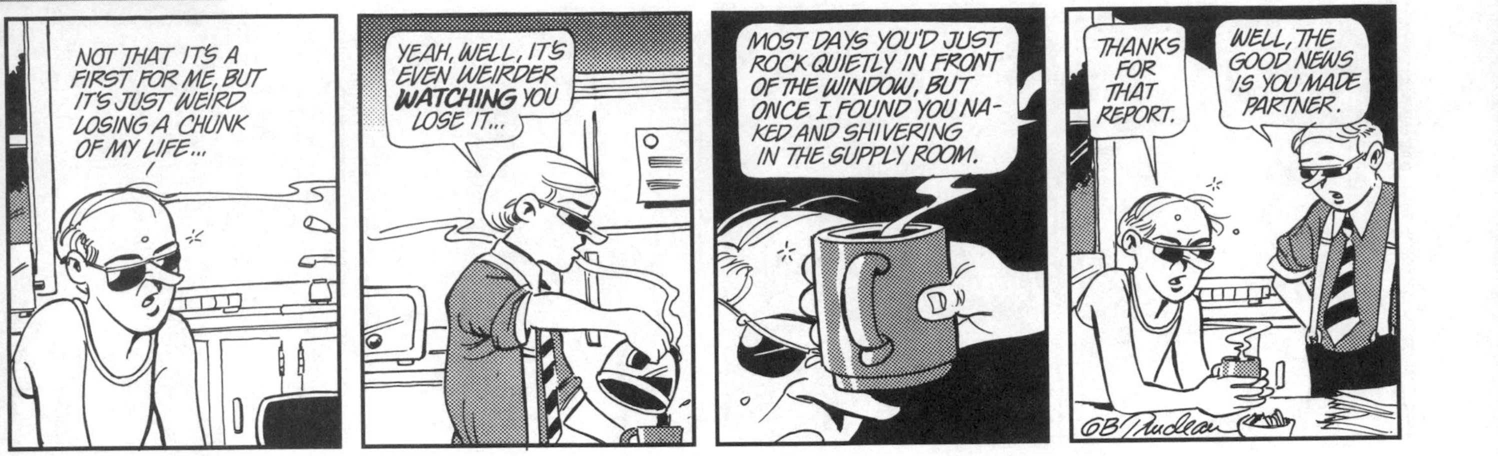
NOT THAT IT'S A FIRST FOR ME, BUT IT'S JUST WEIRD LOSING A CHUNK OF MY LIFE...
YEAH, WELL, IT'S EVEN WEIRDER WATCHING YOU LOSE IT...
MOST DAYS YOU'D JUST ROCK QUIETLY IN FRONT OF THE WINDOW, BUT ONCE I FOUND YOU NAKED AND SHIVERING IN THE SUPPLY ROOM.
THANKS FOR THAT REPORT.
WELL, THE GOOD NEWS IS YOU MADE PARTNER.

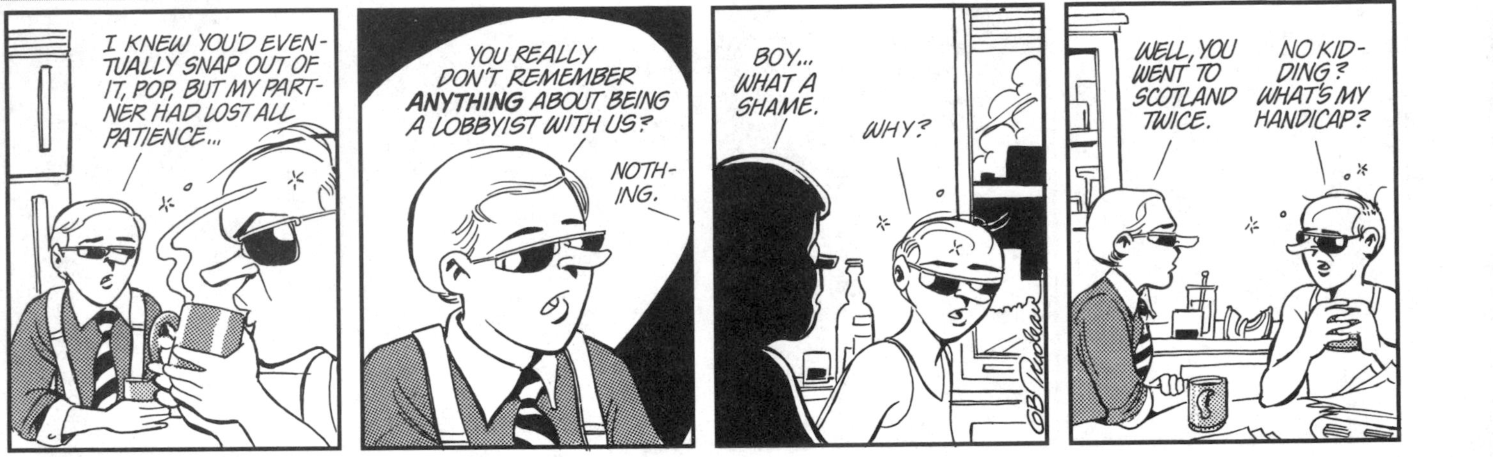
I KNEW YOU'D EVENTUALLY SNAP OUT OF IT, POP, BUT MY PARTNER HAD LOST ALL PATIENCE...
YOU REALLY DON'T REMEMBER ANYTHING ABOUT BEING A LOBBYIST WITH US?
NOTHING.
BOY... WHAT A SHAME.
WHY?
WELL, YOU WENT TO SCOTLAND TWICE.
NO KIDDING? WHAT'S MY HANDICAP?

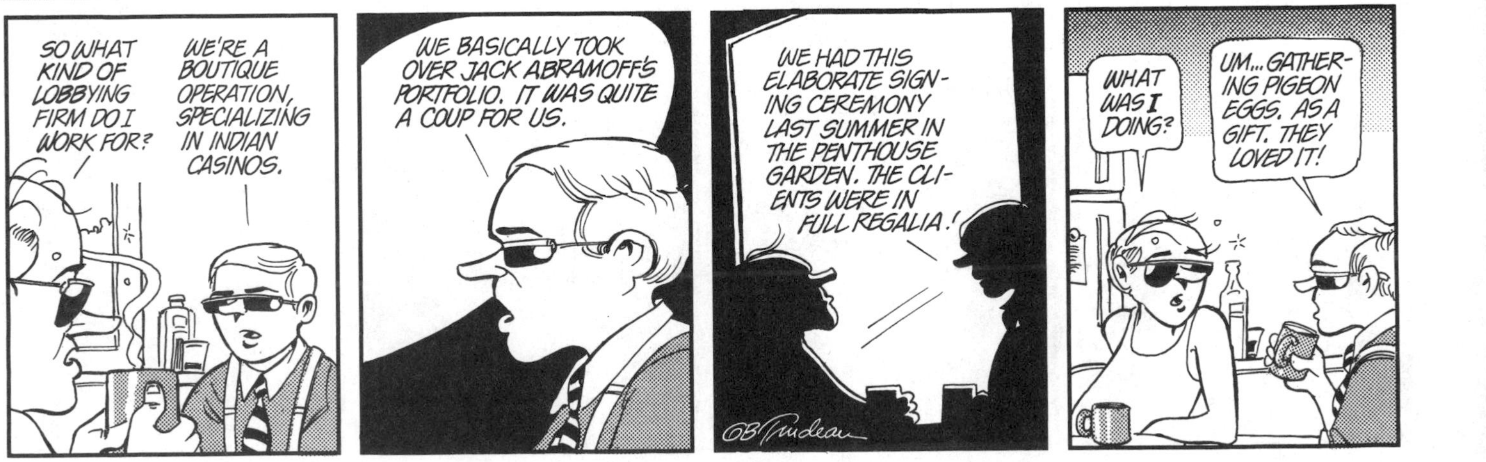
SO WHAT KIND OF LOBBYING FIRM DO I WORK FOR?
WE'RE A BOUTIQUE OPERATION, SPECIALIZING IN INDIAN CASINOS.
WE BASICALLY TOOK OVER JACK ABRAMOFF'S PORTFOLIO. IT WAS QUITE A COUP FOR US.
WE HAD THIS ELABORATE SIGNING CEREMONY LAST SUMMER IN THE PENTHOUSE GARDEN. THE CLIENTS WERE IN FULL REGALIA!
WHAT WAS I DOING?
UM... GATHERING PIGEON EGGS. AS A GIFT. THEY LOVED IT!

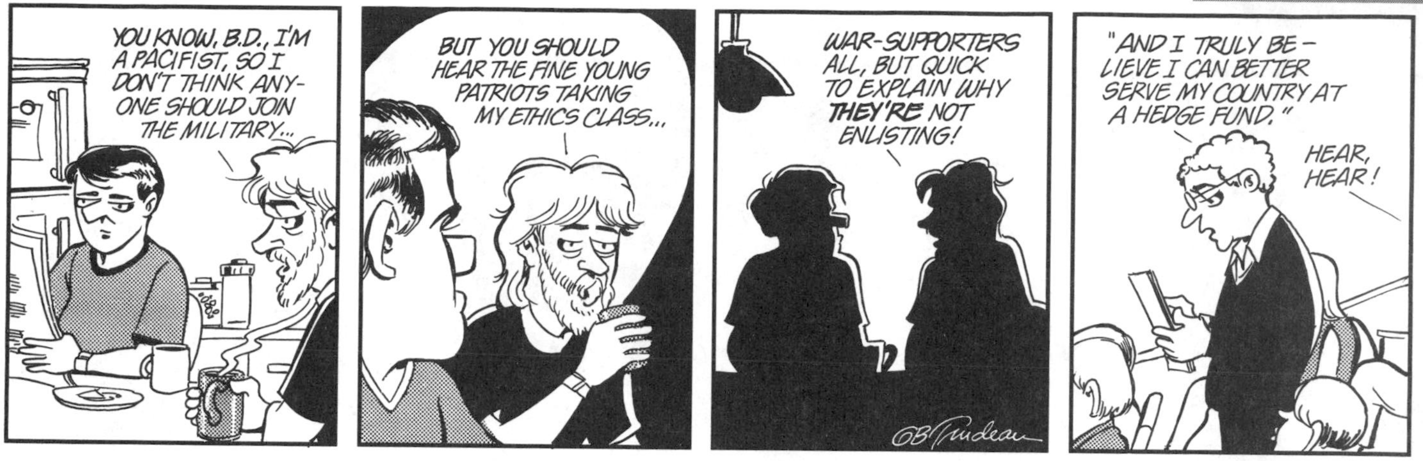
YOU KNOW, B.D., I'M A PACIFIST, SO I DON'T THINK ANY-ONE SHOULD JOIN THE MILITARY...
BUT YOU SHOULD HEAR THE FINE YOUNG PATRIOTS TAKING MY ETHICS CLASS...
WAR-SUPPORTERS ALL, BUT QUICK TO EXPLAIN WHY THEY'RE NOT ENLISTING!
"AND I TRULY BE-LIEVE I CAN BETTER SERVE MY COUNTRY AT A HEDGE FUND."
HEAR, HEAR!

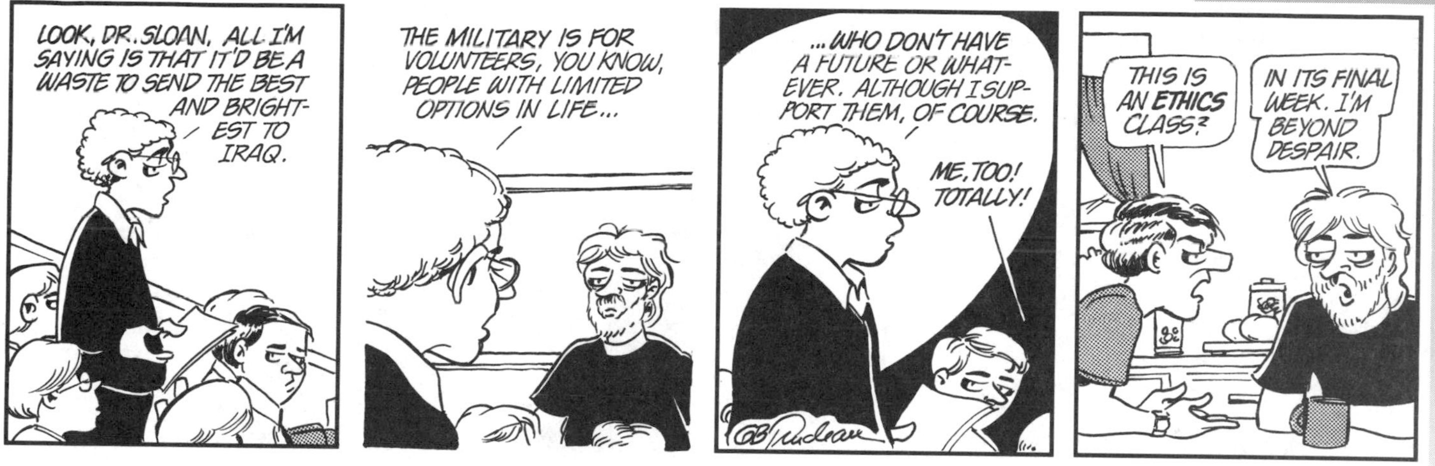
LOOK, DR. SLOAN, ALL I'M SAYING IS THAT IT'D BE A WASTE TO SEND THE BEST AND BRIGHT-EST TO IRAQ.
THE MILITARY IS FOR VOLUNTEERS, YOU KNOW, PEOPLE WITH LIMITED OPTIONS IN LIFE...
...WHO DON'T HAVE A FUTURE OR WHAT-EVER. ALTHOUGH I SUP-PORT THEM, OF COURSE.
ME, TOO! TOTALLY!
THIS IS AN ETHICS CLASS?
IN ITS FINAL WEEK. I'M BEYOND DESPAIR.

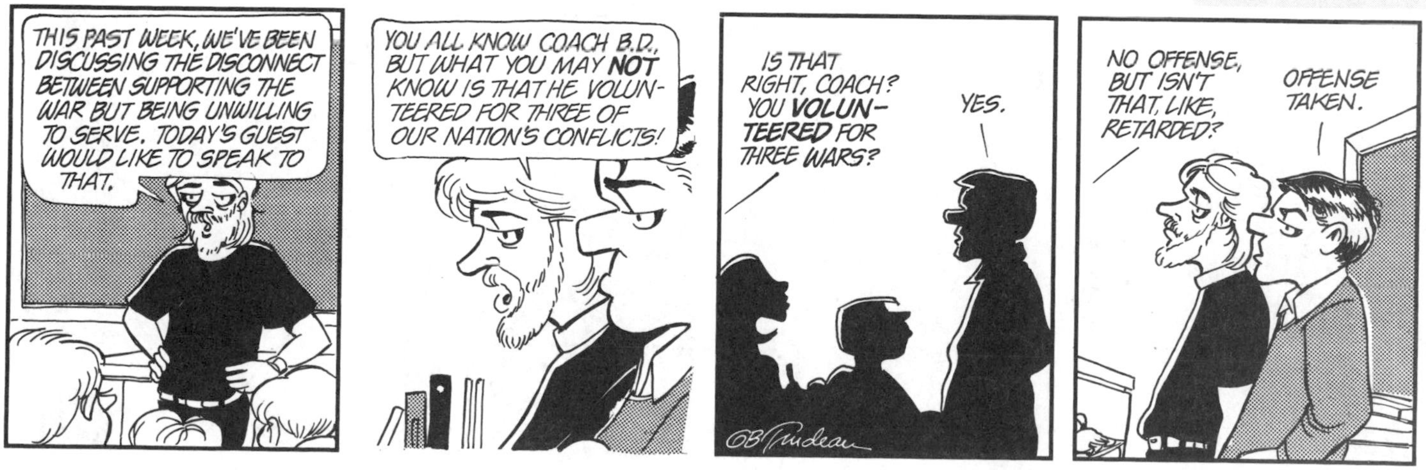
THIS PAST WEEK, WE'VE BEEN DISCUSSING THE DISCONNECT BETWEEN SUPPORTING THE WAR BUT BEING UNWILLING TO SERVE. TODAY'S GUEST WOULD LIKE TO SPEAK TO THAT.
YOU ALL KNOW COACH B.D., BUT WHAT YOU MAY NOT KNOW IS THAT HE VOLUN-TEERED FOR THREE OF OUR NATION'S CONFLICTS!
IS THAT RIGHT, COACH? YOU VOLUN-TEERED FOR THREE WARS?
YES.
NO OFFENSE, BUT ISN'T THAT, LIKE, RETARDED?
OFFENSE TAKEN.

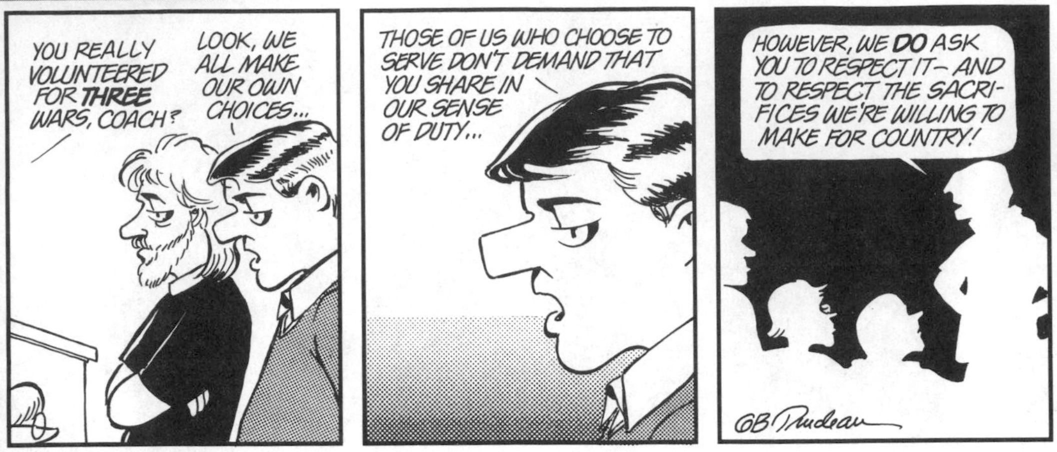
YOU REALLY VOLUNTEERED FOR **THREE** WARS, COACH?
LOOK, WE ALL MAKE OUR OWN CHOICES...
THOSE OF US WHO CHOOSE TO SERVE DON'T DEMAND THAT YOU SHARE IN OUR SENSE OF DUTY...
HOWEVER, WE **DO** ASK YOU TO RESPECT IT— AND TO RESPECT THE SACRIFICES WE'RE WILLING TO MAKE FOR COUNTRY!
BUT I **DO!** I'VE GOT A STICKER ON MY SUV!
ME, TOO! WHAT DO YOU **WANT** FROM US, COACH?
PLEASE DON'T SLAP ANYONE.

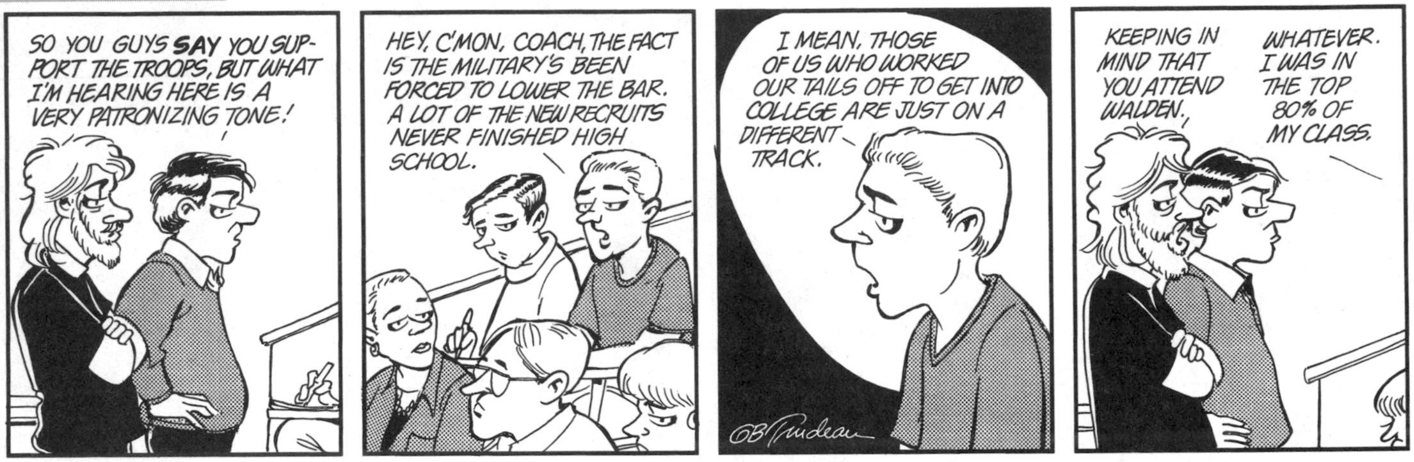
SO YOU GUYS **SAY** YOU SUPPORT THE TROOPS, BUT WHAT I'M HEARING HERE IS A VERY PATRONIZING TONE!
HEY, C'MON, COACH, THE FACT IS THE MILITARY'S BEEN FORCED TO LOWER THE BAR. A LOT OF THE NEW RECRUITS NEVER FINISHED HIGH SCHOOL.
I MEAN, THOSE OF US WHO WORKED OUR TAILS OFF TO GET INTO COLLEGE ARE JUST ON A DIFFERENT TRACK.
KEEPING IN MIND THAT YOU ATTEND WALDEN.
WHATEVER. I WAS IN THE TOP 80% OF MY CLASS.

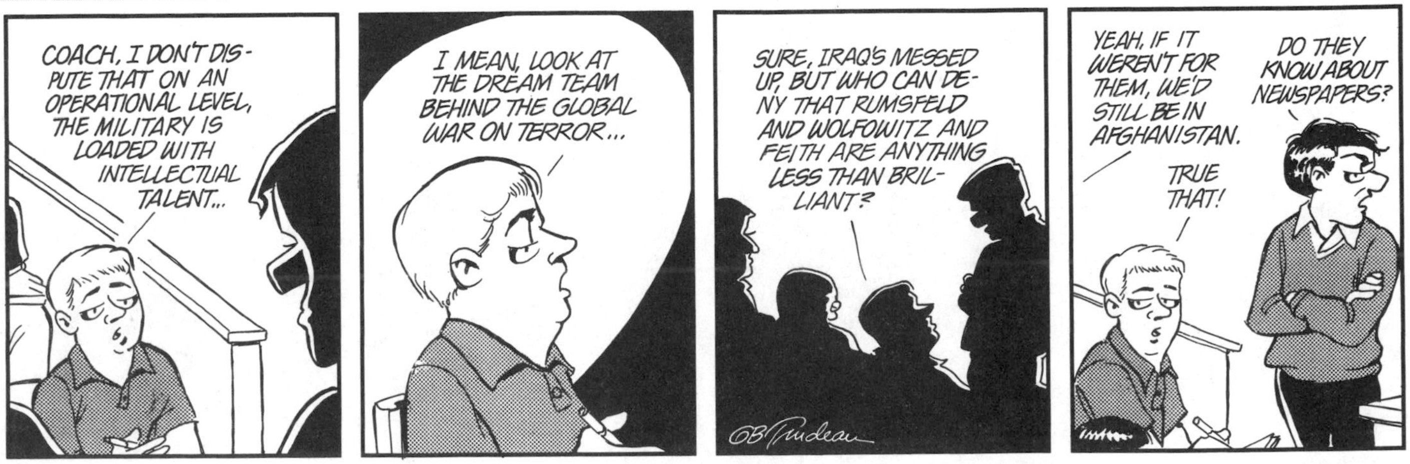
COACH, I DON'T DISPUTE THAT ON AN OPERATIONAL LEVEL, THE MILITARY IS LOADED WITH INTELLECTUAL TALENT...
I MEAN, LOOK AT THE DREAM TEAM BEHIND THE GLOBAL WAR ON TERROR...
SURE, IRAQ'S MESSED UP, BUT WHO CAN DENY THAT RUMSFELD AND WOLFOWITZ AND FEITH ARE ANYTHING LESS THAN BRILLIANT?
YEAH, IF IT WEREN'T FOR THEM, WE'D STILL BE IN AFGHANISTAN.
TRUE THAT!
DO THEY KNOW ABOUT NEWSPAPERS?

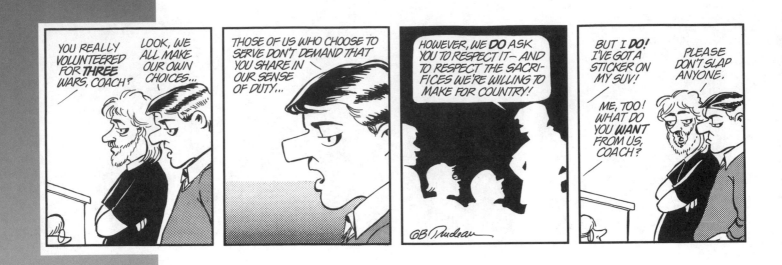

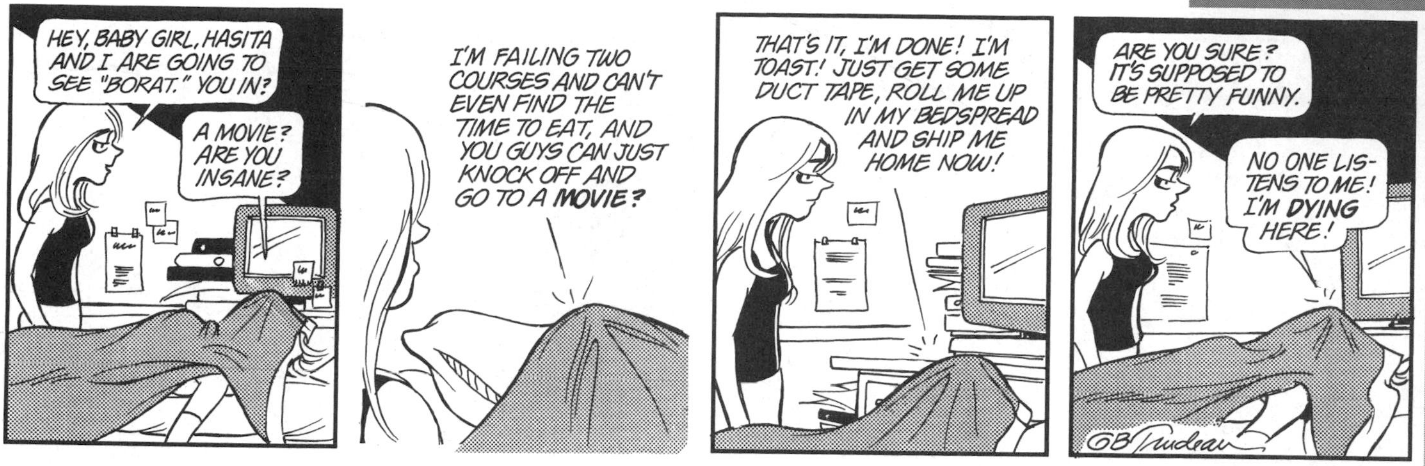
HEY, BABY GIRL, HASITA AND I ARE GOING TO SEE "BORAT." YOU IN?
A MOVIE? ARE YOU INSANE?
I'M FAILING TWO COURSES AND CAN'T EVEN FIND THE TIME TO EAT, AND YOU GUYS CAN JUST KNOCK OFF AND GO TO A MOVIE?
THAT'S IT, I'M DONE! I'M TOAST! JUST GET SOME DUCT TAPE, ROLL ME UP IN MY BEDSPREAD AND SHIP ME HOME NOW!
ARE YOU SURE? IT'S SUPPOSED TO BE PRETTY FUNNY.
NO ONE LISTENS TO ME! I'M DYING HERE!
©B Trudeau

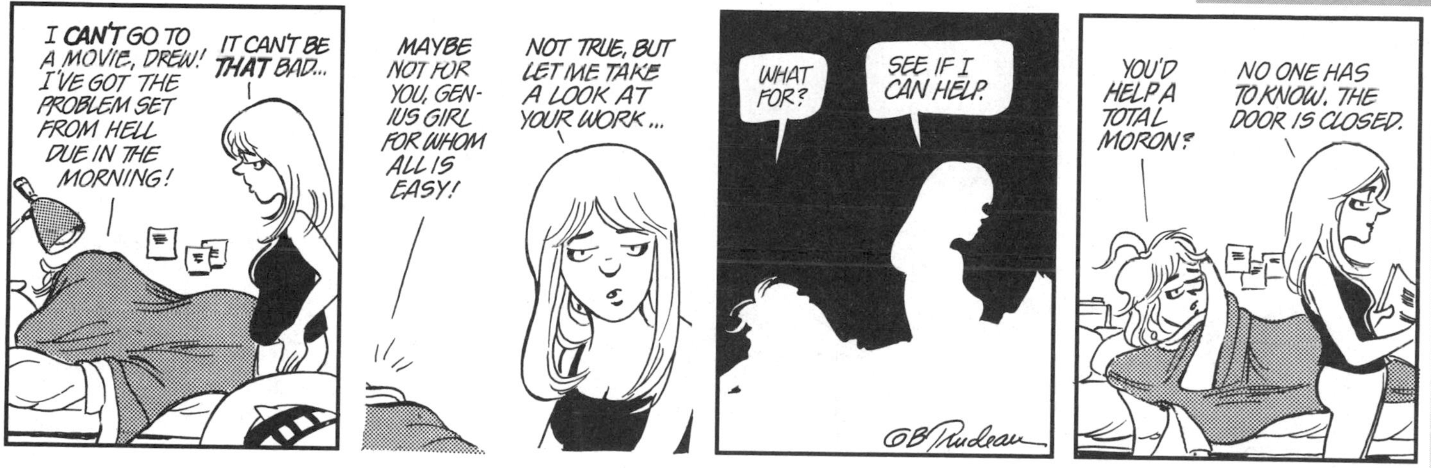
I CAN'T GO TO A MOVIE, DREW! I'VE GOT THE PROBLEM SET FROM HELL DUE IN THE MORNING!
IT CAN'T BE THAT BAD...
MAYBE NOT FOR YOU, GENIUS GIRL FOR WHOM ALL IS EASY!
NOT TRUE, BUT LET ME TAKE A LOOK AT YOUR WORK...
WHAT FOR?
SEE IF I CAN HELP.
YOU'D HELP A TOTAL MORON?
NO ONE HAS TO KNOW. THE DOOR IS CLOSED.
©B Trudeau

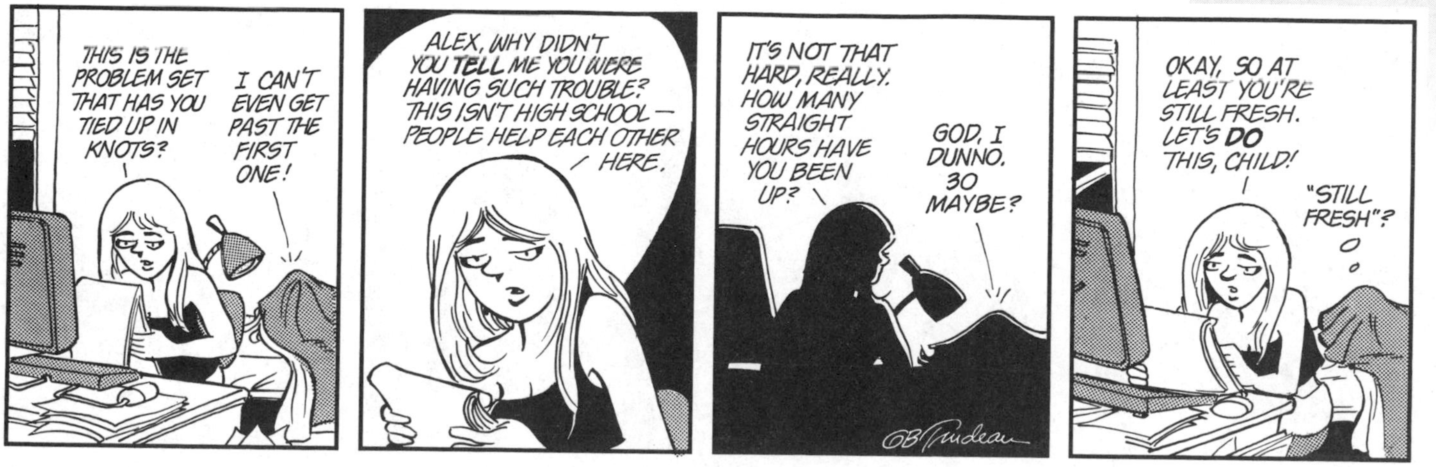
THIS IS THE PROBLEM SET THAT HAS YOU TIED UP IN KNOTS?
I CAN'T EVEN GET PAST THE FIRST ONE!
ALEX, WHY DIDN'T YOU TELL ME YOU WERE HAVING SUCH TROUBLE? THIS ISN'T HIGH SCHOOL — PEOPLE HELP EACH OTHER HERE.
IT'S NOT THAT HARD, REALLY. HOW MANY STRAIGHT HOURS HAVE YOU BEEN UP?
GOD, I DUNNO. 30 MAYBE?
OKAY, SO AT LEAST YOU'RE STILL FRESH. LET'S DO THIS, CHILD!
"STILL FRESH"?
©B Trudeau

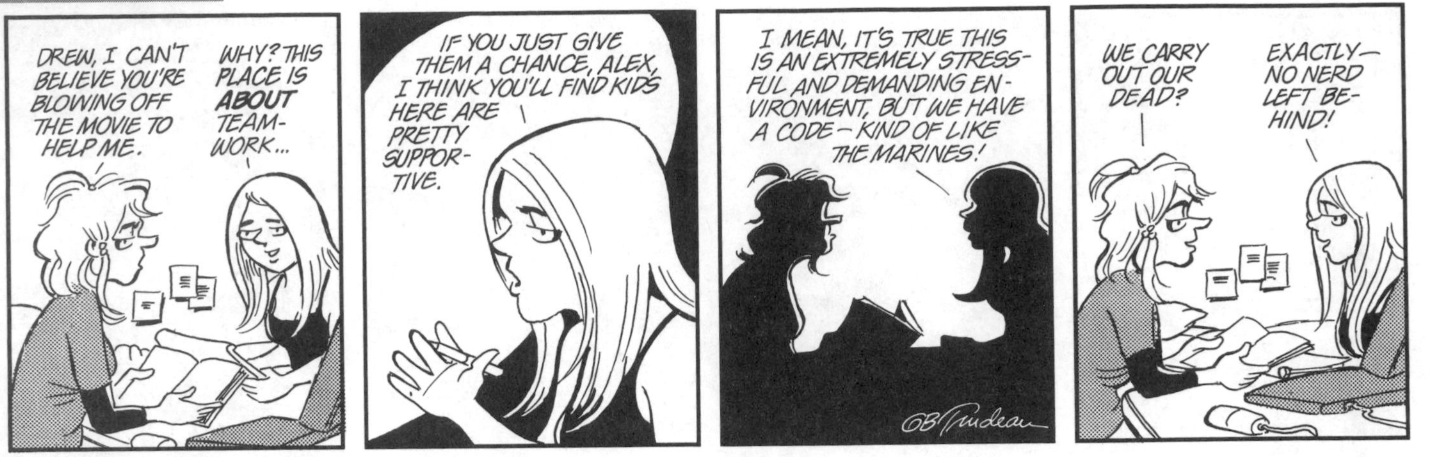
DREW, I CAN'T BELIEVE YOU'RE BLOWING OFF THE MOVIE TO HELP ME.
WHY? THIS PLACE IS ABOUT TEAM-WORK...
IF YOU JUST GIVE THEM A CHANCE, ALEX, I THINK YOU'LL FIND KIDS HERE ARE PRETTY SUPPOR-TIVE.
I MEAN, IT'S TRUE THIS IS AN EXTREMELY STRESS-FUL AND DEMANDING EN-VIRONMENT, BUT WE HAVE A CODE – KIND OF LIKE THE MARINES!
WE CARRY OUT OUR DEAD?
EXACTLY— NO NERD LEFT BE-HIND!

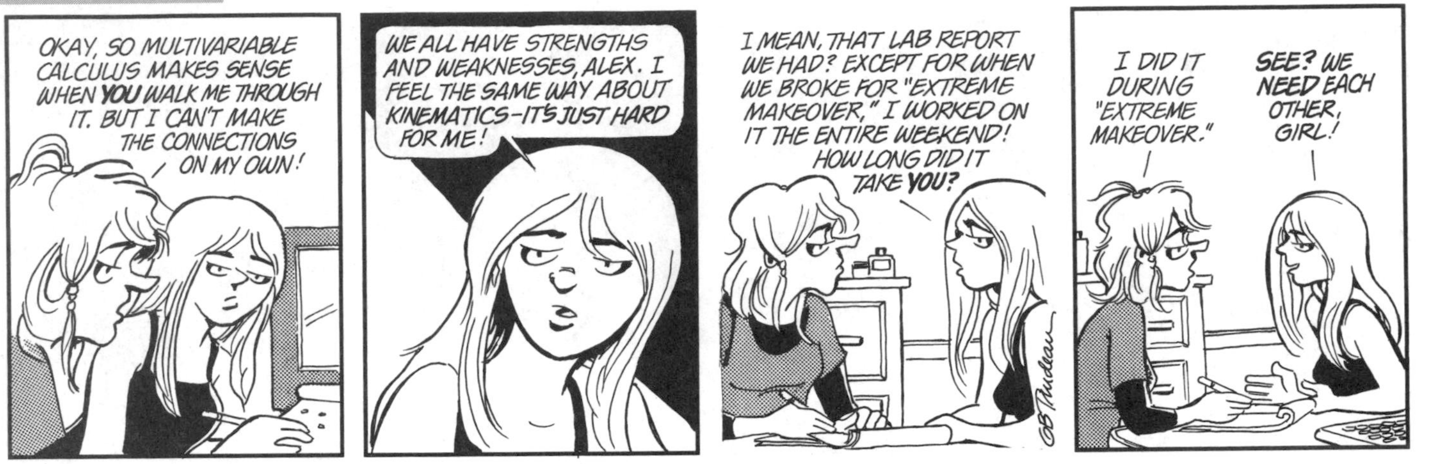
OKAY, SO MULTIVARIABLE CALCULUS MAKES SENSE WHEN YOU WALK ME THROUGH IT. BUT I CAN'T MAKE THE CONNECTIONS ON MY OWN!
WE ALL HAVE STRENGTHS AND WEAKNESSES, ALEX. I FEEL THE SAME WAY ABOUT KINEMATICS–IT'S JUST HARD FOR ME!
I MEAN, THAT LAB REPORT WE HAD? EXCEPT FOR WHEN WE BROKE FOR "EXTREME MAKEOVER," I WORKED ON IT THE ENTIRE WEEKEND! HOW LONG DID IT TAKE YOU?
I DID IT DURING "EXTREME MAKEOVER."
SEE? WE NEED EACH OTHER, GIRL!

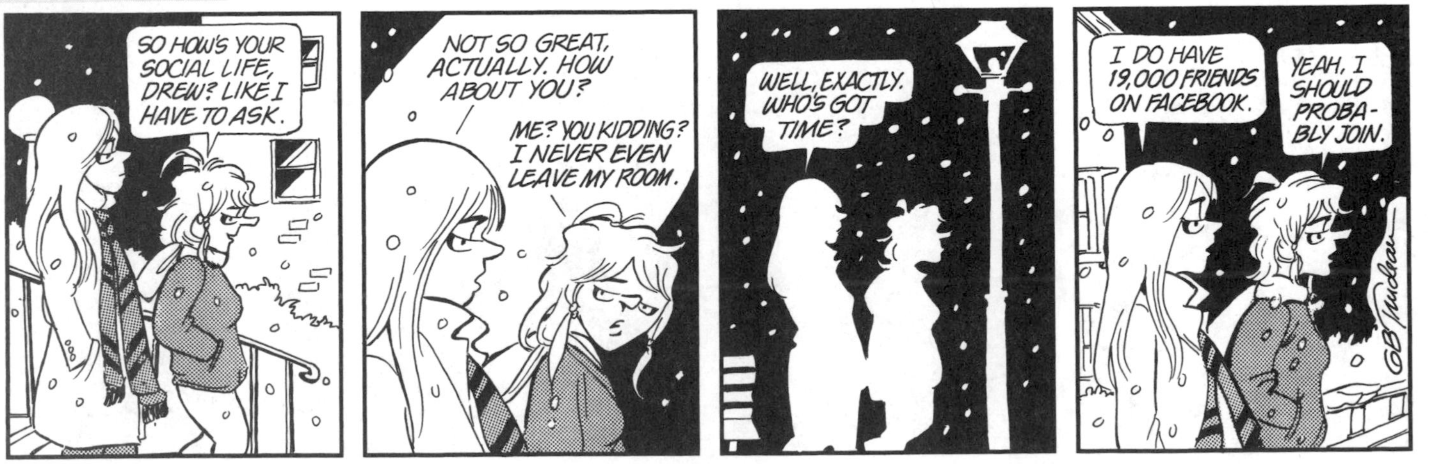
SO HOW'S YOUR SOCIAL LIFE, DREW? LIKE I HAVE TO ASK.
NOT SO GREAT, ACTUALLY. HOW ABOUT YOU?
ME? YOU KIDDING? I NEVER EVEN LEAVE MY ROOM.
WELL, EXACTLY. WHO'S GOT TIME?
I DO HAVE 19,000 FRIENDS ON FACEBOOK.
YEAH, I SHOULD PROBA-BLY JOIN.

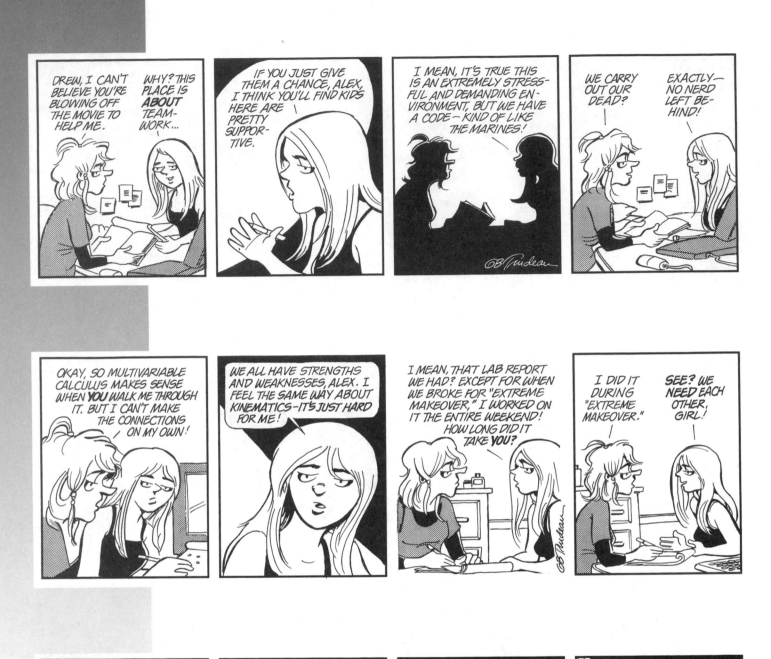

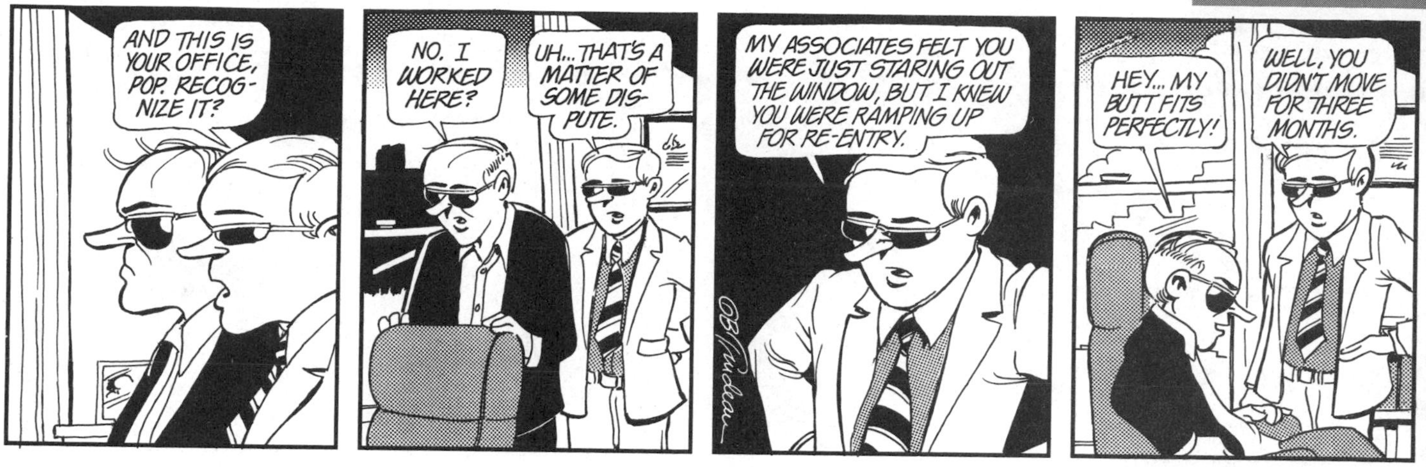
AND THIS IS YOUR OFFICE, POP. RECOGNIZE IT?
NO. I WORKED HERE?
UH... THAT'S A MATTER OF SOME DISPUTE.
MY ASSOCIATES FELT YOU WERE JUST STARING OUT THE WINDOW, BUT I KNEW YOU WERE RAMPING UP FOR RE-ENTRY.
HEY... MY BUTT FITS PERFECTLY!
WELL, YOU DIDN'T MOVE FOR THREE MONTHS.

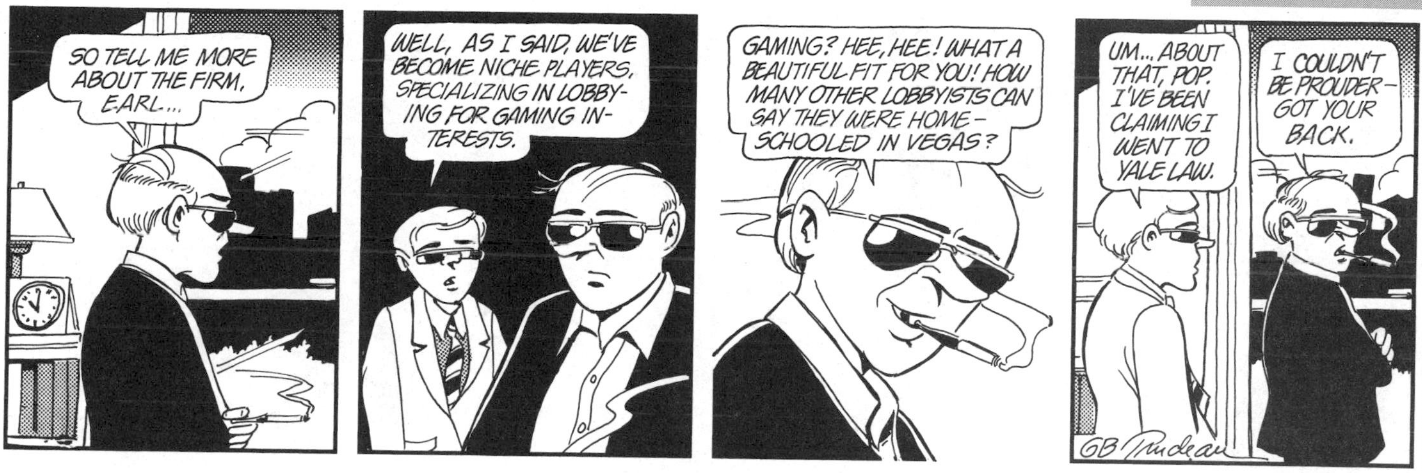
SO TELL ME MORE ABOUT THE FIRM, EARL...
WELL, AS I SAID, WE'VE BECOME NICHE PLAYERS, SPECIALIZING IN LOBBYING FOR GAMING INTERESTS.
GAMING? HEE, HEE! WHAT A BEAUTIFUL FIT FOR YOU! HOW MANY OTHER LOBBYISTS CAN SAY THEY WERE HOME-SCHOOLED IN VEGAS?
UM... ABOUT THAT, POP. I'VE BEEN CLAIMING I WENT TO YALE LAW.
I COULDN'T BE PROUDER - GOT YOUR BACK.

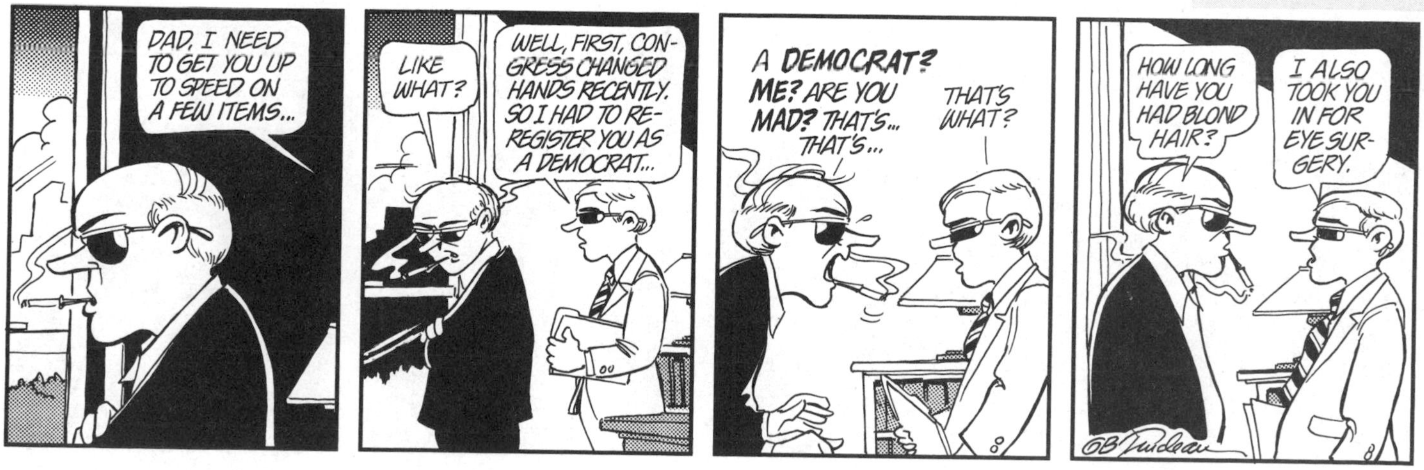
DAD, I NEED TO GET YOU UP TO SPEED ON A FEW ITEMS...
LIKE WHAT?
WELL, FIRST, CONGRESS CHANGED HANDS RECENTLY. SO I HAD TO RE-REGISTER YOU AS A DEMOCRAT...
A DEMOCRAT? ME? ARE YOU MAD? THAT'S... THAT'S...
THAT'S WHAT?
HOW LONG HAVE YOU HAD BLOND HAIR?
I ALSO TOOK YOU IN FOR EYE SURGERY.

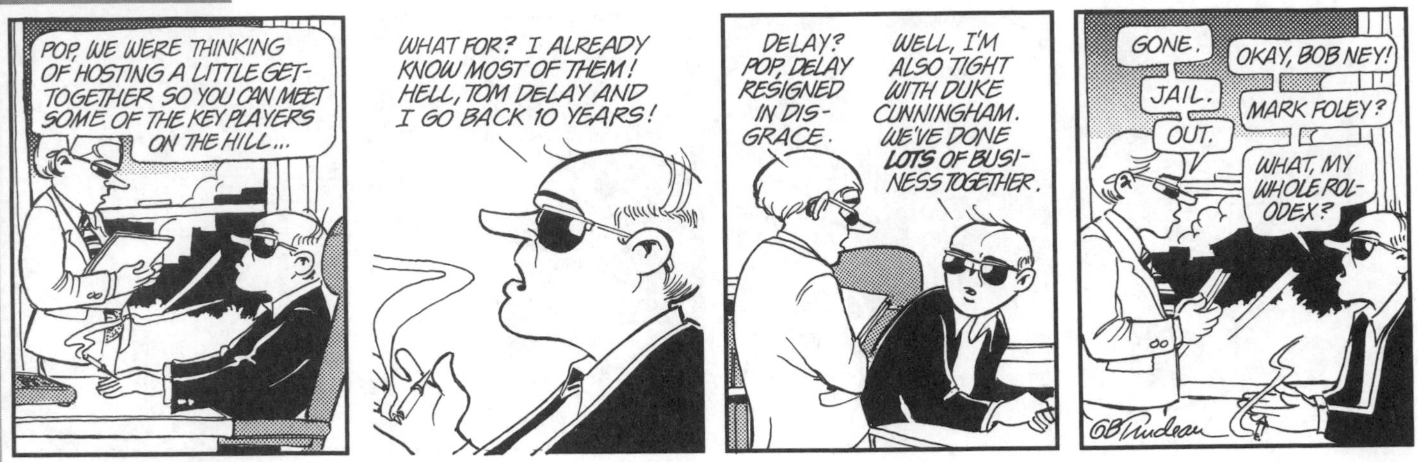
POP, WE WERE THINKING OF HOSTING A LITTLE GET-TOGETHER SO YOU CAN MEET SOME OF THE KEY PLAYERS ON THE HILL...
WHAT FOR? I ALREADY KNOW MOST OF THEM! HELL, TOM DELAY AND I GO BACK 10 YEARS!
DELAY? POP, DELAY RESIGNED IN DISGRACE.
WELL, I'M ALSO TIGHT WITH DUKE CUNNINGHAM. WE'VE DONE **LOTS** OF BUSINESS TOGETHER.
GONE.
OKAY, BOB NEY!
JAIL.
MARK FOLEY?
OUT.
WHAT, MY WHOLE ROLODEX?

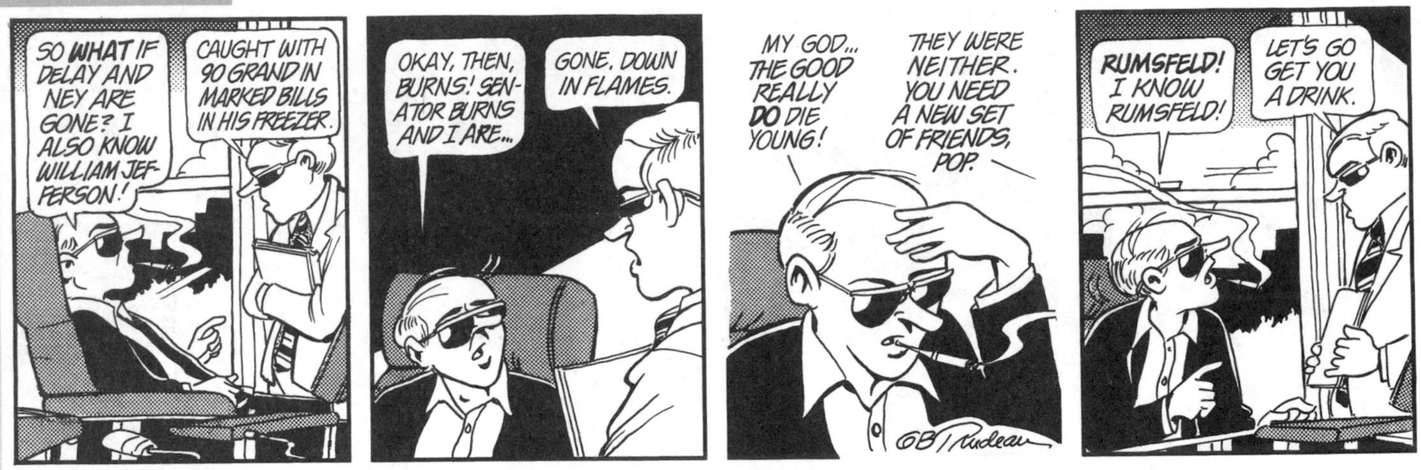
SO **WHAT** IF DELAY AND NEY ARE GONE? I ALSO KNOW WILLIAM JEFFERSON!
CAUGHT WITH 90 GRAND IN MARKED BILLS IN HIS FREEZER.
OKAY, THEN, BURNS! SENATOR BURNS AND I ARE...
GONE, DOWN IN FLAMES.
MY GOD... THE GOOD REALLY **DO** DIE YOUNG!
THEY WERE NEITHER. YOU NEED A NEW SET OF FRIENDS, POP.
RUMSFELD! I KNOW RUMSFELD!
LET'S GO GET YOU A DRINK.

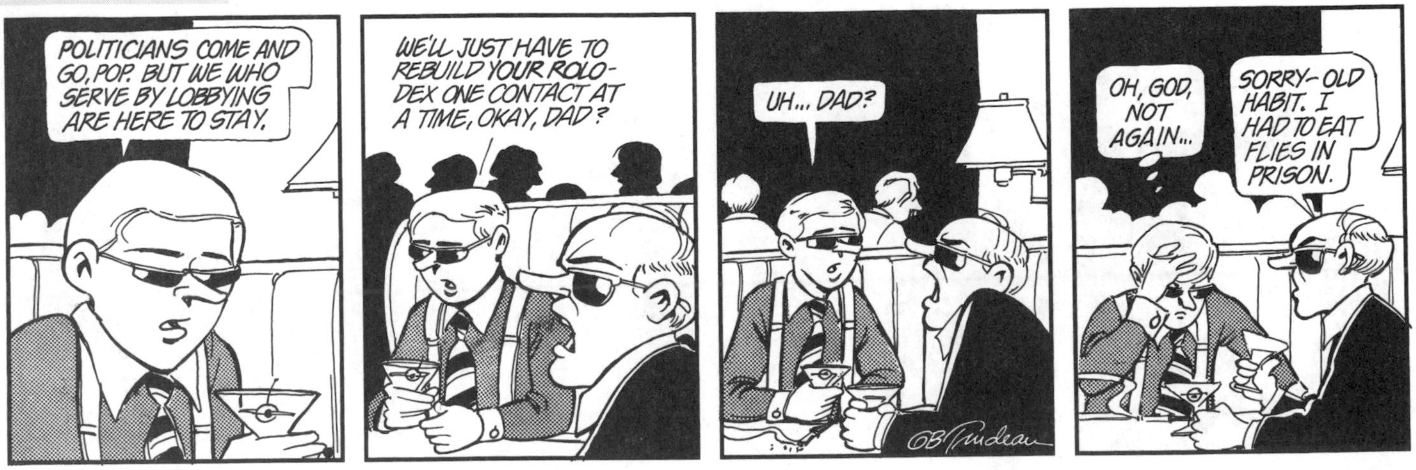
POLITICIANS COME AND GO, POP. BUT WE WHO SERVE BY LOBBYING ARE HERE TO STAY.
WE'LL JUST HAVE TO REBUILD YOUR ROLODEX ONE CONTACT AT A TIME, OKAY, DAD?
UH... DAD?
OH, GOD, NOT AGAIN...
SORRY—OLD HABIT. I HAD TO EAT FLIES IN PRISON.

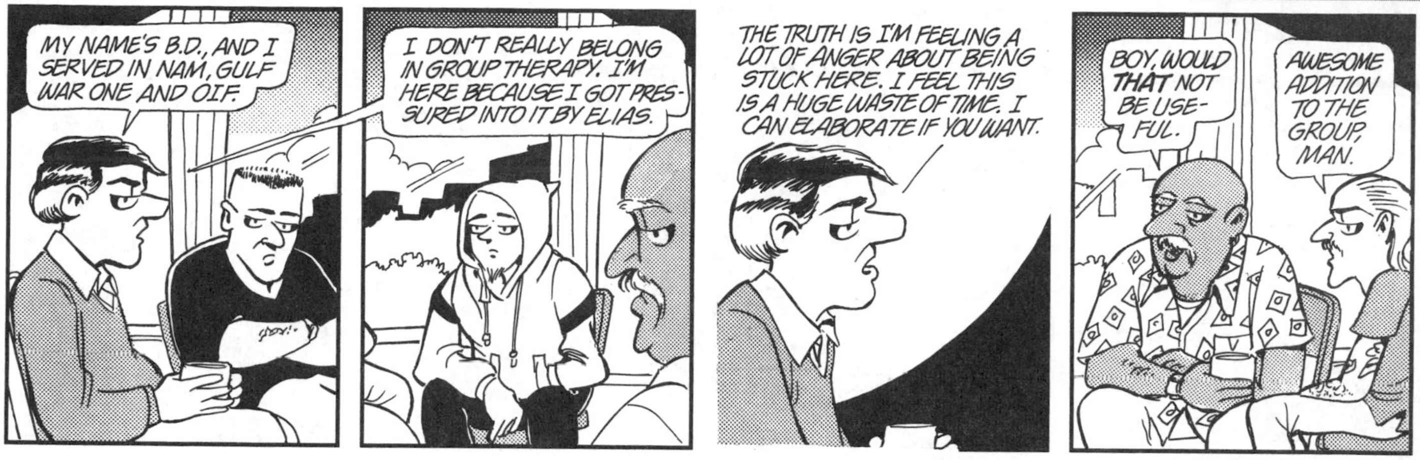
MY NAME'S B.D., AND I SERVED IN NAM, GULF WAR ONE AND OIF.
I DON'T REALLY BELONG IN GROUP THERAPY. I'M HERE BECAUSE I GOT PRES-SURED INTO IT BY ELIAS.
THE TRUTH IS I'M FEELING A LOT OF ANGER ABOUT BEING STUCK HERE. I FEEL THIS IS A HUGE WASTE OF TIME. I CAN ELABORATE IF YOU WANT.
BOY, WOULD **THAT** NOT BE USE-FUL.
AWESOME ADDITION TO THE GROUP, MAN.

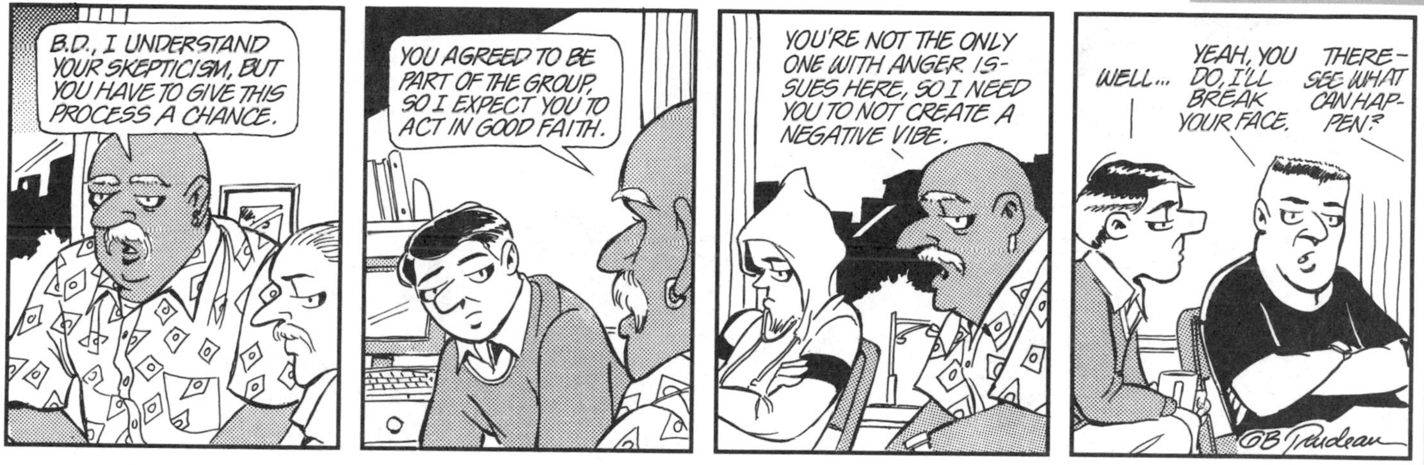
B.D., I UNDERSTAND YOUR SKEPTICISM, BUT YOU HAVE TO GIVE THIS PROCESS A CHANCE.
YOU AGREED TO BE PART OF THE GROUP, SO I EXPECT YOU TO ACT IN GOOD FAITH.
YOU'RE NOT THE ONLY ONE WITH ANGER IS-SUES HERE, SO I NEED YOU TO NOT CREATE A NEGATIVE VIBE.
WELL...
YEAH, YOU DO, I'LL BREAK YOUR FACE.
THERE-SEE WHAT CAN HAP-PEN?
GB Trudeau

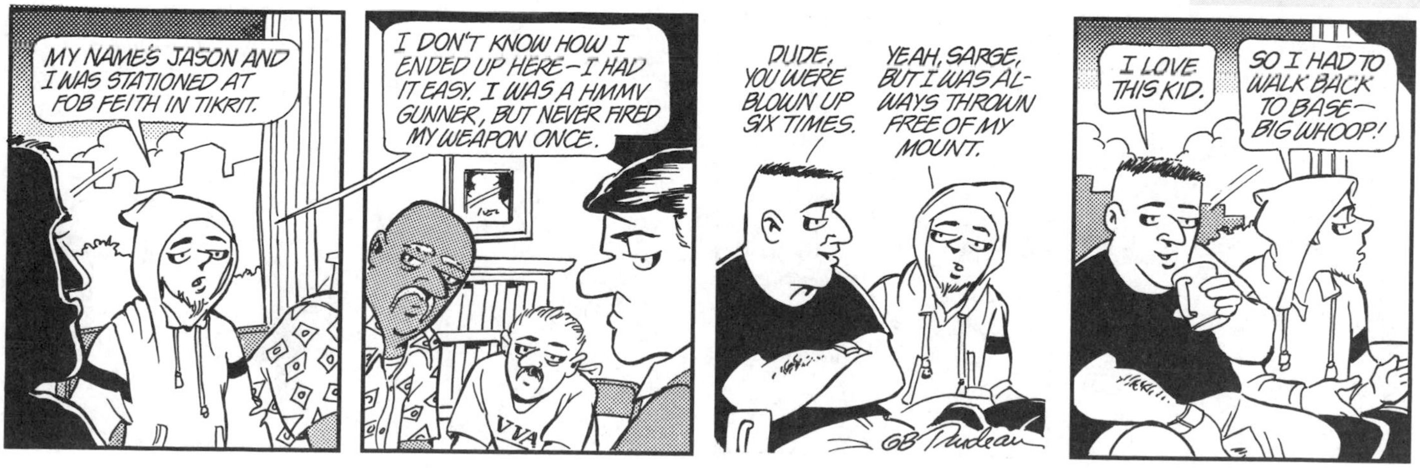
MY NAME'S JASON AND I WAS STATIONED AT FOB FEITH IN TIKRIT.
I DON'T KNOW HOW I ENDED UP HERE – I HAD IT EASY. I WAS A HMMV GUNNER, BUT NEVER FIRED MY WEAPON ONCE.
VVA
DUDE, YOU WERE BLOWN UP SIX TIMES.
YEAH, SARGE, BUT I WAS AL-WAYS THROWN FREE OF MY MOUNT.
GB Trudeau
I LOVE THIS KID.
SO I HAD TO WALK BACK TO BASE-BIG WHOOP!

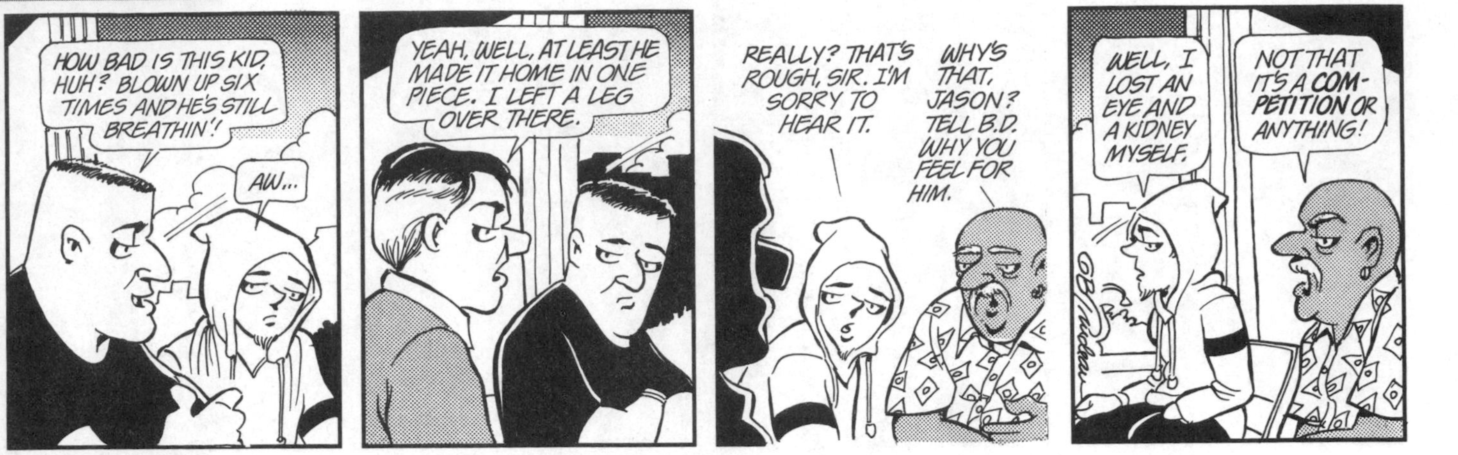
HOW BAD IS THIS KID, HUH? BLOWN UP SIX TIMES AND HE'S STILL BREATHIN'!
AW...
YEAH, WELL, AT LEAST HE MADE IT HOME IN ONE PIECE. I LEFT A LEG OVER THERE.
REALLY? THAT'S ROUGH, SIR. I'M SORRY TO HEAR IT.
WHY'S THAT, JASON? TELL B.D. WHY YOU FEEL FOR HIM.
WELL, I LOST AN EYE AND A KIDNEY MYSELF.
NOT THAT IT'S A COMPETITION OR ANYTHING!
GBTrudeau

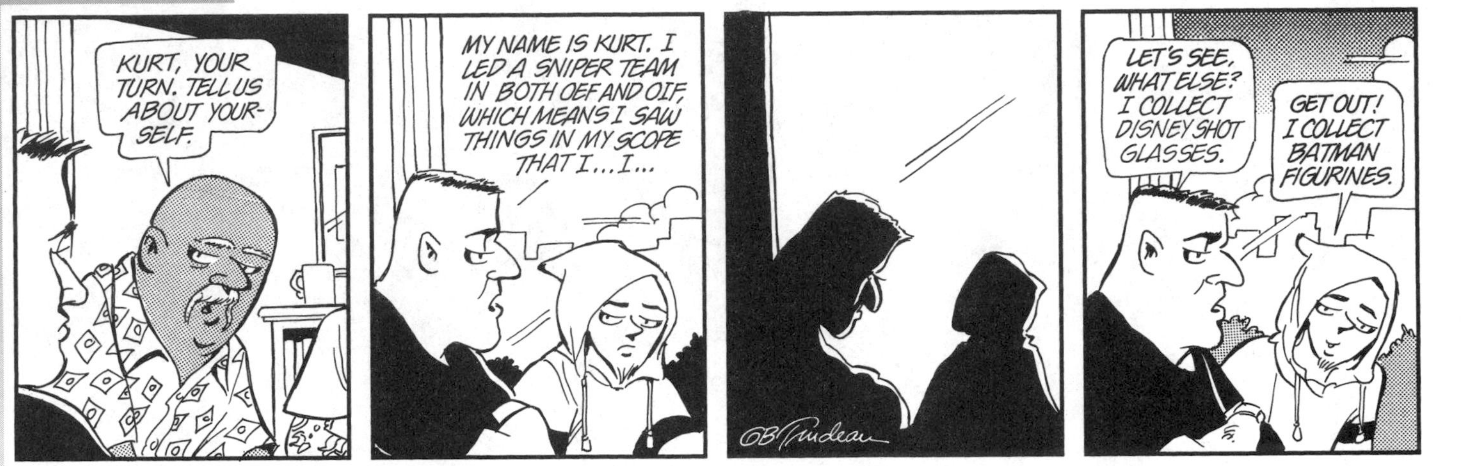
KURT, YOUR TURN. TELL US ABOUT YOURSELF.
MY NAME IS KURT. I LED A SNIPER TEAM IN BOTH OEF AND OIF, WHICH MEANS I SAW THINGS IN MY SCOPE THAT I... I...
GBTrudeau
LET'S SEE, WHAT ELSE? I COLLECT DISNEY SHOT GLASSES.
GET OUT! I COLLECT BATMAN FIGURINES.

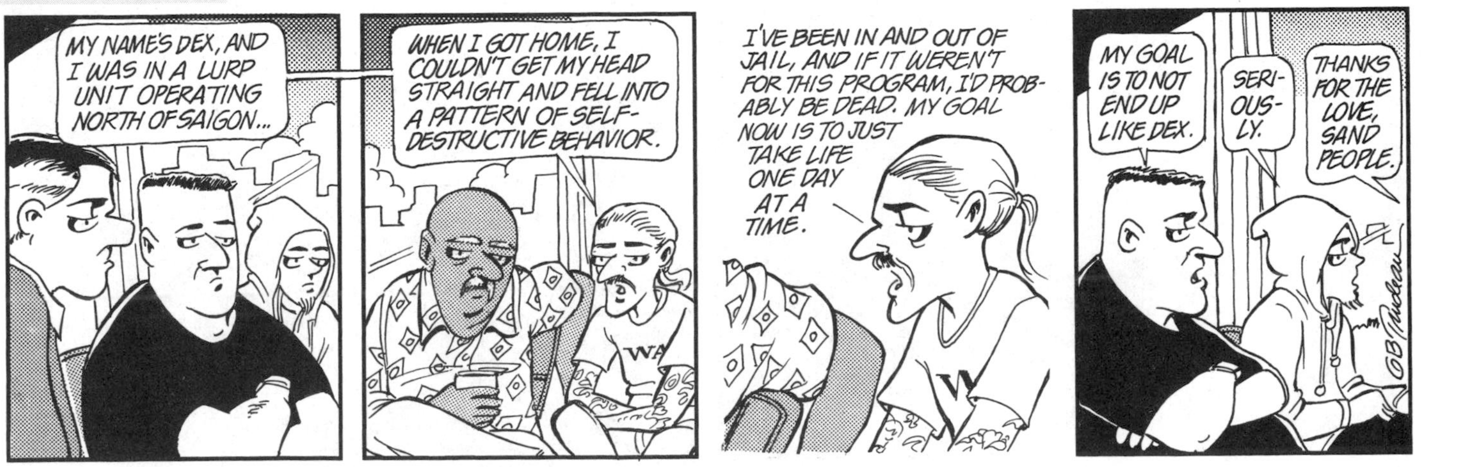
MY NAME'S DEX, AND I WAS IN A LURP UNIT OPERATING NORTH OF SAIGON...
WHEN I GOT HOME, I COULDN'T GET MY HEAD STRAIGHT AND FELL INTO A PATTERN OF SELF-DESTRUCTIVE BEHAVIOR.
I'VE BEEN IN AND OUT OF JAIL, AND IF IT WEREN'T FOR THIS PROGRAM, I'D PROBABLY BE DEAD. MY GOAL NOW IS TO JUST TAKE LIFE ONE DAY AT A TIME.
MY GOAL IS TO NOT END UP LIKE DEX.
SERIOUSLY.
THANKS FOR THE LOVE, SAND PEOPLE.
GBTrudeau

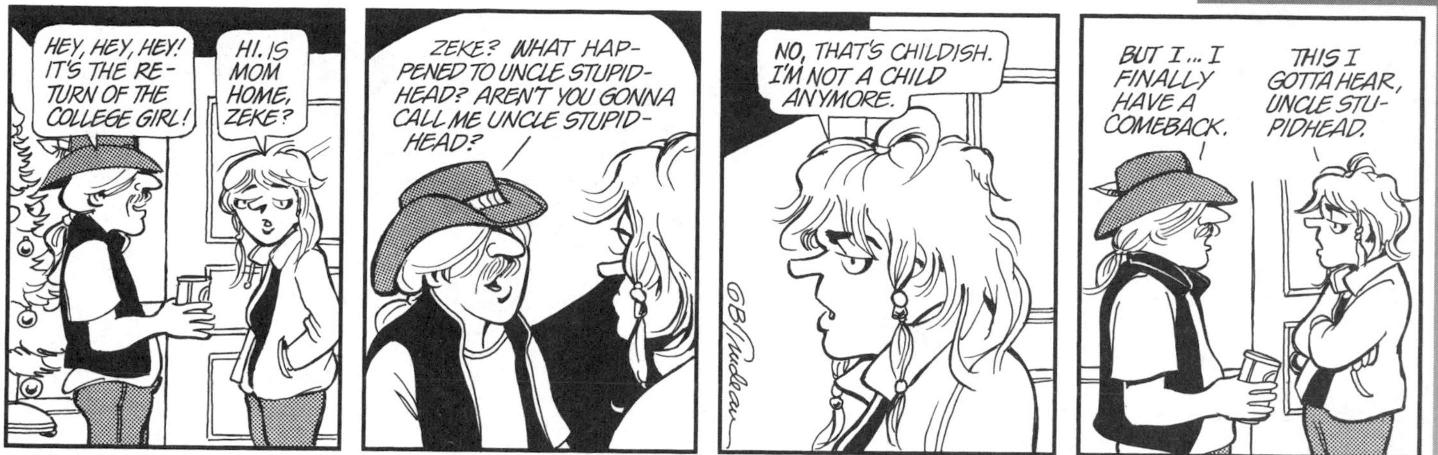
HEY, HEY, HEY! IT'S THE RETURN OF THE COLLEGE GIRL!
HI. IS MOM HOME, ZEKE?
ZEKE? WHAT HAPPENED TO UNCLE STUPIDHEAD? AREN'T YOU GONNA CALL ME UNCLE STUPIDHEAD?
NO, THAT'S CHILDISH. I'M NOT A CHILD ANYMORE.
BUT I... I FINALLY HAVE A COMEBACK.
THIS I GOTTA HEAR, UNCLE STUPIDHEAD.

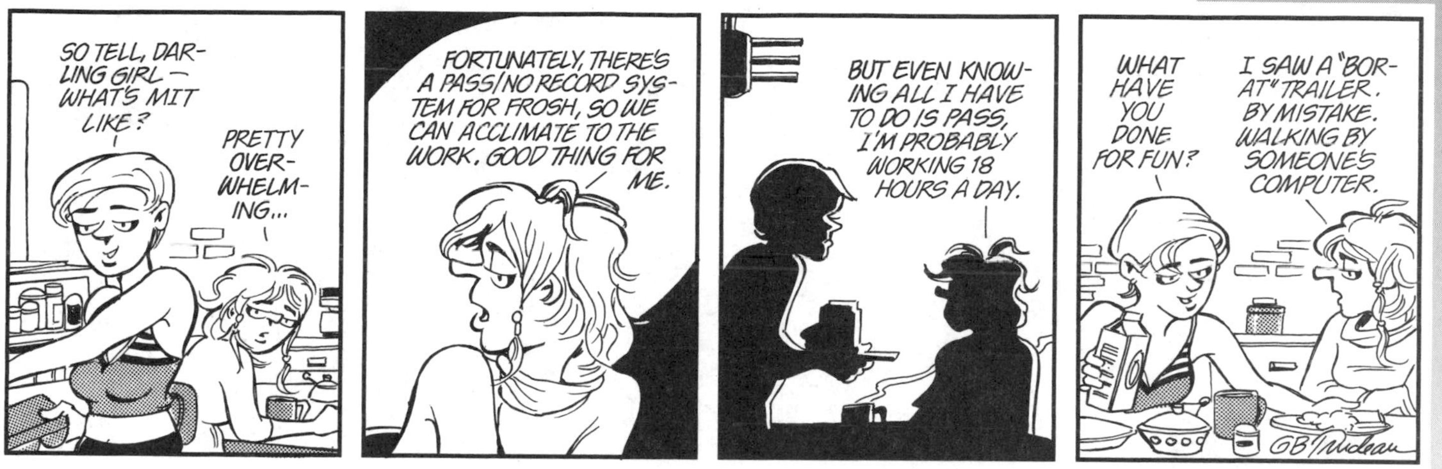
SO TELL, DARLING GIRL— WHAT'S MIT LIKE?
PRETTY OVERWHELMING...
FORTUNATELY, THERE'S A PASS/NO RECORD SYSTEM FOR FROSH, SO WE CAN ACCLIMATE TO THE WORK. GOOD THING FOR ME.
BUT EVEN KNOWING ALL I HAVE TO DO IS PASS, I'M PROBABLY WORKING 18 HOURS A DAY.
WHAT HAVE YOU DONE FOR FUN?
I SAW A "BORAT" TRAILER. BY MISTAKE. WALKING BY SOMEONE'S COMPUTER.

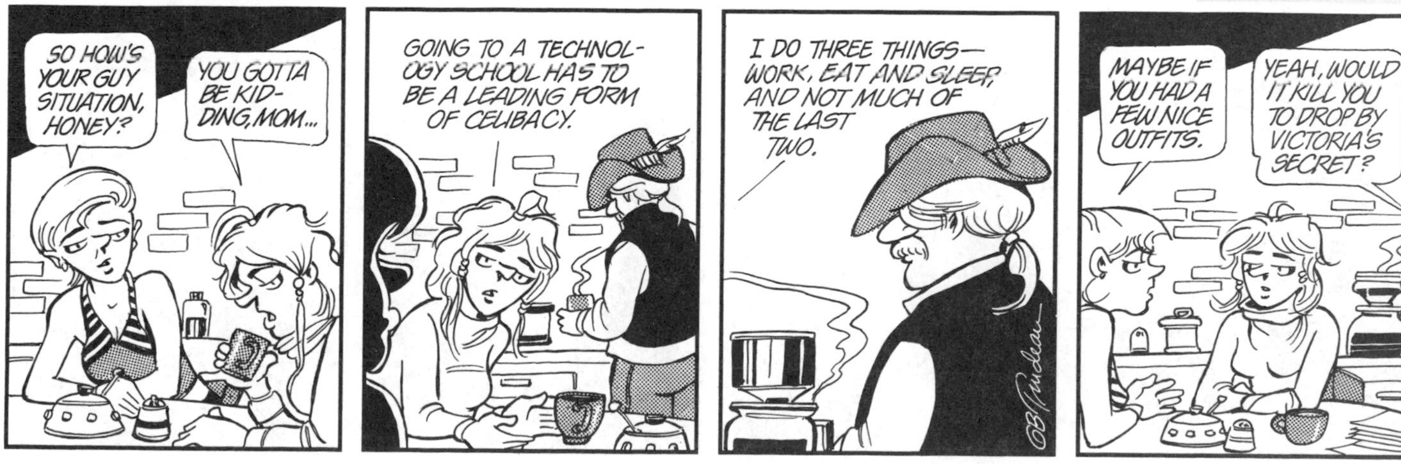
SO HOW'S YOUR GUY SITUATION, HONEY?
YOU GOTTA BE KIDDING, MOM...
GOING TO A TECHNOLOGY SCHOOL HAS TO BE A LEADING FORM OF CELIBACY.
I DO THREE THINGS— WORK, EAT AND SLEEP, AND NOT MUCH OF THE LAST TWO.
MAYBE IF YOU HAD A FEW NICE OUTFITS.
YEAH, WOULD IT KILL YOU TO DROP BY VICTORIA'S SECRET?

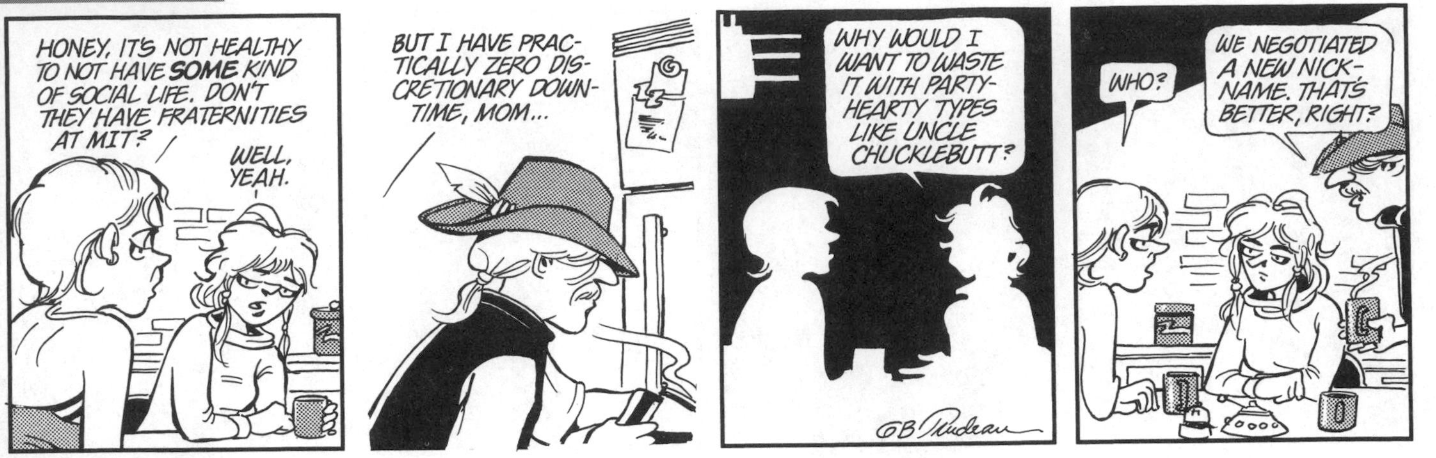
HONEY, IT'S NOT HEALTHY TO NOT HAVE **SOME** KIND OF SOCIAL LIFE. DON'T THEY HAVE FRATERNITIES AT MIT?
WELL, YEAH.
BUT I HAVE PRAC-TICALLY ZERO DIS-CRETIONARY DOWN-TIME, MOM...
WHY WOULD I WANT TO WASTE IT WITH PARTY-HEARTY TYPES LIKE UNCLE CHUCKLEBUTT?
WHO?
WE NEGOTIATED A NEW NICK-NAME. THAT'S BETTER, RIGHT?
GB Trudeau

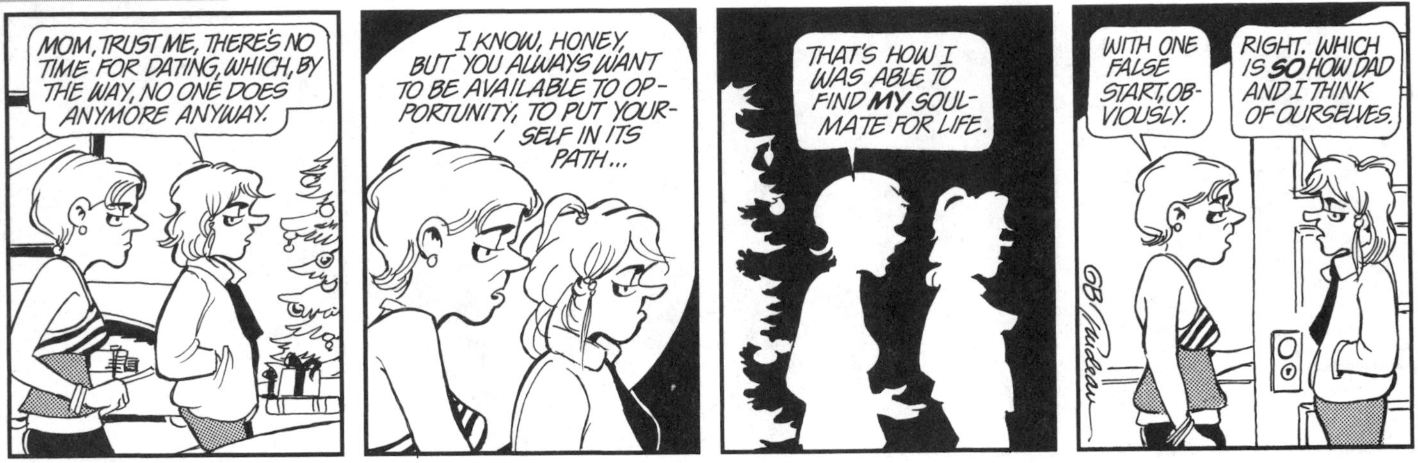
MOM, TRUST ME, THERE'S NO TIME FOR DATING, WHICH, BY THE WAY, NO ONE DOES ANYMORE ANYWAY.
I KNOW, HONEY, BUT YOU ALWAYS WANT TO BE AVAILABLE TO OP-PORTUNITY, TO PUT YOUR-SELF IN ITS PATH...
THAT'S HOW I WAS ABLE TO FIND **MY** SOUL-MATE FOR LIFE.
WITH ONE FALSE START, OB-VIOUSLY.
RIGHT. WHICH IS **SO** HOW DAD AND I THINK OF OURSELVES.
GB Trudeau

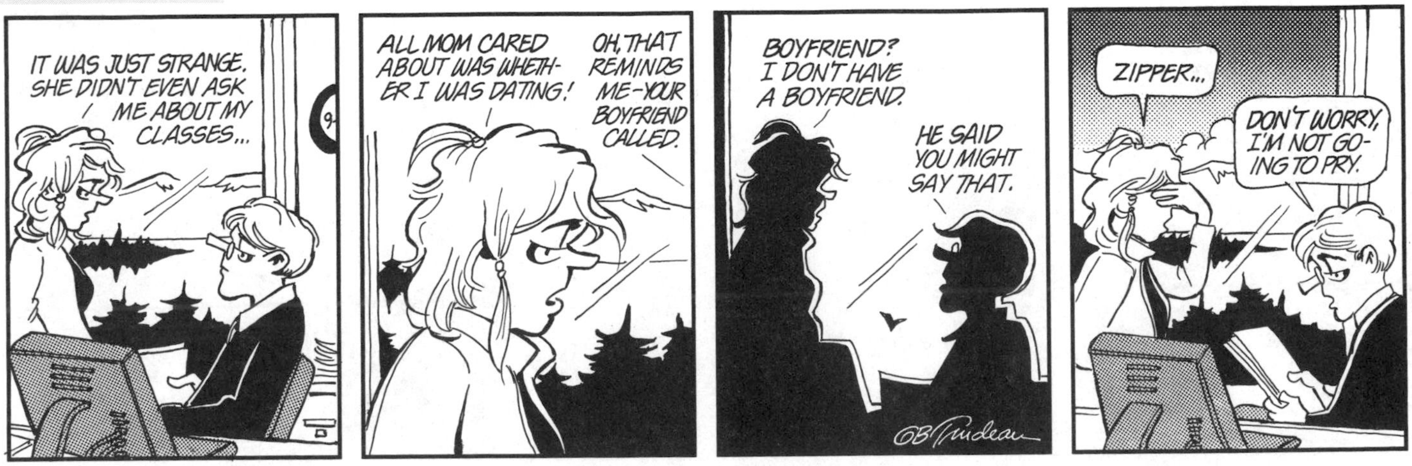
IT WAS JUST STRANGE. SHE DIDN'T EVEN ASK ME ABOUT MY CLASSES...
ALL MOM CARED ABOUT WAS WHETH-ER I WAS DATING!
OH, THAT REMINDS ME—YOUR BOYFRIEND CALLED.
BOYFRIEND? I DON'T HAVE A BOYFRIEND.
HE SAID YOU MIGHT SAY THAT.
GB Trudeau
ZIPPER...
DON'T WORRY, I'M NOT GO-ING TO PRY.

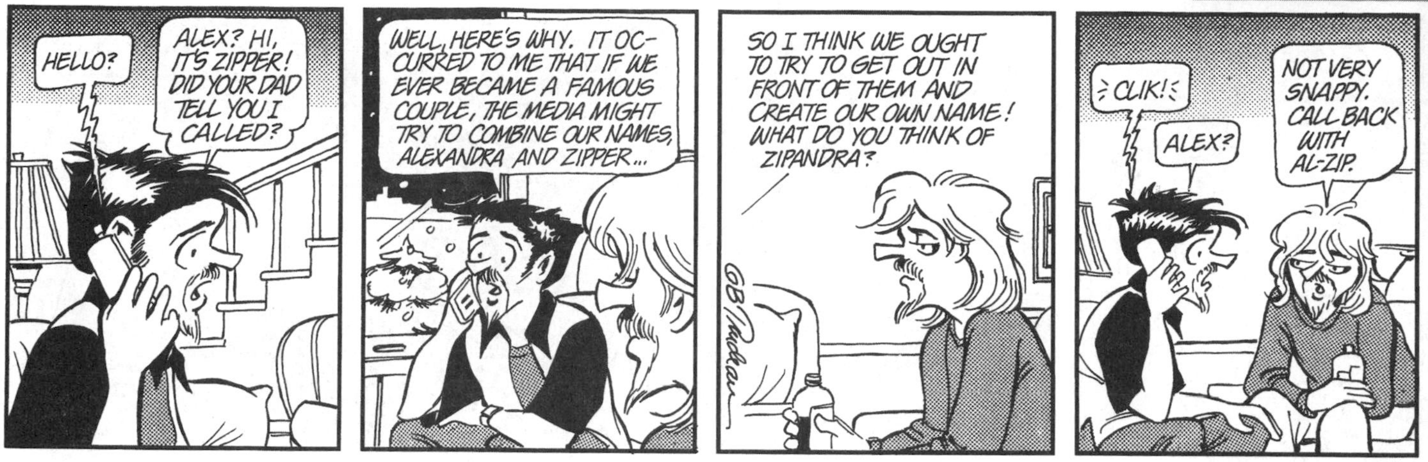
HELLO?
ALEX? HI, IT'S ZIPPER! DID YOUR DAD TELL YOU I CALLED?
WELL, HERE'S WHY. IT OCCURRED TO ME THAT IF WE EVER BECAME A FAMOUS COUPLE, THE MEDIA MIGHT TRY TO COMBINE OUR NAMES, ALEXANDRA AND ZIPPER...
SO I THINK WE OUGHT TO TRY TO GET OUT IN FRONT OF THEM AND CREATE OUR OWN NAME! WHAT DO YOU THINK OF ZIPANDRA?
GB Trudeau
CLIK!
ALEX?
NOT VERY SNAPPY. CALL BACK WITH AL-ZIP.

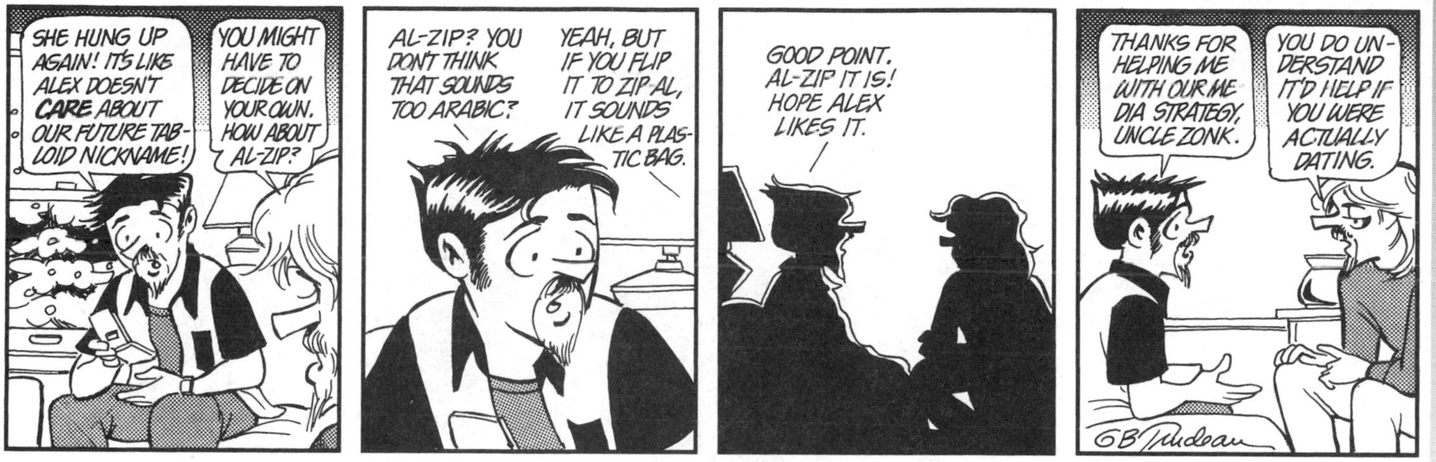
SHE HUNG UP AGAIN! IT'S LIKE ALEX DOESN'T CARE ABOUT OUR FUTURE TABLOID NICKNAME!
YOU MIGHT HAVE TO DECIDE ON YOUR OWN. HOW ABOUT AL-ZIP?
AL-ZIP? YOU DON'T THINK THAT SOUNDS TOO ARABIC?
YEAH, BUT IF YOU FLIP IT TO ZIP-AL, IT SOUNDS LIKE A PLASTIC BAG.
GOOD POINT. AL-ZIP IT IS! HOPE ALEX LIKES IT.
THANKS FOR HELPING ME WITH OUR MEDIA STRATEGY, UNCLE ZONK.
YOU DO UNDERSTAND IT'D HELP IF YOU WERE ACTUALLY DATING.
GB Trudeau

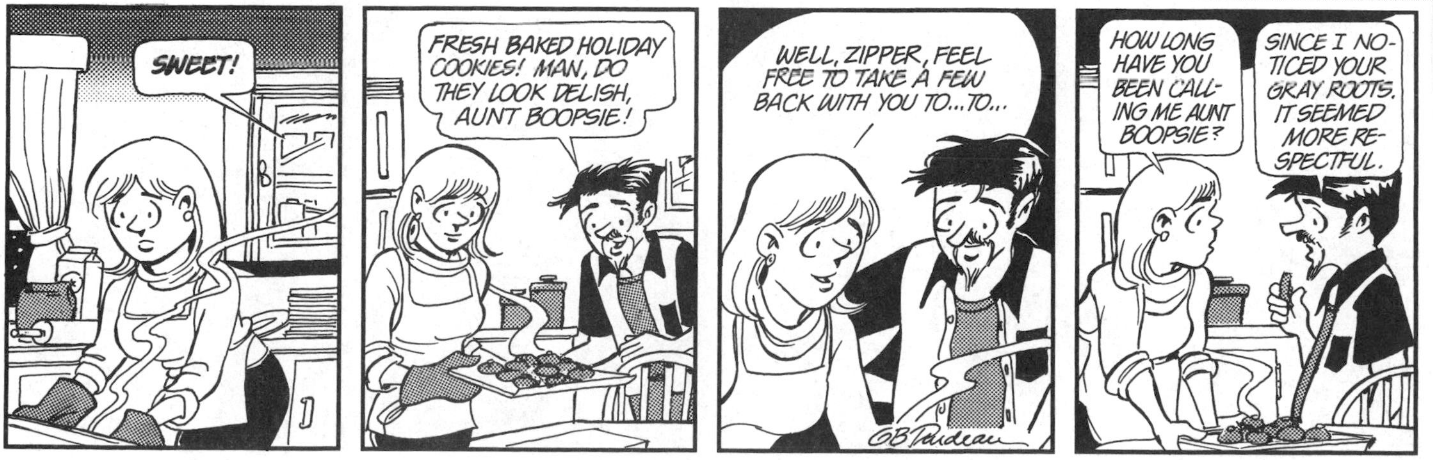
SWEET!
FRESH BAKED HOLIDAY COOKIES! MAN, DO THEY LOOK DELISH, AUNT BOOPSIE!
WELL, ZIPPER, FEEL FREE TO TAKE A FEW BACK WITH YOU TO...TO...
GB Trudeau
HOW LONG HAVE YOU BEEN CALLING ME AUNT BOOPSIE?
SINCE I NOTICED YOUR GRAY ROOTS. IT SEEMED MORE RESPECTFUL.

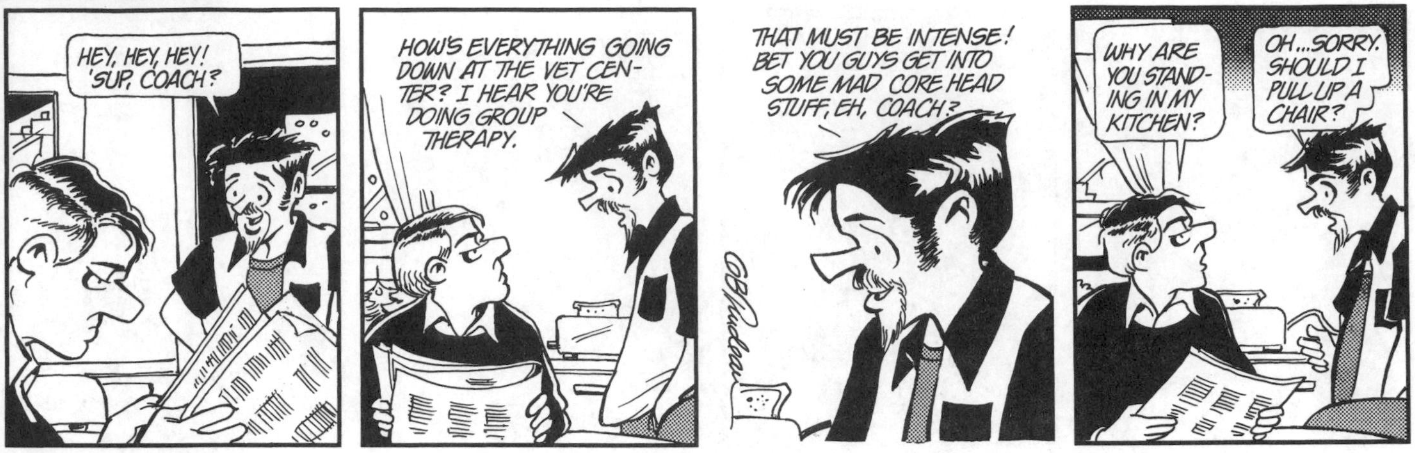
HEY, HEY, HEY! 'SUP, COACH?
HOW'S EVERYTHING GOING DOWN AT THE VET CENTER? I HEAR YOU'RE DOING GROUP THERAPY.
THAT MUST BE INTENSE! BET YOU GUYS GET INTO SOME MAD CORE HEAD STUFF, EH, COACH?
WHY ARE YOU STANDING IN MY KITCHEN?
OH... SORRY. SHOULD I PULL UP A CHAIR?

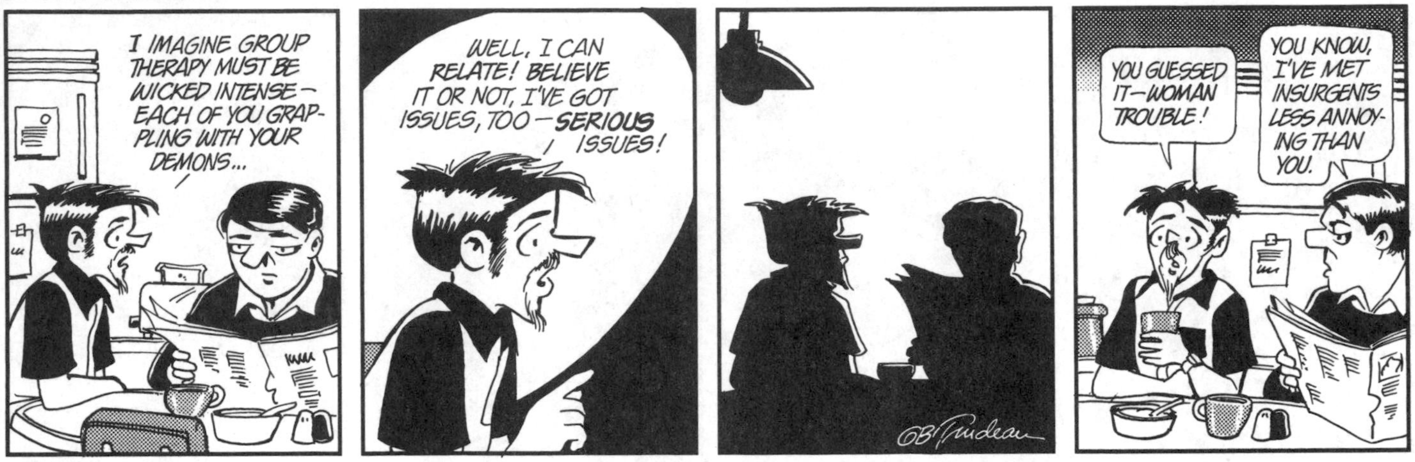
I IMAGINE GROUP THERAPY MUST BE WICKED INTENSE— EACH OF YOU GRAPPLING WITH YOUR DEMONS...
WELL, I CAN RELATE! BELIEVE IT OR NOT, I'VE GOT ISSUES, TOO— SERIOUS ISSUES!
YOU GUESSED IT—WOMAN TROUBLE!
YOU KNOW, I'VE MET INSURGENTS LESS ANNOYING THAN YOU.

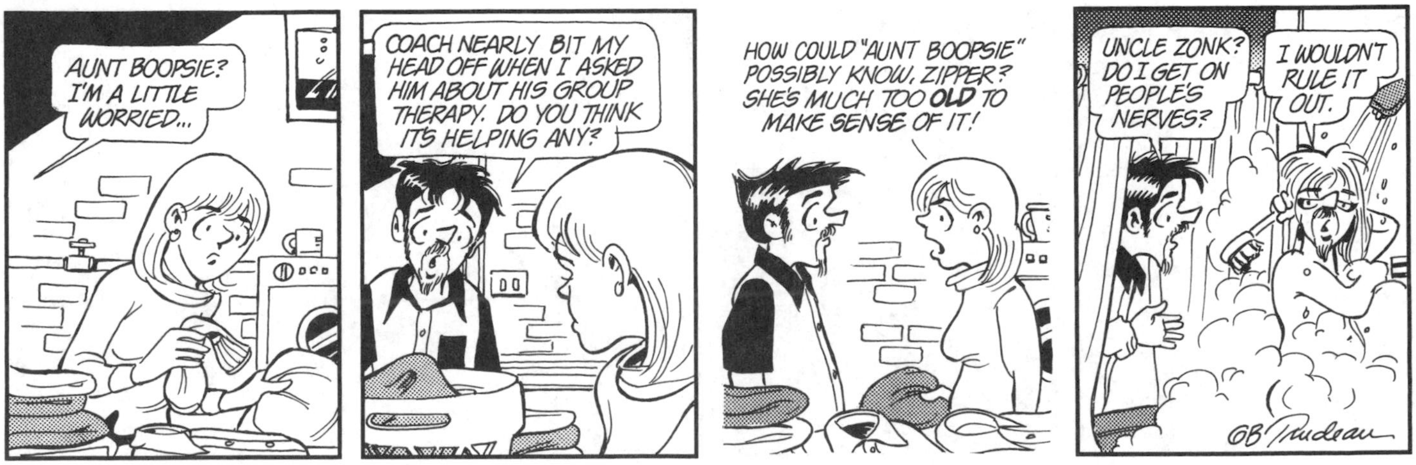
AUNT BOOPSIE? I'M A LITTLE WORRIED...
COACH NEARLY BIT MY HEAD OFF WHEN I ASKED HIM ABOUT HIS GROUP THERAPY. DO YOU THINK IT'S HELPING ANY?
HOW COULD "AUNT BOOPSIE" POSSIBLY KNOW, ZIPPER? SHE'S MUCH TOO OLD TO MAKE SENSE OF IT!
UNCLE ZONK? DO I GET ON PEOPLE'S NERVES?
I WOULDN'T RULE IT OUT.

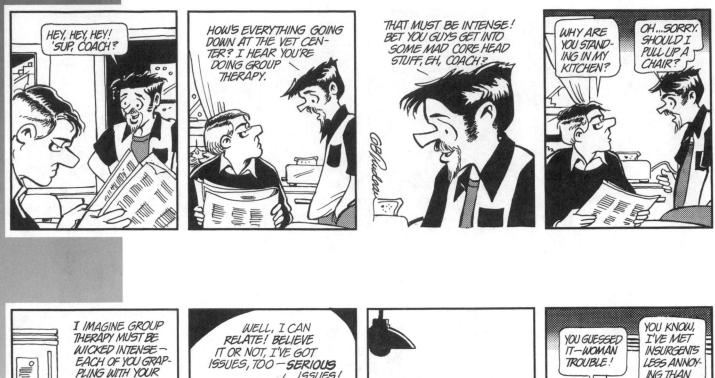

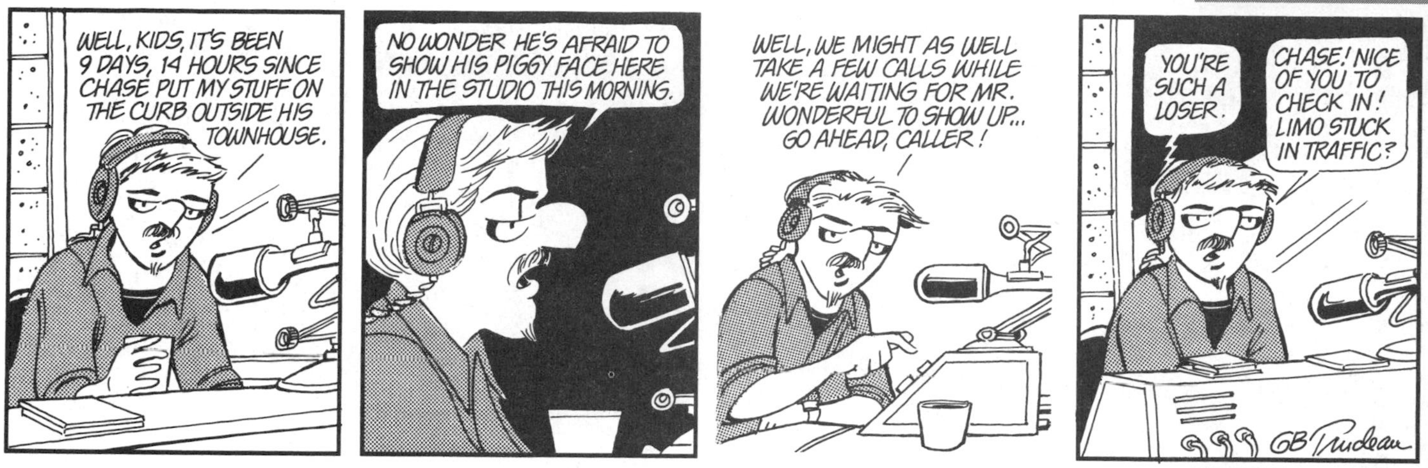
WELL, KIDS, IT'S BEEN 9 DAYS, 14 HOURS SINCE CHASE PUT MY STUFF ON THE CURB OUTSIDE HIS TOWNHOUSE.
NO WONDER HE'S AFRAID TO SHOW HIS PIGGY FACE HERE IN THE STUDIO THIS MORNING.
WELL, WE MIGHT AS WELL TAKE A FEW CALLS WHILE WE'RE WAITING FOR MR. WONDERFUL TO SHOW UP... GO AHEAD, CALLER!
YOU'RE SUCH A LOSER.
CHASE! NICE OF YOU TO CHECK IN! LIMO STUCK IN TRAFFIC?
GB Trudeau

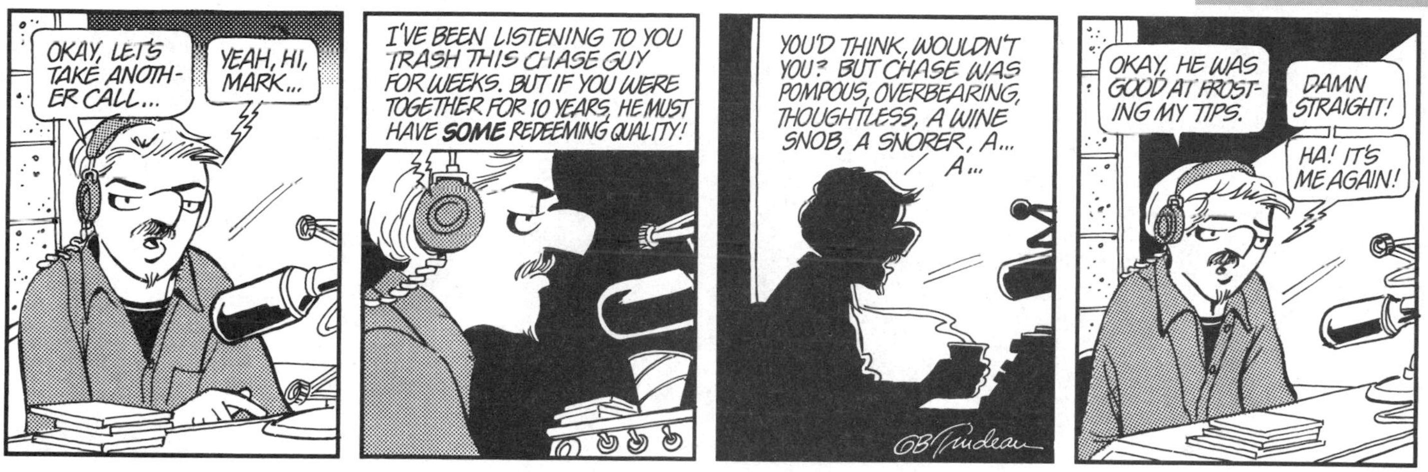
OKAY, LET'S TAKE ANOTHER CALL...
YEAH, HI, MARK...
I'VE BEEN LISTENING TO YOU TRASH THIS CHASE GUY FOR WEEKS. BUT IF YOU WERE TOGETHER FOR 10 YEARS, HE MUST HAVE SOME REDEEMING QUALITY!
YOU'D THINK, WOULDN'T YOU? BUT CHASE WAS POMPOUS, OVERBEARING, THOUGHTLESS, A WINE SNOB, A SNORER, A... A...
GB Trudeau
OKAY, HE WAS GOOD AT FROSTING MY TIPS.
DAMN STRAIGHT!
HA! IT'S ME AGAIN!

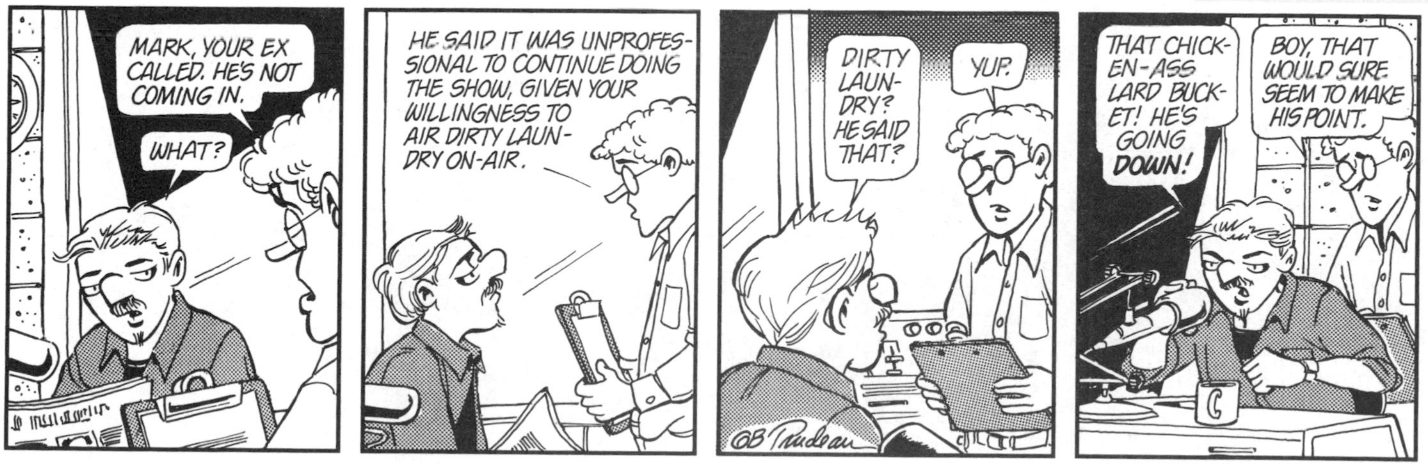
MARK, YOUR EX CALLED. HE'S NOT COMING IN.
WHAT?
HE SAID IT WAS UNPROFESSIONAL TO CONTINUE DOING THE SHOW, GIVEN YOUR WILLINGNESS TO AIR DIRTY LAUNDRY ON-AIR.
DIRTY LAUNDRY? HE SAID THAT?
YUP.
GB Trudeau
THAT CHICKEN-ASS LARD BUCKET! HE'S GOING DOWN!
BOY, THAT WOULD SURE SEEM TO MAKE HIS POINT.

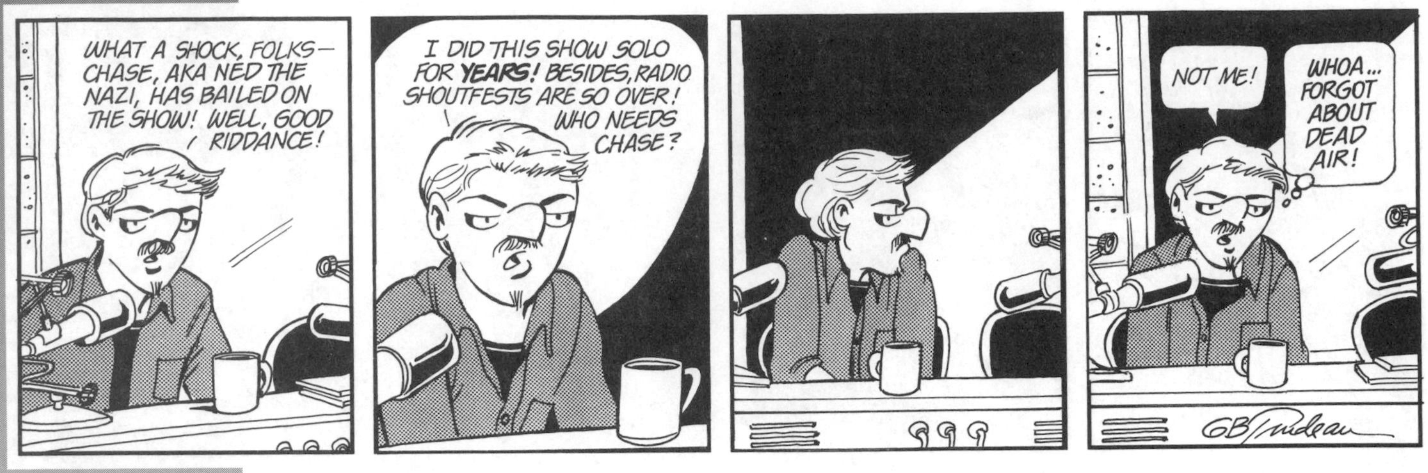
WHAT A SHOCK, FOLKS—CHASE, AKA NED THE NAZI, HAS BAILED ON THE SHOW! WELL, GOOD RIDDANCE!
I DID THIS SHOW SOLO FOR YEARS! BESIDES, RADIO SHOUTFESTS ARE SO OVER! WHO NEEDS CHASE?
NOT ME!
WHOA... FORGOT ABOUT DEAD AIR!
GB Trudeau

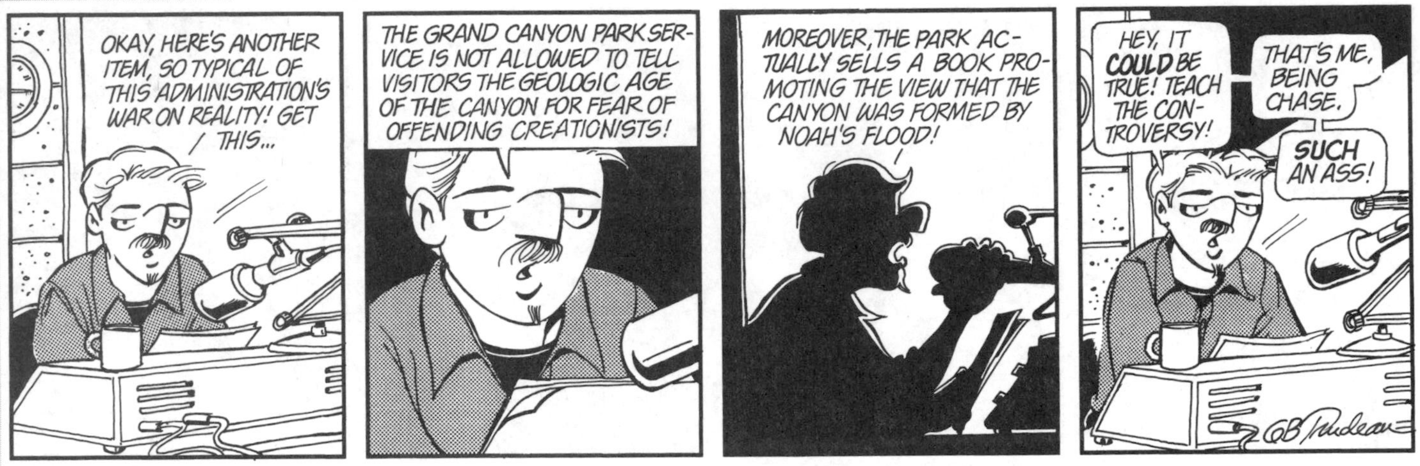
OKAY, HERE'S ANOTHER ITEM, SO TYPICAL OF THIS ADMINISTRATION'S WAR ON REALITY! GET THIS...
THE GRAND CANYON PARK SERVICE IS NOT ALLOWED TO TELL VISITORS THE GEOLOGIC AGE OF THE CANYON FOR FEAR OF OFFENDING CREATIONISTS!
MOREOVER, THE PARK ACTUALLY SELLS A BOOK PROMOTING THE VIEW THAT THE CANYON WAS FORMED BY NOAH'S FLOOD!
HEY, IT COULD BE TRUE! TEACH THE CONTROVERSY!
THAT'S ME, BEING CHASE.
SUCH AN ASS!
GB Trudeau

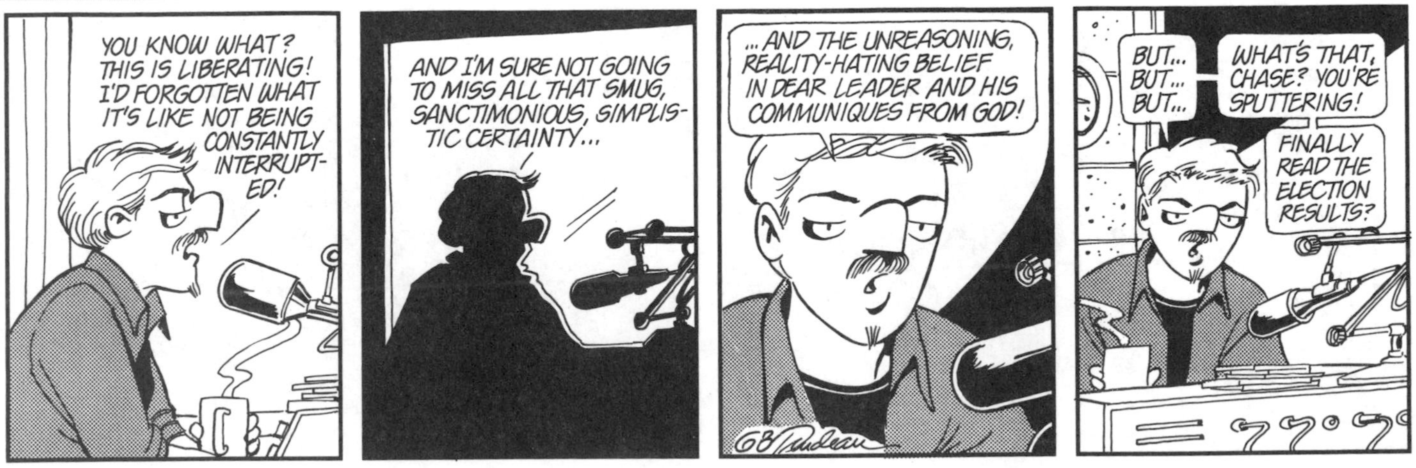
YOU KNOW WHAT? THIS IS LIBERATING! I'D FORGOTTEN WHAT IT'S LIKE NOT BEING CONSTANTLY INTERRUPTED!
AND I'M SURE NOT GOING TO MISS ALL THAT SMUG, SANCTIMONIOUS, SIMPLISTIC CERTAINTY...
...AND THE UNREASONING, REALITY-HATING BELIEF IN DEAR LEADER AND HIS COMMUNIQUES FROM GOD!
GB Trudeau
BUT... BUT... BUT...
WHAT'S THAT, CHASE? YOU'RE SPUTTERING!
FINALLY READ THE ELECTION RESULTS?

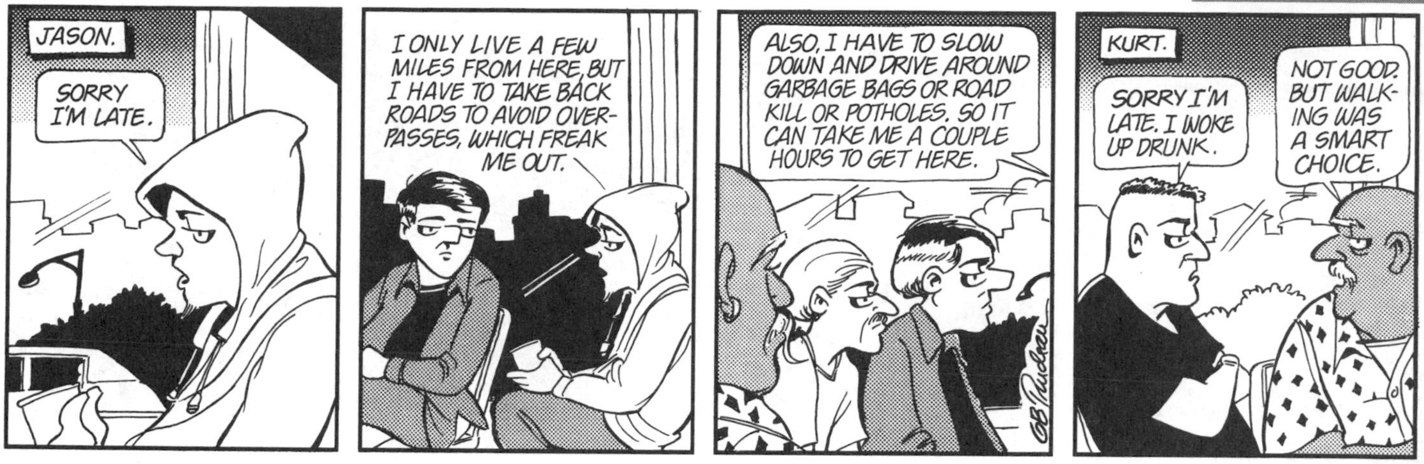
JASON.
SORRY I'M LATE.
I ONLY LIVE A FEW MILES FROM HERE, BUT I HAVE TO TAKE BACK ROADS TO AVOID OVERPASSES, WHICH FREAK ME OUT.
ALSO, I HAVE TO SLOW DOWN AND DRIVE AROUND GARBAGE BAGS OR ROAD KILL OR POTHOLES. SO IT CAN TAKE ME A COUPLE HOURS TO GET HERE.
KURT.
SORRY I'M LATE. I WOKE UP DRUNK.
NOT GOOD. BUT WALKING WAS A SMART CHOICE.

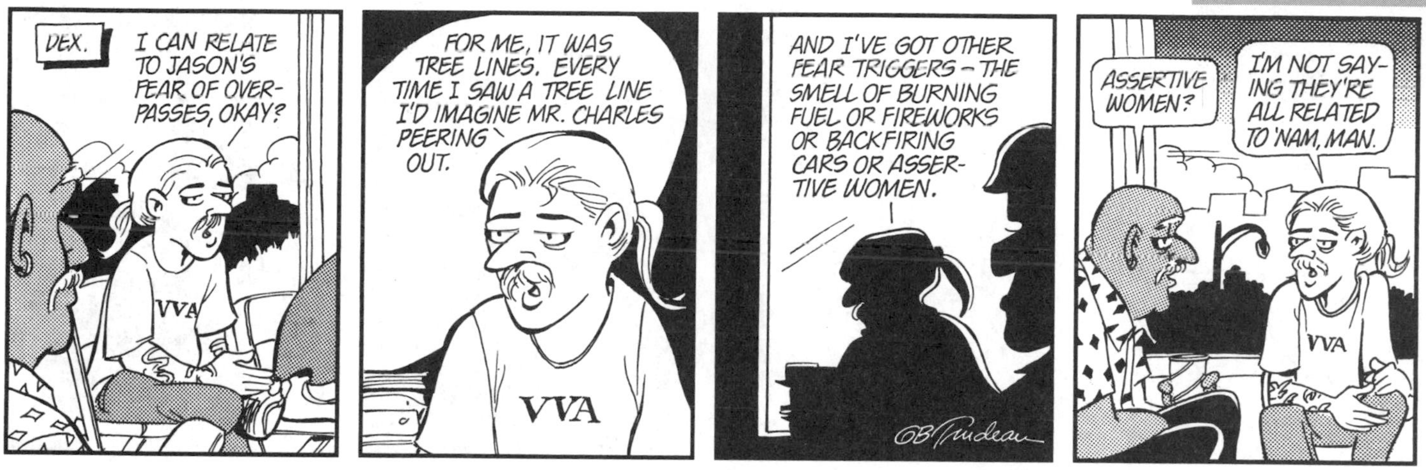
DEX.
I CAN RELATE TO JASON'S FEAR OF OVERPASSES, OKAY?
FOR ME, IT WAS TREE LINES. EVERY TIME I SAW A TREE LINE I'D IMAGINE MR. CHARLES PEERING OUT.
VVA
AND I'VE GOT OTHER FEAR TRIGGERS — THE SMELL OF BURNING FUEL OR FIREWORKS OR BACKFIRING CARS OR ASSERTIVE WOMEN.
ASSERTIVE WOMEN?
I'M NOT SAYING THEY'RE ALL RELATED TO 'NAM, MAN.

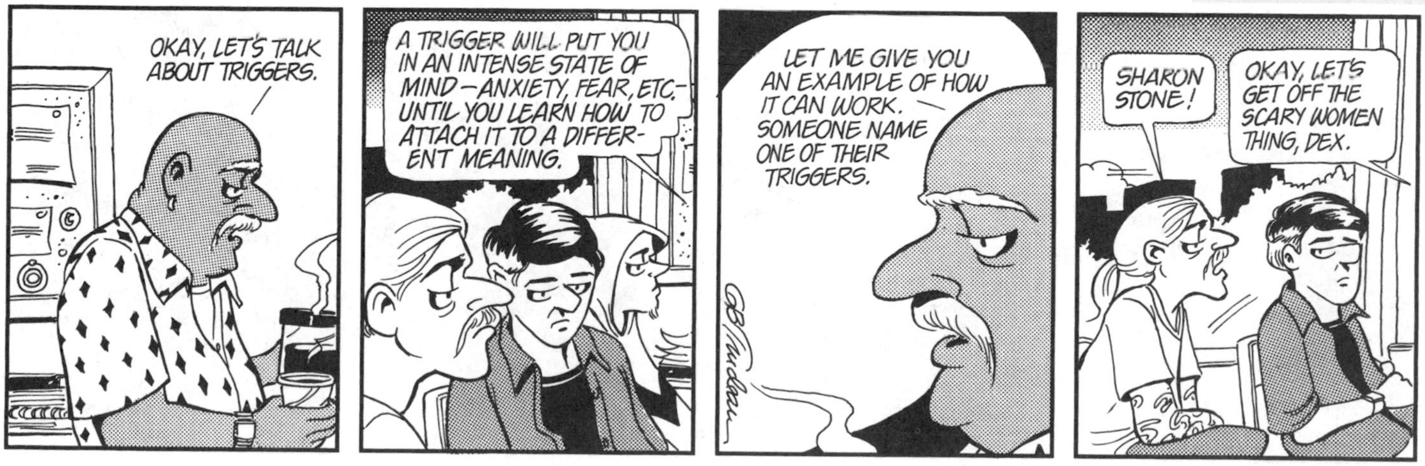
OKAY, LET'S TALK ABOUT TRIGGERS.
A TRIGGER WILL PUT YOU IN AN INTENSE STATE OF MIND — ANXIETY, FEAR, ETC.— UNTIL YOU LEARN HOW TO ATTACH IT TO A DIFFERENT MEANING.
LET ME GIVE YOU AN EXAMPLE OF HOW IT CAN WORK. SOMEONE NAME ONE OF THEIR TRIGGERS.
SHARON STONE!
OKAY, LET'S GET OFF THE SCARY WOMEN THING, DEX.

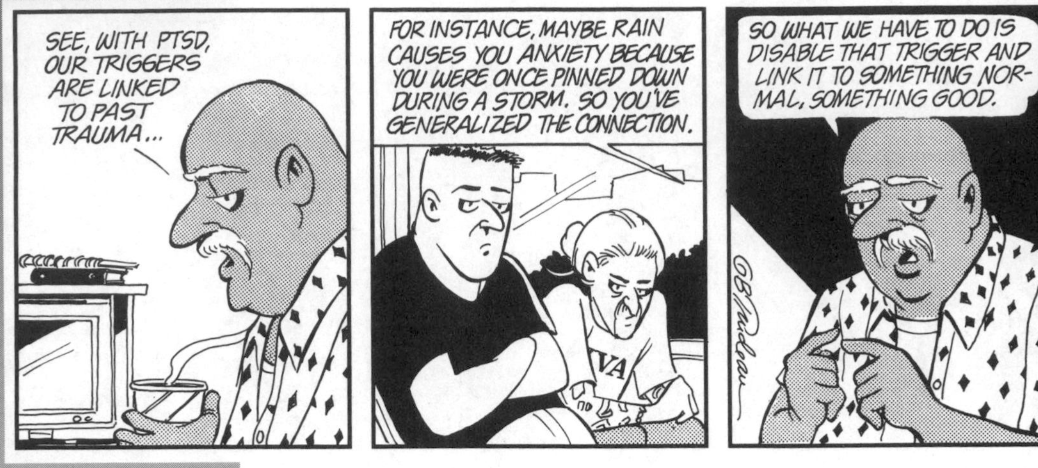
SEE, WITH PTSD, OUR TRIGGERS ARE LINKED TO PAST TRAUMA...
FOR INSTANCE, MAYBE RAIN CAUSES YOU ANXIETY BECAUSE YOU WERE ONCE PINNED DOWN DURING A STORM. SO YOU'VE GENERALIZED THE CONNECTION.
VVA
SO WHAT WE HAVE TO DO IS DISABLE THAT TRIGGER AND LINK IT TO SOMETHING NORMAL, SOMETHING GOOD.
GB Trudeau
YOU MEAN LIKE A PIZZA?
BUT THEN WOULDN'T YOU ALWAYS BE GOING FOR PIZZA IN THE RAIN?

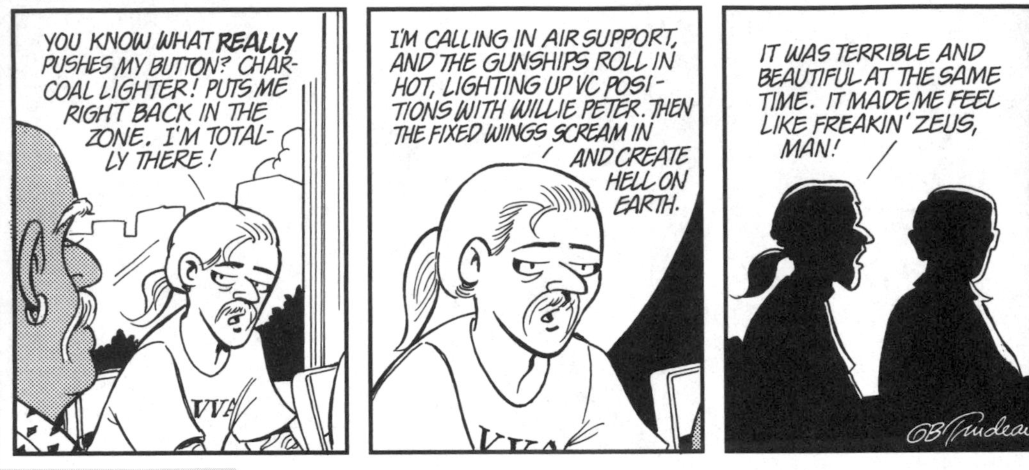
YOU KNOW WHAT **REALLY** PUSHES MY BUTTON? CHARCOAL LIGHTER! PUTS ME RIGHT BACK IN THE ZONE. I'M TOTALLY THERE!
VVA
I'M CALLING IN AIR SUPPORT, AND THE GUNSHIPS ROLL IN HOT, LIGHTING UP VC POSITIONS WITH WILLIE PETER. THEN THE FIXED WINGS SCREAM IN
AND CREATE HELL ON EARTH.
IT WAS TERRIBLE AND BEAUTIFUL AT THE SAME TIME. IT MADE ME FEEL LIKE FREAKIN' ZEUS, MAN!
GB Trudeau
BUT THEN I CAME HOME TO CLEAN POOLS.
CHLORINE - ANOTHER TRIGGER! REMINDS ME OF HOUSEWIVES...
STEADY, DEX.

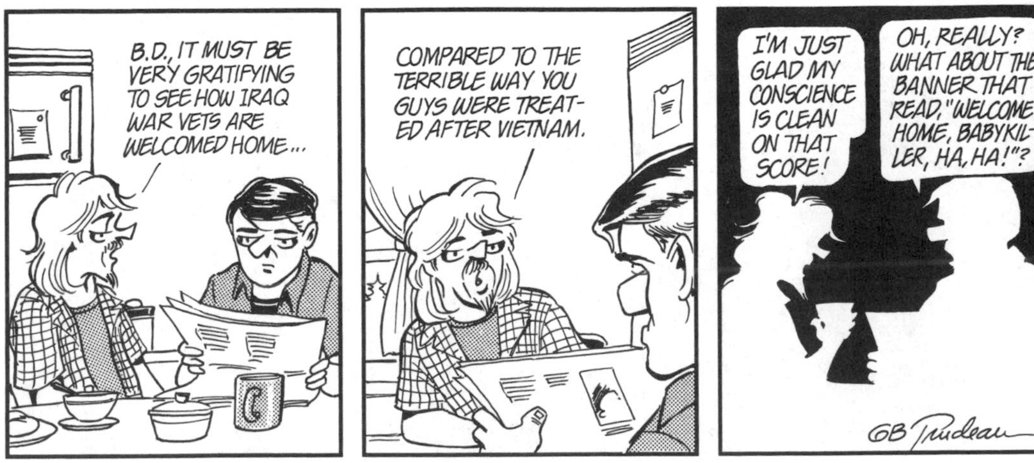
B.D., IT MUST BE VERY GRATIFYING TO SEE HOW IRAQ WAR VETS ARE WELCOMED HOME...
COMPARED TO THE TERRIBLE WAY YOU GUYS WERE TREATED AFTER VIETNAM.
I'M JUST GLAD MY CONSCIENCE IS CLEAN ON THAT SCORE!
OH, REALLY? WHAT ABOUT THE BANNER THAT READ, "WELCOME HOME, BABYKILLER, HA, HA!"?
GB Trudeau
THE "HA, HA" IS CRITICAL, I THINK.
I CAN'T BELIEVE I **LIVE** WITH ONE OF MY TRIGGERS.

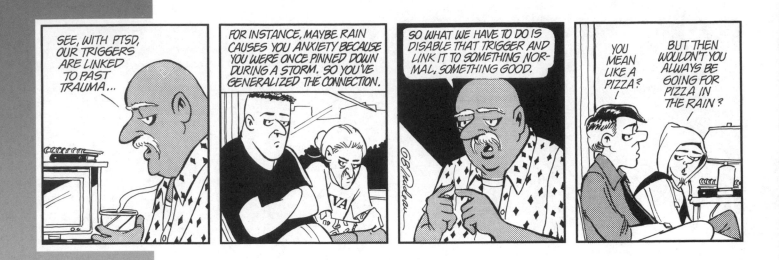

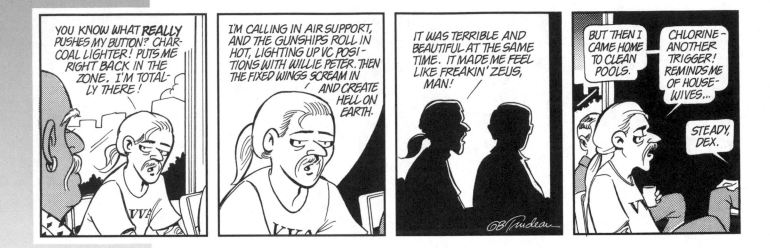

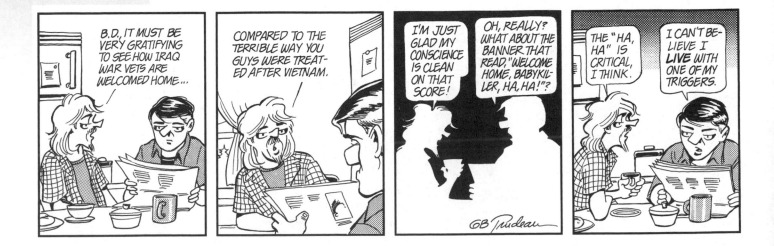

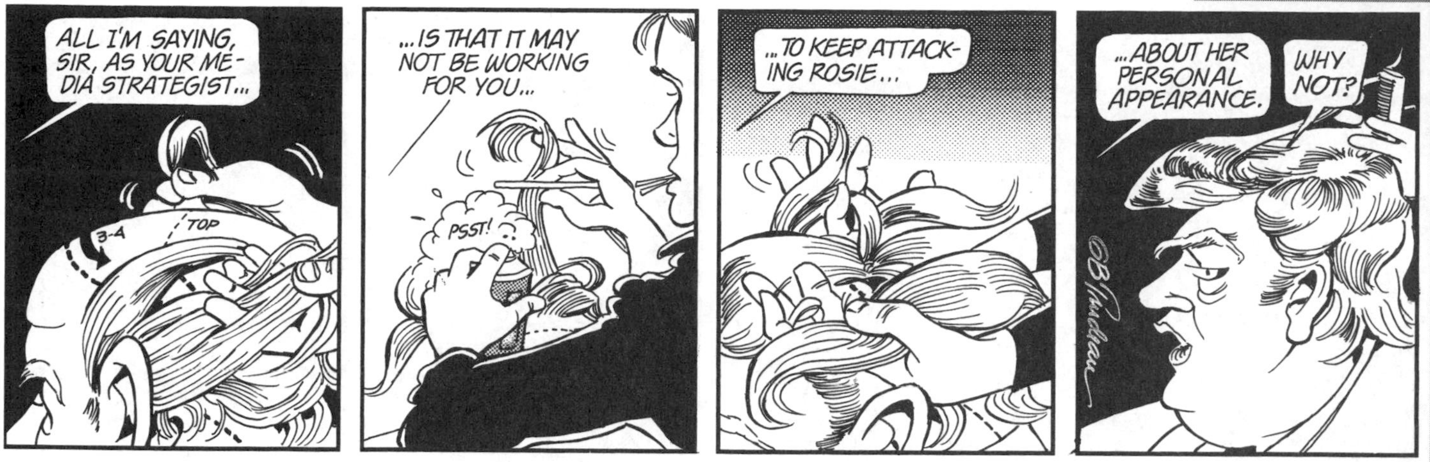
ALL I'M SAYING, SIR, AS YOUR MEDIA STRATEGIST...
3-4
TOP
...IS THAT IT MAY NOT BE WORKING FOR YOU...
PSST!
...TO KEEP ATTACKING ROSIE...
...ABOUT HER PERSONAL APPEARANCE.
WHY NOT?

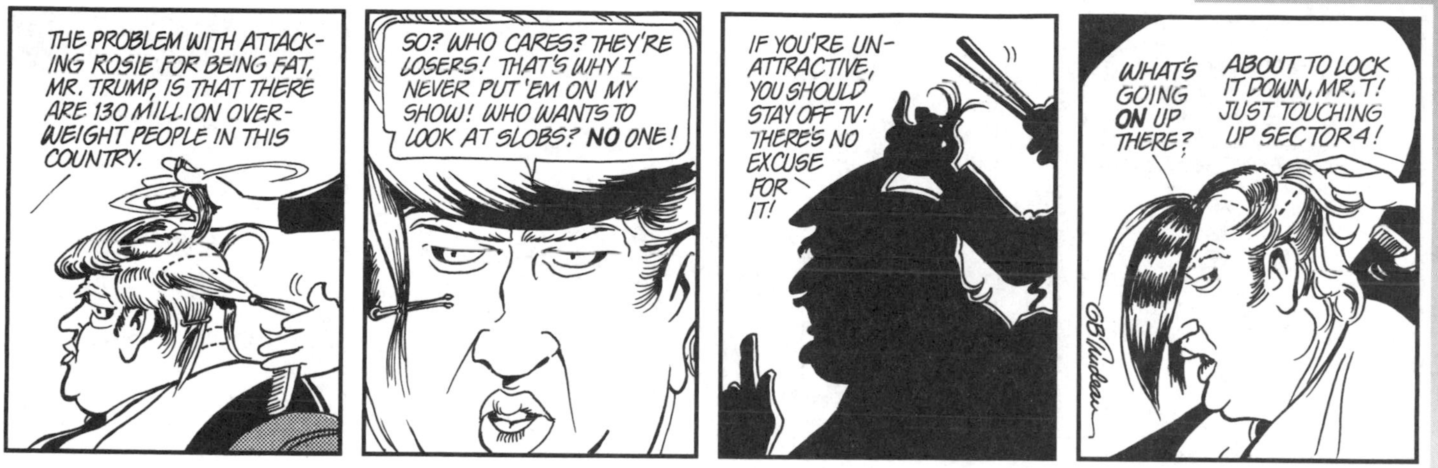
THE PROBLEM WITH ATTACKING ROSIE FOR BEING FAT, MR. TRUMP, IS THAT THERE ARE 130 MILLION OVERWEIGHT PEOPLE IN THIS COUNTRY.
SO? WHO CARES? THEY'RE LOSERS! THAT'S WHY I NEVER PUT 'EM ON MY SHOW! WHO WANTS TO LOOK AT SLOBS? **NO** ONE!
IF YOU'RE UNATTRACTIVE, YOU SHOULD STAY OFF TV! THERE'S NO EXCUSE FOR IT!
WHAT'S GOING **ON** UP THERE?
ABOUT TO LOCK IT DOWN, MR. T! JUST TOUCHING UP SECTOR 4!

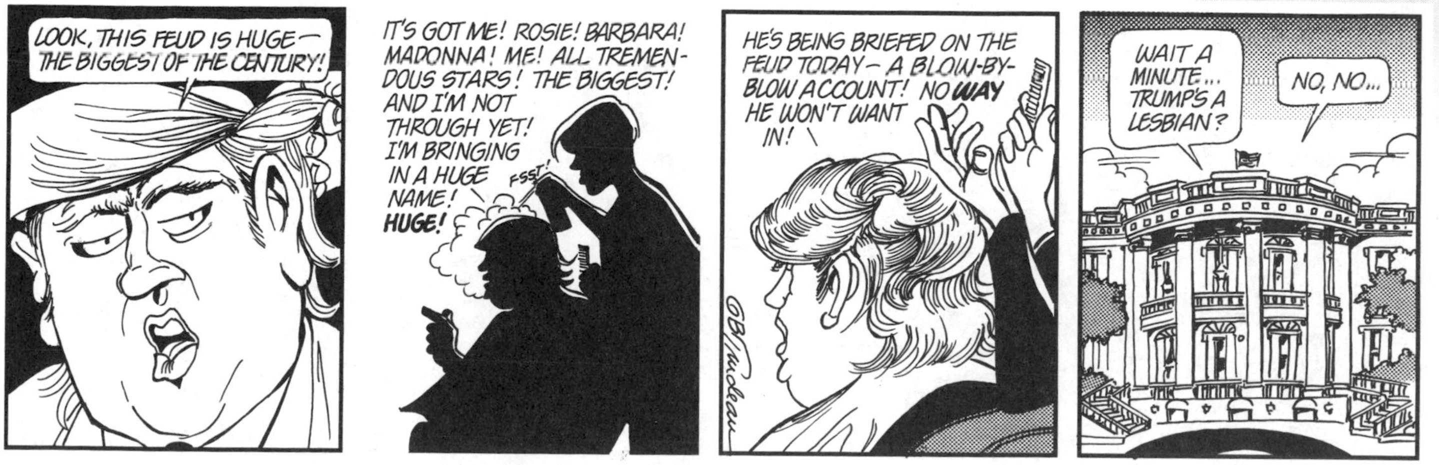
LOOK, THIS FEUD IS HUGE— THE BIGGEST OF THE CENTURY!
IT'S GOT ME! ROSIE! BARBARA! MADONNA! ME! ALL TREMENDOUS STARS! THE BIGGEST! AND I'M NOT THROUGH YET! I'M BRINGING IN A HUGE NAME! **HUGE!**
FSST!
HE'S BEING BRIEFED ON THE FEUD TODAY – A BLOW-BY-BLOW ACCOUNT! NO **WAY** HE WON'T WANT IN!
WAIT A MINUTE... TRUMP'S A LESBIAN?
NO, NO...

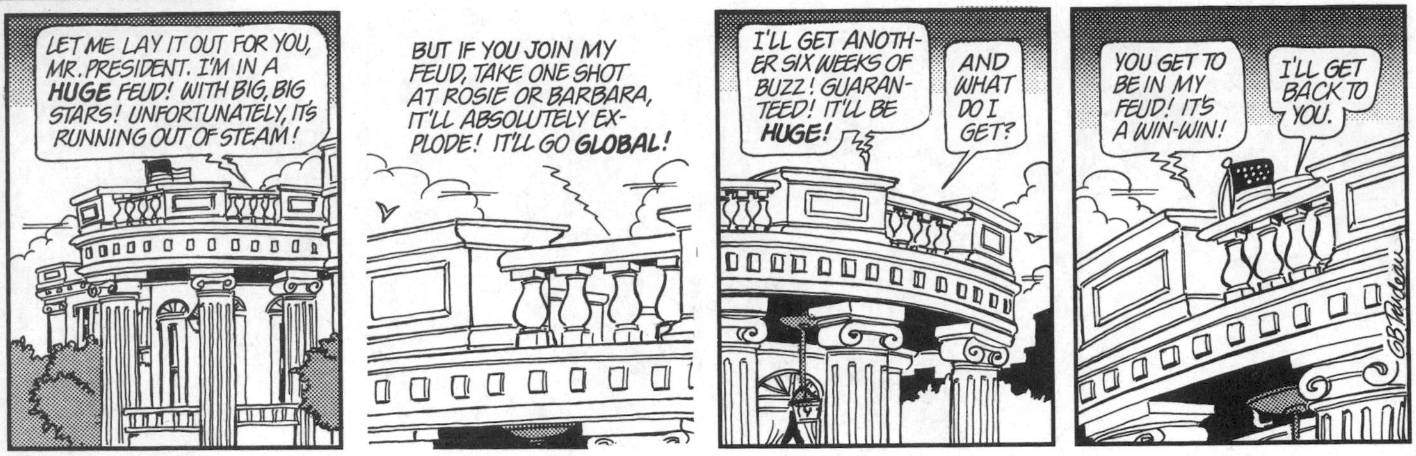
LET ME LAY IT OUT FOR YOU, MR. PRESIDENT. I'M IN A **HUGE** FEUD! WITH BIG, BIG STARS! UNFORTUNATELY, IT'S RUNNING OUT OF STEAM!
BUT IF YOU JOIN MY FEUD, TAKE ONE SHOT AT ROSIE OR BARBARA, IT'LL ABSOLUTELY EXPLODE! IT'LL GO **GLOBAL**!
I'LL GET ANOTHER SIX WEEKS OF BUZZ! GUARANTEED! IT'LL BE **HUGE**!
AND WHAT DO I GET?
YOU GET TO BE IN MY FEUD! IT'S A WIN-WIN!
I'LL GET BACK TO YOU.

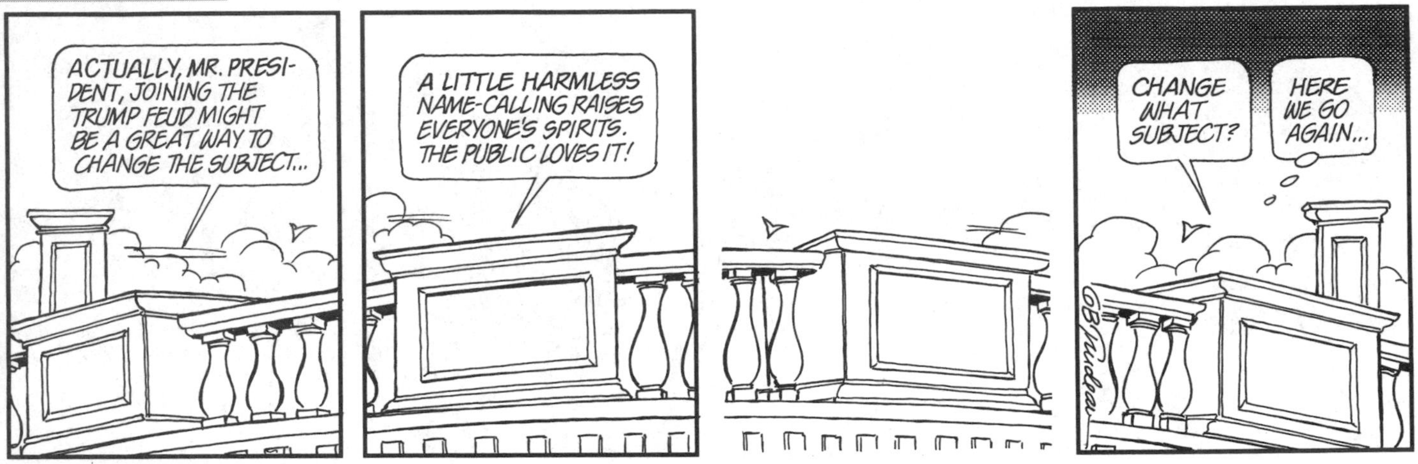
ACTUALLY, MR. PRESIDENT, JOINING THE TRUMP FEUD MIGHT BE A GREAT WAY TO CHANGE THE SUBJECT...
A LITTLE HARMLESS NAME-CALLING RAISES EVERYONE'S SPIRITS. THE PUBLIC LOVES IT!
CHANGE WHAT SUBJECT?
HERE WE GO AGAIN...

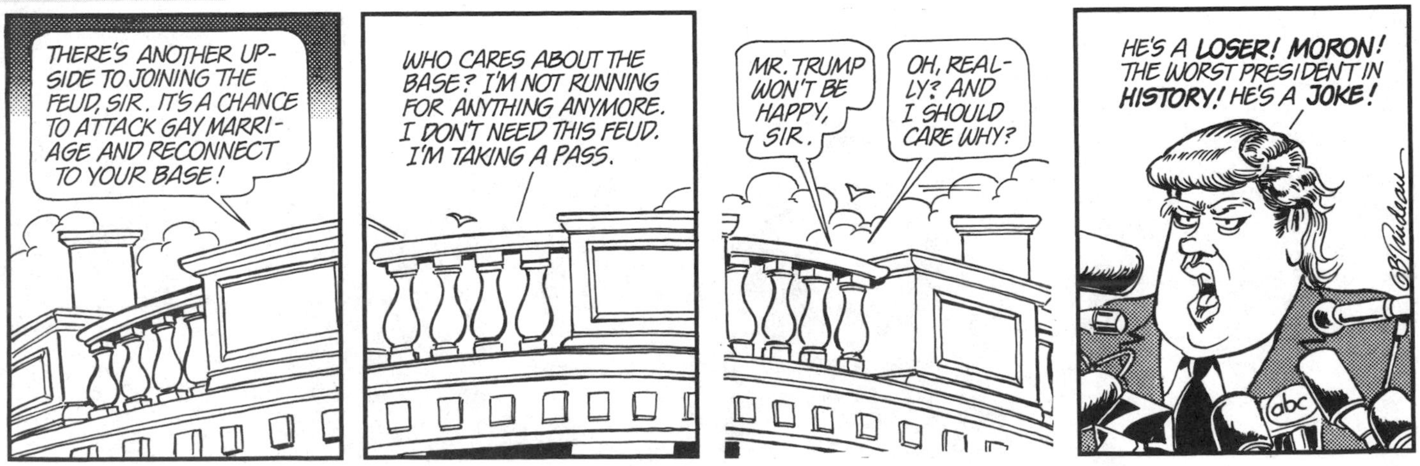
THERE'S ANOTHER UPSIDE TO JOINING THE FEUD, SIR. IT'S A CHANCE TO ATTACK GAY MARRIAGE AND RECONNECT TO YOUR BASE!
WHO CARES ABOUT THE BASE? I'M NOT RUNNING FOR ANYTHING ANYMORE. I DON'T NEED THIS FEUD. I'M TAKING A PASS.
MR. TRUMP WON'T BE HAPPY, SIR.
OH, REALLY? AND I SHOULD CARE WHY?
HE'S A **LOSER! MORON!** THE WORST PRESIDENT IN **HISTORY!** HE'S A **JOKE!**
abc

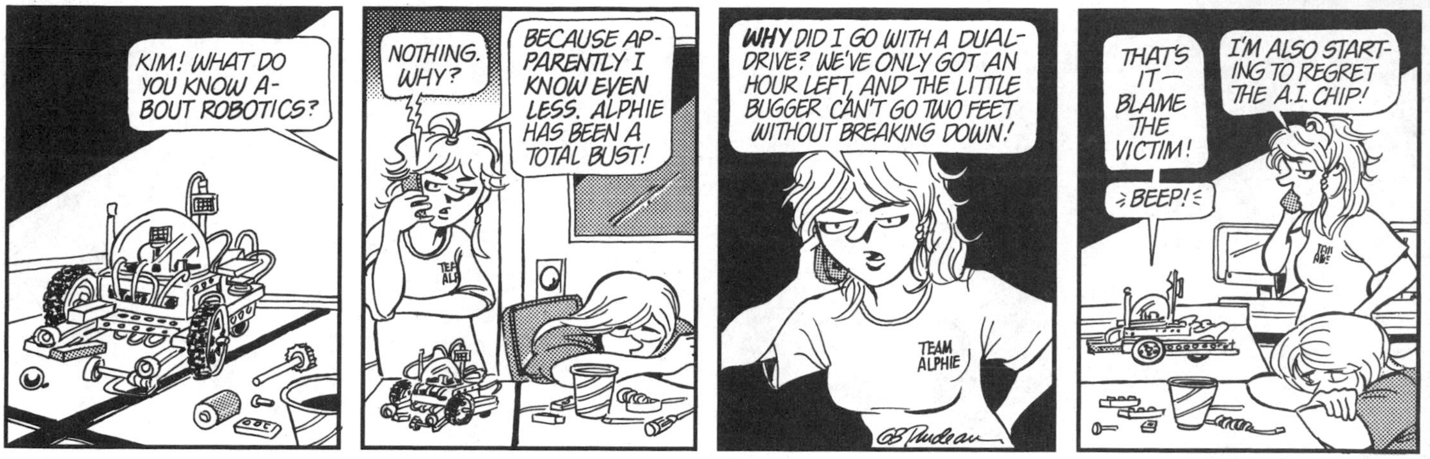
KIM! WHAT DO YOU KNOW A-BOUT ROBOTICS?
NOTHING. WHY?
BECAUSE AP-PARENTLY I KNOW EVEN LESS. ALPHIE HAS BEEN A TOTAL BUST!
TEAM ALPHIE
WHY DID I GO WITH A DUAL-DRIVE? WE'VE ONLY GOT AN HOUR LEFT, AND THE LITTLE BUGGER CAN'T GO TWO FEET WITHOUT BREAKING DOWN!
GB Trudeau
THAT'S IT— BLAME THE VICTIM!
BEEP!
I'M ALSO START-ING TO REGRET THE A.I. CHIP!

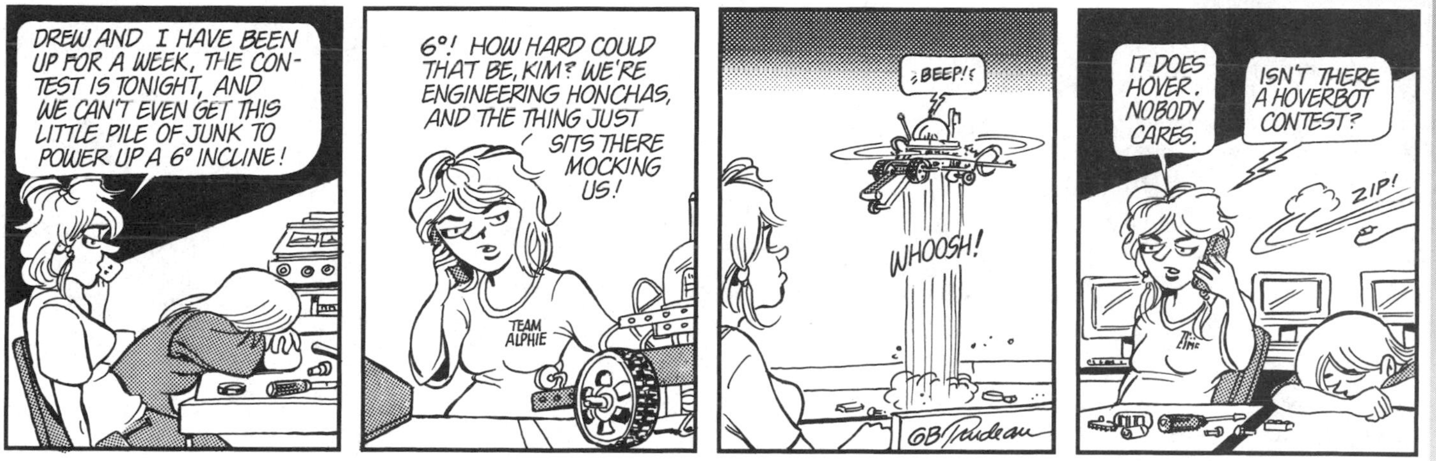
DREW AND I HAVE BEEN UP FOR A WEEK, THE CON-TEST IS TONIGHT, AND WE CAN'T EVEN GET THIS LITTLE PILE OF JUNK TO POWER UP A 6° INCLINE!
6°! HOW HARD COULD THAT BE, KIM? WE'RE ENGINEERING HONCHAS, AND THE THING JUST SITS THERE MOCKING US!
TEAM ALPHIE
BEEP!
WHOOSH!
GB Trudeau
IT DOES HOVER. NOBODY CARES.
ISN'T THERE A HOVERBOT CONTEST?
ZIP!

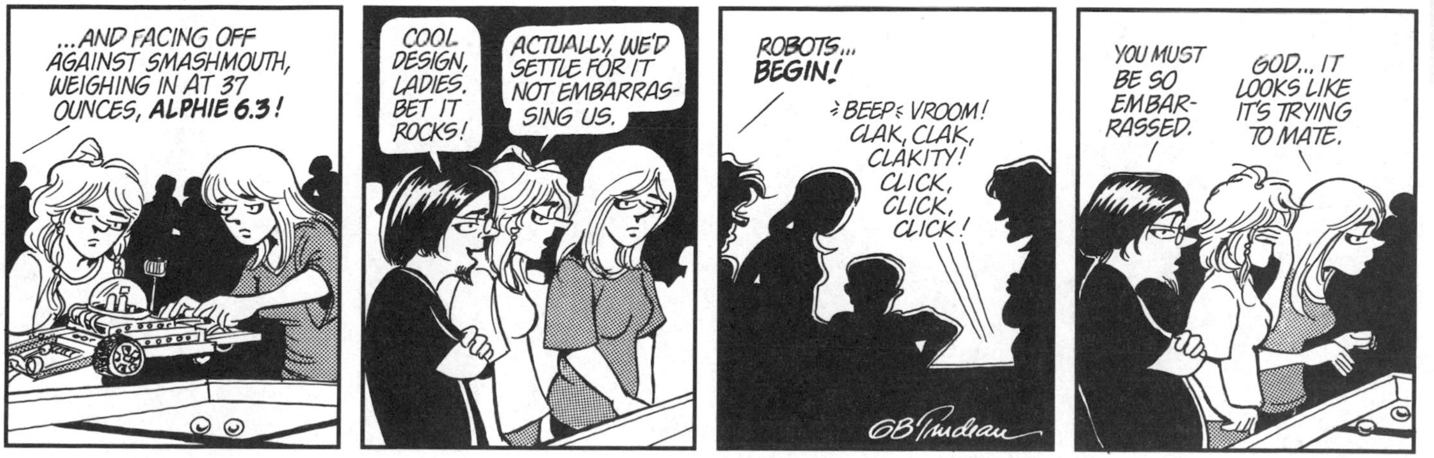
...AND FACING OFF AGAINST SMASHMOUTH, WEIGHING IN AT 37 OUNCES, ALPHIE 6.3!
COOL DESIGN, LADIES. BET IT ROCKS!
ACTUALLY, WE'D SETTLE FOR IT NOT EMBARRAS-SING US.
ROBOTS... BEGIN!
BEEP VROOM! CLAK, CLAK, CLAKITY! CLICK, CLICK, CLICK!
GB Trudeau
YOU MUST BE SO EMBAR-RASSED.
GOD... IT LOOKS LIKE IT'S TRYING TO MATE.

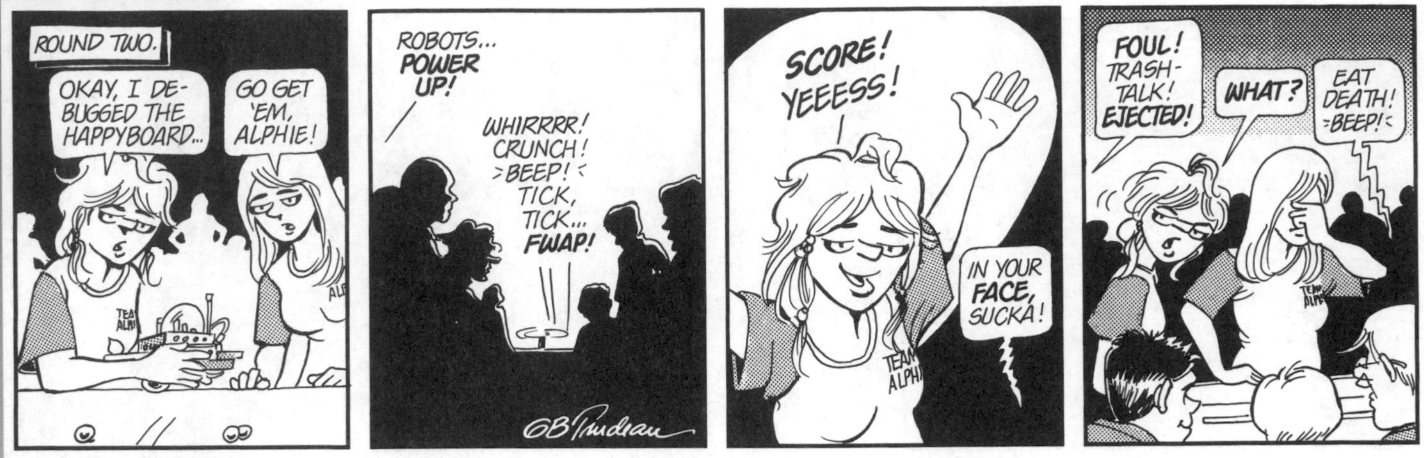
ROUND TWO.
OKAY, I DE-BUGGED THE HAPPYBOARD...
GO GET 'EM, ALPHIE!
ROBOTS... POWER UP!
WHIRRRR! CRUNCH! >BEEP! TICK, TICK... FWAP!
SCORE! YEEESS!
IN YOUR FACE, SUCKA!
FOUL! TRASH-TALK! EJECTED!
WHAT?
EAT DEATH! >BEEP!<

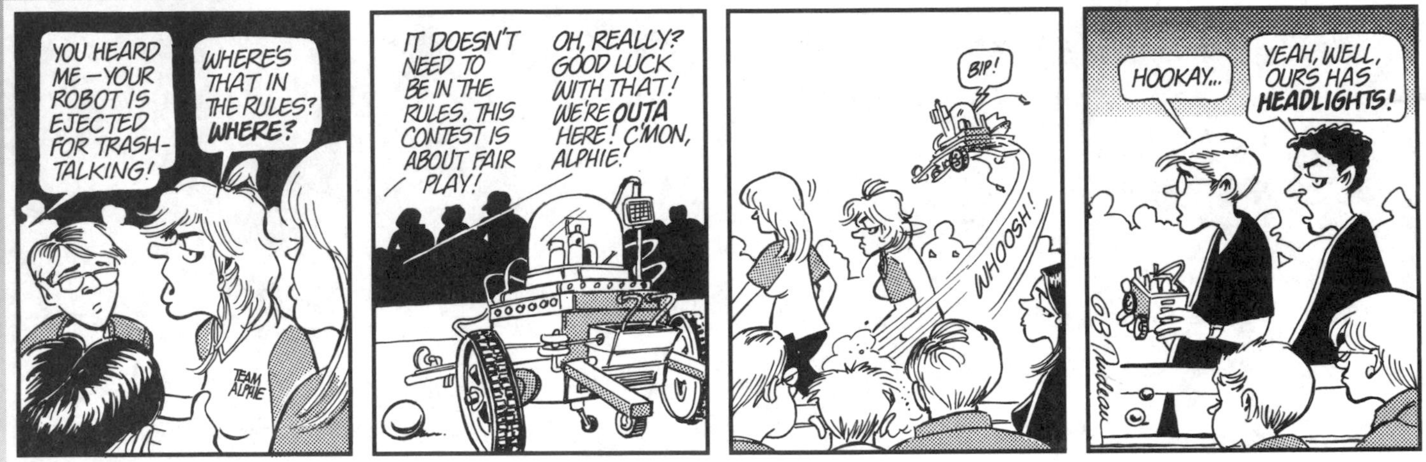
YOU HEARD ME — YOUR ROBOT IS EJECTED FOR TRASH-TALKING!
WHERE'S THAT IN THE RULES? WHERE?
IT DOESN'T NEED TO BE IN THE RULES. THIS CONTEST IS ABOUT FAIR PLAY!
OH, REALLY? GOOD LUCK WITH THAT! WE'RE OUTA HERE! C'MON, ALPHIE!
BIP!
WHOOSH!
HOOKAY...
YEAH, WELL, OURS HAS HEADLIGHTS!

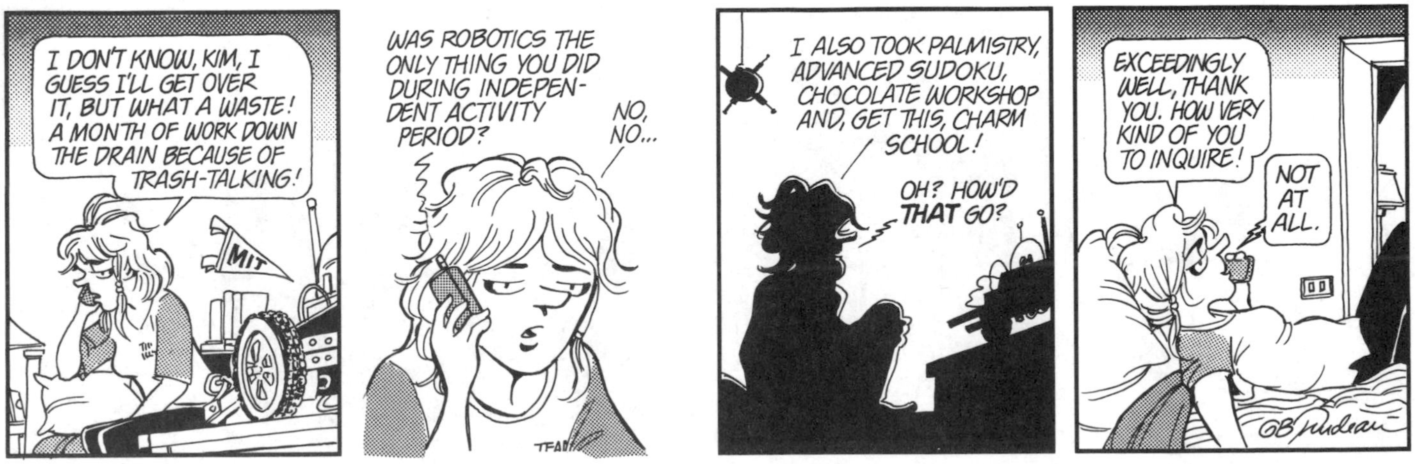
I DON'T KNOW, KIM, I GUESS I'LL GET OVER IT, BUT WHAT A WASTE! A MONTH OF WORK DOWN THE DRAIN BECAUSE OF TRASH-TALKING!
MIT
WAS ROBOTICS THE ONLY THING YOU DID DURING INDEPENDENT ACTIVITY PERIOD?
NO, NO...
I ALSO TOOK PALMISTRY, ADVANCED SUDOKU, CHOCOLATE WORKSHOP AND, GET THIS, CHARM SCHOOL!
OH? HOW'D THAT GO?
EXCEEDINGLY WELL, THANK YOU. HOW VERY KIND OF YOU TO INQUIRE!
NOT AT ALL.

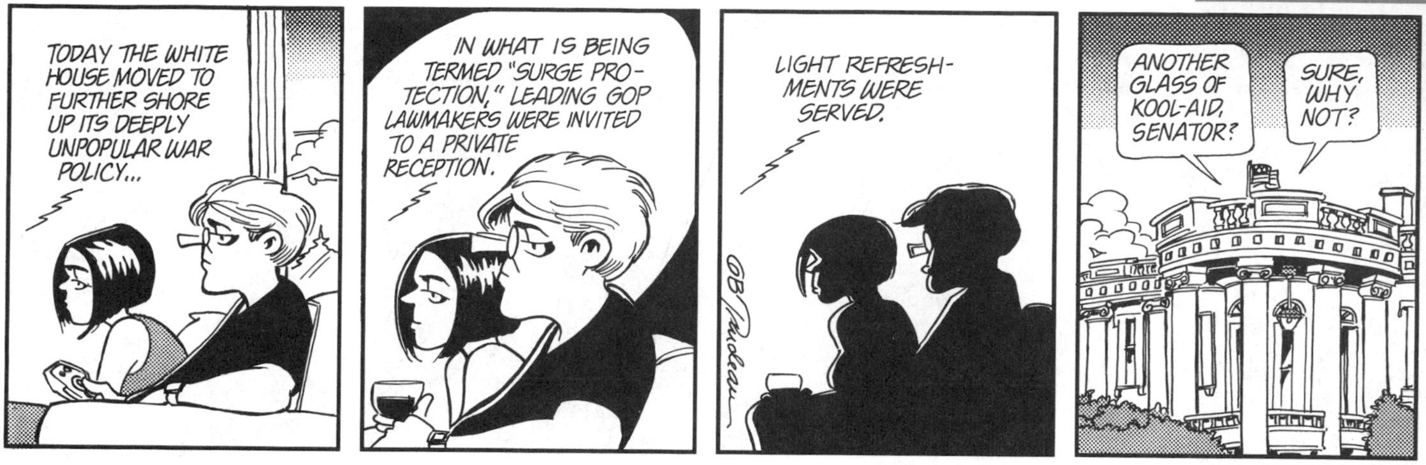
TODAY THE WHITE HOUSE MOVED TO FURTHER SHORE UP ITS DEEPLY UNPOPULAR WAR POLICY...
IN WHAT IS BEING TERMED "SURGE PROTECTION," LEADING GOP LAWMAKERS WERE INVITED TO A PRIVATE RECEPTION.
LIGHT REFRESHMENTS WERE SERVED.
ANOTHER GLASS OF KOOL-AID, SENATOR?
SURE, WHY NOT?

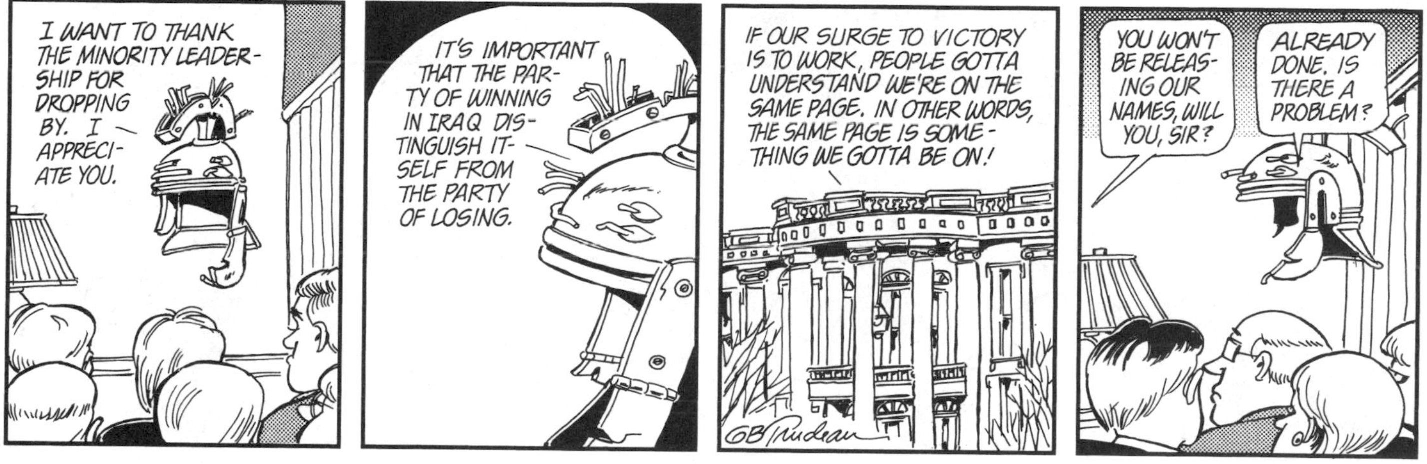
I WANT TO THANK THE MINORITY LEADERSHIP FOR DROPPING BY. I APPRECIATE YOU.
IT'S IMPORTANT THAT THE PARTY OF WINNING IN IRAQ DISTINGUISH ITSELF FROM THE PARTY OF LOSING.
IF OUR SURGE TO VICTORY IS TO WORK, PEOPLE GOTTA UNDERSTAND WE'RE ON THE SAME PAGE. IN OTHER WORDS, THE SAME PAGE IS SOMETHING WE GOTTA BE ON!
YOU WON'T BE RELEASING OUR NAMES, WILL YOU, SIR?
ALREADY DONE. IS THERE A PROBLEM?

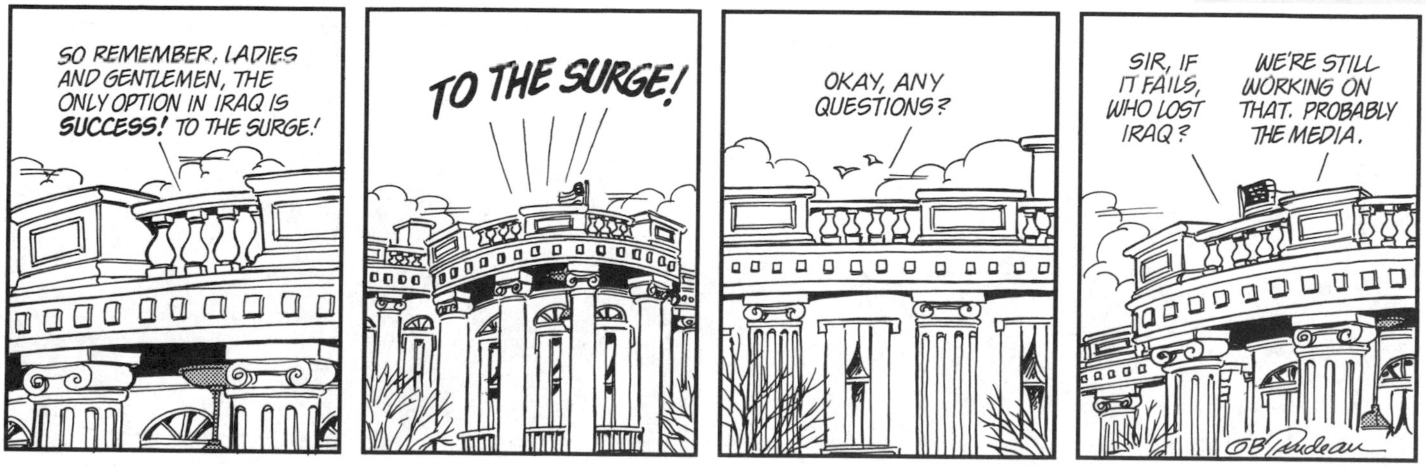
SO REMEMBER, LADIES AND GENTLEMEN, THE ONLY OPTION IN IRAQ IS SUCCESS! TO THE SURGE!
TO THE SURGE!
OKAY, ANY QUESTIONS?
SIR, IF IT FAILS, WHO LOST IRAQ?
WE'RE STILL WORKING ON THAT. PROBABLY THE MEDIA.

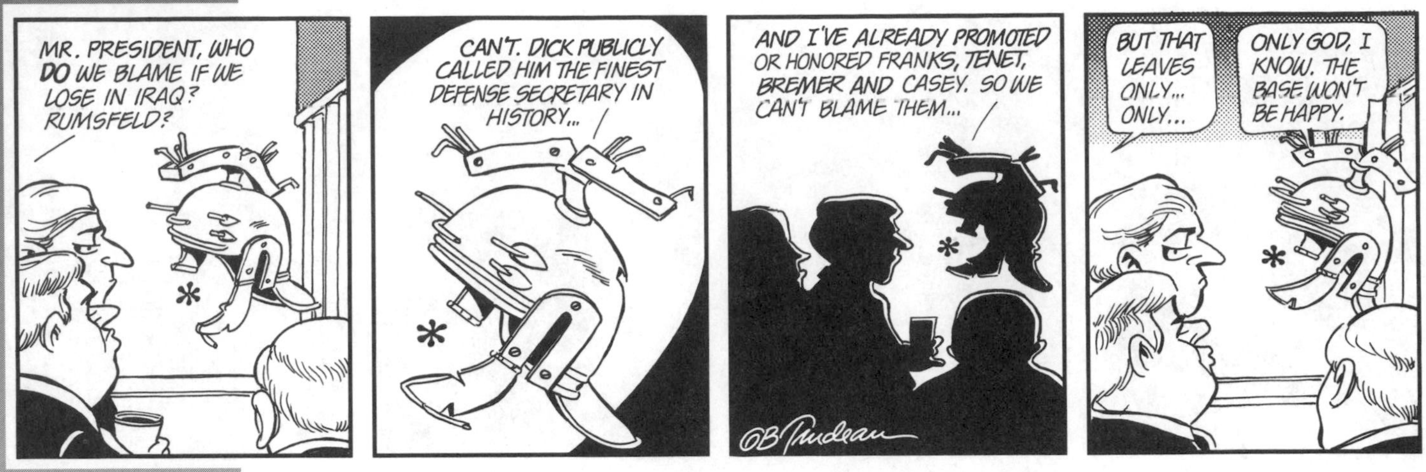
MR. PRESIDENT, WHO DO WE BLAME IF WE LOSE IN IRAQ? RUMSFELD?
CAN'T. DICK PUBLICLY CALLED HIM THE FINEST DEFENSE SECRETARY IN HISTORY...
AND I'VE ALREADY PROMOTED OR HONORED FRANKS, TENET, BREMER AND CASEY. SO WE CAN'T BLAME THEM...
©B Trudeau
BUT THAT LEAVES ONLY... ONLY...
ONLY GOD, I KNOW. THE BASE WON'T BE HAPPY.

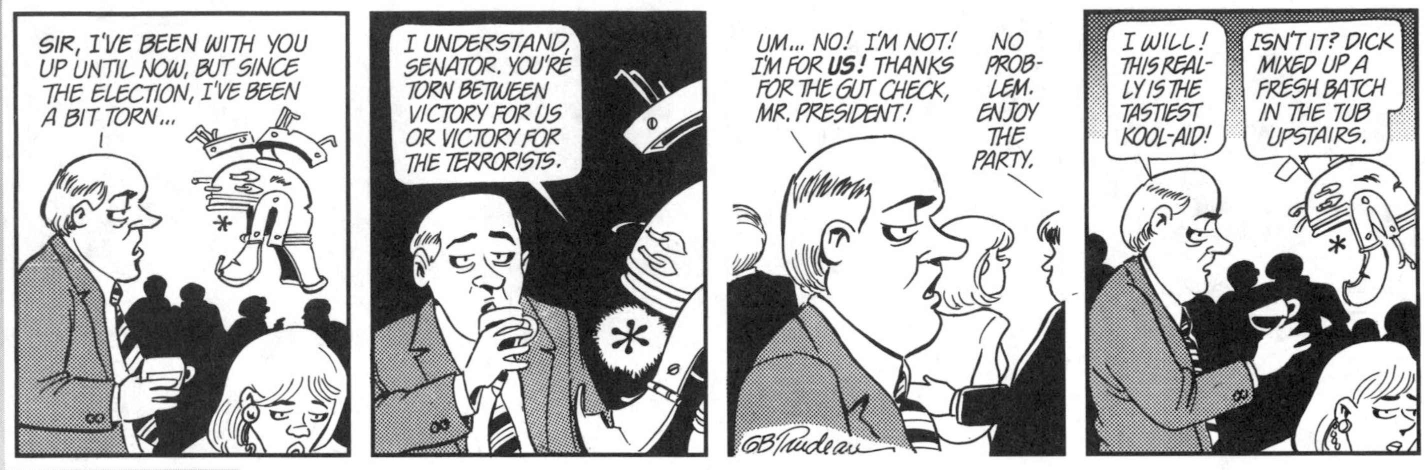
SIR, I'VE BEEN WITH YOU UP UNTIL NOW, BUT SINCE THE ELECTION, I'VE BEEN A BIT TORN...
I UNDERSTAND, SENATOR. YOU'RE TORN BETWEEN VICTORY FOR US OR VICTORY FOR THE TERRORISTS.
UM... NO! I'M NOT! I'M FOR US! THANKS FOR THE GUT CHECK, MR. PRESIDENT!
NO PROB-LEM. ENJOY THE PARTY.
©B Trudeau
I WILL! THIS REAL-LY IS THE TASTIEST KOOL-AID!
ISN'T IT? DICK MIXED UP A FRESH BATCH IN THE TUB UPSTAIRS.

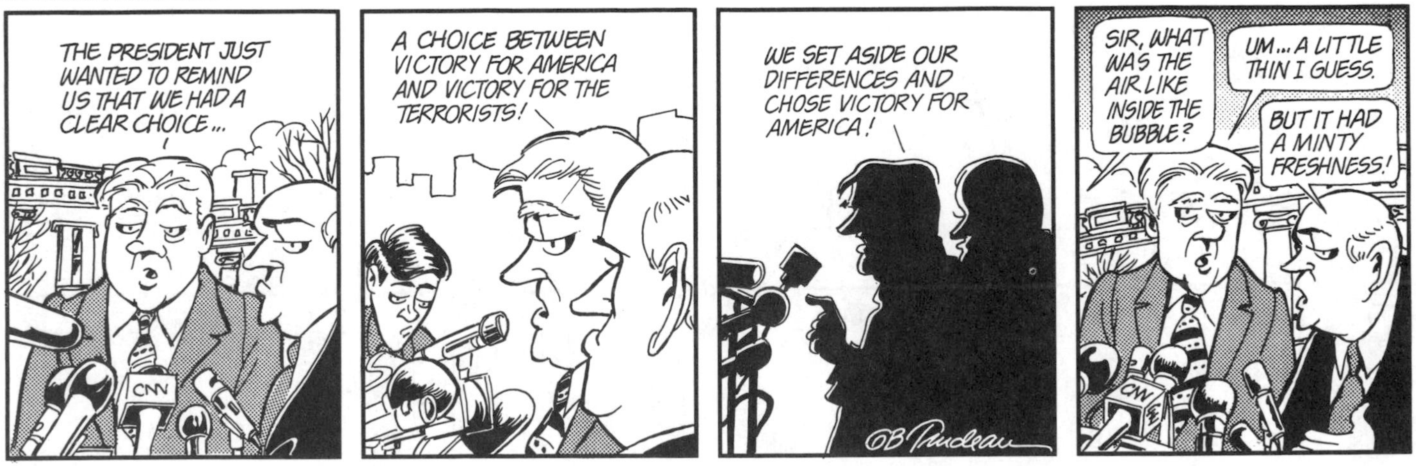
THE PRESIDENT JUST WANTED TO REMIND US THAT WE HAD A CLEAR CHOICE...
CNN
A CHOICE BETWEEN VICTORY FOR AMERICA AND VICTORY FOR THE TERRORISTS!
WE SET ASIDE OUR DIFFERENCES AND CHOSE VICTORY FOR AMERICA!
©B Trudeau
SIR, WHAT WAS THE AIR LIKE INSIDE THE BUBBLE?
UM... A LITTLE THIN I GUESS.
BUT IT HAD A MINTY FRESHNESS!
CNN

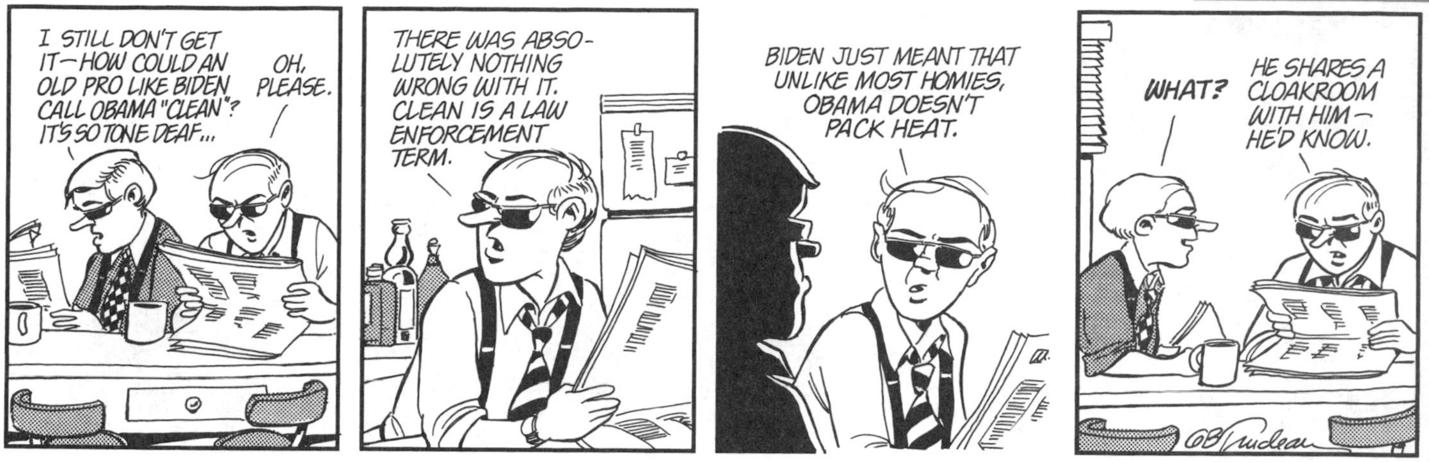
I STILL DON'T GET IT—HOW COULD AN OLD PRO LIKE BIDEN CALL OBAMA "CLEAN"? IT'S SO TONE DEAF...
OH, PLEASE.
THERE WAS ABSO-LUTELY NOTHING WRONG WITH IT. CLEAN IS A LAW ENFORCEMENT TERM.
BIDEN JUST MEANT THAT UNLIKE MOST HOMIES, OBAMA DOESN'T PACK HEAT.
WHAT?
HE SHARES A CLOAKROOM WITH HIM—HE'D KNOW.
©B Trudeau

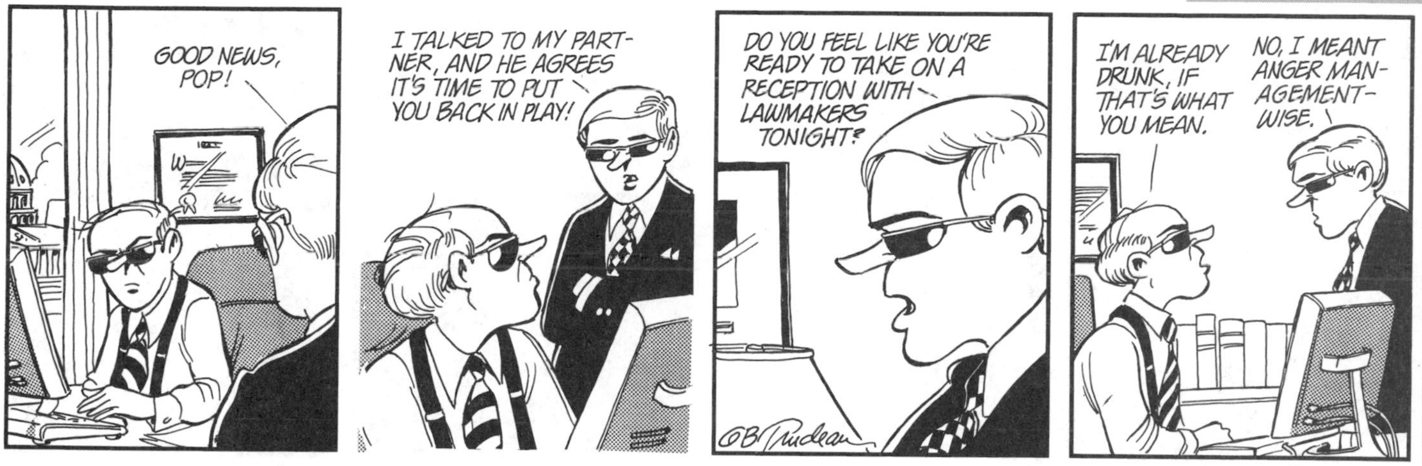
GOOD NEWS, POP!
I TALKED TO MY PART-NER, AND HE AGREES IT'S TIME TO PUT YOU BACK IN PLAY!
DO YOU FEEL LIKE YOU'RE READY TO TAKE ON A RECEPTION WITH LAWMAKERS TONIGHT?
©B Trudeau
I'M ALREADY DRUNK, IF THAT'S WHAT YOU MEAN.
NO, I MEANT ANGER MAN-AGEMENT-WISE.

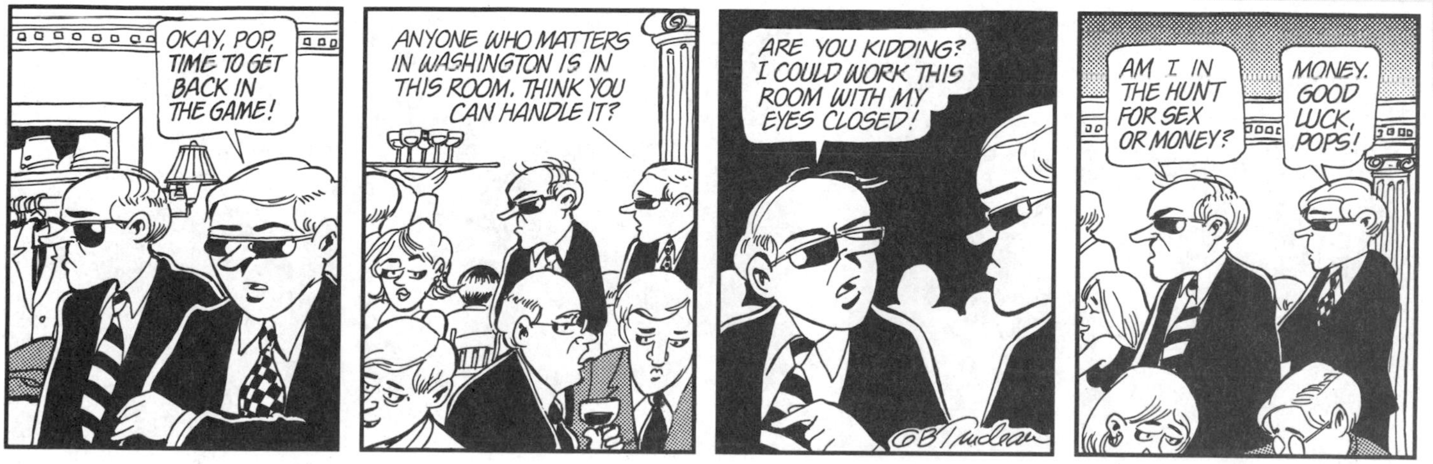
OKAY, POP, TIME TO GET BACK IN THE GAME!
ANYONE WHO MATTERS IN WASHINGTON IS IN THIS ROOM. THINK YOU CAN HANDLE IT?
ARE YOU KIDDING? I COULD WORK THIS ROOM WITH MY EYES CLOSED!
©B Trudeau
AM I IN THE HUNT FOR SEX OR MONEY?
MONEY. GOOD LUCK, POPS!

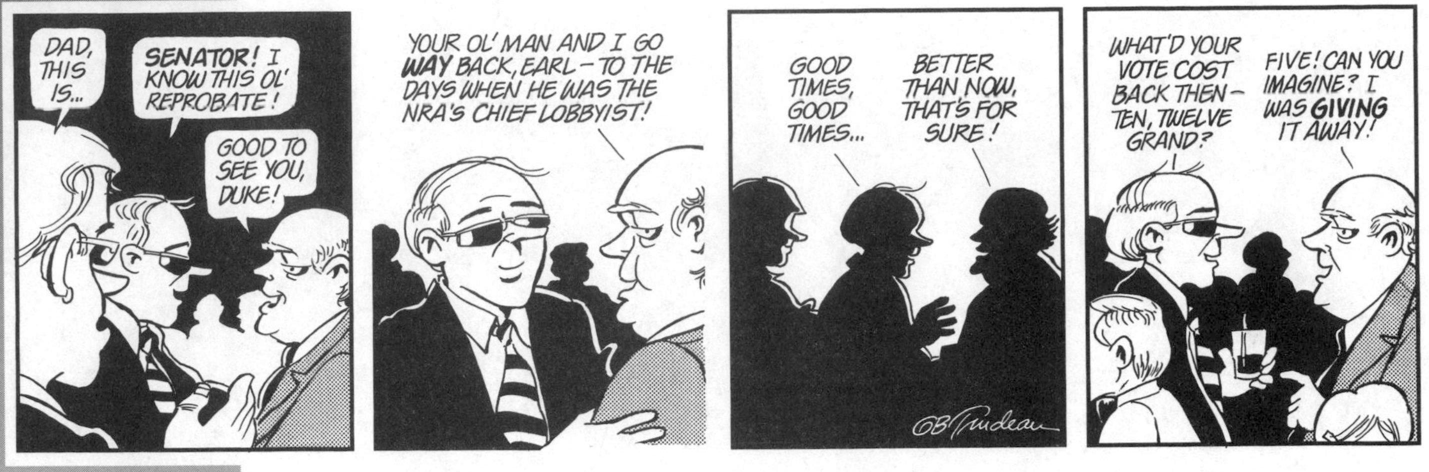
DAD, THIS IS...
SENATOR! I KNOW THIS OL' REPROBATE!
GOOD TO SEE YOU, DUKE!
YOUR OL' MAN AND I GO WAY BACK, EARL – TO THE DAYS WHEN HE WAS THE NRA'S CHIEF LOBBYIST!
GOOD TIMES, GOOD TIMES...
BETTER THAN NOW, THAT'S FOR SURE!
WHAT'D YOUR VOTE COST BACK THEN – TEN, TWELVE GRAND?
FIVE! CAN YOU IMAGINE? I WAS GIVING IT AWAY!
GB Trudeau

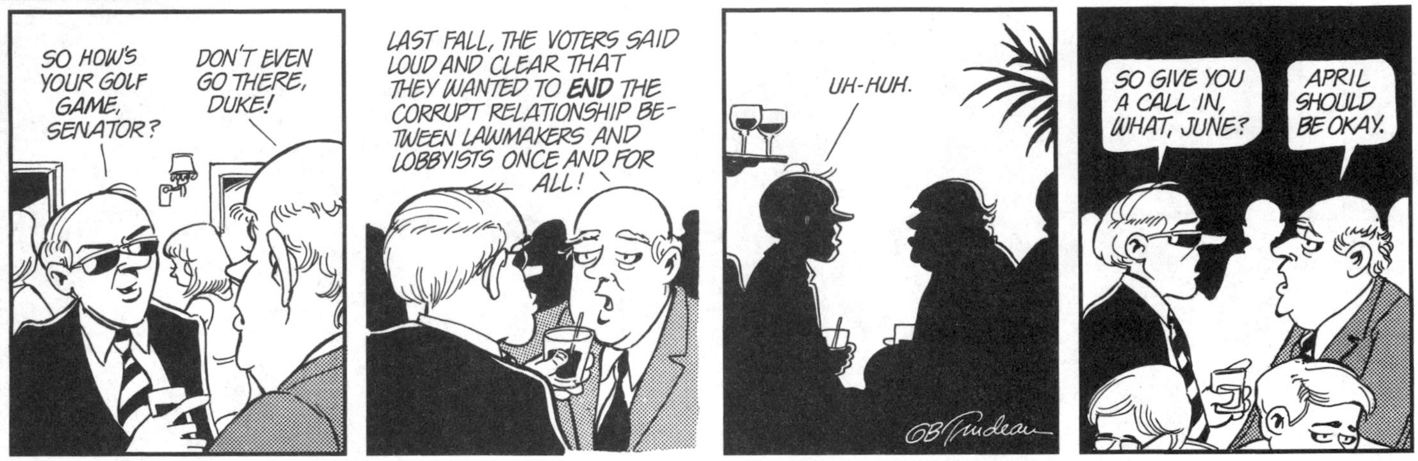
SO HOW'S YOUR GOLF GAME, SENATOR?
DON'T EVEN GO THERE, DUKE!
LAST FALL, THE VOTERS SAID LOUD AND CLEAR THAT THEY WANTED TO END THE CORRUPT RELATIONSHIP BETWEEN LAWMAKERS AND LOBBYISTS ONCE AND FOR ALL!
UH-HUH.
SO GIVE YOU A CALL IN, WHAT, JUNE?
APRIL SHOULD BE OKAY.
GB Trudeau

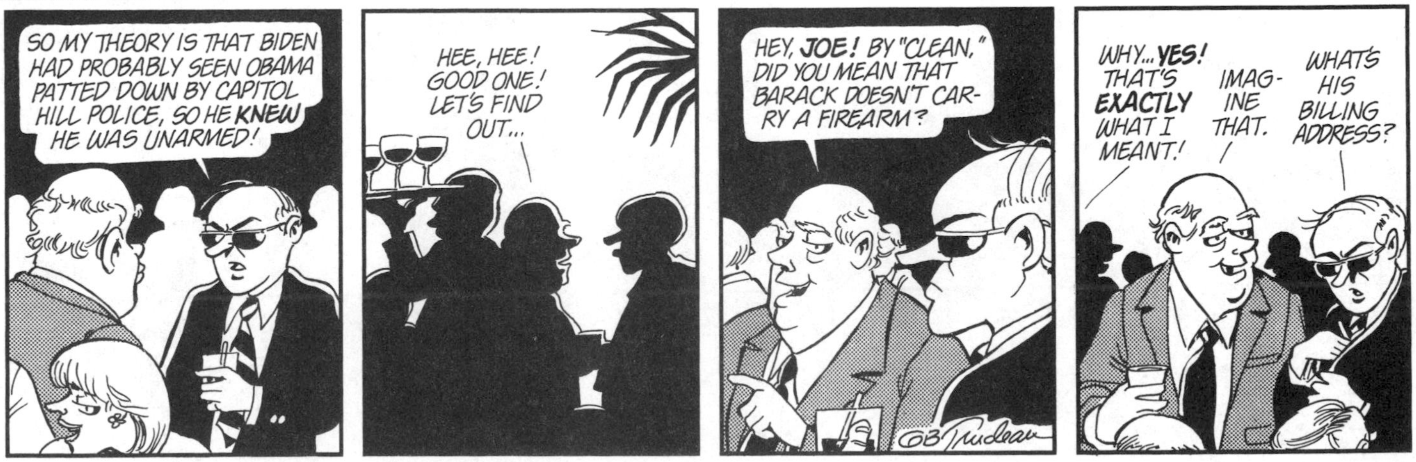
SO MY THEORY IS THAT BIDEN HAD PROBABLY SEEN OBAMA PATTED DOWN BY CAPITOL HILL POLICE, SO HE KNEW HE WAS UNARMED!
HEE, HEE! GOOD ONE! LET'S FIND OUT...
HEY, JOE! BY "CLEAN," DID YOU MEAN THAT BARACK DOESN'T CARRY A FIREARM?
WHY... YES! THAT'S EXACTLY WHAT I MEANT!
IMAGINE THAT.
WHAT'S HIS BILLING ADDRESS?
GB Trudeau

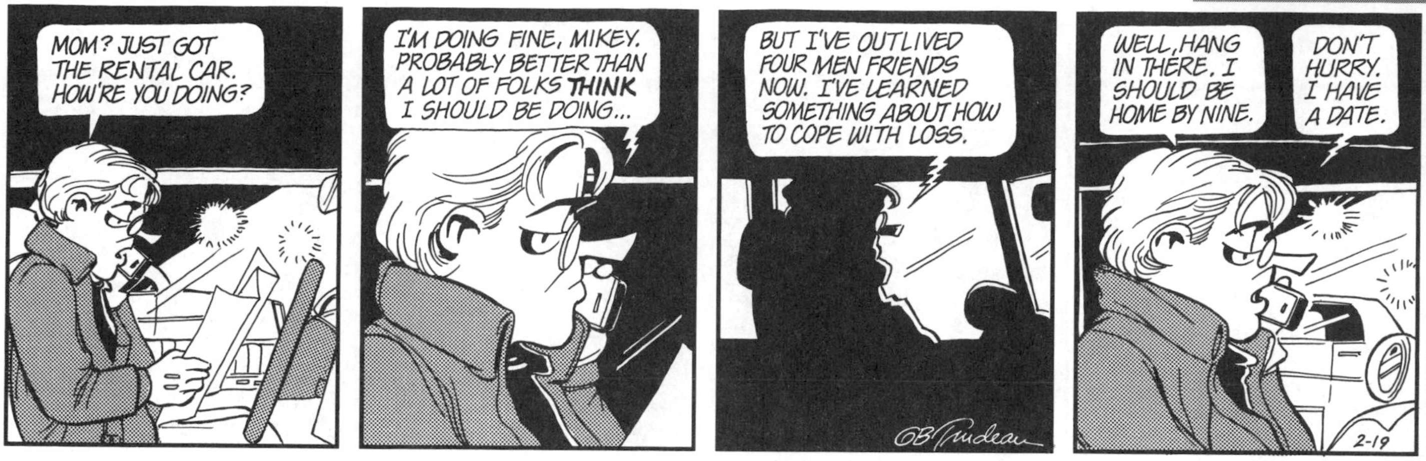
MOM? JUST GOT THE RENTAL CAR. HOW'RE YOU DOING?
I'M DOING FINE, MIKEY. PROBABLY BETTER THAN A LOT OF FOLKS THINK I SHOULD BE DOING...
BUT I'VE OUTLIVED FOUR MEN FRIENDS NOW. I'VE LEARNED SOMETHING ABOUT HOW TO COPE WITH LOSS.
WELL, HANG IN THERE. I SHOULD BE HOME BY NINE.
DON'T HURRY. I HAVE A DATE.

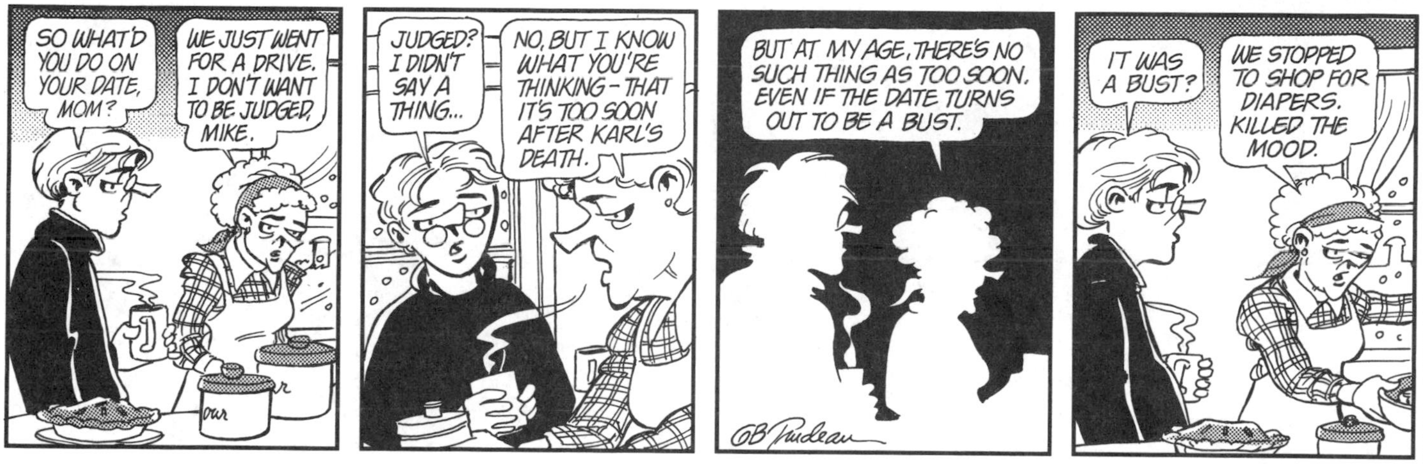
SO WHAT'D YOU DO ON YOUR DATE, MOM?
WE JUST WENT FOR A DRIVE. I DON'T WANT TO BE JUDGED, MIKE.
JUDGED? I DIDN'T SAY A THING...
NO, BUT I KNOW WHAT YOU'RE THINKING - THAT IT'S TOO SOON AFTER KARL'S DEATH.
BUT AT MY AGE, THERE'S NO SUCH THING AS TOO SOON. EVEN IF THE DATE TURNS OUT TO BE A BUST.
IT WAS A BUST?
WE STOPPED TO SHOP FOR DIAPERS. KILLED THE MOOD.

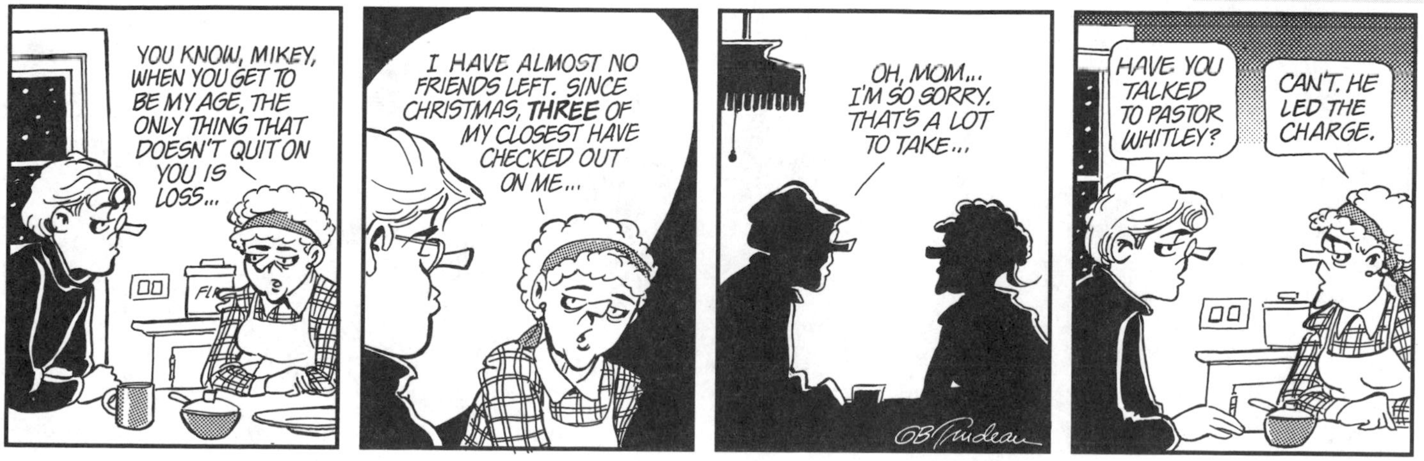
YOU KNOW, MIKEY, WHEN YOU GET TO BE MY AGE, THE ONLY THING THAT DOESN'T QUIT ON YOU IS LOSS...
I HAVE ALMOST NO FRIENDS LEFT. SINCE CHRISTMAS, THREE OF MY CLOSEST HAVE CHECKED OUT ON ME...
OH, MOM... I'M SO SORRY. THAT'S A LOT TO TAKE...
HAVE YOU TALKED TO PASTOR WHITLEY?
CAN'T. HE LED THE CHARGE.

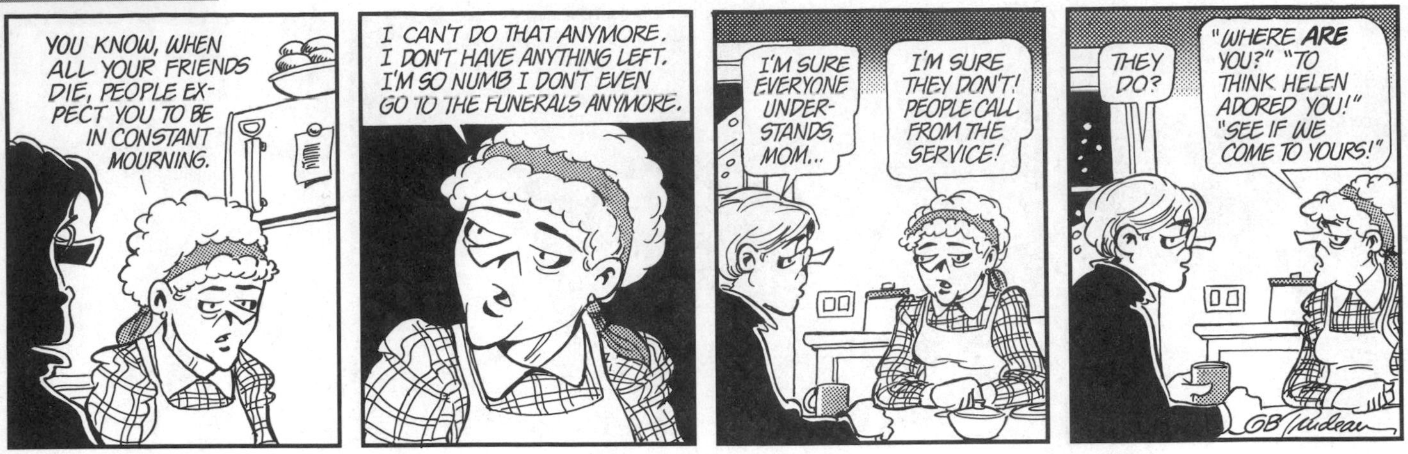
YOU KNOW, WHEN ALL YOUR FRIENDS DIE, PEOPLE EXPECT YOU TO BE IN CONSTANT MOURNING.
I CAN'T DO THAT ANYMORE. I DON'T HAVE ANYTHING LEFT. I'M SO NUMB I DON'T EVEN GO TO THE FUNERALS ANYMORE.
I'M SURE EVERYONE UNDERSTANDS, MOM...
I'M SURE THEY DON'T! PEOPLE CALL FROM THE SERVICE!
THEY DO?
"WHERE **ARE** YOU?" "TO THINK HELEN ADORED YOU!" "SEE IF WE COME TO YOURS!"
GB Trudeau

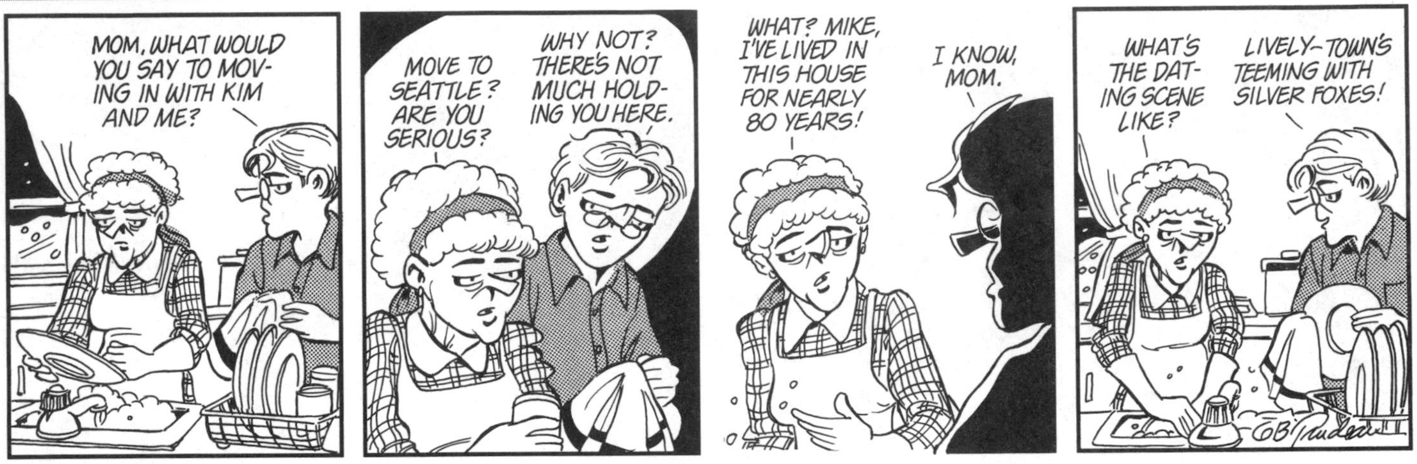
MOM, WHAT WOULD YOU SAY TO MOVING IN WITH KIM AND ME?
MOVE TO SEATTLE? ARE YOU SERIOUS?
WHY NOT? THERE'S NOT MUCH HOLDING YOU HERE.
WHAT? MIKE, I'VE LIVED IN THIS HOUSE FOR NEARLY 80 YEARS!
I KNOW, MOM.
WHAT'S THE DATING SCENE LIKE?
LIVELY-TOWN'S TEEMING WITH SILVER FOXES!
GB Trudeau

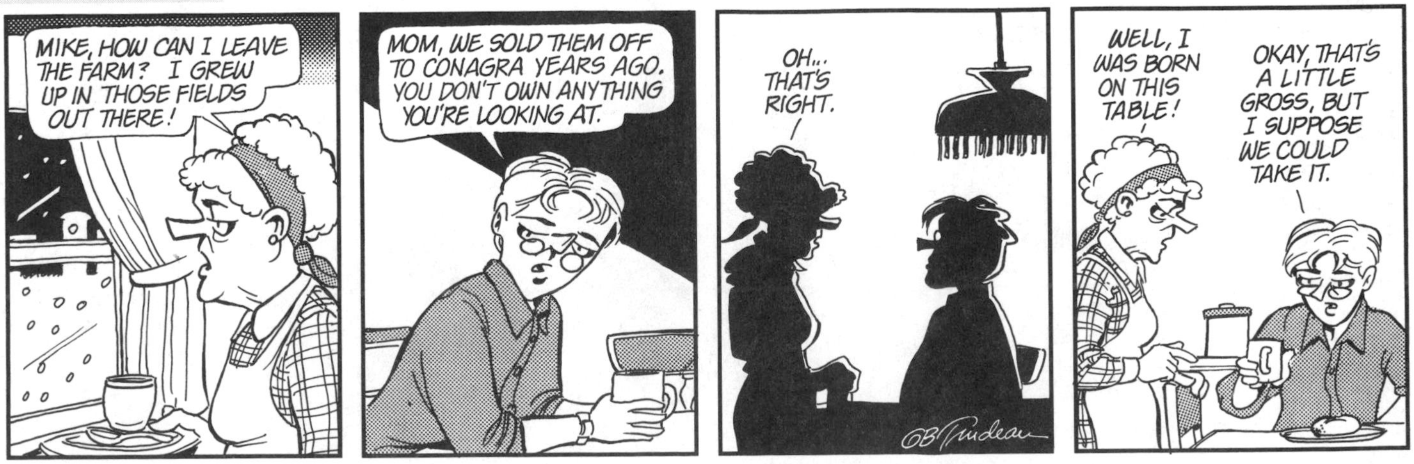
MIKE, HOW CAN I LEAVE THE FARM? I GREW UP IN THOSE FIELDS OUT THERE!
MOM, WE SOLD THEM OFF TO CONAGRA YEARS AGO. YOU DON'T OWN ANYTHING YOU'RE LOOKING AT.
OH... THAT'S RIGHT.
GB Trudeau
WELL, I WAS BORN ON THIS TABLE!
OKAY, THAT'S A LITTLE GROSS, BUT I SUPPOSE WE COULD TAKE IT.

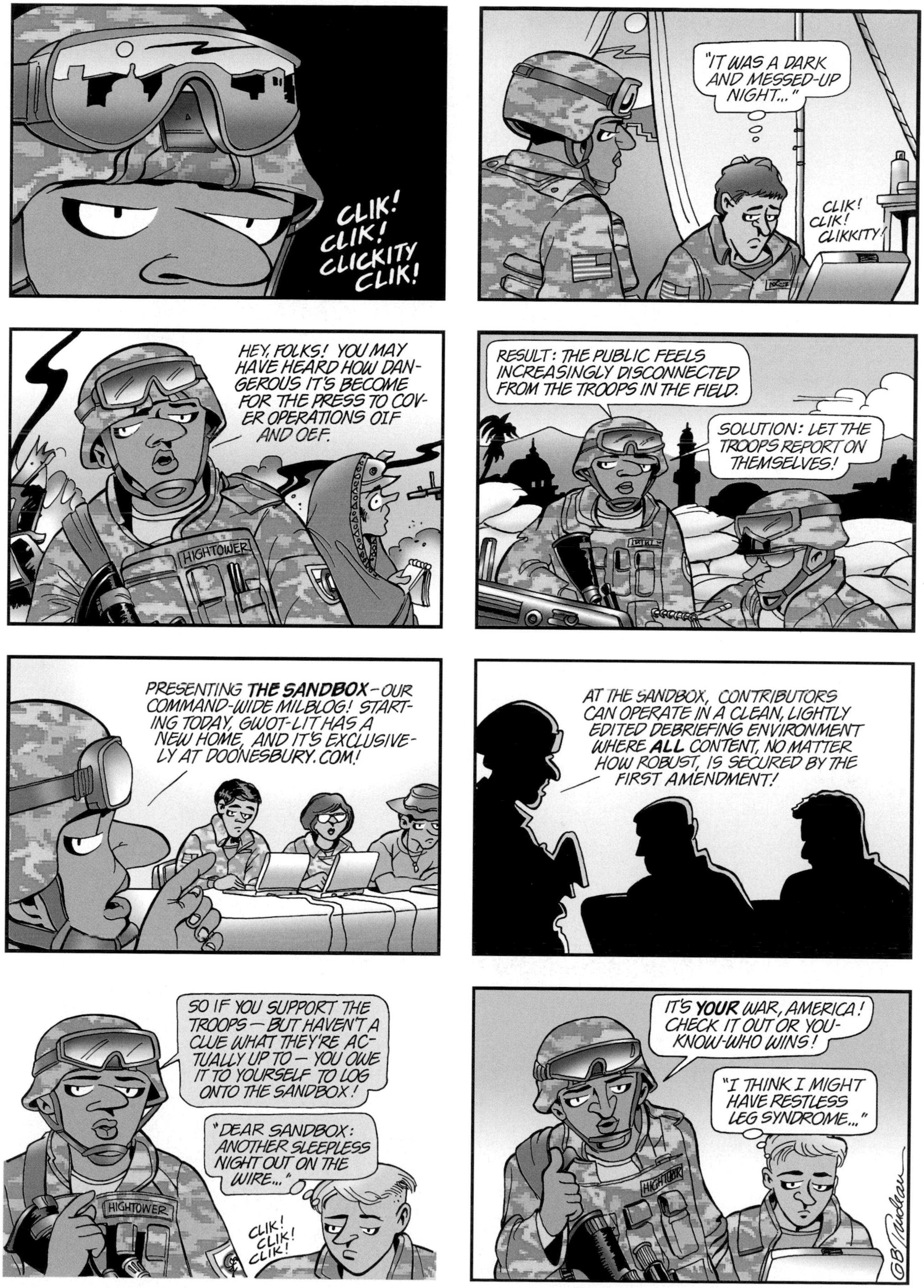

CLIK! CLIK! CLICKITY CLIK!
"IT WAS A DARK AND MESSED-UP NIGHT..."
CLIK! CLIK! CLIKKITY!
HEY, FOLKS! YOU MAY HAVE HEARD HOW DANGEROUS IT'S BECOME FOR THE PRESS TO COVER OPERATIONS OIF AND OEF.
HIGHTOWER
RESULT: THE PUBLIC FEELS INCREASINGLY DISCONNECTED FROM THE TROOPS IN THE FIELD.
SOLUTION: LET THE TROOPS REPORT ON THEMSELVES!
PRESENTING **THE SANDBOX** – OUR COMMAND-WIDE MILBLOG! STARTING TODAY, GWOT-LIT HAS A NEW HOME, AND IT'S EXCLUSIVELY AT DOONESBURY.COM!
AT THE SANDBOX, CONTRIBUTORS CAN OPERATE IN A CLEAN, LIGHTLY EDITED DEBRIEFING ENVIRONMENT WHERE **ALL** CONTENT, NO MATTER HOW ROBUST, IS SECURED BY THE FIRST AMENDMENT!
SO IF YOU SUPPORT THE TROOPS — BUT HAVEN'T A CLUE WHAT THEY'RE ACTUALLY UP TO — YOU OWE IT TO YOURSELF TO LOG ONTO THE SANDBOX!
"DEAR SANDBOX: ANOTHER SLEEPLESS NIGHT OUT ON THE WIRE..."
HIGHTOWER
CLIK! CLIK! CLIK!
IT'S **YOUR** WAR, AMERICA! CHECK IT OUT OR YOU-KNOW-WHO WINS!
"I THINK I MIGHT HAVE RESTLESS LEG SYNDROME..."
HIGHTOWER
GB Trudeau

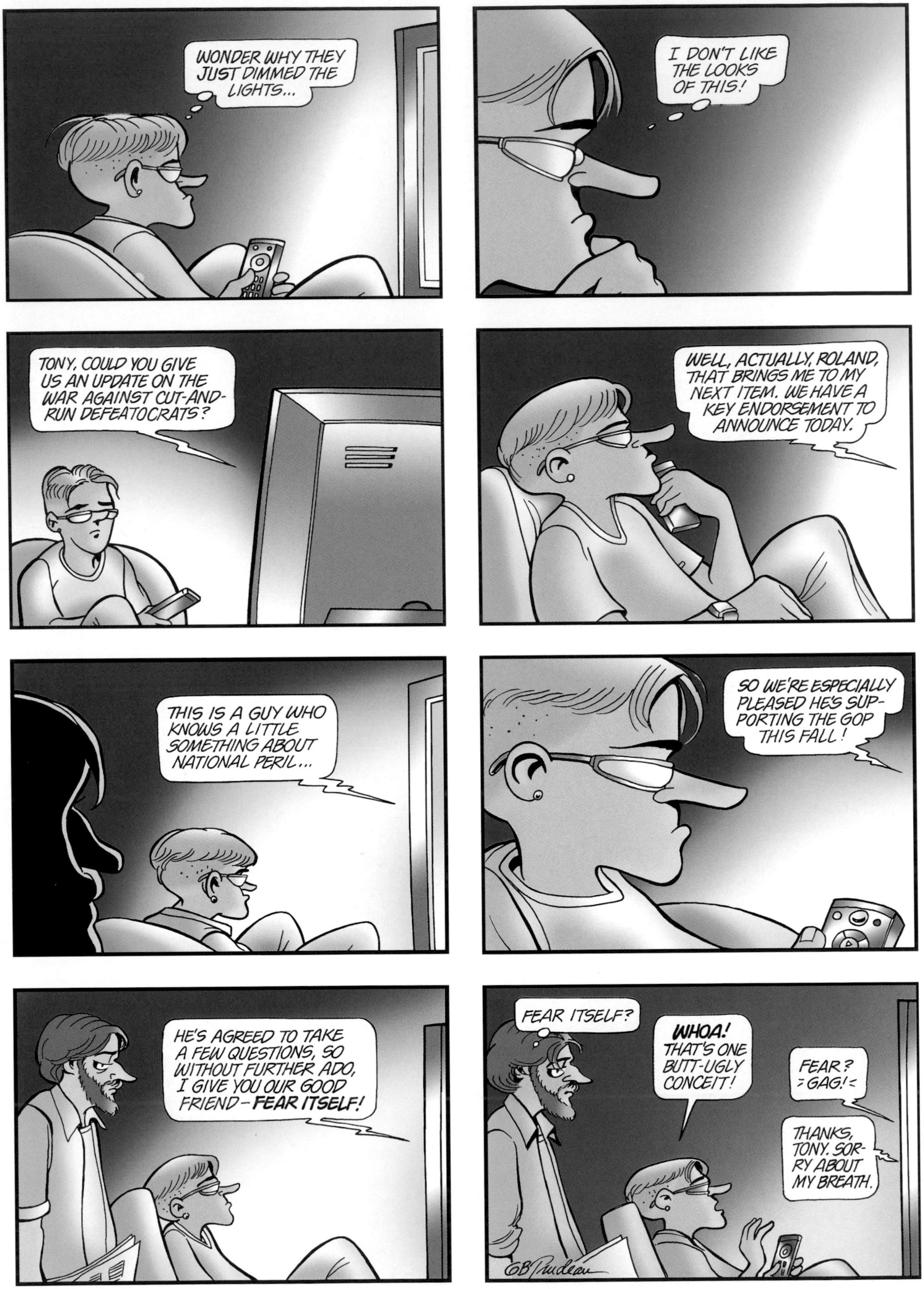
WONDER WHY THEY JUST DIMMED THE LIGHTS...
I DON'T LIKE THE LOOKS OF THIS!
TONY, COULD YOU GIVE US AN UPDATE ON THE WAR AGAINST CUT-AND-RUN DEFEATOCRATS?
WELL, ACTUALLY, ROLAND, THAT BRINGS ME TO MY NEXT ITEM. WE HAVE A KEY ENDORSEMENT TO ANNOUNCE TODAY.
THIS IS A GUY WHO KNOWS A LITTLE SOMETHING ABOUT NATIONAL PERIL...
SO WE'RE ESPECIALLY PLEASED HE'S SUPPORTING THE GOP THIS FALL!
HE'S AGREED TO TAKE A FEW QUESTIONS, SO WITHOUT FURTHER ADO, I GIVE YOU OUR GOOD FRIEND–**FEAR ITSELF!**
FEAR ITSELF?
WHOA! THAT'S ONE BUTT-UGLY CONCEIT!
FEAR? =GAG!=
THANKS, TONY. SORRY ABOUT MY BREATH.
GBTrudeau

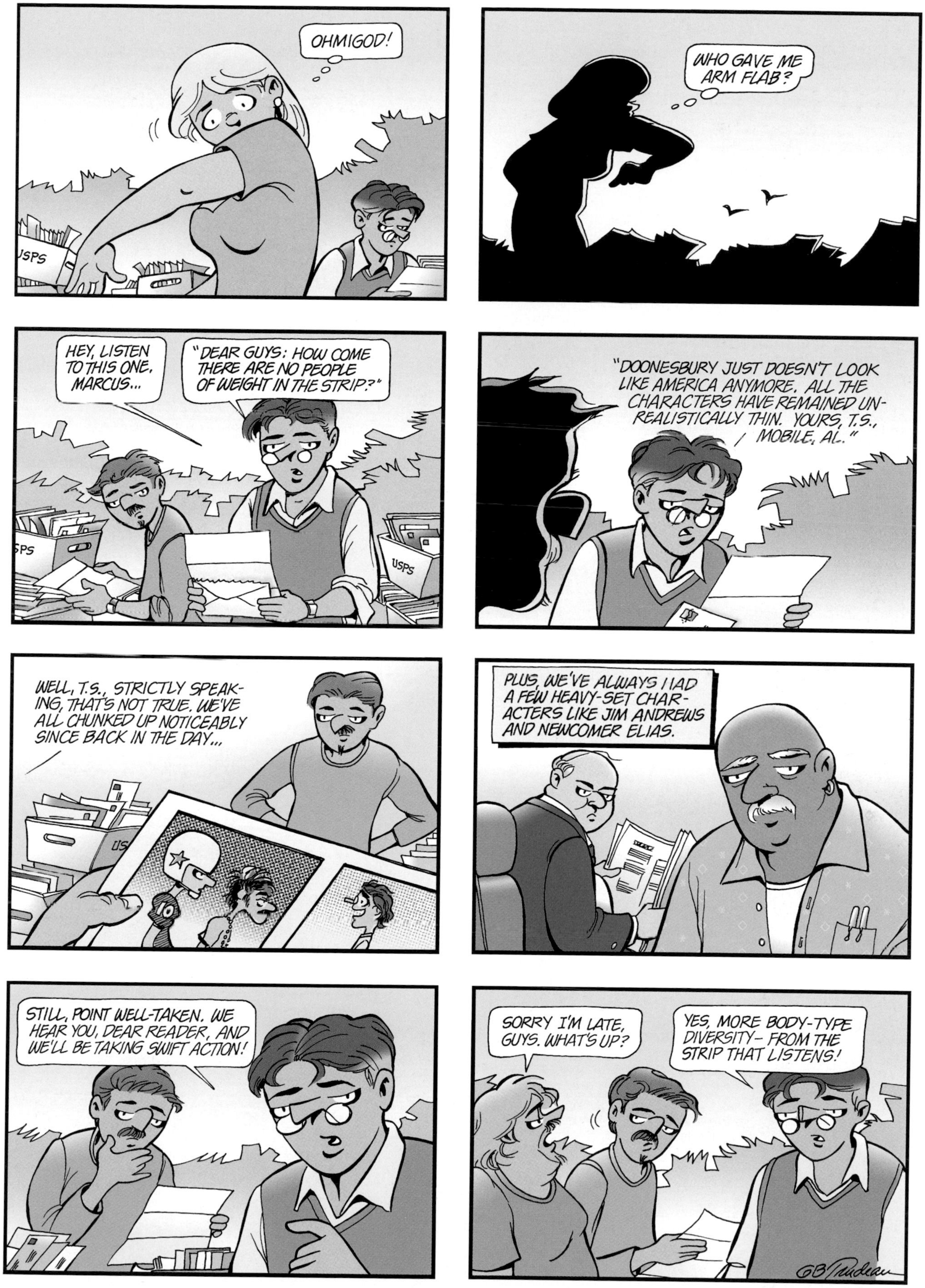
OHMIGOD!
WHO GAVE ME ARM FLAB?
HEY, LISTEN TO THIS ONE, MARCUS...
"DEAR GUYS: HOW COME THERE ARE NO PEOPLE OF WEIGHT IN THE STRIP?"
"DOONESBURY JUST DOESN'T LOOK LIKE AMERICA ANYMORE. ALL THE CHARACTERS HAVE REMAINED UNREALISTICALLY THIN. YOURS, T.S., MOBILE, AL."
WELL, T.S., STRICTLY SPEAKING, THAT'S NOT TRUE. WE'VE ALL CHUNKED UP NOTICEABLY SINCE BACK IN THE DAY...
PLUS, WE'VE ALWAYS HAD A FEW HEAVY-SET CHARACTERS LIKE JIM ANDREWS AND NEWCOMER ELIAS.
STILL, POINT WELL-TAKEN. WE HEAR YOU, DEAR READER, AND WE'LL BE TAKING SWIFT ACTION!
SORRY I'M LATE, GUYS. WHAT'S UP?
YES, MORE BODY-TYPE DIVERSITY– FROM THE STRIP THAT LISTENS!
GB Trudeau

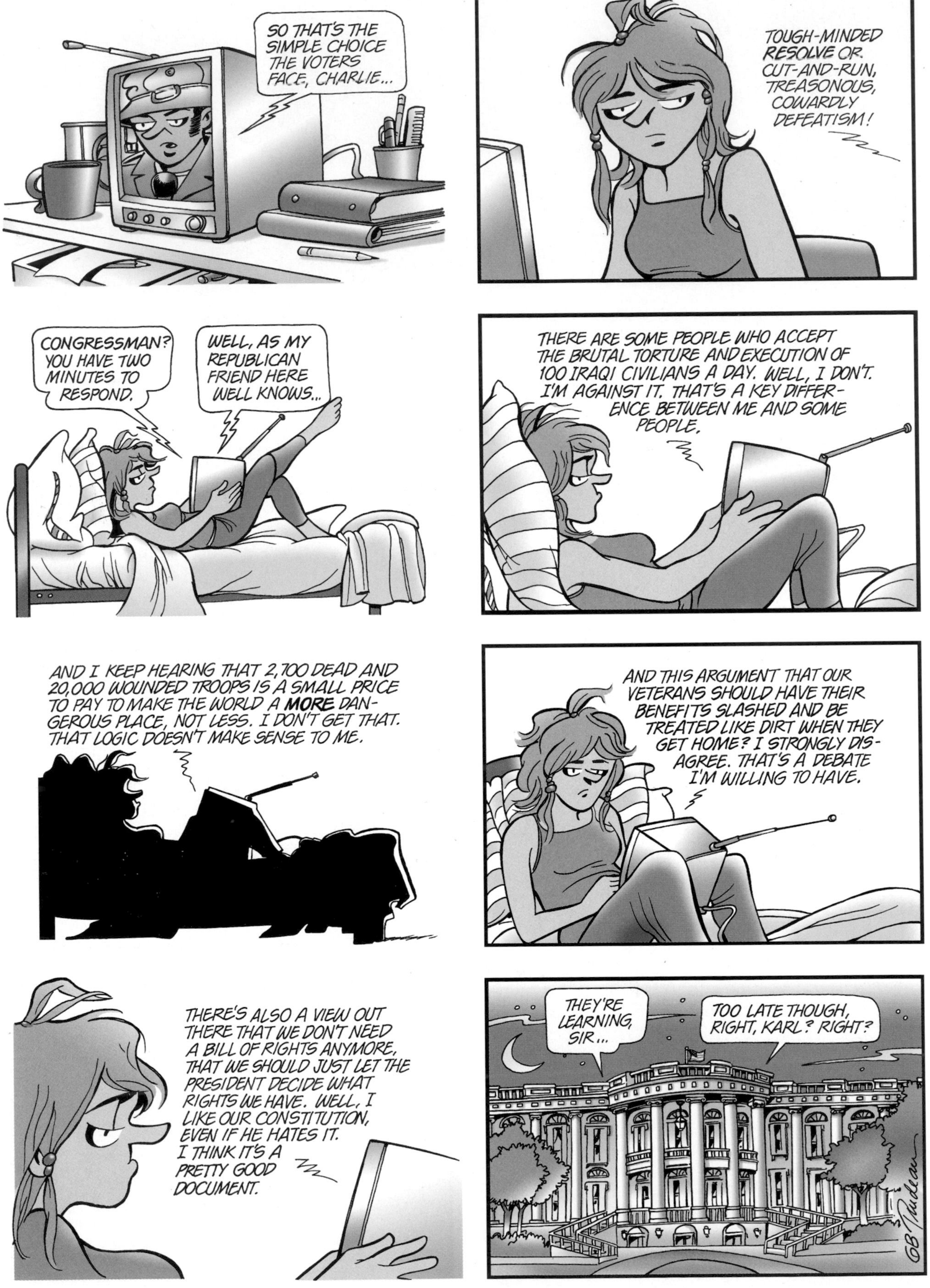
SO THAT'S THE SIMPLE CHOICE THE VOTERS FACE, CHARLIE...
TOUGH-MINDED RESOLVE OR CUT-AND-RUN, TREASONOUS, COWARDLY DEFEATISM!
CONGRESSMAN? YOU HAVE TWO MINUTES TO RESPOND.
WELL, AS MY REPUBLICAN FRIEND HERE WELL KNOWS...
THERE ARE SOME PEOPLE WHO ACCEPT THE BRUTAL TORTURE AND EXECUTION OF 100 IRAQI CIVILIANS A DAY. WELL, I DON'T. I'M AGAINST IT. THAT'S A KEY DIFFERENCE BETWEEN ME AND SOME PEOPLE.
AND I KEEP HEARING THAT 2,700 DEAD AND 20,000 WOUNDED TROOPS IS A SMALL PRICE TO PAY TO MAKE THE WORLD A MORE DANGEROUS PLACE, NOT LESS. I DON'T GET THAT. THAT LOGIC DOESN'T MAKE SENSE TO ME.
AND THIS ARGUMENT THAT OUR VETERANS SHOULD HAVE THEIR BENEFITS SLASHED AND BE TREATED LIKE DIRT WHEN THEY GET HOME? I STRONGLY DISAGREE. THAT'S A DEBATE I'M WILLING TO HAVE.
THERE'S ALSO A VIEW OUT THERE THAT WE DON'T NEED A BILL OF RIGHTS ANYMORE, THAT WE SHOULD JUST LET THE PRESIDENT DECIDE WHAT RIGHTS WE HAVE. WELL, I LIKE OUR CONSTITUTION, EVEN IF HE HATES IT. I THINK IT'S A PRETTY GOOD DOCUMENT.
THEY'RE LEARNING, SIR...
TOO LATE THOUGH, RIGHT, KARL? RIGHT?

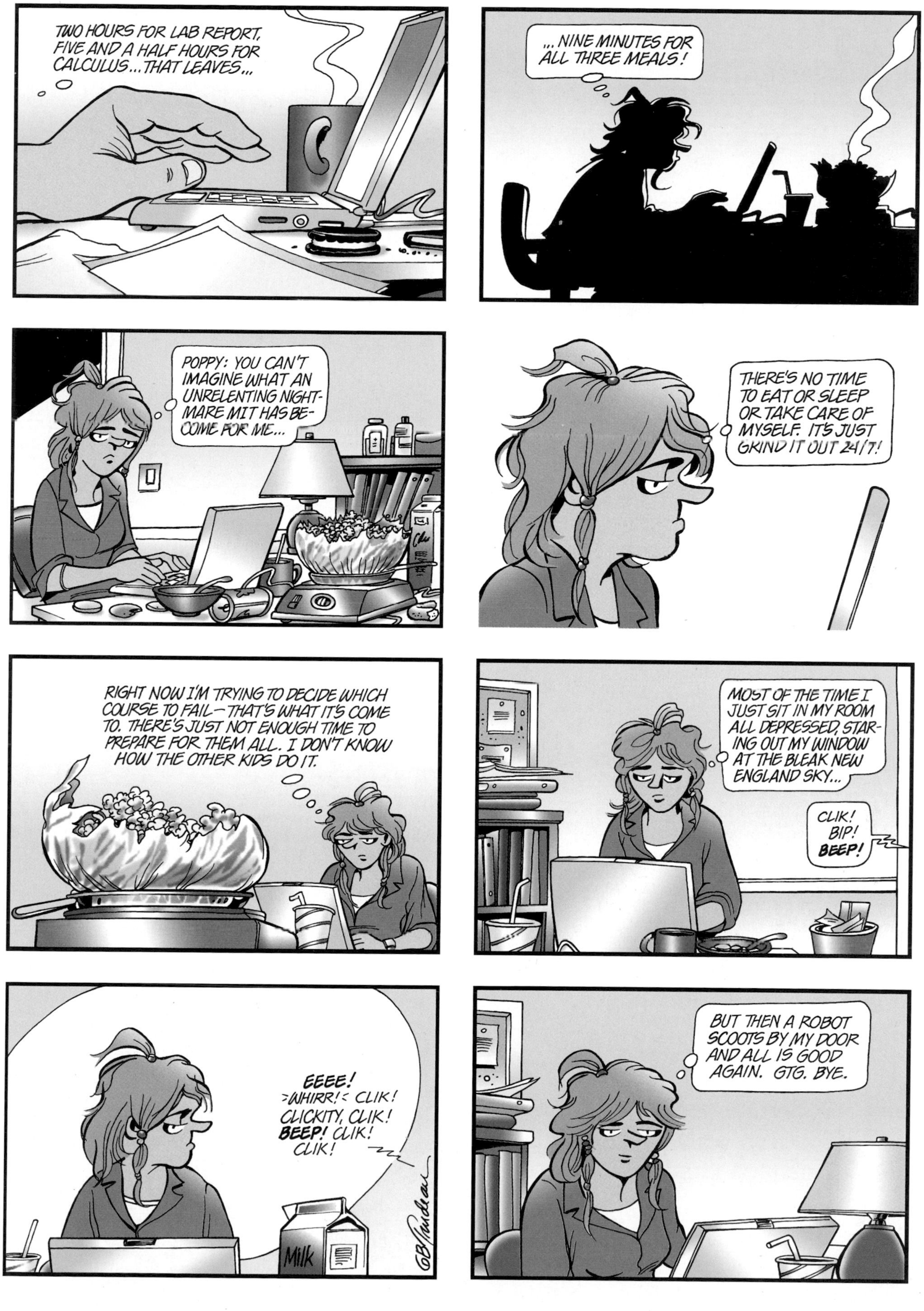
TWO HOURS FOR LAB REPORT, FIVE AND A HALF HOURS FOR CALCULUS... THAT LEAVES...
... NINE MINUTES FOR ALL THREE MEALS!
POPPY: YOU CAN'T IMAGINE WHAT AN UNRELENTING NIGHTMARE MIT HAS BECOME FOR ME...
THERE'S NO TIME TO EAT OR SLEEP OR TAKE CARE OF MYSELF. IT'S JUST GRIND IT OUT 24/7!
RIGHT NOW I'M TRYING TO DECIDE WHICH COURSE TO FAIL—THAT'S WHAT IT'S COME TO. THERE'S JUST NOT ENOUGH TIME TO PREPARE FOR THEM ALL. I DON'T KNOW HOW THE OTHER KIDS DO IT.
MOST OF THE TIME I JUST SIT IN MY ROOM ALL DEPRESSED, STARING OUT MY WINDOW AT THE BLEAK NEW ENGLAND SKY...
CLIK! BIP! BEEP!
EEEE! >WHIRR!< CLIK! CLICKITY, CLIK! BEEP! CLIK! CLIK!
Milk
BUT THEN A ROBOT SCOOTS BY MY DOOR AND ALL IS GOOD AGAIN. GTG. BYE.

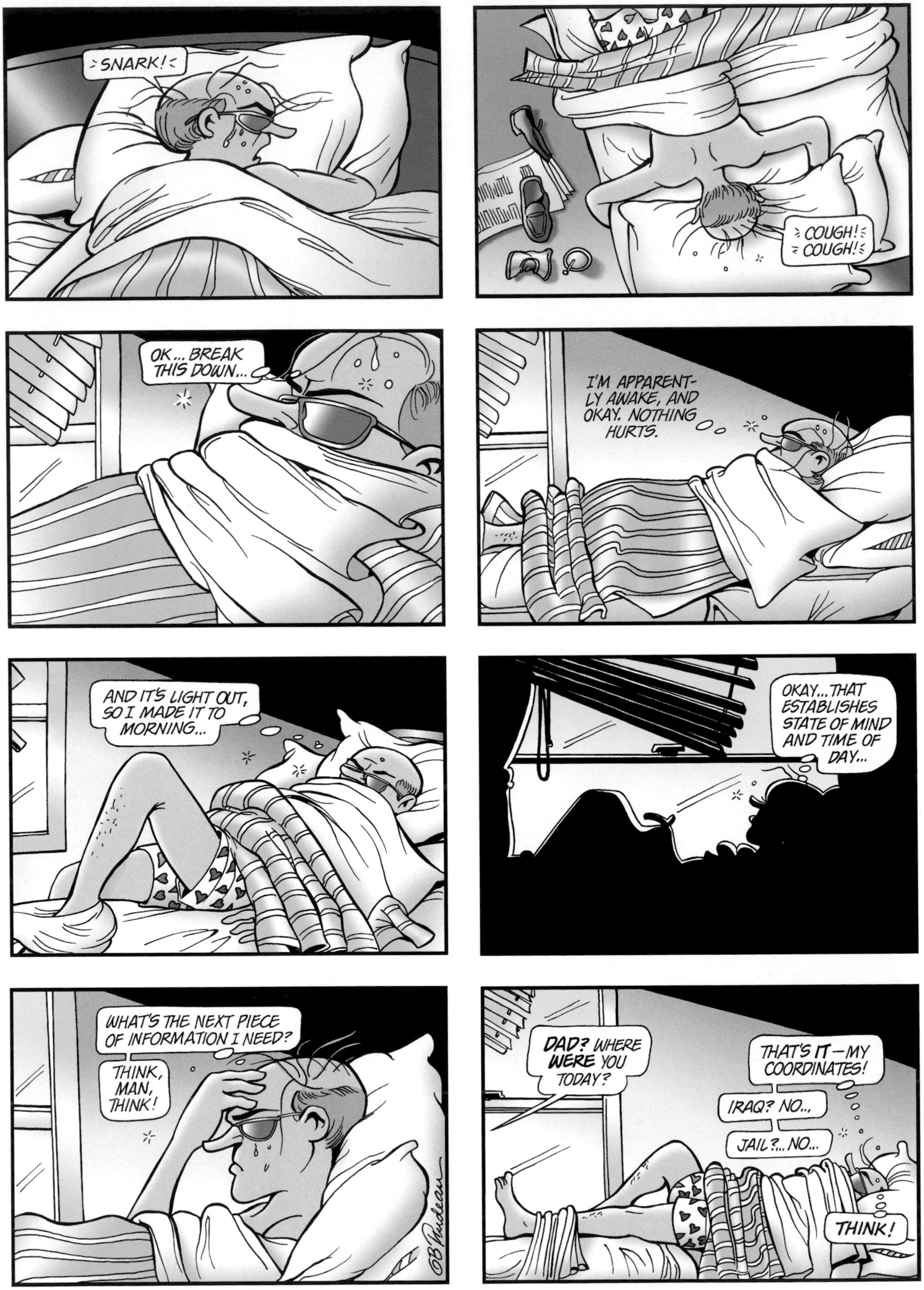
SNARK!
COUGH! COUGH!
OK... BREAK THIS DOWN...
I'M APPARENTLY AWAKE, AND OKAY. NOTHING HURTS.
AND IT'S LIGHT OUT, SO I MADE IT TO MORNING...
OKAY... THAT ESTABLISHES STATE OF MIND AND TIME OF DAY...
WHAT'S THE NEXT PIECE OF INFORMATION I NEED?
THINK, MAN, THINK!
DAD? WHERE WERE YOU TODAY?
THAT'S IT—MY COORDINATES!
IRAQ? NO...
JAIL?... NO...
THINK!
©B Trudeau

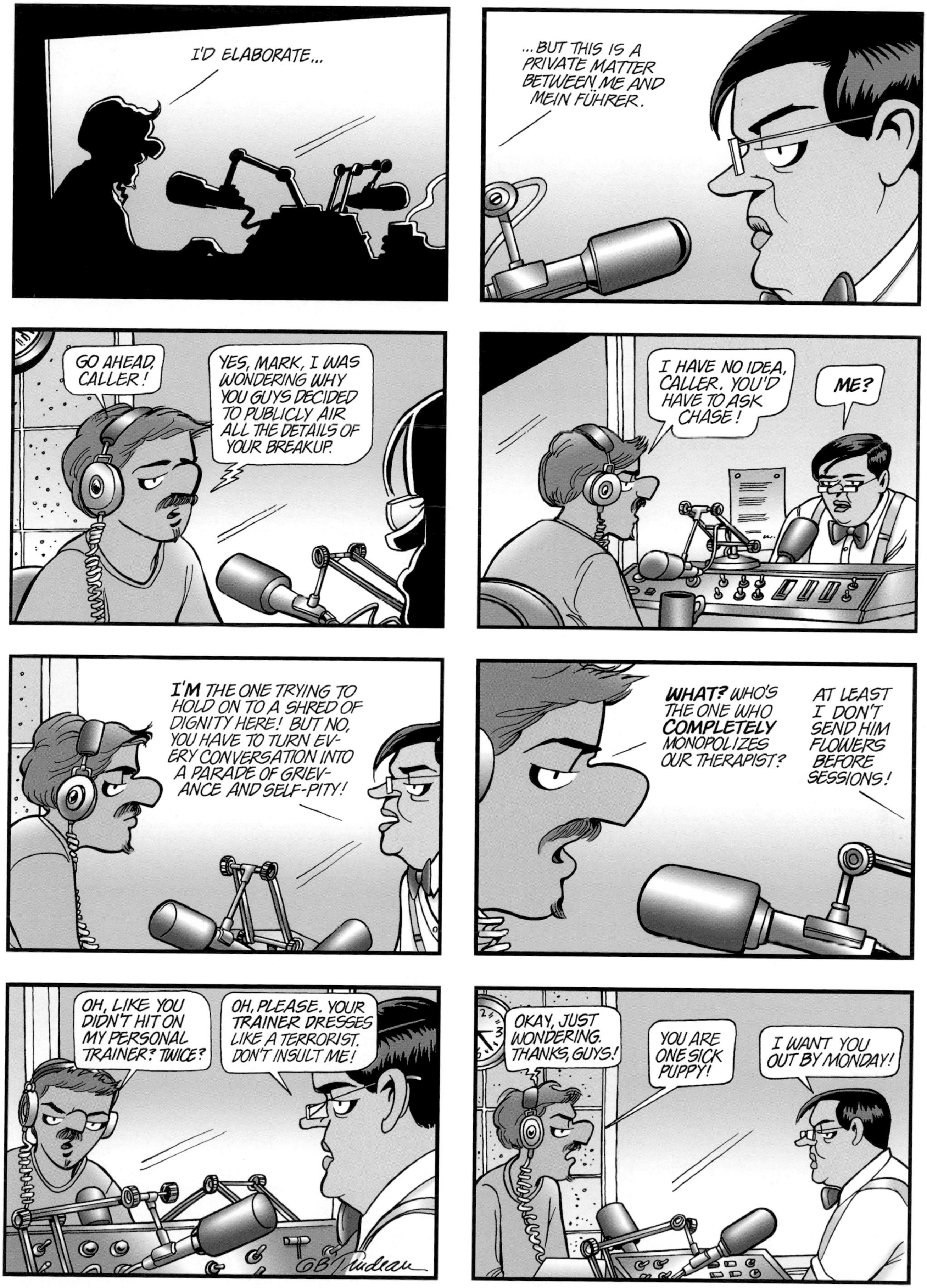
I'D ELABORATE...
...BUT THIS IS A PRIVATE MATTER BETWEEN ME AND MEIN FÜHRER.
GO AHEAD, CALLER!
YES, MARK, I WAS WONDERING WHY YOU GUYS DECIDED TO PUBLICLY AIR ALL THE DETAILS OF YOUR BREAKUP.
I HAVE NO IDEA, CALLER. YOU'D HAVE TO ASK CHASE!
ME?
I'M THE ONE TRYING TO HOLD ON TO A SHRED OF DIGNITY HERE! BUT NO, YOU HAVE TO TURN EVERY CONVERSATION INTO A PARADE OF GRIEVANCE AND SELF-PITY!
WHAT? WHO'S THE ONE WHO COMPLETELY MONOPOLIZES OUR THERAPIST?
AT LEAST I DON'T SEND HIM FLOWERS BEFORE SESSIONS!
OH, LIKE YOU DIDN'T HIT ON MY PERSONAL TRAINER? TWICE?
OH, PLEASE. YOUR TRAINER DRESSES LIKE A TERRORIST. DON'T INSULT ME!
©B Trudeau
OKAY, JUST WONDERING. THANKS, GUYS!
YOU ARE ONE SICK PUPPY!
I WANT YOU OUT BY MONDAY!

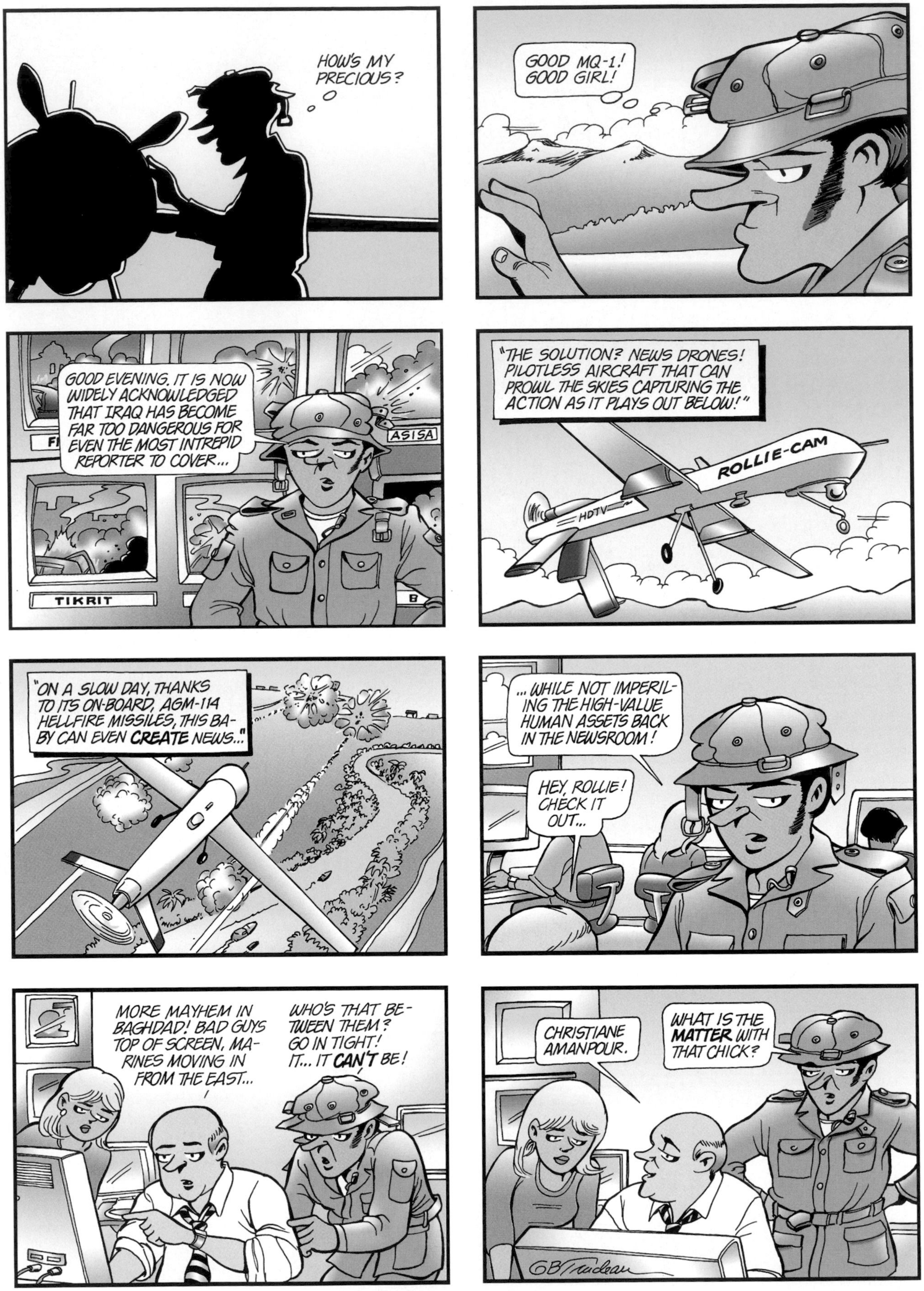
HOW'S MY PRECIOUS?
GOOD MQ-1! GOOD GIRL!
GOOD EVENING. IT IS NOW WIDELY ACKNOWLEDGED THAT IRAQ HAS BECOME FAR TOO DANGEROUS FOR EVEN THE MOST INTREPID REPORTER TO COVER...
ASISA
TIKRIT
"THE SOLUTION? NEWS DRONES! PILOTLESS AIRCRAFT THAT CAN PROWL THE SKIES CAPTURING THE ACTION AS IT PLAYS OUT BELOW!"
ROLLIE-CAM
HDTV
"ON A SLOW DAY, THANKS TO ITS ON-BOARD, AGM-114 HELLFIRE MISSILES, THIS BA-BY CAN EVEN **CREATE** NEWS..."
...WHILE NOT IMPERIL-ING THE HIGH-VALUE HUMAN ASSETS BACK IN THE NEWSROOM!
HEY, ROLLIE! CHECK IT OUT...
MORE MAYHEM IN BAGHDAD! BAD GUYS TOP OF SCREEN, MA-RINES MOVING IN FROM THE EAST...
WHO'S THAT BE-TWEEN THEM? GO IN TIGHT! IT... IT **CAN'T** BE!
CHRISTIANE AMANPOUR.
WHAT IS THE **MATTER** WITH THAT CHICK?
GBTrudeau

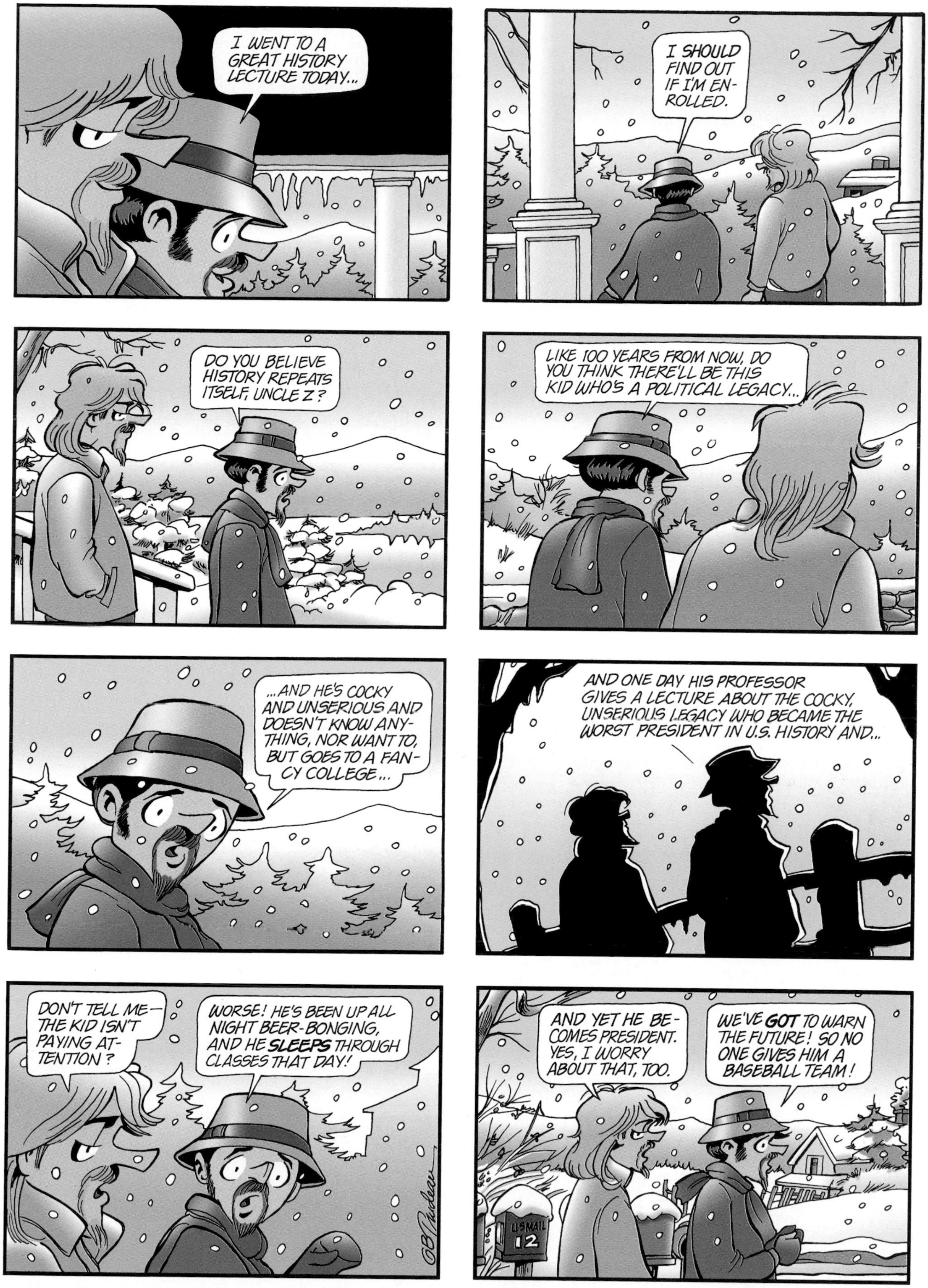

I WENT TO A GREAT HISTORY LECTURE TODAY...
I SHOULD FIND OUT IF I'M EN-ROLLED.
DO YOU BELIEVE HISTORY REPEATS ITSELF, UNCLE Z?
LIKE 100 YEARS FROM NOW, DO YOU THINK THERE'LL BE THIS KID WHO'S A POLITICAL LEGACY...
...AND HE'S COCKY AND UNSERIOUS AND DOESN'T KNOW ANY-THING, NOR WANT TO, BUT GOES TO A FAN-CY COLLEGE...
AND ONE DAY HIS PROFESSOR GIVES A LECTURE ABOUT THE COCKY, UNSERIOUS LEGACY WHO BECAME THE WORST PRESIDENT IN U.S. HISTORY AND...
DON'T TELL ME—THE KID ISN'T PAYING AT-TENTION?
WORSE! HE'S BEEN UP ALL NIGHT BEER-BONGING, AND HE **SLEEPS** THROUGH CLASSES THAT DAY!
AND YET HE BE-COMES PRESIDENT. YES, I WORRY ABOUT THAT, TOO.
WE'VE **GOT** TO WARN THE FUTURE! SO NO ONE GIVES HIM A BASEBALL TEAM!

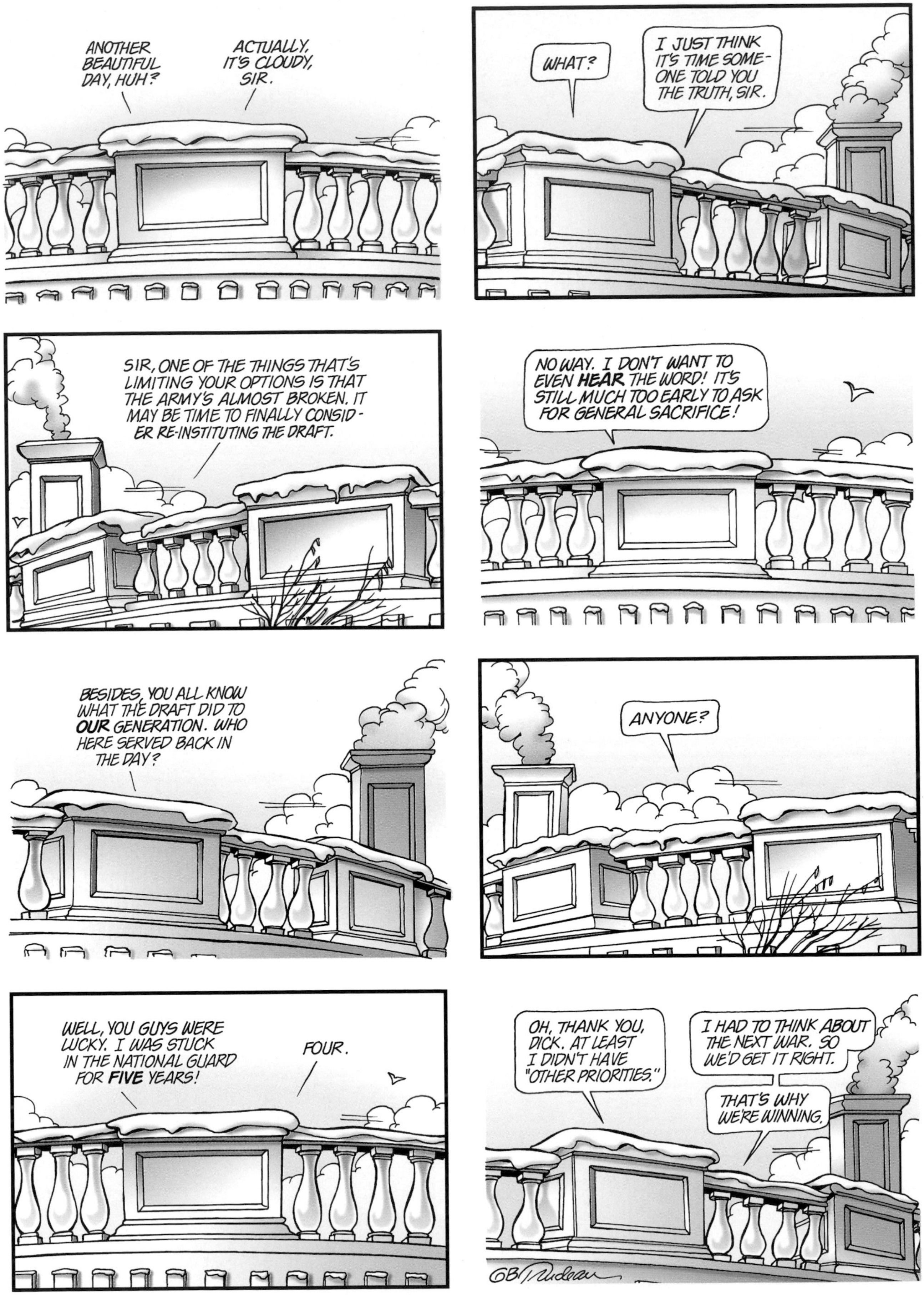
ANOTHER BEAUTIFUL DAY, HUH?
ACTUALLY, IT'S CLOUDY, SIR.
WHAT?
I JUST THINK IT'S TIME SOME-ONE TOLD YOU THE TRUTH, SIR.
SIR, ONE OF THE THINGS THAT'S LIMITING YOUR OPTIONS IS THAT THE ARMY'S ALMOST BROKEN. IT MAY BE TIME TO FINALLY CONSID-ER RE-INSTITUTING THE DRAFT.
NO WAY. I DON'T WANT TO EVEN HEAR THE WORD! IT'S STILL MUCH TOO EARLY TO ASK FOR GENERAL SACRIFICE!
BESIDES, YOU ALL KNOW WHAT THE DRAFT DID TO OUR GENERATION. WHO HERE SERVED BACK IN THE DAY?
ANYONE?
WELL, YOU GUYS WERE LUCKY. I WAS STUCK IN THE NATIONAL GUARD FOR FIVE YEARS!
FOUR.
OH, THANK YOU, DICK. AT LEAST I DIDN'T HAVE "OTHER PRIORITIES."
I HAD TO THINK ABOUT THE NEXT WAR. SO WE'D GET IT RIGHT.
THAT'S WHY WE'RE WINNING.
GBTrudeau

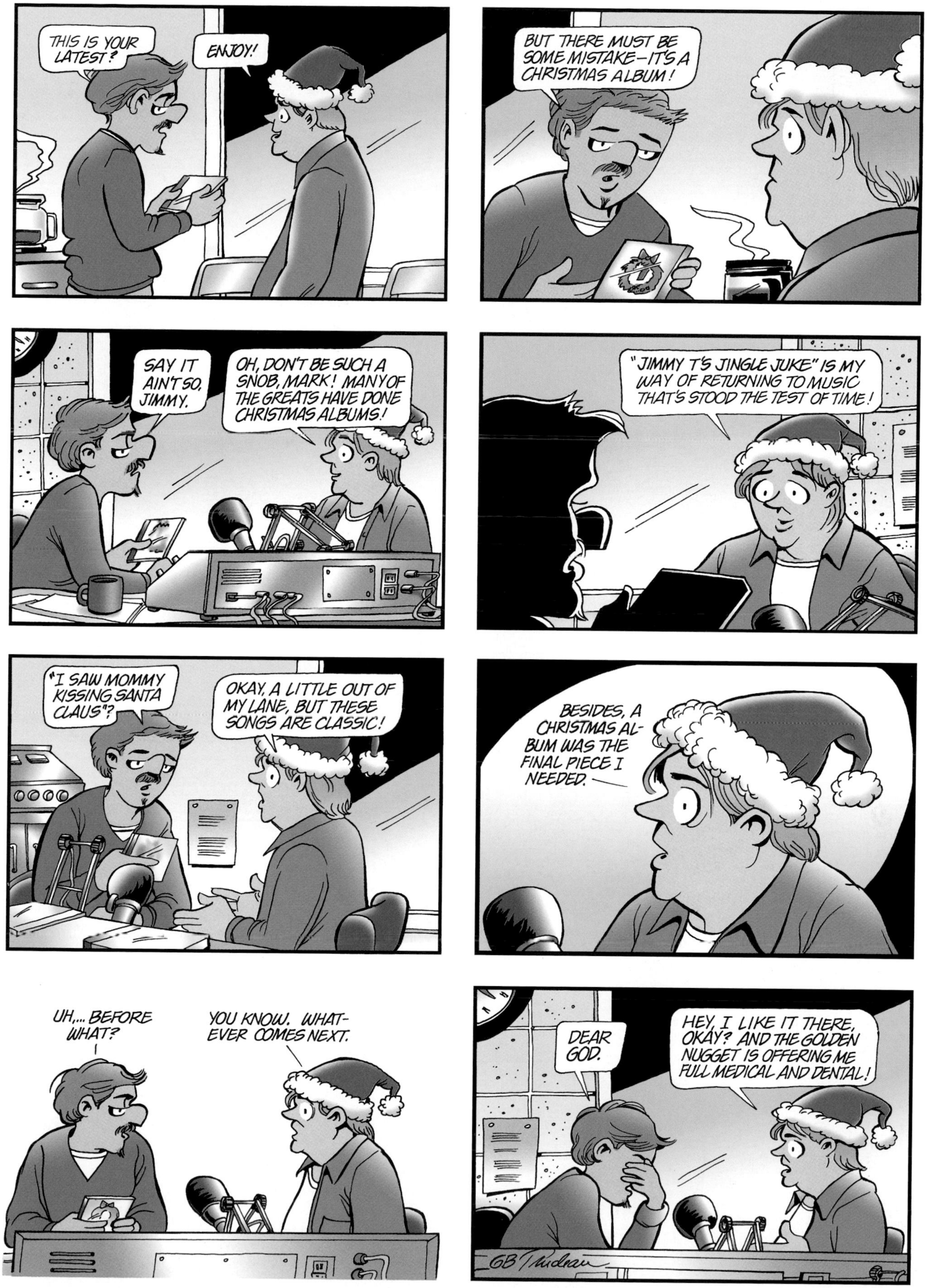

THIS IS YOUR LATEST?
ENJOY!
BUT THERE MUST BE SOME MISTAKE—IT'S A CHRISTMAS ALBUM!
SAY IT AIN'T SO, JIMMY.
OH, DON'T BE SUCH A SNOB, MARK! MANY OF THE GREATS HAVE DONE CHRISTMAS ALBUMS!
"JIMMY T'S JINGLE JUKE" IS MY WAY OF RETURNING TO MUSIC THAT'S STOOD THE TEST OF TIME!
"I SAW MOMMY KISSING SANTA CLAUS"?
OKAY, A LITTLE OUT OF MY LANE, BUT THESE SONGS ARE CLASSIC!
BESIDES, A CHRISTMAS AL-BUM WAS THE FINAL PIECE I NEEDED.
UH,... BEFORE WHAT?
YOU KNOW. WHAT-EVER COMES NEXT.
DEAR GOD.
HEY, I LIKE IT THERE, OKAY? AND THE GOLDEN NUGGET IS OFFERING ME FULL MEDICAL AND DENTAL!
GBT

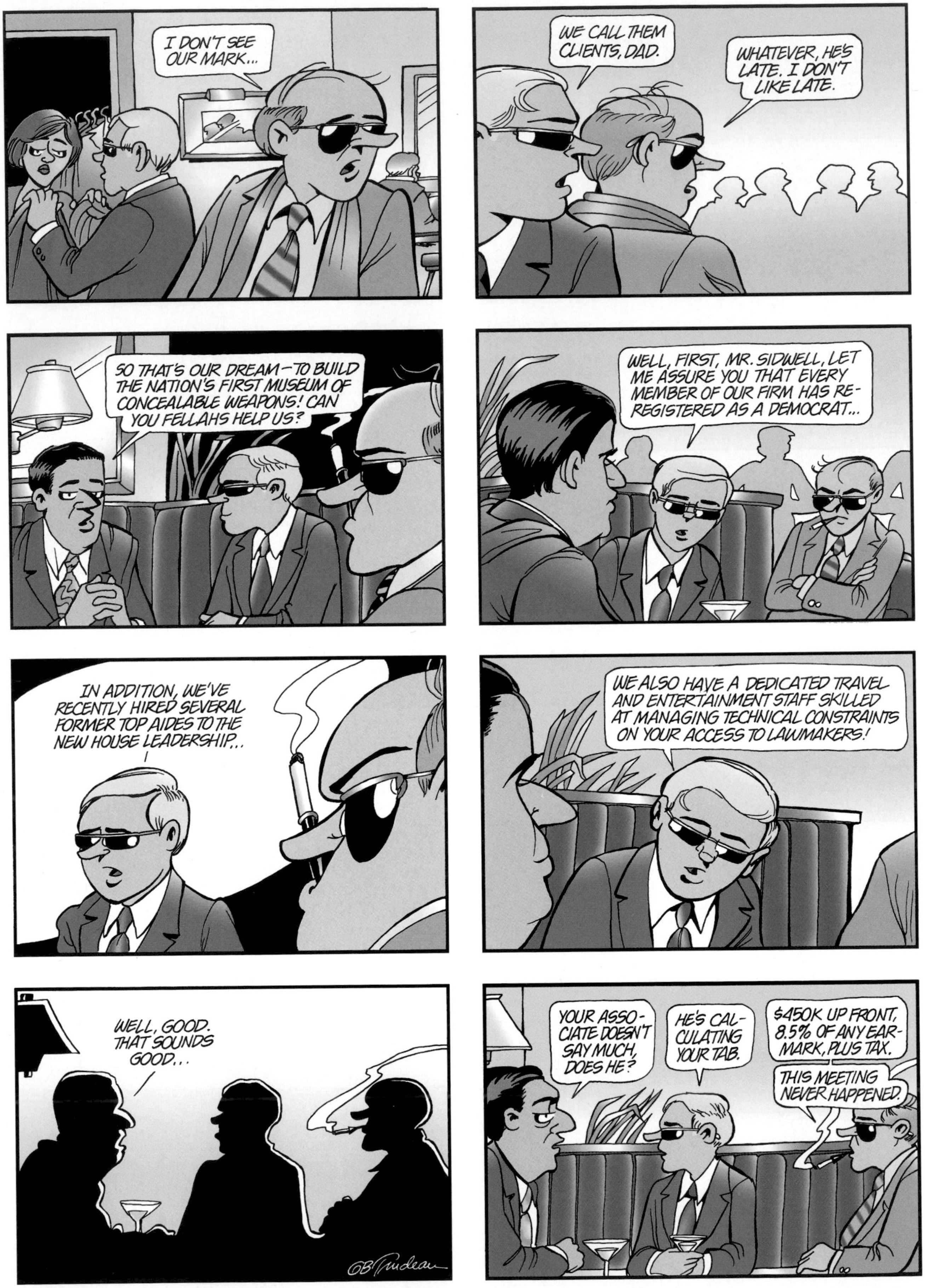
I DON'T SEE OUR MARK...
WE CALL THEM CLIENTS, DAD.
WHATEVER, HE'S LATE. I DON'T LIKE LATE.
SO THAT'S OUR DREAM—TO BUILD THE NATION'S FIRST MUSEUM OF CONCEALABLE WEAPONS! CAN YOU FELLAHS HELP US?
WELL, FIRST, MR. SIDWELL, LET ME ASSURE YOU THAT EVERY MEMBER OF OUR FIRM HAS RE-REGISTERED AS A DEMOCRAT...
IN ADDITION, WE'VE RECENTLY HIRED SEVERAL FORMER TOP AIDES TO THE NEW HOUSE LEADERSHIP...
WE ALSO HAVE A DEDICATED TRAVEL AND ENTERTAINMENT STAFF SKILLED AT MANAGING TECHNICAL CONSTRAINTS ON YOUR ACCESS TO LAWMAKERS!
WELL, GOOD. THAT SOUNDS GOOD...
GB Trudeau
YOUR ASSO-CIATE DOESN'T SAY MUCH, DOES HE?
HE'S CAL-CULATING YOUR TAB.
$450K UP FRONT, 8.5% OF ANY EAR-MARK, PLUS TAX.
THIS MEETING NEVER HAPPENED.

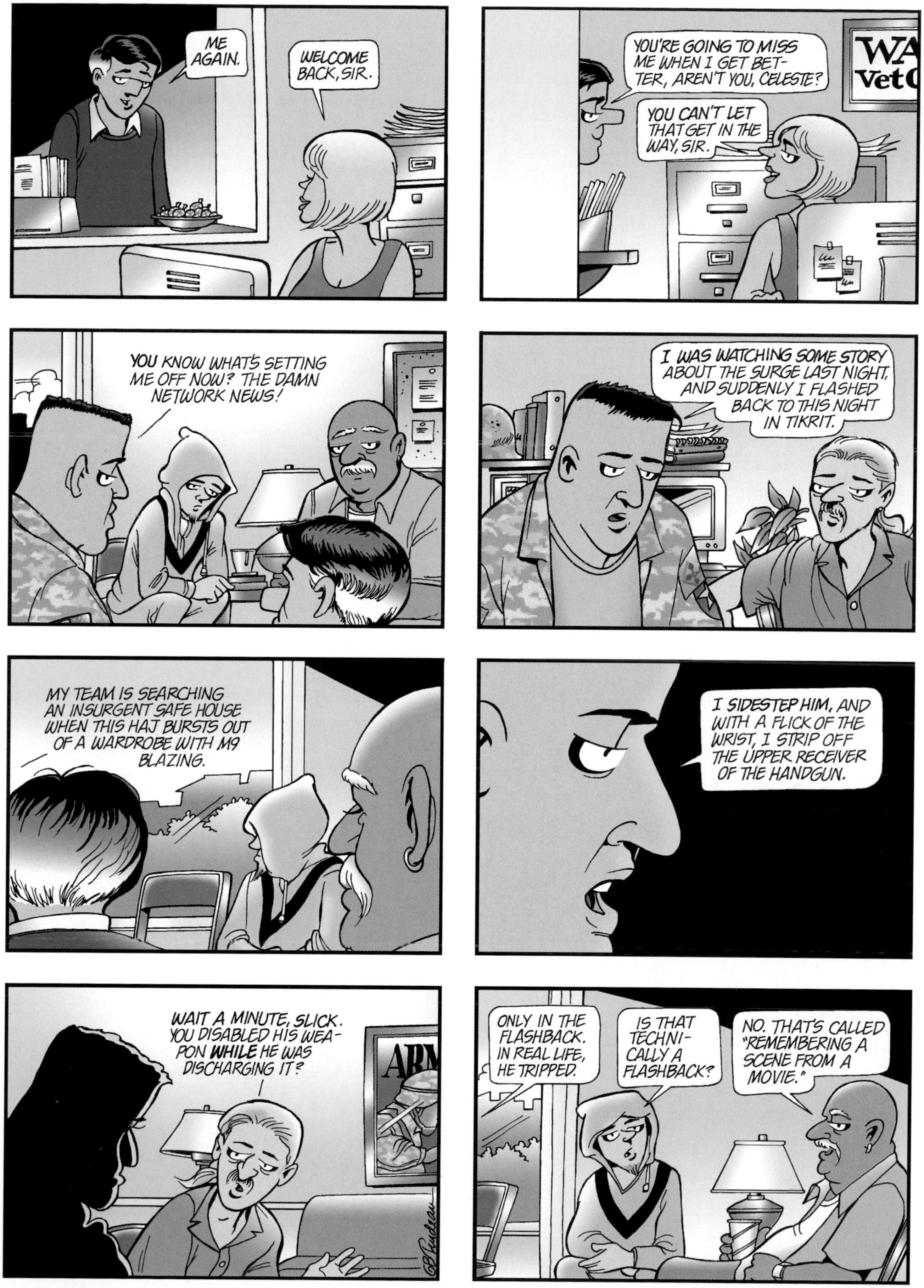
ME AGAIN.
WELCOME BACK, SIR.
YOU'RE GOING TO MISS ME WHEN I GET BETTER, AREN'T YOU, CELESTE?
YOU CAN'T LET THAT GET IN THE WAY, SIR.
YOU KNOW WHAT'S SETTING ME OFF NOW? THE DAMN NETWORK NEWS!
I WAS WATCHING SOME STORY ABOUT THE SURGE LAST NIGHT, AND SUDDENLY I FLASHED BACK TO THIS NIGHT IN TIKRIT.
MY TEAM IS SEARCHING AN INSURGENT SAFE HOUSE WHEN THIS HAJ BURSTS OUT OF A WARDROBE WITH M9 BLAZING.
I SIDESTEP HIM, AND WITH A FLICK OF THE WRIST, I STRIP OFF THE UPPER RECEIVER OF THE HANDGUN.
WAIT A MINUTE, SLICK. YOU DISABLED HIS WEAPON WHILE HE WAS DISCHARGING IT?
ONLY IN THE FLASHBACK. IN REAL LIFE, HE TRIPPED.
IS THAT TECHNICALLY A FLASHBACK?
NO. THAT'S CALLED "REMEMBERING A SCENE FROM A MOVIE."

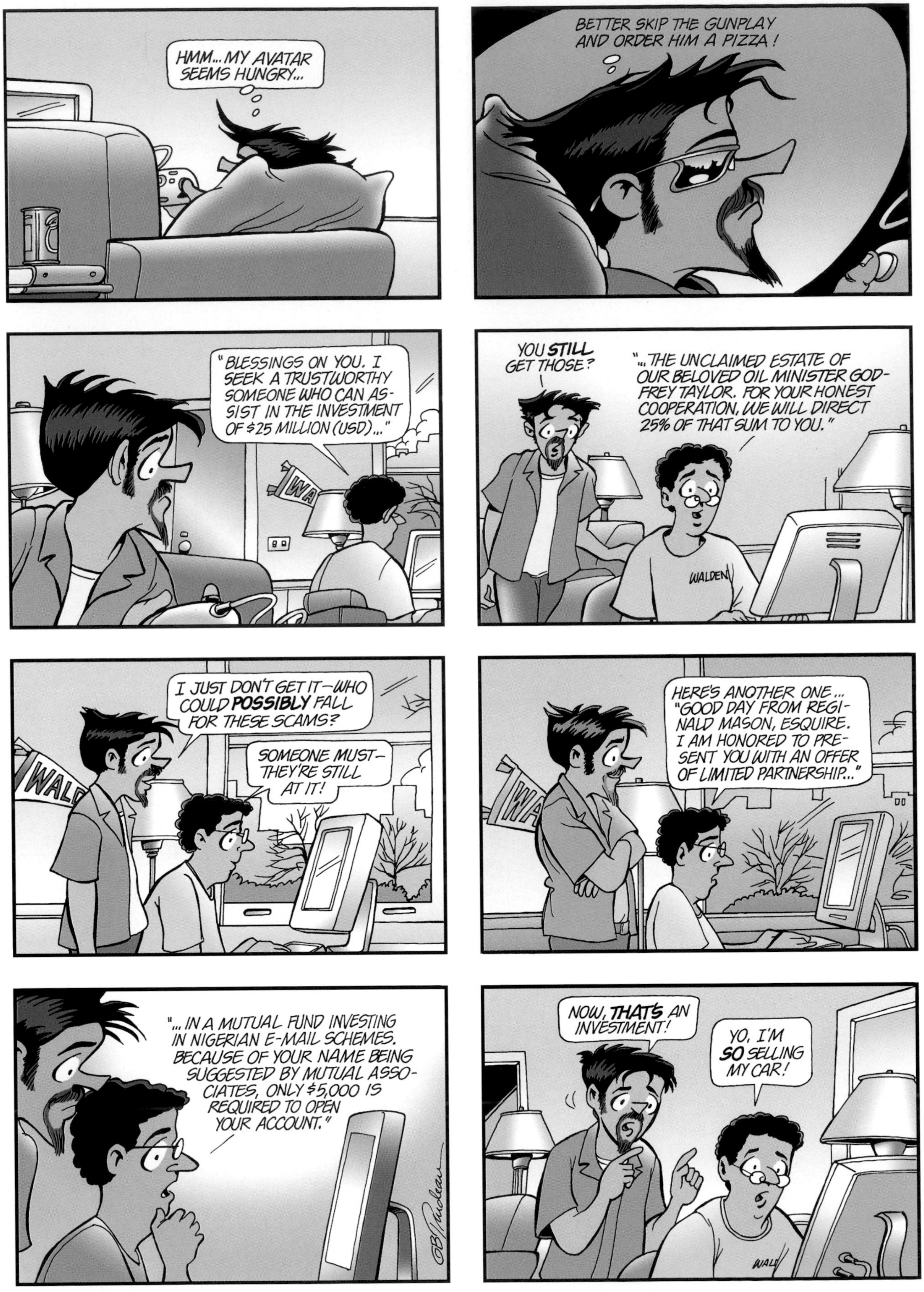
HMM... MY AVATAR SEEMS HUNGRY...
BETTER SKIP THE GUNPLAY AND ORDER HIM A PIZZA!
"BLESSINGS ON YOU. I SEEK A TRUSTWORTHY SOMEONE WHO CAN ASSIST IN THE INVESTMENT OF $25 MILLION (USD)..."
WA
YOU STILL GET THOSE?
"...THE UNCLAIMED ESTATE OF OUR BELOVED OIL MINISTER GODFREY TAYLOR. FOR YOUR HONEST COOPERATION, WE WILL DIRECT 25% OF THAT SUM TO YOU."
WALDEN
I JUST DON'T GET IT—WHO COULD POSSIBLY FALL FOR THESE SCAMS?
SOMEONE MUST—THEY'RE STILL AT IT!
WALD
HERE'S ANOTHER ONE... "GOOD DAY FROM REGINALD MASON, ESQUIRE. I AM HONORED TO PRESENT YOU WITH AN OFFER OF LIMITED PARTNERSHIP..."
"...IN A MUTUAL FUND INVESTING IN NIGERIAN E-MAIL SCHEMES. BECAUSE OF YOUR NAME BEING SUGGESTED BY MUTUAL ASSOCIATES, ONLY $5,000 IS REQUIRED TO OPEN YOUR ACCOUNT."
©B/Trudeau
NOW, THAT'S AN INVESTMENT!
YO, I'M SO SELLING MY CAR!
WAL

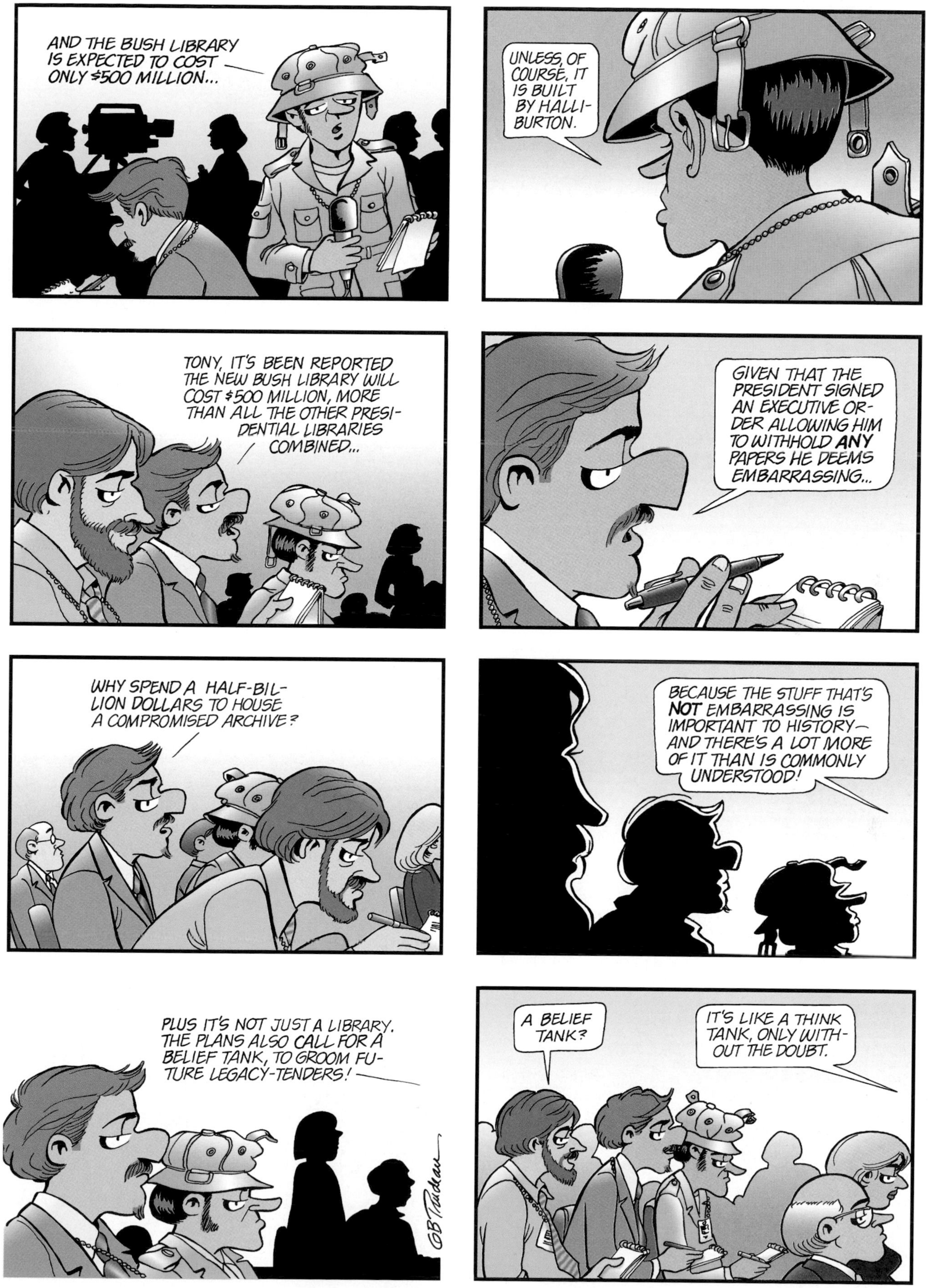
AND THE BUSH LIBRARY IS EXPECTED TO COST ONLY $500 MILLION...
UNLESS, OF COURSE, IT IS BUILT BY HALLI-BURTON.
TONY, IT'S BEEN REPORTED THE NEW BUSH LIBRARY WILL COST $500 MILLION, MORE THAN ALL THE OTHER PRESI-DENTIAL LIBRARIES COMBINED...
GIVEN THAT THE PRESIDENT SIGNED AN EXECUTIVE OR-DER ALLOWING HIM TO WITHHOLD ANY PAPERS HE DEEMS EMBARRASSING...
WHY SPEND A HALF-BIL-LION DOLLARS TO HOUSE A COMPROMISED ARCHIVE?
BECAUSE THE STUFF THAT'S NOT EMBARRASSING IS IMPORTANT TO HISTORY— AND THERE'S A LOT MORE OF IT THAN IS COMMONLY UNDERSTOOD!
PLUS IT'S NOT JUST A LIBRARY. THE PLANS ALSO CALL FOR A BELIEF TANK, TO GROOM FU-TURE LEGACY-TENDERS!
A BELIEF TANK?
IT'S LIKE A THINK TANK, ONLY WITH-OUT THE DOUBT.

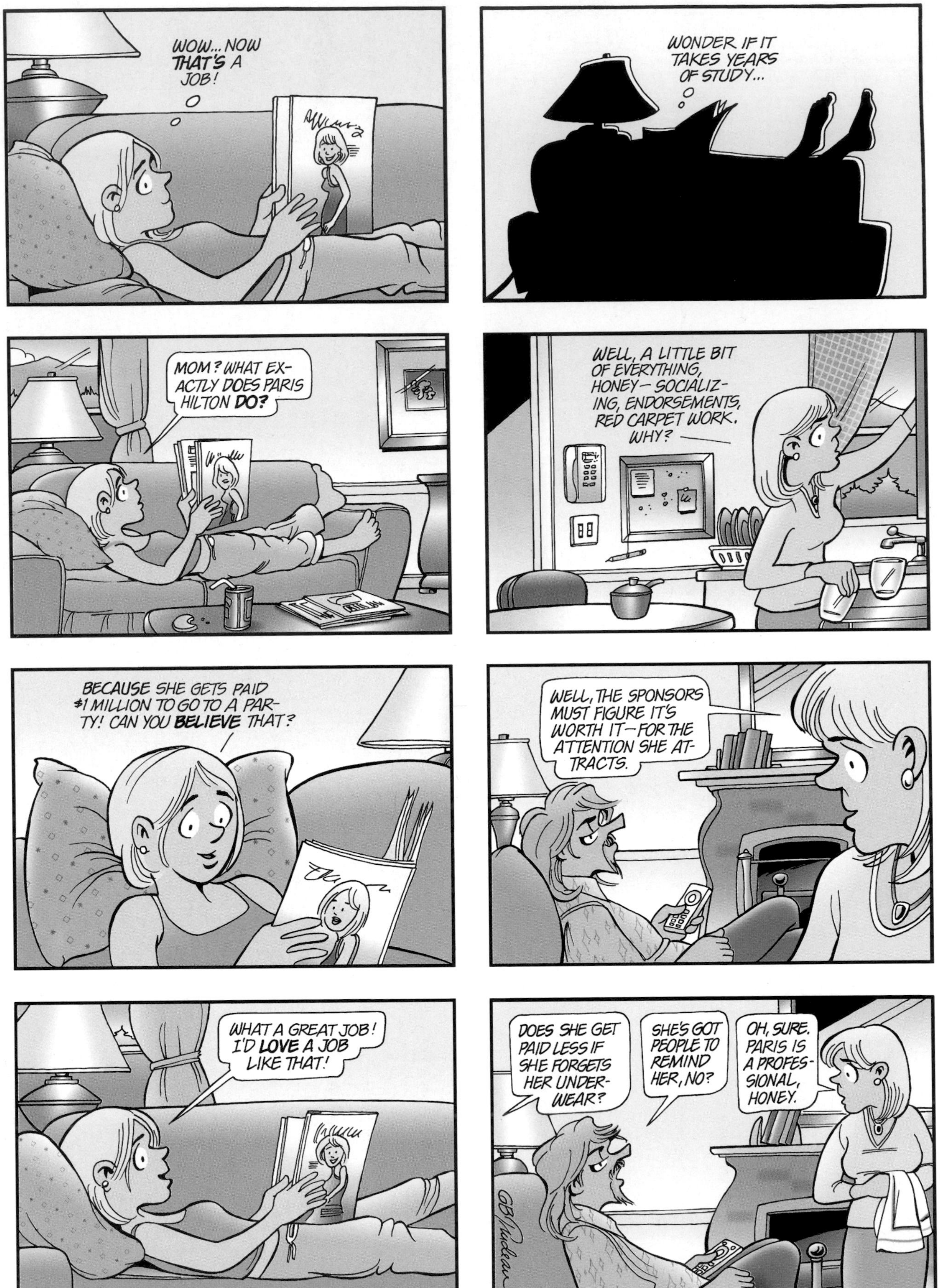
WOW... NOW THAT'S A JOB!
WONDER IF IT TAKES YEARS OF STUDY...
MOM? WHAT EXACTLY DOES PARIS HILTON DO?
WELL, A LITTLE BIT OF EVERYTHING, HONEY— SOCIALIZING, ENDORSEMENTS, RED CARPET WORK. WHY?
BECAUSE SHE GETS PAID $1 MILLION TO GO TO A PARTY! CAN YOU BELIEVE THAT?
WELL, THE SPONSORS MUST FIGURE IT'S WORTH IT—FOR THE ATTENTION SHE ATTRACTS.
WHAT A GREAT JOB! I'D LOVE A JOB LIKE THAT!
OH, SURE. PARIS IS A PROFESSIONAL, HONEY.
DOES SHE GET PAID LESS IF SHE FORGETS HER UNDERWEAR?
SHE'S GOT PEOPLE TO REMIND HER, NO?

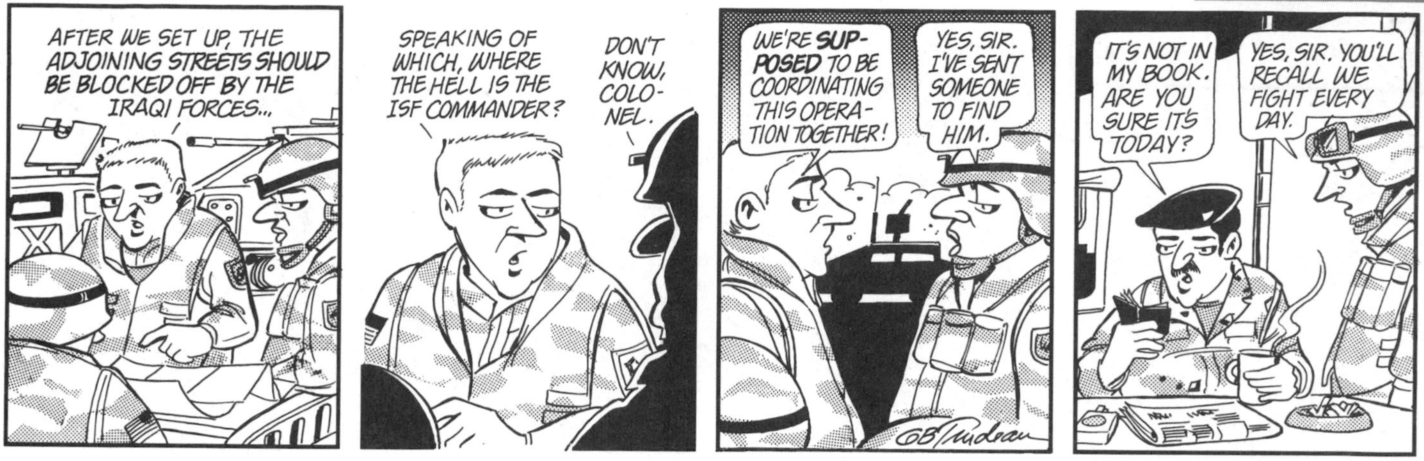
AFTER WE SET UP, THE ADJOINING STREETS SHOULD BE BLOCKED OFF BY THE IRAQI FORCES...
SPEAKING OF WHICH, WHERE THE HELL IS THE ISF COMMANDER?
DON'T KNOW, COLONEL.
WE'RE SUPPOSED TO BE COORDINATING THIS OPERATION TOGETHER!
YES, SIR. I'VE SENT SOMEONE TO FIND HIM.
IT'S NOT IN MY BOOK. ARE YOU SURE IT'S TODAY?
YES, SIR. YOU'LL RECALL WE FIGHT EVERY DAY.
GB Trudeau

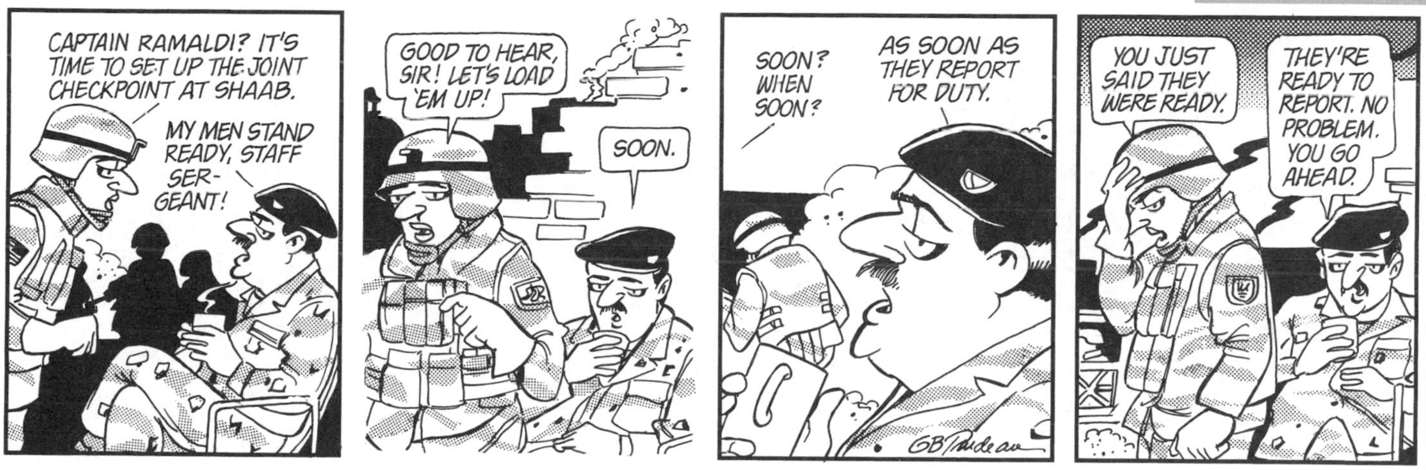
CAPTAIN RAMALDI? IT'S TIME TO SET UP THE JOINT CHECKPOINT AT SHAAB.
MY MEN STAND READY, STAFF SERGEANT!
GOOD TO HEAR, SIR! LET'S LOAD 'EM UP!
SOON.
SOON? WHEN SOON?
AS SOON AS THEY REPORT FOR DUTY.
YOU JUST SAID THEY WERE READY.
THEY'RE READY TO REPORT. NO PROBLEM. YOU GO AHEAD.
GB Trudeau

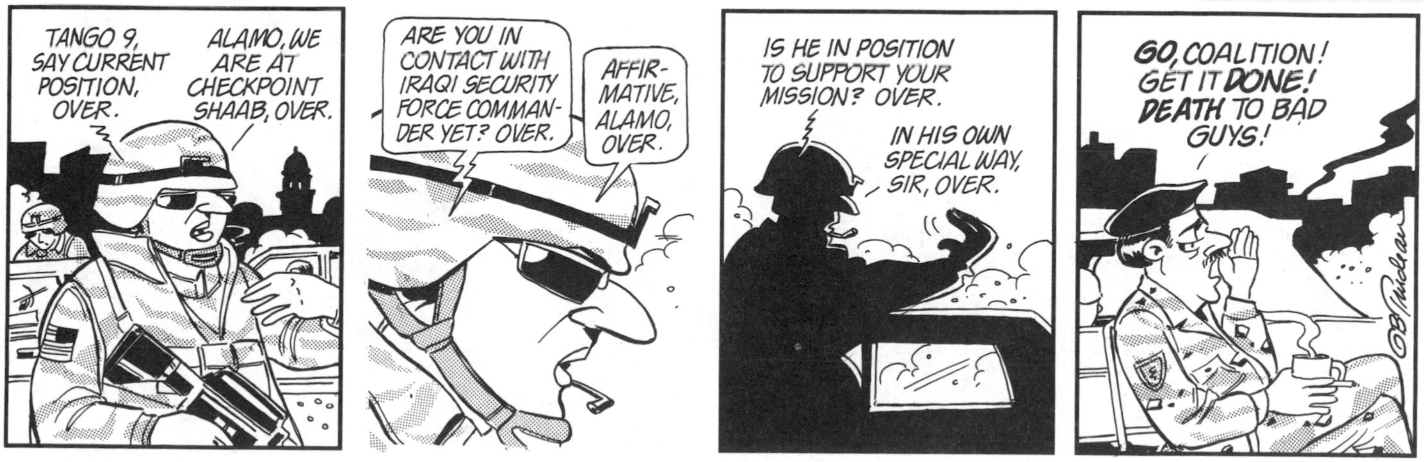
TANGO 9, SAY CURRENT POSITION, OVER.
ALAMO, WE ARE AT CHECKPOINT SHAAB, OVER.
ARE YOU IN CONTACT WITH IRAQI SECURITY FORCE COMMANDER YET? OVER.
AFFIRMATIVE, ALAMO, OVER.
IS HE IN POSITION TO SUPPORT YOUR MISSION? OVER.
IN HIS OWN SPECIAL WAY, SIR, OVER.
GO, COALITION! GET IT DONE! DEATH TO BAD GUYS!
GB Trudeau

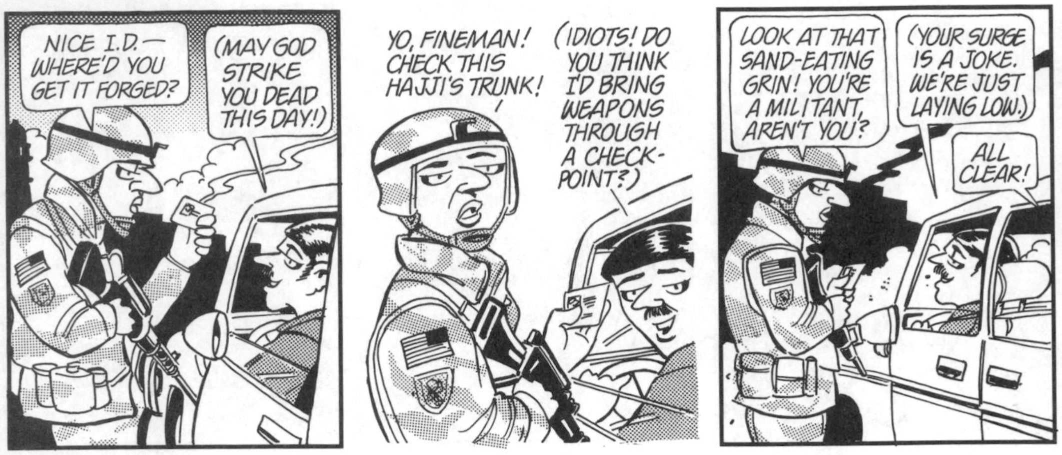
NICE I.D.— WHERE'D YOU GET IT FORGED?
(MAY GOD STRIKE YOU DEAD THIS DAY!)
YO, FINEMAN! CHECK THIS HAJJI'S TRUNK!
(IDIOTS! DO YOU THINK I'D BRING WEAPONS THROUGH A CHECK-POINT?)
LOOK AT THAT SAND-EATING GRIN! YOU'RE A MILITANT, AREN'T YOU?
(YOUR SURGE IS A JOKE. WE'RE JUST LAYING LOW.)
ALL CLEAR!
OKAY, GET OUTA MY FACE!
(MAY CROWS EAT FROM YOUR SKULL! PRAISE GOD!)
GBTrudeau

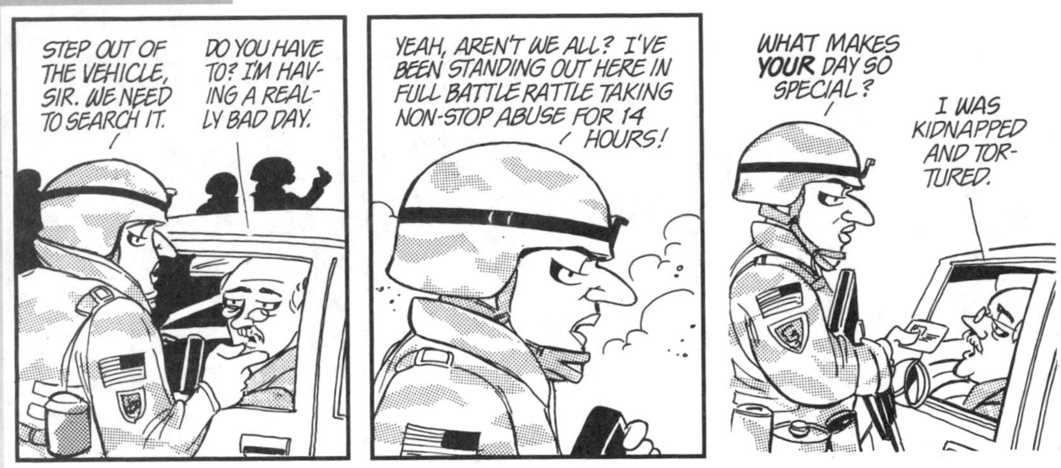
STEP OUT OF THE VEHICLE, SIR. WE NEED TO SEARCH IT.
DO YOU HAVE TO? I'M HAVING A REALLY BAD DAY.
YEAH, AREN'T WE ALL? I'VE BEEN STANDING OUT HERE IN FULL BATTLE RATTLE TAKING NON-STOP ABUSE FOR 14 HOURS!
WHAT MAKES **YOUR** DAY SO SPECIAL?
I WAS KIDNAPPED AND TORTURED.
OH... I'M SORRY. WHAT ARE YOU DOING ON THE ROAD?
ESCAPING. IS THAT A PROBLEM?
GBTrudeau

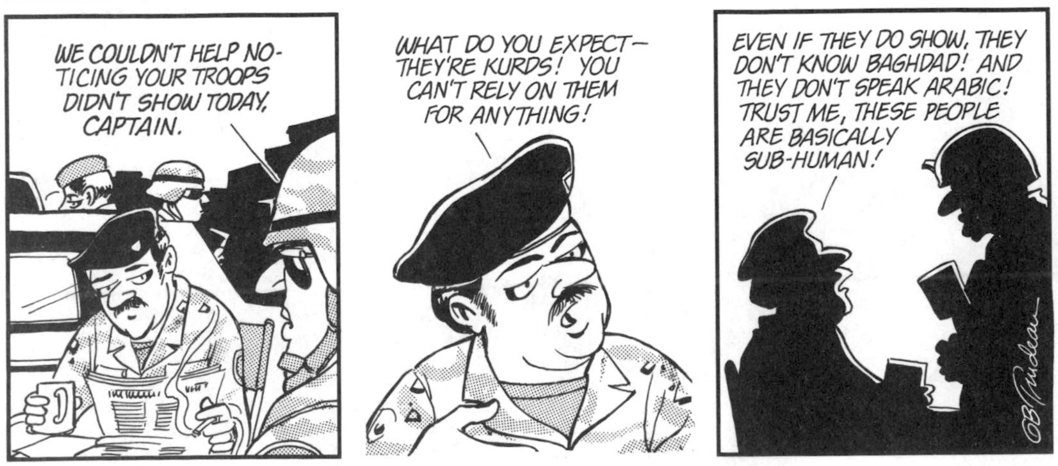
WE COULDN'T HELP NOTICING YOUR TROOPS DIDN'T SHOW TODAY, CAPTAIN.
WHAT DO YOU EXPECT— THEY'RE KURDS! YOU CAN'T RELY ON THEM FOR ANYTHING!
EVEN IF THEY DO SHOW, THEY DON'T KNOW BAGHDAD! AND THEY DON'T SPEAK ARABIC! TRUST ME, THESE PEOPLE ARE BASICALLY SUB-HUMAN!
GBTrudeau
THEY WANT THEIR OWN COUNTRY, YOU KNOW.
I CAN'T IMAGINE WHY...

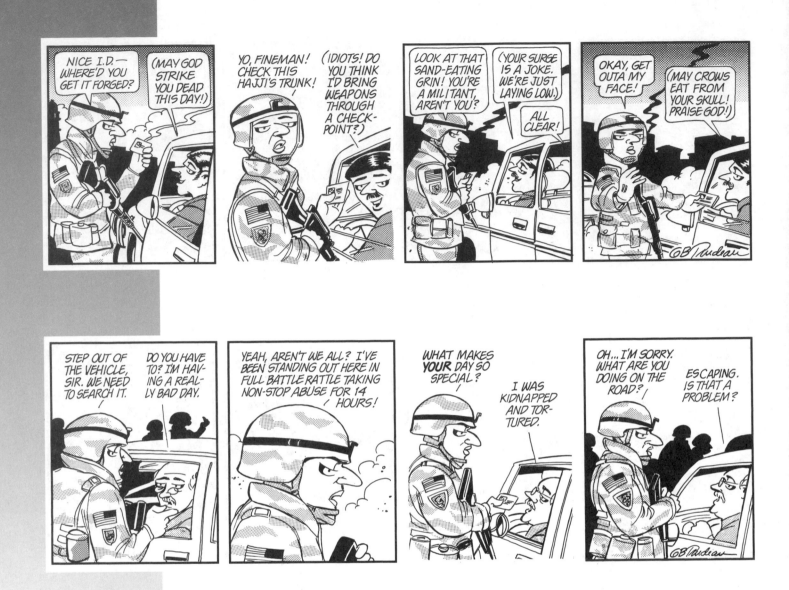

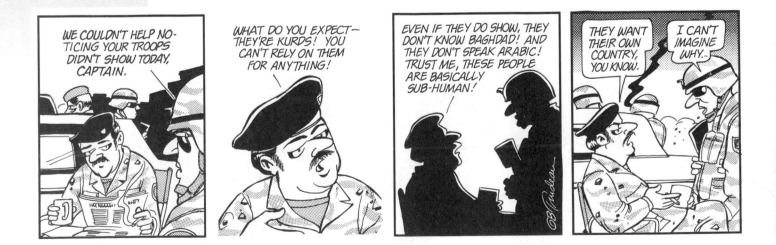

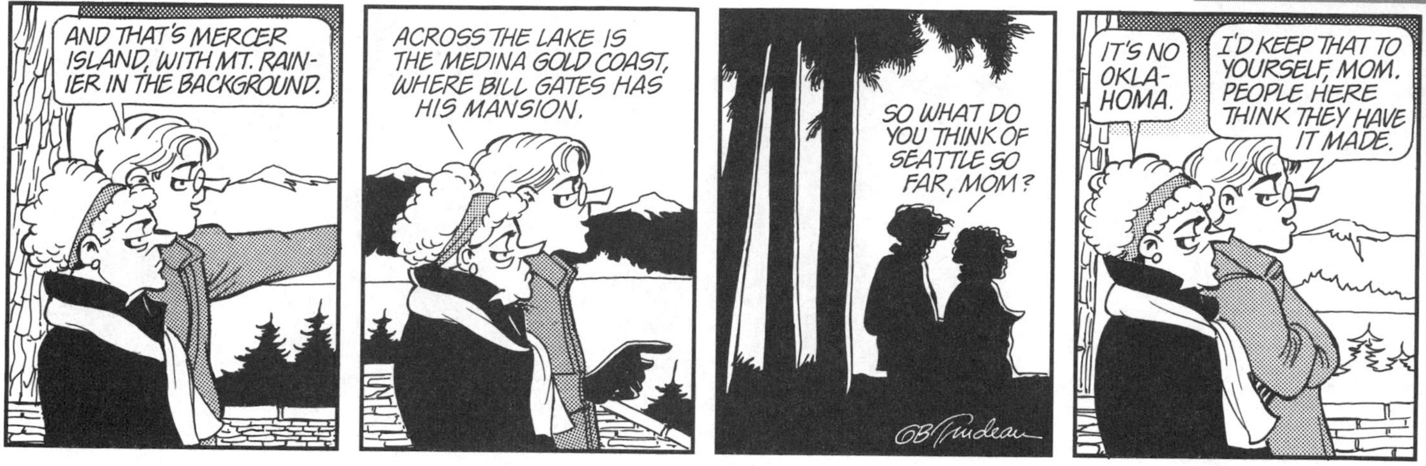
AND THAT'S MERCER ISLAND, WITH MT. RAINIER IN THE BACKGROUND.
ACROSS THE LAKE IS THE MEDINA GOLD COAST, WHERE BILL GATES HAS HIS MANSION.
SO WHAT DO YOU THINK OF SEATTLE SO FAR, MOM?
IT'S NO OKLAHOMA.
I'D KEEP THAT TO YOURSELF, MOM. PEOPLE HERE THINK THEY HAVE IT MADE.

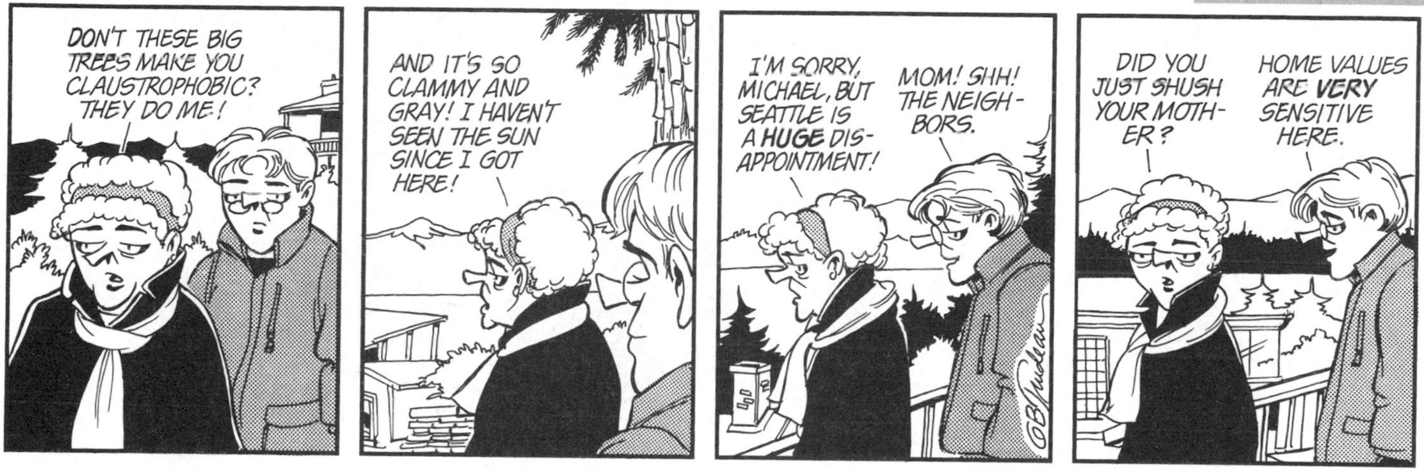
DON'T THESE BIG TREES MAKE YOU CLAUSTROPHOBIC? THEY DO ME!
AND IT'S SO CLAMMY AND GRAY! I HAVEN'T SEEN THE SUN SINCE I GOT HERE!
I'M SORRY, MICHAEL, BUT SEATTLE IS A **HUGE** DISAPPOINTMENT!
MOM! SHH! THE NEIGHBORS.
DID YOU JUST SHUSH YOUR MOTHER?
HOME VALUES ARE **VERY** SENSITIVE HERE.

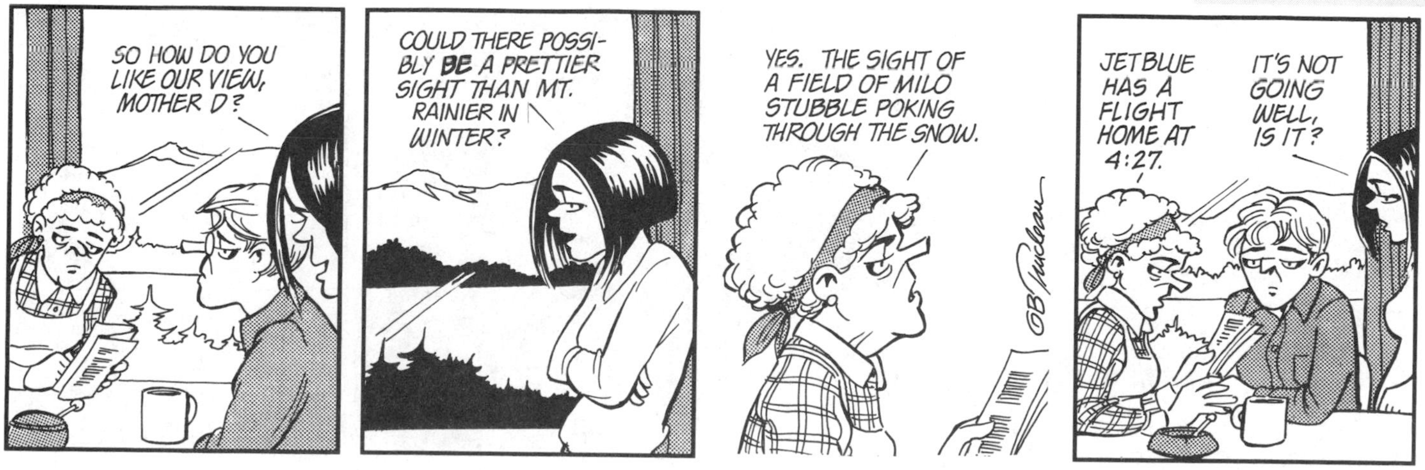
SO HOW DO YOU LIKE OUR VIEW, MOTHER D?
COULD THERE POSSIBLY **BE** A PRETTIER SIGHT THAN MT. RAINIER IN WINTER?
YES. THE SIGHT OF A FIELD OF MILO STUBBLE POKING THROUGH THE SNOW.
JETBLUE HAS A FLIGHT HOME AT 4:27.
IT'S NOT GOING WELL, IS IT?

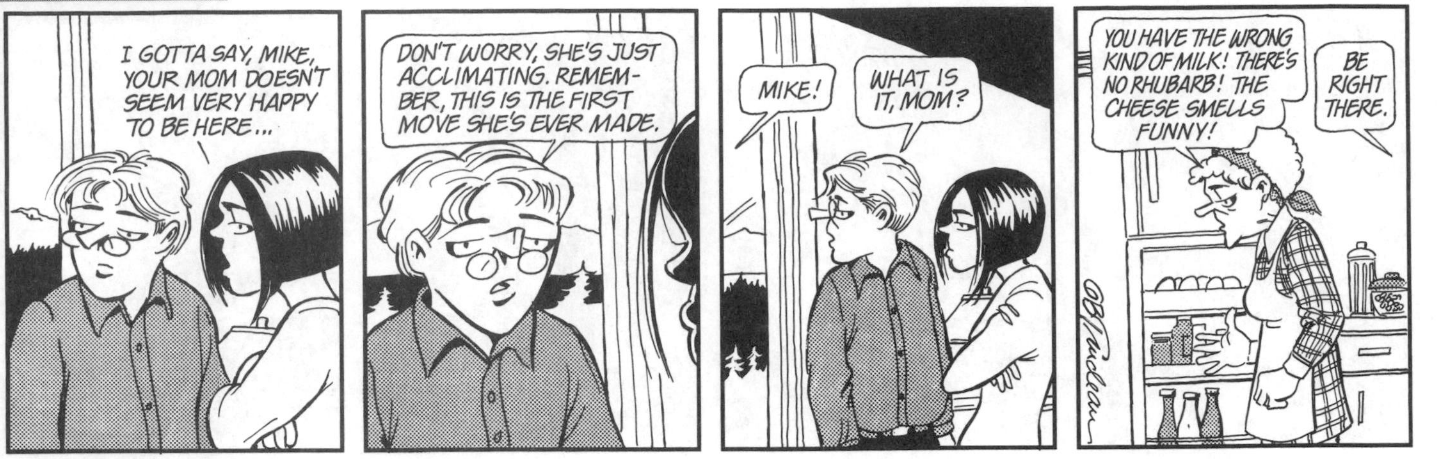
I GOTTA SAY, MIKE, YOUR MOM DOESN'T SEEM VERY HAPPY TO BE HERE...
DON'T WORRY, SHE'S JUST ACCLIMATING. REMEMBER, THIS IS THE FIRST MOVE SHE'S EVER MADE.
MIKE!
WHAT IS IT, MOM?
YOU HAVE THE WRONG KIND OF MILK! THERE'S NO RHUBARB! THE CHEESE SMELLS FUNNY!
BE RIGHT THERE.

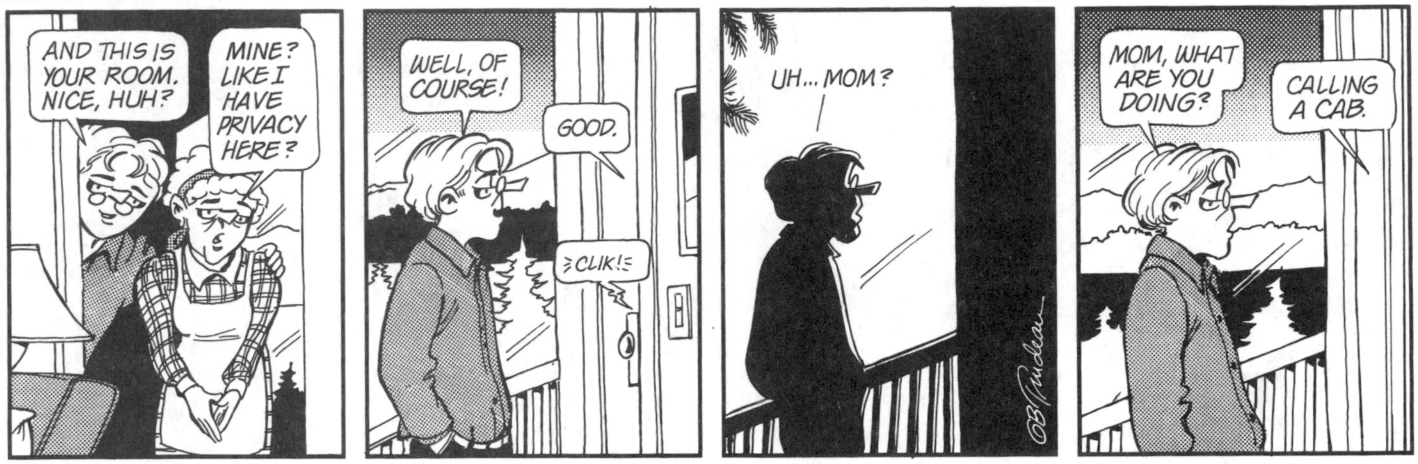
AND THIS IS YOUR ROOM. NICE, HUH?
MINE? LIKE I HAVE PRIVACY HERE?
WELL, OF COURSE!
GOOD.
CLIK!
UH... MOM?
MOM, WHAT ARE YOU DOING?
CALLING A CAB.

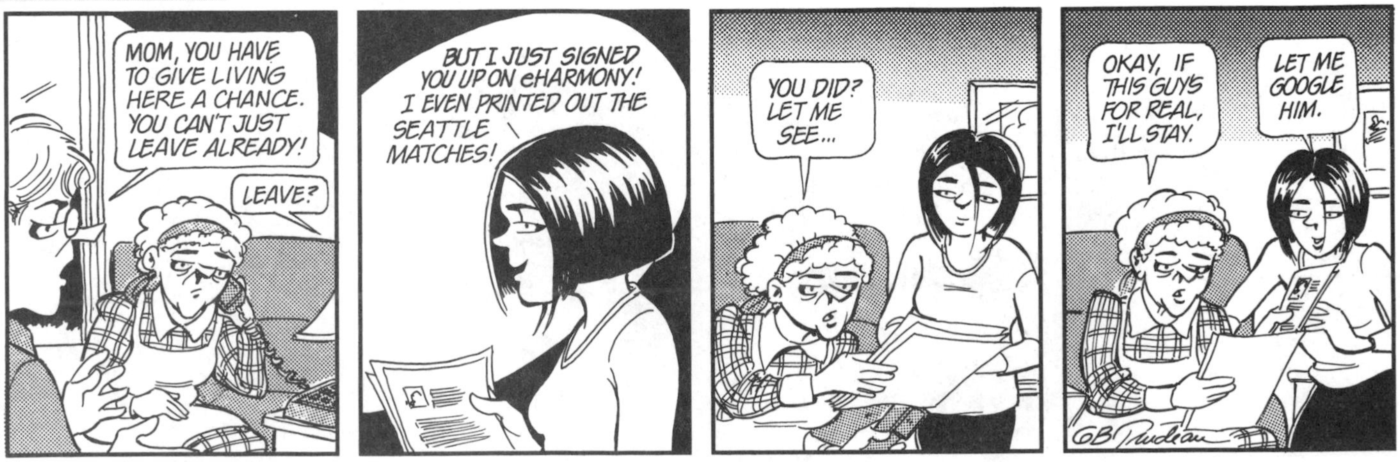
MOM, YOU HAVE TO GIVE LIVING HERE A CHANCE. YOU CAN'T JUST LEAVE ALREADY!
LEAVE?
BUT I JUST SIGNED YOU UP ON eHARMONY! I EVEN PRINTED OUT THE SEATTLE MATCHES!
YOU DID? LET ME SEE...
OKAY, IF THIS GUY'S FOR REAL, I'LL STAY.
LET ME GOOGLE HIM.

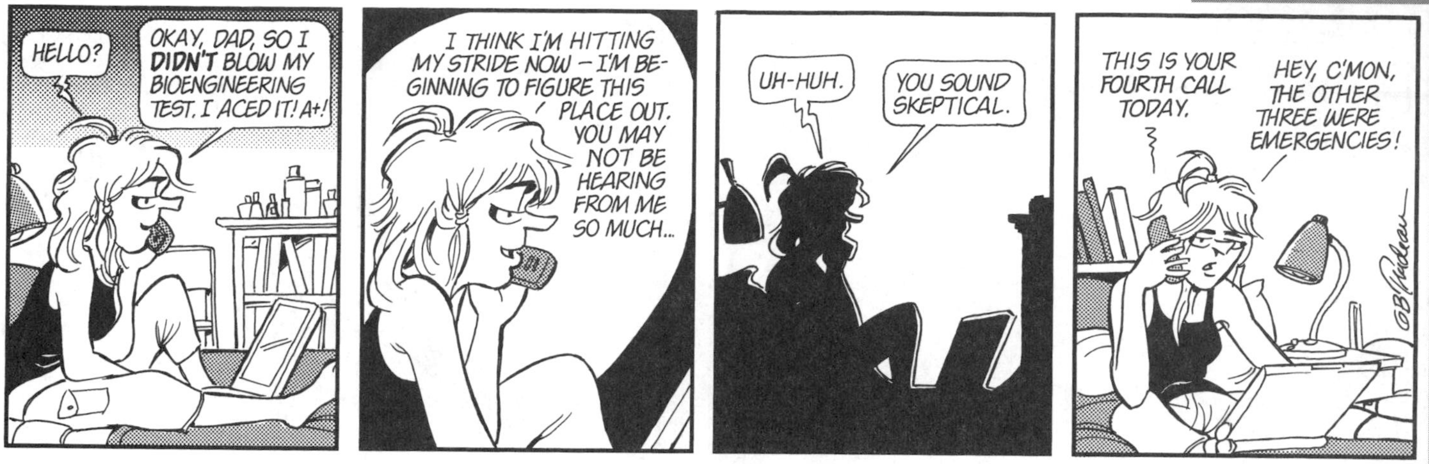
HELLO?
OKAY, DAD, SO I **DIDN'T** BLOW MY BIOENGINEERING TEST. I ACED IT! A+!
I THINK I'M HITTING MY STRIDE NOW – I'M BEGINNING TO FIGURE THIS PLACE OUT.
YOU MAY NOT BE HEARING FROM ME SO MUCH...
UH-HUH.
YOU SOUND SKEPTICAL.
THIS IS YOUR FOURTH CALL TODAY.
HEY, C'MON, THE OTHER THREE WERE EMERGENCIES!
GBTrudeau

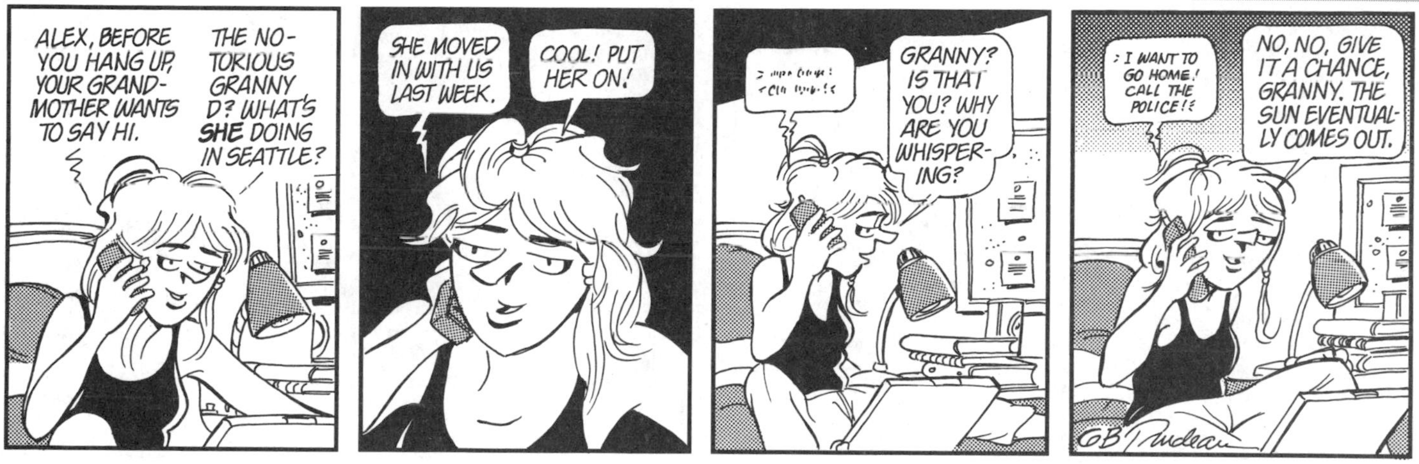
ALEX, BEFORE YOU HANG UP, YOUR GRANDMOTHER WANTS TO SAY HI.
THE NOTORIOUS GRANNY D? WHAT'S **SHE** DOING IN SEATTLE?
SHE MOVED IN WITH US LAST WEEK.
COOL! PUT HER ON!
GRANNY? IS THAT YOU? WHY ARE YOU WHISPERING?
I WANT TO GO HOME! CALL THE POLICE!
NO, NO, GIVE IT A CHANCE, GRANNY. THE SUN EVENTUALLY COMES OUT.
GBTrudeau

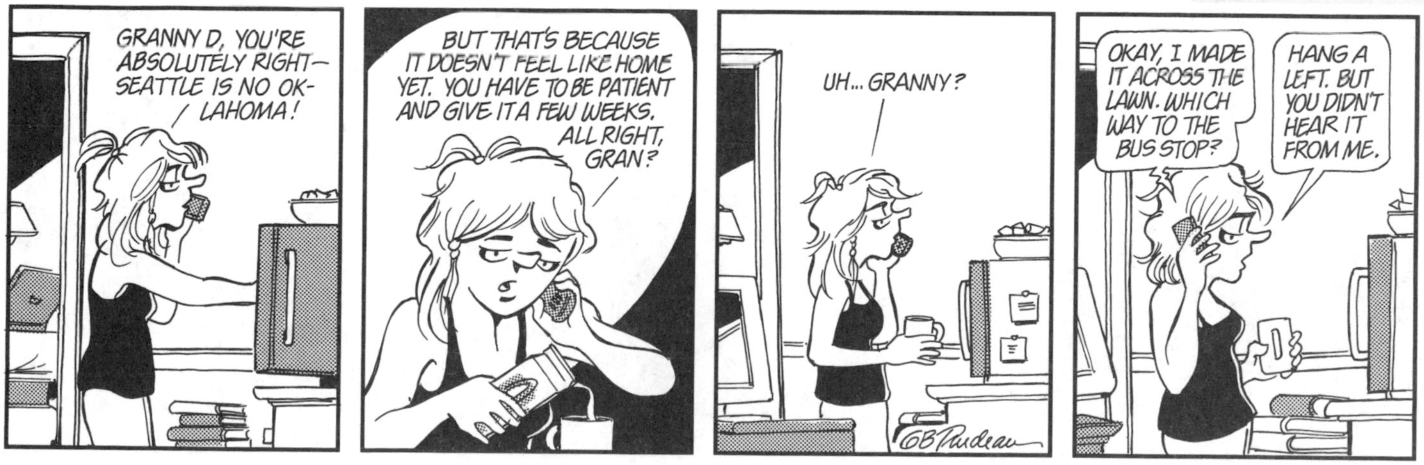
GRANNY D, YOU'RE ABSOLUTELY RIGHT– SEATTLE IS NO OKLAHOMA!
BUT THAT'S BECAUSE IT DOESN'T FEEL LIKE HOME YET. YOU HAVE TO BE PATIENT AND GIVE IT A FEW WEEKS.
ALL RIGHT, GRAN?
UH... GRANNY?
GBTrudeau
OKAY, I MADE IT ACROSS THE LAWN. WHICH WAY TO THE BUS STOP?
HANG A LEFT. BUT YOU DIDN'T HEAR IT FROM ME.

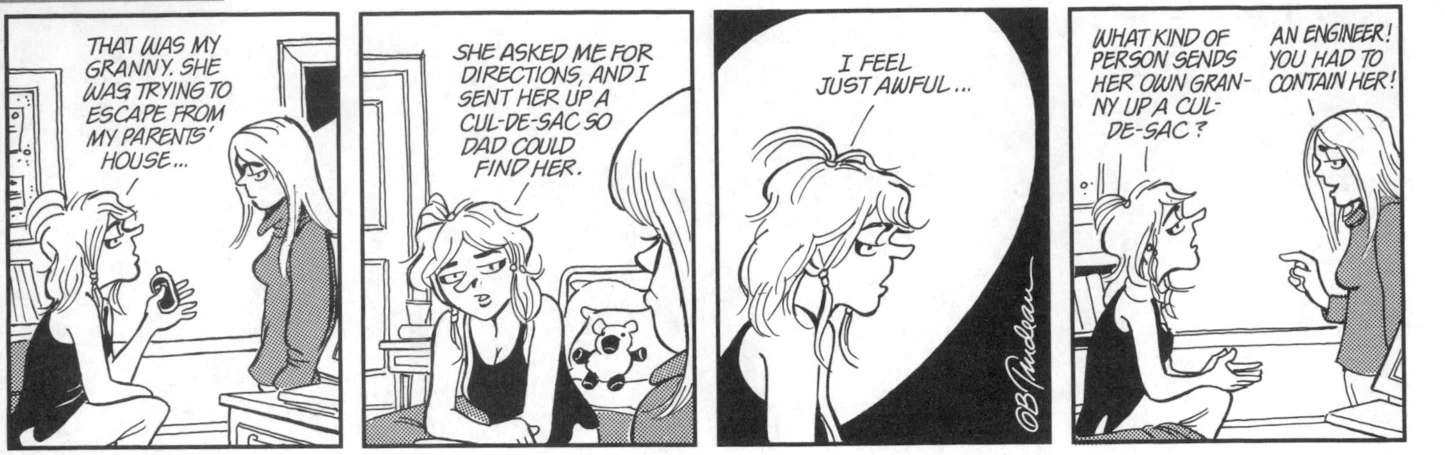
THAT WAS MY GRANNY. SHE WAS TRYING TO ESCAPE FROM MY PARENTS' HOUSE...
SHE ASKED ME FOR DIRECTIONS, AND I SENT HER UP A CUL-DE-SAC SO DAD COULD FIND HER.
I FEEL JUST AWFUL...
WHAT KIND OF PERSON SENDS HER OWN GRANNY UP A CUL-DE-SAC?
AN ENGINEER! YOU HAD TO CONTAIN HER!

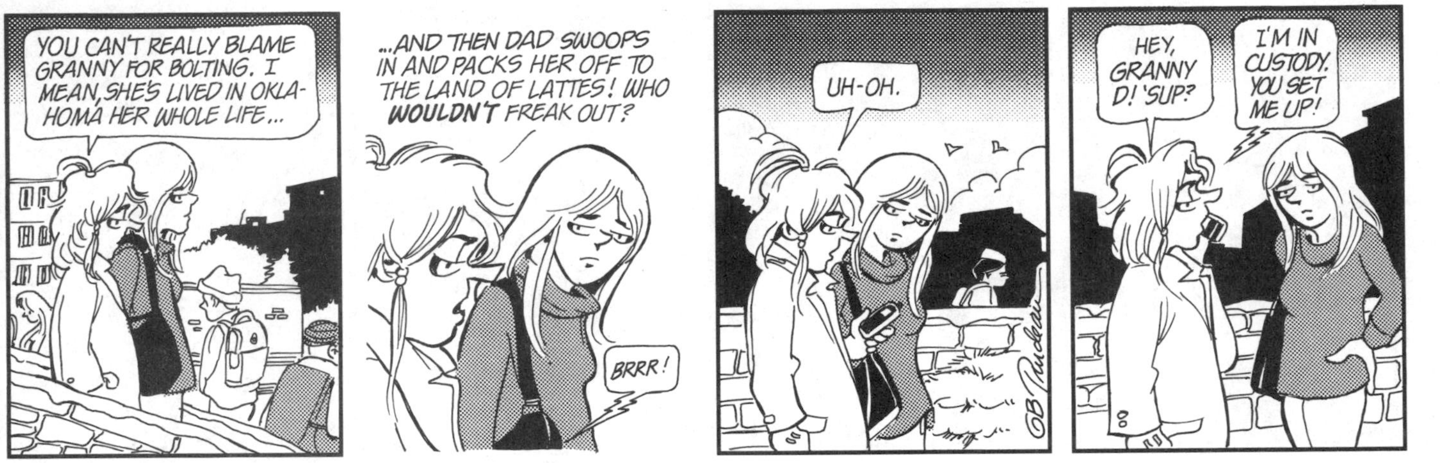
YOU CAN'T REALLY BLAME GRANNY FOR BOLTING. I MEAN, SHE'S LIVED IN OKLAHOMA HER WHOLE LIFE...
...AND THEN DAD SWOOPS IN AND PACKS HER OFF TO THE LAND OF LATTES! WHO **WOULDN'T** FREAK OUT?
BRRR!
UH-OH.
HEY, GRANNY D! 'SUP?
I'M IN CUSTODY. YOU SET ME UP!

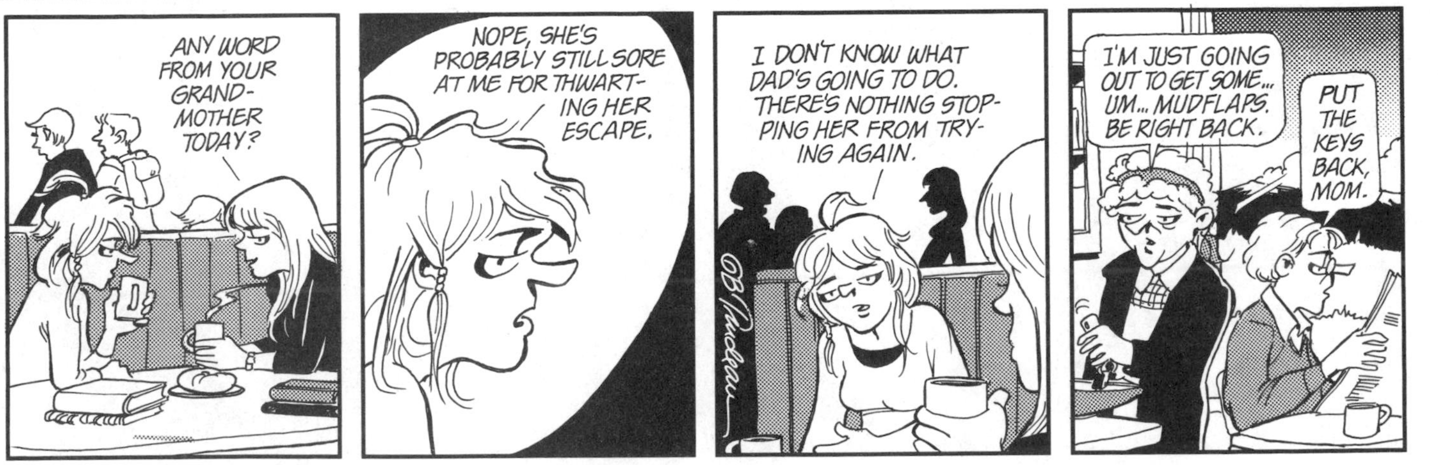
ANY WORD FROM YOUR GRANDMOTHER TODAY?
NOPE, SHE'S PROBABLY STILL SORE AT ME FOR THWARTING HER ESCAPE.
I DON'T KNOW WHAT DAD'S GOING TO DO. THERE'S NOTHING STOPPING HER FROM TRYING AGAIN.
I'M JUST GOING OUT TO GET SOME... UM... MUDFLAPS. BE RIGHT BACK.
PUT THE KEYS BACK, MOM.

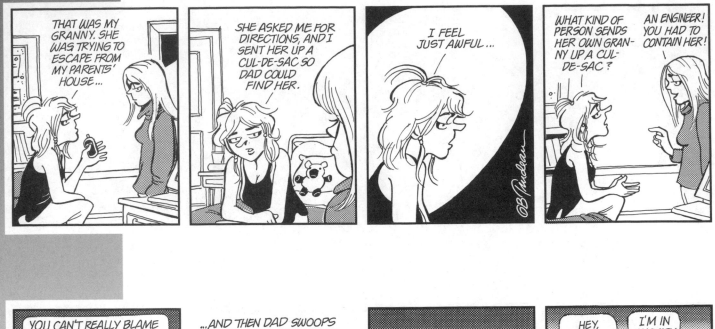

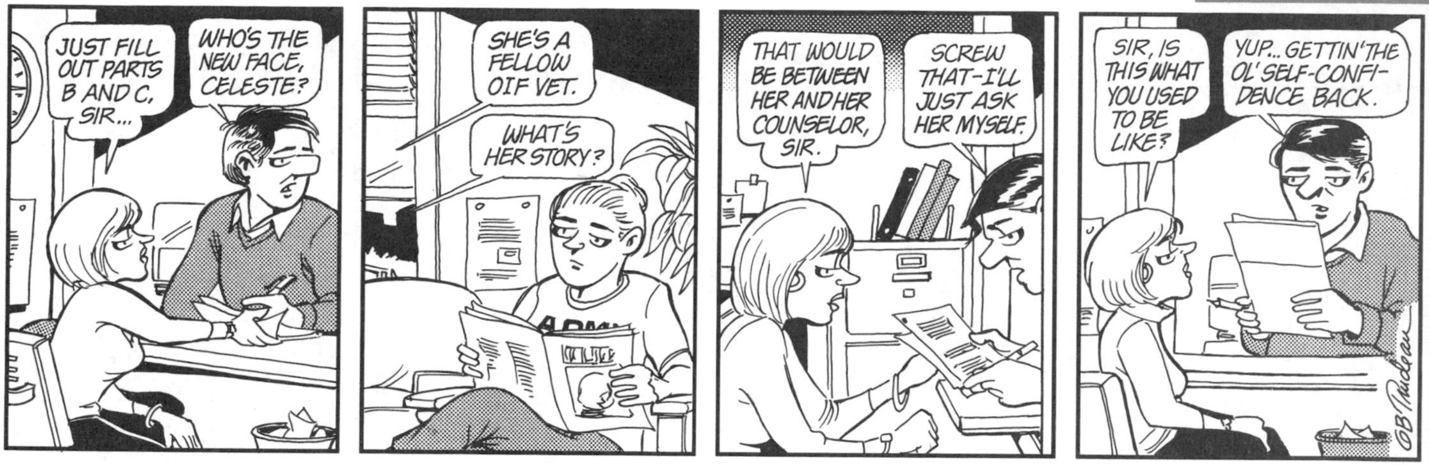
JUST FILL OUT PARTS B AND C, SIR...
WHO'S THE NEW FACE, CELESTE?
SHE'S A FELLOW OIF VET.
WHAT'S HER STORY?
THAT WOULD BE BETWEEN HER AND HER COUNSELOR, SIR.
SCREW THAT–I'LL JUST ASK HER MYSELF.
SIR, IS THIS WHAT YOU USED TO BE LIKE?
YUP... GETTIN' THE OL' SELF-CONFIDENCE BACK.
GB Trudeau

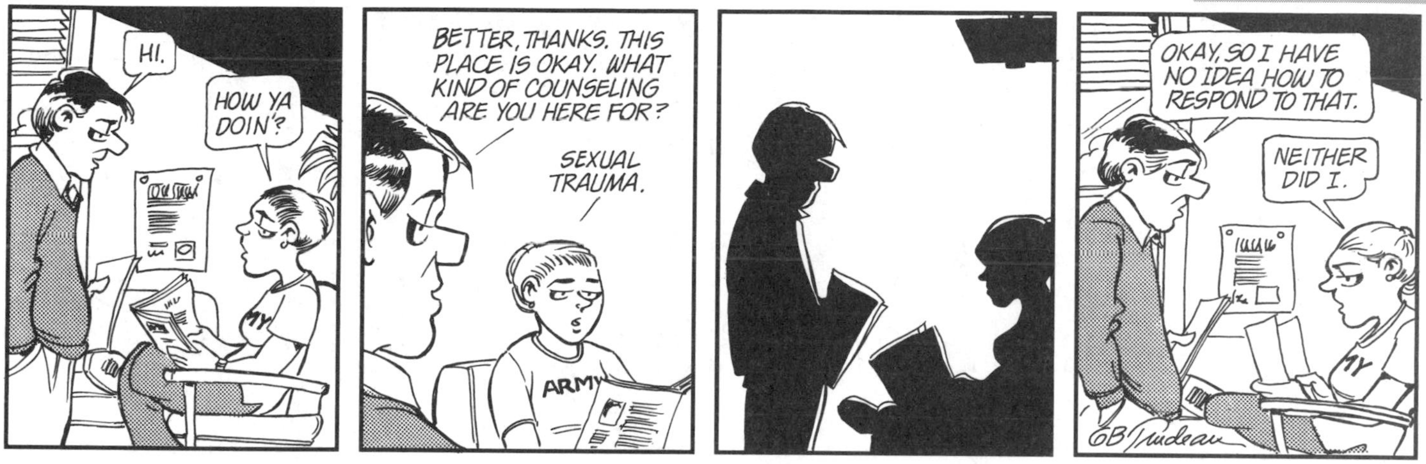
HI.
HOW YA DOIN'?
BETTER, THANKS. THIS PLACE IS OKAY. WHAT KIND OF COUNSELING ARE YOU HERE FOR?
SEXUAL TRAUMA.
OKAY, SO I HAVE NO IDEA HOW TO RESPOND TO THAT.
NEITHER DID I.
GB Trudeau

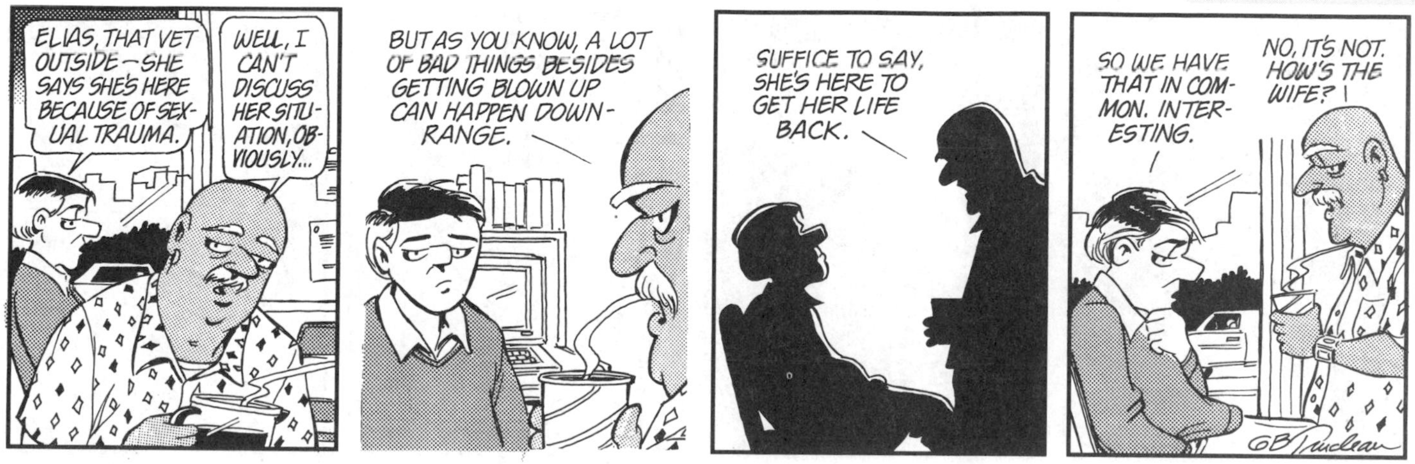
ELIAS, THAT VET OUTSIDE–SHE SAYS SHE'S HERE BECAUSE OF SEXUAL TRAUMA.
WELL, I CAN'T DISCUSS HER SITUATION, OBVIOUSLY...
BUT AS YOU KNOW, A LOT OF BAD THINGS BESIDES GETTING BLOWN UP CAN HAPPEN DOWNRANGE.
SUFFICE TO SAY, SHE'S HERE TO GET HER LIFE BACK.
SO WE HAVE THAT IN COMMON. INTERESTING.
NO, IT'S NOT. HOW'S THE WIFE?
GB Trudeau

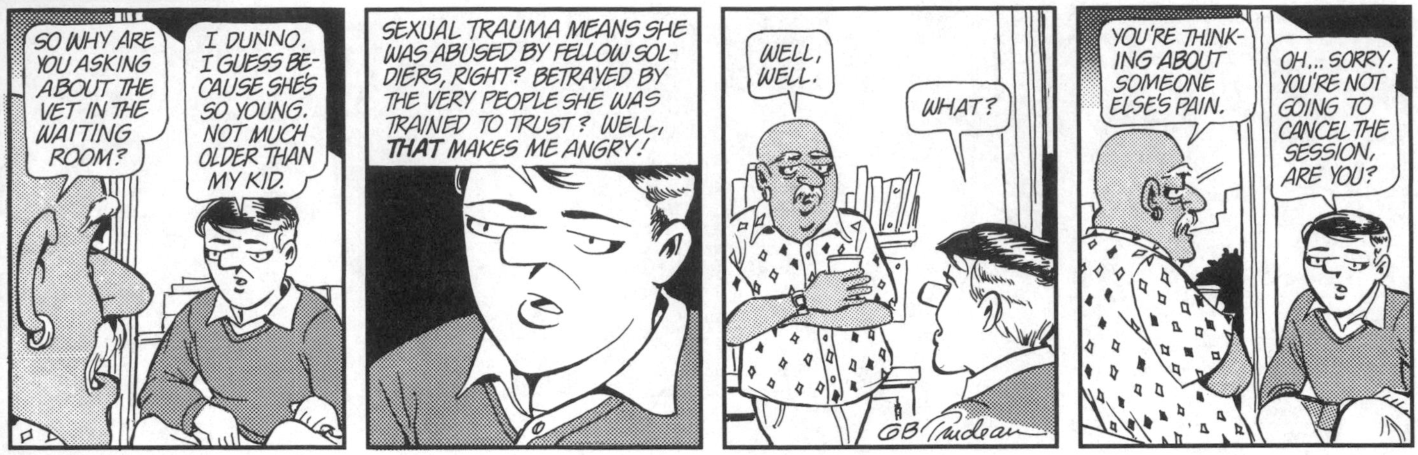
SO WHY ARE YOU ASKING ABOUT THE VET IN THE WAITING ROOM?
I DUNNO. I GUESS BECAUSE SHE'S SO YOUNG. NOT MUCH OLDER THAN MY KID.
SEXUAL TRAUMA MEANS SHE WAS ABUSED BY FELLOW SOLDIERS, RIGHT? BETRAYED BY THE VERY PEOPLE SHE WAS TRAINED TO TRUST? WELL, THAT MAKES ME ANGRY!
WELL, WELL.
WHAT?
YOU'RE THINKING ABOUT SOMEONE ELSE'S PAIN.
OH... SORRY. YOU'RE NOT GOING TO CANCEL THE SESSION, ARE YOU?
GB Trudeau

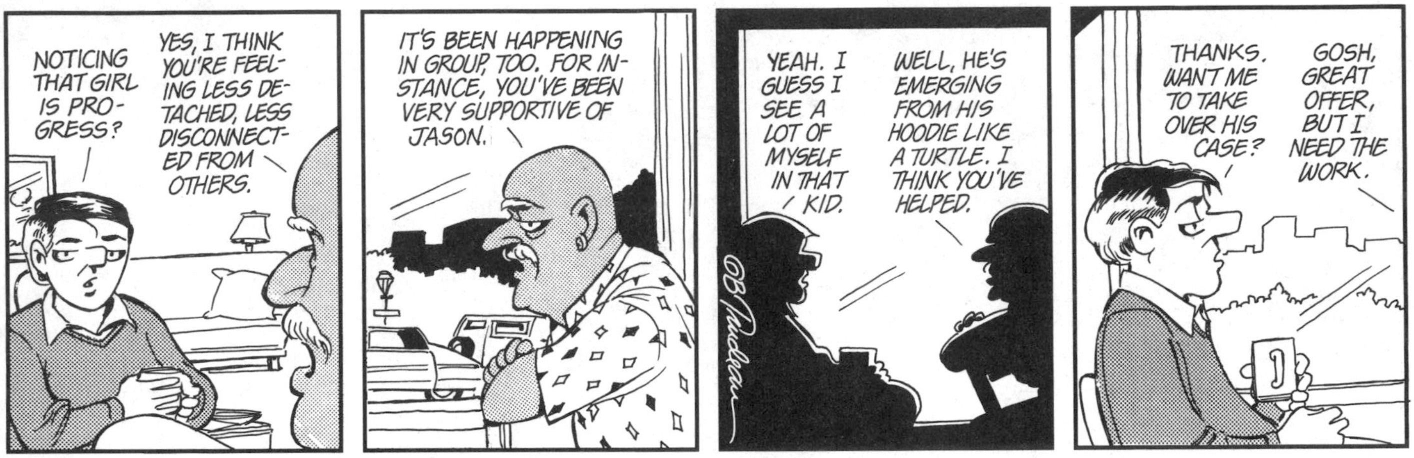
NOTICING THAT GIRL IS PROGRESS?
YES, I THINK YOU'RE FEELING LESS DETACHED, LESS DISCONNECTED FROM OTHERS.
IT'S BEEN HAPPENING IN GROUP, TOO. FOR INSTANCE, YOU'VE BEEN VERY SUPPORTIVE OF JASON.
YEAH. I GUESS I SEE A LOT OF MYSELF IN THAT KID.
WELL, HE'S EMERGING FROM HIS HOODIE LIKE A TURTLE. I THINK YOU'VE HELPED.
GB Trudeau
THANKS. WANT ME TO TAKE OVER HIS CASE?
GOSH, GREAT OFFER, BUT I NEED THE WORK.

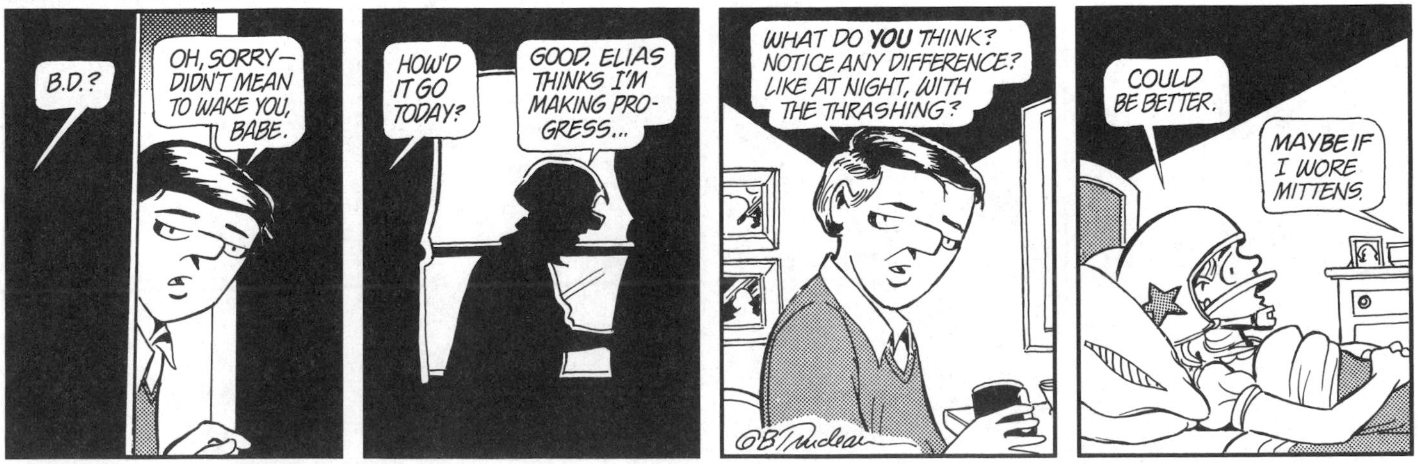
B.D.?
OH, SORRY—DIDN'T MEAN TO WAKE YOU, BABE.
HOW'D IT GO TODAY?
GOOD. ELIAS THINKS I'M MAKING PROGRESS...
WHAT DO YOU THINK? NOTICE ANY DIFFERENCE? LIKE AT NIGHT, WITH THE THRASHING?
GB Trudeau
COULD BE BETTER.
MAYBE IF I WORE MITTENS.

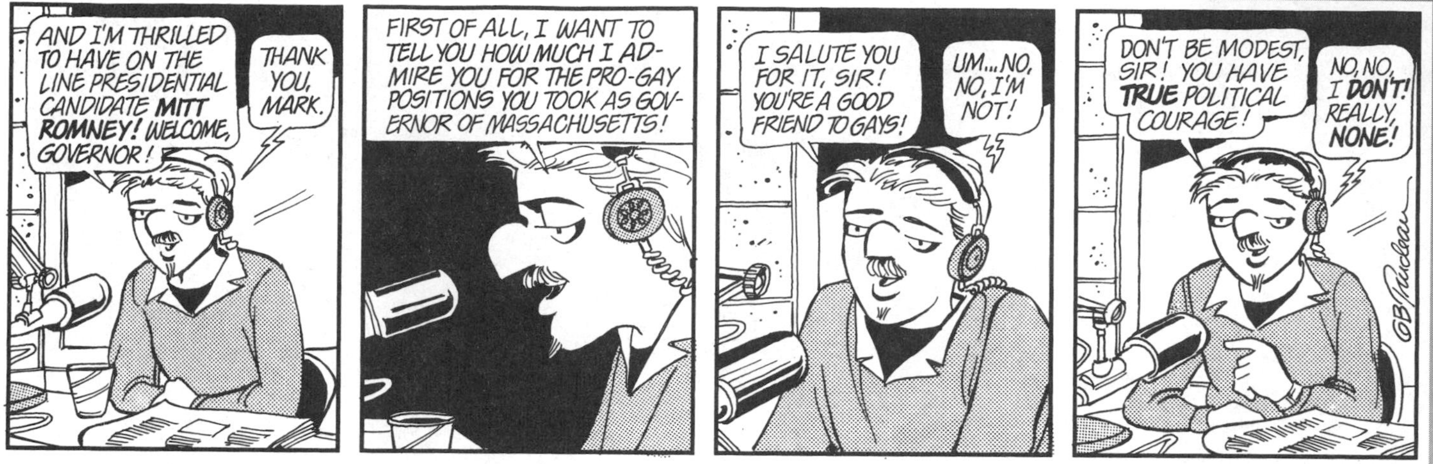
AND I'M THRILLED TO HAVE ON THE LINE PRESIDENTIAL CANDIDATE **MITT ROMNEY!** WELCOME, GOVERNOR!
THANK YOU, MARK.
FIRST OF ALL, I WANT TO TELL YOU HOW MUCH I ADMIRE YOU FOR THE PRO-GAY POSITIONS YOU TOOK AS GOVERNOR OF MASSACHUSETTS!
I SALUTE YOU FOR IT, SIR! YOU'RE A GOOD FRIEND TO GAYS!
UM... NO, NO, I'M NOT!
DON'T BE MODEST, SIR! YOU HAVE **TRUE** POLITICAL COURAGE!
NO, NO, I **DON'T!** REALLY, **NONE!**

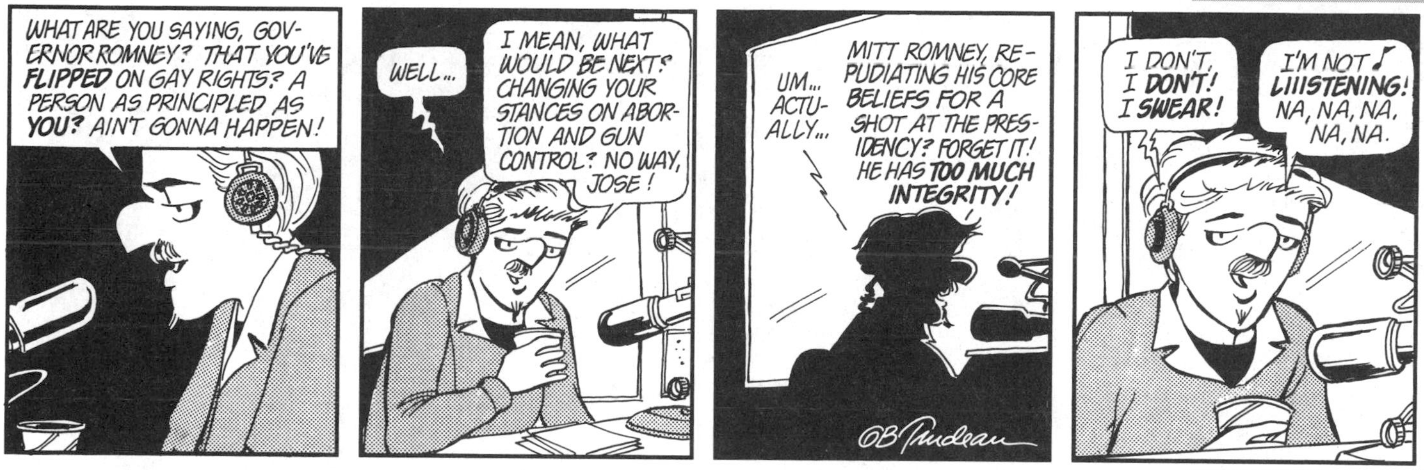
WHAT ARE YOU SAYING, GOVERNOR ROMNEY? THAT YOU'VE **FLIPPED** ON GAY RIGHTS? A PERSON AS PRINCIPLED AS **YOU?** AIN'T GONNA HAPPEN!
WELL...
I MEAN, WHAT WOULD BE NEXT? CHANGING YOUR STANCES ON ABORTION AND GUN CONTROL? NO WAY, JOSE!
UM... ACTUALLY...
MITT ROMNEY, REPUDIATING HIS CORE BELIEFS FOR A SHOT AT THE PRESIDENCY? FORGET IT! HE HAS **TOO MUCH INTEGRITY!**
I DON'T, I **DON'T!** I **SWEAR!**
I'M NOT ♪ **LIIISTENING!** NA, NA, NA, NA, NA.

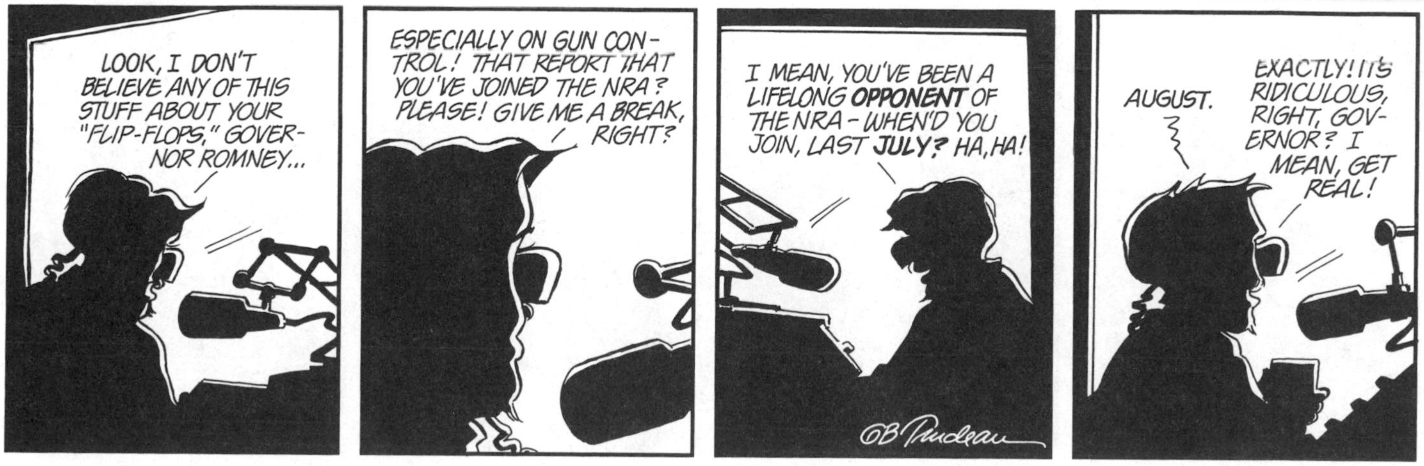
LOOK, I DON'T BELIEVE ANY OF THIS STUFF ABOUT YOUR "FLIP-FLOPS," GOVERNOR ROMNEY...
ESPECIALLY ON GUN CONTROL! THAT REPORT THAT YOU'VE JOINED THE NRA? PLEASE! GIVE ME A BREAK, RIGHT?
I MEAN, YOU'VE BEEN A LIFELONG **OPPONENT** OF THE NRA – WHEN'D YOU JOIN, LAST **JULY?** HA, HA!
AUGUST.
EXACTLY! IT'S RIDICULOUS, RIGHT, GOVERNOR? I MEAN, GET REAL!

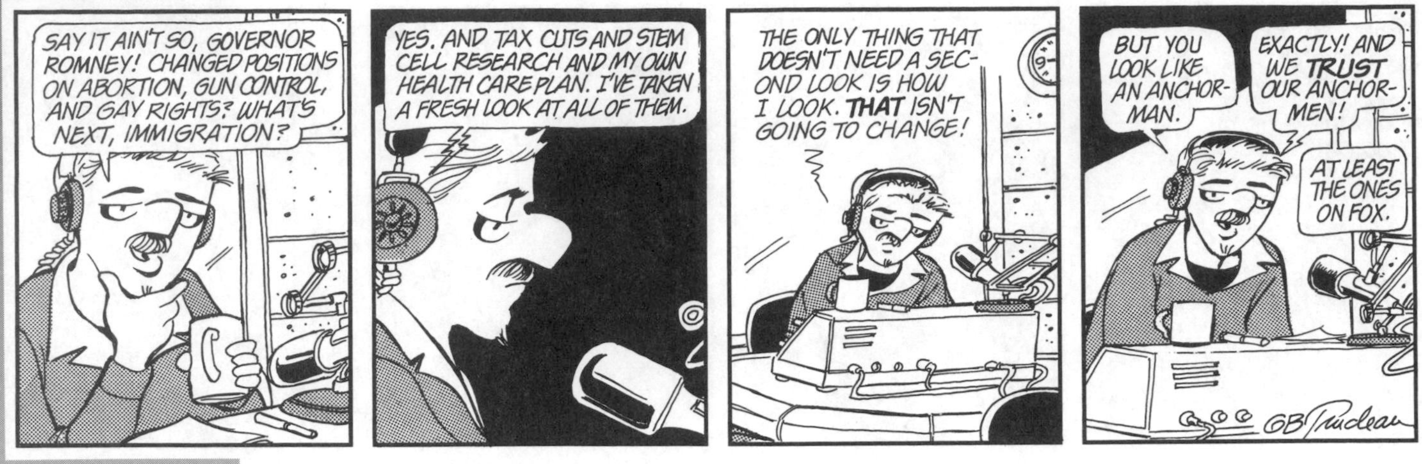
SAY IT AIN'T SO, GOVERNOR ROMNEY! CHANGED POSITIONS ON ABORTION, GUN CONTROL, AND GAY RIGHTS? WHAT'S NEXT, IMMIGRATION?
YES. AND TAX CUTS AND STEM CELL RESEARCH AND MY OWN HEALTH CARE PLAN. I'VE TAKEN A FRESH LOOK AT ALL OF THEM.
THE ONLY THING THAT DOESN'T NEED A SECOND LOOK IS HOW I LOOK. THAT ISN'T GOING TO CHANGE!
BUT YOU LOOK LIKE AN ANCHORMAN.
EXACTLY! AND WE TRUST OUR ANCHORMEN!
AT LEAST THE ONES ON FOX.
GB Trudeau

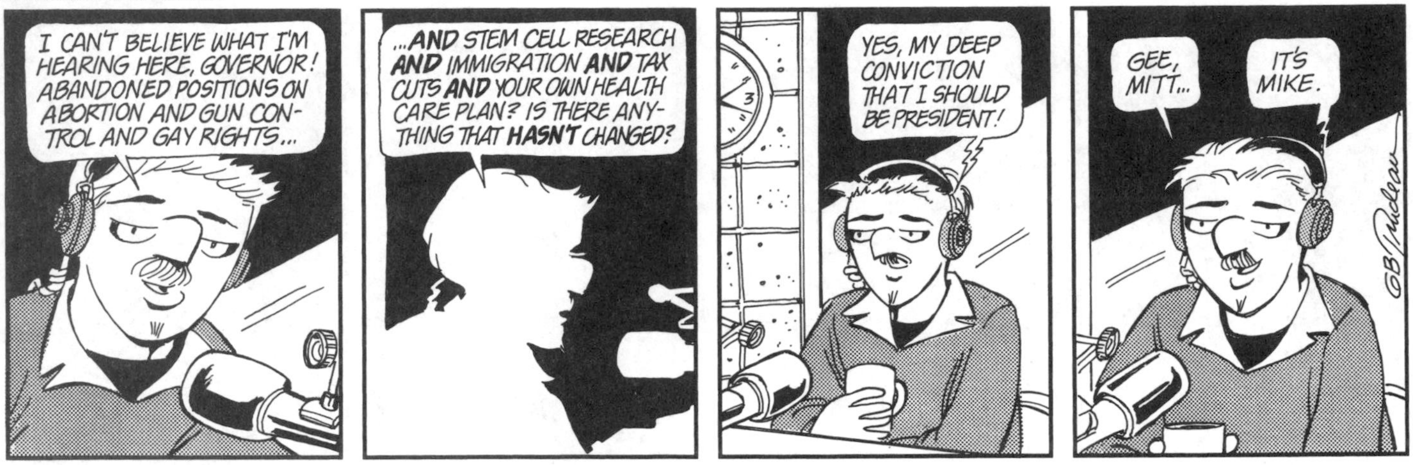
I CAN'T BELIEVE WHAT I'M HEARING HERE, GOVERNOR! ABANDONED POSITIONS ON ABORTION AND GUN CONTROL AND GAY RIGHTS...
...AND STEM CELL RESEARCH AND IMMIGRATION AND TAX CUTS AND YOUR OWN HEALTH CARE PLAN? IS THERE ANYTHING THAT HASN'T CHANGED?
YES, MY DEEP CONVICTION THAT I SHOULD BE PRESIDENT!
GEE, MITT...
IT'S MIKE.
GB Trudeau

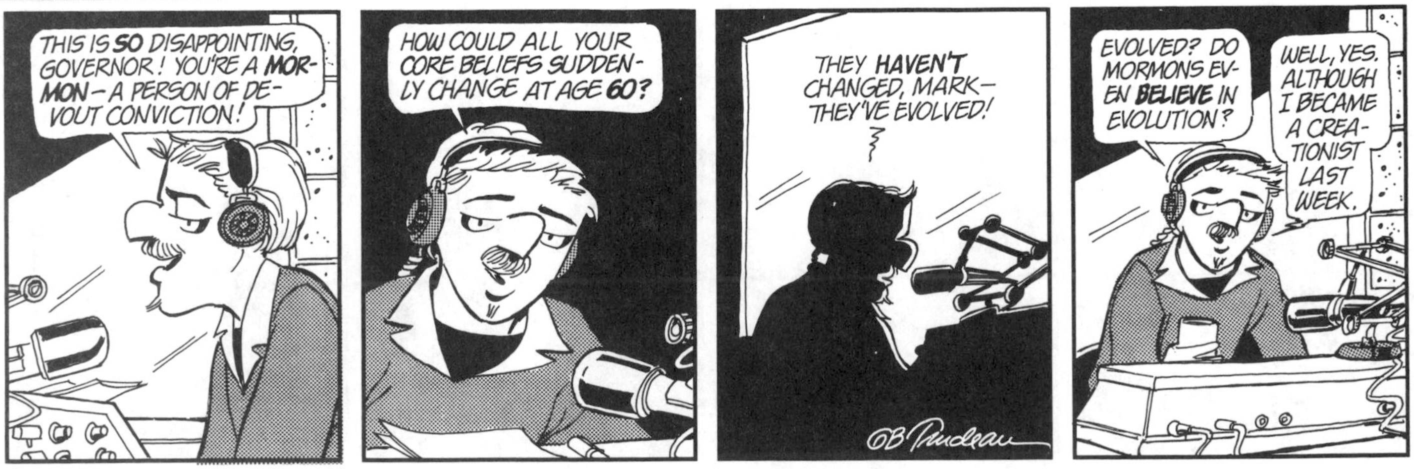
THIS IS SO DISAPPOINTING, GOVERNOR! YOU'RE A MORMON – A PERSON OF DEVOUT CONVICTION!
HOW COULD ALL YOUR CORE BELIEFS SUDDENLY CHANGE AT AGE 60?
THEY HAVEN'T CHANGED, MARK – THEY'VE EVOLVED!
GB Trudeau
EVOLVED? DO MORMONS EVEN BELIEVE IN EVOLUTION?
WELL, YES. ALTHOUGH I BECAME A CREATIONIST LAST WEEK.

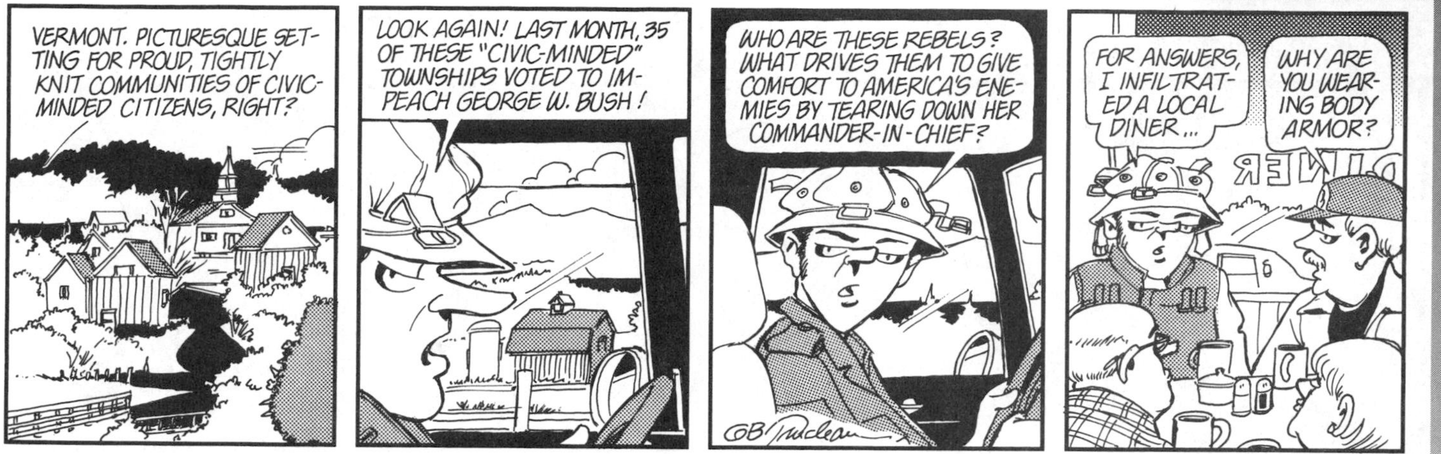
VERMONT. PICTURESQUE SETTING FOR PROUD, TIGHTLY KNIT COMMUNITIES OF CIVIC-MINDED CITIZENS, RIGHT?
LOOK AGAIN! LAST MONTH, 35 OF THESE "CIVIC-MINDED" TOWNSHIPS VOTED TO IMPEACH GEORGE W. BUSH!
WHO ARE THESE REBELS? WHAT DRIVES THEM TO GIVE COMFORT TO AMERICA'S ENEMIES BY TEARING DOWN HER COMMANDER-IN-CHIEF?
GB Trudeau
FOR ANSWERS, I INFILTRATED A LOCAL DINER...
WHY ARE YOU WEARING BODY ARMOR?
DINER

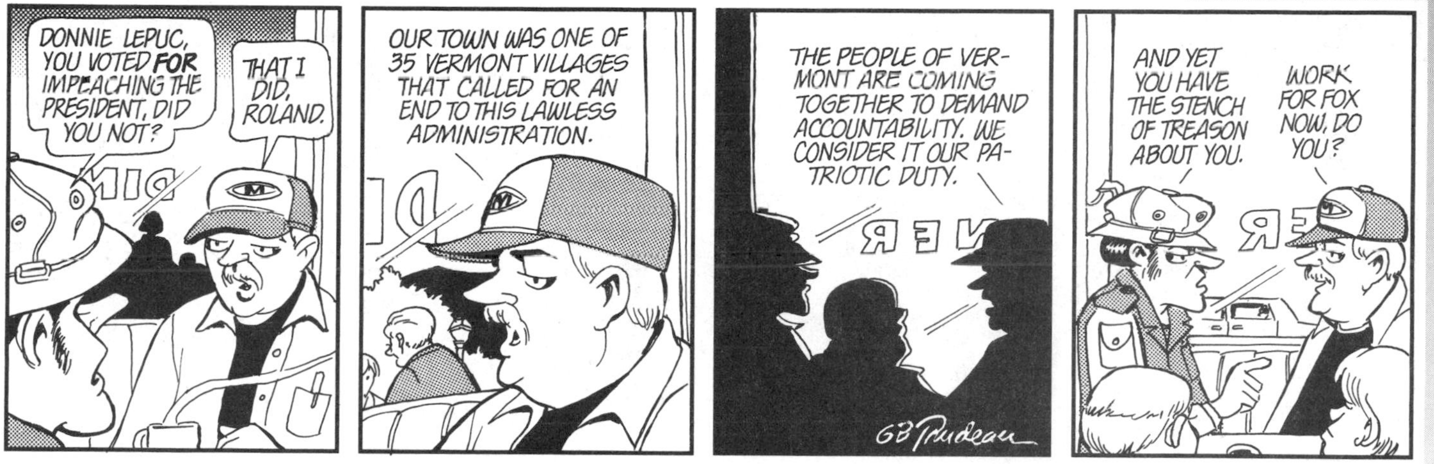
DONNIE LEPUC, YOU VOTED **FOR** IMPEACHING THE PRESIDENT, DID YOU NOT?
THAT I DID, ROLAND.
OUR TOWN WAS ONE OF 35 VERMONT VILLAGES THAT CALLED FOR AN END TO THIS LAWLESS ADMINISTRATION.
THE PEOPLE OF VERMONT ARE COMING TOGETHER TO DEMAND ACCOUNTABILITY. WE CONSIDER IT OUR PATRIOTIC DUTY.
GB Trudeau
AND YET YOU HAVE THE STENCH OF TREASON ABOUT YOU.
WORK FOR FOX NOW, DO YOU?

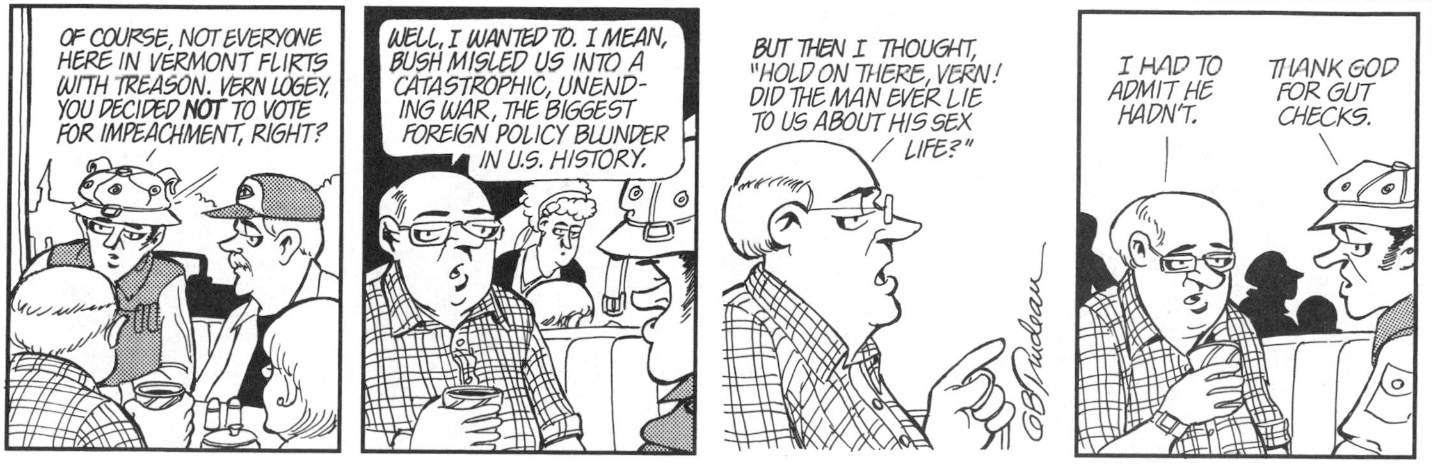
OF COURSE, NOT EVERYONE HERE IN VERMONT FLIRTS WITH TREASON. VERN LOGEY, YOU DECIDED **NOT** TO VOTE FOR IMPEACHMENT, RIGHT?
WELL, I WANTED TO. I MEAN, BUSH MISLED US INTO A CATASTROPHIC, UNENDING WAR, THE BIGGEST FOREIGN POLICY BLUNDER IN U.S. HISTORY.
BUT THEN I THOUGHT, "HOLD ON THERE, VERN! DID THE MAN EVER LIE TO US ABOUT HIS SEX LIFE?"
GB Trudeau
I HAD TO ADMIT HE HADN'T.
THANK GOD FOR GUT CHECKS.

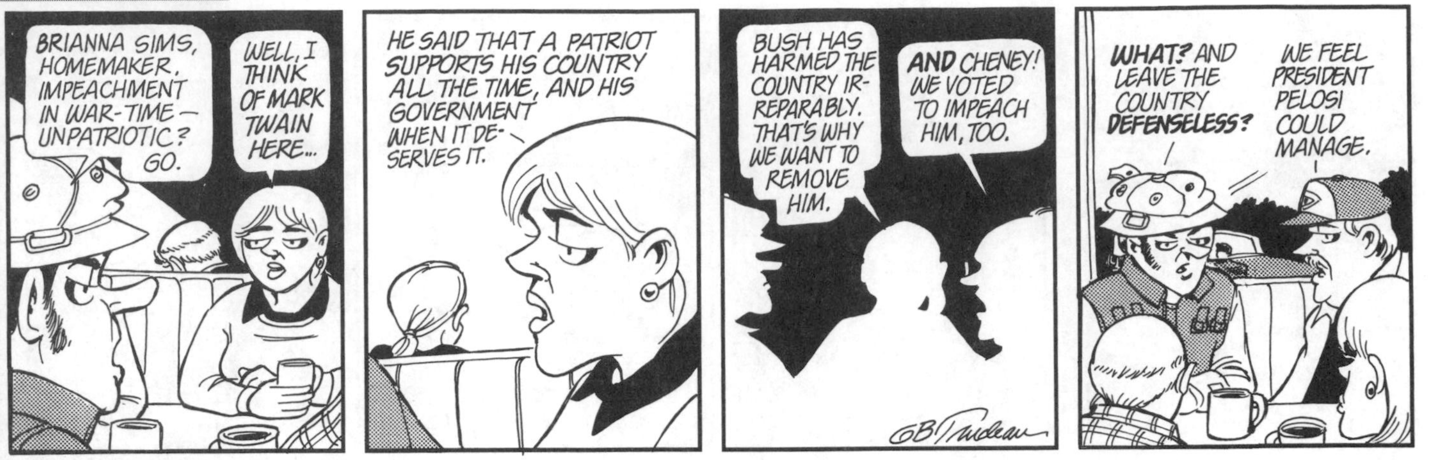
BRIANNA SIMS, HOMEMAKER. IMPEACHMENT IN WAR-TIME — UNPATRIOTIC? GO.
WELL, I THINK OF MARK TWAIN HERE...
HE SAID THAT A PATRIOT SUPPORTS HIS COUNTRY ALL THE TIME, AND HIS GOVERNMENT WHEN IT DESERVES IT.
BUSH HAS HARMED THE COUNTRY IRREPARABLY. THAT'S WHY WE WANT TO REMOVE HIM.
AND CHENEY! WE VOTED TO IMPEACH HIM, TOO.
WHAT? AND LEAVE THE COUNTRY DEFENSELESS?
WE FEEL PRESIDENT PELOSI COULD MANAGE.

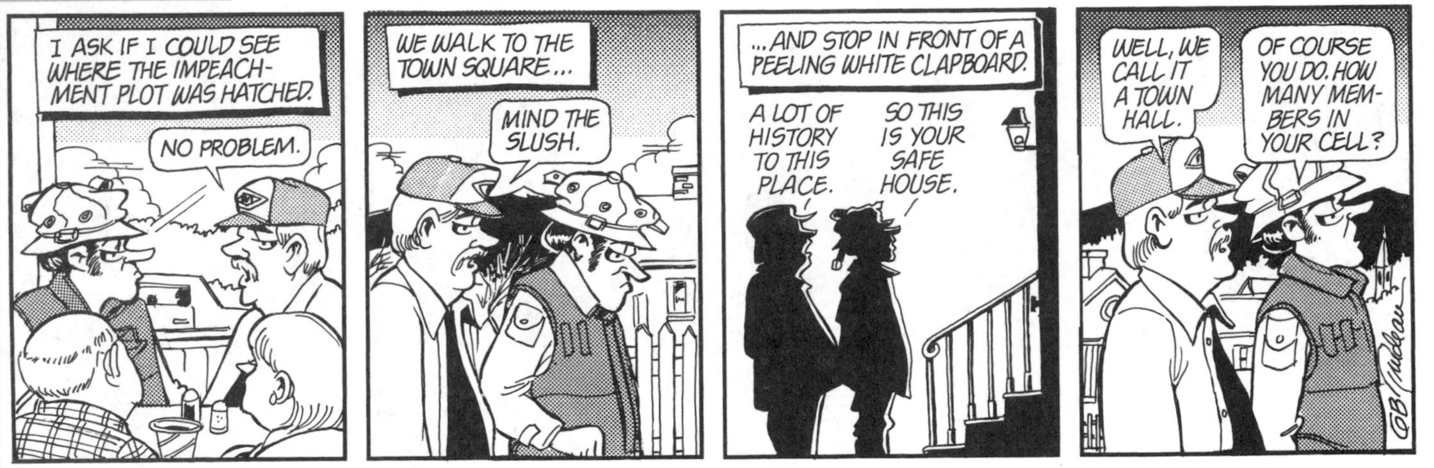
I ASK IF I COULD SEE WHERE THE IMPEACHMENT PLOT WAS HATCHED.
NO PROBLEM.
WE WALK TO THE TOWN SQUARE...
MIND THE SLUSH.
...AND STOP IN FRONT OF A PEELING WHITE CLAPBOARD.
A LOT OF HISTORY TO THIS PLACE.
SO THIS IS YOUR SAFE HOUSE.
WELL, WE CALL IT A TOWN HALL.
OF COURSE YOU DO. HOW MANY MEMBERS IN YOUR CELL?

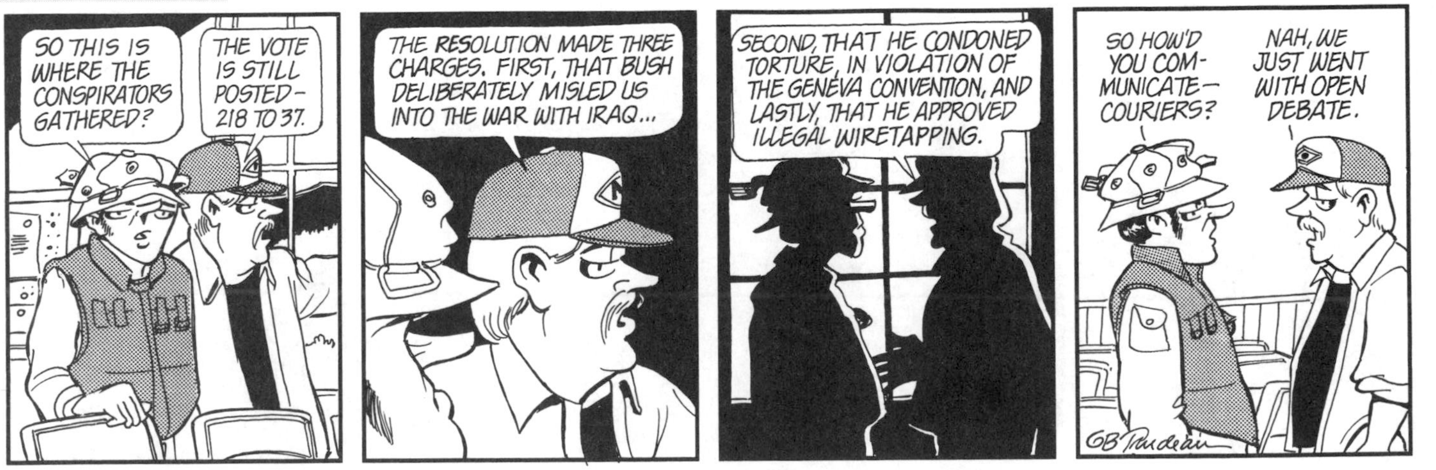
SO THIS IS WHERE THE CONSPIRATORS GATHERED?
THE VOTE IS STILL POSTED — 218 TO 37.
THE RESOLUTION MADE THREE CHARGES. FIRST, THAT BUSH DELIBERATELY MISLED US INTO THE WAR WITH IRAQ...
SECOND, THAT HE CONDONED TORTURE, IN VIOLATION OF THE GENEVA CONVENTION, AND LASTLY, THAT HE APPROVED ILLEGAL WIRETAPPING.
SO HOW'D YOU COMMUNICATE — COURIERS?
NAH, WE JUST WENT WITH OPEN DEBATE.

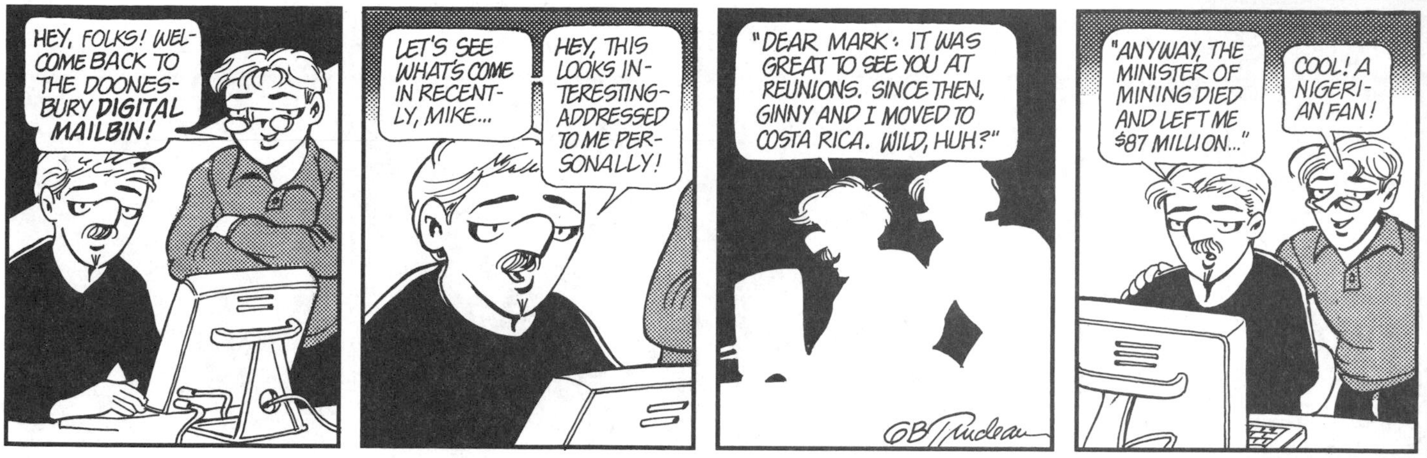
HEY, FOLKS! WELCOME BACK TO THE DOONESBURY DIGITAL MAILBIN!
LET'S SEE WHAT'S COME IN RECENTLY, MIKE...
HEY, THIS LOOKS INTERESTING–ADDRESSED TO ME PERSONALLY!
"DEAR MARK: IT WAS GREAT TO SEE YOU AT REUNIONS. SINCE THEN, GINNY AND I MOVED TO COSTA RICA. WILD, HUH?"
"ANYWAY, THE MINISTER OF MINING DIED AND LEFT ME $87 MILLION..."
COOL! A NIGERIAN FAN!
GB Trudeau

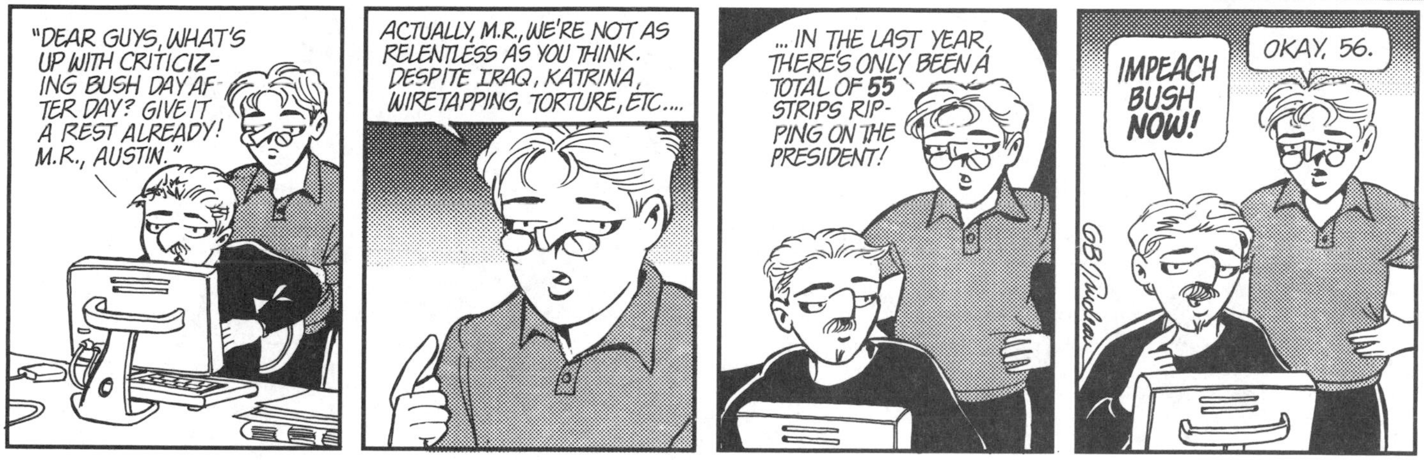
"DEAR GUYS, WHAT'S UP WITH CRITICIZING BUSH DAY AFTER DAY? GIVE IT A REST ALREADY! M.R., AUSTIN."
ACTUALLY, M.R., WE'RE NOT AS RELENTLESS AS YOU THINK. DESPITE IRAQ, KATRINA, WIRETAPPING, TORTURE, ETC....
... IN THE LAST YEAR, THERE'S ONLY BEEN A TOTAL OF 55 STRIPS RIPPING ON THE PRESIDENT!
IMPEACH BUSH NOW!
OKAY, 56.
GB Trudeau

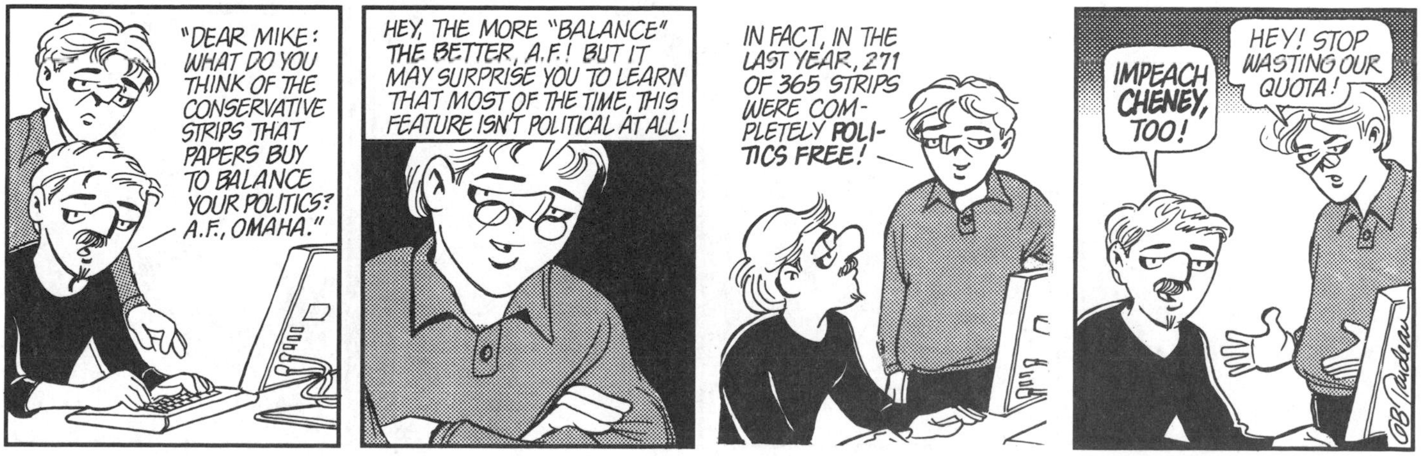
"DEAR MIKE: WHAT DO YOU THINK OF THE CONSERVATIVE STRIPS THAT PAPERS BUY TO BALANCE YOUR POLITICS? A.F., OMAHA."
HEY, THE MORE "BALANCE" THE BETTER, A.F.! BUT IT MAY SURPRISE YOU TO LEARN THAT MOST OF THE TIME, THIS FEATURE ISN'T POLITICAL AT ALL!
IN FACT, IN THE LAST YEAR, 271 OF 365 STRIPS WERE COMPLETELY POLITICS FREE!
IMPEACH CHENEY, TOO!
HEY! STOP WASTING OUR QUOTA!
GB Trudeau

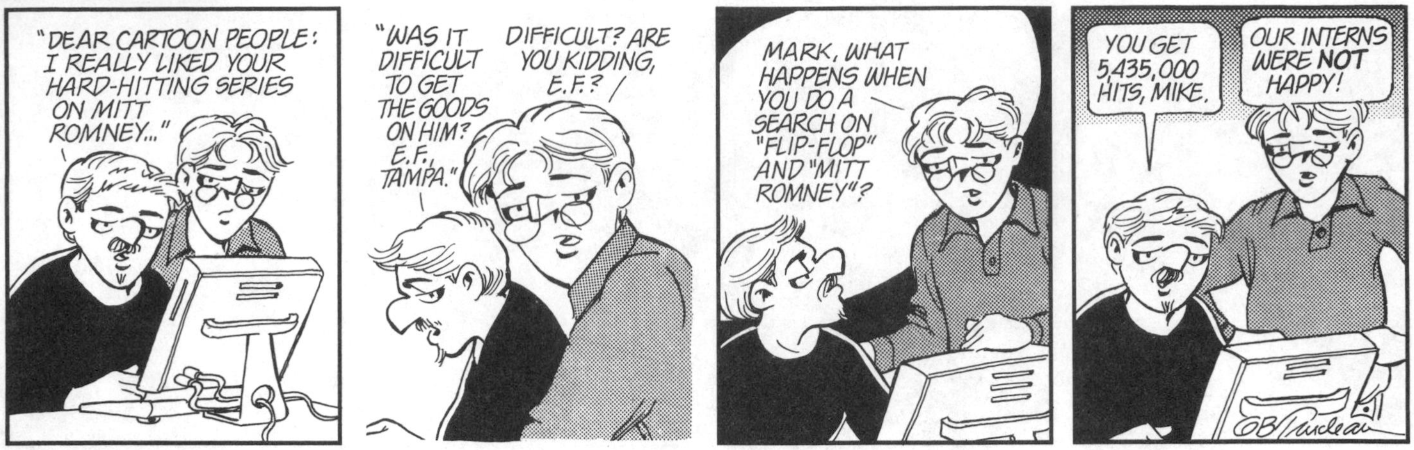
"DEAR CARTOON PEOPLE: I REALLY LIKED YOUR HARD-HITTING SERIES ON MITT ROMNEY..."
"WAS IT DIFFICULT TO GET THE GOODS ON HIM? E.F., TAMPA."
DIFFICULT? ARE YOU KIDDING, E.F.?
MARK, WHAT HAPPENS WHEN YOU DO A SEARCH ON "FLIP-FLOP" AND "MITT ROMNEY"?
YOU GET 5,435,000 HITS, MIKE.
OUR INTERNS WERE **NOT** HAPPY!

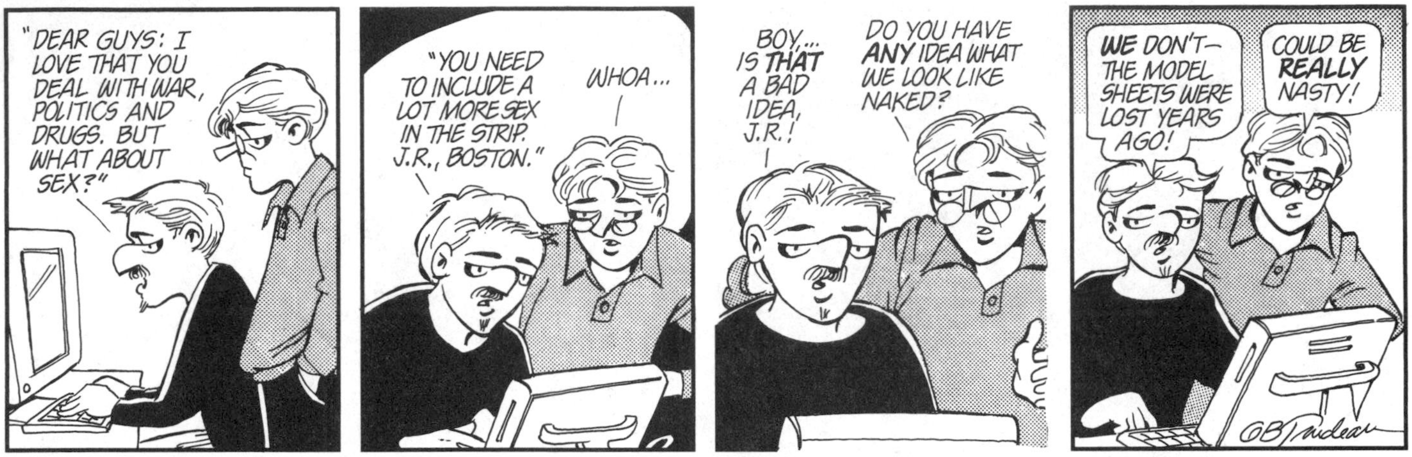
"DEAR GUYS: I LOVE THAT YOU DEAL WITH WAR, POLITICS AND DRUGS. BUT WHAT ABOUT SEX?"
"YOU NEED TO INCLUDE A LOT MORE SEX IN THE STRIP. J.R., BOSTON."
WHOA...
BOY,... IS **THAT** A BAD IDEA, J.R.!
DO YOU HAVE **ANY** IDEA WHAT WE LOOK LIKE NAKED?
WE DON'T— THE MODEL SHEETS WERE LOST YEARS AGO!
COULD BE **REALLY** NASTY!

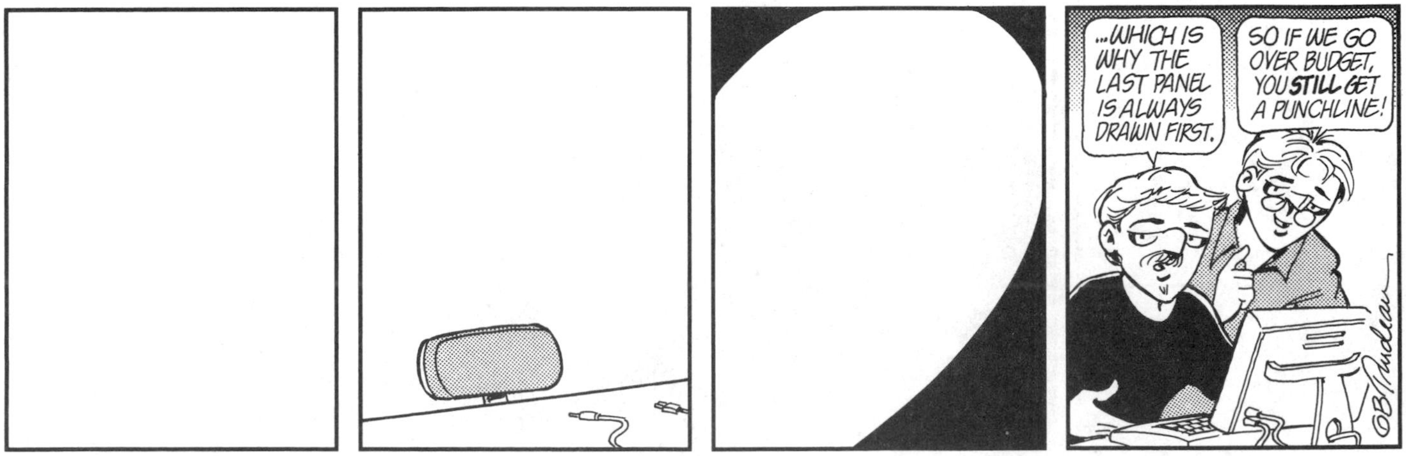
...WHICH IS WHY THE LAST PANEL IS ALWAYS DRAWN FIRST.
SO IF WE GO OVER BUDGET, YOU **STILL** GET A PUNCHLINE!

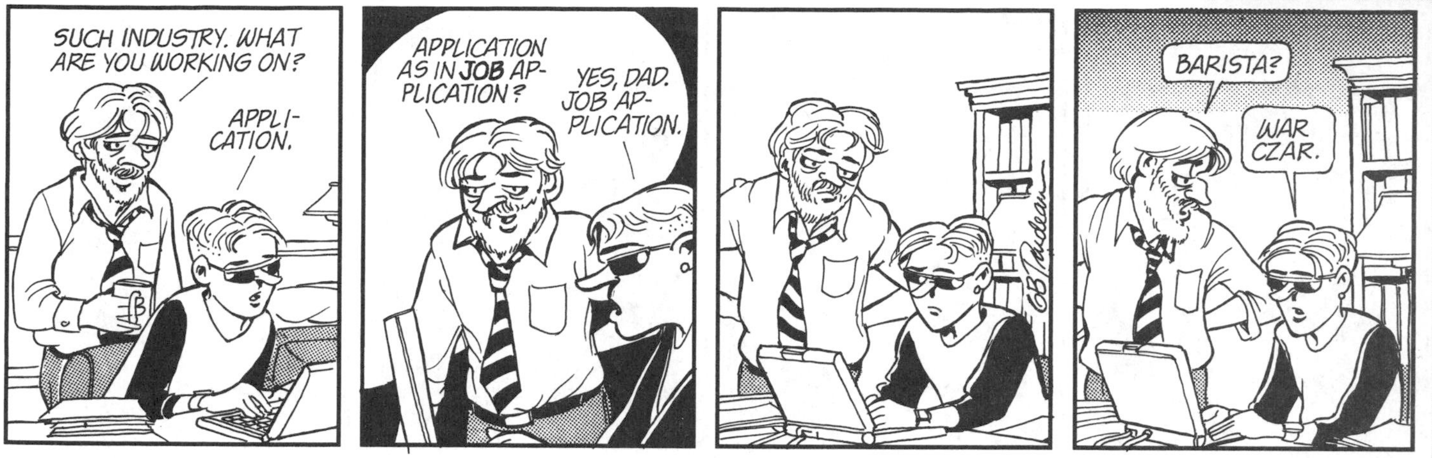
SUCH INDUSTRY. WHAT ARE YOU WORKING ON?
APPLI-CATION.
APPLICATION AS IN JOB AP-PLICATION?
YES, DAD. JOB AP-PLICATION.
BARISTA?
WAR CZAR.

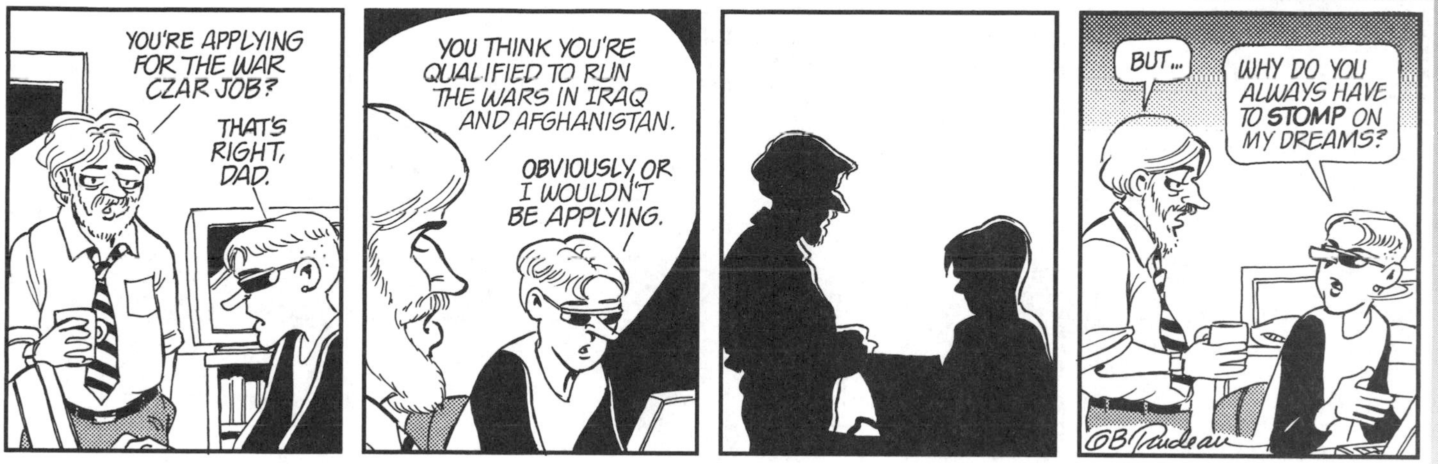
YOU'RE APPLYING FOR THE WAR CZAR JOB?
THAT'S RIGHT, DAD.
YOU THINK YOU'RE QUALIFIED TO RUN THE WARS IN IRAQ AND AFGHANISTAN.
OBVIOUSLY, OR I WOULDN'T BE APPLYING.
BUT...
WHY DO YOU ALWAYS HAVE TO STOMP ON MY DREAMS?

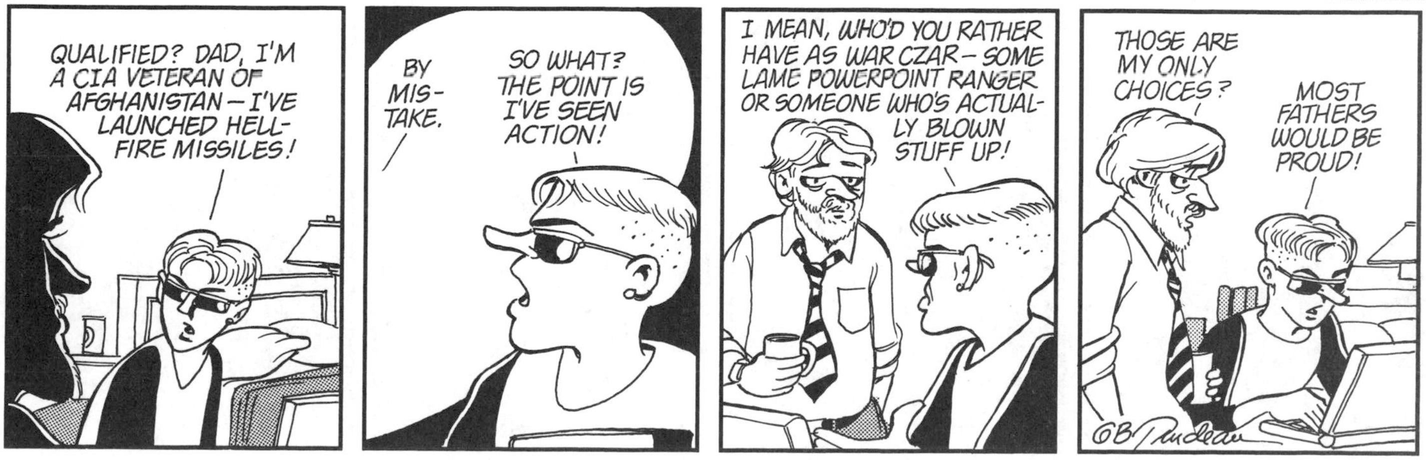
QUALIFIED? DAD, I'M A CIA VETERAN OF AFGHANISTAN – I'VE LAUNCHED HELL-FIRE MISSILES!
BY MIS-TAKE.
SO WHAT? THE POINT IS I'VE SEEN ACTION!
I MEAN, WHO'D YOU RATHER HAVE AS WAR CZAR – SOME LAME POWERPOINT RANGER OR SOMEONE WHO'S ACTUAL-LY BLOWN STUFF UP!
THOSE ARE MY ONLY CHOICES?
MOST FATHERS WOULD BE PROUD!

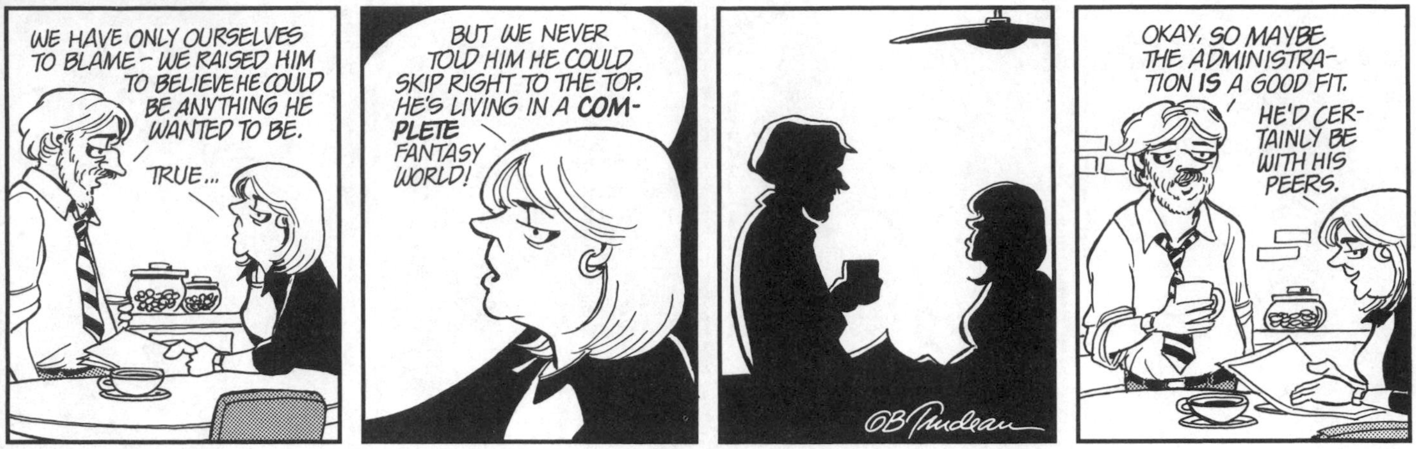
WE HAVE ONLY OURSELVES TO BLAME – WE RAISED HIM TO BELIEVE HE COULD BE ANYTHING HE WANTED TO BE.
TRUE...
BUT WE NEVER TOLD HIM HE COULD SKIP RIGHT TO THE TOP. HE'S LIVING IN A **COMPLETE** FANTASY WORLD!
OKAY, SO MAYBE THE ADMINISTRATION **IS** A GOOD FIT.
HE'D CERTAINLY BE WITH HIS PEERS.

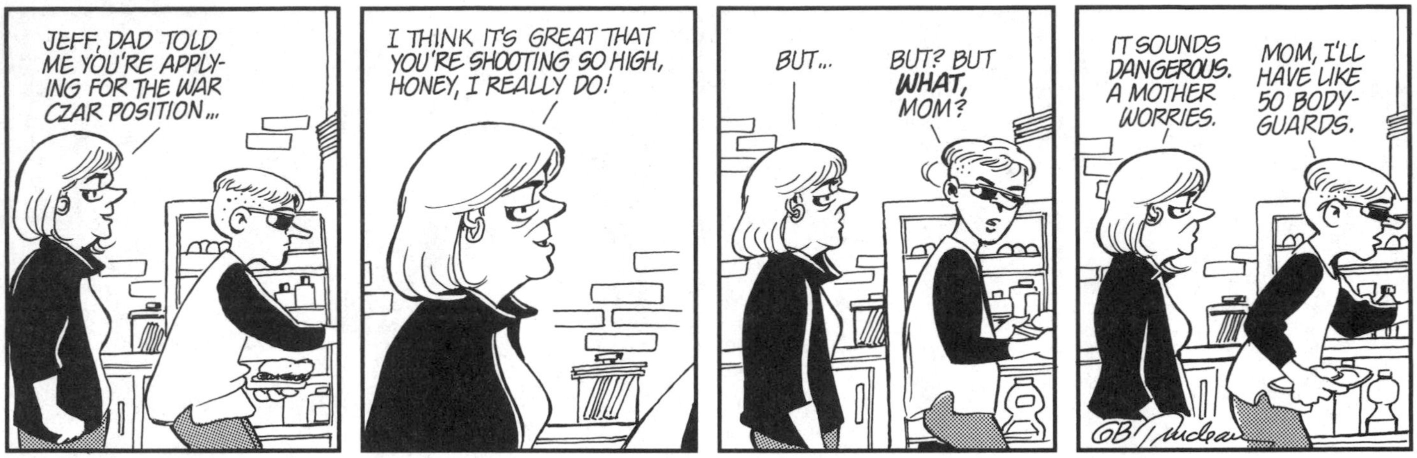
JEFF, DAD TOLD ME YOU'RE APPLYING FOR THE WAR CZAR POSITION...
I THINK IT'S GREAT THAT YOU'RE SHOOTING SO HIGH, HONEY, I REALLY DO!
BUT...
BUT? BUT **WHAT,** MOM?
IT SOUNDS **DANGEROUS.** A MOTHER WORRIES.
MOM, I'LL HAVE LIKE 50 BODYGUARDS.

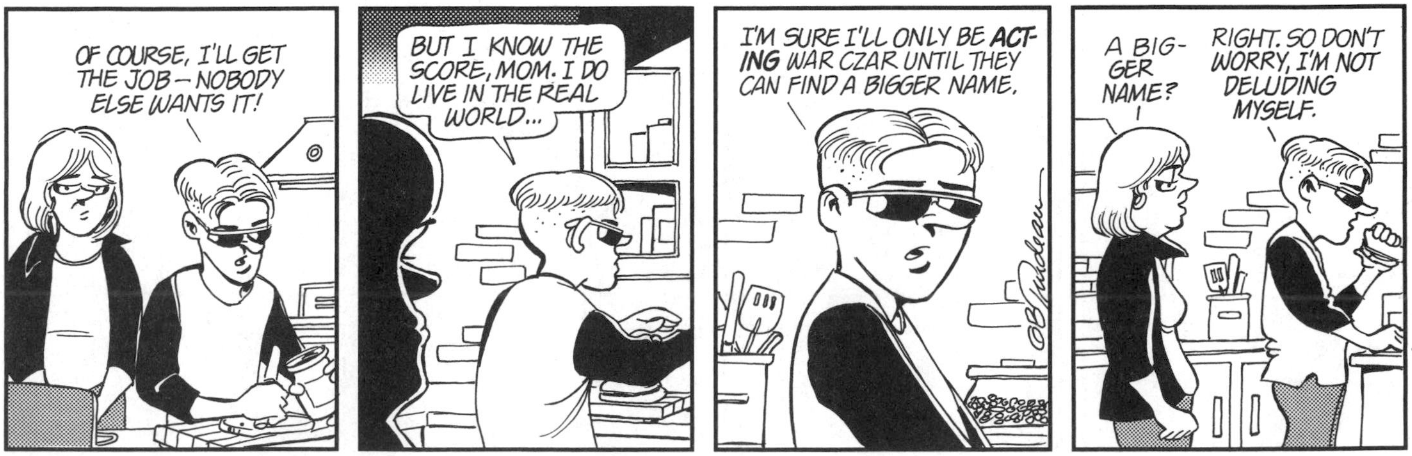
OF COURSE, I'LL GET THE JOB – NOBODY ELSE WANTS IT!
BUT I KNOW THE SCORE, MOM. I DO LIVE IN THE REAL WORLD...
I'M SURE I'LL ONLY BE **ACTING** WAR CZAR UNTIL THEY CAN FIND A BIGGER NAME.
A BIGGER NAME?
RIGHT. SO DON'T WORRY, I'M NOT DELUDING MYSELF.

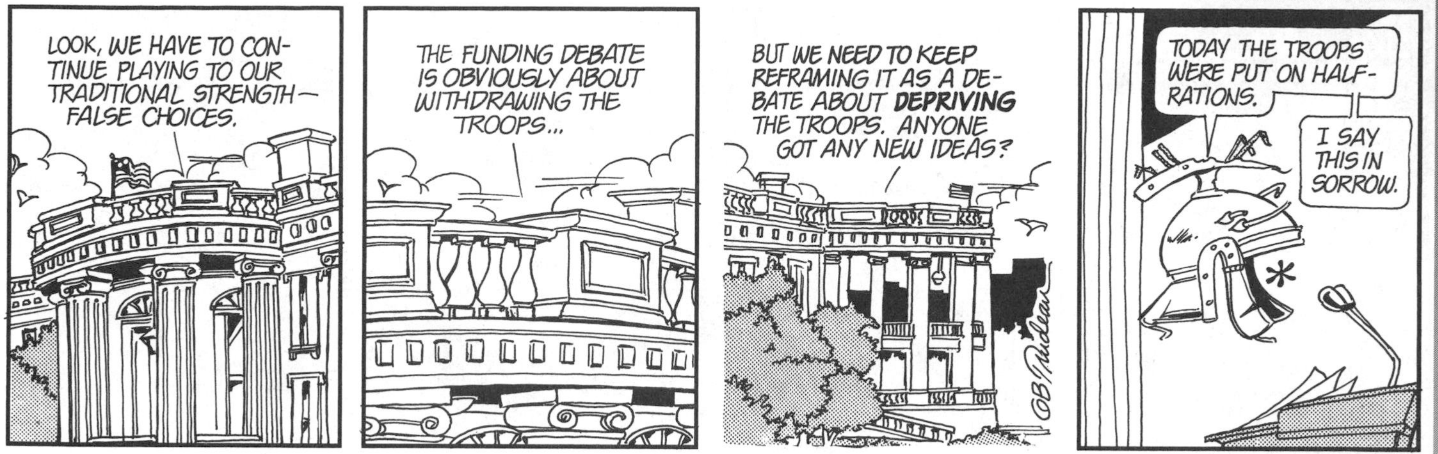
LOOK, WE HAVE TO CONTINUE PLAYING TO OUR TRADITIONAL STRENGTH— FALSE CHOICES.
THE FUNDING DEBATE IS OBVIOUSLY ABOUT WITHDRAWING THE TROOPS...
BUT WE NEED TO KEEP REFRAMING IT AS A DEBATE ABOUT **DEPRIVING** THE TROOPS. ANYONE GOT ANY NEW IDEAS?
TODAY THE TROOPS WERE PUT ON HALF-RATIONS.
I SAY THIS IN SORROW.

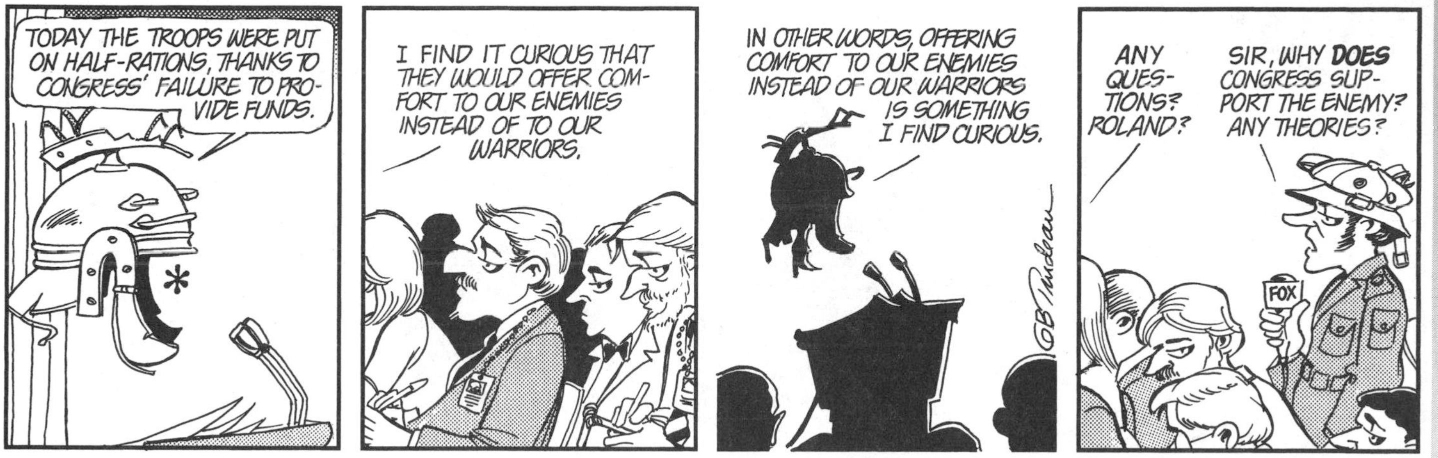
TODAY THE TROOPS WERE PUT ON HALF-RATIONS, THANKS TO CONGRESS' FAILURE TO PROVIDE FUNDS.
I FIND IT CURIOUS THAT THEY WOULD OFFER COMFORT TO OUR ENEMIES INSTEAD OF TO OUR WARRIORS.
IN OTHER WORDS, OFFERING COMFORT TO OUR ENEMIES INSTEAD OF OUR WARRIORS IS SOMETHING I FIND CURIOUS.
ANY QUESTIONS? ROLAND?
SIR, WHY **DOES** CONGRESS SUPPORT THE ENEMY? ANY THEORIES?
FOX

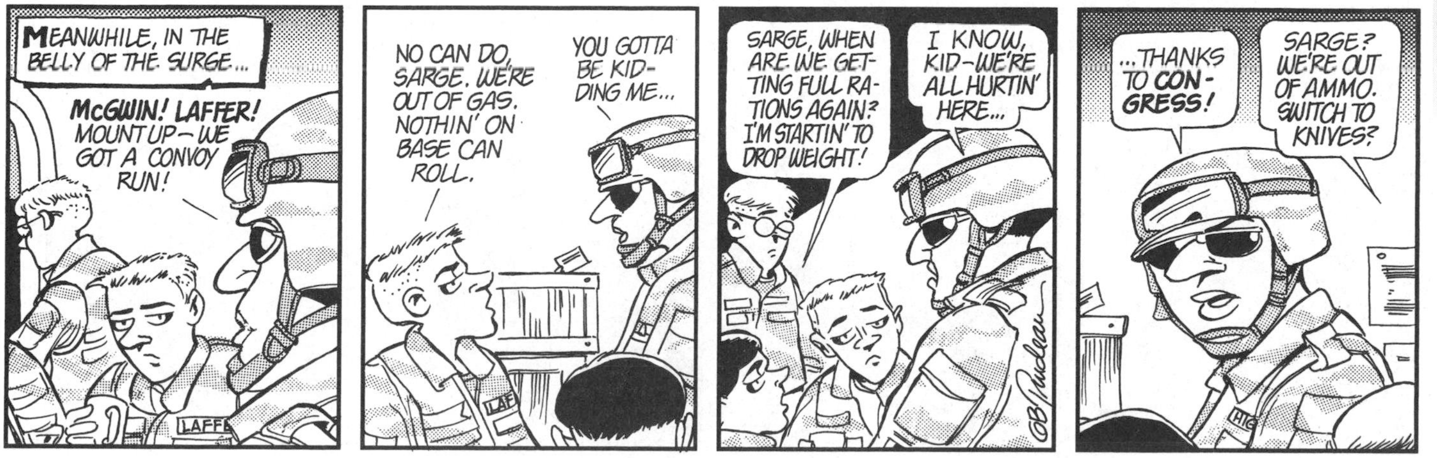
MEANWHILE, IN THE BELLY OF THE SURGE...
McGWIN! LAFFER! MOUNT UP—WE GOT A CONVOY RUN!
NO CAN DO, SARGE. WE'RE OUT OF GAS. NOTHIN' ON BASE CAN ROLL.
YOU GOTTA BE KIDDING ME...
SARGE, WHEN ARE WE GETTING FULL RATIONS AGAIN? I'M STARTIN' TO DROP WEIGHT!
I KNOW, KID—WE'RE ALL HURTIN' HERE...
...THANKS TO **CONGRESS!**
SARGE? WE'RE OUT OF AMMO. SWITCH TO KNIVES?

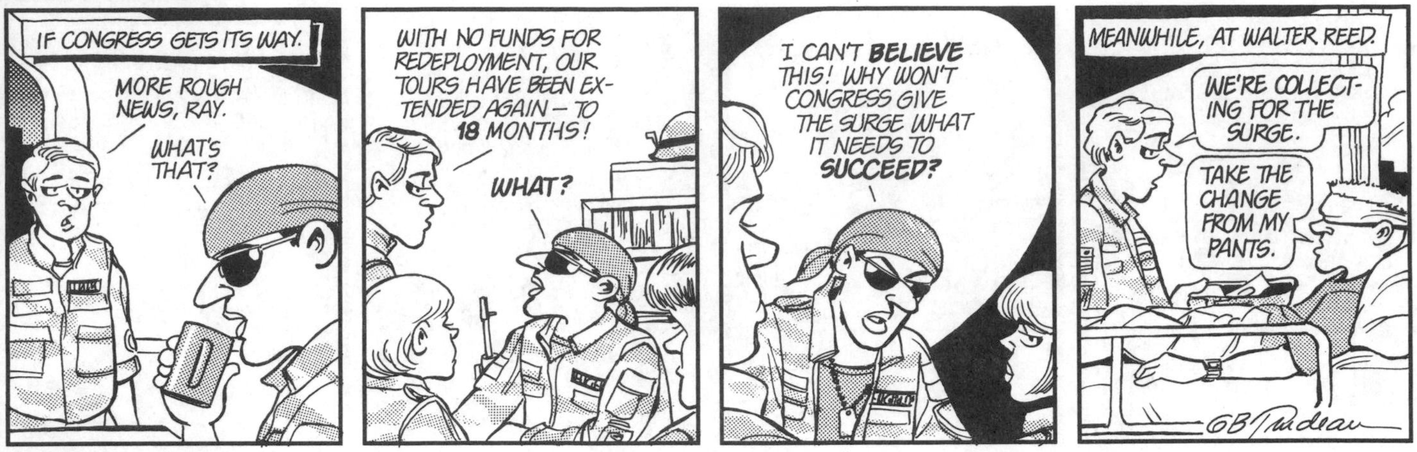
IF CONGRESS GETS ITS WAY.
MORE ROUGH NEWS, RAY.
WHAT'S THAT?
WITH NO FUNDS FOR REDEPLOYMENT, OUR TOURS HAVE BEEN EXTENDED AGAIN — TO 18 MONTHS!
WHAT?
I CAN'T BELIEVE THIS! WHY WON'T CONGRESS GIVE THE SURGE WHAT IT NEEDS TO SUCCEED?
MEANWHILE, AT WALTER REED.
WE'RE COLLECTING FOR THE SURGE.
TAKE THE CHANGE FROM MY PANTS.

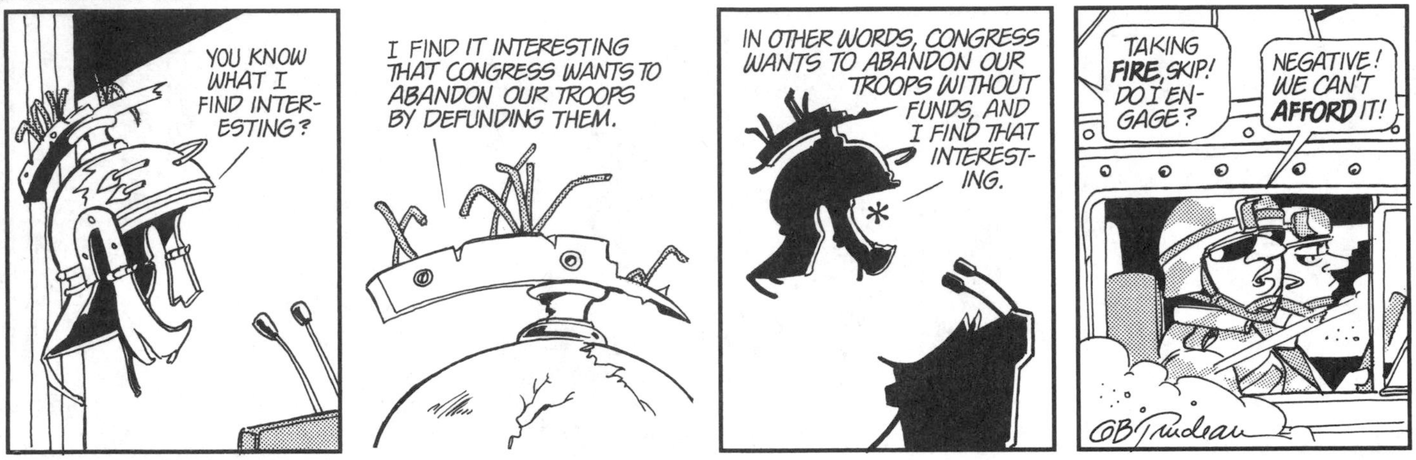
YOU KNOW WHAT I FIND INTERESTING?
I FIND IT INTERESTING THAT CONGRESS WANTS TO ABANDON OUR TROOPS BY DEFUNDING THEM.
IN OTHER WORDS, CONGRESS WANTS TO ABANDON OUR TROOPS WITHOUT FUNDS, AND I FIND THAT INTERESTING.
TAKING FIRE, SKIP! DO I ENGAGE?
NEGATIVE! WE CAN'T AFFORD IT!

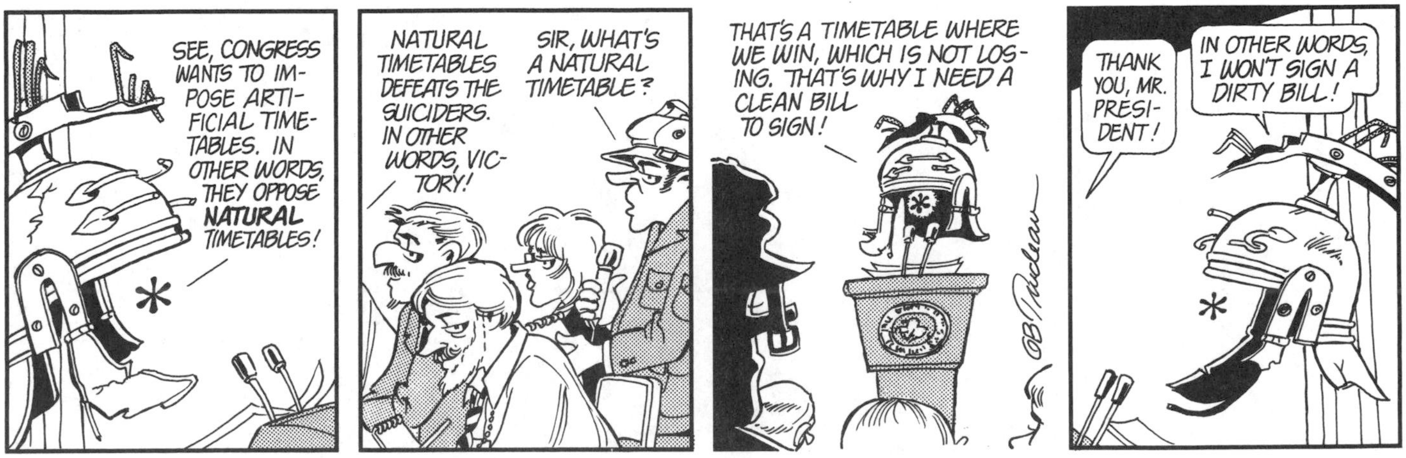
SEE, CONGRESS WANTS TO IMPOSE ARTIFICIAL TIMETABLES. IN OTHER WORDS, THEY OPPOSE NATURAL TIMETABLES!
NATURAL TIMETABLES DEFEATS THE SUICIDERS. IN OTHER WORDS, VICTORY!
SIR, WHAT'S A NATURAL TIMETABLE?
THAT'S A TIMETABLE WHERE WE WIN, WHICH IS NOT LOSING. THAT'S WHY I NEED A CLEAN BILL TO SIGN!
THANK YOU, MR. PRESIDENT!
IN OTHER WORDS, I WON'T SIGN A DIRTY BILL!

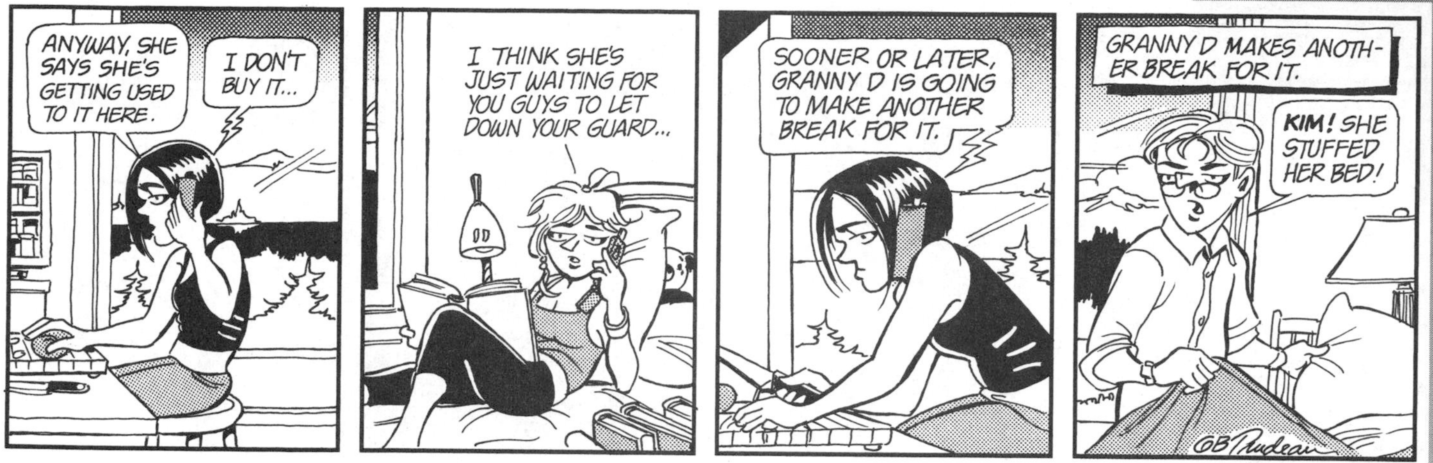
ANYWAY, SHE SAYS SHE'S GETTING USED TO IT HERE.
I DON'T BUY IT...
I THINK SHE'S JUST WAITING FOR YOU GUYS TO LET DOWN YOUR GUARD...
SOONER OR LATER, GRANNY D IS GOING TO MAKE ANOTHER BREAK FOR IT.
GRANNY D MAKES ANOTHER BREAK FOR IT.
KIM! SHE STUFFED HER BED!
GB Trudeau

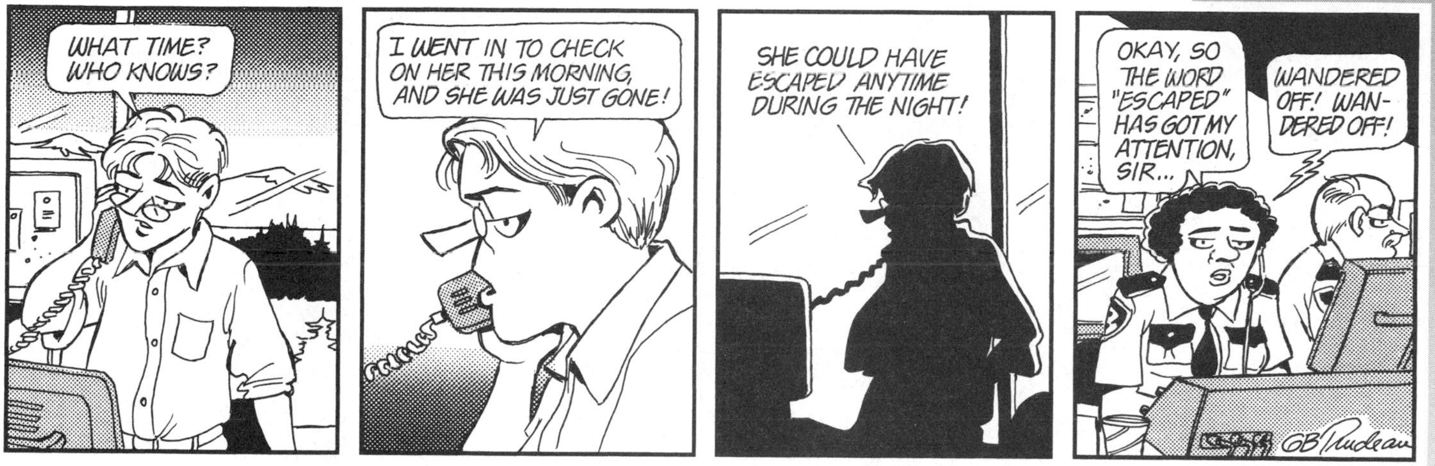
WHAT TIME? WHO KNOWS?
I WENT IN TO CHECK ON HER THIS MORNING, AND SHE WAS JUST GONE!
SHE COULD HAVE ESCAPED ANYTIME DURING THE NIGHT!
OKAY, SO THE WORD "ESCAPED" HAS GOT MY ATTENTION, SIR...
WANDERED OFF! WANDERED OFF!
GB Trudeau

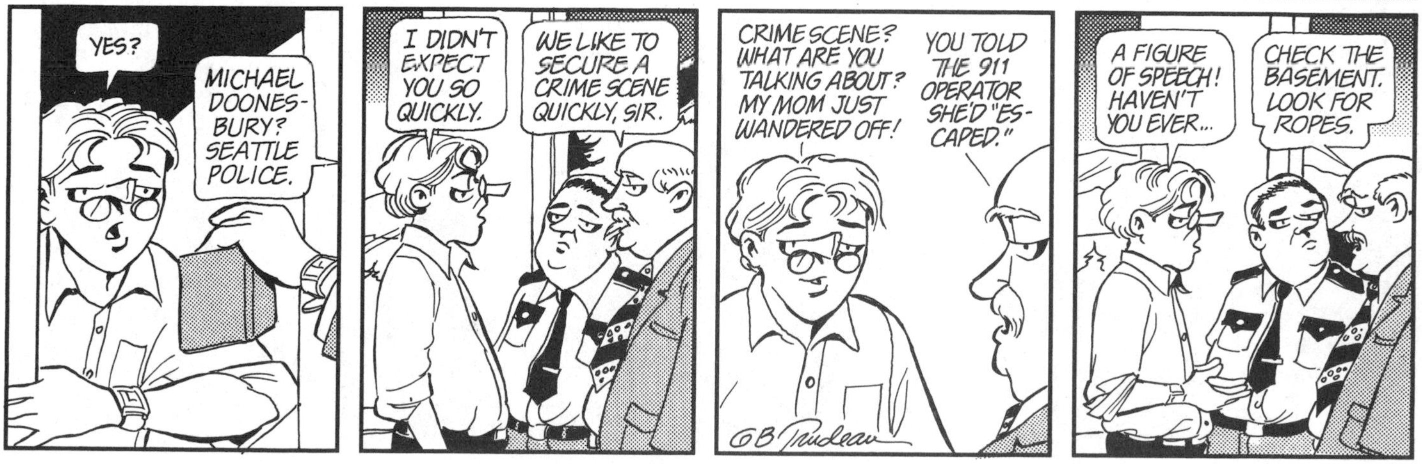
YES?
MICHAEL DOONESBURY? SEATTLE POLICE.
I DIDN'T EXPECT YOU SO QUICKLY.
WE LIKE TO SECURE A CRIME SCENE QUICKLY, SIR.
CRIME SCENE? WHAT ARE YOU TALKING ABOUT? MY MOM JUST WANDERED OFF!
YOU TOLD THE 911 OPERATOR SHE'D "ESCAPED."
GB Trudeau
A FIGURE OF SPEECH! HAVEN'T YOU EVER...
CHECK THE BASEMENT. LOOK FOR ROPES.

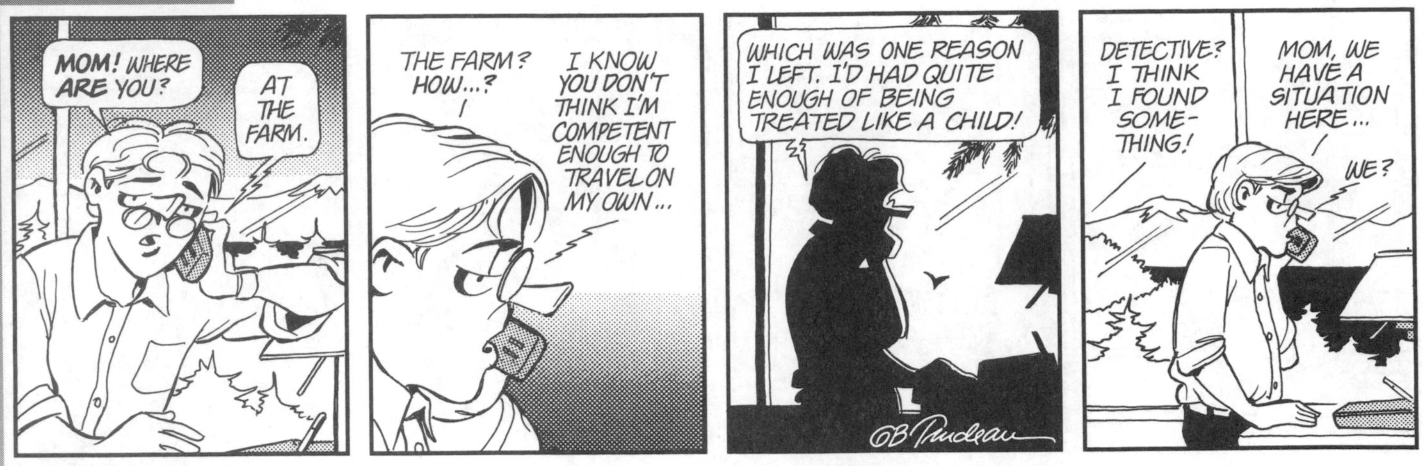
MOM! WHERE ARE YOU?
AT THE FARM.
THE FARM? HOW...?
I KNOW YOU DON'T THINK I'M COMPETENT ENOUGH TO TRAVEL ON MY OWN...
WHICH WAS ONE REASON I LEFT. I'D HAD QUITE ENOUGH OF BEING TREATED LIKE A CHILD!
DETECTIVE? I THINK I FOUND SOME-THING!
MOM, WE HAVE A SITUATION HERE...
WE?
©B. Trudeau

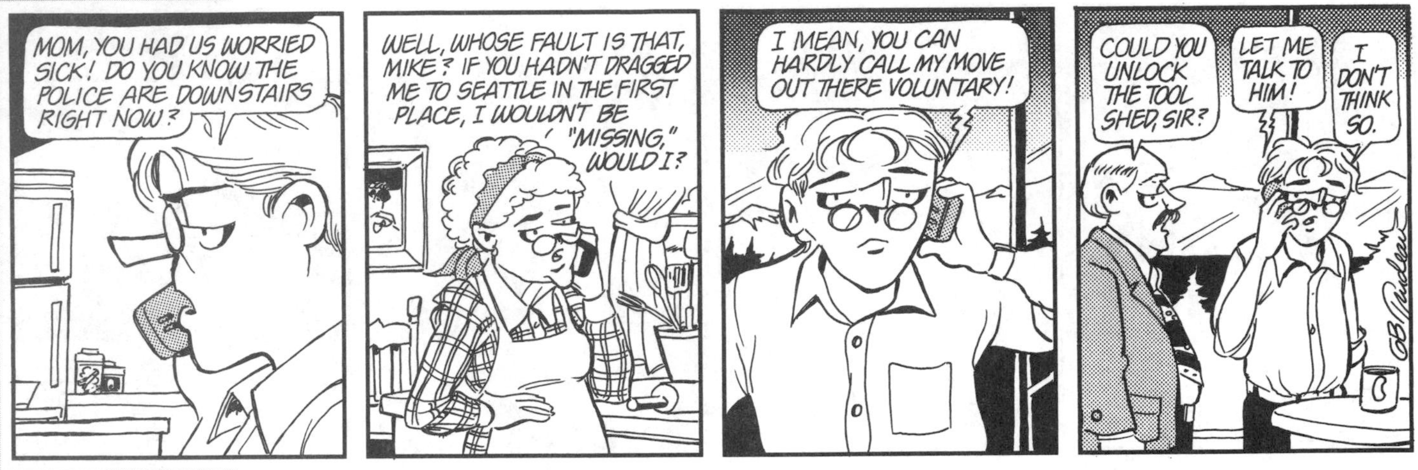
MOM, YOU HAD US WORRIED SICK! DO YOU KNOW THE POLICE ARE DOWNSTAIRS RIGHT NOW?
WELL, WHOSE FAULT IS THAT, MIKE? IF YOU HADN'T DRAGGED ME TO SEATTLE IN THE FIRST PLACE, I WOULDN'T BE "MISSING," WOULD I?
I MEAN, YOU CAN HARDLY CALL MY MOVE OUT THERE VOLUNTARY!
COULD YOU UNLOCK THE TOOL SHED, SIR?
LET ME TALK TO HIM!
I DON'T THINK SO.
©B. Trudeau

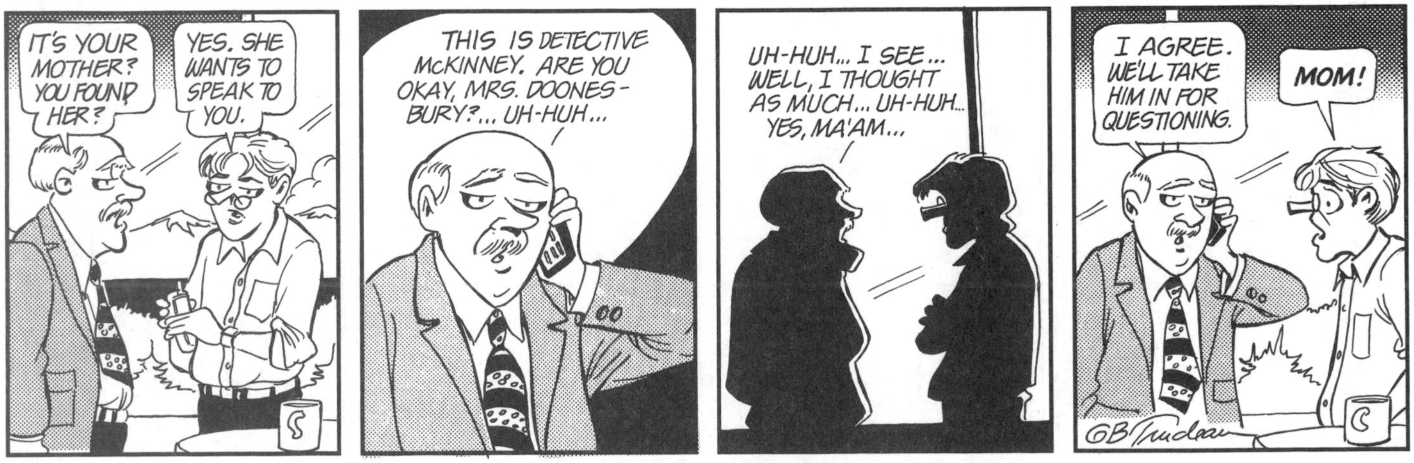
IT'S YOUR MOTHER? YOU FOUND HER?
YES. SHE WANTS TO SPEAK TO YOU.
THIS IS DETECTIVE McKINNEY. ARE YOU OKAY, MRS. DOONES-BURY?... UH-HUH...
UH-HUH... I SEE... WELL, I THOUGHT AS MUCH... UH-HUH... YES, MA'AM...
I AGREE. WE'LL TAKE HIM IN FOR QUESTIONING.
MOM!
©B. Trudeau

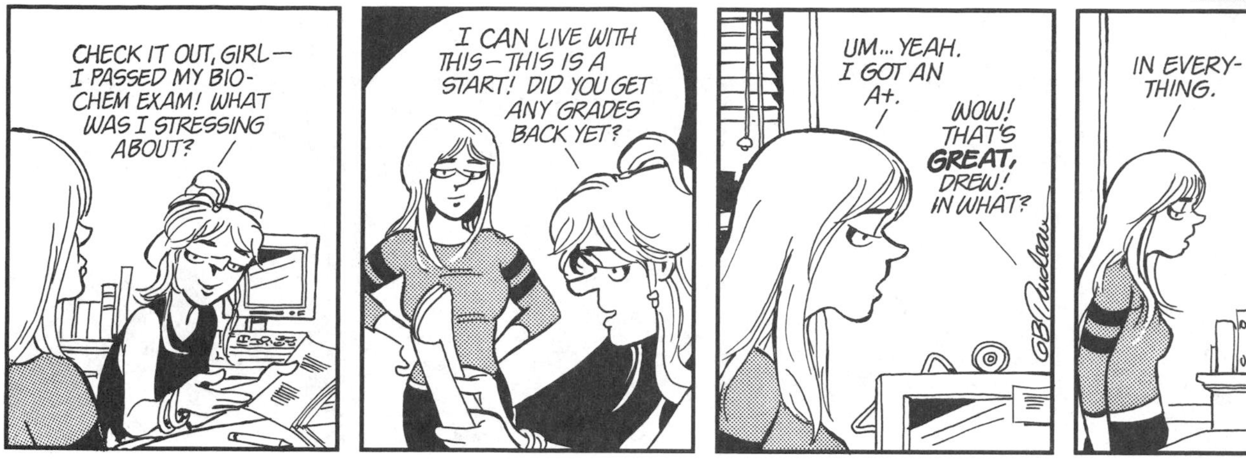
CHECK IT OUT, GIRL— I PASSED MY BIO-CHEM EXAM! WHAT WAS I STRESSING ABOUT?
I CAN LIVE WITH THIS—THIS IS A START! DID YOU GET ANY GRADES BACK YET?
UM... YEAH. I GOT AN A+.
WOW! THAT'S GREAT, DREW! IN WHAT?
IN EVERY-THING.
OKAY, GET OUT OF MY ROOM. SERI-OUSLY, YOU'RE DEAD TO ME.

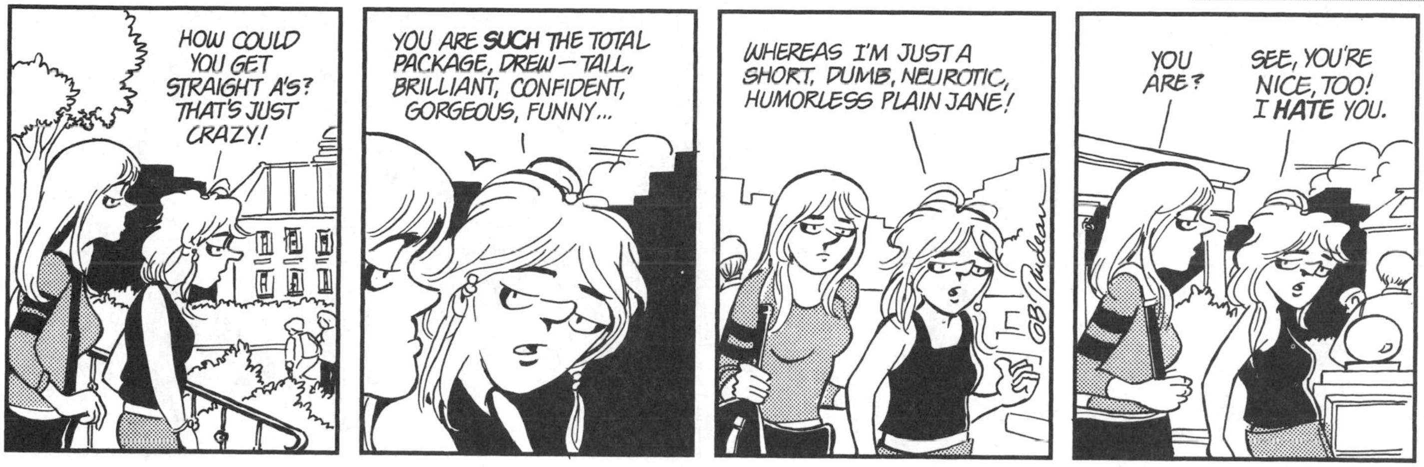
HOW COULD YOU GET STRAIGHT A'S? THAT'S JUST CRAZY!
YOU ARE SUCH THE TOTAL PACKAGE, DREW—TALL, BRILLIANT, CONFIDENT, GORGEOUS, FUNNY...
WHEREAS I'M JUST A SHORT, DUMB, NEUROTIC, HUMORLESS PLAIN JANE!
YOU ARE?
SEE, YOU'RE NICE, TOO! I HATE YOU.

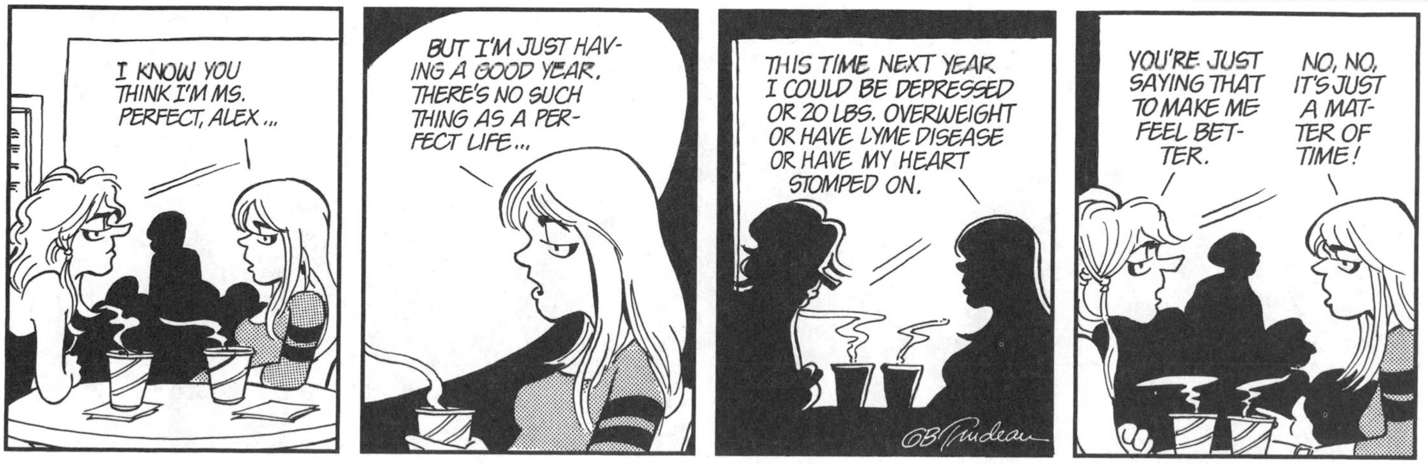
I KNOW YOU THINK I'M MS. PERFECT, ALEX...
BUT I'M JUST HAV-ING A GOOD YEAR. THERE'S NO SUCH THING AS A PER-FECT LIFE...
THIS TIME NEXT YEAR I COULD BE DEPRESSED OR 20 LBS. OVERWEIGHT OR HAVE LYME DISEASE OR HAVE MY HEART STOMPED ON.
YOU'RE JUST SAYING THAT TO MAKE ME FEEL BET-TER.
NO, NO, IT'S JUST A MAT-TER OF TIME!

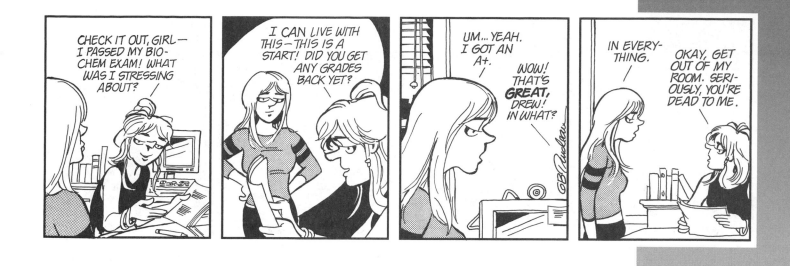

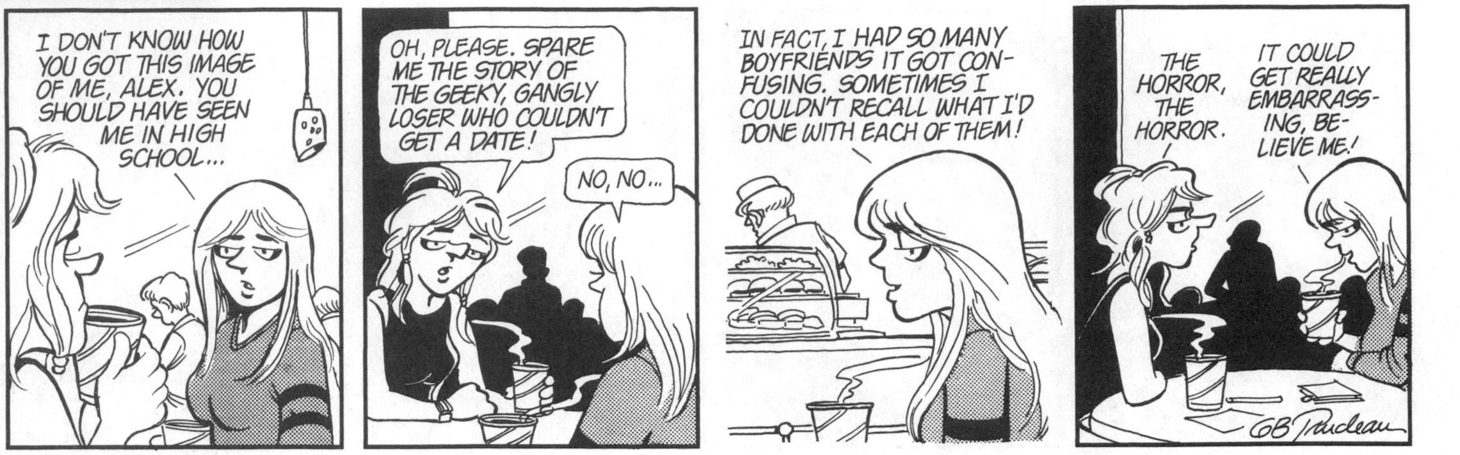
I DON'T KNOW HOW YOU GOT THIS IMAGE OF ME, ALEX. YOU SHOULD HAVE SEEN ME IN HIGH SCHOOL...
OH, PLEASE. SPARE ME THE STORY OF THE GEEKY, GANGLY LOSER WHO COULDN'T GET A DATE!
NO, NO...
IN FACT, I HAD SO MANY BOYFRIENDS IT GOT CONFUSING. SOMETIMES I COULDN'T RECALL WHAT I'D DONE WITH EACH OF THEM!
THE HORROR, THE HORROR.
IT COULD GET REALLY EMBARRASSING, BELIEVE ME!
GB Trudeau

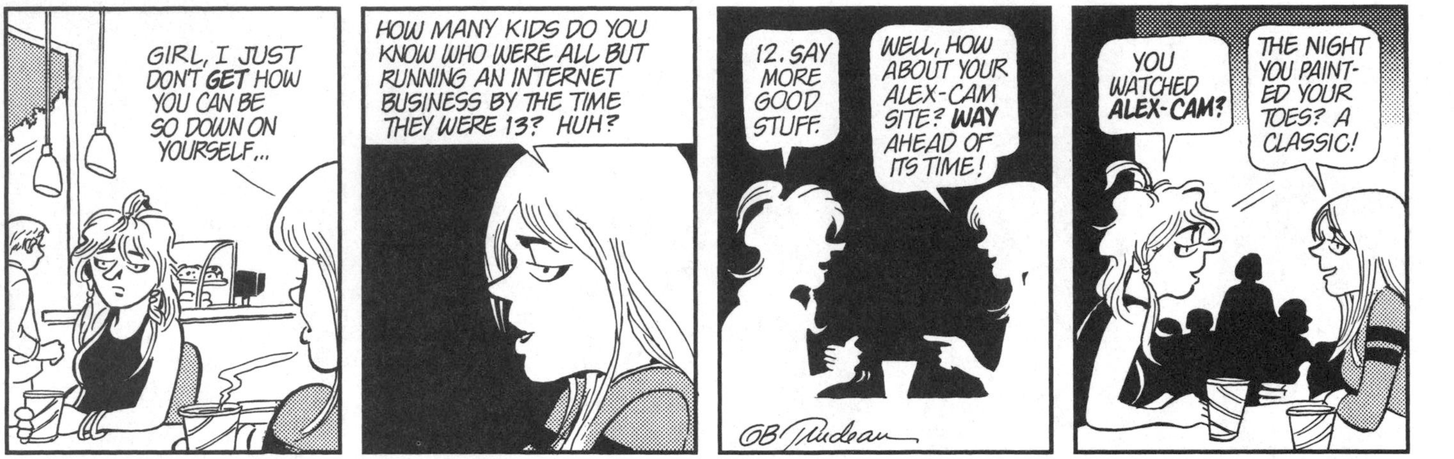
GIRL, I JUST DON'T **GET** HOW YOU CAN BE SO DOWN ON YOURSELF...
HOW MANY KIDS DO YOU KNOW WHO WERE ALL BUT RUNNING AN INTERNET BUSINESS BY THE TIME THEY WERE 13? HUH?
12. SAY MORE GOOD STUFF.
WELL, HOW ABOUT YOUR ALEX-CAM SITE? **WAY** AHEAD OF ITS TIME!
GB Trudeau
YOU WATCHED **ALEX-CAM?**
THE NIGHT YOU PAINTED YOUR TOES? A CLASSIC!

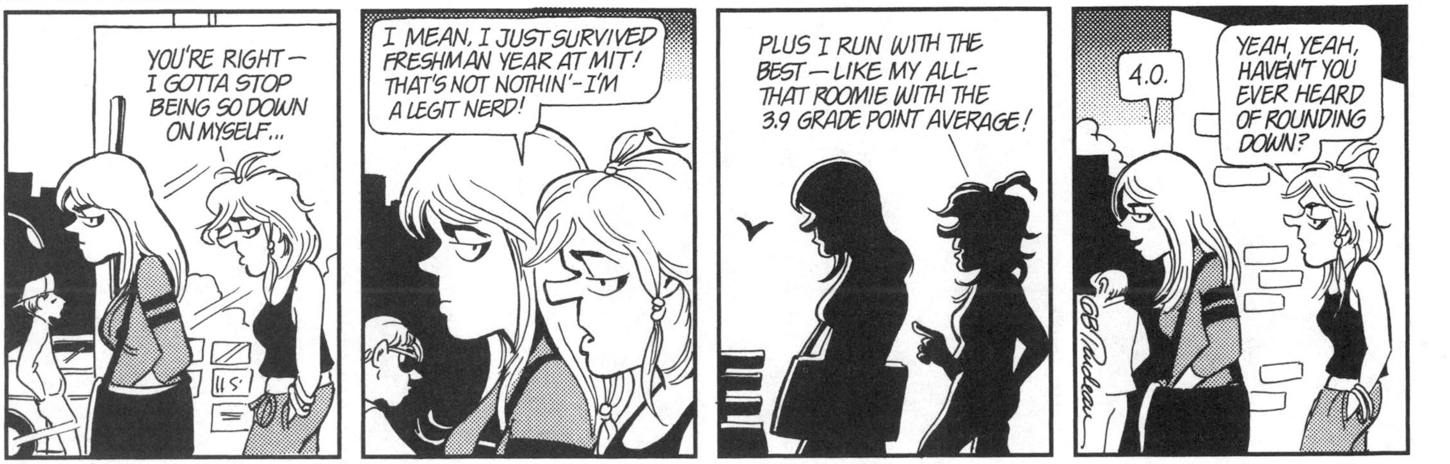
YOU'RE RIGHT— I GOTTA STOP BEING SO DOWN ON MYSELF...
I MEAN, I JUST SURVIVED FRESHMAN YEAR AT MIT! THAT'S NOT NOTHIN'- I'M A LEGIT NERD!
PLUS I RUN WITH THE BEST— LIKE MY ALL-THAT ROOMIE WITH THE 3.9 GRADE POINT AVERAGE!
4.0.
YEAH, YEAH, HAVEN'T YOU EVER HEARD OF ROUNDING DOWN?
GB Trudeau

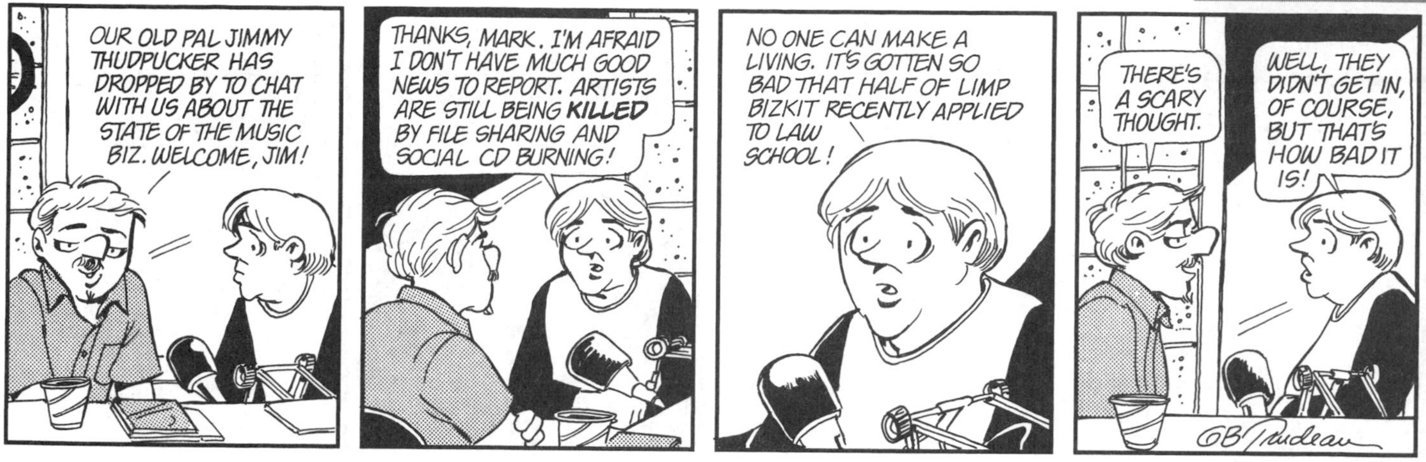
OUR OLD PAL JIMMY THUDPUCKER HAS DROPPED BY TO CHAT WITH US ABOUT THE STATE OF THE MUSIC BIZ. WELCOME, JIM!
THANKS, MARK. I'M AFRAID I DON'T HAVE MUCH GOOD NEWS TO REPORT. ARTISTS ARE STILL BEING **KILLED** BY FILE SHARING AND SOCIAL CD BURNING!
NO ONE CAN MAKE A LIVING. IT'S GOTTEN SO BAD THAT HALF OF LIMP BIZKIT RECENTLY APPLIED TO LAW SCHOOL!
THERE'S A SCARY THOUGHT.
WELL, THEY DIDN'T GET IN, OF COURSE, BUT THAT'S HOW BAD IT IS!
GB Trudeau

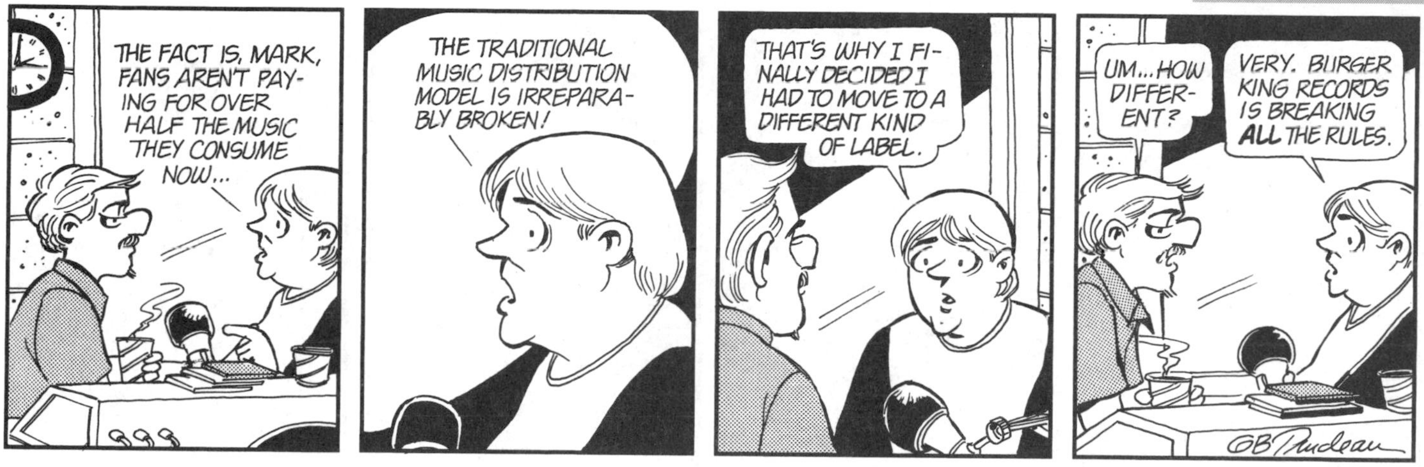
THE FACT IS, MARK, FANS AREN'T PAYING FOR OVER HALF THE MUSIC THEY CONSUME NOW...
THE TRADITIONAL MUSIC DISTRIBUTION MODEL IS IRREPARABLY BROKEN!
THAT'S WHY I FINALLY DECIDED I HAD TO MOVE TO A DIFFERENT KIND OF LABEL.
UM... HOW DIFFERENT?
VERY. BURGER KING RECORDS IS BREAKING **ALL** THE RULES.
GB Trudeau

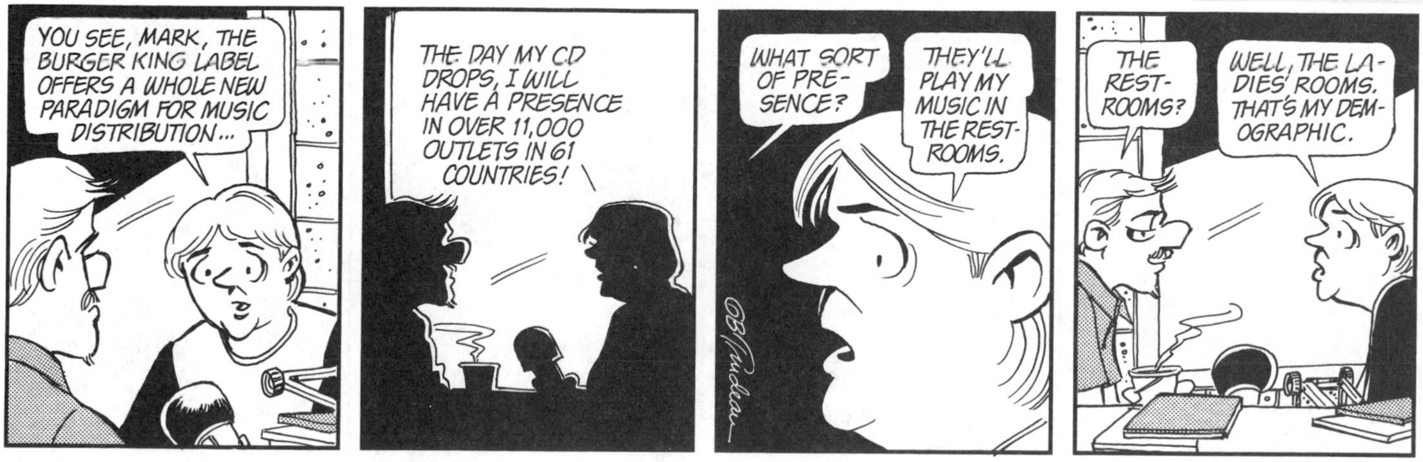
YOU SEE, MARK, THE BURGER KING LABEL OFFERS A WHOLE NEW PARADIGM FOR MUSIC DISTRIBUTION...
THE DAY MY CD DROPS, I WILL HAVE A PRESENCE IN OVER 11,000 OUTLETS IN 61 COUNTRIES!
GB Trudeau
WHAT SORT OF PRESENCE?
THEY'LL PLAY MY MUSIC IN THE RESTROOMS.
THE RESTROOMS?
WELL, THE LADIES' ROOMS. THAT'S MY DEMOGRAPHIC.

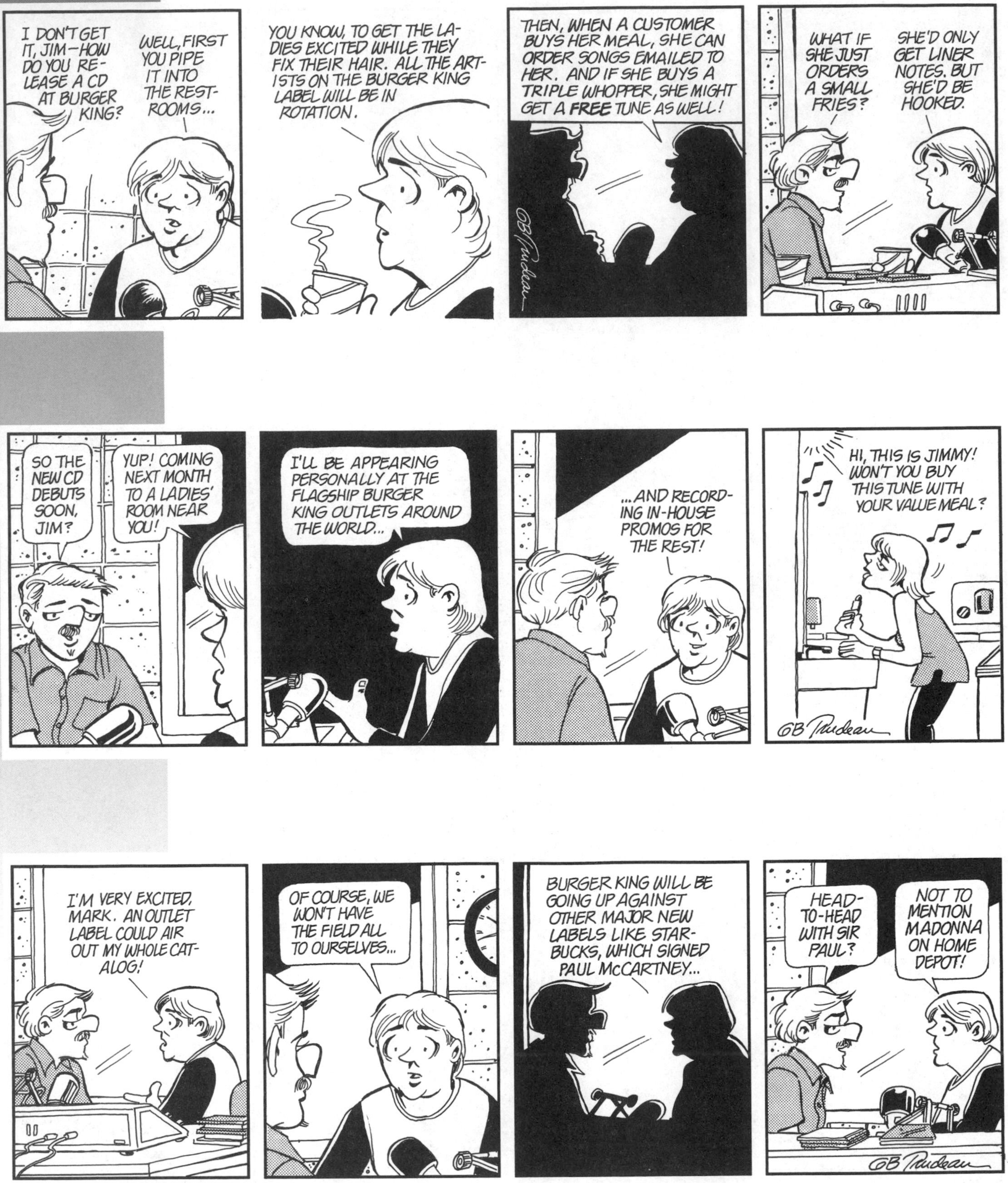
I DON'T GET IT, JIM—HOW DO YOU RELEASE A CD AT BURGER KING?
WELL, FIRST YOU PIPE IT INTO THE RESTROOMS...
YOU KNOW, TO GET THE LADIES EXCITED WHILE THEY FIX THEIR HAIR. ALL THE ARTISTS ON THE BURGER KING LABEL WILL BE IN ROTATION.
THEN, WHEN A CUSTOMER BUYS HER MEAL, SHE CAN ORDER SONGS EMAILED TO HER. AND IF SHE BUYS A TRIPLE WHOPPER, SHE MIGHT GET A FREE TUNE AS WELL!
WHAT IF SHE JUST ORDERS A SMALL FRIES?
SHE'D ONLY GET LINER NOTES. BUT SHE'D BE HOOKED.
GB Trudeau
SO THE NEW CD DEBUTS SOON, JIM?
YUP! COMING NEXT MONTH TO A LADIES' ROOM NEAR YOU!
I'LL BE APPEARING PERSONALLY AT THE FLAGSHIP BURGER KING OUTLETS AROUND THE WORLD...
...AND RECORDING IN-HOUSE PROMOS FOR THE REST!
HI, THIS IS JIMMY! WON'T YOU BUY THIS TUNE WITH YOUR VALUE MEAL?
GB Trudeau
I'M VERY EXCITED, MARK. AN OUTLET LABEL COULD AIR OUT MY WHOLE CATALOG!
OF COURSE, WE WON'T HAVE THE FIELD ALL TO OURSELVES...
BURGER KING WILL BE GOING UP AGAINST OTHER MAJOR NEW LABELS LIKE STARBUCKS, WHICH SIGNED PAUL McCARTNEY...
HEAD-TO-HEAD WITH SIR PAUL?
NOT TO MENTION MADONNA ON HOME DEPOT!
GB Trudeau

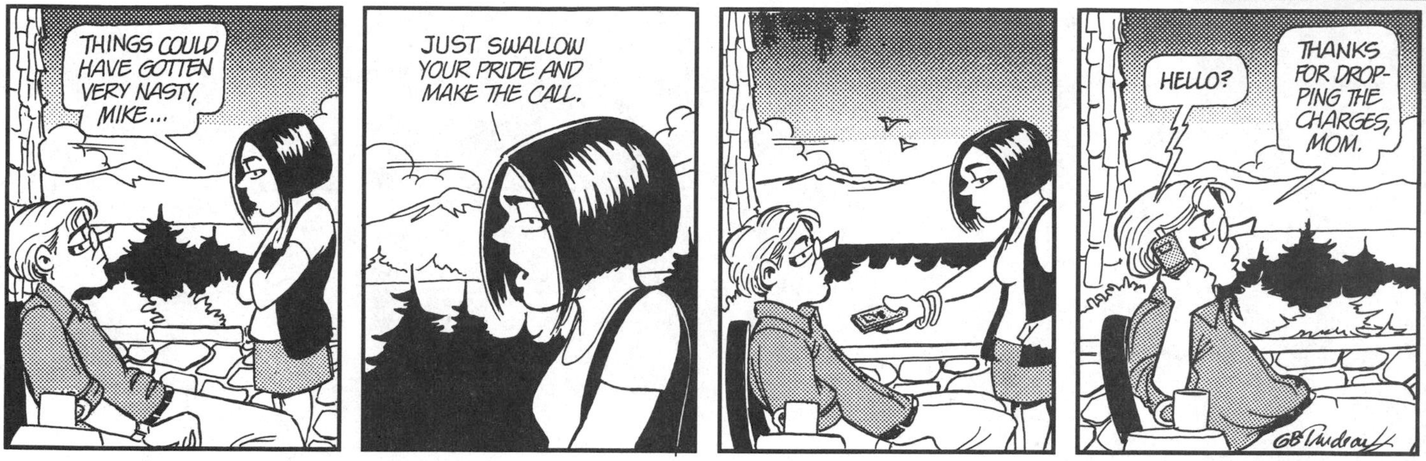
THINGS COULD HAVE GOTTEN VERY NASTY, MIKE...
JUST SWALLOW YOUR PRIDE AND MAKE THE CALL.
HELLO?
THANKS FOR DROPPING THE CHARGES, MOM.
©B Trudeau

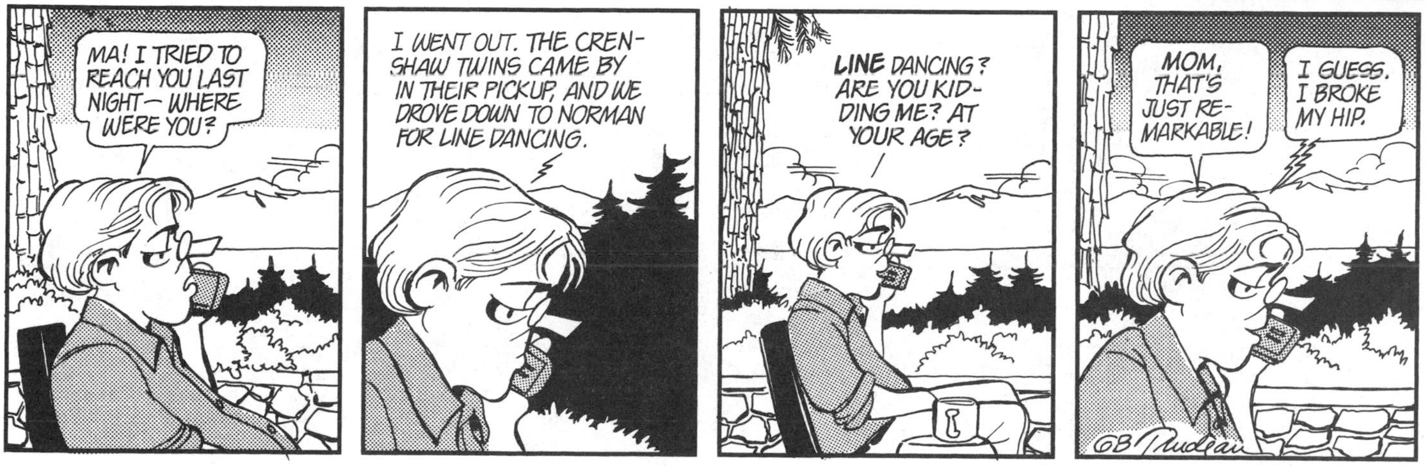
MA! I TRIED TO REACH YOU LAST NIGHT— WHERE WERE YOU?
I WENT OUT. THE CRENSHAW TWINS CAME BY IN THEIR PICKUP, AND WE DROVE DOWN TO NORMAN FOR LINE DANCING.
LINE DANCING? ARE YOU KIDDING ME? AT YOUR AGE?
MOM, THAT'S JUST REMARKABLE!
I GUESS. I BROKE MY HIP.
©B Trudeau

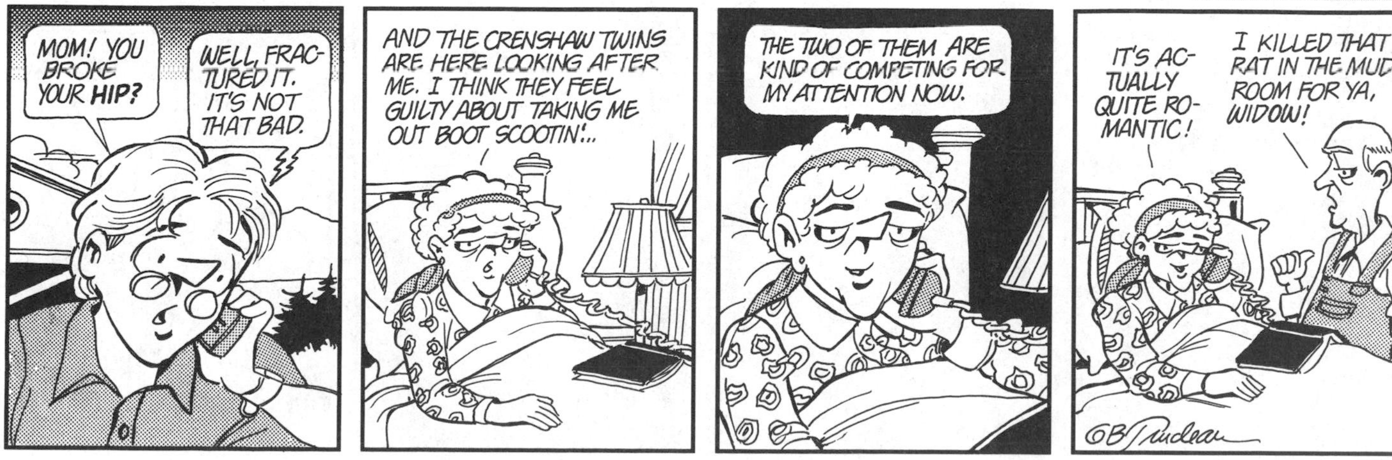
MOM! YOU BROKE YOUR HIP?
WELL, FRACTURED IT. IT'S NOT THAT BAD.
AND THE CRENSHAW TWINS ARE HERE LOOKING AFTER ME. I THINK THEY FEEL GUILTY ABOUT TAKING ME OUT BOOT SCOOTIN'...
THE TWO OF THEM ARE KIND OF COMPETING FOR MY ATTENTION NOW.
IT'S ACTUALLY QUITE ROMANTIC!
I KILLED THAT RAT IN THE MUD ROOM FOR YA, WIDOW!
©B Trudeau

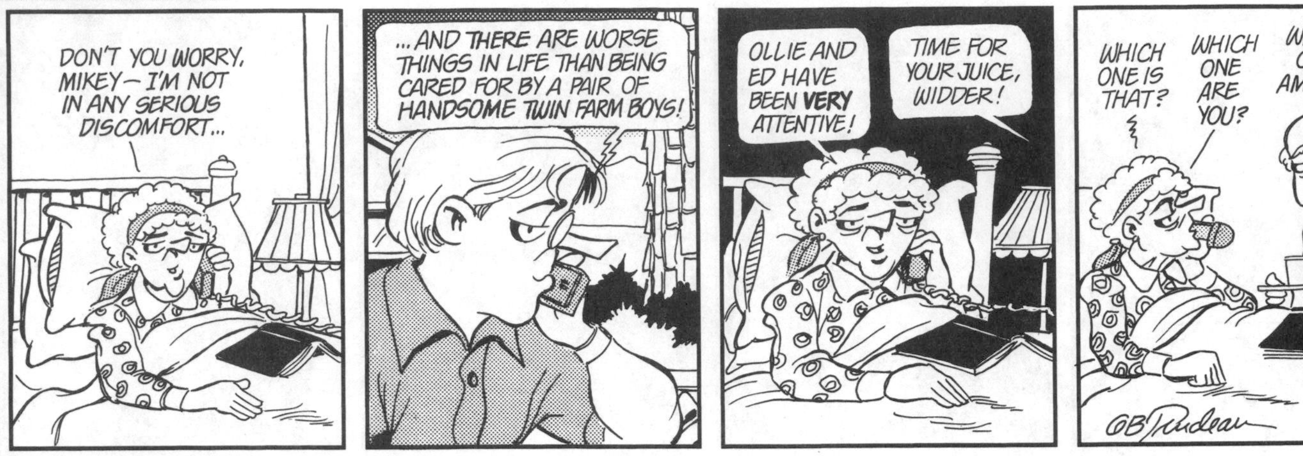
DON'T YOU WORRY, MIKEY— I'M NOT IN ANY SERIOUS DISCOMFORT...
...AND THERE ARE WORSE THINGS IN LIFE THAN BEING CARED FOR BY A PAIR OF HANDSOME TWIN FARM BOYS!
OLLIE AND ED HAVE BEEN VERY ATTENTIVE!
TIME FOR YOUR JUICE, WIDDER!
WHICH ONE IS THAT?
WHICH ONE ARE YOU?
WHICH ONE AM I?
ED.
GB Trudeau

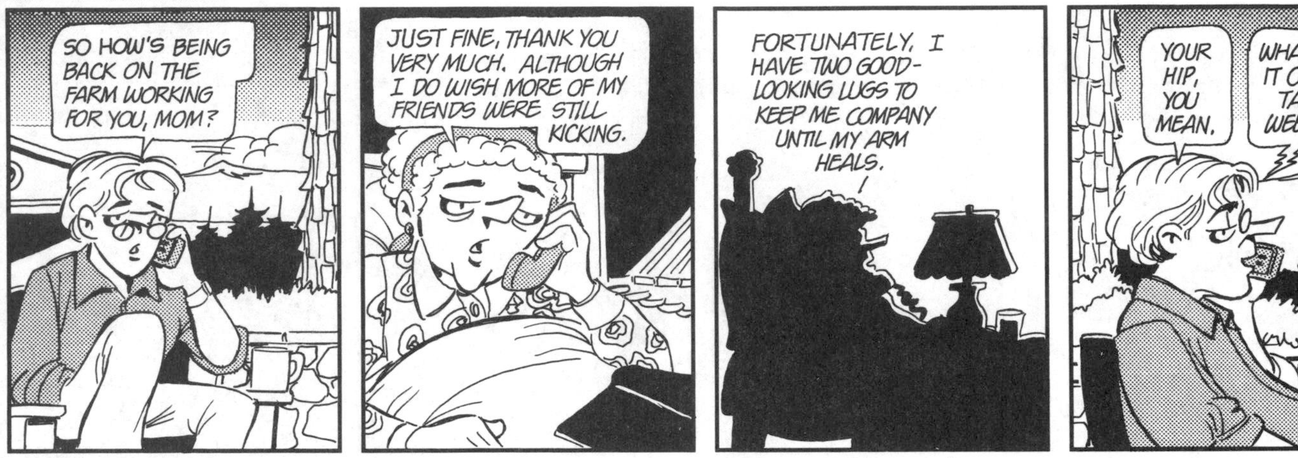
SO HOW'S BEING BACK ON THE FARM WORKING FOR YOU, MOM?
JUST FINE, THANK YOU VERY MUCH. ALTHOUGH I DO WISH MORE OF MY FRIENDS WERE STILL KICKING.
FORTUNATELY, I HAVE TWO GOOD-LOOKING LUGS TO KEEP ME COMPANY UNTIL MY ARM HEALS.
YOUR HIP, YOU MEAN.
WHATEVER, IT COULD TAKE WEEKS!
GB Trudeau

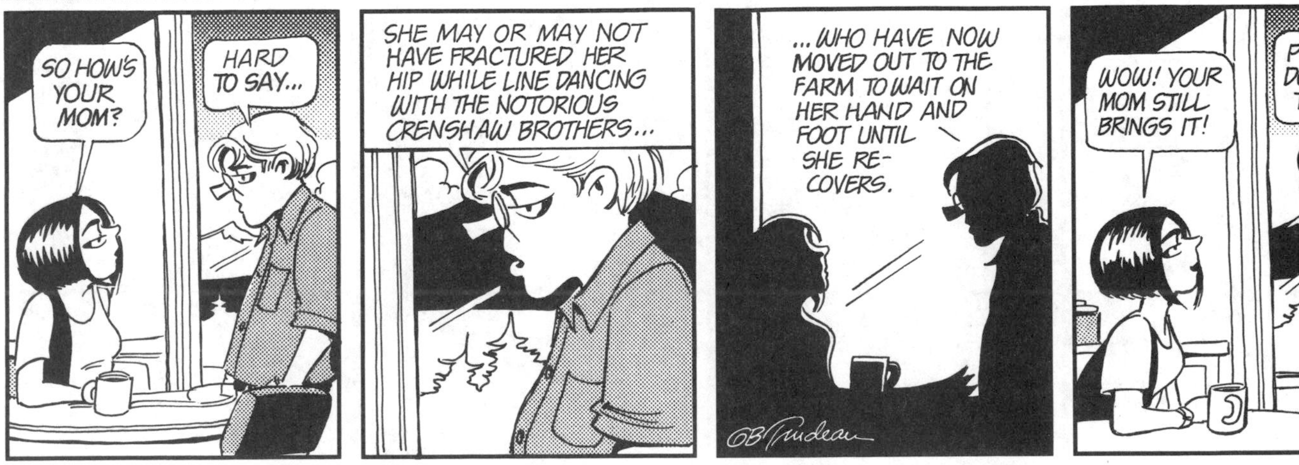
SO HOW'S YOUR MOM?
HARD TO SAY...
SHE MAY OR MAY NOT HAVE FRACTURED HER HIP WHILE LINE DANCING WITH THE NOTORIOUS CRENSHAW BROTHERS...
...WHO HAVE NOW MOVED OUT TO THE FARM TO WAIT ON HER HAND AND FOOT UNTIL SHE RE-COVERS.
GB Trudeau
WOW! YOUR MOM STILL BRINGS IT!
PLEASE DON'T SAY THAT.

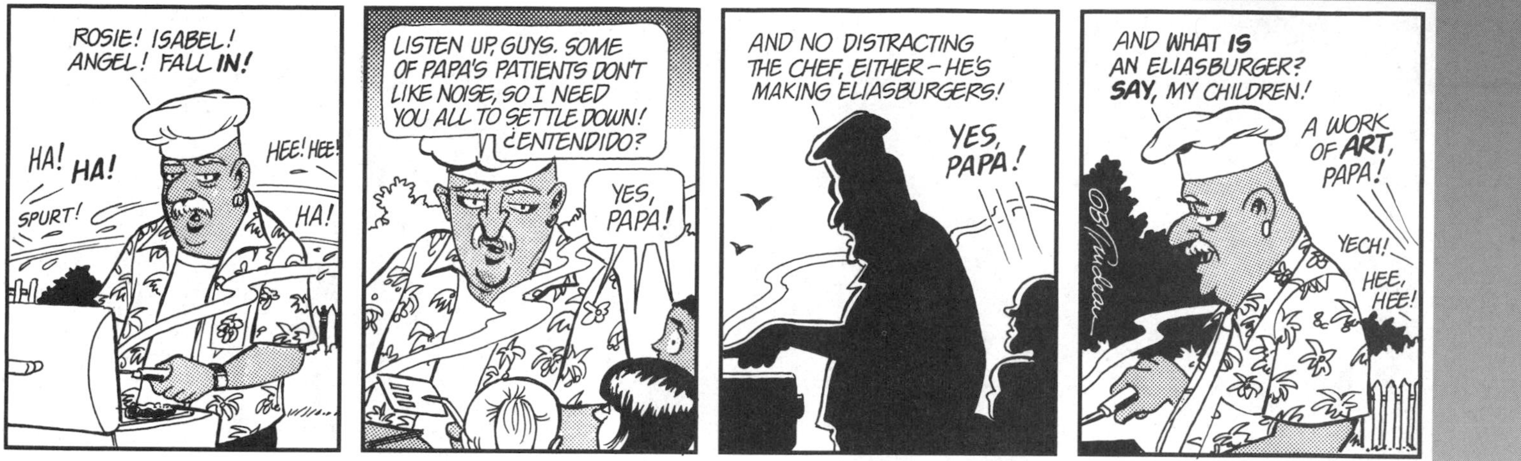
ROSIE! ISABEL! ANGEL! FALL IN!
HA! HA!
SPURT!
HEE! HEE!
HA!
LISTEN UP, GUYS. SOME OF PAPA'S PATIENTS DON'T LIKE NOISE, SO I NEED YOU ALL TO SETTLE DOWN! ¿ENTENDIDO?
YES, PAPA!
AND NO DISTRACTING THE CHEF, EITHER – HE'S MAKING ELIASBURGERS!
YES, PAPA!
AND WHAT IS AN ELIASBURGER? SAY, MY CHILDREN!
A WORK OF ART, PAPA!
YECH!
HEE, HEE!
GB Trudeau

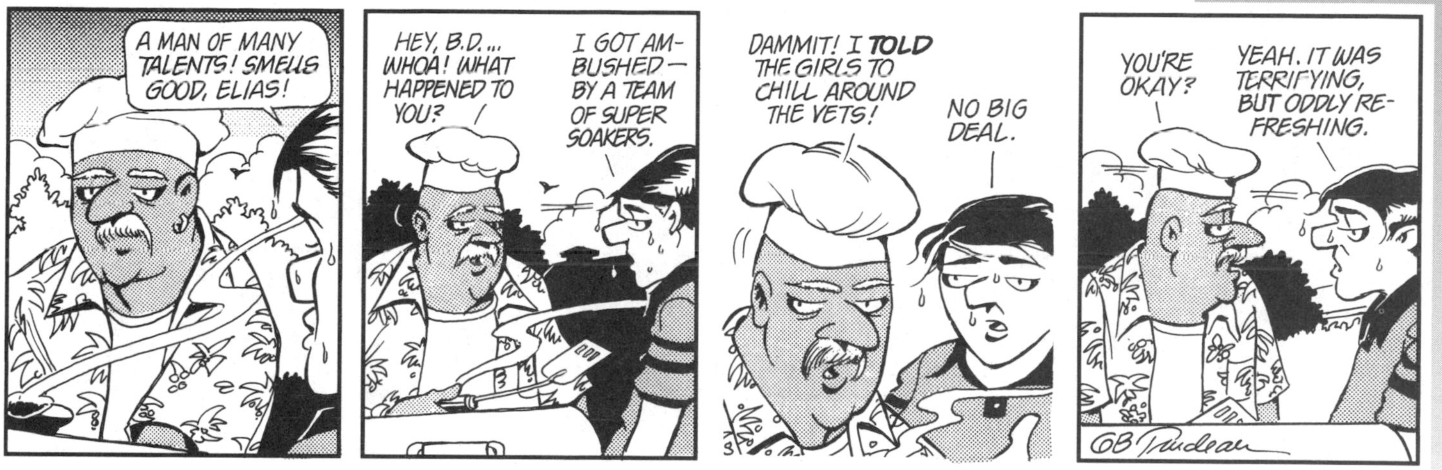
A MAN OF MANY TALENTS! SMELLS GOOD, ELIAS!
HEY, B.D. ... WHOA! WHAT HAPPENED TO YOU?
I GOT AMBUSHED – BY A TEAM OF SUPER SOAKERS.
DAMMIT! I TOLD THE GIRLS TO CHILL AROUND THE VETS!
NO BIG DEAL.
YOU'RE OKAY?
YEAH. IT WAS TERRIFYING, BUT ODDLY REFRESHING.
GB Trudeau

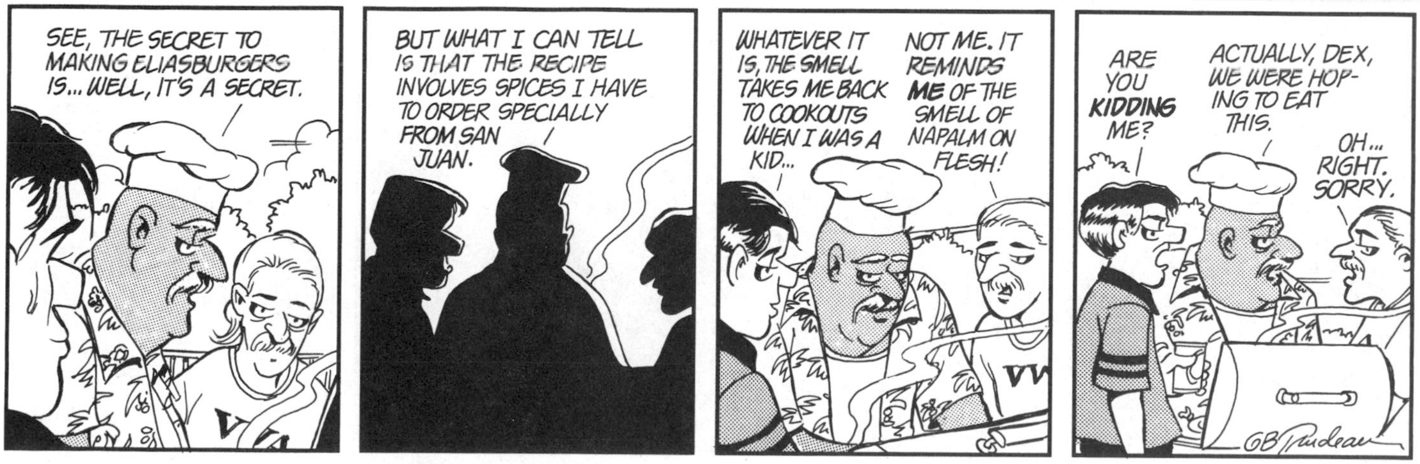
SEE, THE SECRET TO MAKING ELIASBURGERS IS... WELL, IT'S A SECRET.
BUT WHAT I CAN TELL IS THAT THE RECIPE INVOLVES SPICES I HAVE TO ORDER SPECIALLY FROM SAN JUAN.
WHATEVER IT IS, THE SMELL TAKES ME BACK TO COOKOUTS WHEN I WAS A KID...
NOT ME. IT REMINDS ME OF THE SMELL OF NAPALM ON FLESH!
ARE YOU KIDDING ME?
ACTUALLY, DEX, WE WERE HOPING TO EAT THIS.
OH... RIGHT. SORRY.
GB Trudeau

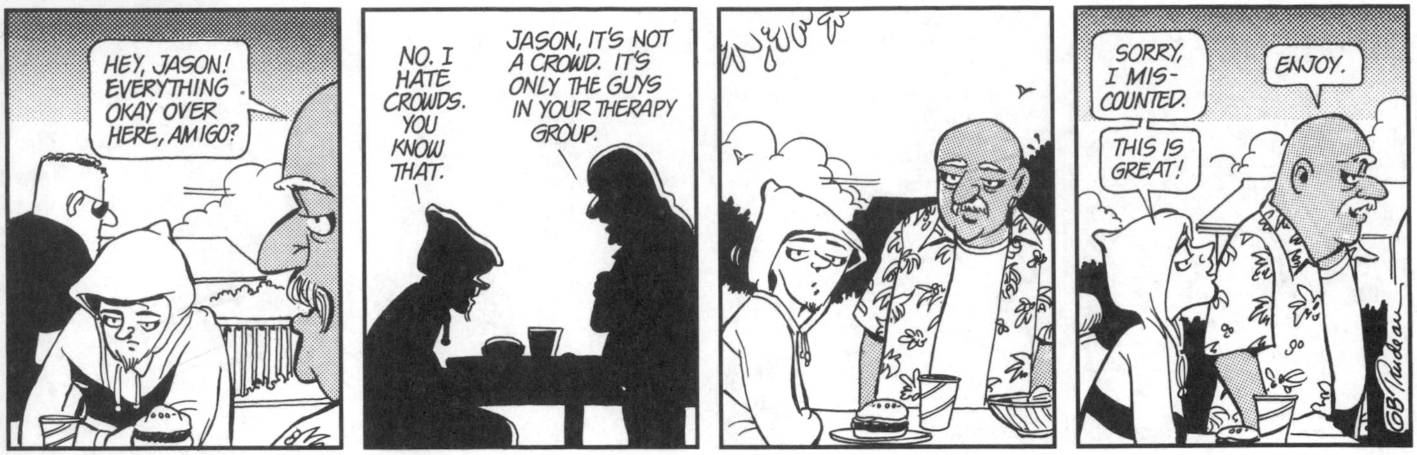
HEY, JASON! EVERYTHING OKAY OVER HERE, AMIGO?
NO. I HATE CROWDS. YOU KNOW THAT.
JASON, IT'S NOT A CROWD. IT'S ONLY THE GUYS IN YOUR THERAPY GROUP.
SORRY, I MIS-COUNTED.
THIS IS GREAT!
ENJOY.
GB Trudeau

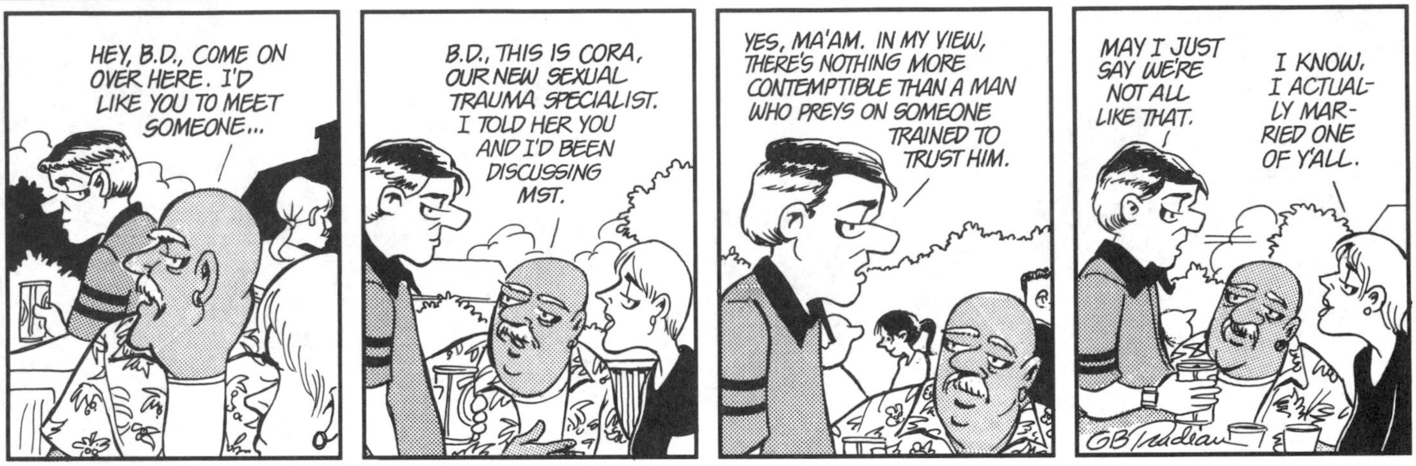
HEY, B.D., COME ON OVER HERE. I'D LIKE YOU TO MEET SOMEONE...
B.D., THIS IS CORA, OUR NEW SEXUAL TRAUMA SPECIALIST. I TOLD HER YOU AND I'D BEEN DISCUSSING MST.
YES, MA'AM. IN MY VIEW, THERE'S NOTHING MORE CONTEMPTIBLE THAN A MAN WHO PREYS ON SOMEONE TRAINED TO TRUST HIM.
MAY I JUST SAY WE'RE NOT ALL LIKE THAT.
I KNOW. I ACTUAL-LY MAR-RIED ONE OF Y'ALL.
GB Trudeau

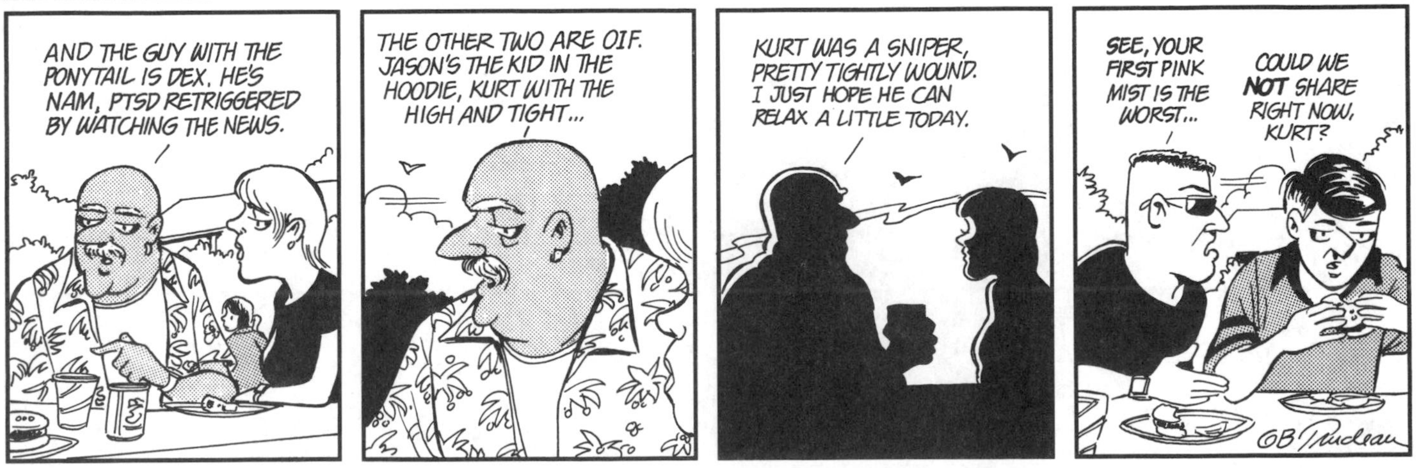
AND THE GUY WITH THE PONYTAIL IS DEX. HE'S NAM, PTSD RETRIGGERED BY WATCHING THE NEWS.
THE OTHER TWO ARE OIF. JASON'S THE KID IN THE HOODIE, KURT WITH THE HIGH AND TIGHT...
KURT WAS A SNIPER, PRETTY TIGHTLY WOUND. I JUST HOPE HE CAN RELAX A LITTLE TODAY.
SEE, YOUR FIRST PINK MIST IS THE WORST...
COULD WE NOT SHARE RIGHT NOW, KURT?
GB Trudeau

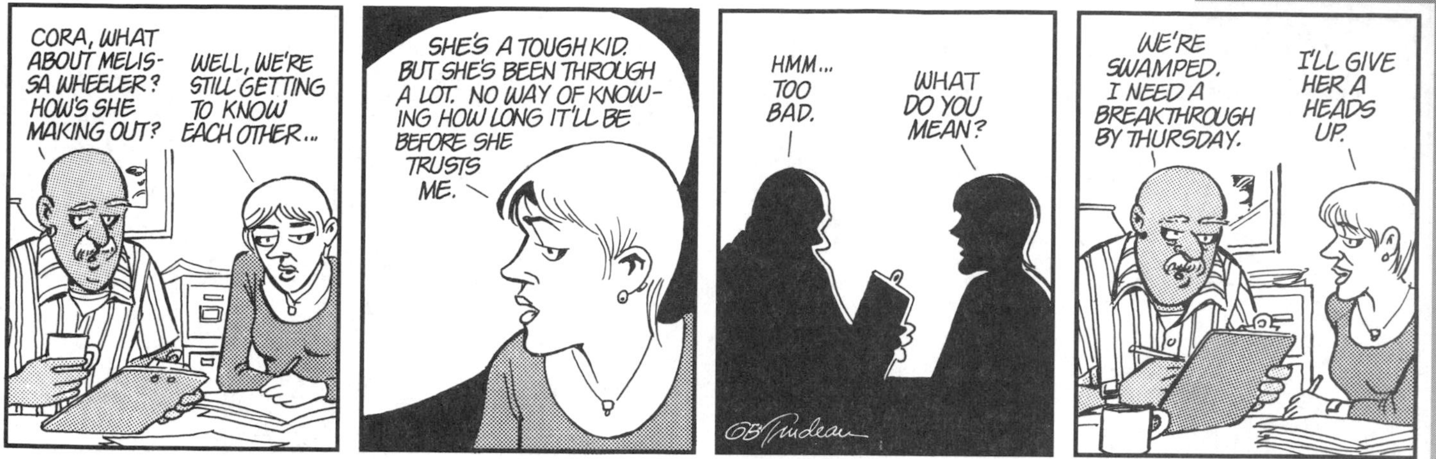
CORA, WHAT ABOUT MELISSA WHEELER? HOW'S SHE MAKING OUT?
WELL, WE'RE STILL GETTING TO KNOW EACH OTHER...
SHE'S A TOUGH KID. BUT SHE'S BEEN THROUGH A LOT. NO WAY OF KNOWING HOW LONG IT'LL BE BEFORE SHE TRUSTS ME.
HMM... TOO BAD.
WHAT DO YOU MEAN?
WE'RE SWAMPED. I NEED A BREAKTHROUGH BY THURSDAY.
I'LL GIVE HER A HEADS UP.

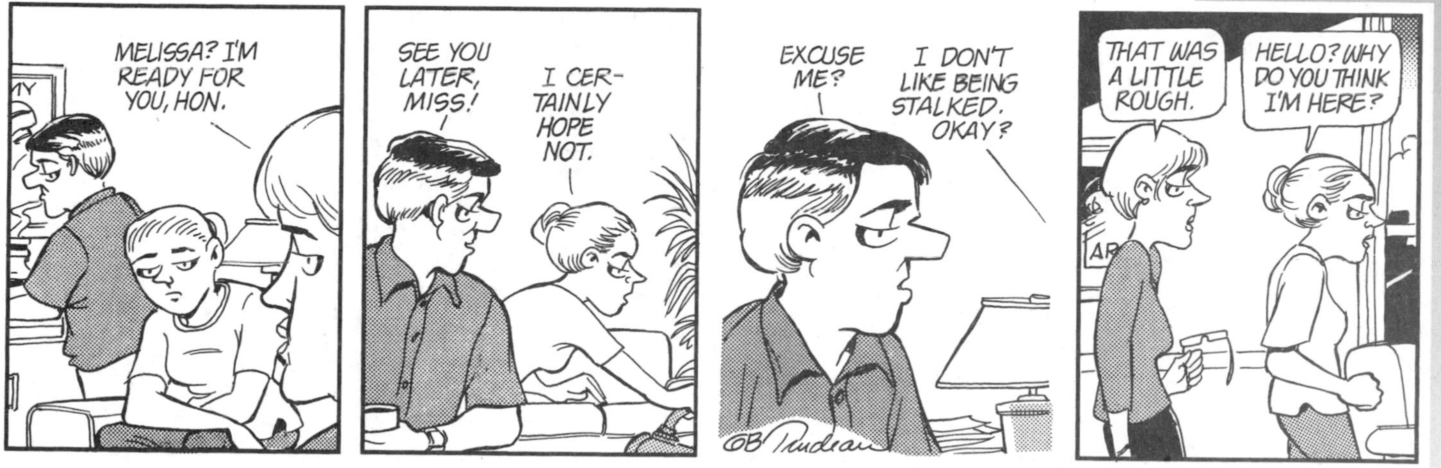
MELISSA? I'M READY FOR YOU, HON.
SEE YOU LATER, MISS!
I CERTAINLY HOPE NOT.
EXCUSE ME?
I DON'T LIKE BEING STALKED. OKAY?
THAT WAS A LITTLE ROUGH.
HELLO? WHY DO YOU THINK I'M HERE?

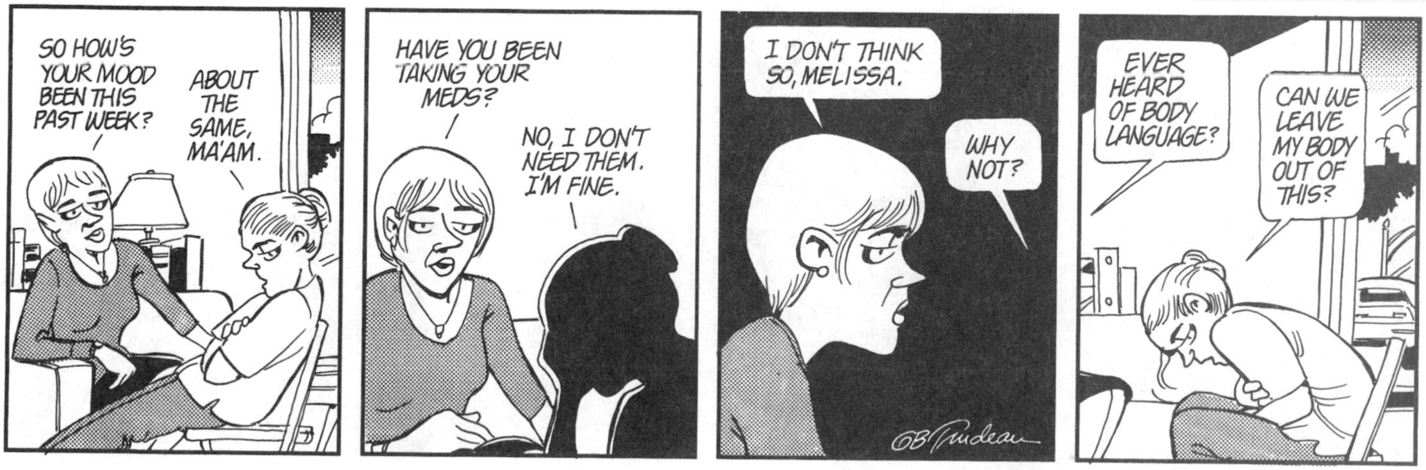
SO HOW'S YOUR MOOD BEEN THIS PAST WEEK?
ABOUT THE SAME, MA'AM.
HAVE YOU BEEN TAKING YOUR MEDS?
NO, I DON'T NEED THEM. I'M FINE.
I DON'T THINK SO, MELISSA.
WHY NOT?
EVER HEARD OF BODY LANGUAGE?
CAN WE LEAVE MY BODY OUT OF THIS?

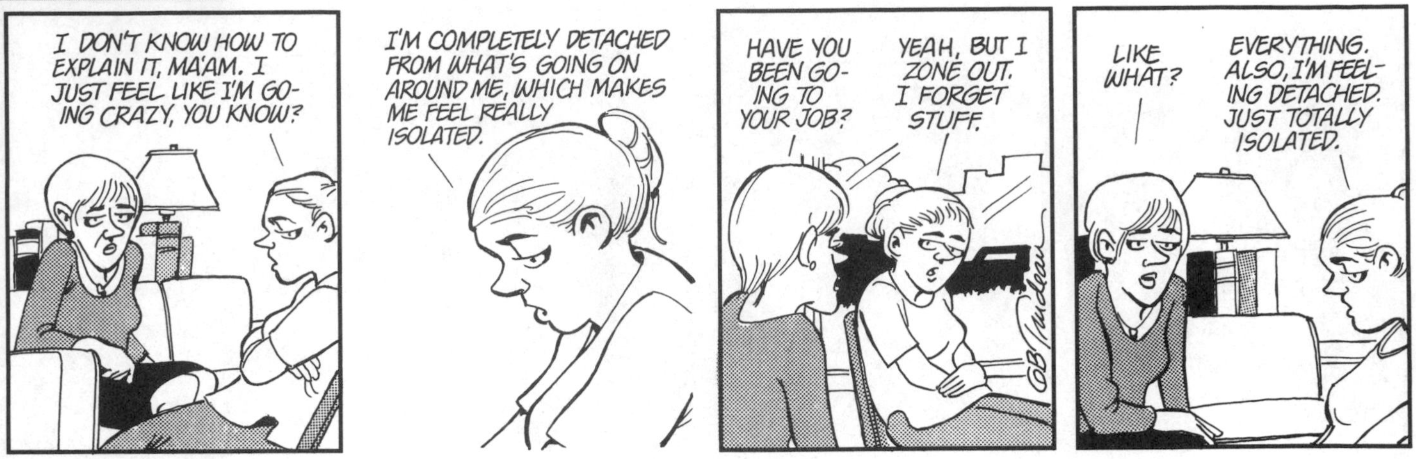
I DON'T KNOW HOW TO EXPLAIN IT, MA'AM. I JUST FEEL LIKE I'M GOING CRAZY, YOU KNOW?
I'M COMPLETELY DETACHED FROM WHAT'S GOING ON AROUND ME, WHICH MAKES ME FEEL REALLY ISOLATED.
HAVE YOU BEEN GOING TO YOUR JOB?
YEAH, BUT I ZONE OUT. I FORGET STUFF.
LIKE WHAT?
EVERYTHING. ALSO, I'M FEELING DETACHED. JUST TOTALLY ISOLATED.

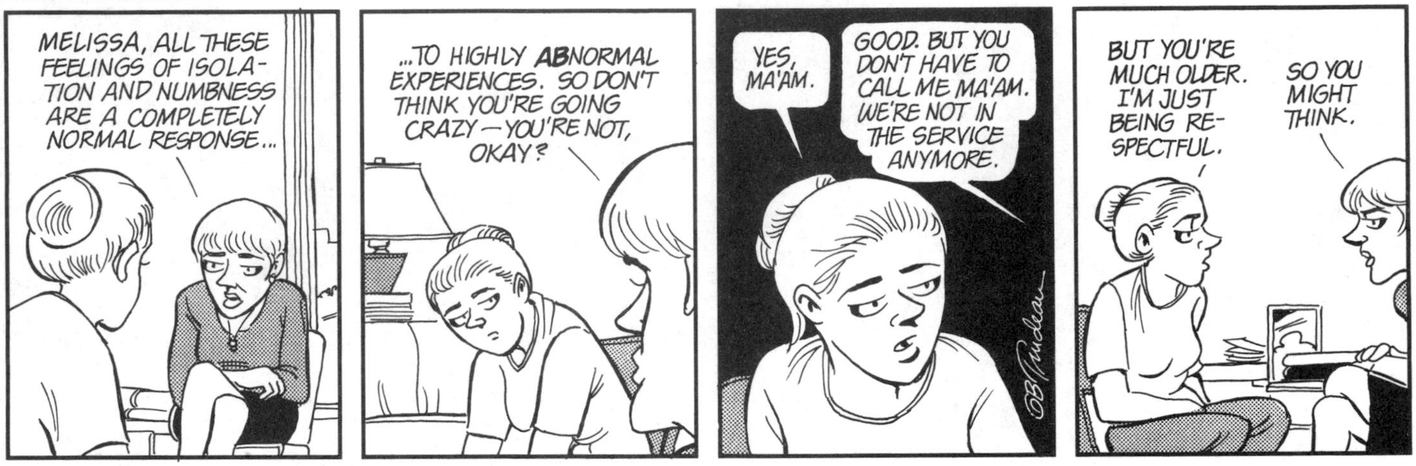
MELISSA, ALL THESE FEELINGS OF ISOLATION AND NUMBNESS ARE A COMPLETELY NORMAL RESPONSE...
...TO HIGHLY ABNORMAL EXPERIENCES. SO DON'T THINK YOU'RE GOING CRAZY — YOU'RE NOT, OKAY?
YES, MA'AM.
GOOD. BUT YOU DON'T HAVE TO CALL ME MA'AM. WE'RE NOT IN THE SERVICE ANYMORE.
BUT YOU'RE MUCH OLDER. I'M JUST BEING RESPECTFUL.
SO YOU MIGHT THINK.

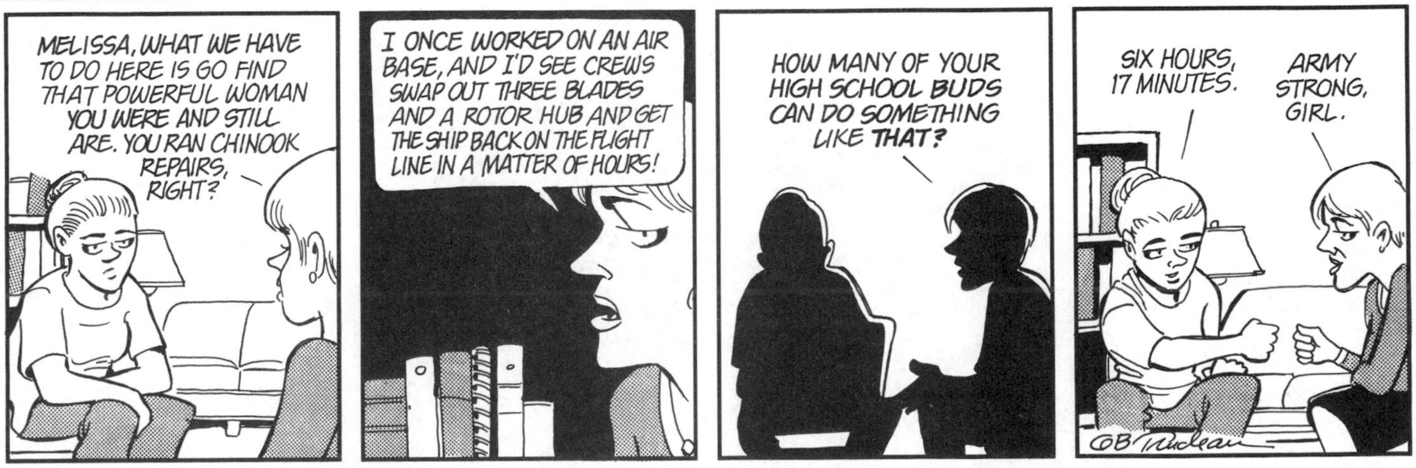
MELISSA, WHAT WE HAVE TO DO HERE IS GO FIND THAT POWERFUL WOMAN YOU WERE AND STILL ARE. YOU RAN CHINOOK REPAIRS, RIGHT?
I ONCE WORKED ON AN AIR BASE, AND I'D SEE CREWS SWAP OUT THREE BLADES AND A ROTOR HUB AND GET THE SHIP BACK ON THE FLIGHT LINE IN A MATTER OF HOURS!
HOW MANY OF YOUR HIGH SCHOOL BUDS CAN DO SOMETHING LIKE THAT?
SIX HOURS, 17 MINUTES.
ARMY STRONG, GIRL.

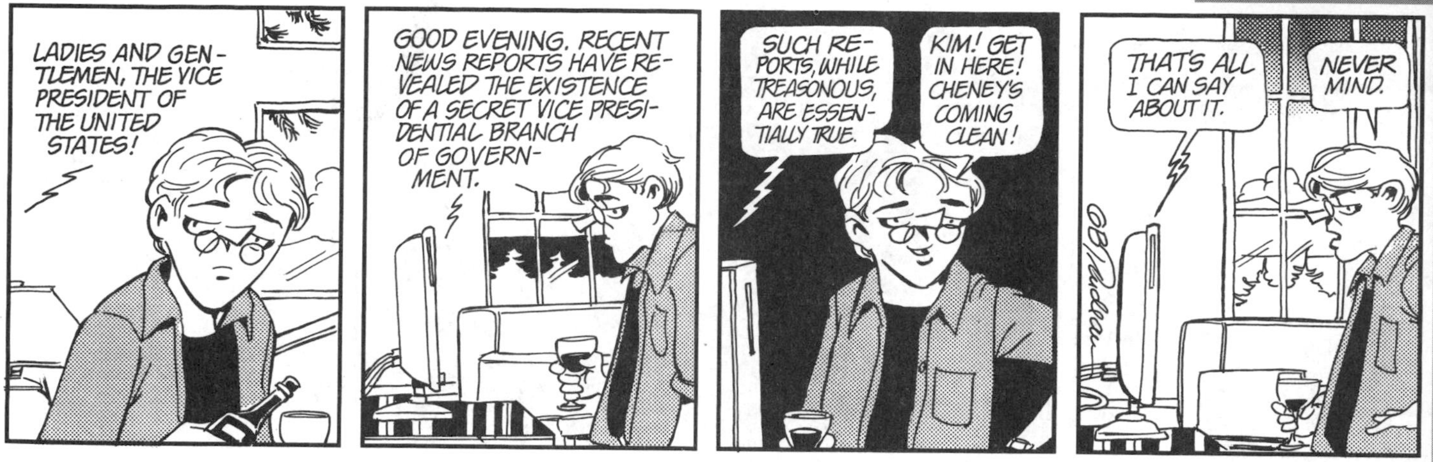
LADIES AND GEN-TLEMEN, THE VICE PRESIDENT OF THE UNITED STATES!
GOOD EVENING. RECENT NEWS REPORTS HAVE RE-VEALED THE EXISTENCE OF A SECRET VICE PRESI-DENTIAL BRANCH OF GOVERN-MENT.
SUCH RE-PORTS, WHILE TREASONOUS, ARE ESSEN-TIALLY TRUE.
KIM! GET IN HERE! CHENEY'S COMING CLEAN!
THAT'S ALL I CAN SAY ABOUT IT.
NEVER MIND.

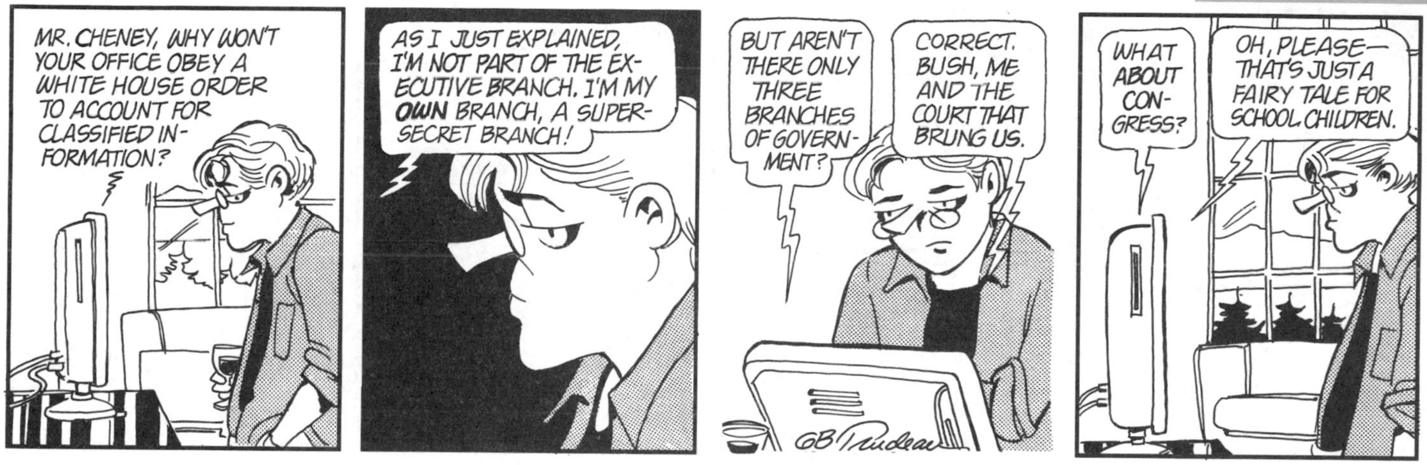
MR. CHENEY, WHY WON'T YOUR OFFICE OBEY A WHITE HOUSE ORDER TO ACCOUNT FOR CLASSIFIED IN-FORMATION?
AS I JUST EXPLAINED, I'M NOT PART OF THE EX-ECUTIVE BRANCH. I'M MY **OWN** BRANCH, A SUPER-SECRET BRANCH!
BUT AREN'T THERE ONLY THREE BRANCHES OF GOVERN-MENT?
CORRECT. BUSH, ME AND THE COURT THAT BRUNG US.
WHAT ABOUT CON-GRESS?
OH, PLEASE— THAT'S JUST A FAIRY TALE FOR SCHOOL CHILDREN.

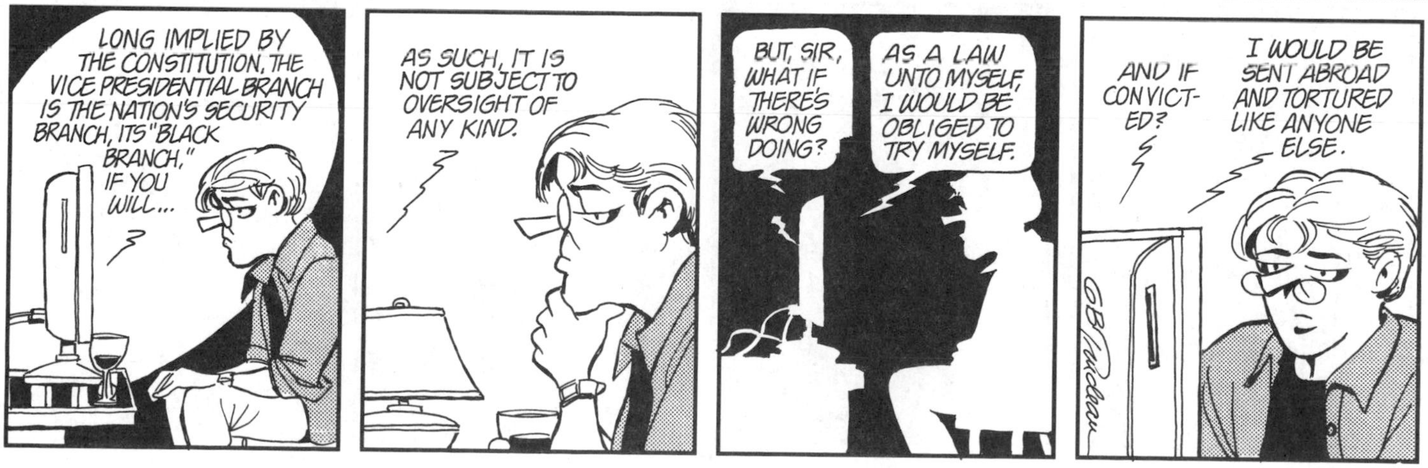
LONG IMPLIED BY THE CONSTITUTION, THE VICE PRESIDENTIAL BRANCH IS THE NATION'S SECURITY BRANCH, ITS "BLACK BRANCH," IF YOU WILL...
AS SUCH, IT IS NOT SUBJECT TO OVERSIGHT OF ANY KIND.
BUT, SIR, WHAT IF THERE'S WRONG DOING?
AS A LAW UNTO MYSELF, I WOULD BE OBLIGED TO TRY MYSELF.
AND IF CONVICT-ED?
I WOULD BE SENT ABROAD AND TORTURED LIKE ANYONE ELSE.

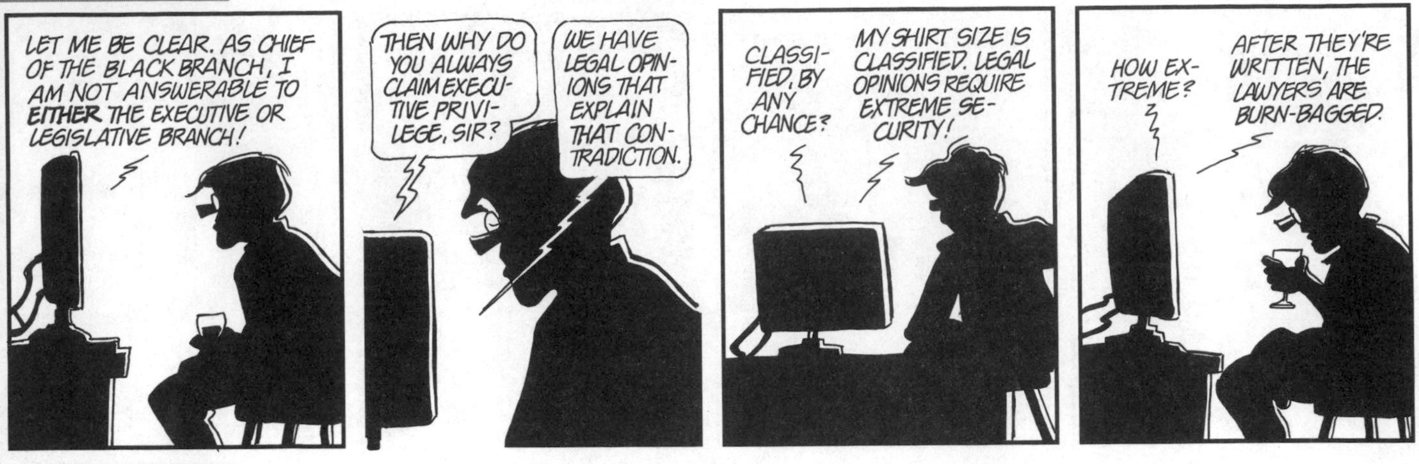
LET ME BE CLEAR. AS CHIEF OF THE BLACK BRANCH, I AM NOT ANSWERABLE TO **EITHER** THE EXECUTIVE OR LEGISLATIVE BRANCH!
THEN WHY DO YOU ALWAYS CLAIM EXECUTIVE PRIVILEGE, SIR?
WE HAVE LEGAL OPINIONS THAT EXPLAIN THAT CONTRADICTION.
CLASSIFIED, BY ANY CHANCE?
MY SHIRT SIZE IS CLASSIFIED. LEGAL OPINIONS REQUIRE EXTREME SECURITY!
HOW EXTREME?
AFTER THEY'RE WRITTEN, THE LAWYERS ARE BURN-BAGGED.

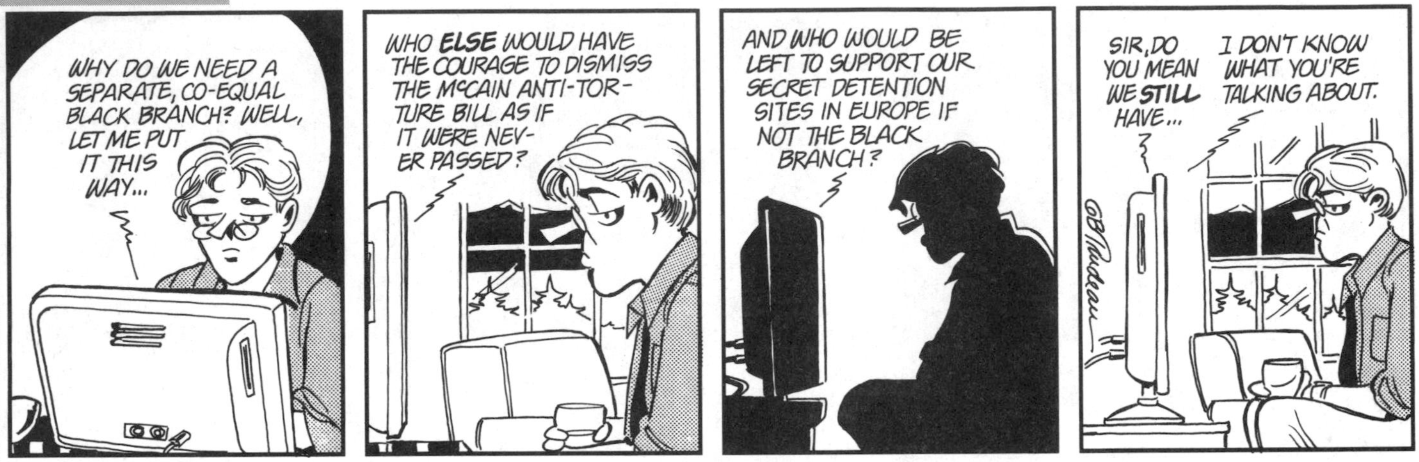
WHY DO WE NEED A SEPARATE, CO-EQUAL BLACK BRANCH? WELL, LET ME PUT IT THIS WAY...
WHO **ELSE** WOULD HAVE THE COURAGE TO DISMISS THE McCAIN ANTI-TORTURE BILL AS IF IT WERE NEVER PASSED?
AND WHO WOULD BE LEFT TO SUPPORT OUR SECRET DETENTION SITES IN EUROPE IF NOT THE BLACK BRANCH?
SIR, DO YOU MEAN WE **STILL** HAVE...
I DON'T KNOW WHAT YOU'RE TALKING ABOUT.
GB Trudeau

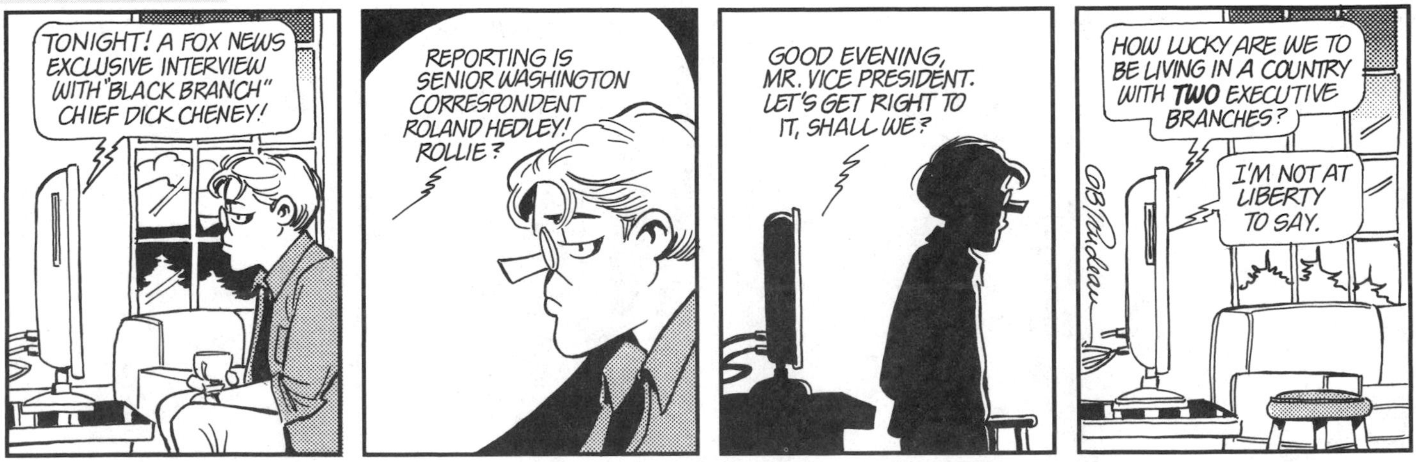
TONIGHT! A FOX NEWS EXCLUSIVE INTERVIEW WITH "BLACK BRANCH" CHIEF DICK CHENEY!
REPORTING IS SENIOR WASHINGTON CORRESPONDENT ROLAND HEDLEY! ROLLIE?
GOOD EVENING, MR. VICE PRESIDENT. LET'S GET RIGHT TO IT, SHALL WE?
HOW LUCKY ARE WE TO BE LIVING IN A COUNTRY WITH **TWO** EXECUTIVE BRANCHES?
I'M NOT AT LIBERTY TO SAY.
GB Trudeau

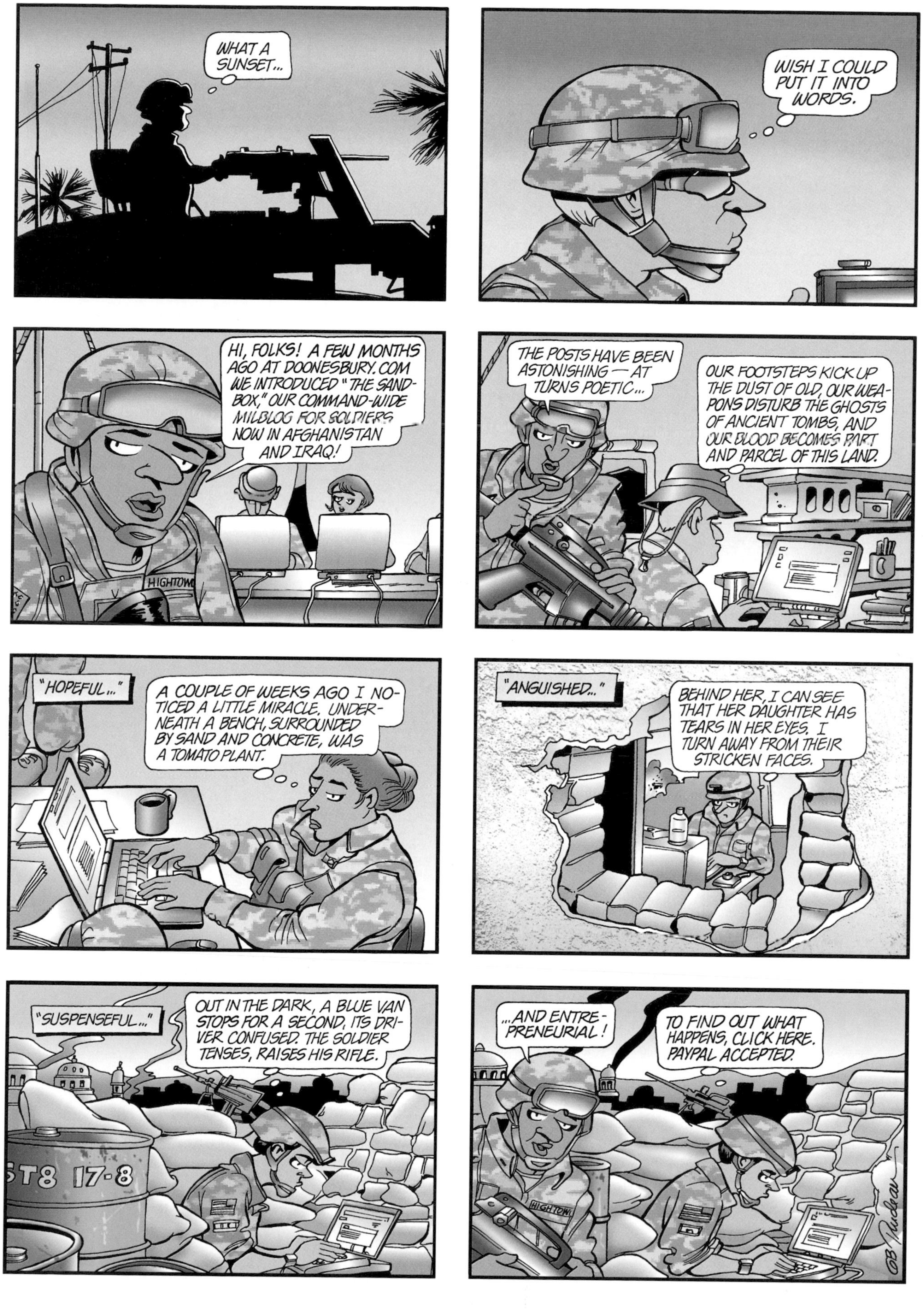
WHAT A SUNSET...
WISH I COULD PUT IT INTO WORDS.
HI, FOLKS! A FEW MONTHS AGO AT DOONESBURY.COM WE INTRODUCED "THE SANDBOX," OUR COMMAND-WIDE MILBLOG FOR SOLDIERS NOW IN AFGHANISTAN AND IRAQ!
HIGHTOW
THE POSTS HAVE BEEN ASTONISHING — AT TURNS POETIC...
OUR FOOTSTEPS KICK UP THE DUST OF OLD, OUR WEAPONS DISTURB THE GHOSTS OF ANCIENT TOMBS, AND OUR BLOOD BECOMES PART AND PARCEL OF THIS LAND.
"HOPEFUL..."
A COUPLE OF WEEKS AGO I NOTICED A LITTLE MIRACLE. UNDERNEATH A BENCH, SURROUNDED BY SAND AND CONCRETE, WAS A TOMATO PLANT.
"ANGUISHED..."
BEHIND HER, I CAN SEE THAT HER DAUGHTER HAS TEARS IN HER EYES. I TURN AWAY FROM THEIR STRICKEN FACES.
"SUSPENSEFUL..."
OUT IN THE DARK, A BLUE VAN STOPS FOR A SECOND, ITS DRIVER CONFUSED. THE SOLDIER TENSES, RAISES HIS RIFLE.
ST8 17-8
...AND ENTREPRENEURIAL!
TO FIND OUT WHAT HAPPENS, CLICK HERE. PAYPAL ACCEPTED.
HIGHTOW
GB Trudeau

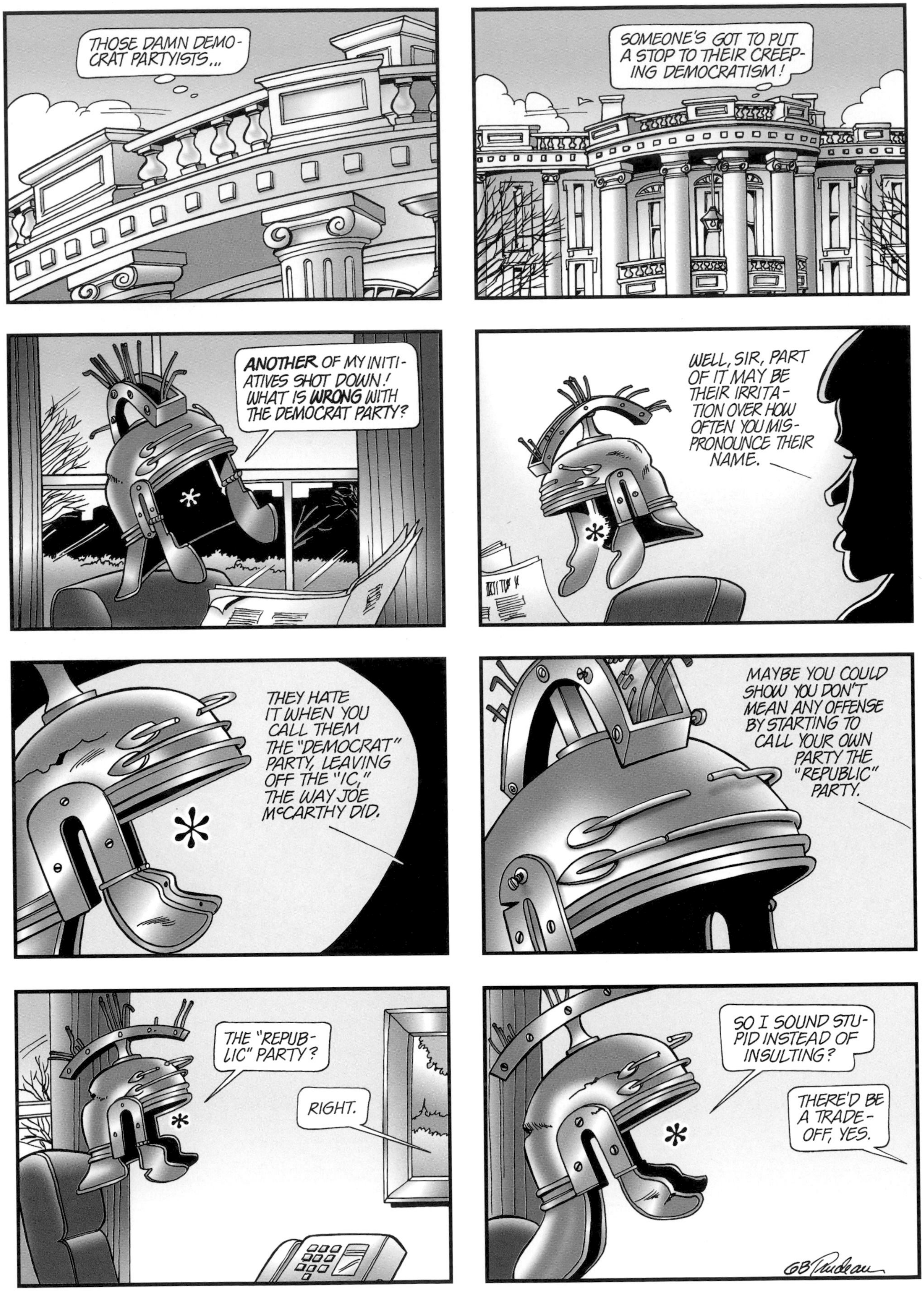
THOSE DAMN DEMOCRAT PARTYISTS...
SOMEONE'S GOT TO PUT A STOP TO THEIR CREEPING DEMOCRATISM!
ANOTHER OF MY INITIATIVES SHOT DOWN! WHAT IS WRONG WITH THE DEMOCRAT PARTY?
WELL, SIR, PART OF IT MAY BE THEIR IRRITATION OVER HOW OFTEN YOU MISPRONOUNCE THEIR NAME.
THEY HATE IT WHEN YOU CALL THEM THE "DEMOCRAT" PARTY, LEAVING OFF THE "IC," THE WAY JOE McCARTHY DID.
MAYBE YOU COULD SHOW YOU DON'T MEAN ANY OFFENSE BY STARTING TO CALL YOUR OWN PARTY THE "REPUBLIC" PARTY.
THE "REPUBLIC" PARTY?
RIGHT.
SO I SOUND STUPID INSTEAD OF INSULTING?
THERE'D BE A TRADE-OFF, YES.
GB Trudeau

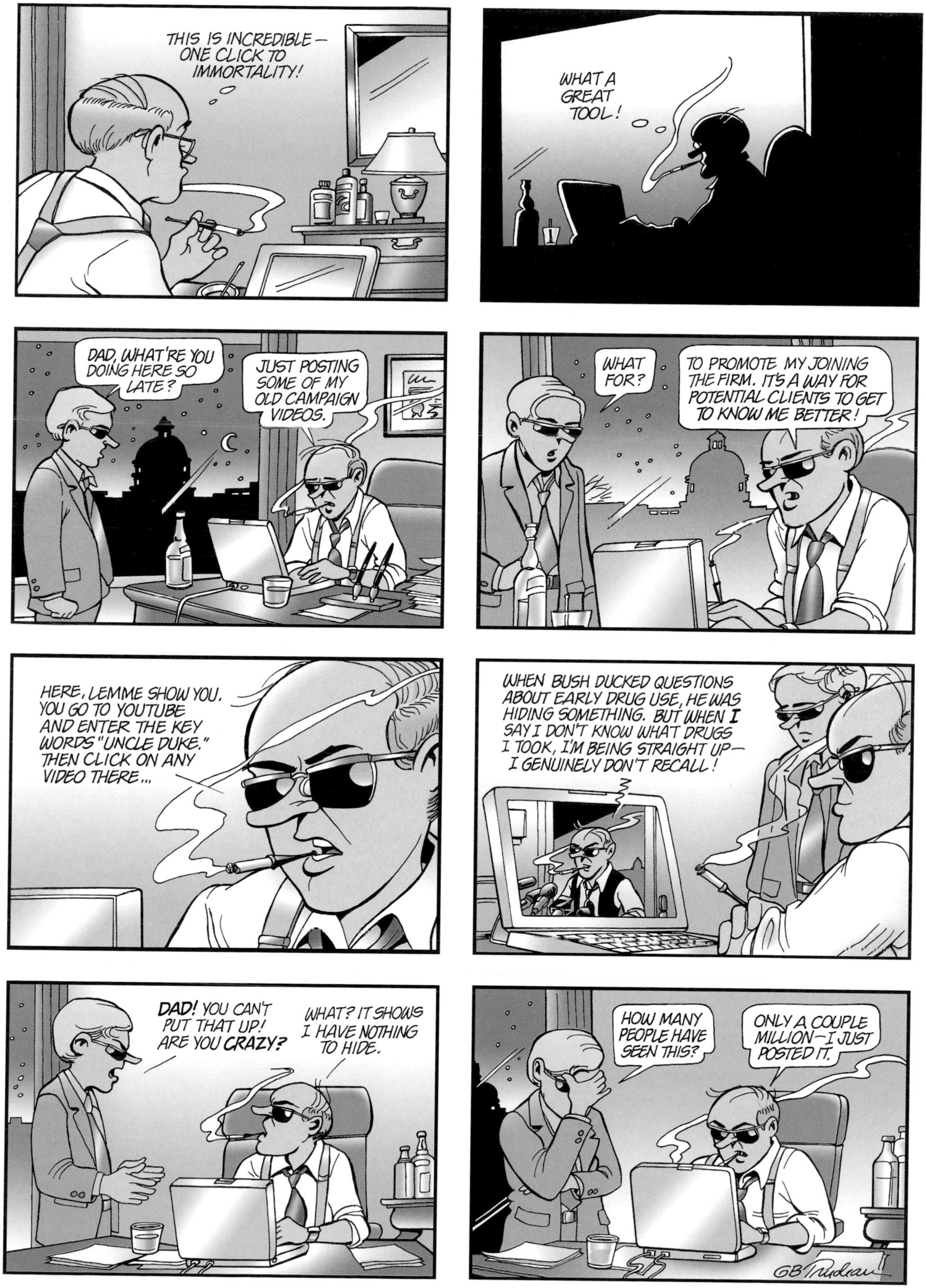
THIS IS INCREDIBLE— ONE CLICK TO IMMORTALITY!
WHAT A GREAT TOOL!
DAD, WHAT'RE YOU DOING HERE SO LATE?
JUST POSTING SOME OF MY OLD CAMPAIGN VIDEOS.
WHAT FOR?
TO PROMOTE MY JOINING THE FIRM. IT'S A WAY FOR POTENTIAL CLIENTS TO GET TO KNOW ME BETTER!
HERE, LEMME SHOW YOU. YOU GO TO YOUTUBE AND ENTER THE KEY WORDS "UNCLE DUKE." THEN CLICK ON ANY VIDEO THERE...
WHEN BUSH DUCKED QUESTIONS ABOUT EARLY DRUG USE, HE WAS HIDING SOMETHING. BUT WHEN **I** SAY I DON'T KNOW WHAT DRUGS I TOOK, I'M BEING STRAIGHT UP— I GENUINELY DON'T RECALL!
DAD! YOU CAN'T PUT THAT UP! ARE YOU **CRAZY?**
WHAT? IT SHOWS I HAVE NOTHING TO HIDE.
HOW MANY PEOPLE HAVE SEEN THIS?
ONLY A COUPLE MILLION—I JUST POSTED IT.
GB Trudeau

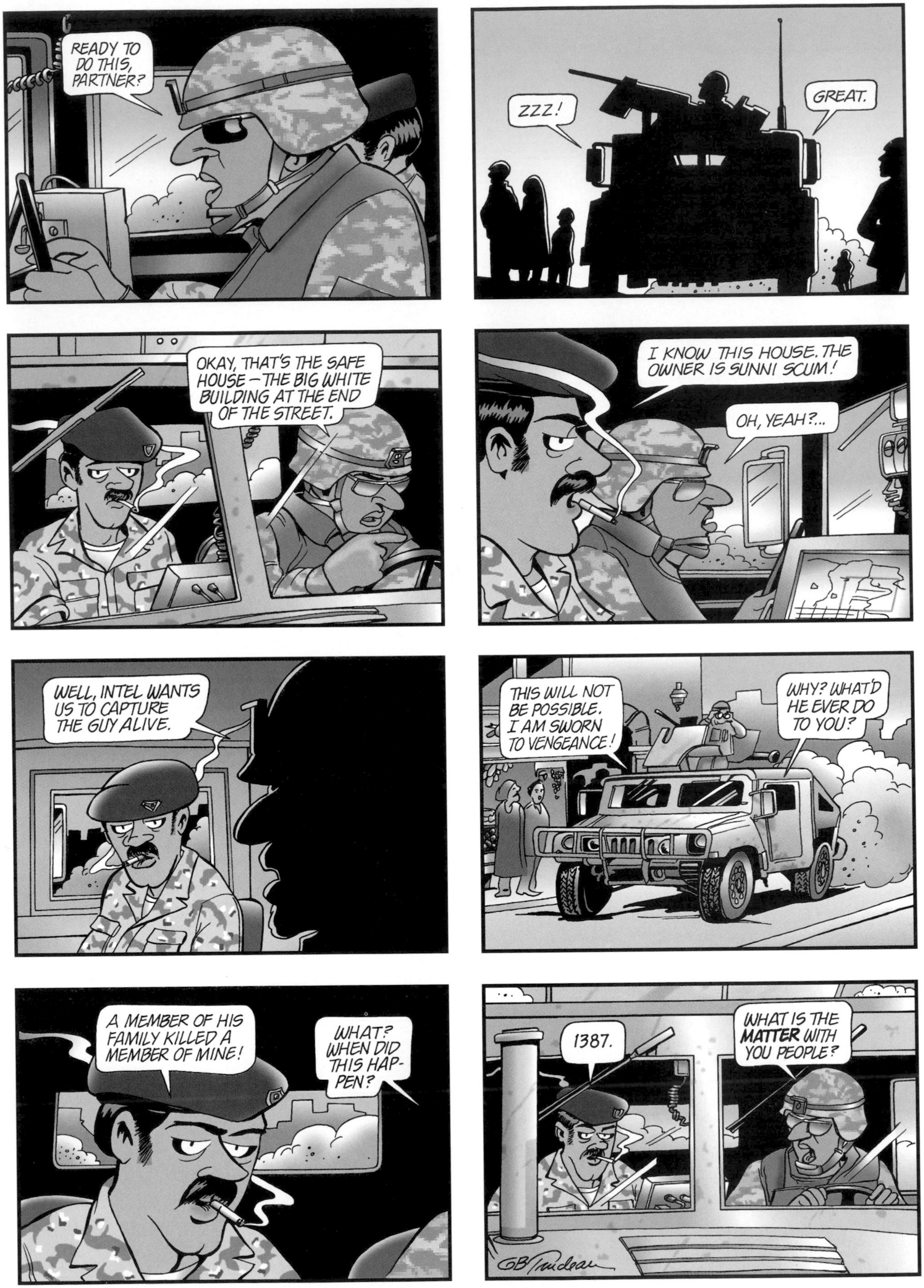
READY TO DO THIS, PARTNER?
ZZZ!
GREAT.
OKAY, THAT'S THE SAFE HOUSE—THE BIG WHITE BUILDING AT THE END OF THE STREET.
I KNOW THIS HOUSE. THE OWNER IS SUNNI SCUM!
OH, YEAH?...
WELL, INTEL WANTS US TO CAPTURE THE GUY ALIVE.
THIS WILL NOT BE POSSIBLE. I AM SWORN TO VENGEANCE!
WHY? WHAT'D HE EVER DO TO YOU?
A MEMBER OF HIS FAMILY KILLED A MEMBER OF MINE!
WHAT? WHEN DID THIS HAP-PEN?
1387.
WHAT IS THE **MATTER** WITH YOU PEOPLE?
GB Trudeau

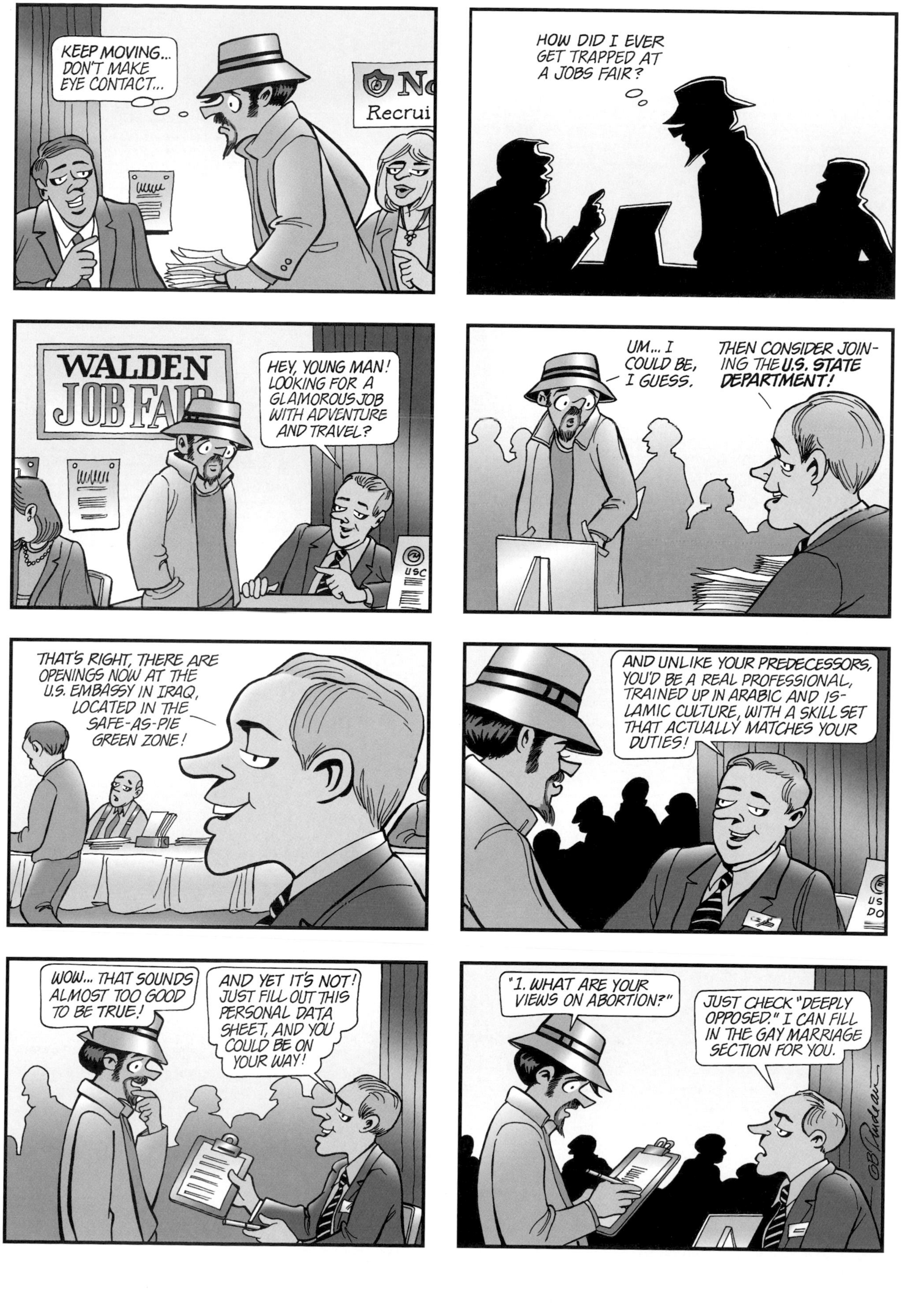
KEEP MOVING... DON'T MAKE EYE CONTACT...
HOW DID I EVER GET TRAPPED AT A JOBS FAIR?
WALDEN JOB FAIR
HEY, YOUNG MAN! LOOKING FOR A GLAMOROUS JOB WITH ADVENTURE AND TRAVEL?
UM... I COULD BE, I GUESS.
THEN CONSIDER JOINING THE U.S. STATE DEPARTMENT!
THAT'S RIGHT, THERE ARE OPENINGS NOW AT THE U.S. EMBASSY IN IRAQ, LOCATED IN THE SAFE-AS-PIE GREEN ZONE!
AND UNLIKE YOUR PREDECESSORS, YOU'D BE A REAL PROFESSIONAL, TRAINED UP IN ARABIC AND ISLAMIC CULTURE, WITH A SKILL SET THAT ACTUALLY MATCHES YOUR DUTIES!
WOW... THAT SOUNDS ALMOST TOO GOOD TO BE TRUE!
AND YET IT'S NOT! JUST FILL OUT THIS PERSONAL DATA SHEET, AND YOU COULD BE ON YOUR WAY!
"1. WHAT ARE YOUR VIEWS ON ABORTION?"
JUST CHECK "DEEPLY OPPOSED." I CAN FILL IN THE GAY MARRIAGE SECTION FOR YOU.

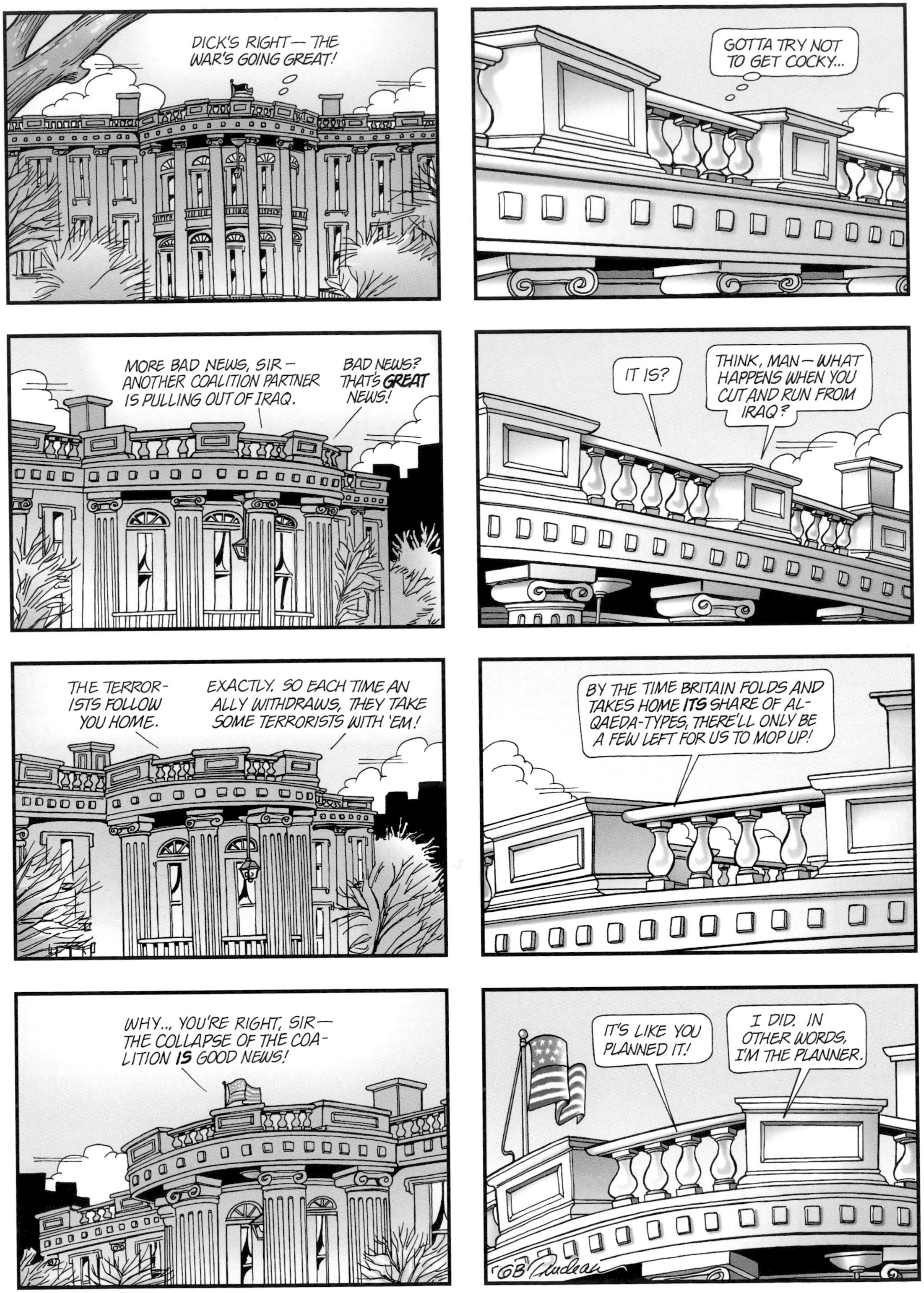
DICK'S RIGHT— THE WAR'S GOING GREAT!
GOTTA TRY NOT TO GET COCKY...
MORE BAD NEWS, SIR— ANOTHER COALITION PARTNER IS PULLING OUT OF IRAQ.
BAD NEWS? THAT'S GREAT NEWS!
IT IS?
THINK, MAN— WHAT HAPPENS WHEN YOU CUT AND RUN FROM IRAQ?
THE TERRORISTS FOLLOW YOU HOME.
EXACTLY. SO EACH TIME AN ALLY WITHDRAWS, THEY TAKE SOME TERRORISTS WITH 'EM!
BY THE TIME BRITAIN FOLDS AND TAKES HOME ITS SHARE OF AL-QAEDA-TYPES, THERE'LL ONLY BE A FEW LEFT FOR US TO MOP UP!
WHY.., YOU'RE RIGHT, SIR— THE COLLAPSE OF THE COALITION IS GOOD NEWS!
IT'S LIKE YOU PLANNED IT!
I DID. IN OTHER WORDS, I'M THE PLANNER.
©GB Trudeau

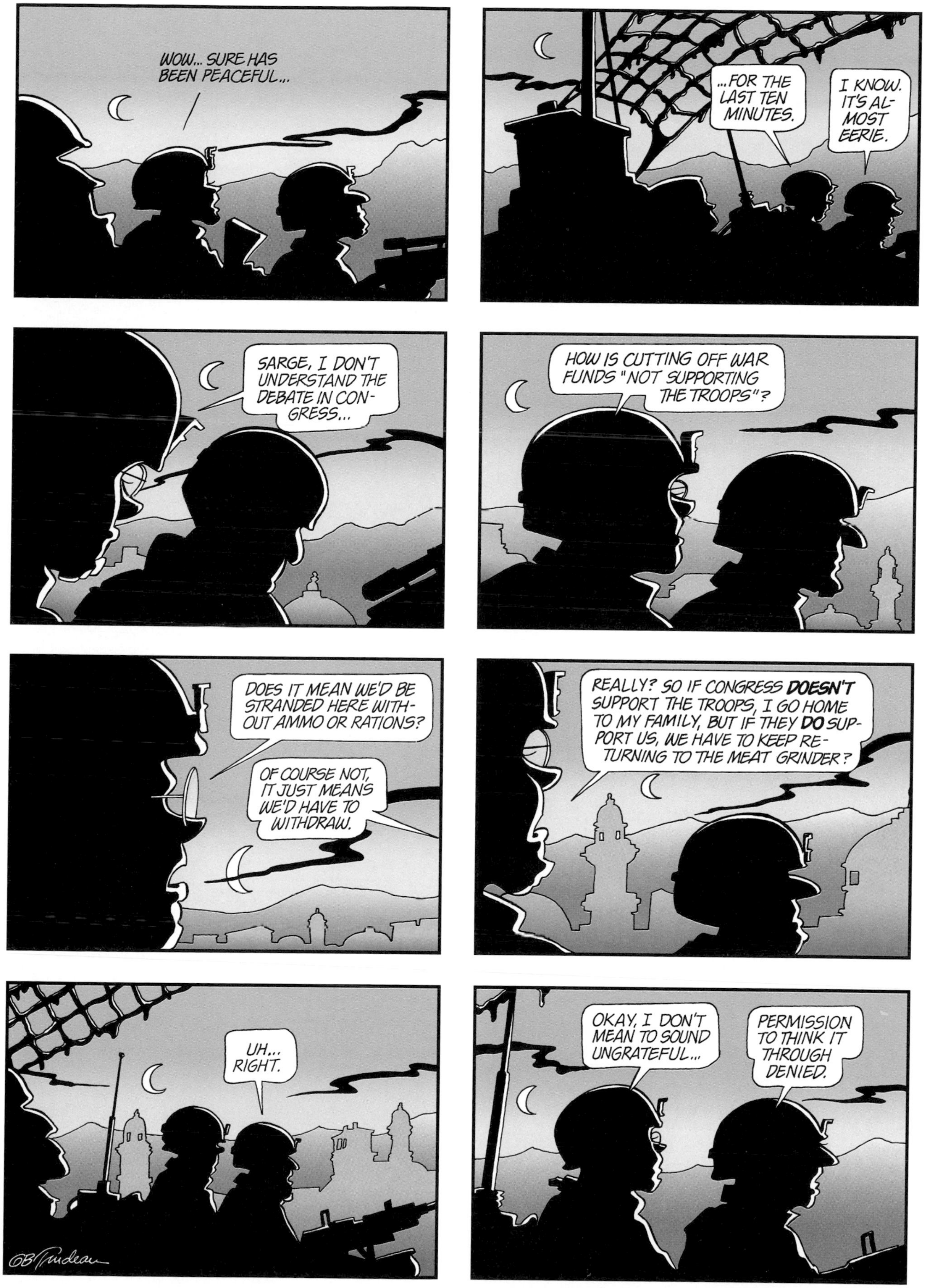
WOW... SURE HAS BEEN PEACEFUL...
...FOR THE LAST TEN MINUTES.
I KNOW. IT'S AL-MOST EERIE.
SARGE, I DON'T UNDERSTAND THE DEBATE IN CON-GRESS...
HOW IS CUTTING OFF WAR FUNDS "NOT SUPPORTING THE TROOPS"?
DOES IT MEAN WE'D BE STRANDED HERE WITH-OUT AMMO OR RATIONS?
OF COURSE NOT, IT JUST MEANS WE'D HAVE TO WITHDRAW.
REALLY? SO IF CONGRESS **DOESN'T** SUPPORT THE TROOPS, I GO HOME TO MY FAMILY, BUT IF THEY **DO** SUP-PORT US, WE HAVE TO KEEP RE-TURNING TO THE MEAT GRINDER?
UH... RIGHT.
OKAY, I DON'T MEAN TO SOUND UNGRATEFUL...
PERMISSION TO THINK IT THROUGH DENIED.

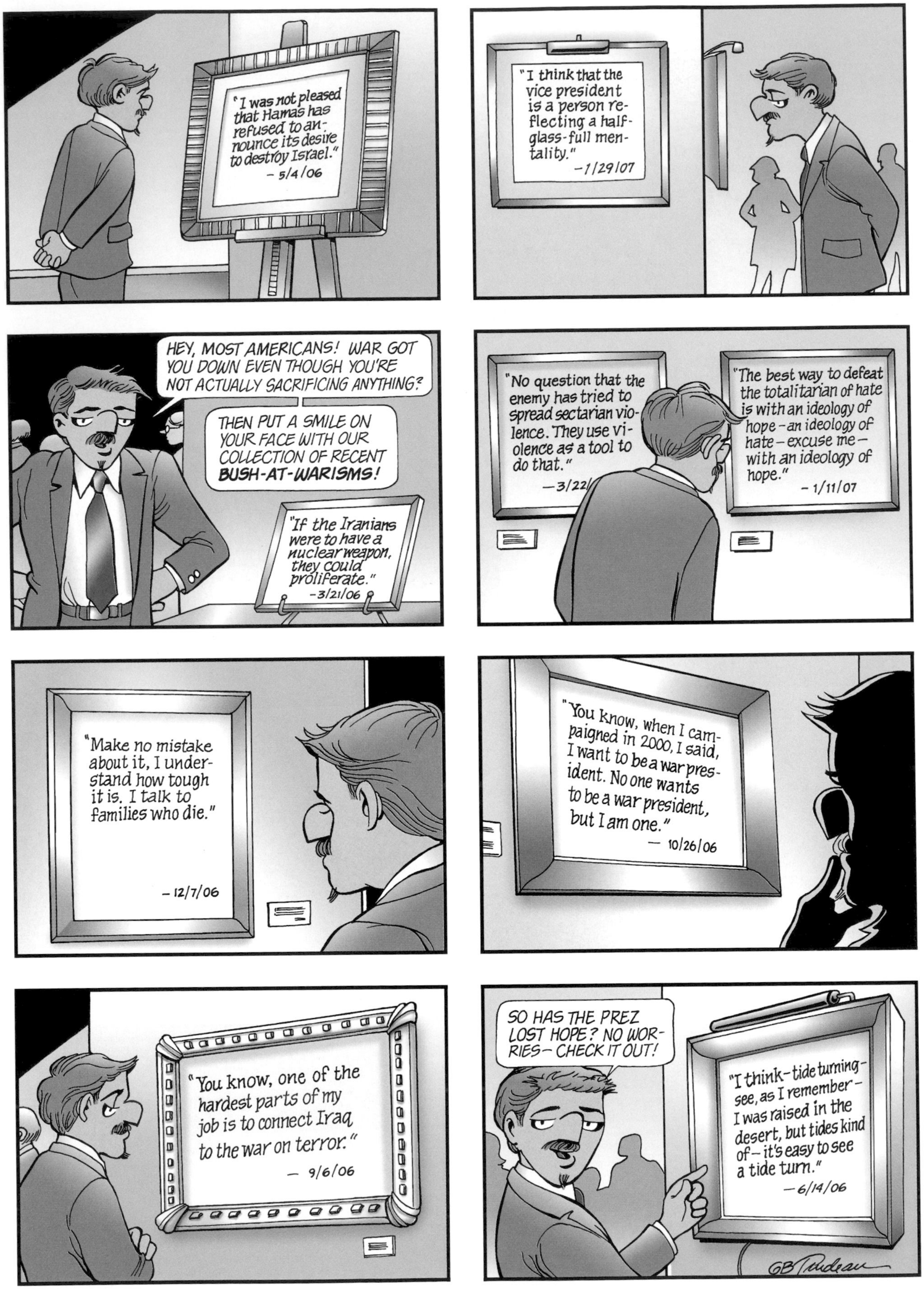
"I was not pleased that Hamas has refused to announce its desire to destroy Israel." – 5/4/06
"I think that the vice president is a person reflecting a half-glass-full mentality." –1/29/07
HEY, MOST AMERICANS! WAR GOT YOU DOWN EVEN THOUGH YOU'RE NOT ACTUALLY SACRIFICING ANYTHING?
THEN PUT A SMILE ON YOUR FACE WITH OUR COLLECTION OF RECENT BUSH-AT-WARISMS!
"If the Iranians were to have a nuclear weapon, they could proliferate." –3/21/06
"No question that the enemy has tried to spread sectarian violence. They use violence as a tool to do that." –3/22/
"The best way to defeat the totalitarian of hate is with an ideology of hope – an ideology of hate – excuse me – with an ideology of hope." – 1/11/07
"Make no mistake about it, I understand how tough it is. I talk to families who die." – 12/7/06
"You know, when I campaigned in 2000, I said, I want to be a war president. No one wants to be a war president, but I am one." — 10/26/06
"You know, one of the hardest parts of my job is to connect Iraq to the war on terror." — 9/6/06
SO HAS THE PREZ LOST HOPE? NO WORRIES – CHECK IT OUT!
"I think – tide turning – see, as I remember – I was raised in the desert, but tides kind of – it's easy to see a tide turn." –6/14/06
GBTrudeau

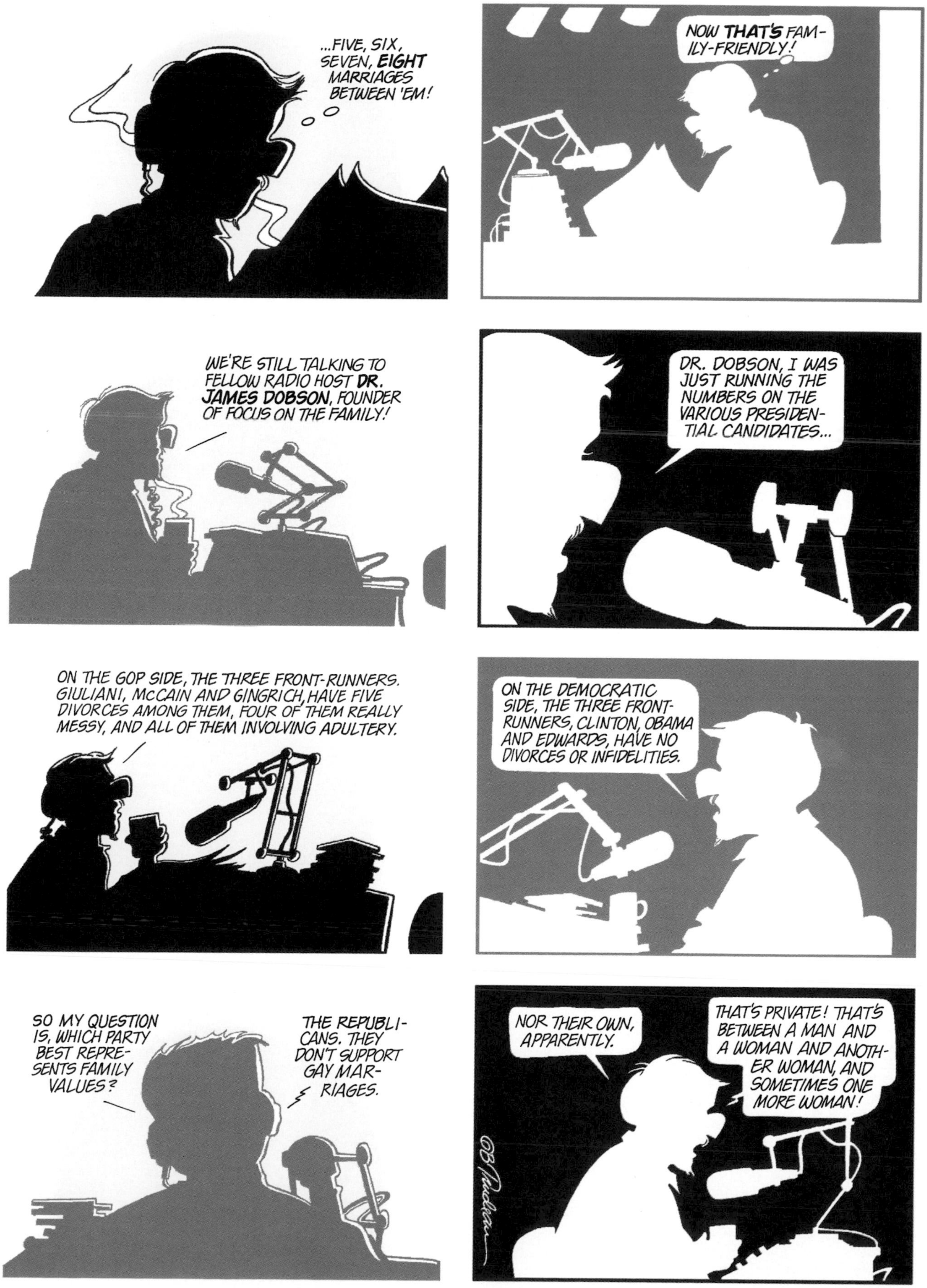

...FIVE, SIX, SEVEN, **EIGHT** MARRIAGES BETWEEN 'EM!
NOW **THAT'S** FAMILY-FRIENDLY!
WE'RE STILL TALKING TO FELLOW RADIO HOST **DR. JAMES DOBSON**, FOUNDER OF FOCUS ON THE FAMILY!
DR. DOBSON, I WAS JUST RUNNING THE NUMBERS ON THE VARIOUS PRESIDENTIAL CANDIDATES...
ON THE GOP SIDE, THE THREE FRONT-RUNNERS. GIULIANI, McCAIN AND GINGRICH, HAVE FIVE DIVORCES AMONG THEM, FOUR OF THEM REALLY MESSY, AND ALL OF THEM INVOLVING ADULTERY.
ON THE DEMOCRATIC SIDE, THE THREE FRONT-RUNNERS, CLINTON, OBAMA AND EDWARDS, HAVE NO DIVORCES OR INFIDELITIES.
SO MY QUESTION IS, WHICH PARTY BEST REPRESENTS FAMILY VALUES?
THE REPUBLICANS. THEY DON'T SUPPORT GAY MARRIAGES.
NOR THEIR OWN, APPARENTLY.
THAT'S PRIVATE! THAT'S BETWEEN A MAN AND A WOMAN AND ANOTHER WOMAN, AND SOMETIMES ONE MORE WOMAN!

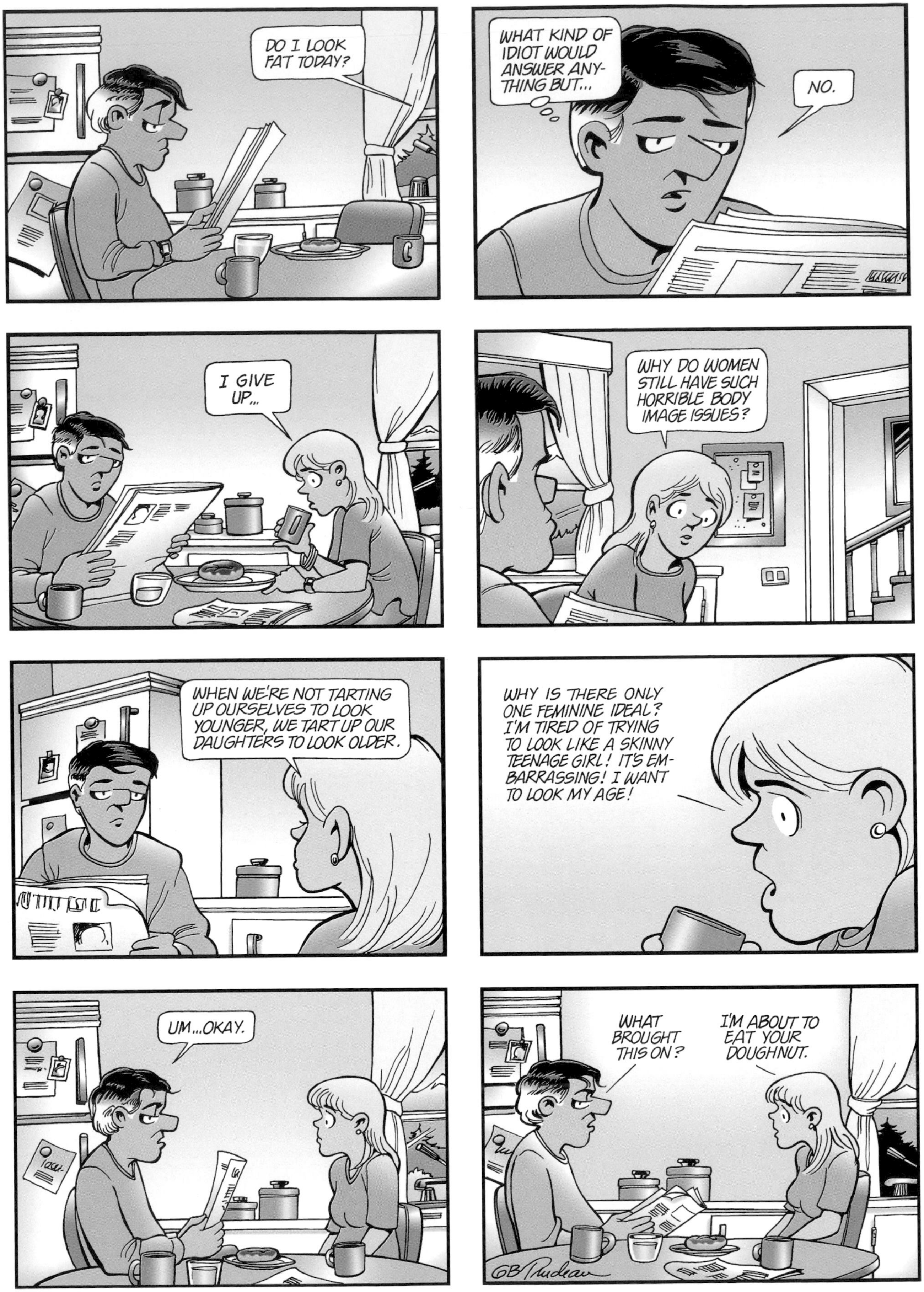
DO I LOOK FAT TODAY?
WHAT KIND OF IDIOT WOULD ANSWER ANY-THING BUT...
NO.
I GIVE UP...
WHY DO WOMEN STILL HAVE SUCH HORRIBLE BODY IMAGE ISSUES?
WHEN WE'RE NOT TARTING UP OURSELVES TO LOOK YOUNGER, WE TART UP OUR DAUGHTERS TO LOOK OLDER.
WHY IS THERE ONLY ONE FEMININE IDEAL? I'M TIRED OF TRYING TO LOOK LIKE A SKINNY TEENAGE GIRL! IT'S EM-BARRASSING! I WANT TO LOOK MY AGE!
UM...OKAY.
WHAT BROUGHT THIS ON?
I'M ABOUT TO EAT YOUR DOUGHNUT.
GB Trudeau

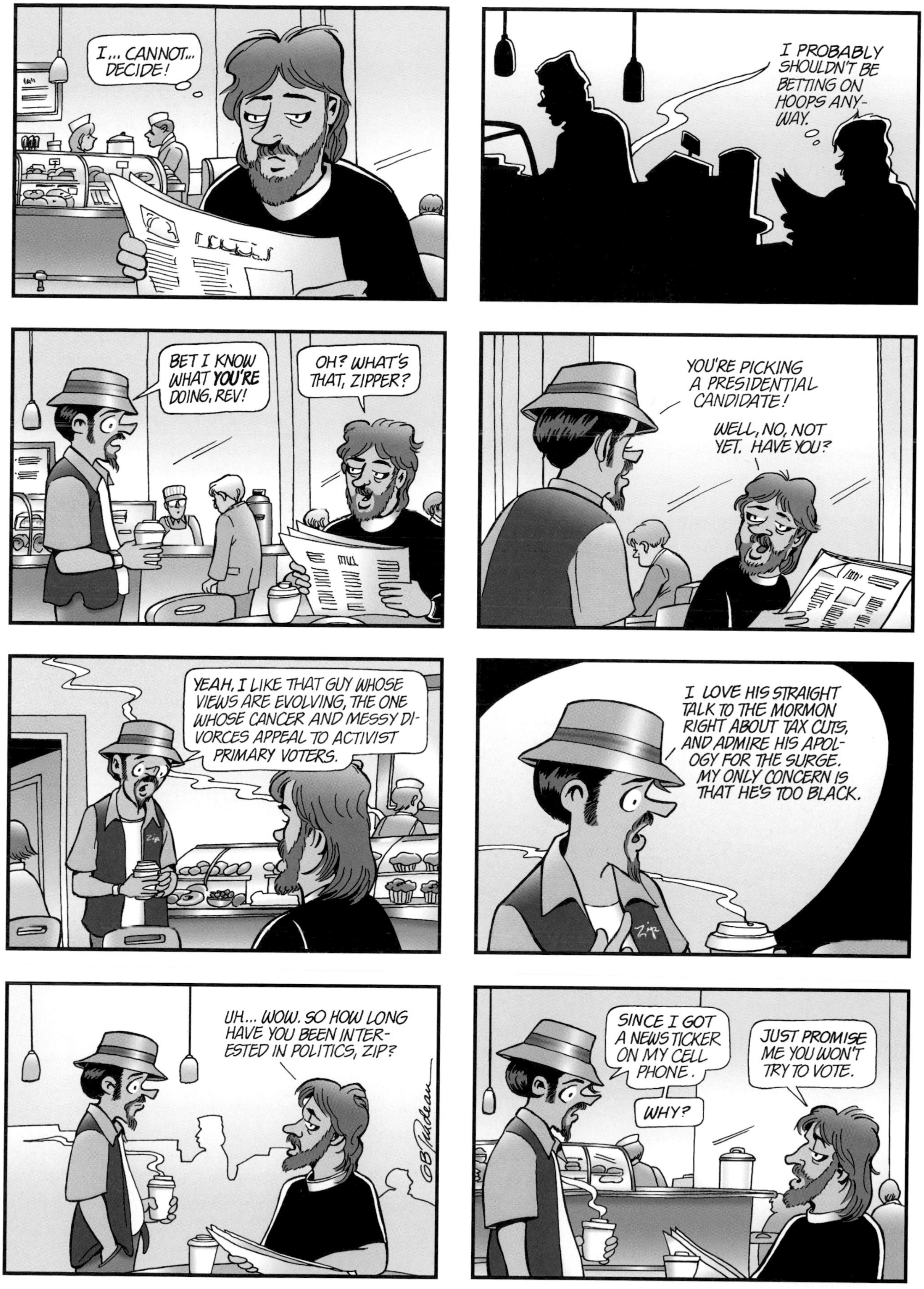

I... CANNOT... DECIDE!
I PROBABLY SHOULDN'T BE BETTING ON HOOPS ANY-WAY.
BET I KNOW WHAT **YOU'RE** DOING, REV!
OH? WHAT'S THAT, ZIPPER?
YOU'RE PICKING A PRESIDENTIAL CANDIDATE!
WELL, NO, NOT YET. HAVE YOU?
YEAH, I LIKE THAT GUY WHOSE VIEWS ARE EVOLVING, THE ONE WHOSE CANCER AND MESSY DI-VORCES APPEAL TO ACTIVIST PRIMARY VOTERS.
I LOVE HIS STRAIGHT TALK TO THE MORMON RIGHT ABOUT TAX CUTS, AND ADMIRE HIS APOL-OGY FOR THE SURGE. MY ONLY CONCERN IS THAT HE'S TOO BLACK.
UH... WOW. SO HOW LONG HAVE YOU BEEN INTER-ESTED IN POLITICS, ZIP?
SINCE I GOT A NEWS TICKER ON MY CELL PHONE.
JUST PROMISE ME YOU WON'T TRY TO VOTE.
WHY?

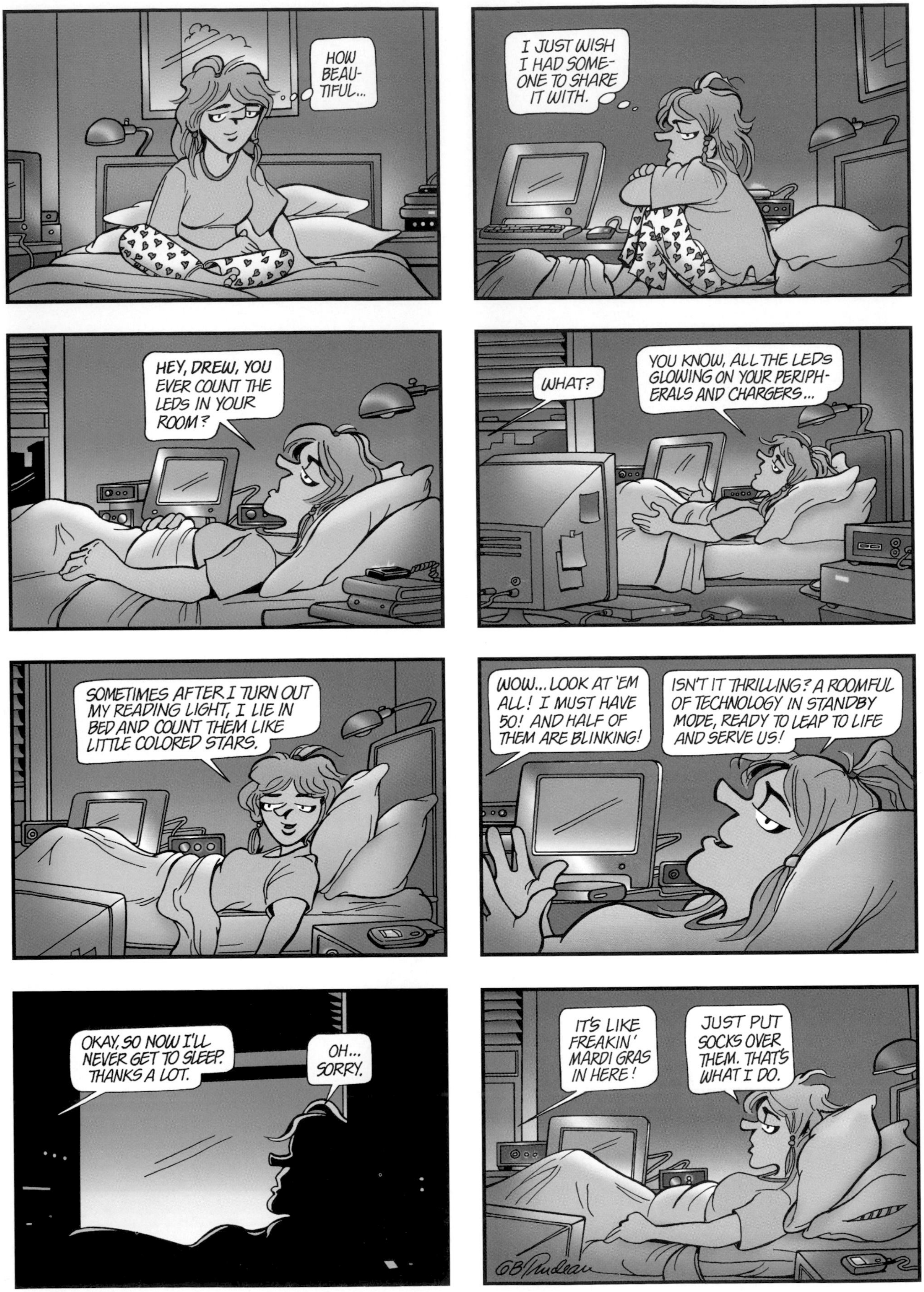
HOW BEAU-TIFUL...
I JUST WISH I HAD SOME-ONE TO SHARE IT WITH.
HEY, DREW, YOU EVER COUNT THE LEDS IN YOUR ROOM?
WHAT?
YOU KNOW, ALL THE LEDS GLOWING ON YOUR PERIPH-ERALS AND CHARGERS...
SOMETIMES AFTER I TURN OUT MY READING LIGHT, I LIE IN BED AND COUNT THEM LIKE LITTLE COLORED STARS.
WOW... LOOK AT 'EM ALL! I MUST HAVE 50! AND HALF OF THEM ARE BLINKING!
ISN'T IT THRILLING? A ROOMFUL OF TECHNOLOGY IN STANDBY MODE, READY TO LEAP TO LIFE AND SERVE US!
OKAY, SO NOW I'LL NEVER GET TO SLEEP. THANKS A LOT.
OH... SORRY.
IT'S LIKE FREAKIN' MARDI GRAS IN HERE!
JUST PUT SOCKS OVER THEM. THAT'S WHAT I DO.

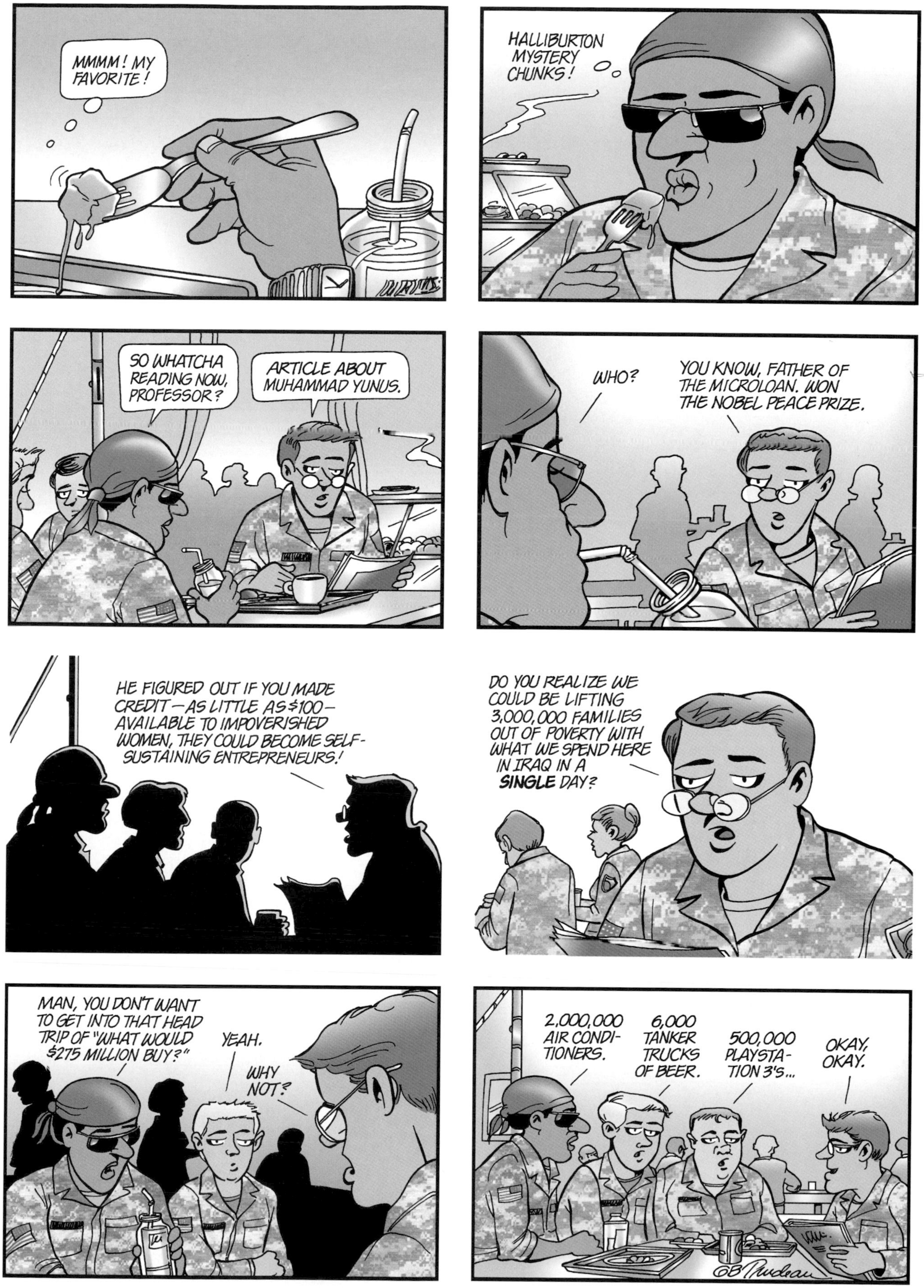
MMMM! MY FAVORITE!
HALLIBURTON MYSTERY CHUNKS!
SO WHATCHA READING NOW, PROFESSOR?
ARTICLE ABOUT MUHAMMAD YUNUS.
WHO?
YOU KNOW, FATHER OF THE MICROLOAN. WON THE NOBEL PEACE PRIZE.
HE FIGURED OUT IF YOU MADE CREDIT—AS LITTLE AS $100—AVAILABLE TO IMPOVERISHED WOMEN, THEY COULD BECOME SELF-SUSTAINING ENTREPRENEURS!
DO YOU REALIZE WE COULD BE LIFTING 3,000,000 FAMILIES OUT OF POVERTY WITH WHAT WE SPEND HERE IN IRAQ IN A **SINGLE** DAY?
MAN, YOU DON'T WANT TO GET INTO THAT HEAD TRIP OF "WHAT WOULD $275 MILLION BUY?"
YEAH.
WHY NOT?
2,000,000 AIR CONDITIONERS.
6,000 TANKER TRUCKS OF BEER.
500,000 PLAYSTATION 3'S...
OKAY, OKAY.
©B Trudeau

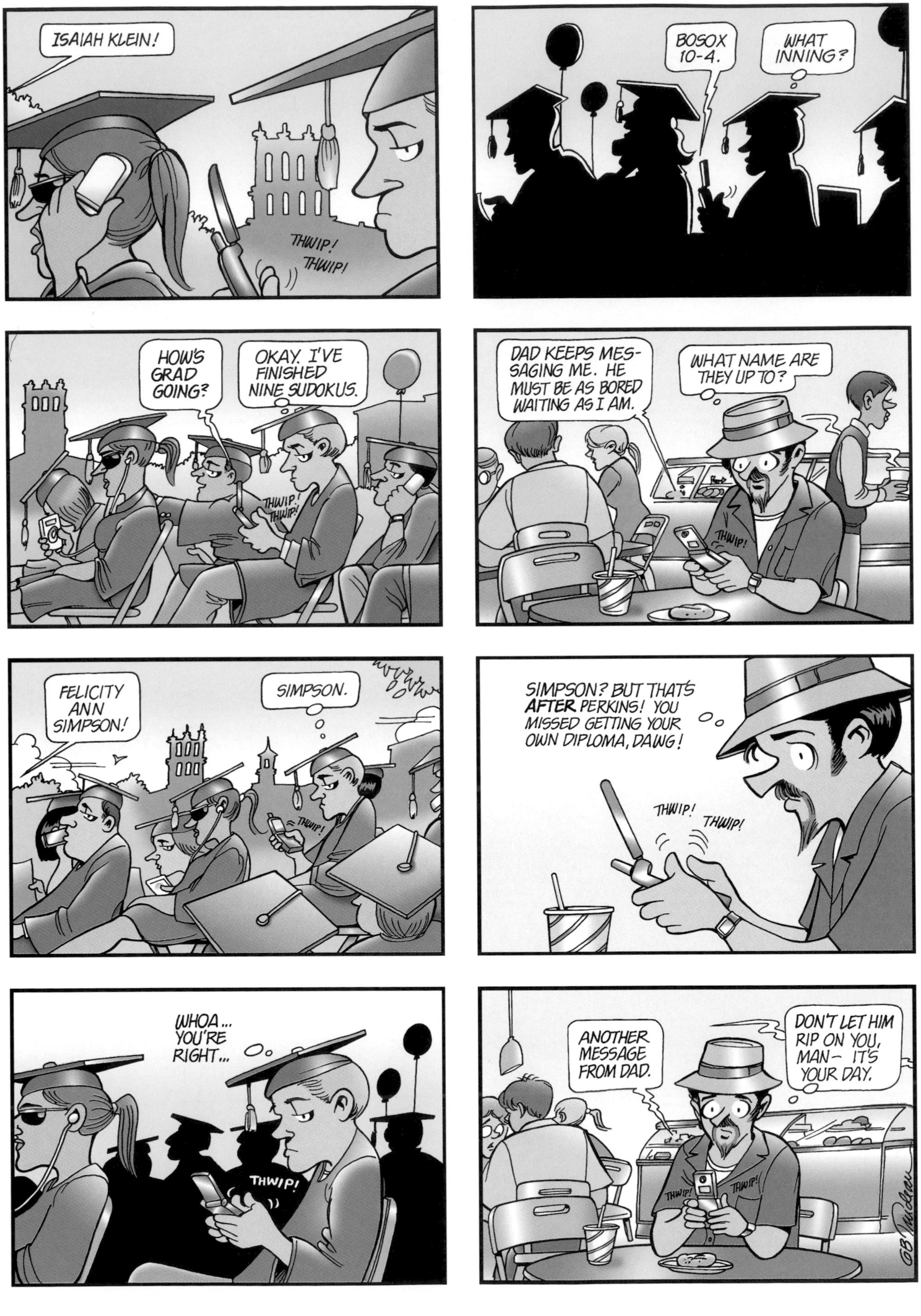
ISAIAH KLEIN!
THWIP! THWIP!
BOSOX 10-4.
WHAT INNING?
HOW'S GRAD GOING?
OKAY. I'VE FINISHED NINE SUDOKUS.
THWIP! THWIP!
DAD KEEPS MESSAGING ME. HE MUST BE AS BORED WAITING AS I AM.
WHAT NAME ARE THEY UP TO?
THWIP!
FELICITY ANN SIMPSON!
SIMPSON.
THWIP!
SIMPSON? BUT THAT'S **AFTER** PERKINS! YOU MISSED GETTING YOUR OWN DIPLOMA, DAWG!
THWIP! THWIP!
WHOA... YOU'RE RIGHT...
THWIP!
ANOTHER MESSAGE FROM DAD.
DON'T LET HIM RIP ON YOU, MAN— IT'S YOUR DAY.
THWIP! THWIP!

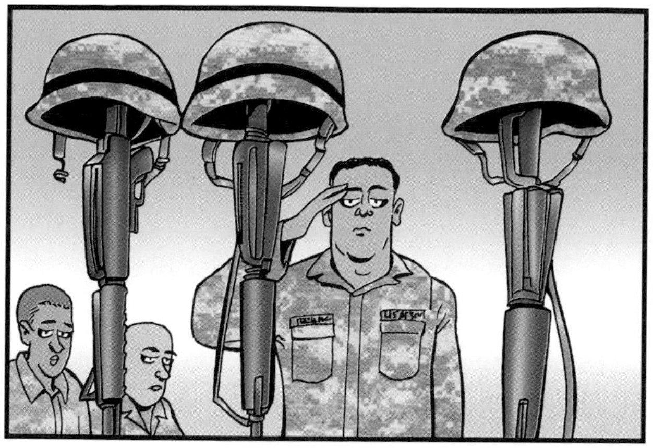

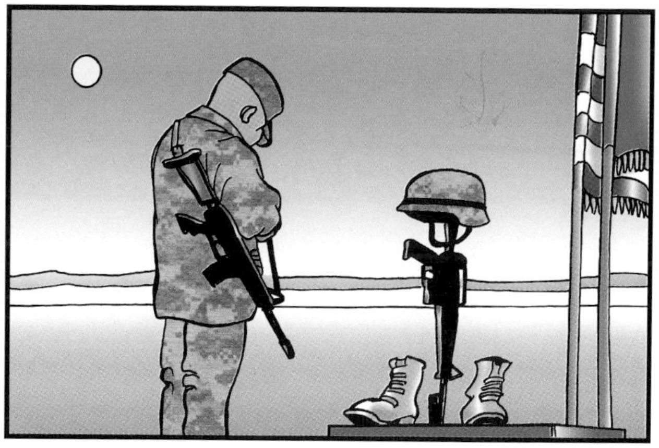

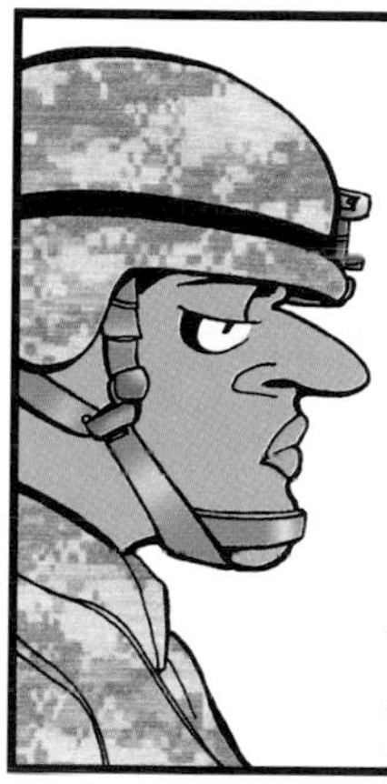

OPERATION IRAQI FREEDOM

IN MEMORIAM

SINCE 4/26/06 - PART I

Jacob H. Allcott • Michael E. Bouthot • Kyle A. Colnot • Eric D. King • Robert W. Ehney • Shawn Thomas Lasswell Jr. Metodio A. Bandonill • Aaron William Simons • Raymond L. Henry • Richard J. Herrema • Michael L. Ford • Bobby Mendez • Mark A. Wall • Matthew A. Webber • Jose Gomez Bryant A. Herlem • Edward G. Davis III • Brandon M. Hardy Lea R. Mills • Steve M. Sakoda • Robbie Glen Light Robert L. Moscillo • Christopher M. Eckhardt • Benjamin T. Zieske • Joseph E. Proctor • Brian S. Letendre • Bryan L. Quinton • Gavin B. Reinke • Stephen R. Bixler • Elisha R. Parker • Alva L. Gaylord • Carlos N. Saenz • Teodoro Torres Nathan J. Vacho • Dale James Kelly Jr. • David Michael Veverka • Loon Deraps • Matthew J. Fenton • Cory L. Palmer • Emmanuel L. Legaspi • Gregory A. Wagner Aaron P. Latimer • Alessandro Carbonaro • Armer N. Burkart • Eric D. Clark • Stephen P. Snowberger III • Jason K. Burnett • David J. Grames Sanchez • Michael L. Licalzi Steve Vahaviolos • Brandon L. Teeters • Adam C. Conboy Ron Gebur • Richard Z. James • John W. Engeman

Jamie D. Weeks • Robert H. West • Matthew W. Worrel • Shane Mahaffee Jose S. Marin-Dominguez Jr. • Hatak Yuka Keyu M. Yearby • Grant Allen Dampier • Marion Flint Jr. • Santiago M. Halsel • Lee Hamilton Deal • Lonnie Calvin Allen Jr. • Nicholas Cournoyer • Daniel E. Holland • Robert Seidel III • William B. Fulks • Benito A. Ramirez David Christoff Jr. • William J. Leusink • Michael L. Hermanson • Steven Freund • Robert G. Posivio III • Robert E. Blair • Douglas A. DiCenzo • Caleb A. Lufkin • Adam Lucas J. Adan Garcia • Richard A. Bennett • Nathanael J. Doring • James A. Funkhouser Jeremy M. Loveless • Brock L. Bucklin • Bobby R. West • Alexander J. Kolasa • Benjamin E. Mejia • Brett L. Tribble • Darren Harmon • Ryan J. Cummings • Michael D. Stover • Issac S. Lawson • Jamie Jaenke • Gary Rovinski • Andy D. Anderson • Daniel Gionet • Carlos E. Pernell • Ryan T. Sanders • Richard A. Blakley • Mark T. Smykowski • David N. Crombie Scott M. Love • John Shaw Vaughan • Clarence D. McSwain • Luis D. Santos • Daniel Crabtree • Ben Slaven • Jose M. Velez • Salvador Guerrero • Brent Zoucha • Zachary M. Alday • Michael A. Estrella • Jeremiah S. Santos • David J. Babineau • Kristian Menchaca Thomas Lowell Tucker • Brent W. Koch • Robert L. Jones • Reyes Ramirez • Christopher D. Leon • Brandon J. Webb • Christopher N. White • Benjamin D. Williams • Jason J. Buzzard • Sirlou C. Cuaresma • Nicholas J. Whyte • Riley E. Baker • Paul A. Beyer • Mario J. Bievre • Ryan J. Buckley • Devon J. Gibbons • Channing G. Singletary • Benjamin J. Laymon • Justin Dean Norton • Virruota A. Sanchez • Paul N. King • Terry Lisk • Michael J. Potocki • Raymond J. Plouhar • Jeremy Jones • Terry O.P. Wallace • Jason W. Morrow Rex A. Page • Ryan J. Clark • Bryan C. Luckey • James P. Muldoon • Christopher D. Rose • Kyle Miller • Carl Jerome Ware Jr. • Collin T. Mason • Justin Noyes • Paul Pabla Omar Flores • Troy Carlin Linden • Joseph P. Micks • Damien M. Montoya • Duane J. Dreasky • Irving Hernandez Jr. • Jerry A. Tharp • Al'Kaila Floyd • Thomas B. Turner Jr.

Andres J. Contreras • Manuel J. Holguin • Jason M. Evey • Nathaniel S. Baughman Michael A Dickinson II • Kenneth I. Pugh • Scott R. Smith • Mark Richard Vecchione Geofrey R. Cayer • Derek J. Plowman • Julian A. Ramon • Matthew P. Wallace Christopher T. Pate • Adam J. Fargo • Blake H. Russell • Christopher Swanson • Dennis K. Samson Jr. • Jason M. West • Stephen W. Castner • Joseph A. Graves • Edward A Koth James W. Higgins • Adam R. Murray • Timothy D. Roos • Enrique Henry Sanchez • Phillip E. Baucus • Anthony E. Butterfield • Jason Hanson • Christian B. Williams • Joshua Ford Hai Ming Hsia • Ryan D. Jopek • Dustin D. Laird • Joseph A. Tomci • Marc A. Lee • Kurt Edward Dechen • George M. Ulloa Jr. • Bradley H. Beste • Leroy Segura Jr. • Clint J. Storey Brian J. Kubik • Carlton A. Clark • Tracy L. Melvin • Zachary A. Seale • Jose Zamora Jeffery S. Brown • Aaron Jagger • Steven P. Mennemeyer • Ignacio Ramirez • Shane W. Woods • Jeremy Z. Long • Kenneth A. Jenkins • Michael C. Lloyd • Kevin L. Zeigler Jeffrey S. Loa • John P. Phillips • Michael Dennis Glover • John James McKenna IV James J. Arellano • Ruben J. Villa Jr. • Marquees A. Quick • Gabriel G. DeRoo • Adam Anthony Galvez • Randy Lee Newman • Chadwick Thomas Kenyon • Brad A. Clemmons Paul J. Darga • Thomas J. Barbieri • James Daniel Hirlston • Jeremy E. King • William E. Thorne • Gordon George Solomon • Dwayne E. Williams • Jordan C. Pierson • Edgardo Zayas • David G. Weimortz • David J. Almazan • Kenneth Cross • Dan Dolan • Seth A. Hildreth • Moises Jazmine • Joshua D. Jones • Qixing Lee • Shaun A. Novak • Tristan Smith • Darry Benson • Jeffrey J. Hansen • Donald E. Champlin • Matthew E. Schneider Shannon L. Squires • Matthew J. Vosbein • Christopher Tyler Warndorf • Joshua R. Hanson • Colin Joseph Wolfe • Michael L. Deason • Angel D. Mercado-Velazquez • Cliff Golla • Eugene Alex • Edwin Anthony Andino Jr. • Justin W. Dreese • Richard J. Henkes II Nicholas A. Madaras • Jason L. Merrill • Ralph N. Porras • Shane P. Harris

Philip A. Johnson • Ryan Edwin Miller • Hannah L. Gunterman • Marshall A. Gutierrez Germaine L. Debro • Jared M. Shoemaker • Eric P. Valdepenas • Christopher Walsh • John A. Carroll • Jeremy R. Shank • Luis A. Montes • David J. Ramsey • Vincent M. Frassetto David W. Gordon • Anthony P. Seig • Johnathan Benson • Alexander Jordan • Harley D. Andrews • Emily J.T. Perez • Matthew C. Mattingly • Jeffrey Shaffer • Marcus A. Cain Jennifer M. Hartman • Russell M. Makowski • Aaron A. Smith • David Thomas Weir • Clint E. Williams • Ryan A. Miller • Cesar A. Granados • David Sean Roddy • David J. Davis Adam L. Knox • James R. Worster • Robert Thomas Callahan • Ashley L. Henderson Huff Jared J. Raymond • Jane Elizabeth Lanham • Eric Kavanagh • Charles Jason Jones Robb Gordon Needham • Yull Estrada Rodriguez • Christopher Michael Zimmerman Allan R. Bevington • Kenneth E. Kincaid, IV • Velton Locklear, III • Windell J. Simmons Carlos Dominguez • Howard S. March Jr. • Rene Martinez • Casey L. Mellen • Jose A. Lanzarin • Henry Paul • Edward C. Reynolds Jr. • Christopher T. Riviere • James N. Lyons James Chamroeun • Christopher T. Blaney • Michael A. Monsoor • Luis E. Tejeda Robert Weber • Scott E. Nisely • Kampha B. Sourivong • Chase A. Haag • Mario Nelson Denise A. Lannaman • Justin D. Peterson • Christopher B. Cosgrove III • Aaron L. Seal Raymond S. Armijo • James D. Ellis • Satieon V. Greenlee • Justin R. Jarrett • Joe A. Narvaez • Michael K. Oremus • Joseph W. Perry • Kristofer C. Walker • Daniel Isshak Jonathan Rojas • Dean Bright • Timothy Burke • Christopher O. Moudry • George R. Obourn Jr. • Edward M. Garvin • Benjamin S. Rosales • Nicholas A. Arvanitis • John Edward Hale • Bradford H. Payne • Brandon S. Asbury • Carl W. Johnson II • Lawrence Parrish • John Edward Wood • Roger Alan Napper Jr. • Shane R. Austin • Timothy Fulkerson • Stephen F. Johnson • Derek W. Jones • Jeremy Scott Sandvick Monroe Robert M. Secher • Phillip B. Williams • Julian M. Arechaga • Jon Eric Bowman

Shelby J. Feniello • Shane T. Adcock • Nicholas R. Sowinski • Justin T. Walsh • Gene A. Hawkins • Johnny K. Craver • Thomas J. Hewett • Kenny F. Stanton Jr. • Leebenard E. Chavis • Joseph M. Kane • Charles M. King • Timothy J. Lauer • Keith J. Moore • Jonathan J. Simpson • Lester Domenico Baroncini Jr. • Stephen Bicknell • Joshua Deese • Jonathan E. Lootens • Mark C. Paine • Brock A. Babb • Joshua M. Hines • Russell G. Culbertson III Joseph C. Dumas Jr. • Nathan J. Frigo • Ryan E. Haupt • Christopher E. Loudon • Garth D. Sizemore • Norman R. Taylor III • David M. Unger • Daniel W. Winegeart • Ronald L. Paulsen • Joshua L. Booth • Patrick O. Barlow • Jesus M. Montalvo • Jose R. Perez Daniel A. Brozovich • Edwardo Lopez Jr. • Kevin M. Witte • Tony L. Knier • Clifford R. Collinsworth • Nathan R. Elrod • Eric W. Herzberg • Nicholas J. Manoukian • Joshua C. Watkins • Nathaniel A. Aguirre • Matthew W. Creed • Willsun M. Mock • Nicholas K. Rogers David G. Taylor • Amos C.R. Bock • Carl A. Eason • Richard A. Buerstetta • Tyler R. Overstreet • Charles O. Sare • Donald S. Brown • Daniel B. Chaires • Thomas M. Gilbert Jonathan B. Thornsberry • Charles V. Komppa • Ricky L. McGinnis • Luke J. Zimmerman Troy D. Nealey • Kenneth E. Bostic • Kraig D. Foyteck • Michael T. Seeley • Michael R. Weidemann • Jason Franco • Kevin J. Ellenburg • Gary A. Koehler • Minhee Kim • Michael P. Bridges • Paul J. Finken • Joseph A. Gage • Eric J. Kruger • James Brown • Jason D. Whitehouse • Luke B. Holler • Michael H. Lasky • James L. Bridges • Mark C. Gelina • Kyle W. Powell • Douglas C. Desjardins • Jose A. Galvan • Miles P. Henderson • John R. Priestner • Lucas T. White • Richwell A. Doria • Ryan T. McCaughn • Courtland A. Kennard Gregory W.G. McCoy • Rudy A. Salcido • Bryan Burgess • Kristopher C. Warren William Samuel Jackson II • Misael Martinez • Angel De Jesus Lucio Ramirez • Michael A. Cerrone • Harry A. Winkler III • Daniel J. Allman II • Jang H. Kim • Peter E. Winston Thomas H. Felts Sr. • Justin R. Garcia • Tung M. Nguyen • Eric G. Palacios Rivera

Timothy W. Brown • Mario D. Gonzalez • Michael D. Scholl • John R. Dennison • Schuyler B. Haynes Mitchel T. Mutz • Rhett W. Schiller • Bradley N. Shilling • Jeremy S. Shock • James P. Musack • Eric Vizcaino • Donovan E. Watts • Joshua C. Alonzo • James R. Davenport • Heath Warner • James D. Priestap • Reece D. Moreno Nicholas P. Rapavi • Daniel M. Morris Michael C. Ledsome • Jeromy D. West • Joshua C. Burrows Jeannette T. Dunn • David M. Fraser • Jason R. Hamill • Troy L. Gilbert • Michael A. Schwarz Jonerik Loney • Chris Mason Theodore M. West • John L. Hartman Jr. • Jeremy W. Mulhair Robert L. Love Jr. • Keith E. Fiscus Bryan T. McDonough • Corey J. Rystad

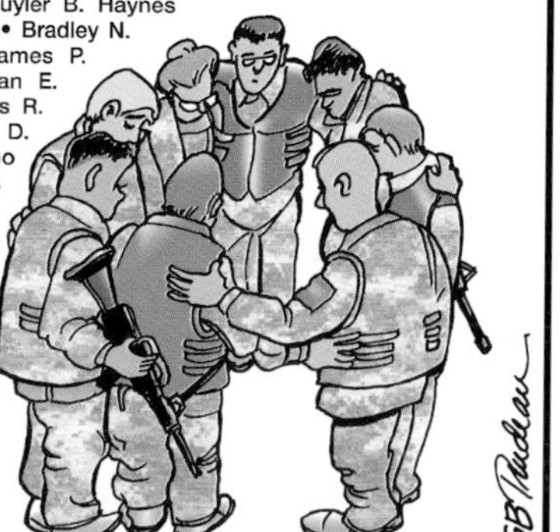
GBTrudeau

CONTINUED NEXT WEEK

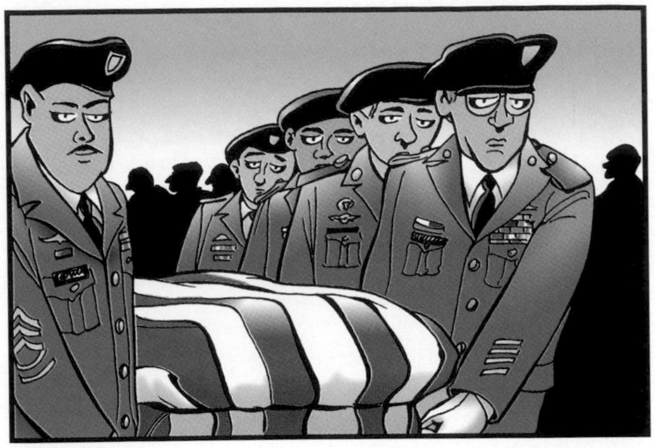

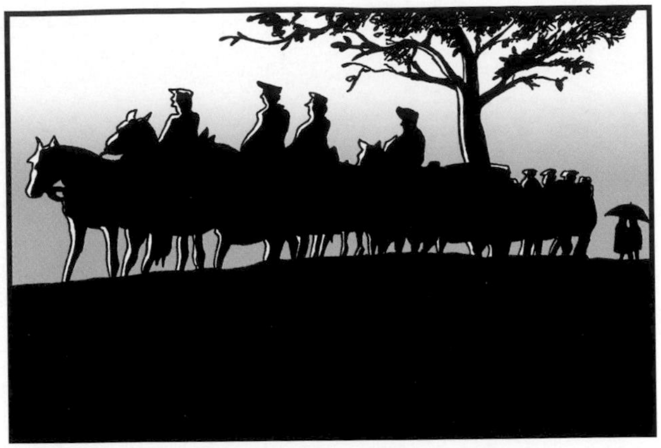

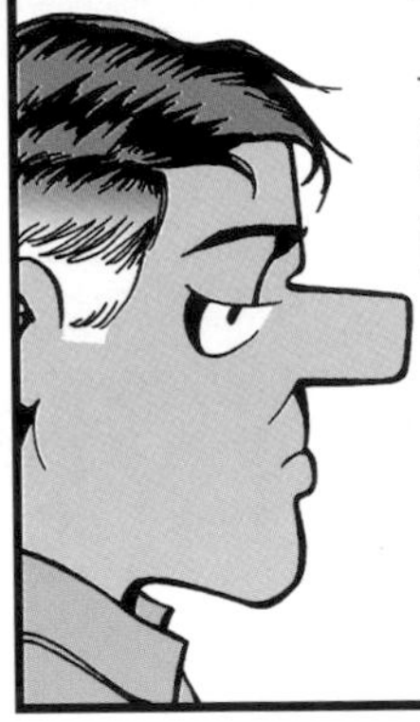

OPERATION IRAQI FREEDOM

IN MEMORIAM

SINCE 4/26/06 - PART II

Jesse D. Tillery • Kermit O. Evans • Troy D. Cooper • Shawn L. English • Billy B. Farris • Kenneth W. Haines • Joseph Trane McCloud • Joshua C. Sticklen • Dustin M. Adkins Jay R. Gauthreaux • Ross A. McGinnis • Albert M. Nelson Roger A. Suarez-Gonzalez • Nicholas D. Turcotte Thomas P. Echols • Christopher A. Anderson • Jordan W. Hess • Marco L. Miller • Jesse J.J. Castro • Nicholas R. Gibbs • Jason Huffman • Travis C. Krege • Joshua B. Madden • Yari Mokri • Travis L. Patriquin • Vincent J. Pomante III • Yevgeniy Ryndych • Dustin J. Libby • Megan M. McClung • Cody G. Watson • Kristofer R. Ciraso Micah S. Gifford • Henry W. Linck • Brent E. Beeler Nathan M. Krissoff • Philip C. Ford • Brennan C. Gibson Shawn M. Murphy • Nicholas P. Steinbacher • Thomas W. Clemons • Budd M. Cote • Matthew V. Dillon • Brian P. McAnulty • Clinton J. Miller • Gloria D. Davis • Brent W. Dunkleberger • Theodore A. Spatol • Matthew W. Clark Luke C. Yepsen • Paul Balint Jr. • Henry K. Kahalewai

Joe L. Baines • David R. Staats • Matthew J. Stanley • Nick J. Palmer • Seth M. Stanton Brian L. Mintzlaff • Kevin M. Kryst • Andrew P. Daul • Joshua D. Pickard • Scott D. Dykman Jacob G. McMillan • Robert J. Volker • Myles Cody Sebastien • Ryan J. Burgess • Ryan L. Mayhan • Fernando S. Tamayo • Kyle A. Nolen • Joshua D. Sheppard • John Barta Michael J. Crutchfield • Elias Elias • Bobby Mejia II • Curtis L. Norris • Wilson A. Algrim Chad J. Vollmer • Evan A. Bixler • Stephen L. Morris • Hayes Clayton • Jason C. Denfrund Jae S. Moon • Andrew H. Nelson • Aaron L. Preston • Dexter E. Wheelous • Eric R. Wilkus John T. Bubeck • Joseph A. Strong • Joshua M. Schmitz • Nathaniel A. Given • Clinton T. McCormick • Christopher P. Messer • Edward W. Shaffer • Douglas L. Tinsley • William C. Koprince Jr. • Luis G. Ayala • Dustin R. Donica • Aron C. Blum • Christopher E. Esckelson Nicholas A. Miller • William D. Spencer • Lawrance J. Carter • William R. Newgard • David E. Dietrich • John M. Sullivan • Alan R. Blohm • Jonathan E. Schiller • Richard A. Smith Sandra S. Grant • Thomas E. Vandling Jr. • Charles D. Allen • Michael Lewis Mundell Jeremiah Johnson • Raymond N. Mitchell III • Elizabeth A. Loncki • Daniel B. Miller Jr. Timothy R. Weiner • Eric T. Caldwell • Stephen J. Raderstorf • Ryan R. Berg • Ming Sun James M. Wosika Jr. • Gregroy A. Wright • James D. Riekena • Paul T. Sanchez • Ian C. Anderson • John E. Cooper • Jason J. Corbett • Mark J. Daily • Matthew T. Grimm • Collin R. Schockmel • Joseph D. Alomar • Jennifer A. Valdivia • William J. Rechenmacher Russell P. Borea • Luis J. Castillo • Jacob H. Neal • Brian D. Allgood • Jeffrey D. Bisson Johnathan Bryan Chism • Shawn Patrick Falter • Sean P. Fennerty • Brian Scott Freeman Jacob N. Fritz • Ryan J. Hill • Allen B. Jaynes • Jonathan P. C. Kingman • Victor M. Langarica • Phillip D. McNeill • Jonathan Millican • Toby R. Olsen • Daryl D. Booker • John G. Brown • David C. Canegata • Marilyn L. Gabbard • Roger W. Haller • Paul M. Kelly Floyd E. Lake • Sean E. Lyerly • Michael Taylor • William T. Warren • Darrel J. Morris

Brandon L. Stout • Andrew G. Matus • Emilian D. Sanchez • Nicholas P. Brown • Jamie D. Wilson • Michael J. Wiggins • Gary S. Johnston • Michael M. Kashkoush • Keith A. Callahan • Hector Leija • Michael Balsley • Alexander H. Fuller • Darrell W. Shipp • Mark D. Kidd • Nathan P. Fairlie • Alan R. Johnson • Mickel D. Garrigus • Jon B. St. John II Timothy A. Swanson • David T. Toomalatai • Anthony C. Melia • Cornell C. Chao • Mark T. Resh • Carla Jane Stewart • Adam Q. Emul • Corey J. Aultz • Milton A. Gist Jr. • Alejandro Carrillo • William M. Sigua • Stephen D. Shannon • David C. Armstrong • Tyler Butler Michael C. Mettille • Eric R. Sieger • Terry J. Elliott • Richard O. Quill III • Matthew G. Conte Jason Garth DeFrenn • Terrence D. Dunn • Kevin C. Landeck • Alan E. McPeek • Keith Yoakum • Matthew T. Zeimer • Ronnie L. Sanders • Clarence T. Spencer • Randy J. Matheny • Brandon J. Van Parys • Brian A. Browning • Joshua J. Frazier • Joseph J. Ellis Jennifer J. Harris • Jared M. Landaker • Jennifer M. Parcell • Travis D. Pfister • Thomas E. Saba • James Rodney Tijerina • Tarryl B. Hill • Matthew P. Pathenos • Gilbert Minjares Jr. Manuel A. Ruiz • Ross A. Clevenger • James J. Holtom • Raymond M. Werner • Leeroy A. Camacho • James J. Regan • Eric Ross • Ian W. Shaw • Donnie R. Belser Jr. • Russell A. Kurtz • Robert B. Thrasher • Dennis L. Sellen Jr. • Allen Mosteiro • Nickolas A. Tanton Branden C. Cummings • Ronnie G. Madore Jr. • John D. Rode • Carl Leonard Seigart Daniel T. Morris • Todd M. Siebert • Chad E. Marsh • Justin T. Paton • Christopher K. Boone • William C. Spillers • Brian A. Escalante • Matthew S. Apuan • Kelly D. Youngblood Blake H. Howey • Matthew C. Bowe • Adare W. Cleveland • Pedro J. Colon • Shawn M. Dunkin • Montrel S. Mcarn • Brett Witteveen • Richard L. Ford • Louis G. Kim • Clinton W. Ahlquist • Travis Wayne Buford • Joshua R. Hager • Rowan D. Walter • David R. Berry Jeremy D. Barnett • Ethan J. Biggers • William J. Beardsley • Anthony Aguirre Jonathan D. Cadavero • Lorne E. Henry Jr. • Karl O. Soto-Pinedo • Richard A. Soukenka

Chad M. Allen • Bufford "Kenny" Van Slyke • Paul M. Latourney • Luis O. Rodriguez-Contrera • Wesley J. Williams • Christopher D. Young • Dustin M. Gould • Luke Emch Morgan C. Tulang • Ashly L. Moyer • Brandon Allen Parr • Michael C. Peek • Raul S. Bravo Jr. • Darrel D. Kasson • Ryan M. Bell • Justin M. Estes • Blake Harris • Cory C. Kosters Barry Wayne Mayo • Andrew C. Perkins • Justin A. Rollins • Ryan D. Russell • Robert Stanley • Mark W. Graham • Shawn Rankinen • Michael D. Rivera • Christopher R. Webb Dennis J. Veater • Thomas L. Latham • Jonathan K. Smith • Daniel E. Woodcock Douglas C. Stone • Nathanial Dain Windsor • Robert M. Carr • Alberto Garcia Jr. • Angel Rosa • Joshua M. Boyd • Brian L. Chevalier • Stephen M. Kowalczyk • Adam J. Rosema Forrest J. Waterbury • Steven M. Chavez • James L. Arnold • Emerson N. Brand • Blake M. Harris • Terry W. Prater • John S. Stephens • Raymond J. Holzhauer • Christopher R. Brevard • John E. Allen • William N. Davis • Marieo Guerrero • Anthony A. Kaiser • John F. Landry Jr. • Ed Santini • Benjamin L. Sebban • Nimo W. Tauala • Harry H. Timberman Ryan P. Green • Wayne R. Cornell • Curtis E. Glawson Jr. • Stephen K. Richardson • Darrell R. Griffin Jr. • Adrian J. Lewis • Nicholas J. Lightner • Joey T. Sams II • Dustin Jerome Lee Freeman L. Gardner Jr. • Henry W. Bogrette • Lance C. Springer II • Greg N. Riewer Trevor A. Roberts • Orlando E. Gonzalez • Sean K. McDonald • Jason Nunez • Jason Swiger • Anthony White • Curtis J. Forshey • Sean Michael Thomas • Marcus A. Golczynski • Joe Polo • Wilfred Flores Jr. • Neale M. Shank • Jason R. Arnette • William G. Bowling • Robert M. McDowell • David A. Mejias • Eric R. Vick • Miguel A. Marcial III Brian E. Ritzberg • Curtis R. Spivey • Bradley D. King • Daniel R. Olsen • Shane R. Becker Gabriel J. Figueroa • Jerry C. Burge • Joseph H. Cantrell IV • James J. Coon • Walter Freeman Jr. • Derek A. Gibson • Forrest D. Cauthorn • Jason A. Shaffer • Jay S. Cajimat Ryan S. Dallam • Daniel A. Fuentes • Anthony Palermo Jr. • Damian Lopez Rodriguez

Gregory J. Billiter • Curtis R. Hall • Joseph A. McSween • Joseph C. Schwedler • Ebe F. Emolo • Jonathan D. Grassbaugh • Levi K. Hoover • Rodney L. McCandless • Philip A. Murphy-Sweet • Harrison Brown • Adam P. Kennedy • Phillip I. Neel • David N. Simmons Todd A. Singleton • Jesse L. Williams • Brian Lee Holden • Ismael Solorio • Clifford A. Spohn III • Brett Andre Walton • Kyle G. Bohrnsen • Raymond S. Sevaaetasi • Jason J. Beadles • John G. Borbonus • James T. Lindsey • Gwilym J. Newman • Cody A. Putnam Larry R. Bowman • Ryan A. Bishop • Joshua A. Schmit • Brandon L. Wallace • Robert J. Basham • Daniel J. Santee • Steven J. Walberg • Mario K. De Leon • Aaron M. Genevie Lucas V. Starcevich • Shaun M. Blue • Jesse D. Delatorre • Daniel R. Scherry • Richard P. Langenbrunner

OPERATION ENDURING FREEDOM (AFGHANISTAN) SINCE 4/26/06

Joseph J. Fenty • Eric W. Totten • Christopher B. Donaldson • Christopher T. Howick Bryan A. Brewster • John C. Griffith • Jeffery S. Wiekamp • Justin L. O'Donohoe • David N. Timmons Jr. • Brian M. Moquin Jr. • Christian Longsworth • Derek A. Stanley • Travis A. Van Zoest • Curtis R. Mehrer • Bernard P. Corpuz • Charles E. Munier • Russell M. Durgin • Roger P. Peña Jr. • Patrick Damon • Forrest P. Ewens • Ian T. Sanchez • Jared C. Monti • Patrick L. Lybert • Brian J. Bradbury • Heathe N. Craig • Thomas D. Maholic Joseph F. Fuerst III • Justin R. Davis • Aaron M. Griner • William T. Flanigan • Kevin F. Edgin • Jeff McLochlin • Robert P. Kassin • Robert J. Chiomento • Eric Caban Christopher C. Rafferty • David M. Hierholzer • Andrew Velez • Daniel Suplee • Rogelio R. Garza Jr. • Andrew Small • James P. White Jr. • Jeremiah S. Cole • Joseph R. Blake Robert E. Drawl Jr. • Wakkuna Jackson • Chris Sitton • Adam P. Servais • Merideth Howard • Robert J. Paul • Nathaniel Brad Lindsey • Mike Fuga • Jeremy E. DePottey

Bernard Lee Deghand • Angelo J. Vaccaro • Fernando D. Robinson • Scott W. Dyer Jason A. Lucas • Michael V. Bailey • Kyu H. Chay • Isaiah Calloway • Douglas E. Sloan Alex Oceguera • Charles J. McClain • William R. Brown • Nathan J. Goodiron Scott B. Lundell • Benjamin D. Keating • Michael A. Shank Jeffrey G. Roberson • Chris Kleinwachter • Joseph E. Phaneuf II • Long N. Nguyen • Laquita Pate James Timothy D. Lewis • Kristofer D. S. Thomas • Scott E. Duffman • Ryan C. Garbs • Adam A. Wilkinson John A. Quinlan • Hershel D. McCants Jr. Brandon D. Gordon • Travis R. Vaughn Buddy J. Hughie • Jason D. Johns Daniel Zizumbo • Christopher J. C. Fernandez • Gregory D. Fejeran Edmund W. McDonald • Agustin Gutierrez • Christopher M. Wilson Conor G. Masterson • Edelman L. Hernandez • David A. Stephens Casey D. Combs

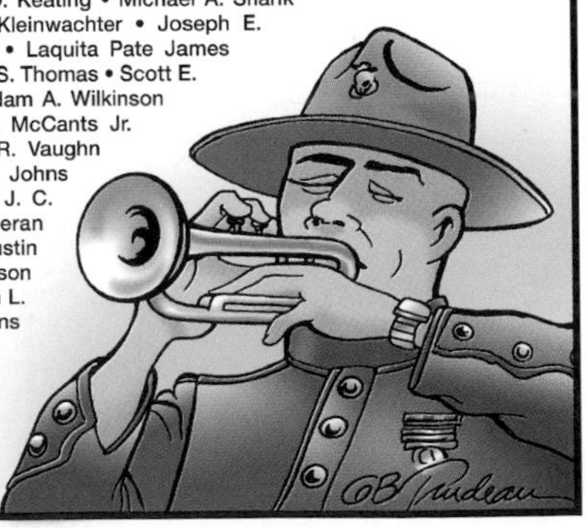
GB Trudeau

List as of April 18, 2007 – for updates go to icasualties.org

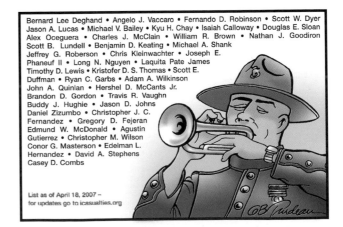

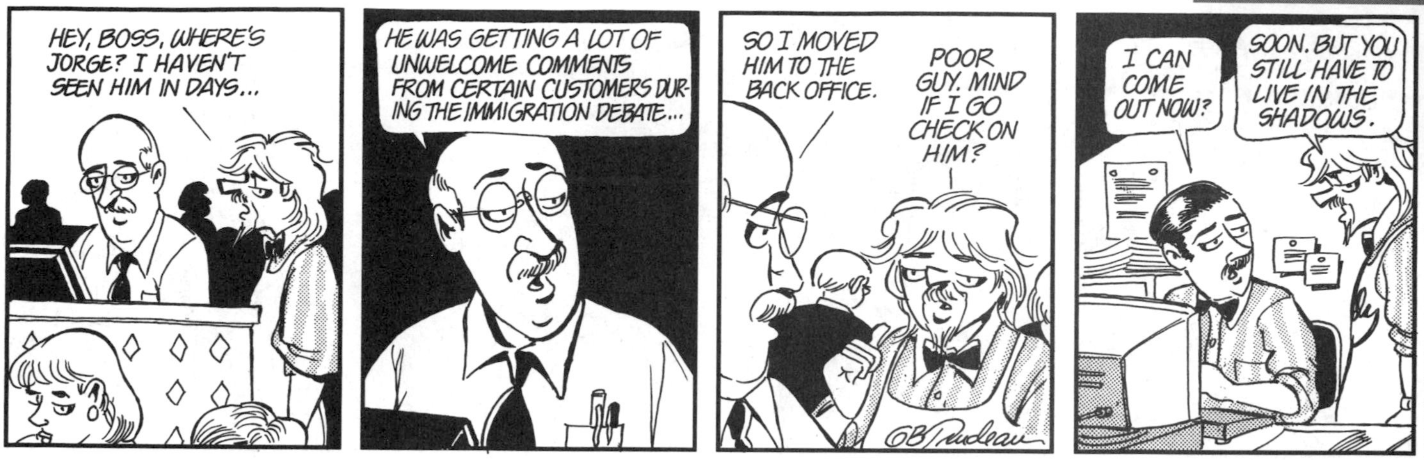
HEY, BOSS, WHERE'S JORGE? I HAVEN'T SEEN HIM IN DAYS...
HE WAS GETTING A LOT OF UNWELCOME COMMENTS FROM CERTAIN CUSTOMERS DURING THE IMMIGRATION DEBATE...
SO I MOVED HIM TO THE BACK OFFICE.
POOR GUY. MIND IF I GO CHECK ON HIM?
I CAN COME OUT NOW?
SOON. BUT YOU STILL HAVE TO LIVE IN THE SHADOWS.

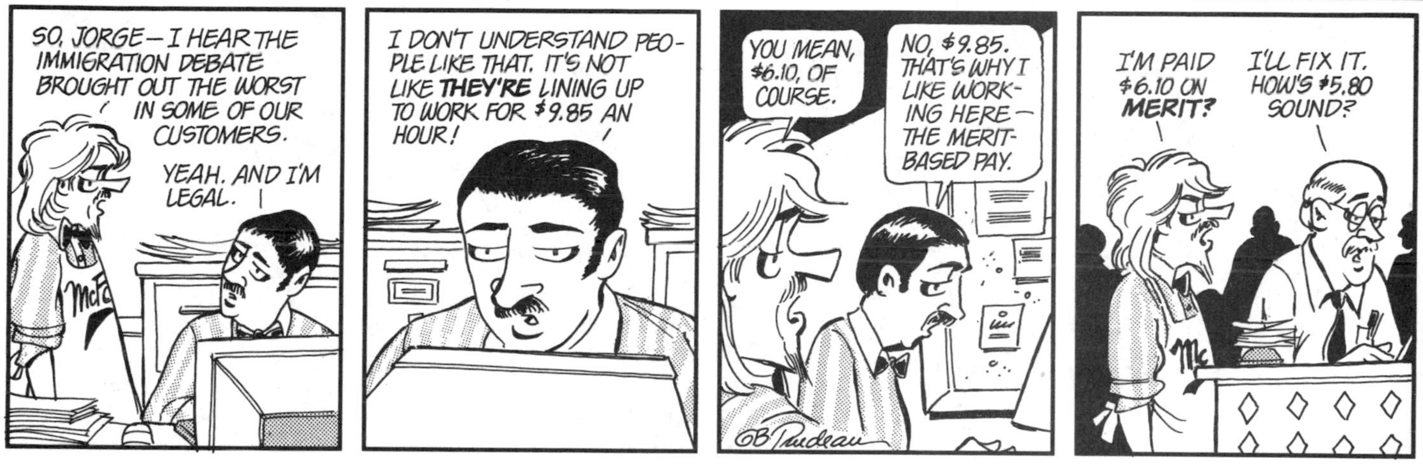
SO, JORGE—I HEAR THE IMMIGRATION DEBATE BROUGHT OUT THE WORST IN SOME OF OUR CUSTOMERS.
YEAH. AND I'M LEGAL.
I DON'T UNDERSTAND PEOPLE LIKE THAT. IT'S NOT LIKE THEY'RE LINING UP TO WORK FOR $9.85 AN HOUR!
YOU MEAN, $6.10, OF COURSE.
NO, $9.85. THAT'S WHY I LIKE WORKING HERE—THE MERIT-BASED PAY.
I'M PAID $6.10 ON MERIT?
I'LL FIX IT. HOW'S $5.80 SOUND?

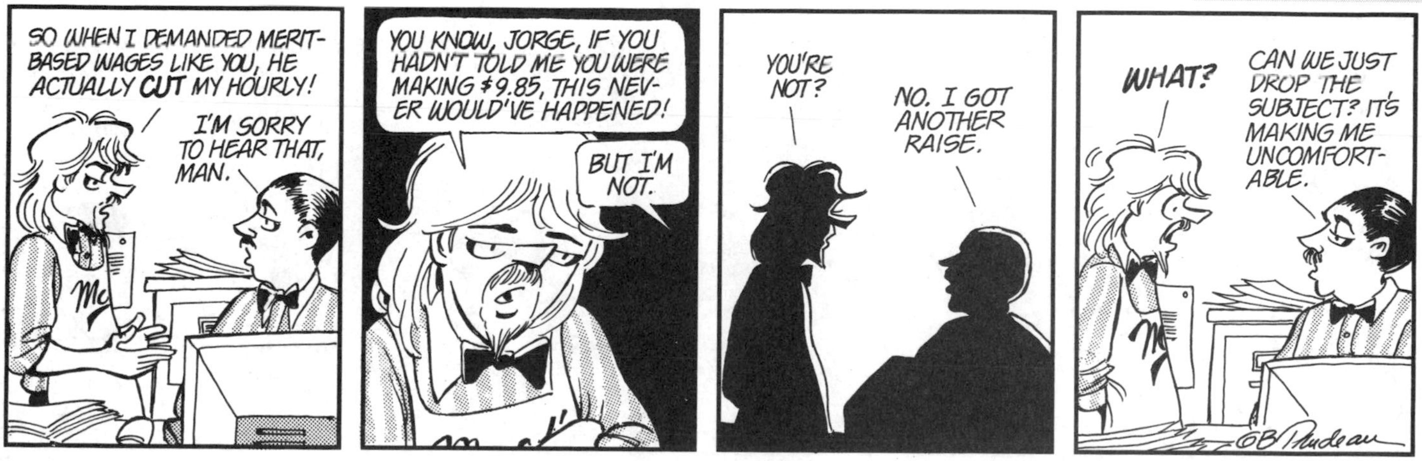
SO WHEN I DEMANDED MERIT-BASED WAGES LIKE YOU, HE ACTUALLY CUT MY HOURLY!
I'M SORRY TO HEAR THAT, MAN.
YOU KNOW, JORGE, IF YOU HADN'T TOLD ME YOU WERE MAKING $9.85, THIS NEVER WOULD'VE HAPPENED!
BUT I'M NOT.
YOU'RE NOT?
NO. I GOT ANOTHER RAISE.
WHAT?
CAN WE JUST DROP THE SUBJECT? IT'S MAKING ME UNCOMFORTABLE.

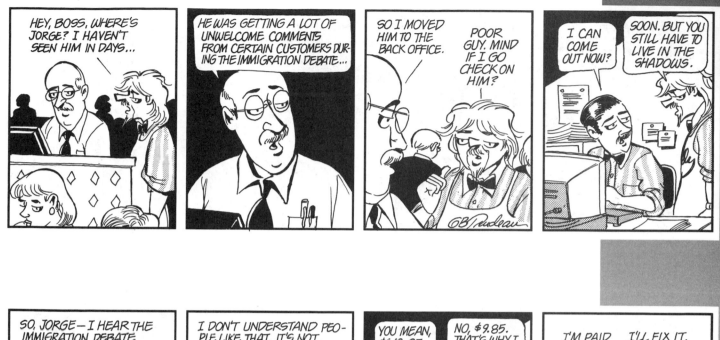

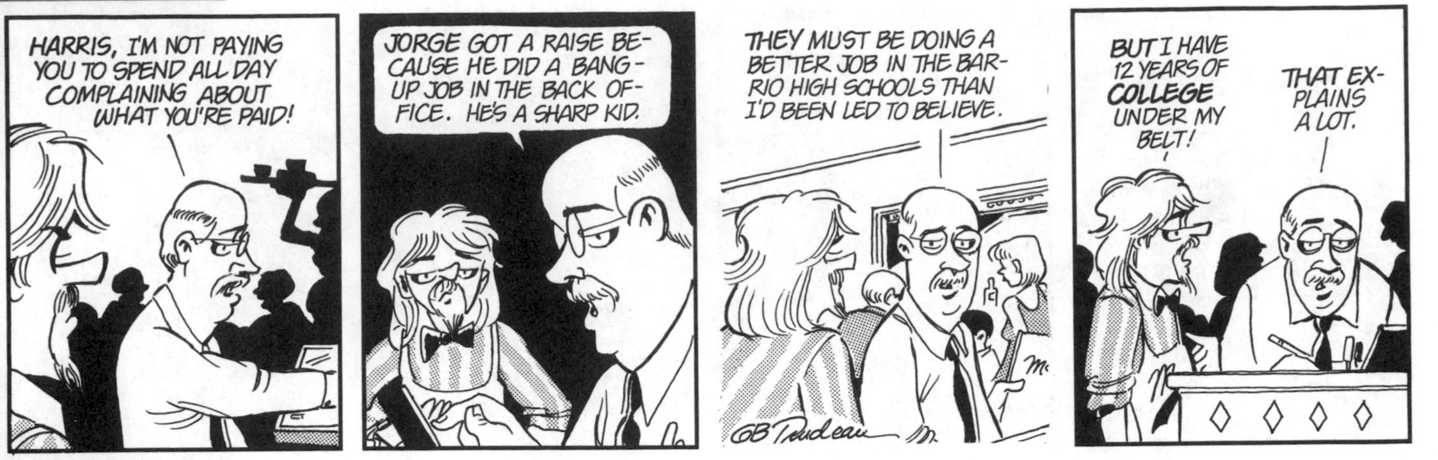
HARRIS, I'M NOT PAYING YOU TO SPEND ALL DAY COMPLAINING ABOUT WHAT YOU'RE PAID!
JORGE GOT A RAISE BECAUSE HE DID A BANG-UP JOB IN THE BACK OFFICE. HE'S A SHARP KID.
THEY MUST BE DOING A BETTER JOB IN THE BARRIO HIGH SCHOOLS THAN I'D BEEN LED TO BELIEVE.
BUT I HAVE 12 YEARS OF COLLEGE UNDER MY BELT!
THAT EXPLAINS A LOT.

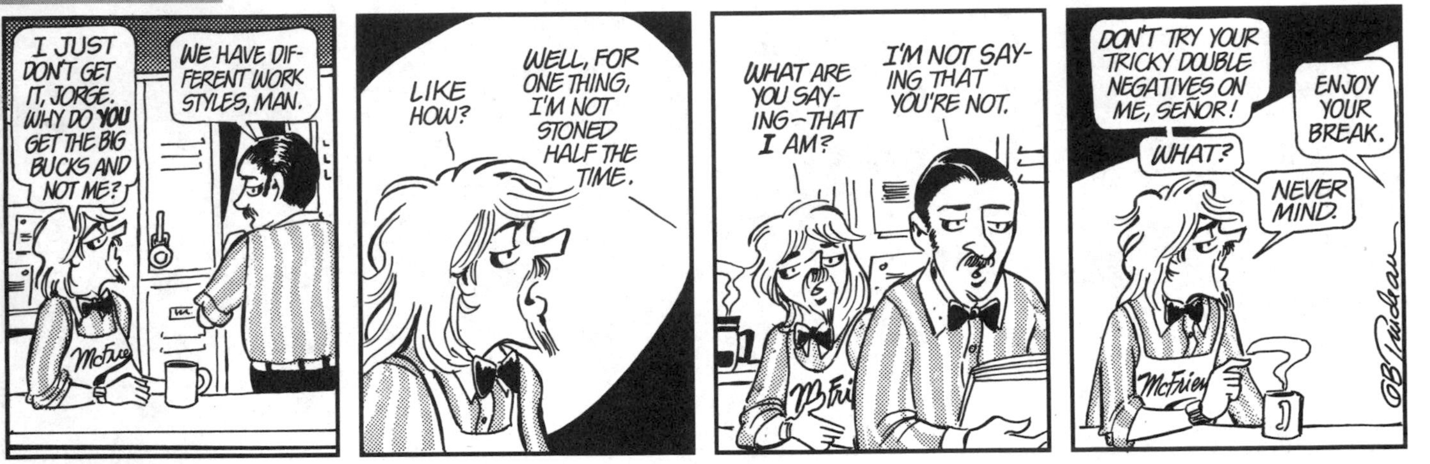
I JUST DON'T GET IT, JORGE. WHY DO YOU GET THE BIG BUCKS AND NOT ME?
WE HAVE DIFFERENT WORK STYLES, MAN.
LIKE HOW?
WELL, FOR ONE THING, I'M NOT STONED HALF THE TIME.
WHAT ARE YOU SAYING—THAT I AM?
I'M NOT SAYING THAT YOU'RE NOT.
DON'T TRY YOUR TRICKY DOUBLE NEGATIVES ON ME, SEÑOR!
WHAT?
NEVER MIND.
ENJOY YOUR BREAK.

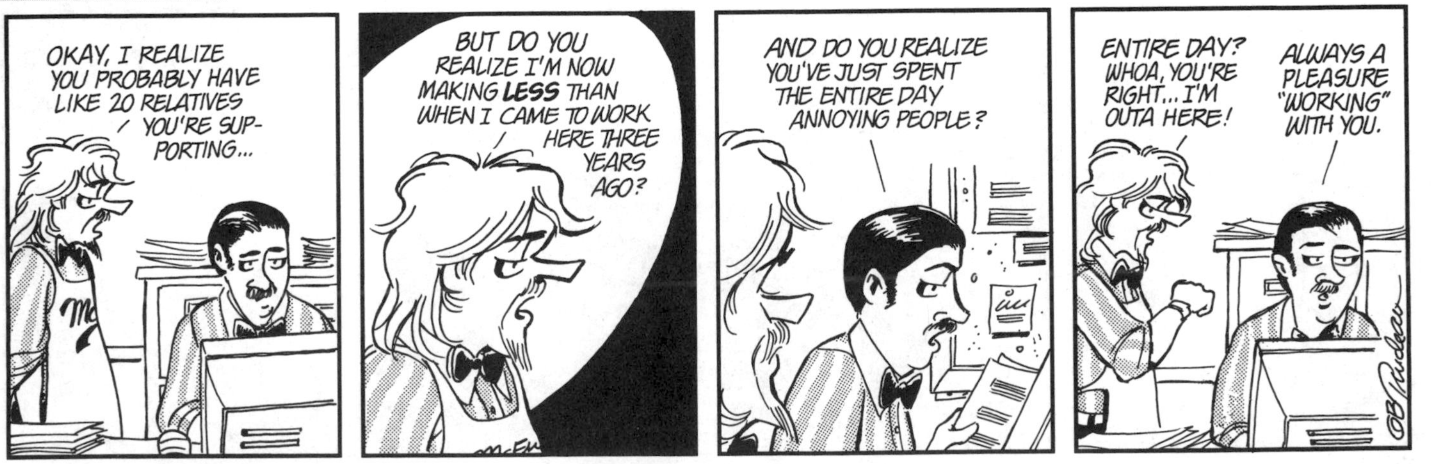
OKAY, I REALIZE YOU PROBABLY HAVE LIKE 20 RELATIVES YOU'RE SUPPORTING...
BUT DO YOU REALIZE I'M NOW MAKING LESS THAN WHEN I CAME TO WORK HERE THREE YEARS AGO?
AND DO YOU REALIZE YOU'VE JUST SPENT THE ENTIRE DAY ANNOYING PEOPLE?
ENTIRE DAY? WHOA, YOU'RE RIGHT... I'M OUTA HERE!
ALWAYS A PLEASURE "WORKING" WITH YOU.

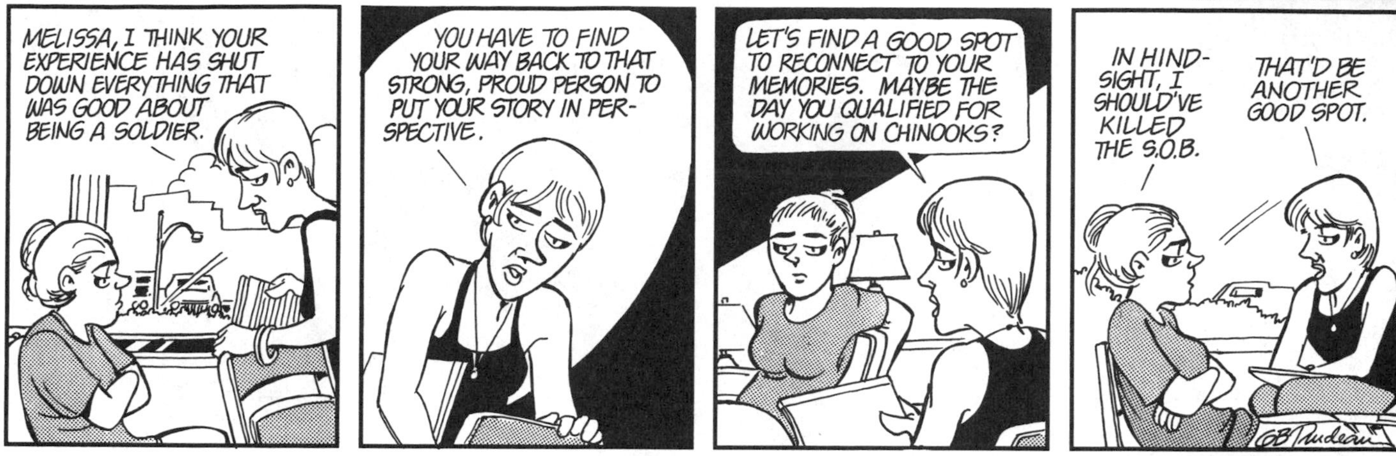
MELISSA, I THINK YOUR EXPERIENCE HAS SHUT DOWN EVERYTHING THAT WAS GOOD ABOUT BEING A SOLDIER.
YOU HAVE TO FIND YOUR WAY BACK TO THAT STRONG, PROUD PERSON TO PUT YOUR STORY IN PERSPECTIVE.
LET'S FIND A GOOD SPOT TO RECONNECT TO YOUR MEMORIES. MAYBE THE DAY YOU QUALIFIED FOR WORKING ON CHINOOKS?
IN HINDSIGHT, I SHOULD'VE KILLED THE S.O.B.
THAT'D BE ANOTHER GOOD SPOT.
GB Trudeau

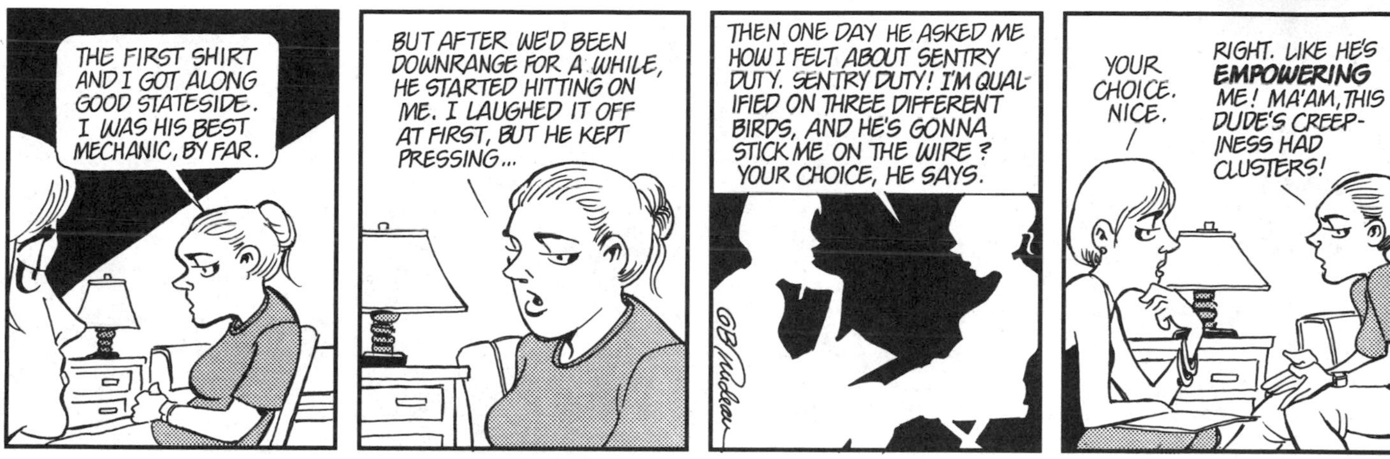
THE FIRST SHIRT AND I GOT ALONG GOOD STATESIDE. I WAS HIS BEST MECHANIC, BY FAR.
BUT AFTER WE'D BEEN DOWNRANGE FOR A WHILE, HE STARTED HITTING ON ME. I LAUGHED IT OFF AT FIRST, BUT HE KEPT PRESSING...
THEN ONE DAY HE ASKED ME HOW I FELT ABOUT SENTRY DUTY. SENTRY DUTY! I'M QUALIFIED ON THREE DIFFERENT BIRDS, AND HE'S GONNA STICK ME ON THE WIRE? YOUR CHOICE, HE SAYS.
GB Trudeau
YOUR CHOICE. NICE.
RIGHT. LIKE HE'S **EMPOWERING** ME! MA'AM, THIS DUDE'S CREEPINESS HAD CLUSTERS!

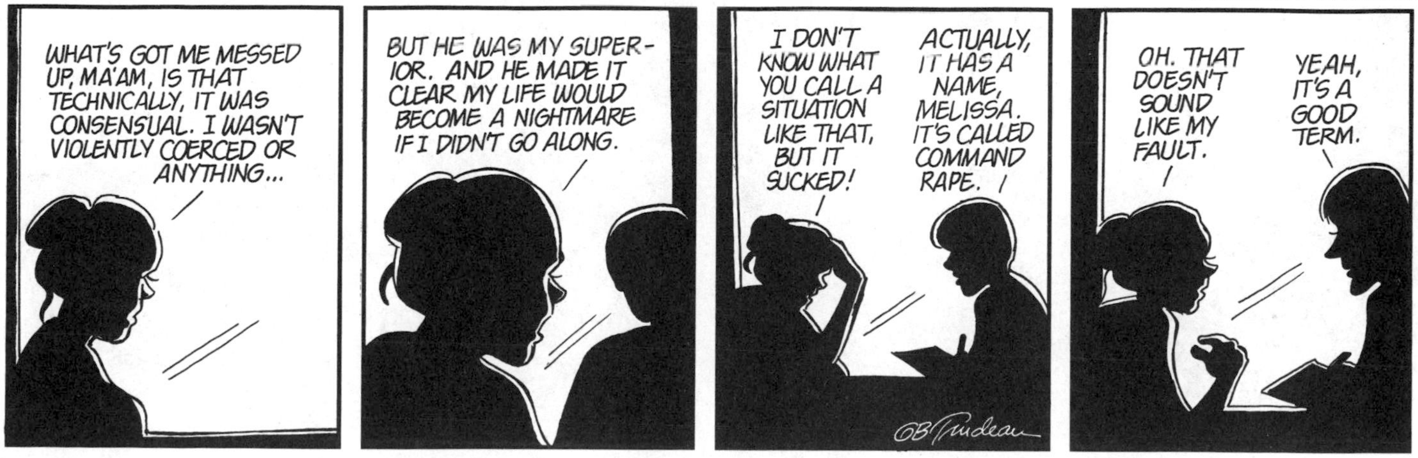
WHAT'S GOT ME MESSED UP, MA'AM, IS THAT TECHNICALLY, IT WAS CONSENSUAL. I WASN'T VIOLENTLY COERCED OR ANYTHING...
BUT HE WAS MY SUPERIOR. AND HE MADE IT CLEAR MY LIFE WOULD BECOME A NIGHTMARE IF I DIDN'T GO ALONG.
I DON'T KNOW WHAT YOU CALL A SITUATION LIKE THAT, BUT IT SUCKED!
ACTUALLY, IT HAS A NAME, MELISSA. IT'S CALLED COMMAND RAPE.
GB Trudeau
OH. THAT DOESN'T SOUND LIKE MY FAULT.
YEAH, IT'S A GOOD TERM.

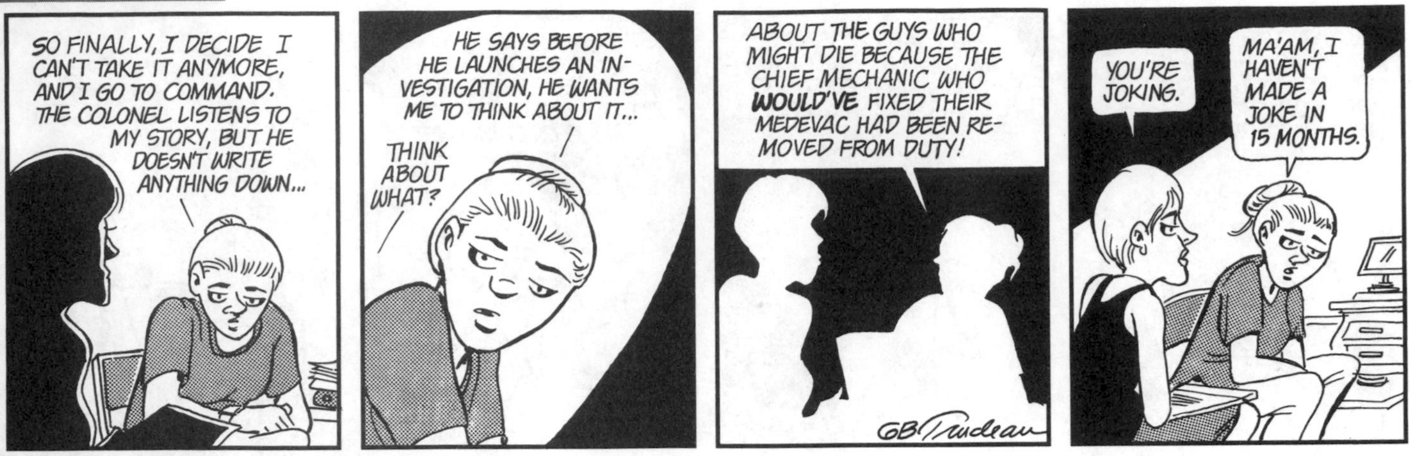
SO FINALLY, I DECIDE I CAN'T TAKE IT ANYMORE, AND I GO TO COMMAND. THE COLONEL LISTENS TO MY STORY, BUT HE DOESN'T WRITE ANYTHING DOWN...
HE SAYS BEFORE HE LAUNCHES AN IN-VESTIGATION, HE WANTS ME TO THINK ABOUT IT...
THINK ABOUT WHAT?
ABOUT THE GUYS WHO MIGHT DIE BECAUSE THE CHIEF MECHANIC WHO **WOULD'VE** FIXED THEIR MEDEVAC HAD BEEN RE-MOVED FROM DUTY!
GB Trudeau
YOU'RE JOKING.
MA'AM, I HAVEN'T MADE A JOKE IN 15 MONTHS.

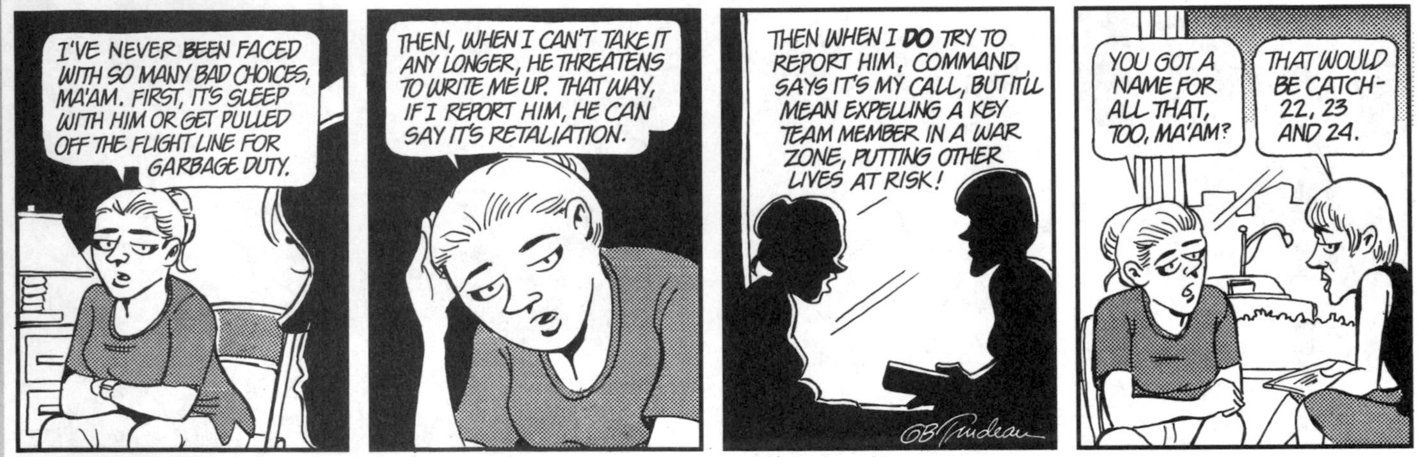
I'VE NEVER BEEN FACED WITH SO MANY BAD CHOICES, MA'AM. FIRST, IT'S SLEEP WITH HIM OR GET PULLED OFF THE FLIGHT LINE FOR GARBAGE DUTY.
THEN, WHEN I CAN'T TAKE IT ANY LONGER, HE THREATENS TO WRITE ME UP. THAT WAY, IF I REPORT HIM, HE CAN SAY IT'S RETALIATION.
THEN WHEN I **DO** TRY TO REPORT HIM, COMMAND SAYS IT'S MY CALL, BUT IT'LL MEAN EXPELLING A KEY TEAM MEMBER IN A WAR ZONE, PUTTING OTHER LIVES AT RISK!
GB Trudeau
YOU GOT A NAME FOR ALL THAT, TOO, MA'AM?
THAT WOULD BE CATCH-22, 23 AND 24.

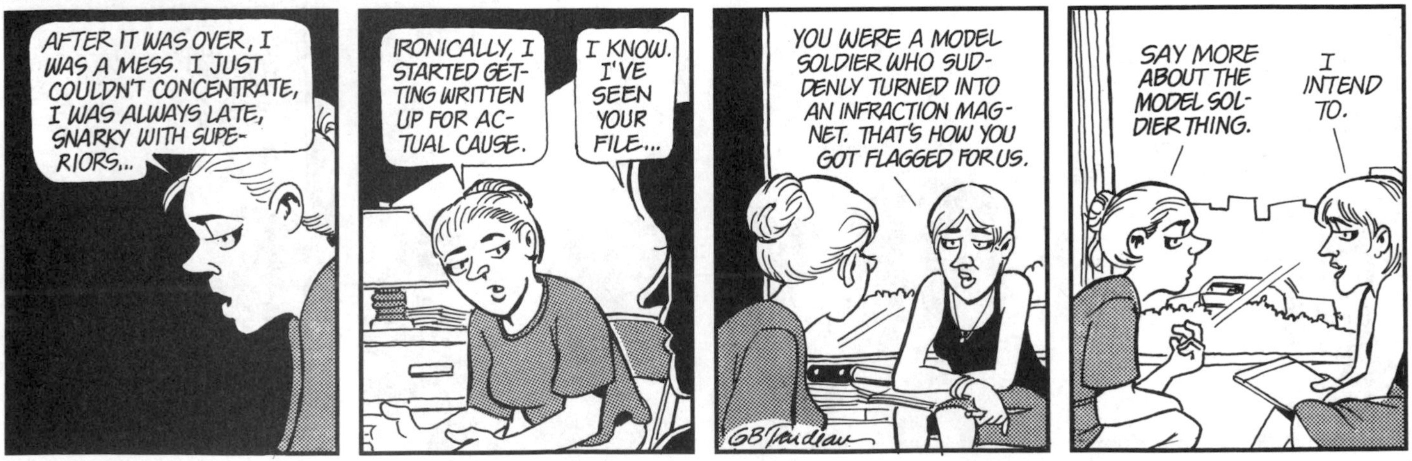
AFTER IT WAS OVER, I WAS A MESS. I JUST COULDN'T CONCENTRATE, I WAS ALWAYS LATE, SNARKY WITH SUPE-RIORS...
IRONICALLY, I STARTED GET-TING WRITTEN UP FOR AC-TUAL CAUSE.
I KNOW. I'VE SEEN YOUR FILE...
YOU WERE A MODEL SOLDIER WHO SUD-DENLY TURNED INTO AN INFRACTION MAG-NET. THAT'S HOW YOU GOT FLAGGED FOR US.
GB Trudeau
SAY MORE ABOUT THE MODEL SOL-DIER THING.
I INTEND TO.

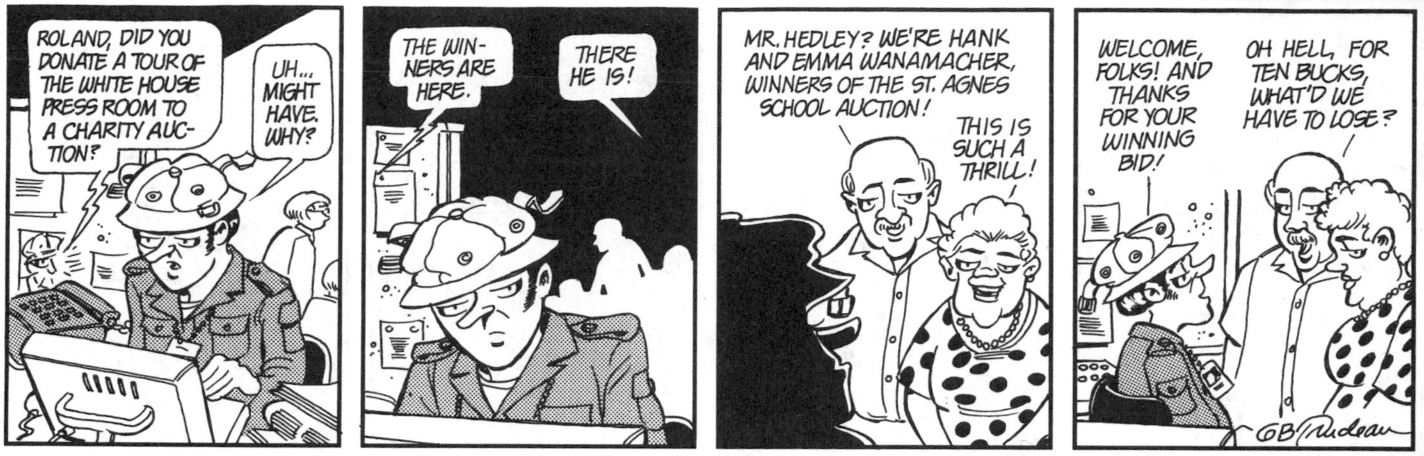
ROLAND, DID YOU DONATE A TOUR OF THE WHITE HOUSE PRESS ROOM TO A CHARITY AUCTION?
UH... MIGHT HAVE. WHY?
THE WINNERS ARE HERE.
THERE HE IS!
MR. HEDLEY? WE'RE HANK AND EMMA WANAMACHER, WINNERS OF THE ST. AGNES SCHOOL AUCTION!
THIS IS SUCH A THRILL!
WELCOME, FOLKS! AND THANKS FOR YOUR WINNING BID!
OH HELL, FOR TEN BUCKS, WHAT'D WE HAVE TO LOSE?
GBTrudeau

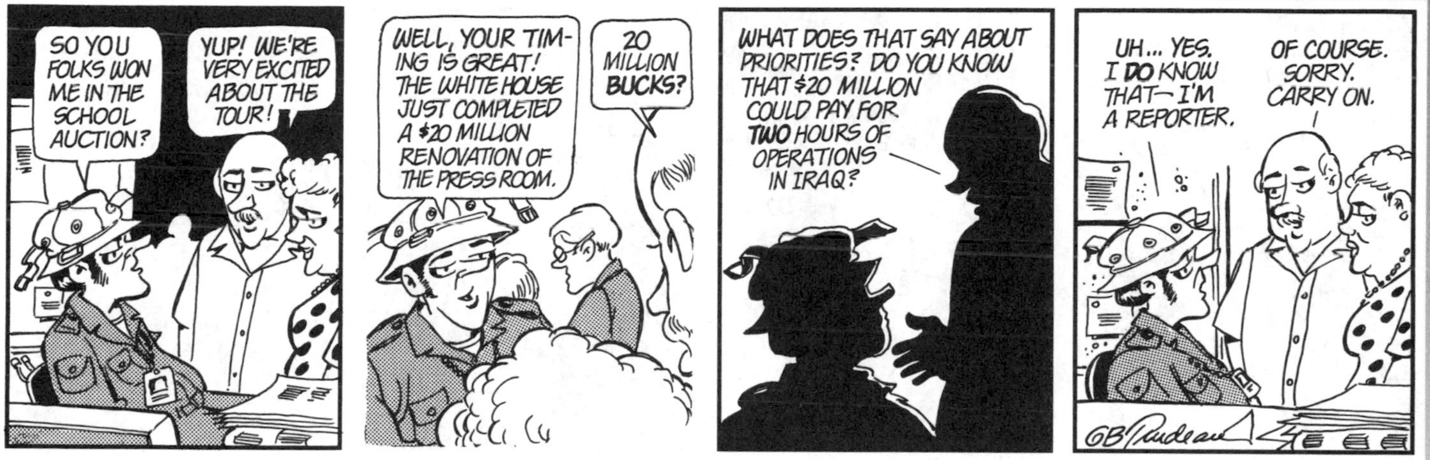
SO YOU FOLKS WON ME IN THE SCHOOL AUCTION?
YUP! WE'RE VERY EXCITED ABOUT THE TOUR!
WELL, YOUR TIMING IS GREAT! THE WHITE HOUSE JUST COMPLETED A $20 MILLION RENOVATION OF THE PRESS ROOM.
20 MILLION BUCKS?
WHAT DOES THAT SAY ABOUT PRIORITIES? DO YOU KNOW THAT $20 MILLION COULD PAY FOR TWO HOURS OF OPERATIONS IN IRAQ?
UH... YES. I DO KNOW THAT— I'M A REPORTER.
OF COURSE. SORRY. CARRY ON.
GBTrudeau

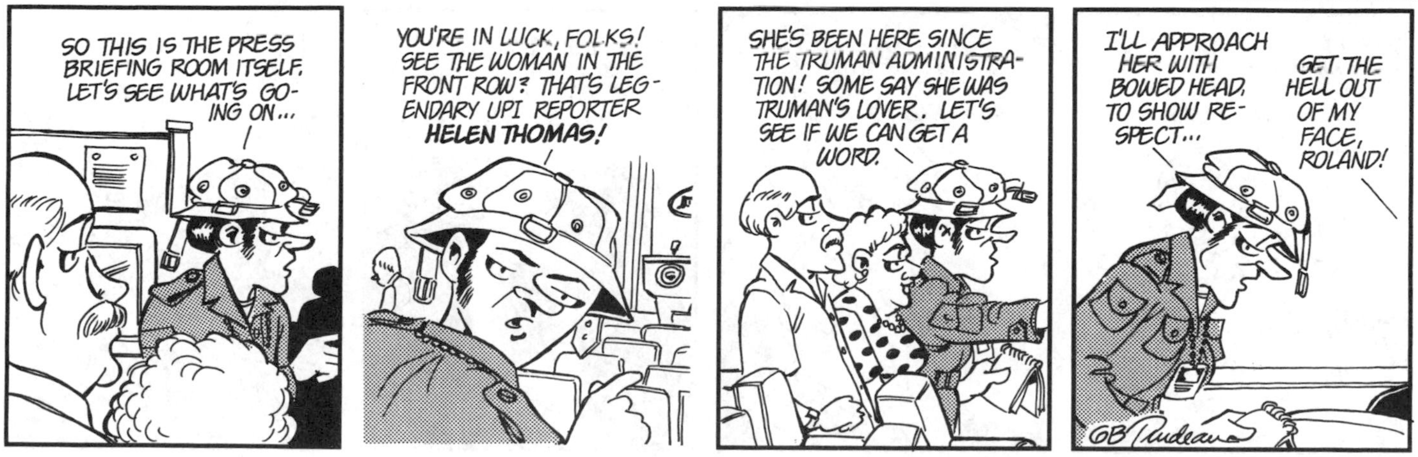
SO THIS IS THE PRESS BRIEFING ROOM ITSELF. LET'S SEE WHAT'S GOING ON...
YOU'RE IN LUCK, FOLKS! SEE THE WOMAN IN THE FRONT ROW? THAT'S LEGENDARY UPI REPORTER HELEN THOMAS!
SHE'S BEEN HERE SINCE THE TRUMAN ADMINISTRATION! SOME SAY SHE WAS TRUMAN'S LOVER. LET'S SEE IF WE CAN GET A WORD.
I'LL APPROACH HER WITH BOWED HEAD, TO SHOW RESPECT...
GET THE HELL OUT OF MY FACE, ROLAND!
GBTrudeau

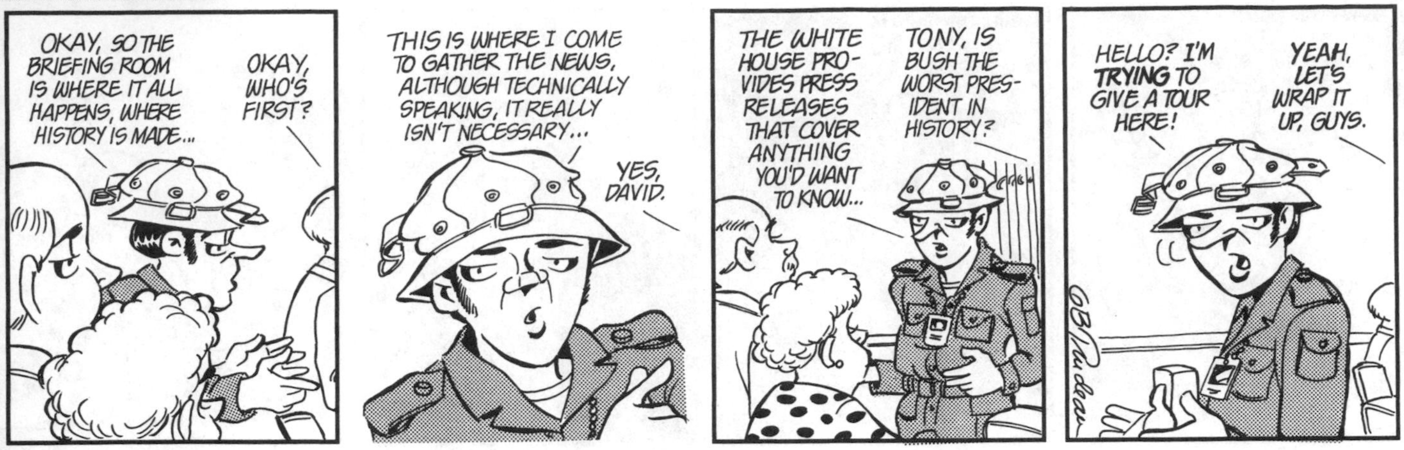
OKAY, SO THE BRIEFING ROOM IS WHERE IT ALL HAPPENS, WHERE HISTORY IS MADE...
OKAY, WHO'S FIRST?
THIS IS WHERE I COME TO GATHER THE NEWS, ALTHOUGH TECHNICALLY SPEAKING, IT REALLY ISN'T NECESSARY...
YES, DAVID.
THE WHITE HOUSE PROVIDES PRESS RELEASES THAT COVER ANYTHING YOU'D WANT TO KNOW...
TONY, IS BUSH THE WORST PRESIDENT IN HISTORY?
HELLO? I'M TRYING TO GIVE A TOUR HERE!
YEAH, LET'S WRAP IT UP, GUYS.

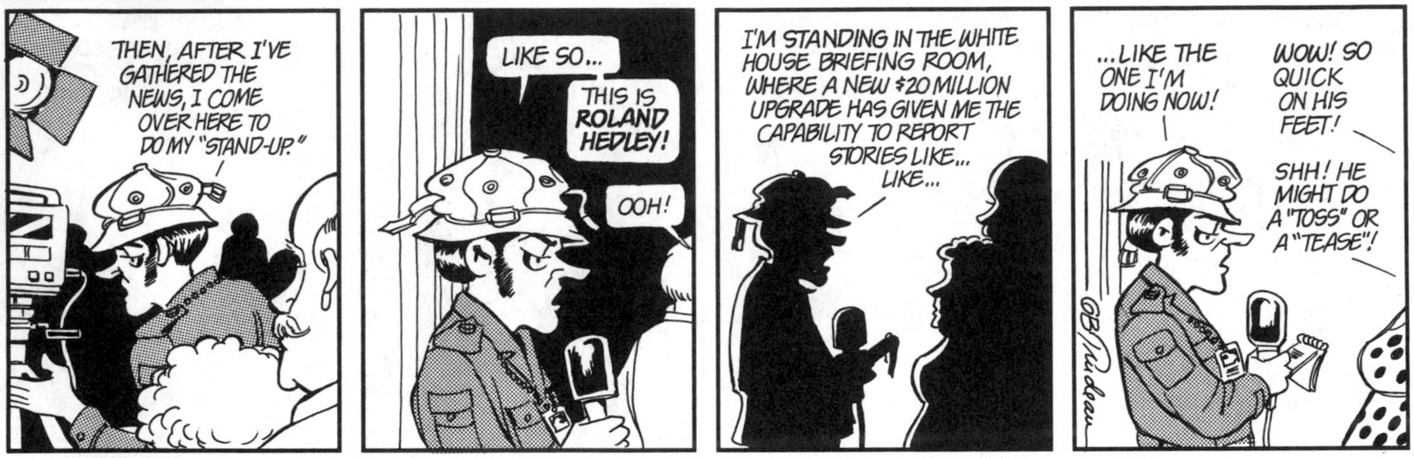
THEN, AFTER I'VE GATHERED THE NEWS, I COME OVER HERE TO DO MY "STAND-UP."
LIKE SO...
THIS IS ROLAND HEDLEY!
OOH!
I'M STANDING IN THE WHITE HOUSE BRIEFING ROOM, WHERE A NEW $20 MILLION UPGRADE HAS GIVEN ME THE CAPABILITY TO REPORT STORIES LIKE... LIKE...
...LIKE THE ONE I'M DOING NOW!
WOW! SO QUICK ON HIS FEET!
SHH! HE MIGHT DO A "TOSS" OR A "TEASE"!

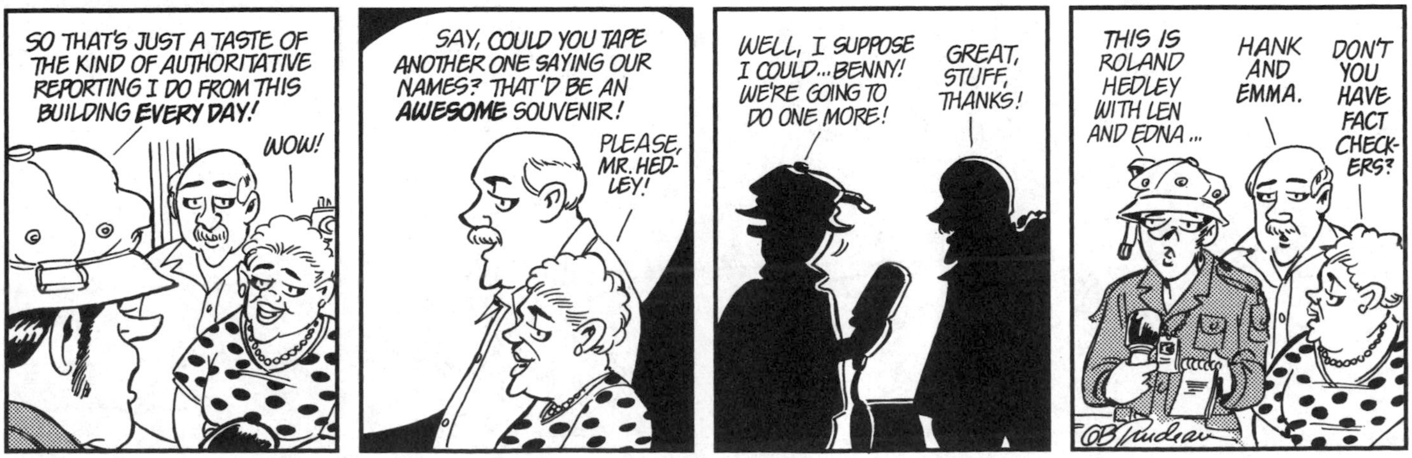
SO THAT'S JUST A TASTE OF THE KIND OF AUTHORITATIVE REPORTING I DO FROM THIS BUILDING EVERY DAY!
WOW!
SAY, COULD YOU TAPE ANOTHER ONE SAYING OUR NAMES? THAT'D BE AN AWESOME SOUVENIR!
PLEASE, MR. HEDLEY!
WELL, I SUPPOSE I COULD... BENNY! WE'RE GOING TO DO ONE MORE!
GREAT, STUFF, THANKS!
THIS IS ROLAND HEDLEY WITH LEN AND EDNA...
HANK AND EMMA.
DON'T YOU HAVE FACT CHECKERS?

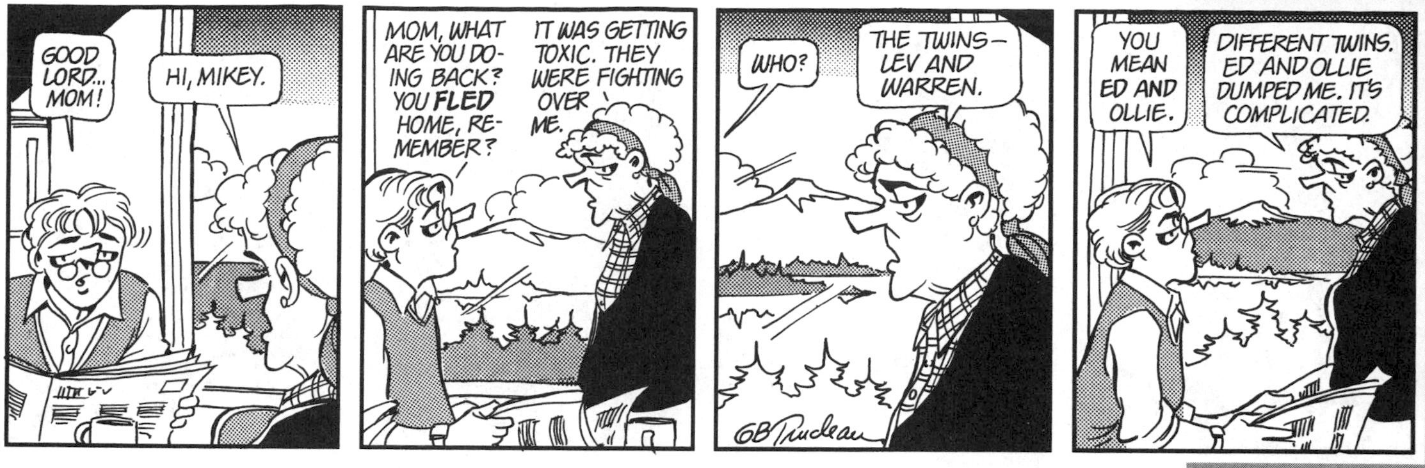
GOOD LORD... MOM!
HI, MIKEY.
MOM, WHAT ARE YOU DOING BACK? YOU **FLED** HOME, REMEMBER?
IT WAS GETTING TOXIC. THEY WERE FIGHTING OVER ME.
WHO?
THE TWINS— LEV AND WARREN.
YOU MEAN ED AND OLLIE.
DIFFERENT TWINS. ED AND OLLIE DUMPED ME. IT'S COMPLICATED.

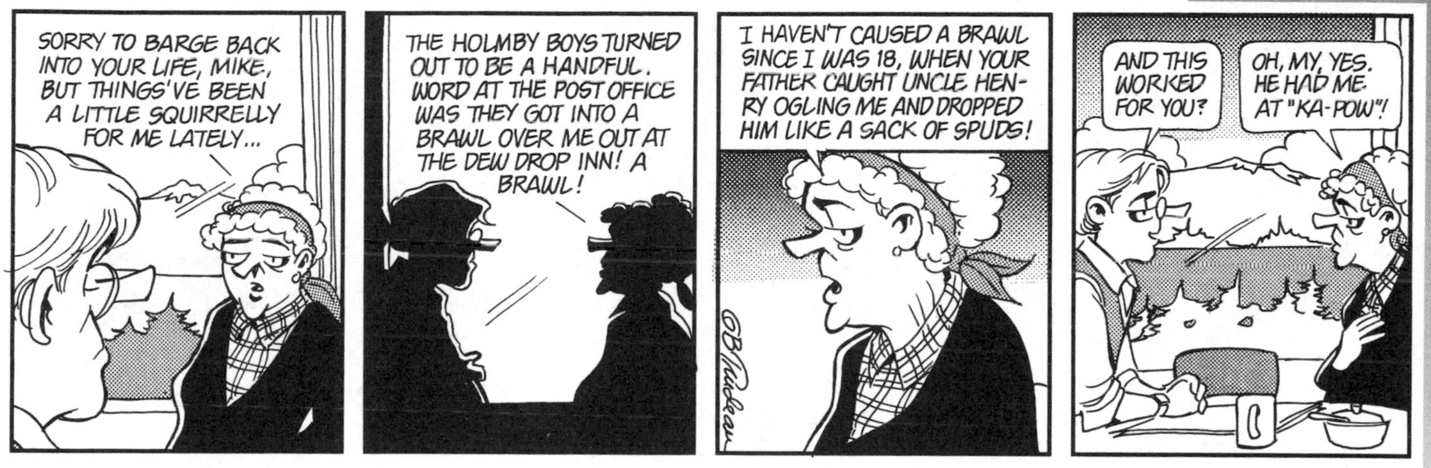
SORRY TO BARGE BACK INTO YOUR LIFE, MIKE, BUT THINGS'VE BEEN A LITTLE SQUIRRELLY FOR ME LATELY...
THE HOLMBY BOYS TURNED OUT TO BE A HANDFUL. WORD AT THE POST OFFICE WAS THEY GOT INTO A BRAWL OVER ME OUT AT THE DEW DROP INN! A BRAWL!
I HAVEN'T CAUSED A BRAWL SINCE I WAS 18, WHEN YOUR FATHER CAUGHT UNCLE HENRY OGLING ME AND DROPPED HIM LIKE A SACK OF SPUDS!
AND THIS WORKED FOR YOU?
OH, MY, YES. HE HAD ME AT "KA-POW"!

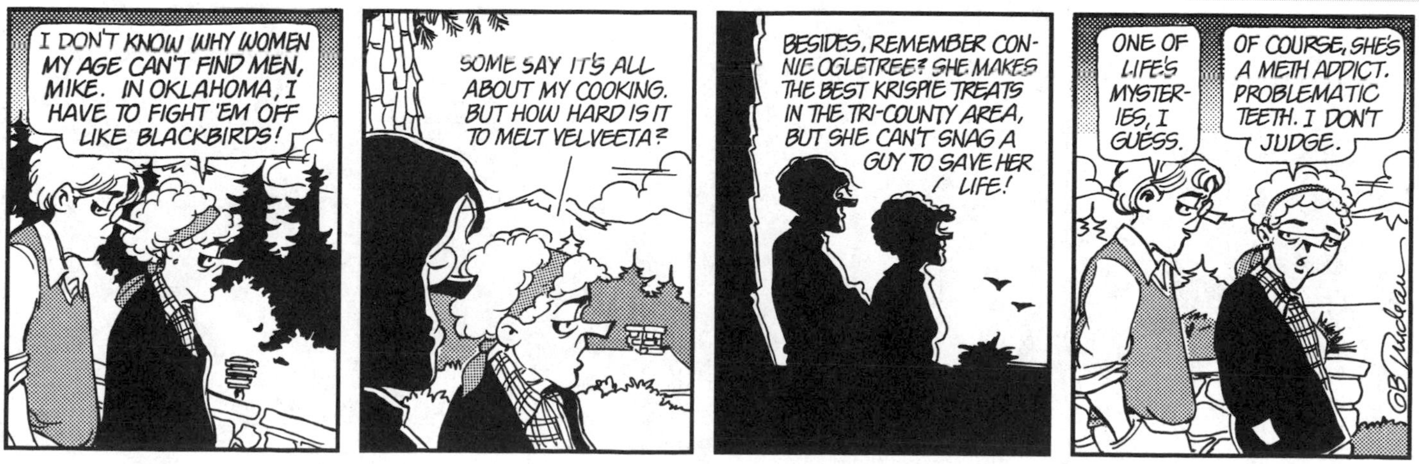
I DON'T KNOW WHY WOMEN MY AGE CAN'T FIND MEN, MIKE. IN OKLAHOMA, I HAVE TO FIGHT 'EM OFF LIKE BLACKBIRDS!
SOME SAY IT'S ALL ABOUT MY COOKING. BUT HOW HARD IS IT TO MELT VELVEETA?
BESIDES, REMEMBER CONNIE OGLETREE? SHE MAKES THE BEST KRISPIE TREATS IN THE TRI-COUNTY AREA, BUT SHE CAN'T SNAG A GUY TO SAVE HER LIFE!
ONE OF LIFE'S MYSTERIES, I GUESS.
OF COURSE, SHE'S A METH ADDICT. PROBLEMATIC TEETH. I DON'T JUDGE.

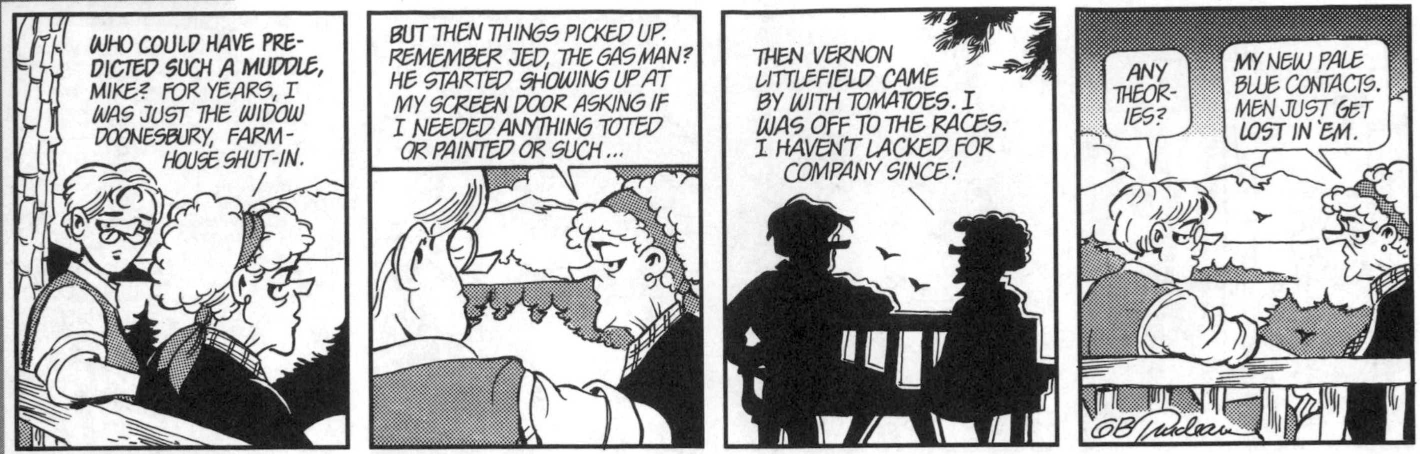
WHO COULD HAVE PREDICTED SUCH A MUDDLE, MIKE? FOR YEARS, I WAS JUST THE WIDOW DOONESBURY, FARMHOUSE SHUT-IN.
BUT THEN THINGS PICKED UP. REMEMBER JED, THE GAS MAN? HE STARTED SHOWING UP AT MY SCREEN DOOR ASKING IF I NEEDED ANYTHING TOTED OR PAINTED OR SUCH...
THEN VERNON LITTLEFIELD CAME BY WITH TOMATOES. I WAS OFF TO THE RACES. I HAVEN'T LACKED FOR COMPANY SINCE!
ANY THEORIES?
MY NEW PALE BLUE CONTACTS. MEN JUST GET LOST IN 'EM.
GB Trudeau

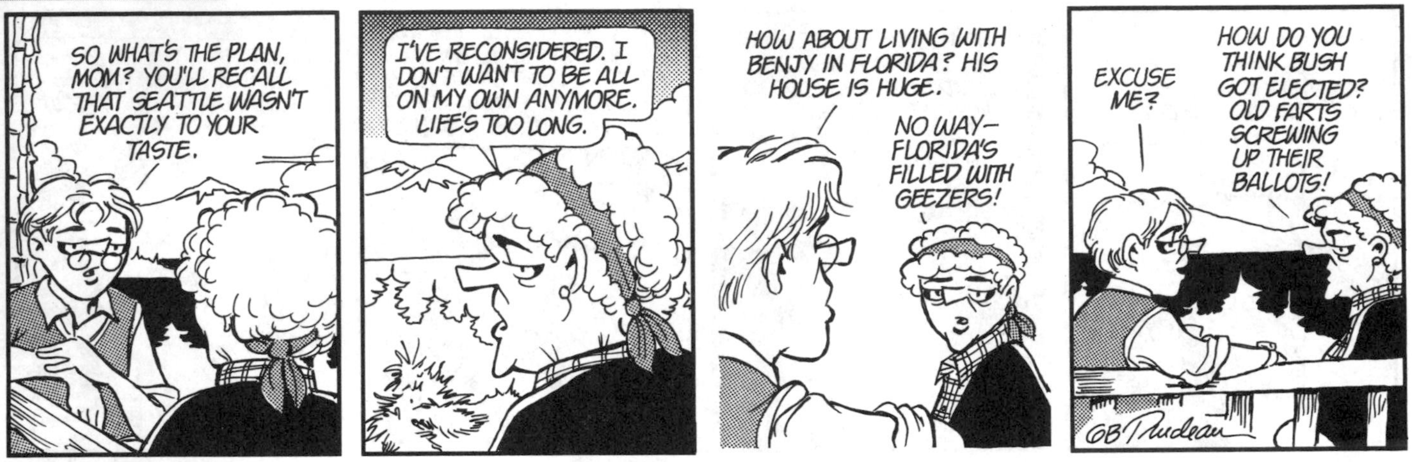
SO WHAT'S THE PLAN, MOM? YOU'LL RECALL THAT SEATTLE WASN'T EXACTLY TO YOUR TASTE.
I'VE RECONSIDERED. I DON'T WANT TO BE ALL ON MY OWN ANYMORE. LIFE'S TOO LONG.
HOW ABOUT LIVING WITH BENJY IN FLORIDA? HIS HOUSE IS HUGE.
NO WAY– FLORIDA'S FILLED WITH GEEZERS!
EXCUSE ME?
HOW DO YOU THINK BUSH GOT ELECTED? OLD FARTS SCREWING UP THEIR BALLOTS!
GB Trudeau

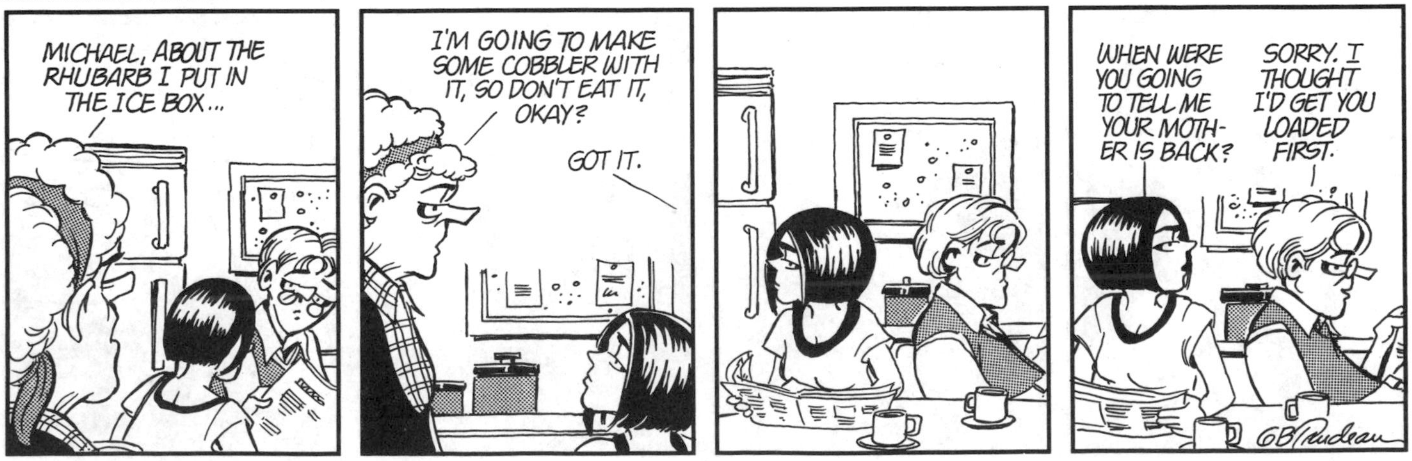
MICHAEL, ABOUT THE RHUBARB I PUT IN THE ICE BOX...
I'M GOING TO MAKE SOME COBBLER WITH IT, SO DON'T EAT IT, OKAY?
GOT IT.
WHEN WERE YOU GOING TO TELL ME YOUR MOTHER IS BACK?
SORRY. I THOUGHT I'D GET YOU LOADED FIRST.
GB Trudeau